THE BIG BOOK OF CAT

An ASK A CAT Omnibus by Charles Brubaker

SMALLBUG PRESS

Martin, TN

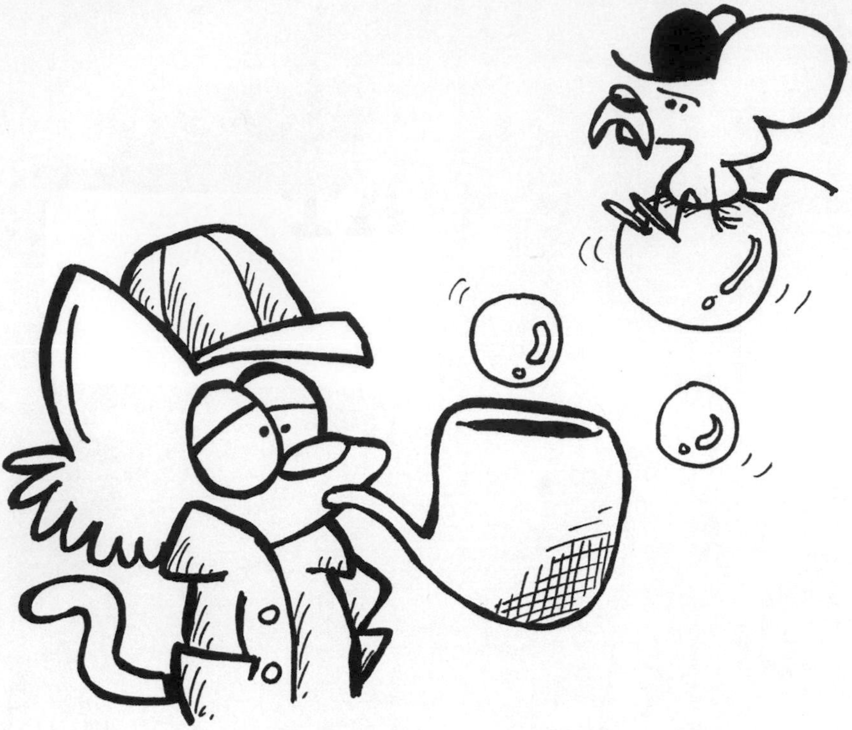

Support on Patreon
www.patreon.com/smallbug

www.smallbugstudio.com
cbrubaker@gmail.com

Printed in the United States of America
10 9 8 7 6 5 4 3 2 1

Library of Congress Control Number: 2022901184
ISBN: 978-0-9989482-6-3

Published by Smallbug Press, Martin, TN.

ASK A CAT

I drew "Ask a Cat" for five years, from 2014 to 2019. This represents most of the run. Hope you enjoy!

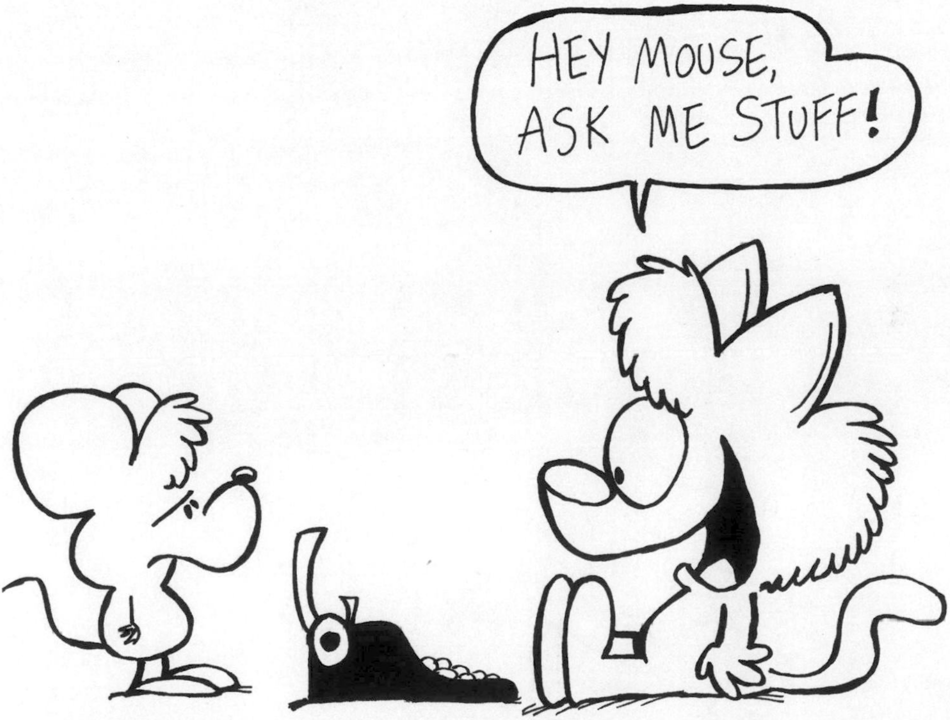
HEY MOUSE, ASK ME STUFF!

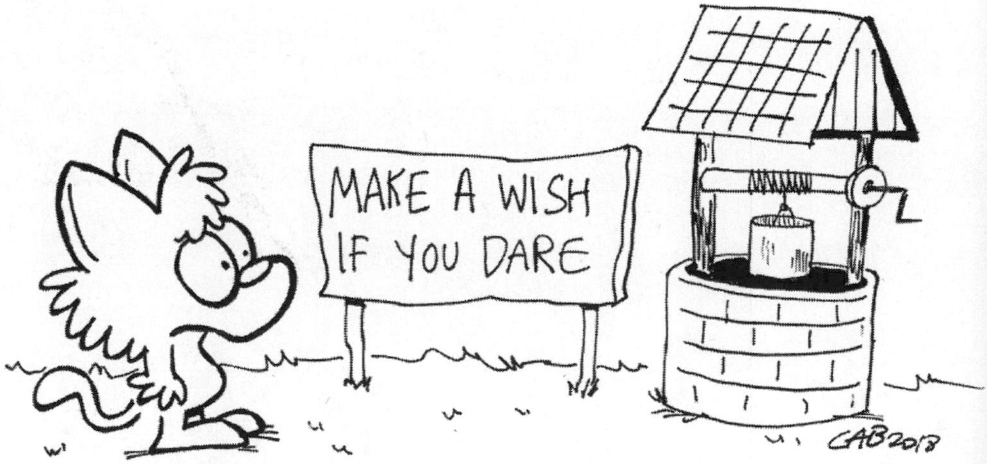
MAKE A WISH
IF YOU DARE
CAB 2018

Mr. Cat:

Counter Logic Gaming of League of Legends esports was recently fined $10,000 for tampering and poaching.

What are your thoughts?

- A Perilous Persian

I THINK IT'S A BLESSING IN DISGUISE, PERSONALLY. WITH $10,000 NOW IN THEIR POCKETS, THEY CAN USE IT TO FUND A GREAT NEW GAME US CATS CAME UP WITH. IT'S CALLED...

THE LEAGUE of LOAF

YOU CONTROL A CAT, AND YOU GET TO ACT OUT OUR NORMAL LIVES, INCLUDING EATING...

SLEEPING

BECOMING A NINJA

COMMITTING TERRORISM

BOOM!

PUSHING A BMW OFF A TALL BUILDING

MEOW

BEING AN INTERNET CELEBRITY

CAB 2014

THE POSSIBILITIES ARE ENDLESS! CALL RIOT GAMES NOW AND SAY YOU WANT CATS!

...BUT WE ONLY MAKE LOL...

JUST DO IT, MAN! CAAATS!

5

Dear Cat,

What should I make for dinner?

-Crafty Calico

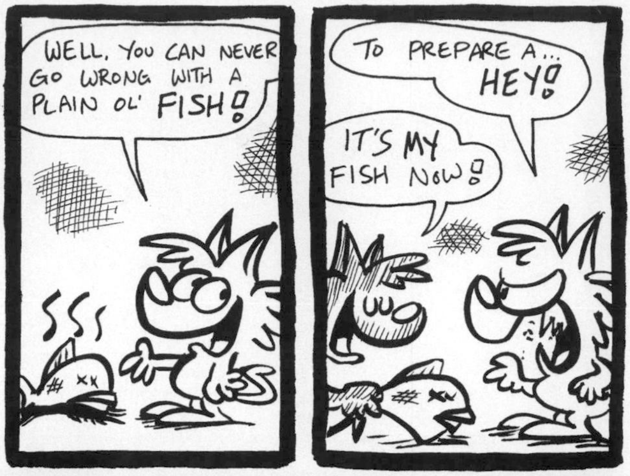
WELL, YOU CAN NEVER GO WRONG WITH A PLAIN OL' FISH!
TO PREPARE A... HEY!
IT'S MY FISH NOW!

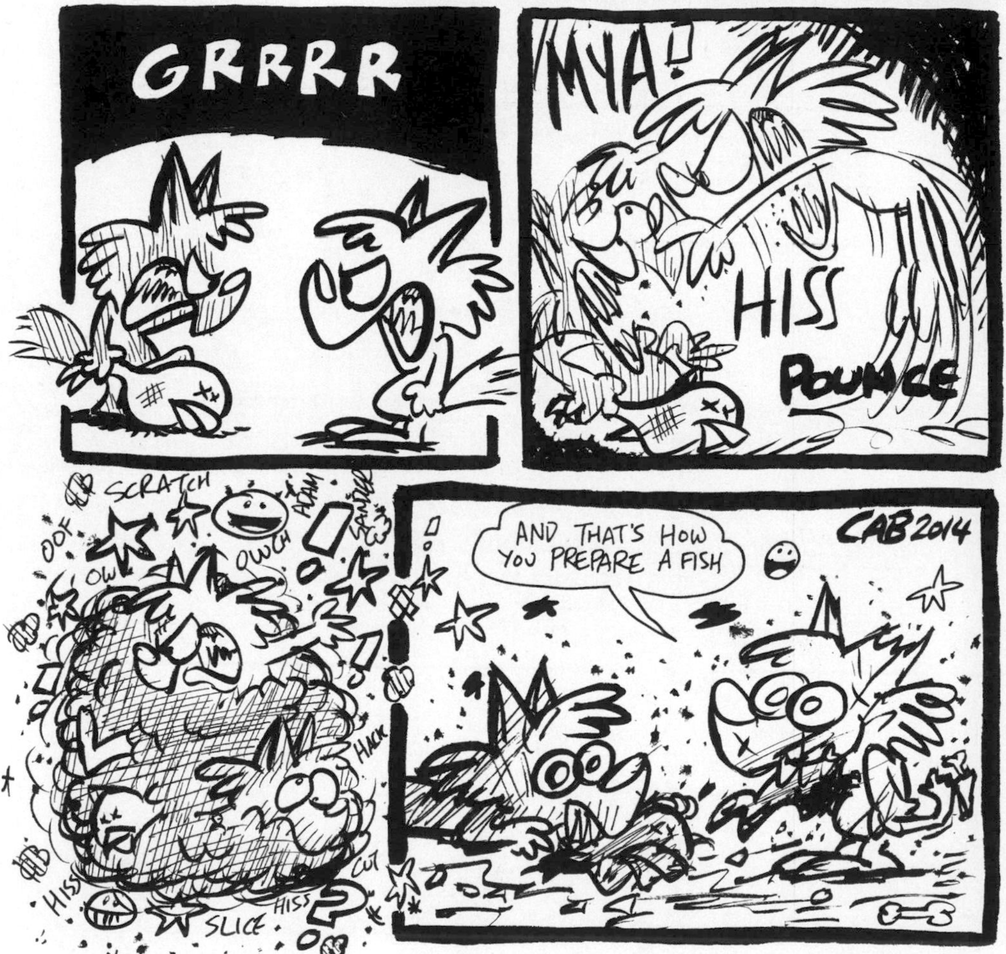
GRRRR
MYA!
HISS
POUNCE
SCRATCH
OOF
OW
OUCH
HACK
HISS
CUT
SLICE
HISS
AND THAT'S HOW YOU PREPARE A FISH
CAB 2014

Dear Cat,
Did humans really land on the moon?

-Tabby with a Treat

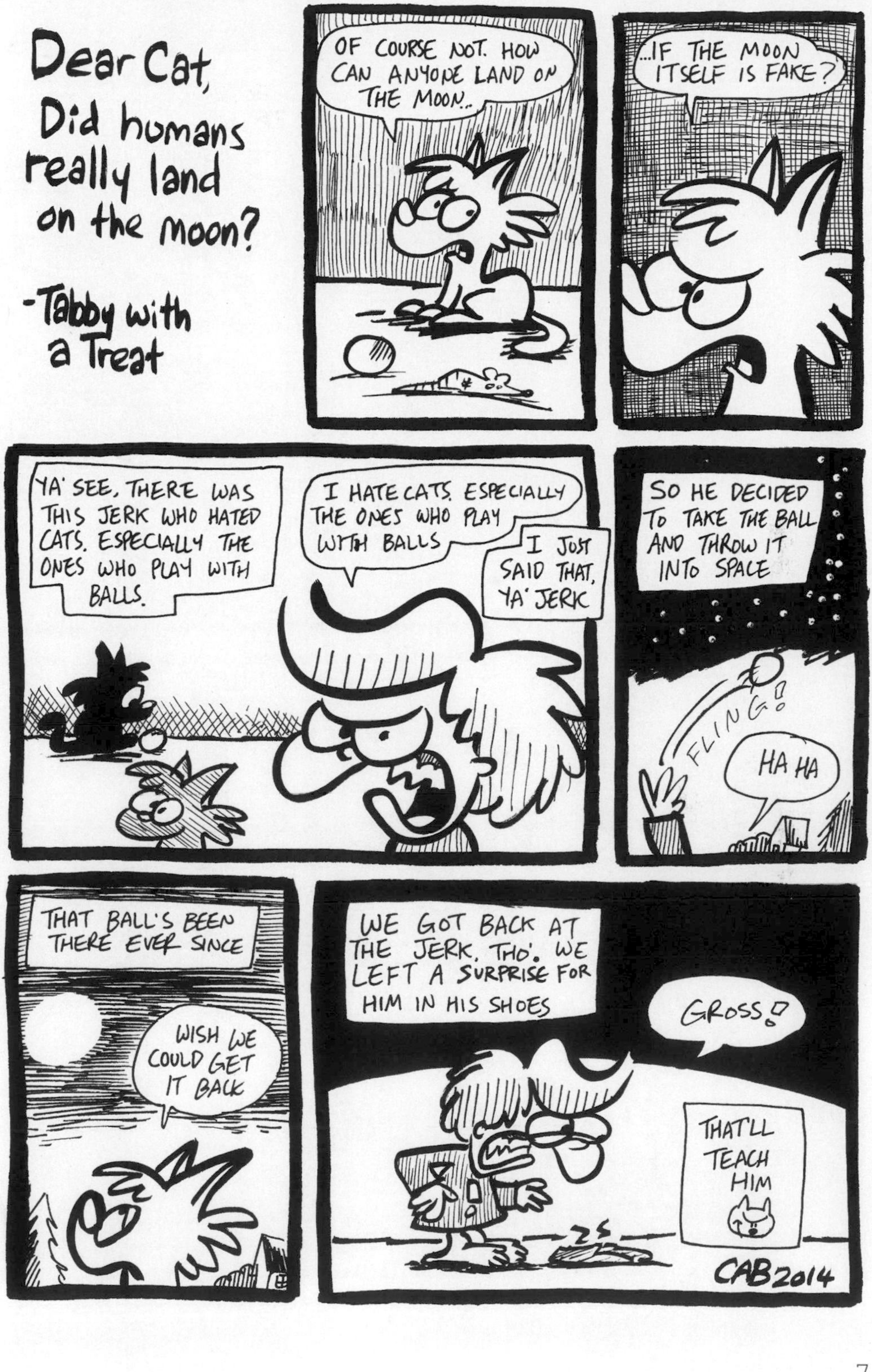
OF COURSE NOT. HOW CAN ANYONE LAND ON THE MOON...
...IF THE MOON ITSELF IS FAKE?
YA' SEE, THERE WAS THIS JERK WHO HATED CATS. ESPECIALLY THE ONES WHO PLAY WITH BALLS.
I HATE CATS. ESPECIALLY THE ONES WHO PLAY WITH BALLS
I JUST SAID THAT, YA' JERK
SO HE DECIDED TO TAKE THE BALL AND THROW IT INTO SPACE
FLING!
HA HA
THAT BALL'S BEEN THERE EVER SINCE
WISH WE COULD GET IT BACK
WE GOT BACK AT THE JERK, THO'. WE LEFT A SURPRISE FOR HIM IN HIS SHOES
GROSS!
THAT'LL TEACH HIM
CAB 2014

Dear Cat, What should we do with a drunken Sailor?
-A Still Living Curious Cat

THAT'S A GOOD QUESTION. WHAT SHOULD WE DO WITH THEM?
PAW PAW
JUNK
I SUPPOSE WE CAN STEAL HIS CLOTHES AND USE IT TO POSE AS HUMANS
good Pants
WITH THIS, WE CAN DO HUMAN ACTIVITIES, LIKE DRIVING A CAR...
wee
BRIDGE OUT
...MAKE MONEY...
Yo, GIMME MONEY
AH! BANK ROBBERY!
TELLER
ESCAPING POLICE
BANG
HALT!
ON SECOND THOUGHT, THIS IS A BAD IDEA
hands up, perv
TO HELL WITH THIS
I'M KEEPIN' THE PANTS, THO
CAB 2014

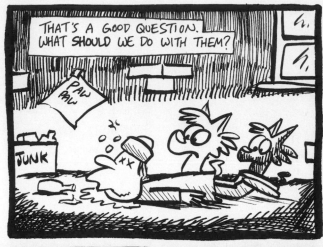

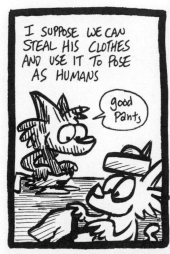

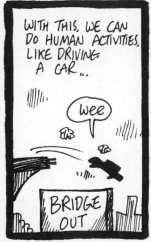

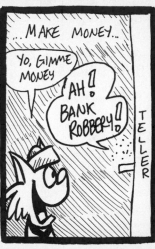

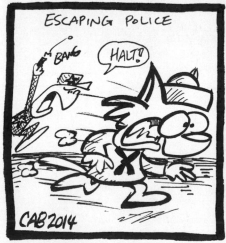

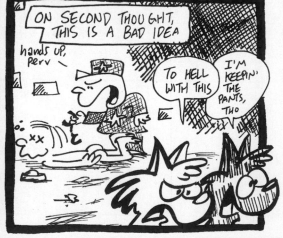

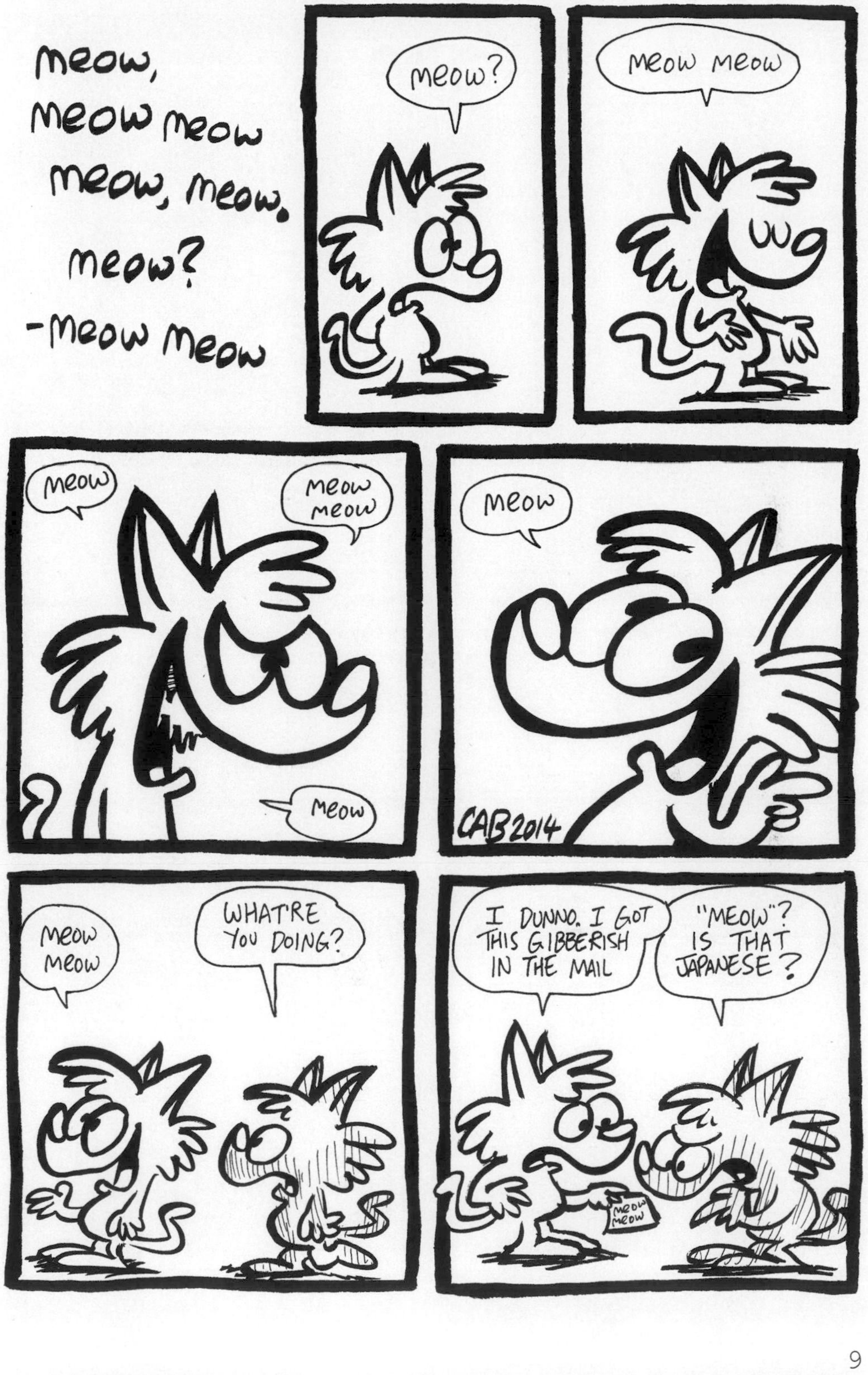
meow,
meow meow
meow, meow.
meow?
-Meow meow
meow?
meow meow
meow
meow meow
meow
meow
meow meow
WHAT'RE YOU DOING?
I DUNNO. I GOT THIS GIBBERISH IN THE MAIL
MEOW MEOW
"MEOW"? IS THAT JAPANESE?
CAB 2014

Dear Cat,

How accurate is the 1978 movie "The Cat from Outer Space"?

-Saucy Siamese

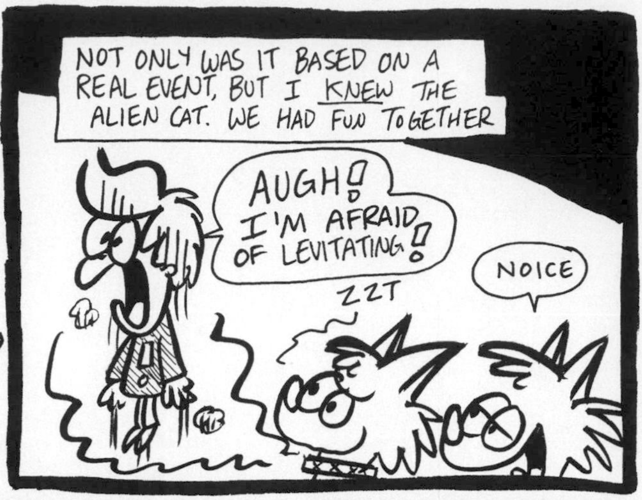

NOT ONLY WAS IT BASED ON A REAL EVENT, BUT I KNEW THE ALIEN CAT. WE HAD FUN TOGETHER
AUGH! I'M AFRAID OF LEVITATING!
ZZT
NOICE

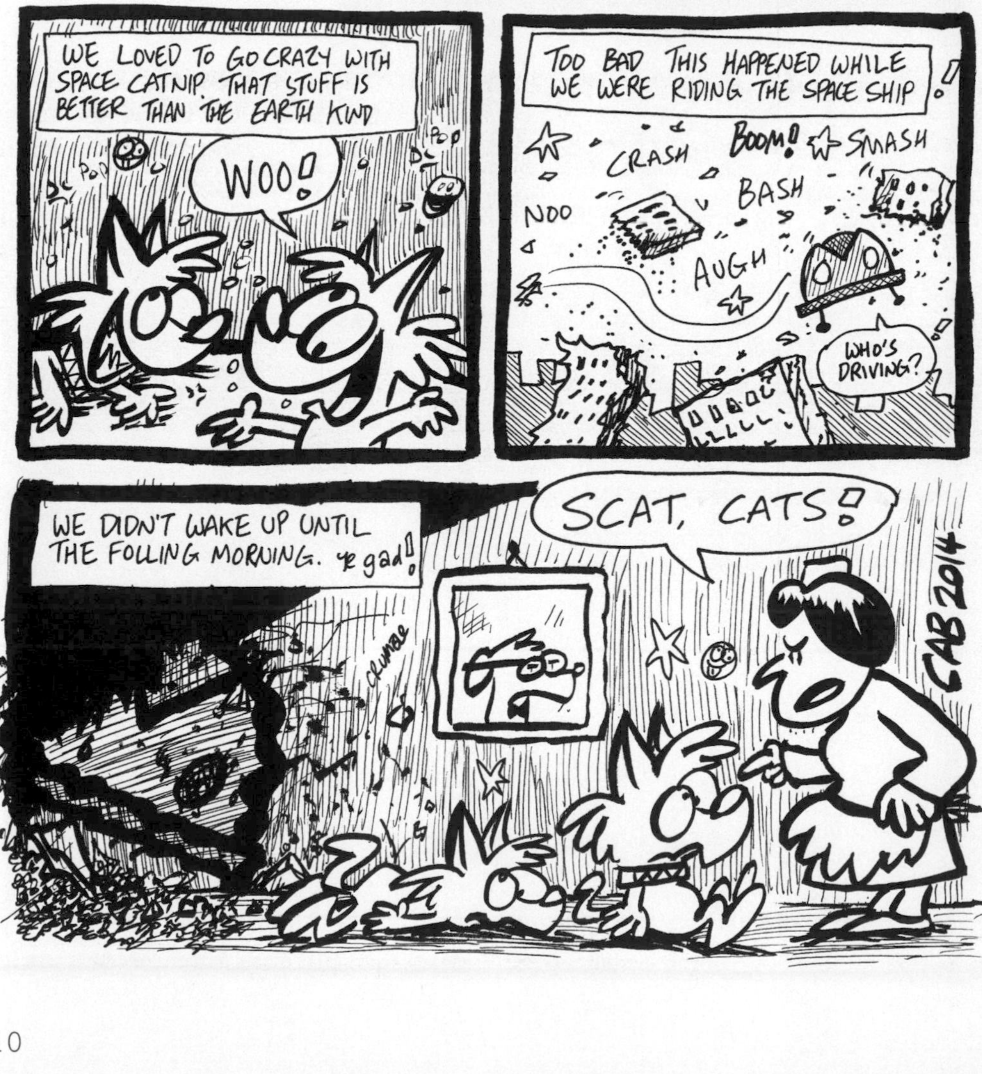

WE LOVED TO GO CRAZY WITH SPACE CATNIP. THAT STUFF IS BETTER THAN THE EARTH KIND
WOO!
TOO BAD THIS HAPPENED WHILE WE WERE RIDING THE SPACE SHIP!
CRASH
BOOM!
SMASH
BASH
NOO
AUGH
WHO'S DRIVING?
WE DIDN'T WAKE UP UNTIL THE FOLLING MORNING. ye gad!
SCAT, CATS!
CRUMBLE
CAB 2014

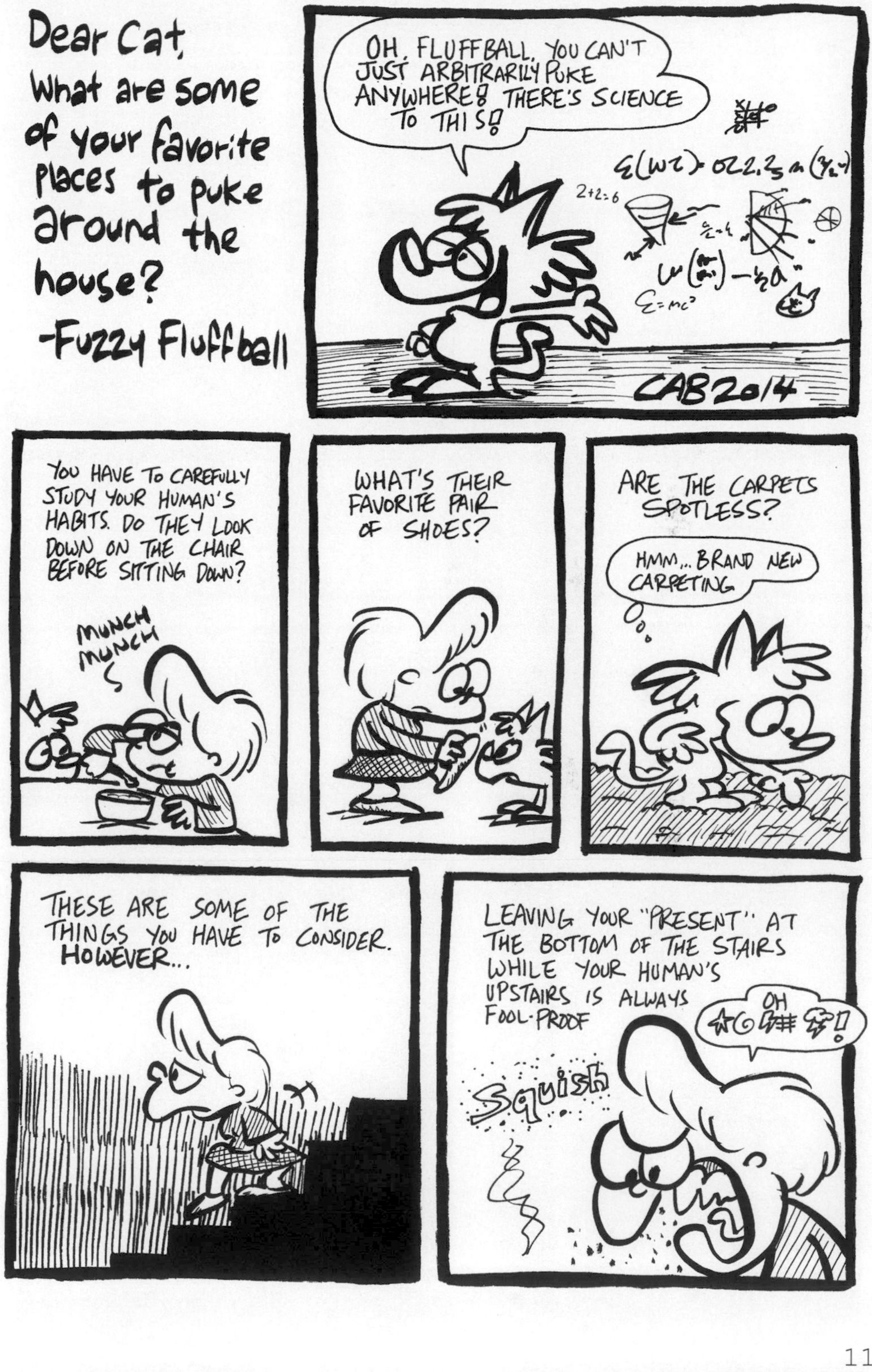
Dear Cat,
What are some of your favorite places to puke around the house?
-Fuzzy Fluffball
OH, FLUFFBALL, YOU CAN'T JUST ARBITRARILY PUKE ANYWHERE! THERE'S SCIENCE TO THIS!
2+2=6
E=mc²
CAB 2014
YOU HAVE TO CAREFULLY STUDY YOUR HUMAN'S HABITS. DO THEY LOOK DOWN ON THE CHAIR BEFORE SITTING DOWN?
MUNCH MUNCH
WHAT'S THEIR FAVORITE PAIR OF SHOES?
ARE THE CARPETS SPOTLESS?
HMM... BRAND NEW CARPETING
THESE ARE SOME OF THE THINGS YOU HAVE TO CONSIDER. HOWEVER...
LEAVING YOUR "PRESENT" AT THE BOTTOM OF THE STAIRS WHILE YOUR HUMAN'S UPSTAIRS IS ALWAYS FOOL-PROOF
SQUISH
OH ☆@#$!

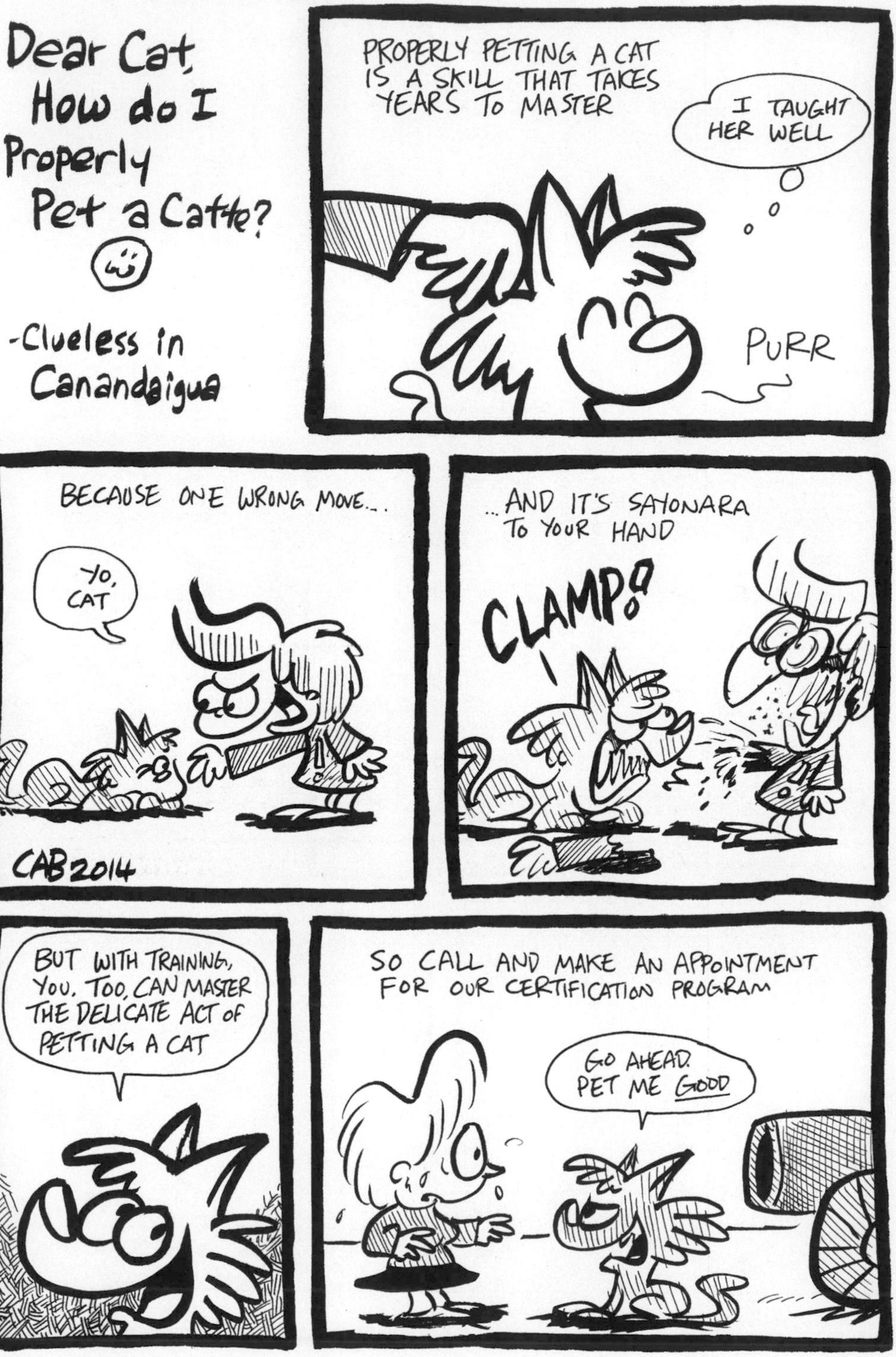
Dear Cat, How do I Properly Pet a Catte?
-Clueless in Canandaigua
PROPERLY PETTING A CAT IS A SKILL THAT TAKES YEARS TO MASTER
I TAUGHT HER WELL
PURR
BECAUSE ONE WRONG MOVE...
YO, CAT
CAB 2014
...AND IT'S SAYONARA TO YOUR HAND
CLAMP!
BUT WITH TRAINING, YOU, TOO, CAN MASTER THE DELICATE ACT OF PETTING A CAT
SO CALL AND MAKE AN APPOINTMENT FOR OUR CERTIFICATION PROGRAM
GO AHEAD. PET ME GOOD

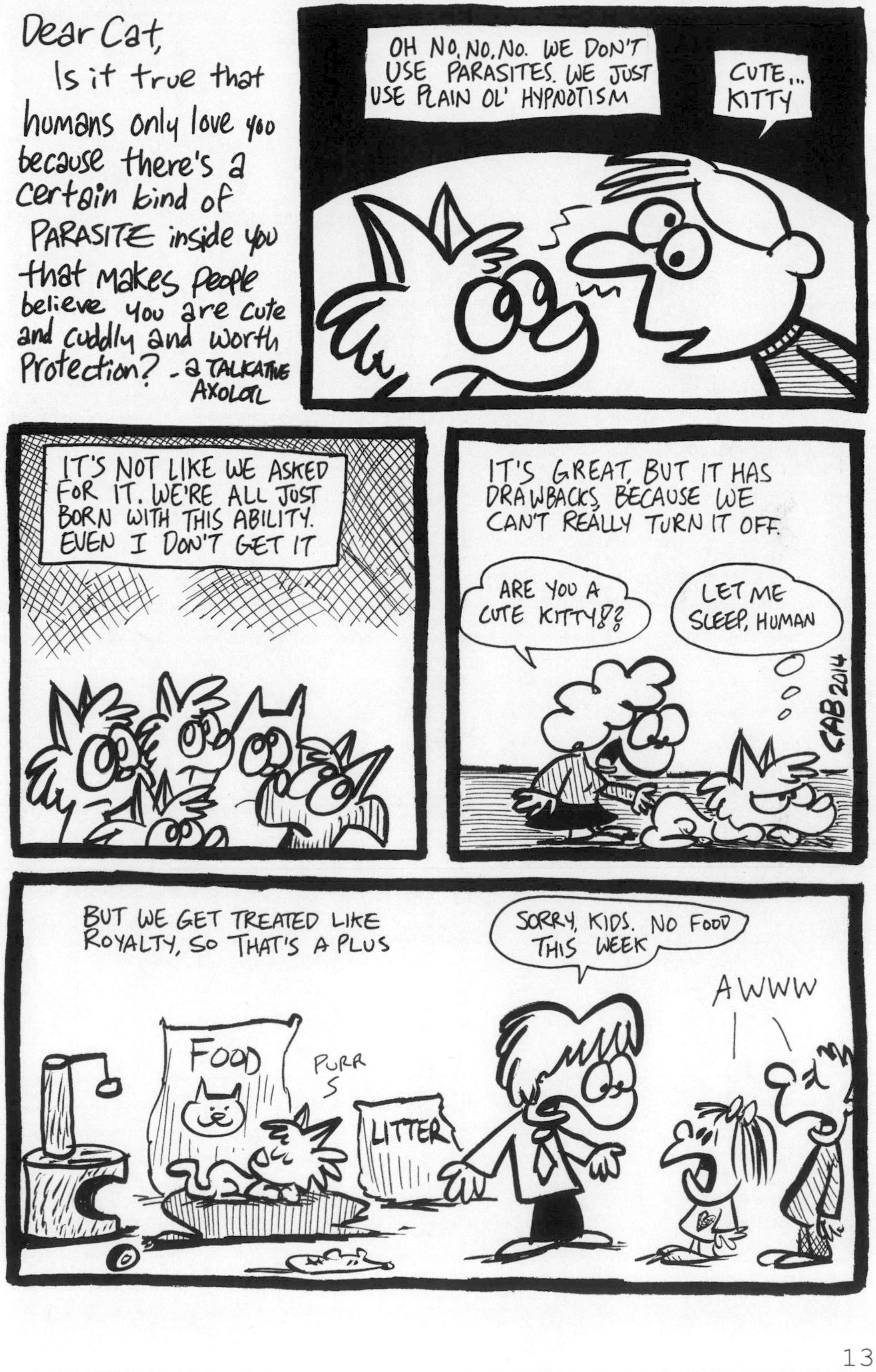
Dear Cat,
Is it true that humans only love you because there's a certain kind of PARASITE inside you that makes people believe you are cute and cuddly and worth Protection? - a TALKATIVE AXOLOTL
OH NO, NO, NO. WE DON'T USE PARASITES. WE JUST USE PLAIN OL' HYPNOTISM
CUTE... KITTY
IT'S NOT LIKE WE ASKED FOR IT. WE'RE ALL JUST BORN WITH THIS ABILITY. EVEN I DON'T GET IT
IT'S GREAT, BUT IT HAS DRAWBACKS, BECAUSE WE CAN'T REALLY TURN IT OFF.
ARE YOU A CUTE KITTY!?
LET ME SLEEP, HUMAN
CAB 2014
BUT WE GET TREATED LIKE ROYALTY, SO THAT'S A PLUS
SORRY, KIDS. NO FOOD THIS WEEK
AWWW
FOOD
PURR S
LITTER

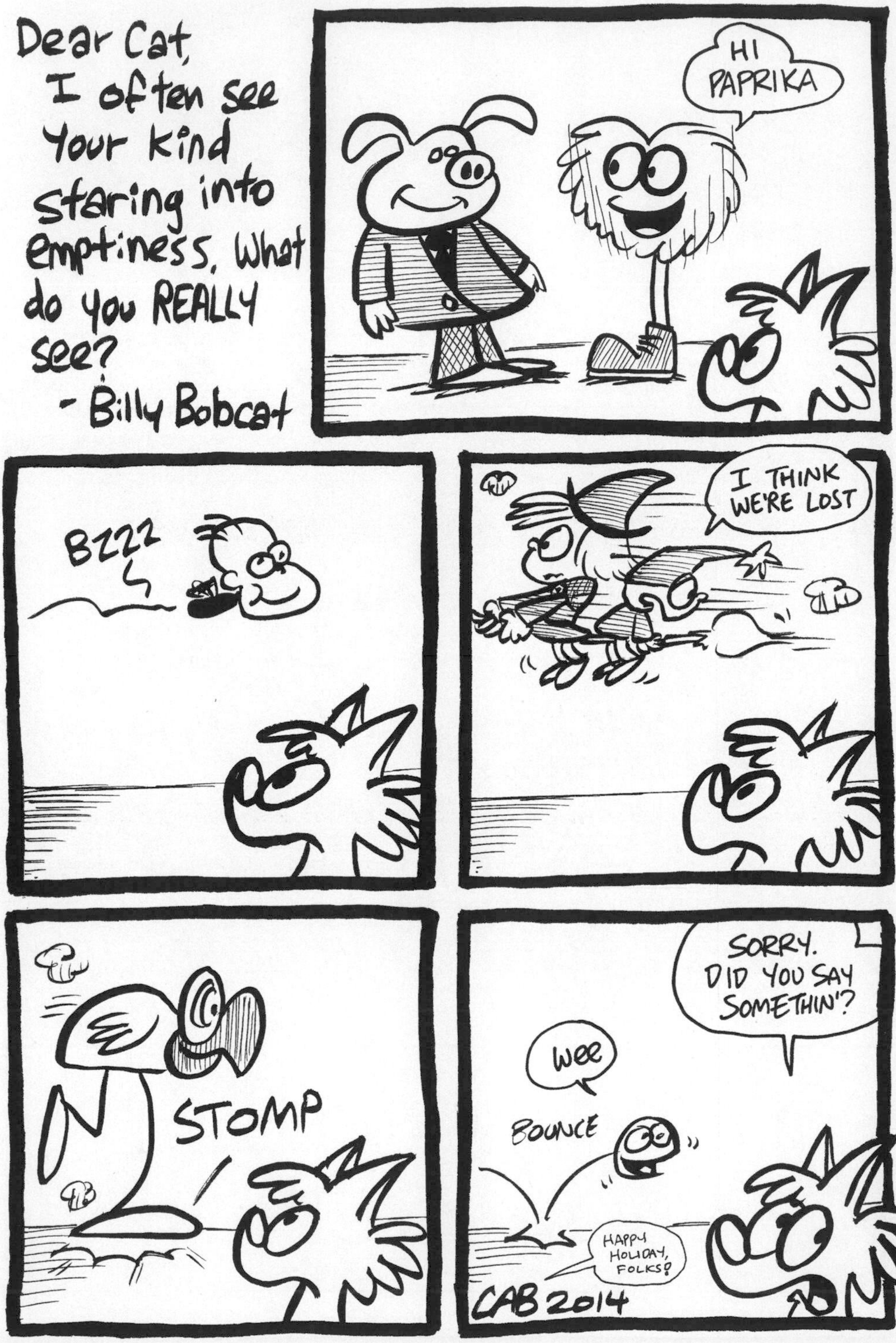
Dear Cat,
I often see your kind staring into emptiness. What do you REALLY see?
- Billy Bobcat
HI PAPRIKA
BZZZ
I THINK WE'RE LOST
STOMP
SORRY. DID YOU SAY SOMETHIN'?
wee
BOUNCE
HAPPY HOLIDAY, FOLKS!
CAB 2014

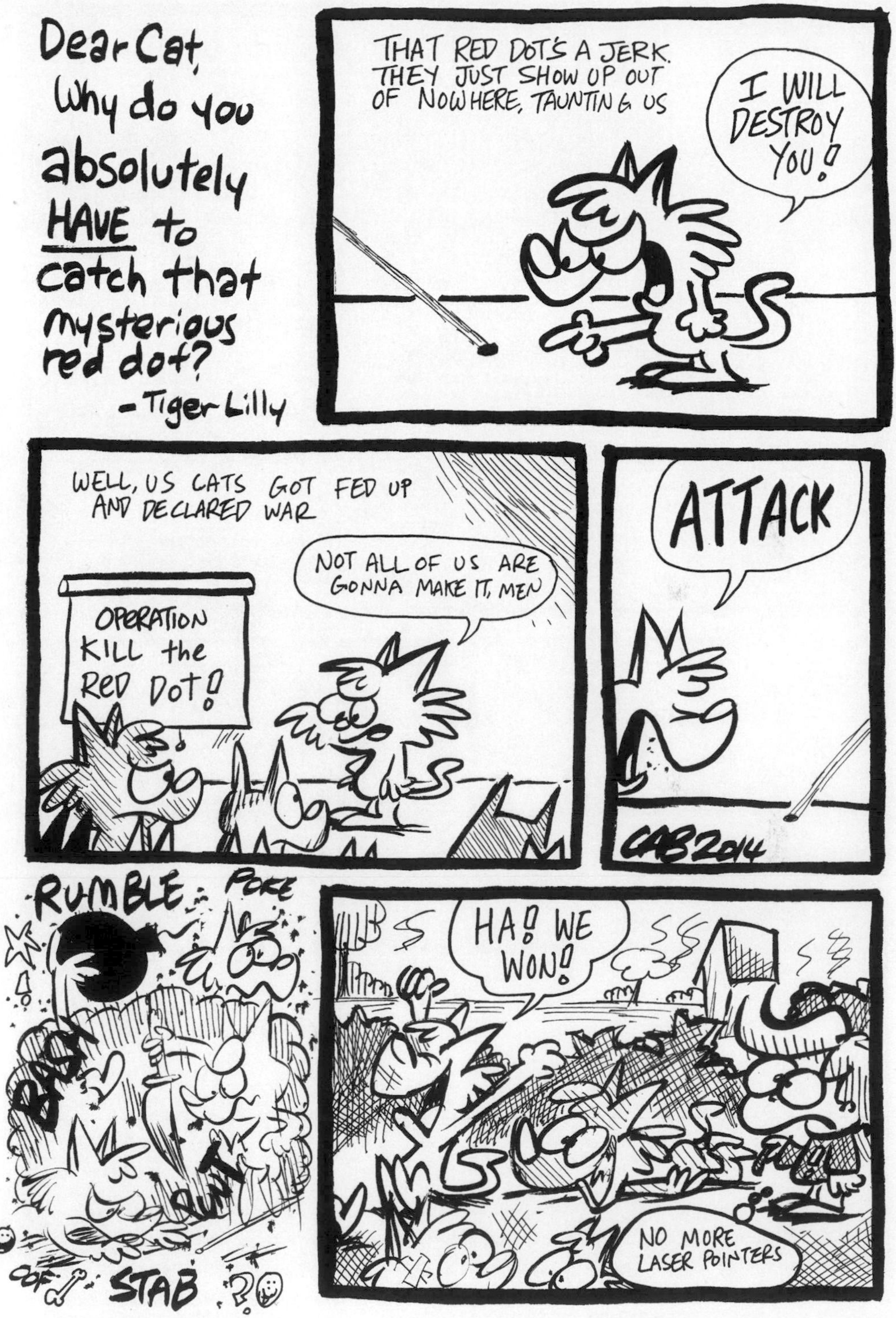
Dear Cat,
Why do you absolutely HAVE to catch that mysterious red dot?
-Tiger Lilly
THAT RED DOT'S A JERK. THEY JUST SHOW UP OUT OF NOWHERE, TAUNTING US
I WILL DESTROY YOU!
WELL, US CATS GOT FED UP AND DECLARED WAR
OPERATION KILL the RED DOT!
NOT ALL OF US ARE GONNA MAKE IT, MEN
ATTACK
CAB 2014
RUMBLE
POKE
BASH
STAB
HA! WE WON!
NO MORE LASER POINTERS

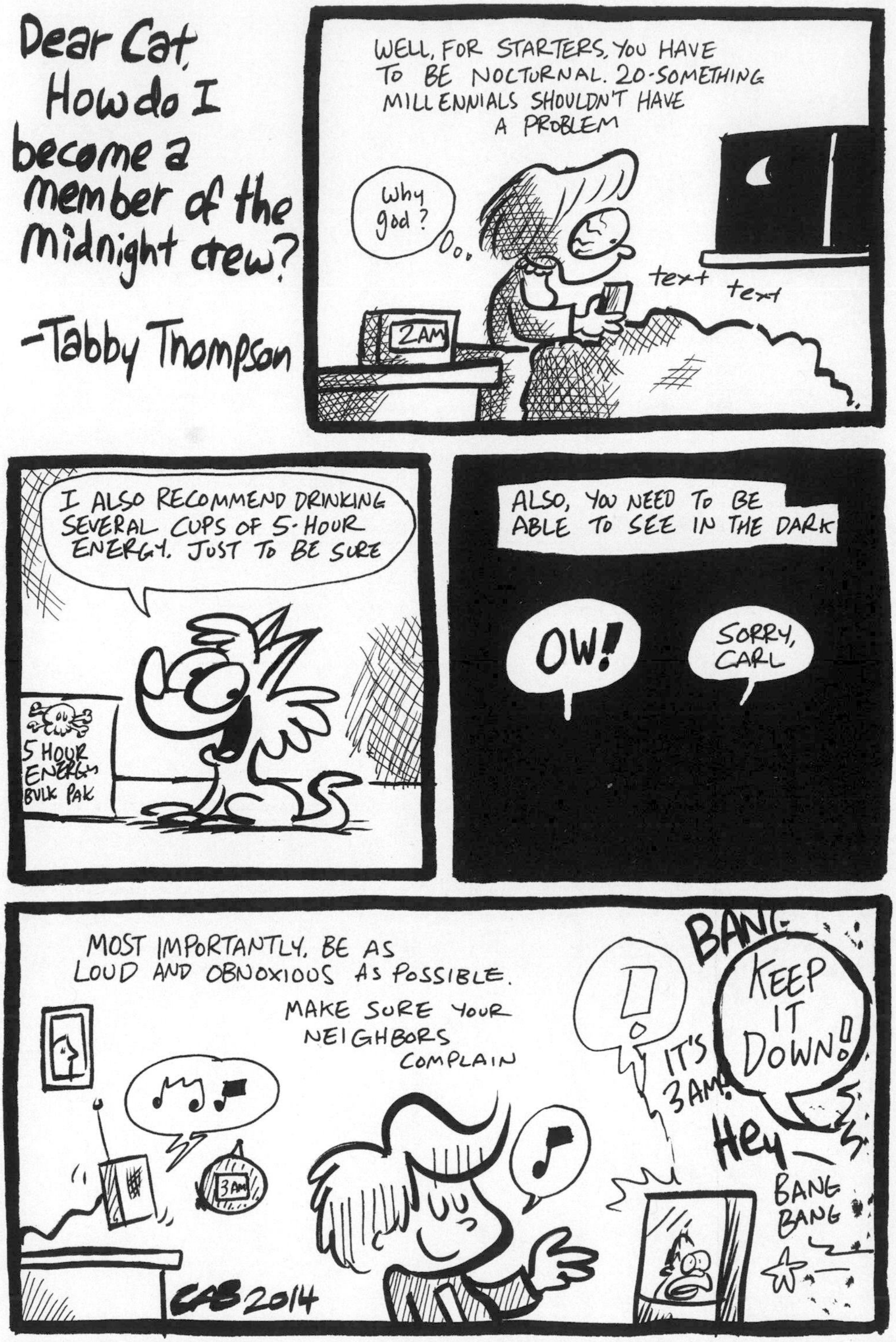

Dear Cat,
How do I become a member of the midnight crew?
-Tabby Thompson
WELL, FOR STARTERS, YOU HAVE TO BE NOCTURNAL. 20-SOMETHING MILLENNIALS SHOULDN'T HAVE A PROBLEM
Why god?
2AM
text text
I ALSO RECOMMEND DRINKING SEVERAL CUPS OF 5-HOUR ENERGY. JUST TO BE SURE
5 HOUR ENERGY BULK PAK
ALSO, YOU NEED TO BE ABLE TO SEE IN THE DARK
OW!
SORRY, CARL
MOST IMPORTANTLY, BE AS LOUD AND OBNOXIOUS AS POSSIBLE.
MAKE SURE YOUR NEIGHBORS COMPLAIN
3AM
BANG
KEEP IT DOWN!!
IT'S 3AM!
Hey
BANG BANG
CAB 2014

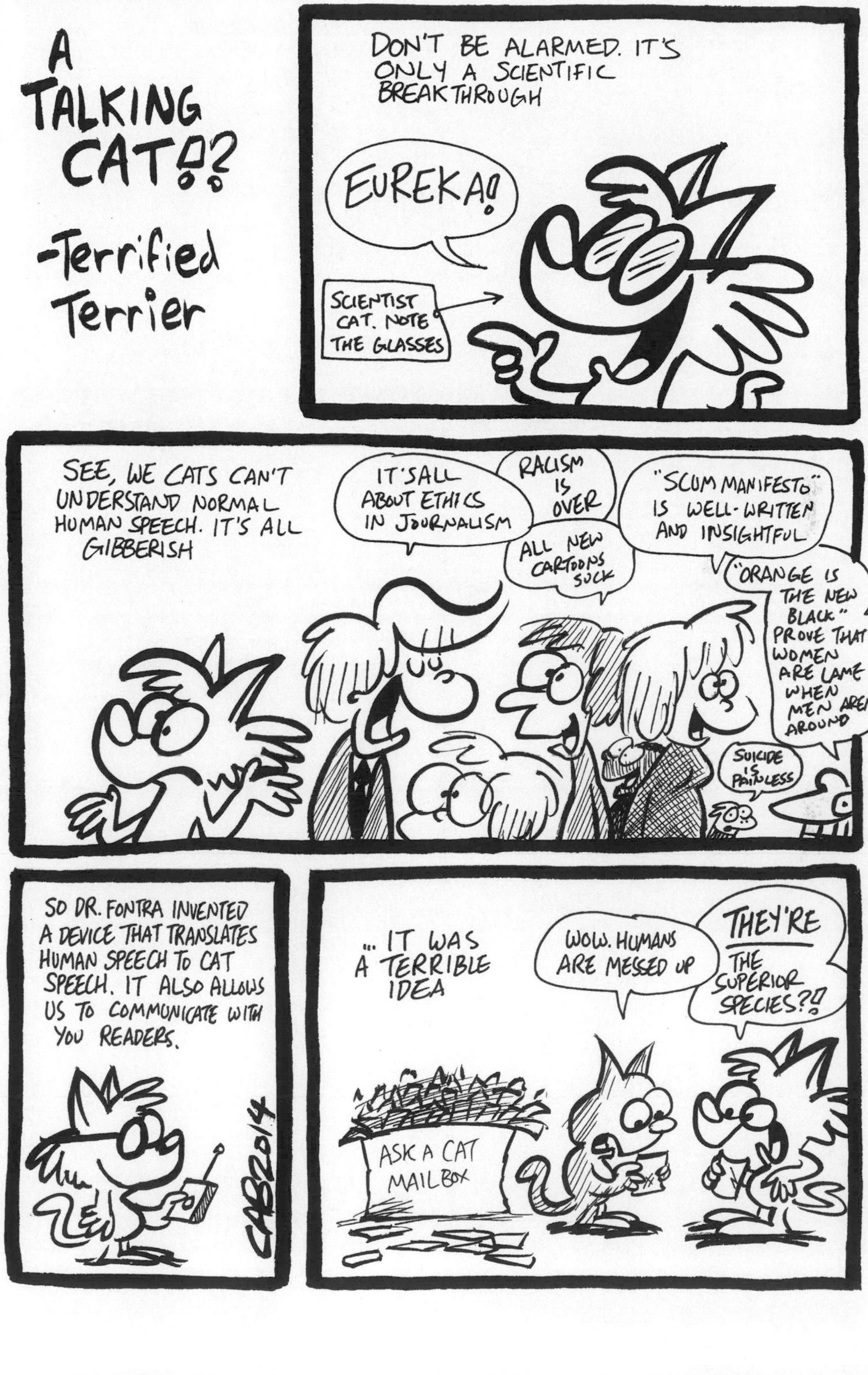
A TALKING CAT!?
-Terrified Terrier
DON'T BE ALARMED. IT'S ONLY A SCIENTIFIC BREAKTHROUGH
EUREKA!
SCIENTIST CAT. NOTE THE GLASSES
SEE, WE CATS CAN'T UNDERSTAND NORMAL HUMAN SPEECH. IT'S ALL GIBBERISH
IT'S ALL ABOUT ETHICS IN JOURNALISM
RACISM IS OVER
ALL NEW CARTOONS SUCK
"SCUM MANIFESTO" IS WELL-WRITTEN AND INSIGHTFUL
"ORANGE IS THE NEW BLACK" PROVE THAT WOMEN ARE LAME WHEN MEN AREN'T AROUND
SUICIDE IS PAINLESS
SO DR. FONTRA INVENTED A DEVICE THAT TRANSLATES HUMAN SPEECH TO CAT SPEECH. IT ALSO ALLOWS US TO COMMUNICATE WITH YOU READERS.
CAB 2014
... IT WAS A TERRIBLE IDEA
WOW. HUMANS ARE MESSED UP
THEY'RE THE SUPERIOR SPECIES?!
ASK A CAT MAILBOX

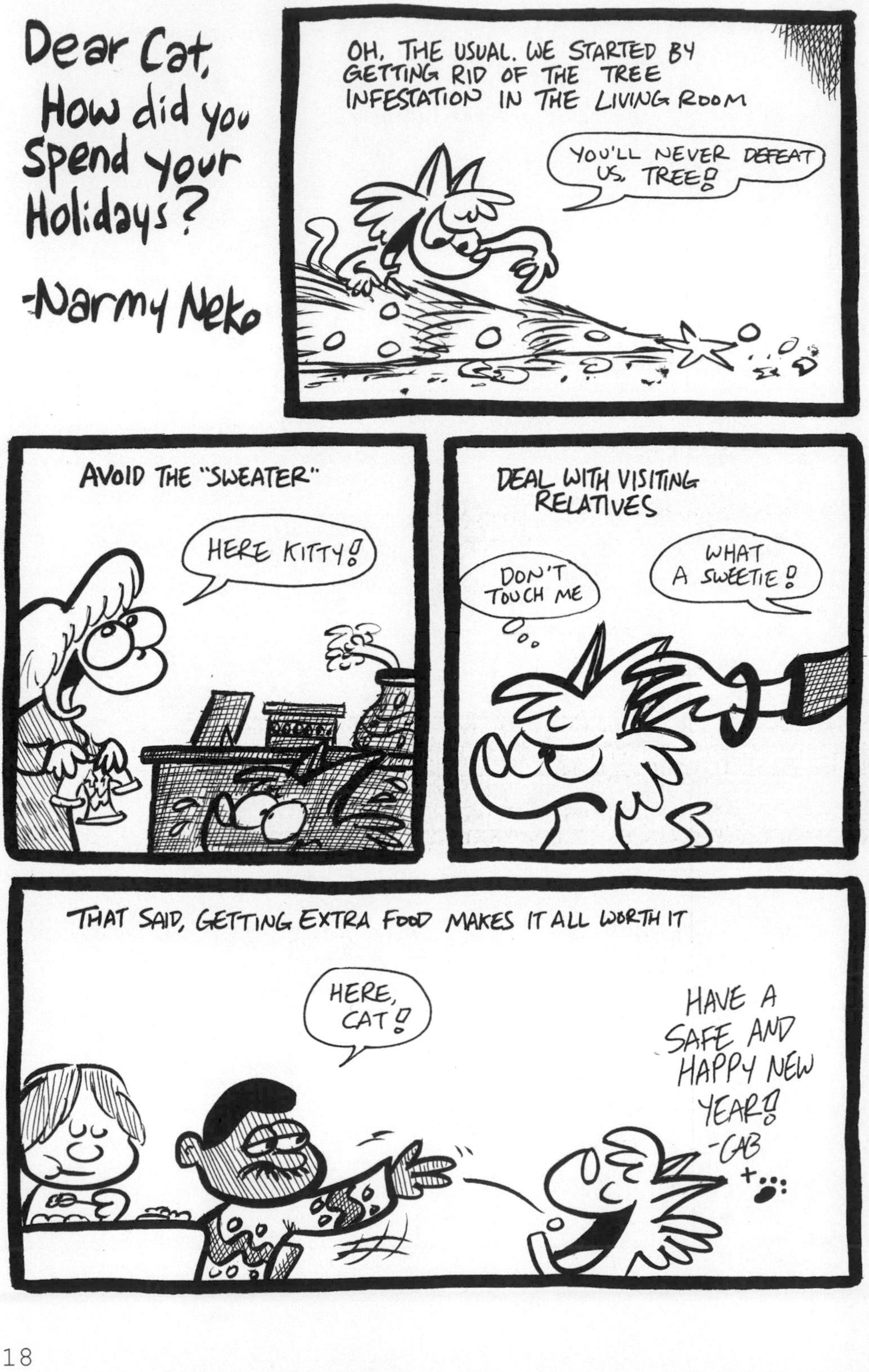
Dear Cat, How did you Spend your Holidays? -Narmy Neko
OH, THE USUAL. WE STARTED BY GETTING RID OF THE TREE INFESTATION IN THE LIVING ROOM
YOU'LL NEVER DEFEAT US, TREE!
AVOID THE "SWEATER"
HERE KITTY!
DEAL WITH VISITING RELATIVES
DON'T TOUCH ME
WHAT A SWEETIE!
THAT SAID, GETTING EXTRA FOOD MAKES IT ALL WORTH IT
HERE, CAT!
HAVE A SAFE AND HAPPY NEW YEAR! -GAB

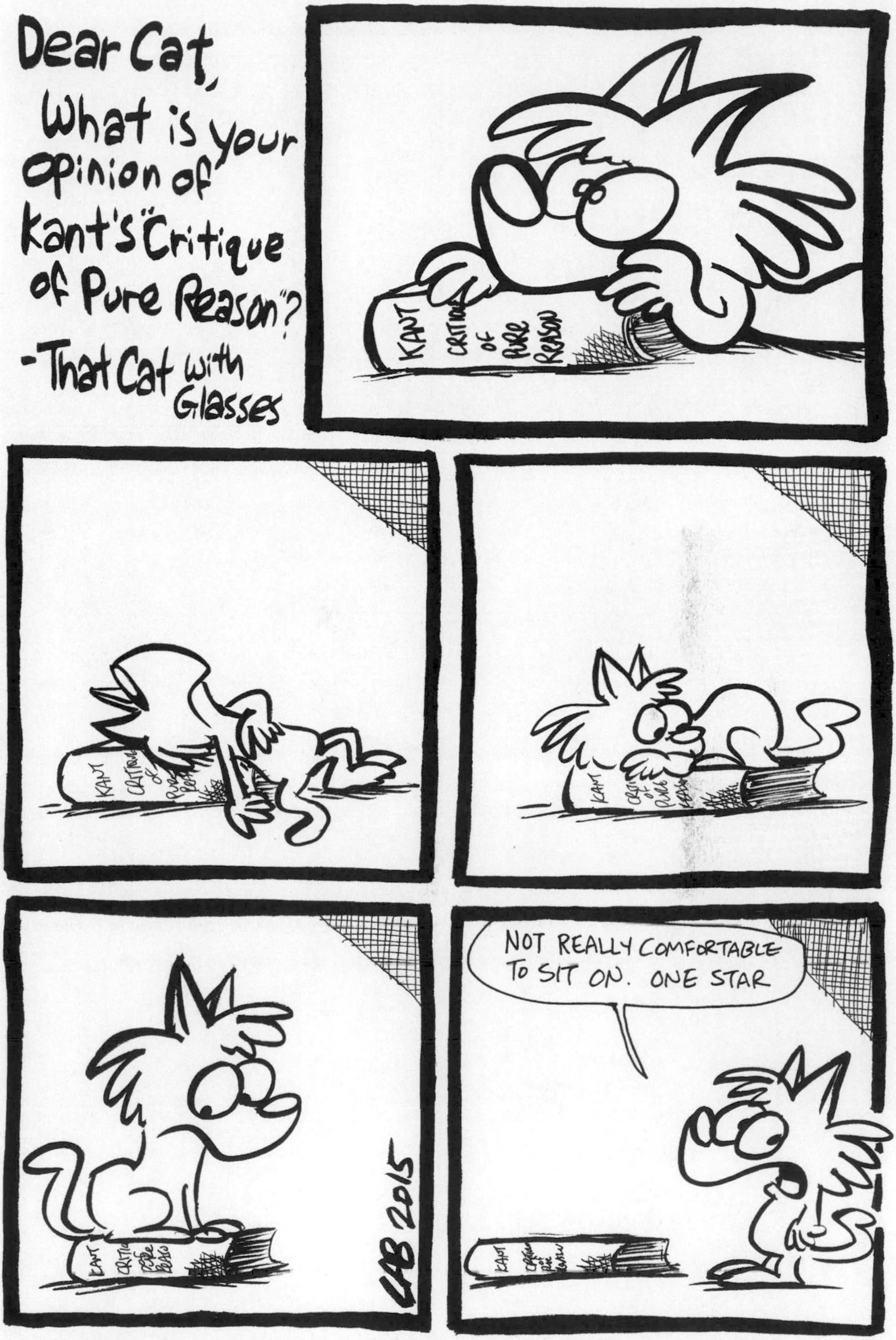
Dear Cat,
What is your opinion of Kant's "Critique of Pure Reason"?
-That Cat with Glasses
KANT CRITIQUE OF PURE REASON
CAB 2015
NOT REALLY COMFORTABLE TO SIT ON. ONE STAR

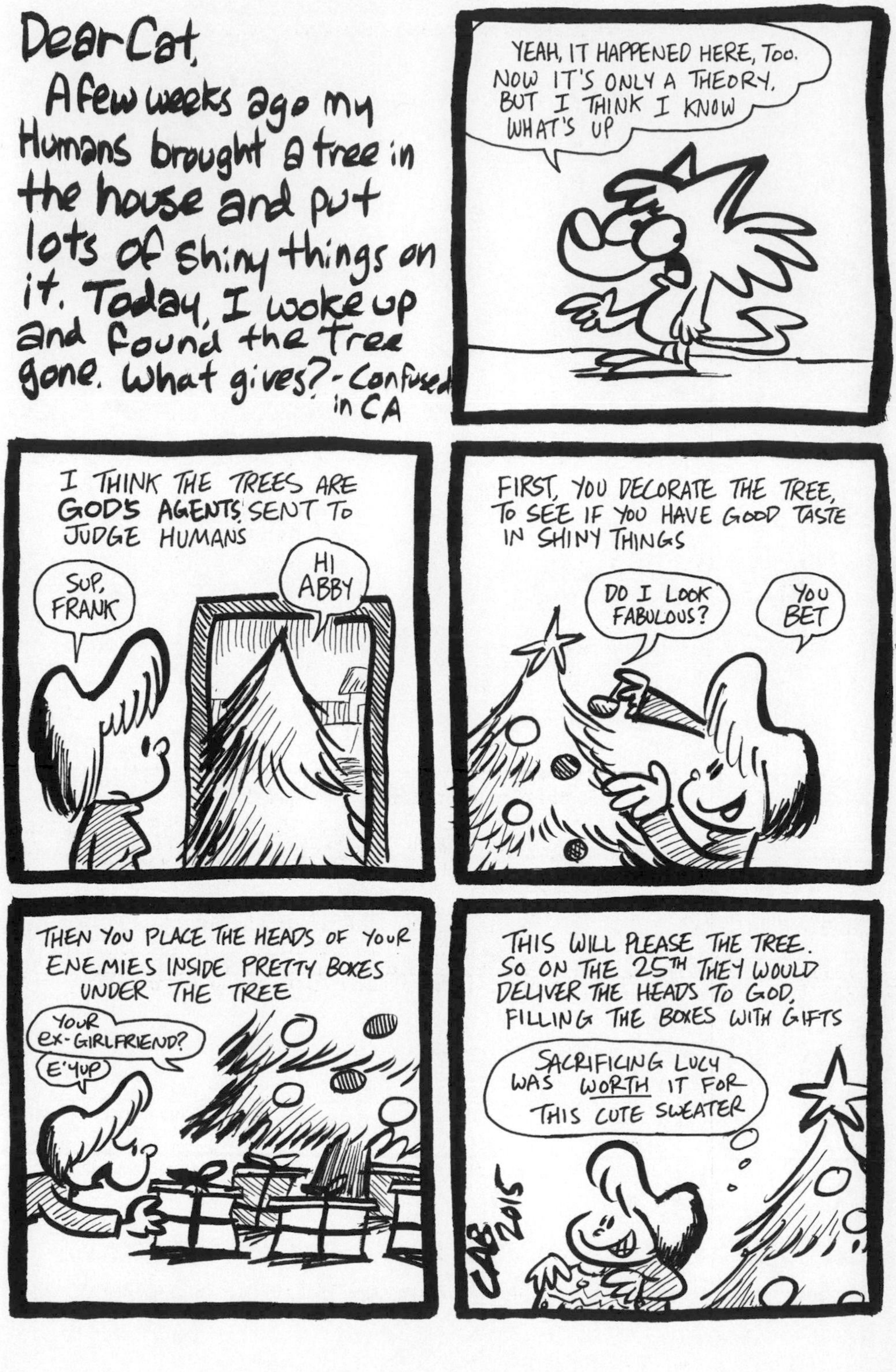

Dear Cat,
A few weeks ago my Humans brought a tree in the house and put lots of shiny things on it. Today, I woke up and found the tree gone. What gives? - Confused in CA
YEAH, IT HAPPENED HERE, TOO. NOW IT'S ONLY A THEORY, BUT I THINK I KNOW WHAT'S UP
I THINK THE TREES ARE GOD'S AGENTS SENT TO JUDGE HUMANS
SUP, FRANK
HI ABBY
FIRST, YOU DECORATE THE TREE, TO SEE IF YOU HAVE GOOD TASTE IN SHINY THINGS
DO I LOOK FABULOUS?
YOU BET
THEN YOU PLACE THE HEADS OF YOUR ENEMIES INSIDE PRETTY BOXES UNDER THE TREE
YOUR EX-GIRLFRIEND?
E'YUP
THIS WILL PLEASE THE TREE. SO ON THE 25TH THEY WOULD DELIVER THE HEADS TO GOD, FILLING THE BOXES WITH GIFTS
SACRIFICING LUCY WAS WORTH IT FOR THIS CUTE SWEATER
CAB 2015

Dear Cat,
If all dogs go to heaven, where do cats go?

-Righteous Ragdoll

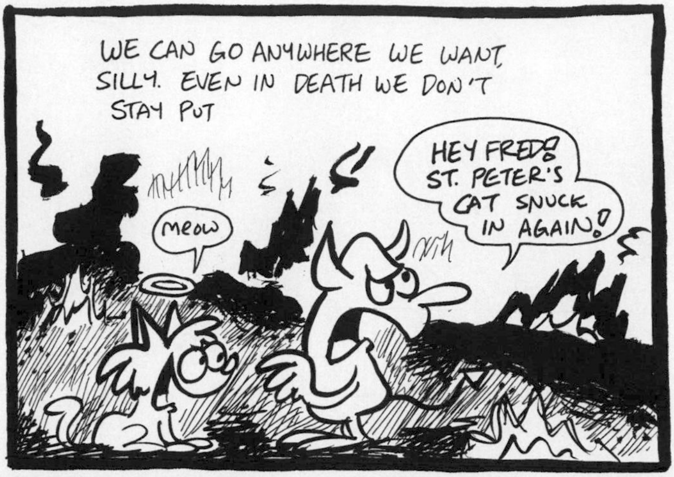
WE CAN GO ANYWHERE WE WANT, SILLY. EVEN IN DEATH WE DON'T STAY PUT
MEOW
HEY FRED! ST. PETER'S CAT SNUCK IN AGAIN!

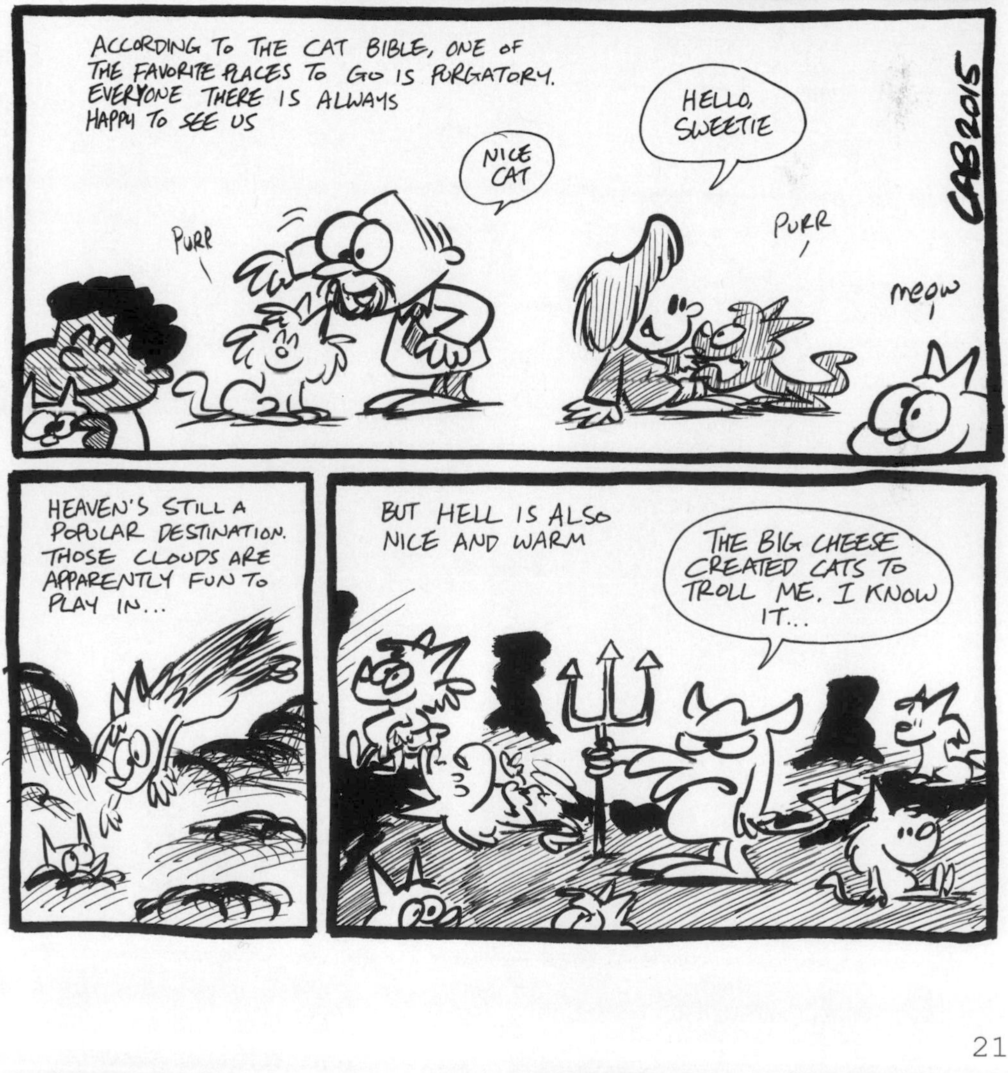
ACCORDING TO THE CAT BIBLE, ONE OF THE FAVORITE PLACES TO GO IS PURGATORY. EVERYONE THERE IS ALWAYS HAPPY TO SEE US
CAB2015
HELLO, SWEETIE
NICE CAT
PURR
PURR
MEOW
HEAVEN'S STILL A POPULAR DESTINATION. THOSE CLOUDS ARE APPARENTLY FUN TO PLAY IN...
BUT HELL IS ALSO NICE AND WARM
THE BIG CHEESE CREATED CATS TO TROLL ME. I KNOW IT...

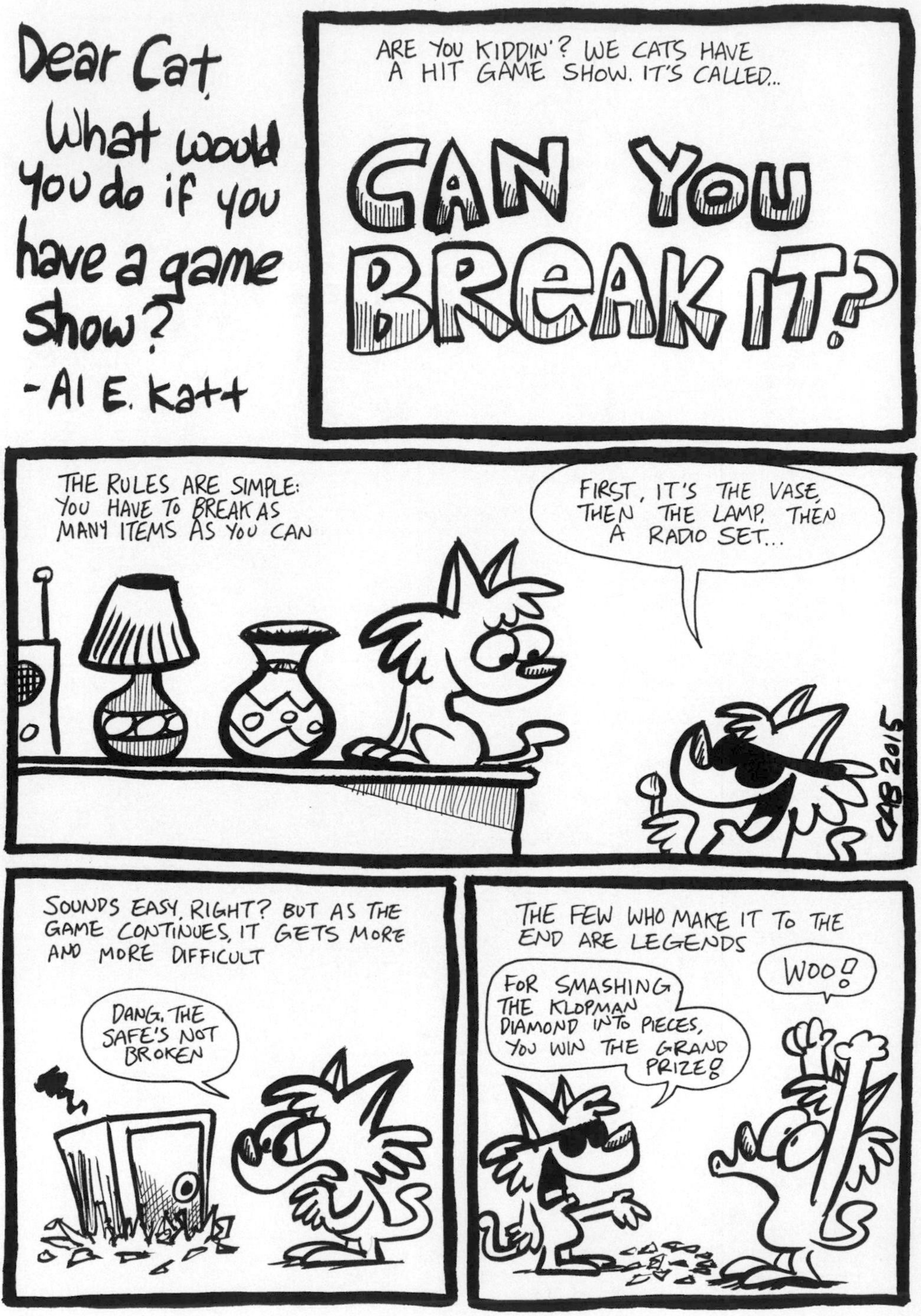
Dear Cat,
What would you do if you have a game show?
-Al E. Katt
ARE YOU KIDDIN'? WE CATS HAVE A HIT GAME SHOW. IT'S CALLED...
CAN YOU BREAK IT?
THE RULES ARE SIMPLE: YOU HAVE TO BREAK AS MANY ITEMS AS YOU CAN
FIRST, IT'S THE VASE, THEN THE LAMP, THEN A RADIO SET...
CAB 2015
SOUNDS EASY, RIGHT? BUT AS THE GAME CONTINUES, IT GETS MORE AND MORE DIFFICULT
DANG. THE SAFE'S NOT BROKEN
THE FEW WHO MAKE IT TO THE END ARE LEGENDS
FOR SMASHING THE KLOPMAN DIAMOND INTO PIECES, YOU WIN THE GRAND PRIZE!
WOO!

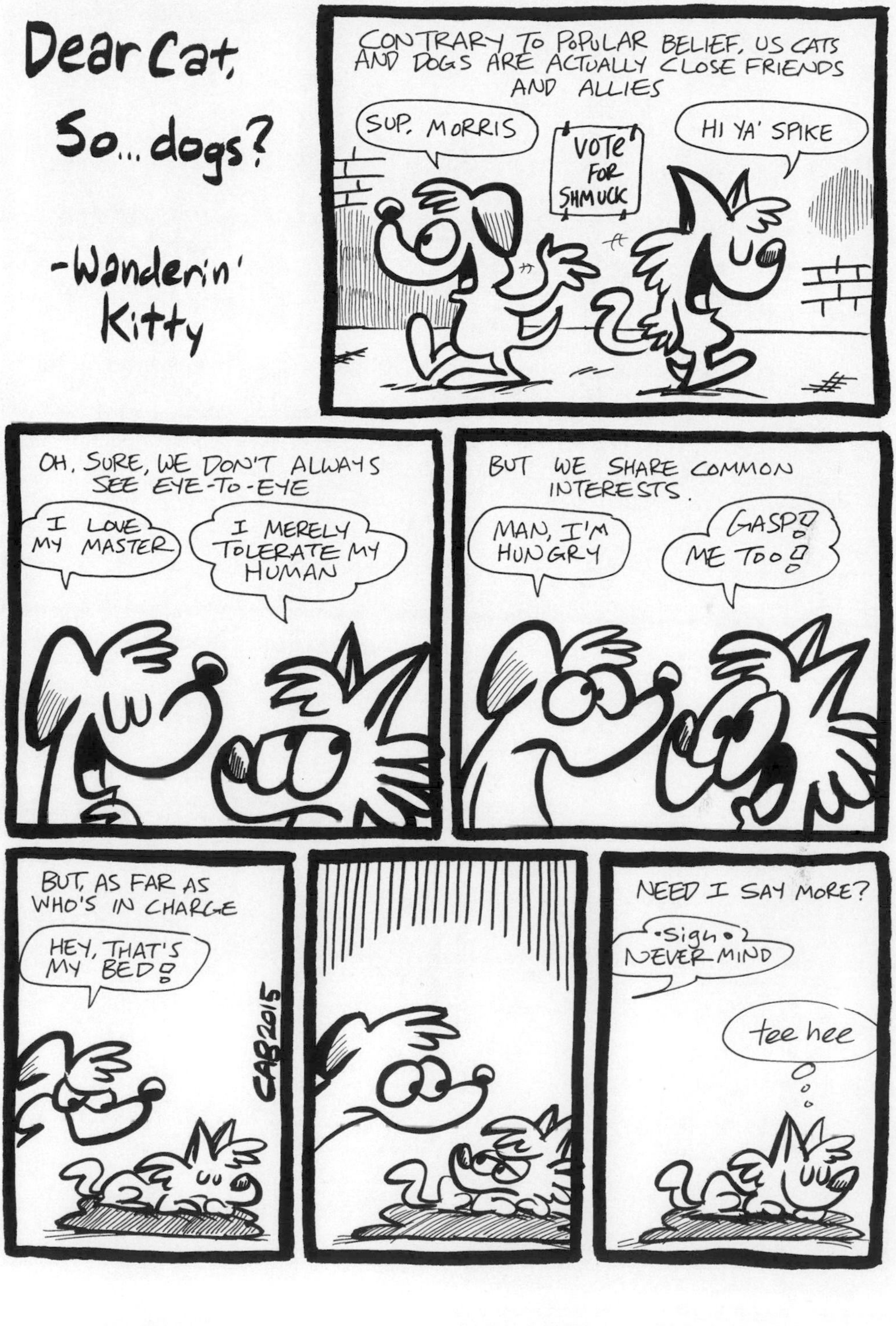
Dear Cat,
So... dogs?
-Wanderin' Kitty
CONTRARY TO POPULAR BELIEF, US CATS AND DOGS ARE ACTUALLY CLOSE FRIENDS AND ALLIES
SUP, MORRIS
VOTE FOR SHMUCK
HI YA' SPIKE
OH, SURE, WE DON'T ALWAYS SEE EYE-TO-EYE
I LOVE MY MASTER
I MERELY TOLERATE MY HUMAN
BUT WE SHARE COMMON INTERESTS.
MAN, I'M HUNGRY
GASP!! ME TOO!!
BUT, AS FAR AS WHO'S IN CHARGE
HEY, THAT'S MY BED!!
CAB2015
NEED I SAY MORE?
•sigh• NEVER MIND
tee hee

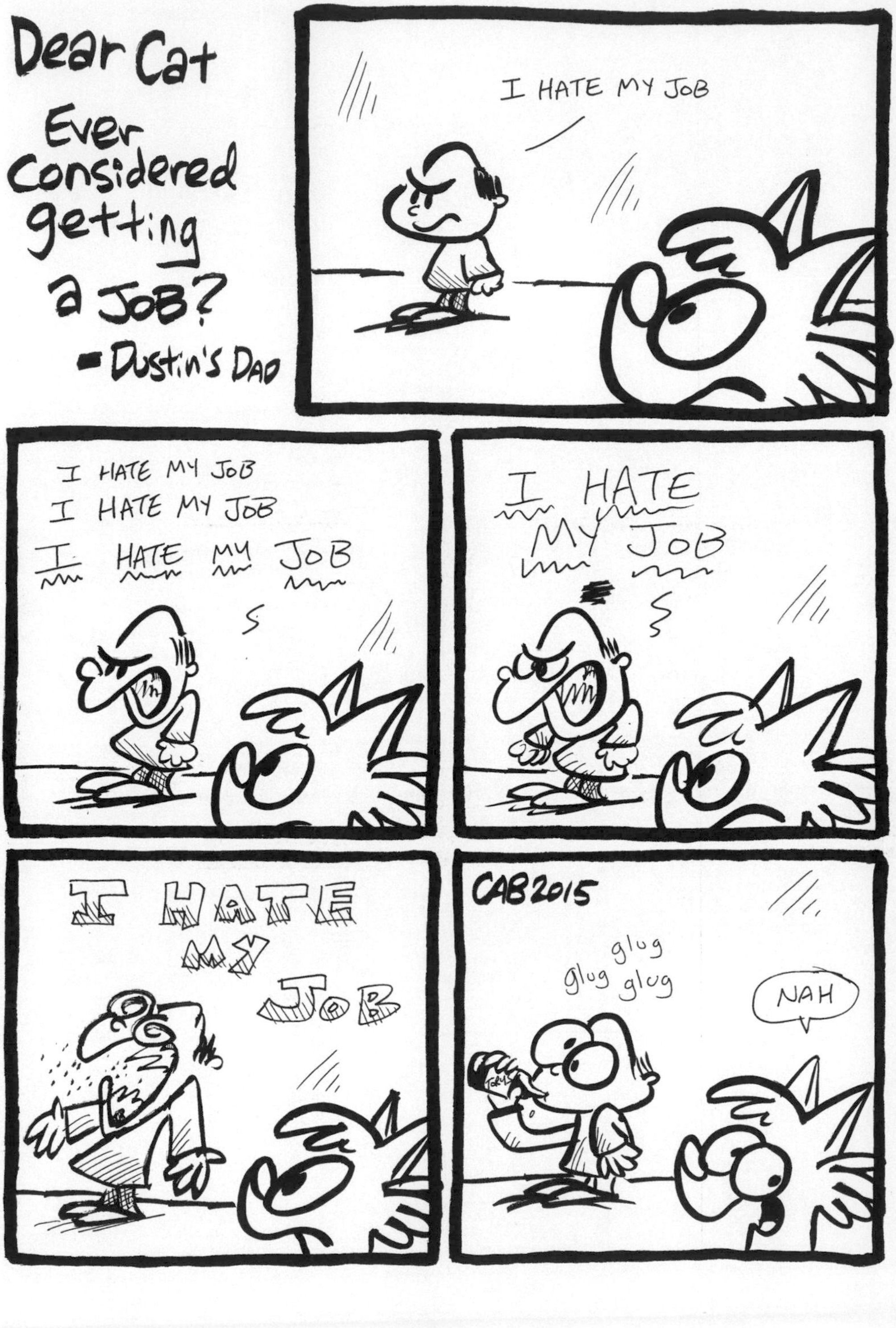
Dear Cat
Ever considered getting a JOB?
- Dustin's Dad
I HATE MY JOB
I HATE MY JOB
I HATE MY JOB
I HATE MY JOB
I HATE MY JOB
I HATE MY JOB
CAB 2015
glug glug glug
NAH

Dear Cat,
Why do you want a door to be opened, only to return shortly after?

It's kinda annoying

- Disgruntled David

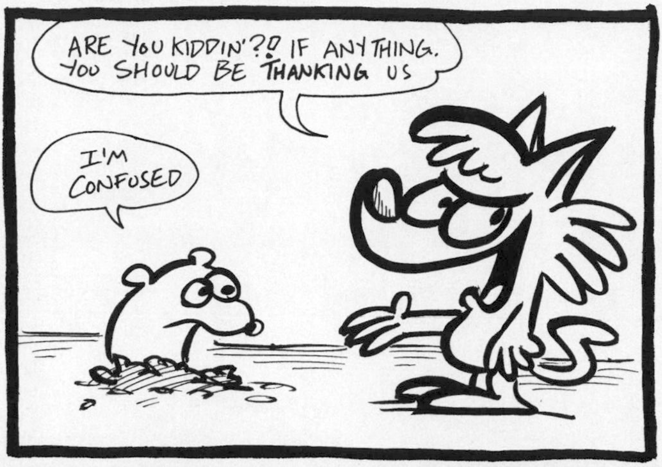
ARE YOU KIDDIN'?!? IF ANYTHING, YOU SHOULD BE THANKING US
I'M CONFUSED

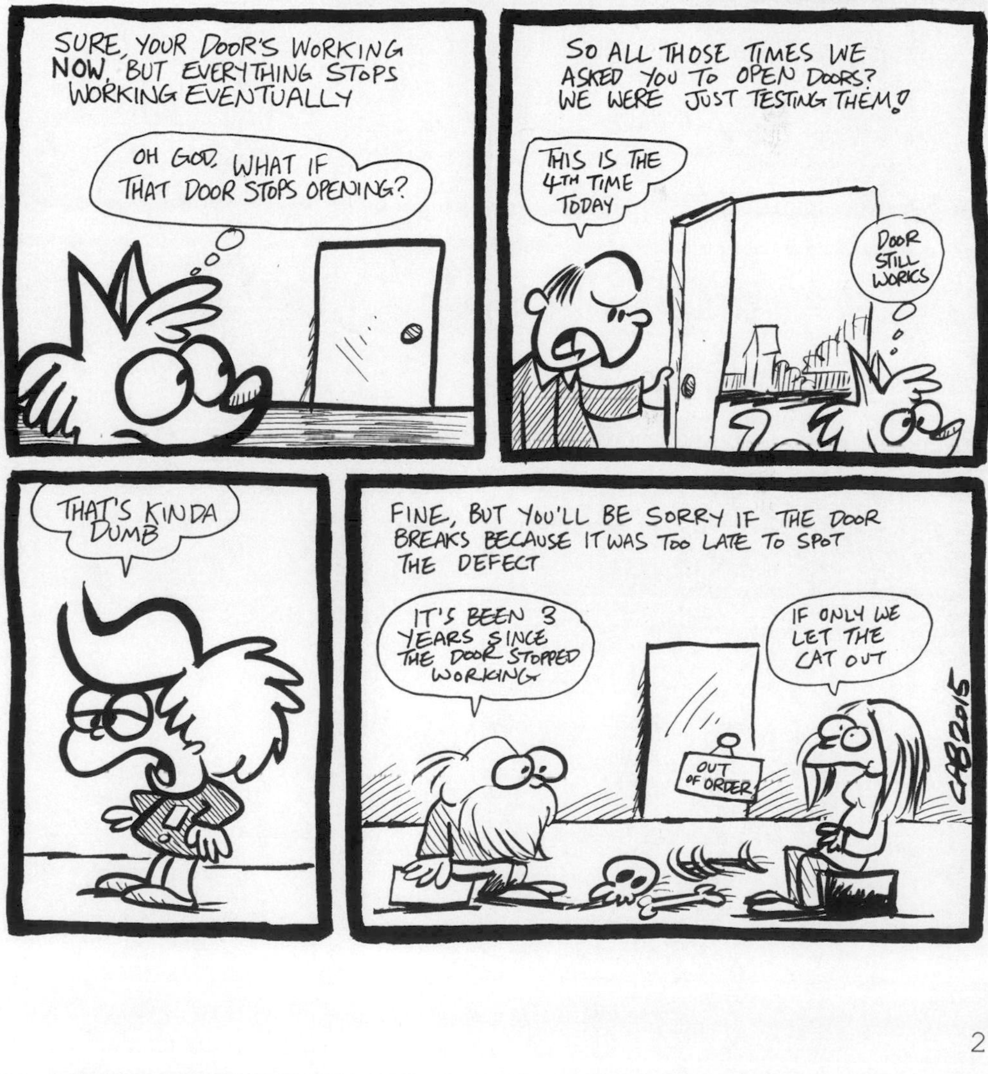
SURE, YOUR DOOR'S WORKING NOW, BUT EVERYTHING STOPS WORKING EVENTUALLY
OH GOD. WHAT IF THAT DOOR STOPS OPENING?
SO ALL THOSE TIMES WE ASKED YOU TO OPEN DOORS? WE WERE JUST TESTING THEM!
THIS IS THE 4TH TIME TODAY
DOOR STILL WORKS
THAT'S KINDA DUMB
FINE, BUT YOU'LL BE SORRY IF THE DOOR BREAKS BECAUSE IT WAS TOO LATE TO SPOT THE DEFECT
IT'S BEEN 3 YEARS SINCE THE DOOR STOPPED WORKING
IF ONLY WE LET THE CAT OUT
OUT OF ORDER
CAB2015

Dear Cat,
Why do you knead on people?
-Wanderin' Kitten

US CATS FANTASIZE ABOUT MAKING BREAD. THE PART WHERE YOU KNEAD BREAD LOOKS SO MUCH FUN
SOOO JEALOUS
FLOUR
MILK
WE TRIED TO MAKE OUR OWN BREAD. BUT WE COULDN'T COMPREHEND FLOUR
HOW DO YOU FLOUR?
FLOUR
CAB 2015
SO WE JUST KNEAD ON YOU GUYS INSTEAD
GOOD 'NUFF
THANKS TO JOEY PLUNK
KNEAD KNEAD
YOU'RE STARTING TO CREEP ME OUT, CAT

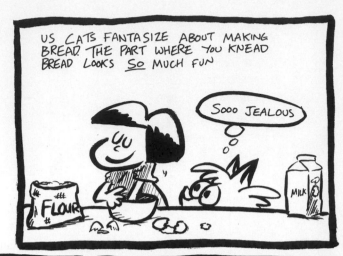

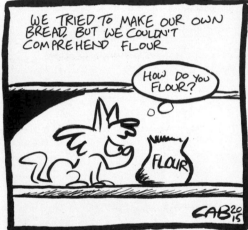

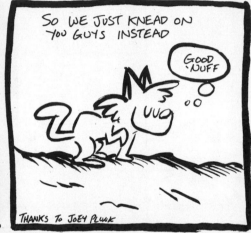

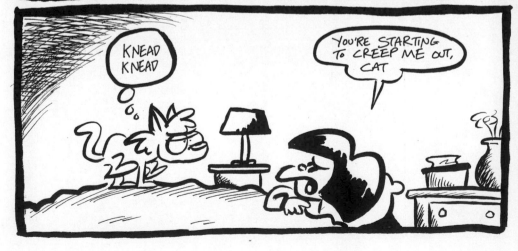

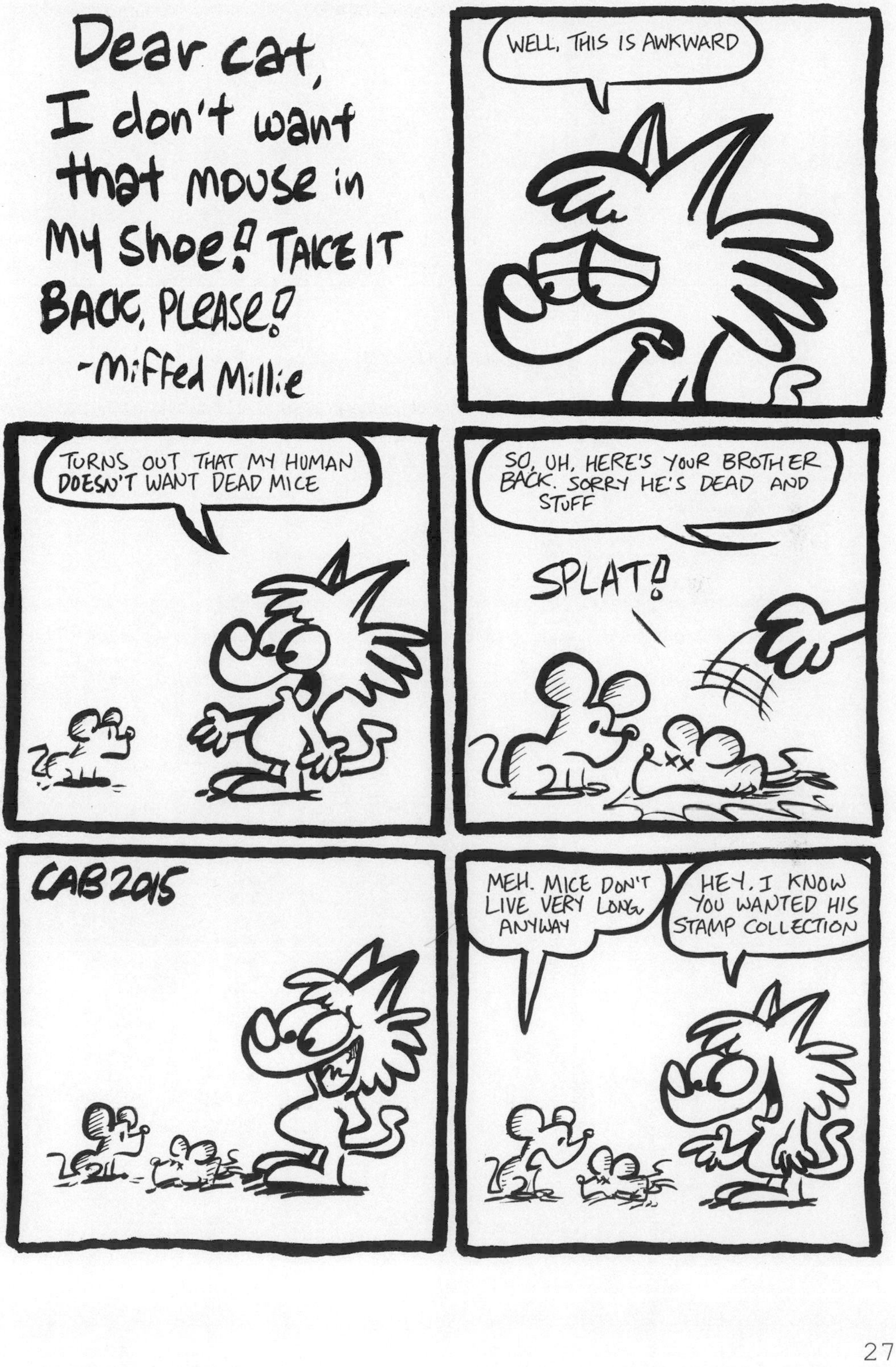
Dear cat,
I don't want that mouse in my shoe!! TAKE IT BACK, PLEASE!!
-Miffed Millie
WELL, THIS IS AWKWARD
TURNS OUT THAT MY HUMAN DOESN'T WANT DEAD MICE
SO, UH, HERE'S YOUR BROTHER BACK. SORRY HE'S DEAD AND STUFF
SPLAT!!
CAB 2015
MEH. MICE DON'T LIVE VERY LONG ANYWAY
HEY, I KNOW YOU WANTED HIS STAMP COLLECTION

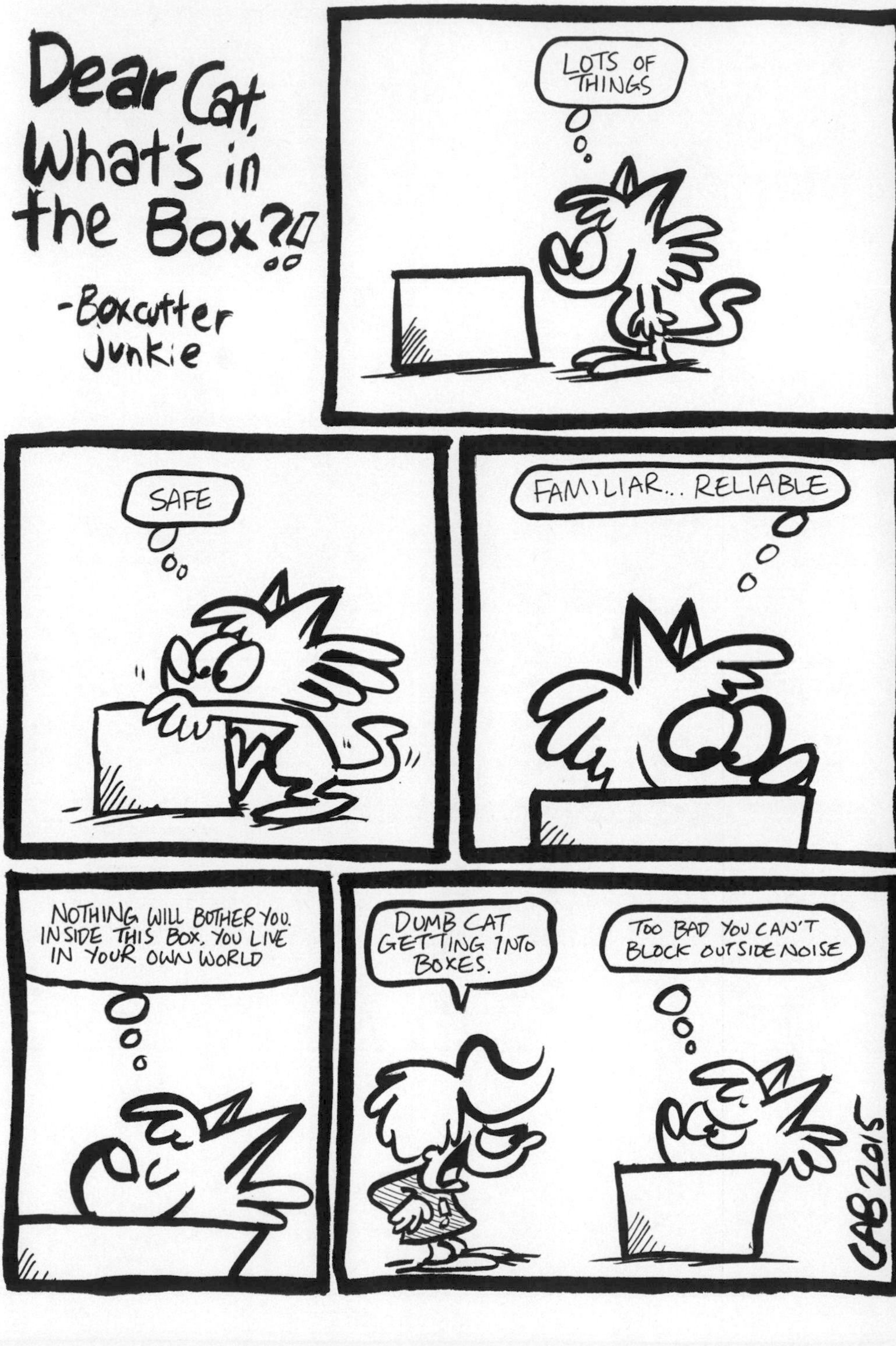
Dear Cat, What's in the Box?!
-Boxcutter Junkie
LOTS OF THINGS
SAFE
FAMILIAR... RELIABLE
NOTHING WILL BOTHER YOU. INSIDE THIS BOX, YOU LIVE IN YOUR OWN WORLD
DUMB CAT GETTING INTO BOXES.
TOO BAD YOU CAN'T BLOCK OUTSIDE NOISE
CAB 2015

DEAR CAT,

WHAT'S WITH THE ~~ATTITUDE~~ CATTITUDE?

-AN EIGHT LEGGED MUSICIAN

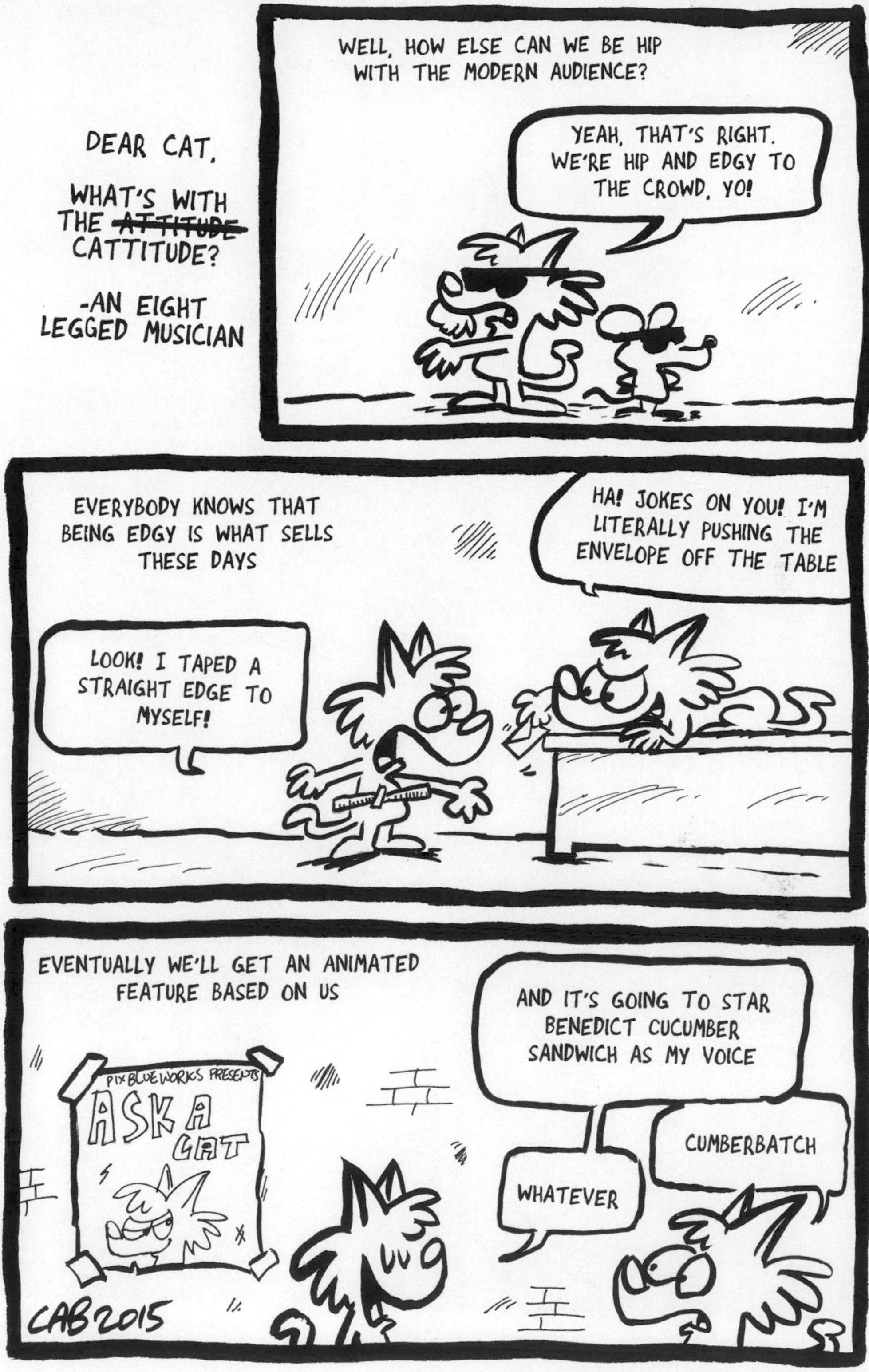
WELL, HOW ELSE CAN WE BE HIP WITH THE MODERN AUDIENCE?
YEAH, THAT'S RIGHT. WE'RE HIP AND EDGY TO THE CROWD, YO!
EVERYBODY KNOWS THAT BEING EDGY IS WHAT SELLS THESE DAYS
HA! JOKES ON YOU! I'M LITERALLY PUSHING THE ENVELOPE OFF THE TABLE
LOOK! I TAPED A STRAIGHT EDGE TO MYSELF!
EVENTUALLY WE'LL GET AN ANIMATED FEATURE BASED ON US
PIXBLUEWORKS PRESENTS
ASK A CAT
AND IT'S GOING TO STAR BENEDICT CUCUMBER SANDWICH AS MY VOICE
CUMBERBATCH
WHATEVER
CAB 2015

DEAR CAT.

WHY DO YOU HATE WATER SO MUCH?

-MAGICAL DOLPHIN

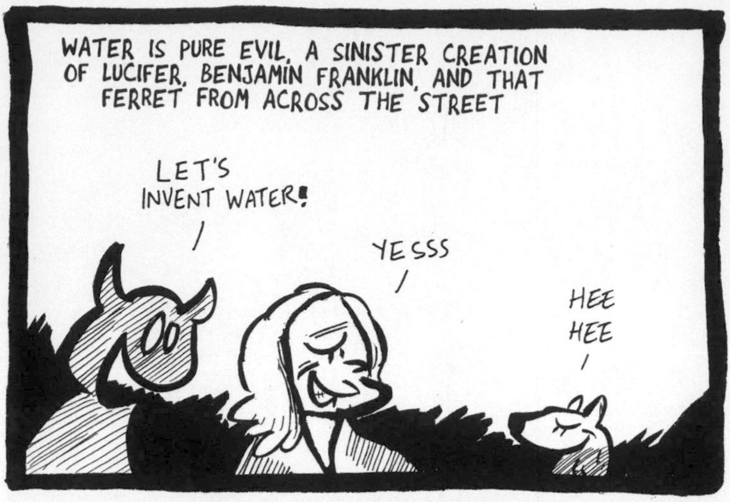
WATER IS PURE EVIL. A SINISTER CREATION OF LUCIFER, BENJAMIN FRANKLIN, AND THAT FERRET FROM ACROSS THE STREET
LET'S INVENT WATER!
YESSS
HEE HEE

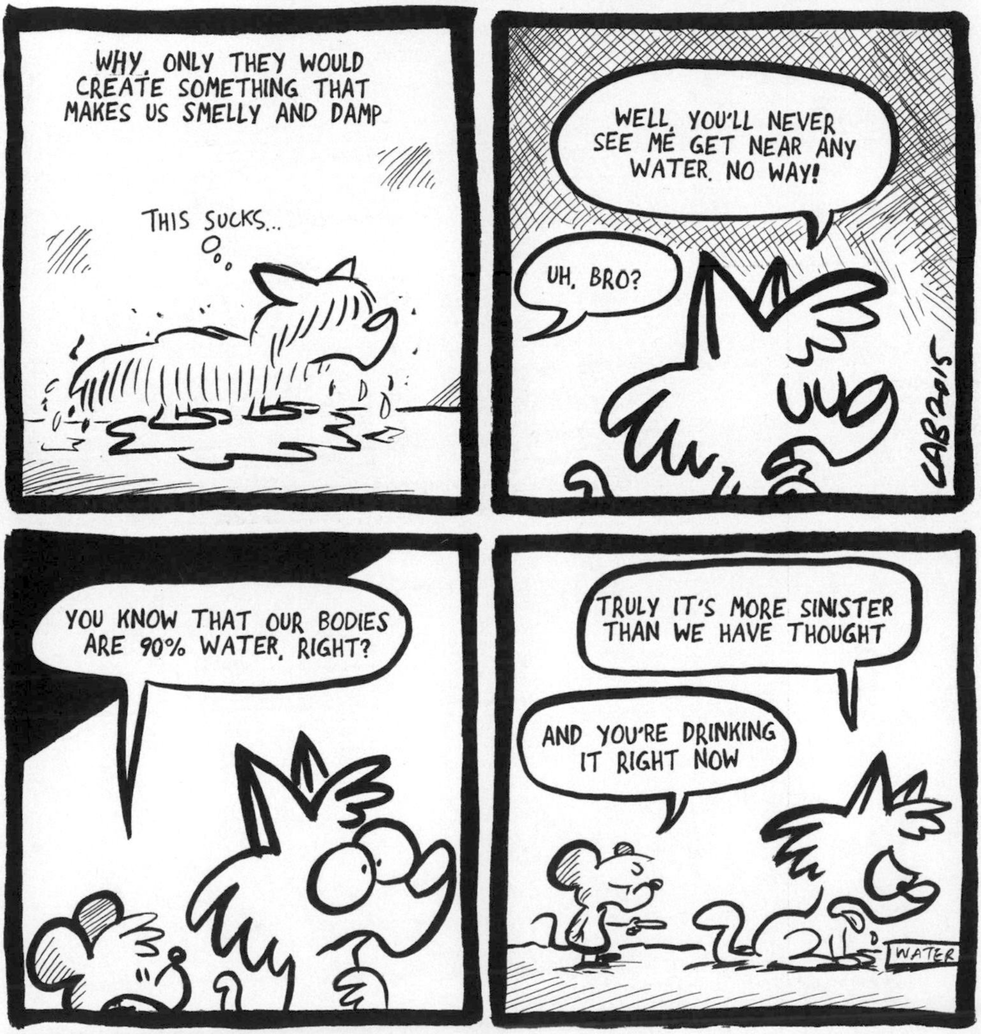
WHY, ONLY THEY WOULD CREATE SOMETHING THAT MAKES US SMELLY AND DAMP
THIS SUCKS...
WELL, YOU'LL NEVER SEE ME GET NEAR ANY WATER. NO WAY!
UH, BRO?
CAB2015
YOU KNOW THAT OUR BODIES ARE 90% WATER, RIGHT?
TRULY IT'S MORE SINISTER THAN WE HAVE THOUGHT
AND YOU'RE DRINKING IT RIGHT NOW
WATER

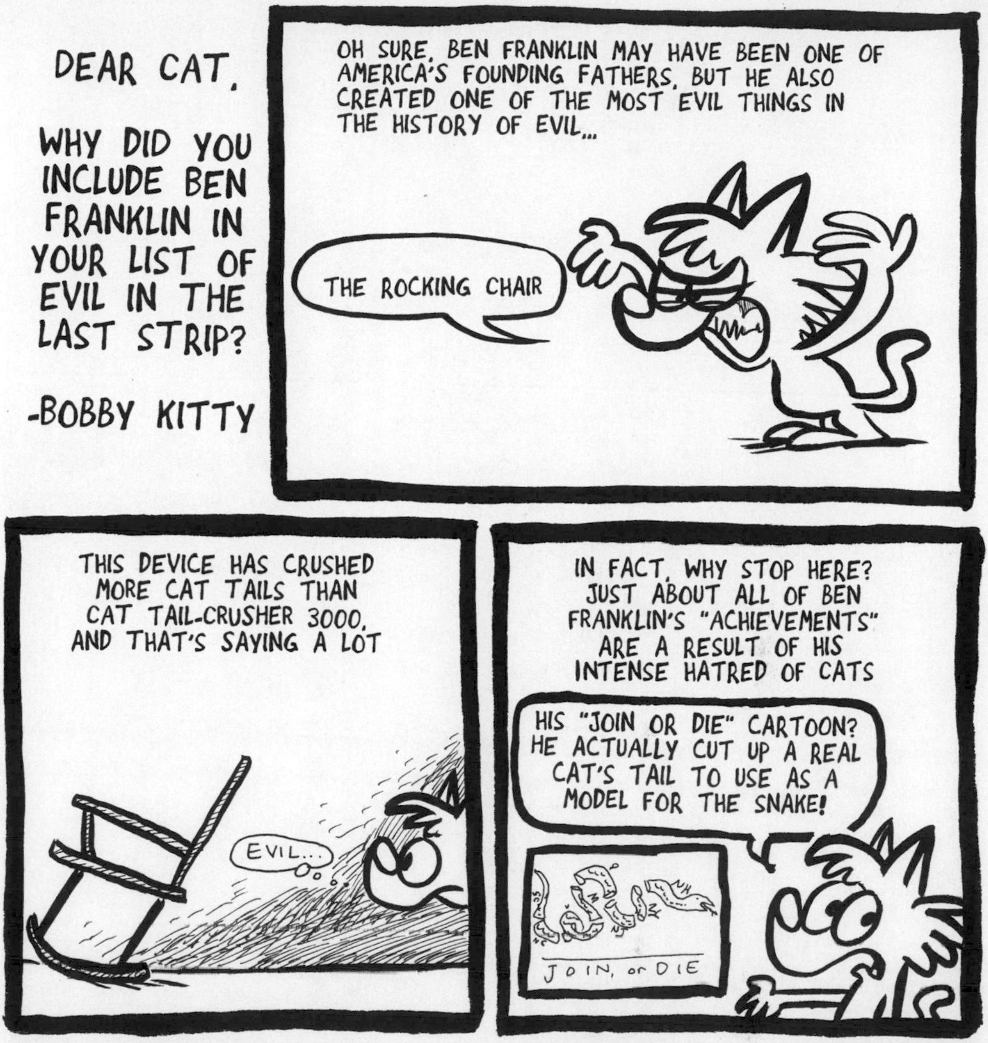
DEAR CAT,
WHY DID YOU INCLUDE BEN FRANKLIN IN YOUR LIST OF EVIL IN THE LAST STRIP?
-BOBBY KITTY
OH SURE, BEN FRANKLIN MAY HAVE BEEN ONE OF AMERICA'S FOUNDING FATHERS, BUT HE ALSO CREATED ONE OF THE MOST EVIL THINGS IN THE HISTORY OF EVIL...
THE ROCKING CHAIR
THIS DEVICE HAS CRUSHED MORE CAT TAILS THAN CAT TAIL-CRUSHER 3000, AND THAT'S SAYING A LOT
EVIL...
IN FACT, WHY STOP HERE? JUST ABOUT ALL OF BEN FRANKLIN'S "ACHIEVEMENTS" ARE A RESULT OF HIS INTENSE HATRED OF CATS
HIS "JOIN OR DIE" CARTOON? HE ACTUALLY CUT UP A REAL CAT'S TAIL TO USE AS A MODEL FOR THE SNAKE!
JOIN, or DIE
WELL, WE'RE NOT GOING TO PUT UP WITH HIS ANTI-CAT LEGACY ANYMORE!
CAB2015
WHO SHREDDED MY $100 BILLS!?
JUSTICE...
UUG

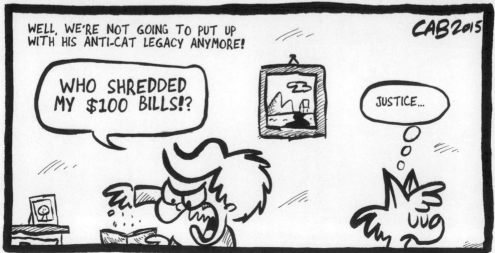

DEAR CAT,

WHY DO YOU ASK FOR BELLY RUBS WHEN YOU CLEARLY DON'T WANT THEM?

- MR. RUB OUT

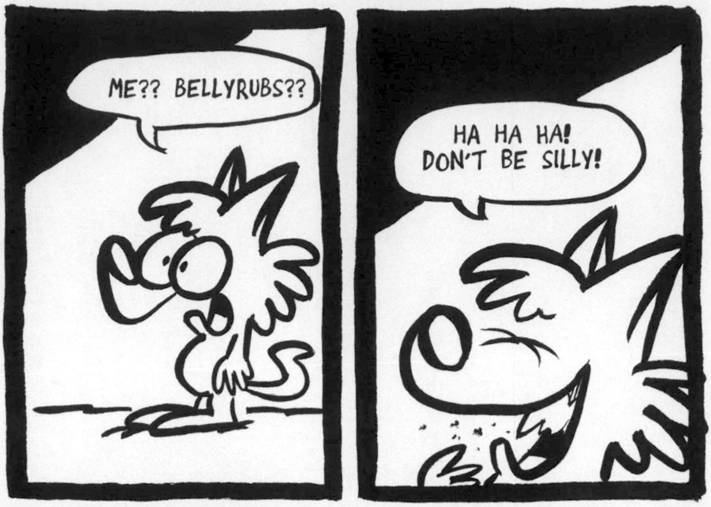

ME?? BELLYRUBS??
HA HA HA! DON'T BE SILLY!

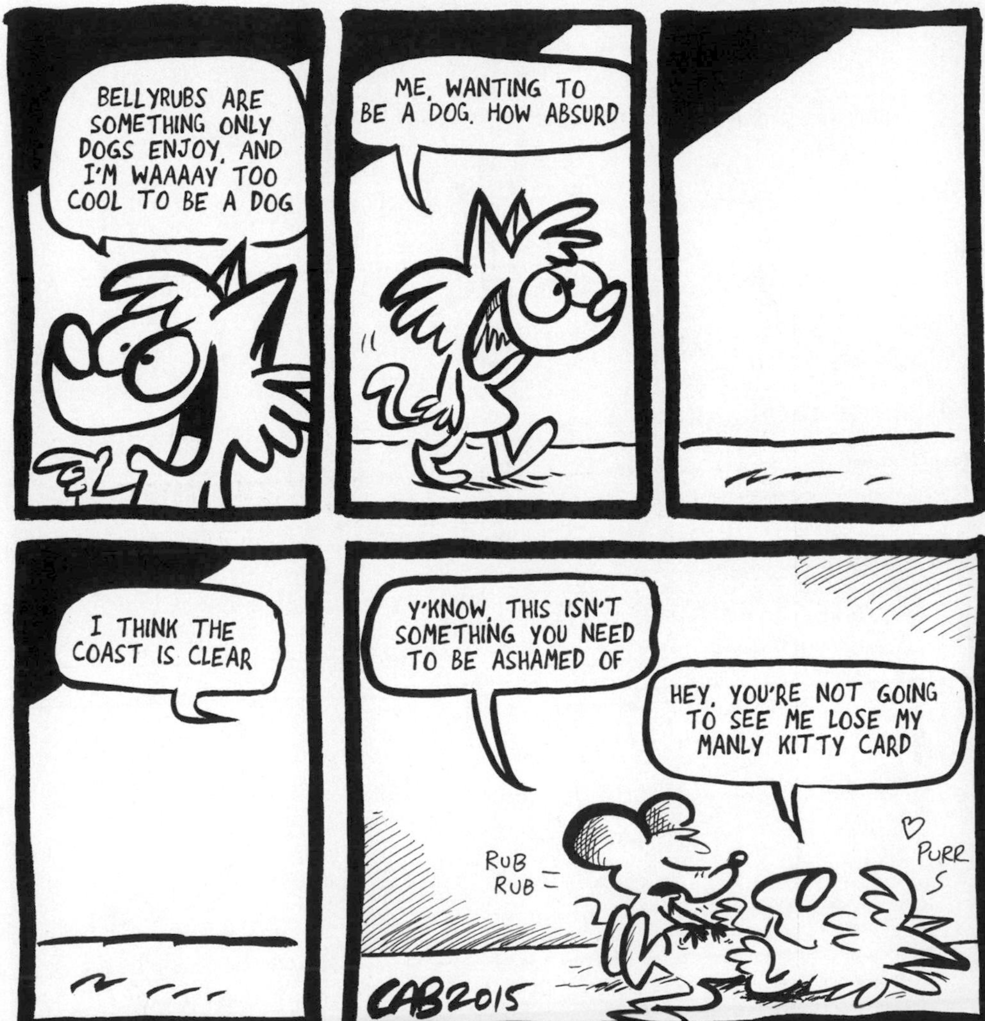

BELLYRUBS ARE SOMETHING ONLY DOGS ENJOY, AND I'M WAAAAY TOO COOL TO BE A DOG
ME, WANTING TO BE A DOG. HOW ABSURD
I THINK THE COAST IS CLEAR
Y'KNOW, THIS ISN'T SOMETHING YOU NEED TO BE ASHAMED OF
HEY, YOU'RE NOT GOING TO SEE ME LOSE MY MANLY KITTY CARD
RUB RUB
PURR
CAB2015

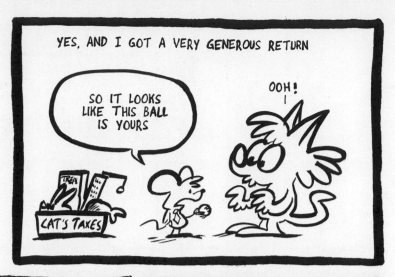

DEAR CAT,

DID YOU FILE YOUR TAXES THIS YEAR?

-MR. L. SHARK

YES, AND I GOT A VERY GENEROUS RETURN
SO IT LOOKS LIKE THIS BALL IS YOURS
OOH!
CAT'S TAXES

I LOVE THESE BALLS. THEY'RE JUST SO...ROUND
MAJESTIC...
YOU CAN JUST BAP THEM AROUND ENDLESSLY. THEY'RE SO MUCH FUN
BAP
BINK
WATER
BONK
BUP
TILT
BONK
ALSO...
CAB2015
TRIP!
AUGH!
IT'S FUN WITH PEOPLE, TOO
AND ANOTHER POINT TO THE BALL
OUCH
OOF
EEK!
AUGH!

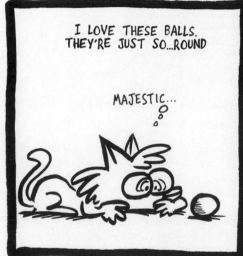

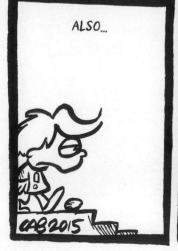

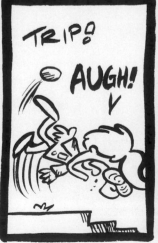

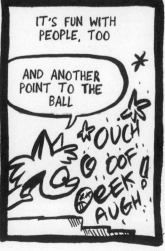

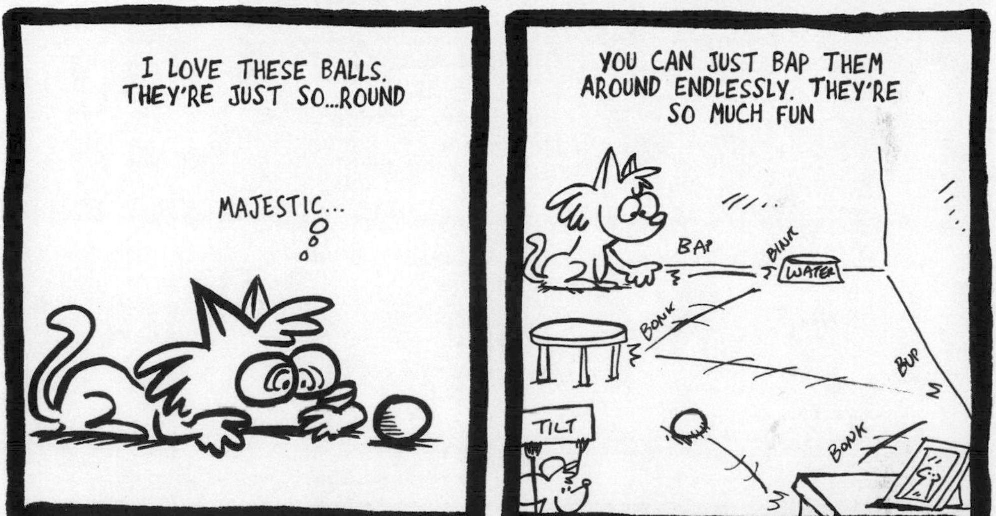

DEAR CAT,

YOU GET SO MANY QUESTIONS, HOW DO YOU FIND TIME TO ANSWER THEM ALL?

-MR. SOMECAT

HERE'S OUR SECRET: WE'RE ACTUALLY TWO CATS FILLING IN FOR EACH OTHER DURING SHIFTS!

ALL YOURS!

ONE OF US WOULD ANSWER QUESTIONS, WHILE ANOTHER EATS AND SLEEP

DEAR CAT, HOW DO YOU TYPE WITH MITTENS... WHAT IS THIS?!

CAT #2

CAB 2015

SOMETIMES, THOUGH, WE'RE BOTH UNAVAILABLE AT THE SAME TIME

YES...

THAT'S WHEN OUR MOUSE FRIEND COMES IN

THE BEST PART IS I GET TO JUMP ON KEYBOARDS. WEEEEE!

DEAR CAT,

DO YOU THINK YOU'D BE A GOOD SUPERHERO?

-MR. CALVED

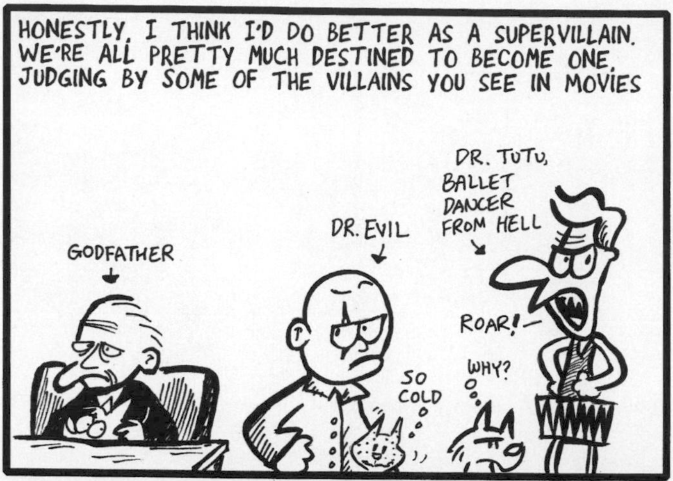
HONESTLY, I THINK I'D DO BETTER AS A SUPERVILLAIN. WE'RE ALL PRETTY MUCH DESTINED TO BECOME ONE, JUDGING BY SOME OF THE VILLAINS YOU SEE IN MOVIES
GODFATHER
DR. EVIL
DR. TUTU, BALLET DANCER FROM HELL
ROAR!
SO COLD
WHY?

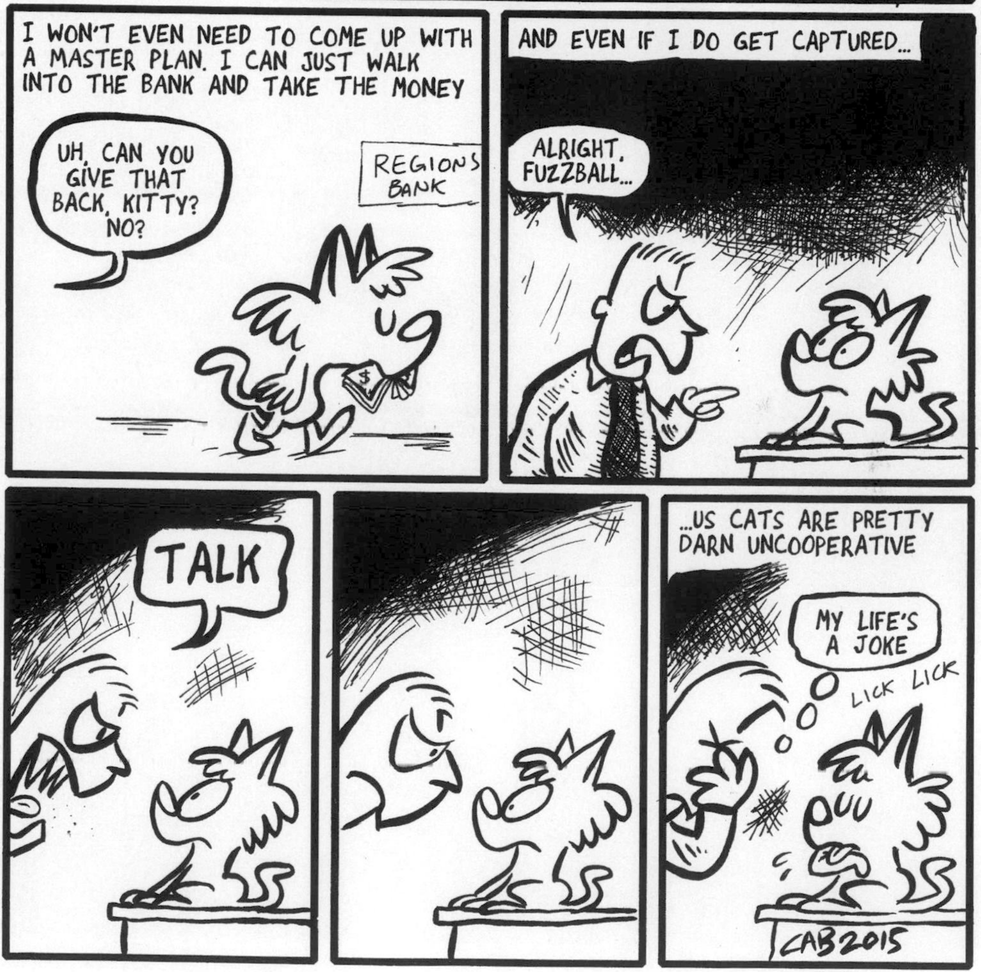
I WON'T EVEN NEED TO COME UP WITH A MASTER PLAN. I CAN JUST WALK INTO THE BANK AND TAKE THE MONEY
UH, CAN YOU GIVE THAT BACK, KITTY? NO?
REGIONS BANK
AND EVEN IF I DO GET CAPTURED...
ALRIGHT, FUZZBALL...
TALK
...US CATS ARE PRETTY DARN UNCOOPERATIVE
MY LIFE'S A JOKE
LICK LICK
CAB 2015

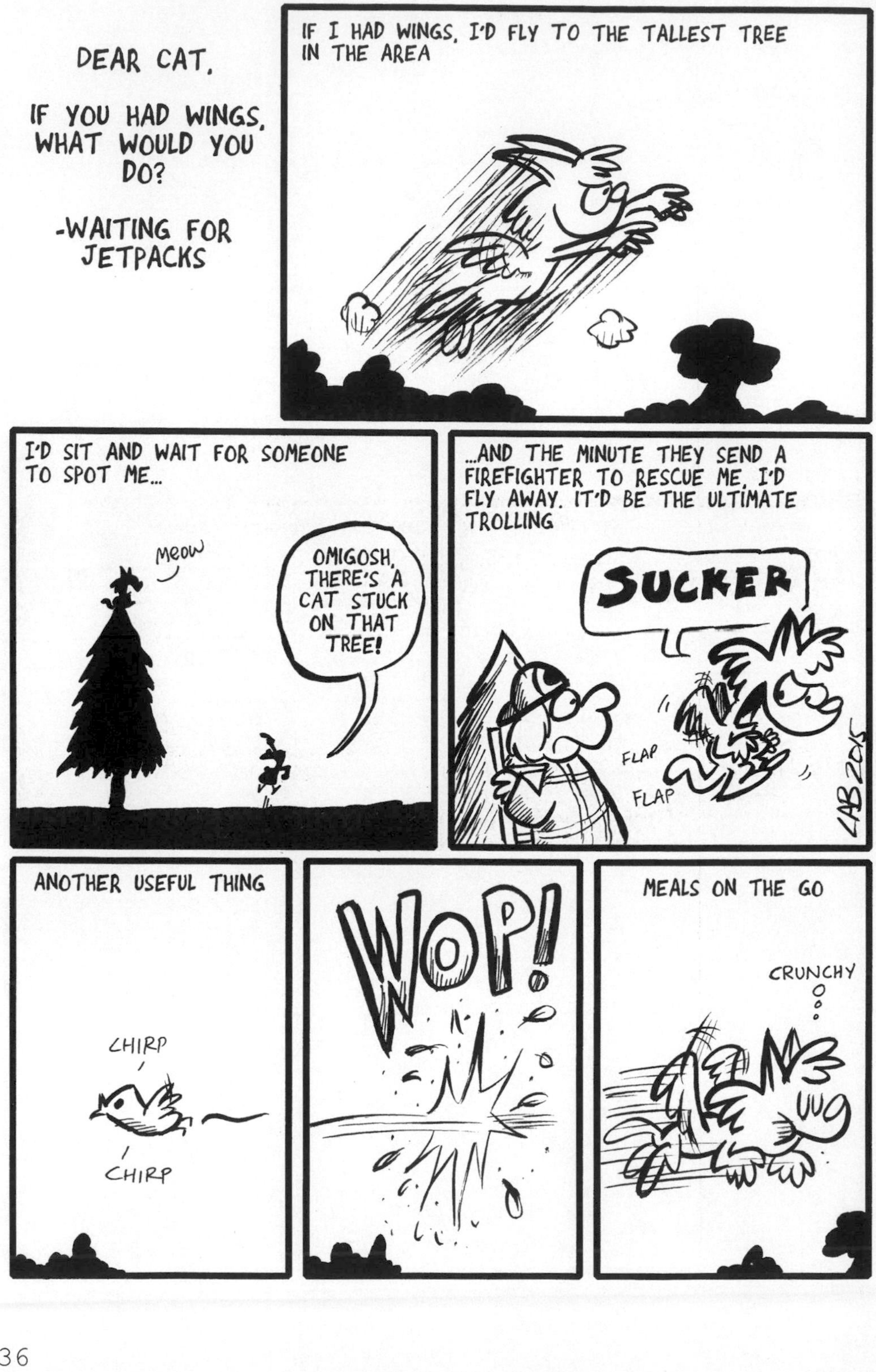
DEAR CAT,
IF YOU HAD WINGS, WHAT WOULD YOU DO?
-WAITING FOR JETPACKS
IF I HAD WINGS, I'D FLY TO THE TALLEST TREE IN THE AREA
I'D SIT AND WAIT FOR SOMEONE TO SPOT ME...
MEOW
OMIGOSH, THERE'S A CAT STUCK ON THAT TREE!
...AND THE MINUTE THEY SEND A FIREFIGHTER TO RESCUE ME, I'D FLY AWAY. IT'D BE THE ULTIMATE TROLLING
SUCKER
FLAP
FLAP
LAB 2015
ANOTHER USEFUL THING
CHIRP
CHIRP
WOP!
MEALS ON THE GO
CRUNCHY

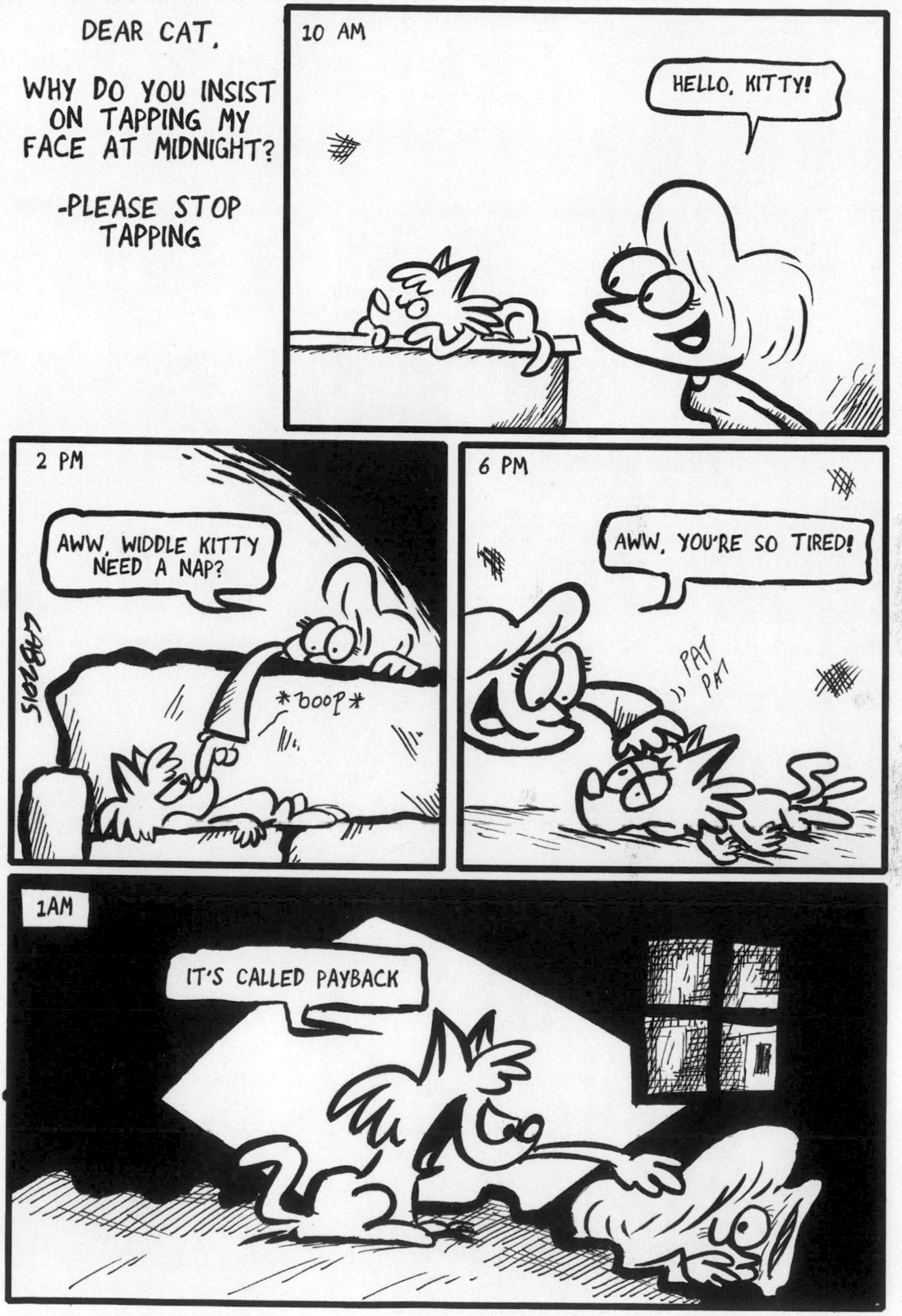
DEAR CAT,
WHY DO YOU INSIST ON TAPPING MY FACE AT MIDNIGHT?
-PLEASE STOP TAPPING
10 AM
HELLO, KITTY!
2 PM
AWW, WIDDLE KITTY NEED A NAP?
BOOP
6 PM
AWW, YOU'RE SO TIRED!
PAT PAT
1AM
IT'S CALLED PAYBACK

DEAR CAT,

WHAT ACTUALLY HAPPENED TO SCHRODINGER'S CAT?

-OUT OF THE BOX

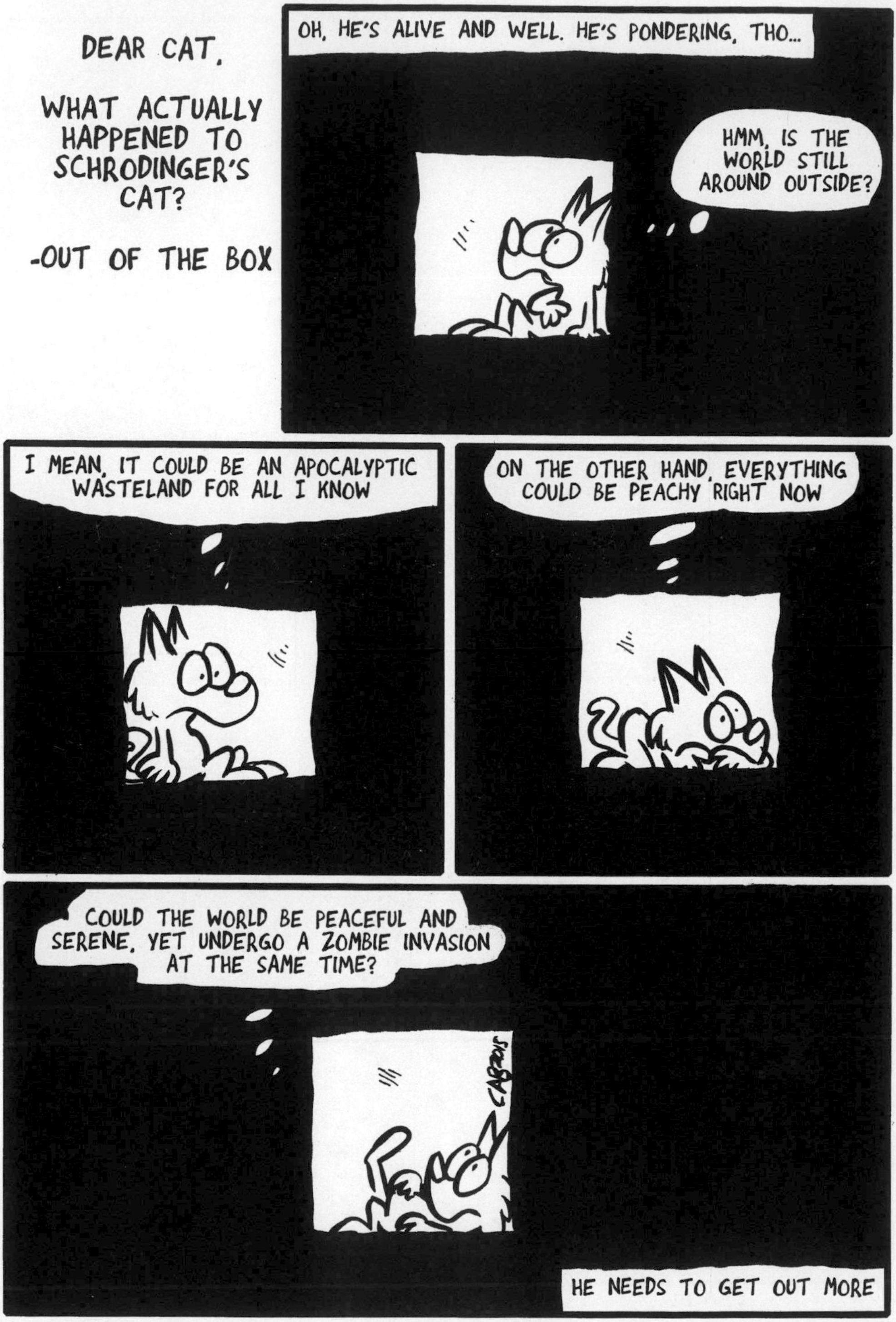
OH, HE'S ALIVE AND WELL. HE'S PONDERING, THO...
HMM, IS THE WORLD STILL AROUND OUTSIDE?
I MEAN, IT COULD BE AN APOCALYPTIC WASTELAND FOR ALL I KNOW
ON THE OTHER HAND, EVERYTHING COULD BE PEACHY RIGHT NOW
COULD THE WORLD BE PEACEFUL AND SERENE, YET UNDERGO A ZOMBIE INVASION AT THE SAME TIME?
HE NEEDS TO GET OUT MORE

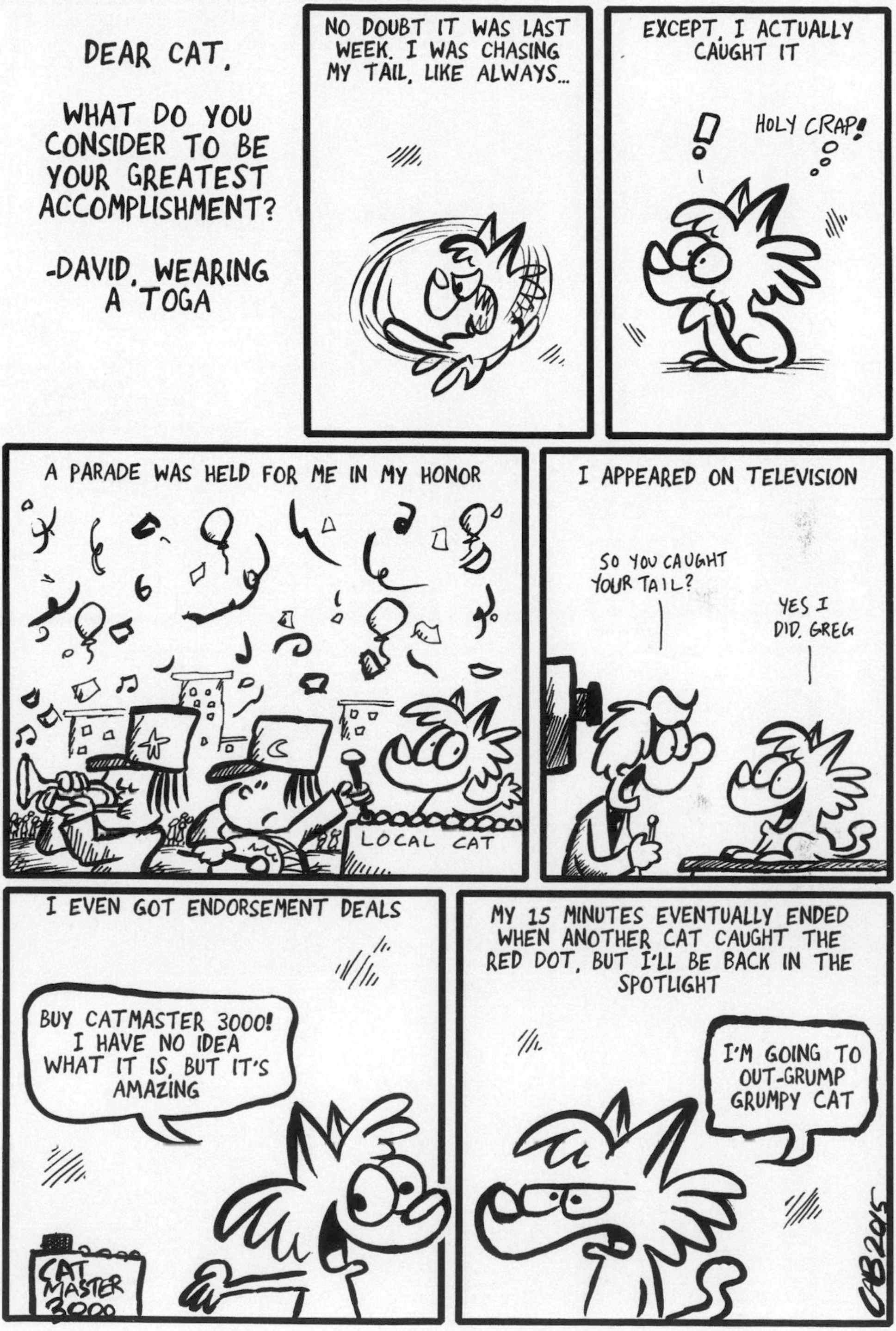
DEAR CAT,
WHAT DO YOU CONSIDER TO BE YOUR GREATEST ACCOMPLISHMENT?
-DAVID, WEARING A TOGA
NO DOUBT IT WAS LAST WEEK. I WAS CHASING MY TAIL, LIKE ALWAYS...
EXCEPT, I ACTUALLY CAUGHT IT
!
HOLY CRAP!
A PARADE WAS HELD FOR ME IN MY HONOR
LOCAL CAT
I APPEARED ON TELEVISION
SO YOU CAUGHT YOUR TAIL?
YES I DID, GREG
I EVEN GOT ENDORSEMENT DEALS
BUY CATMASTER 3000! I HAVE NO IDEA WHAT IT IS, BUT IT'S AMAZING
CAT MASTER 3000
MY 15 MINUTES EVENTUALLY ENDED WHEN ANOTHER CAT CAUGHT THE RED DOT, BUT I'LL BE BACK IN THE SPOTLIGHT
I'M GOING TO OUT-GRUMP GRUMPY CAT
CAB 2015

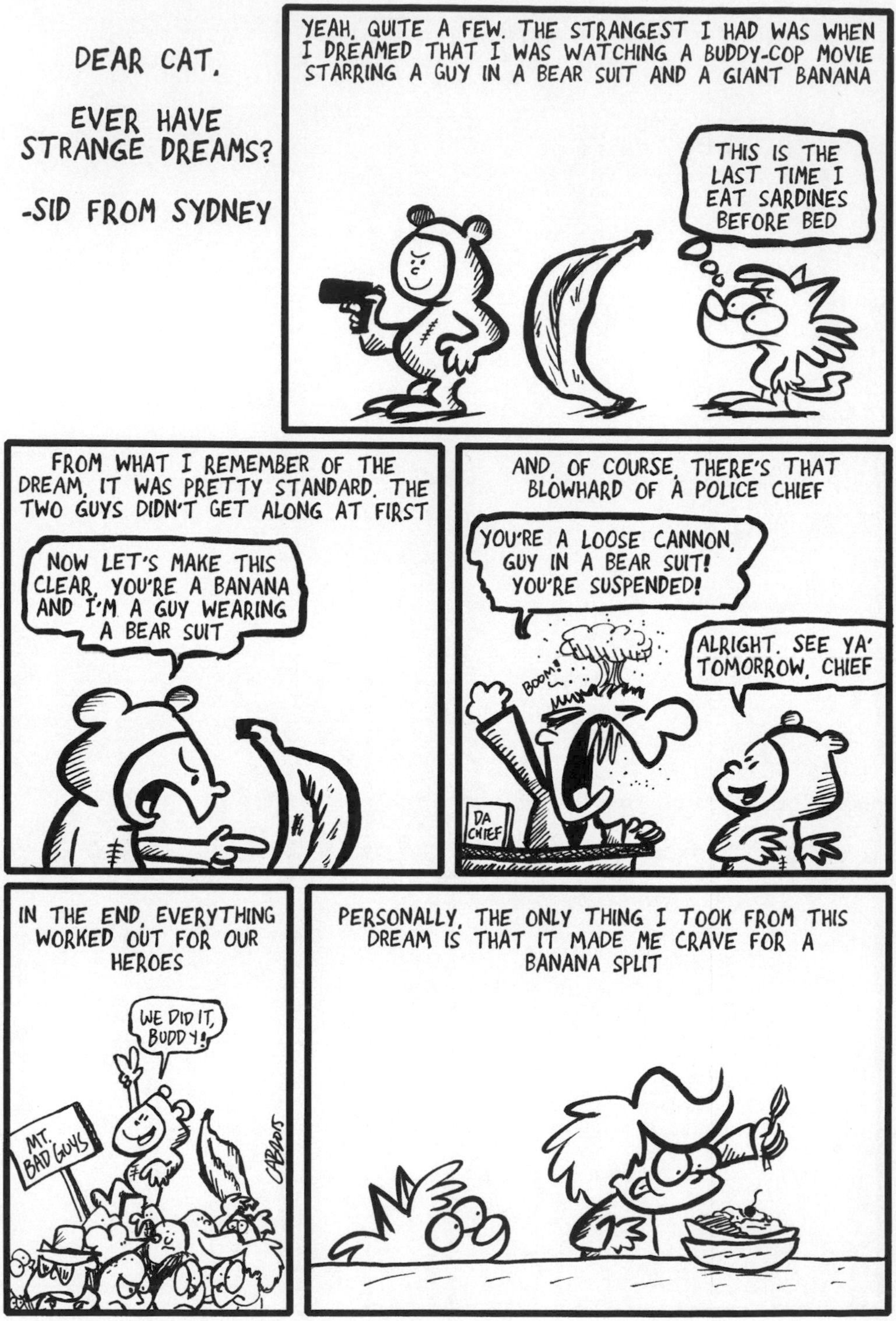
DEAR CAT,
EVER HAVE STRANGE DREAMS?
-SID FROM SYDNEY
YEAH, QUITE A FEW. THE STRANGEST I HAD WAS WHEN I DREAMED THAT I WAS WATCHING A BUDDY-COP MOVIE STARRING A GUY IN A BEAR SUIT AND A GIANT BANANA
THIS IS THE LAST TIME I EAT SARDINES BEFORE BED
FROM WHAT I REMEMBER OF THE DREAM, IT WAS PRETTY STANDARD. THE TWO GUYS DIDN'T GET ALONG AT FIRST
NOW LET'S MAKE THIS CLEAR, YOU'RE A BANANA AND I'M A GUY WEARING A BEAR SUIT
AND, OF COURSE, THERE'S THAT BLOWHARD OF A POLICE CHIEF
YOU'RE A LOOSE CANNON, GUY IN A BEAR SUIT! YOU'RE SUSPENDED!
BOOM!
DA CHIEF
ALRIGHT. SEE YA' TOMORROW, CHIEF
IN THE END, EVERYTHING WORKED OUT FOR OUR HEROES
WE DID IT, BUDDY!
MT. BAD GUYS
PERSONALLY, THE ONLY THING I TOOK FROM THIS DREAM IS THAT IT MADE ME CRAVE FOR A BANANA SPLIT

DEAR CAT.

WHAT WAS THE WORST RIDE YOU'VE EVER BEEN ON?

-A WACKY RACER

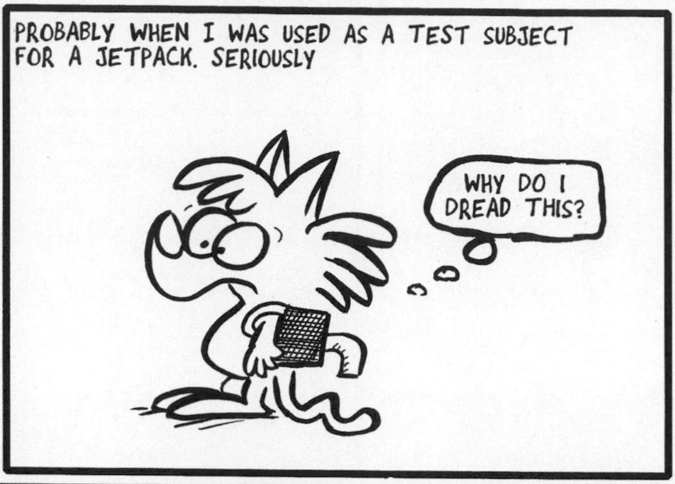
PROBABLY WHEN I WAS USED AS A TEST SUBJECT FOR A JETPACK. SERIOUSLY
WHY DO I DREAD THIS?

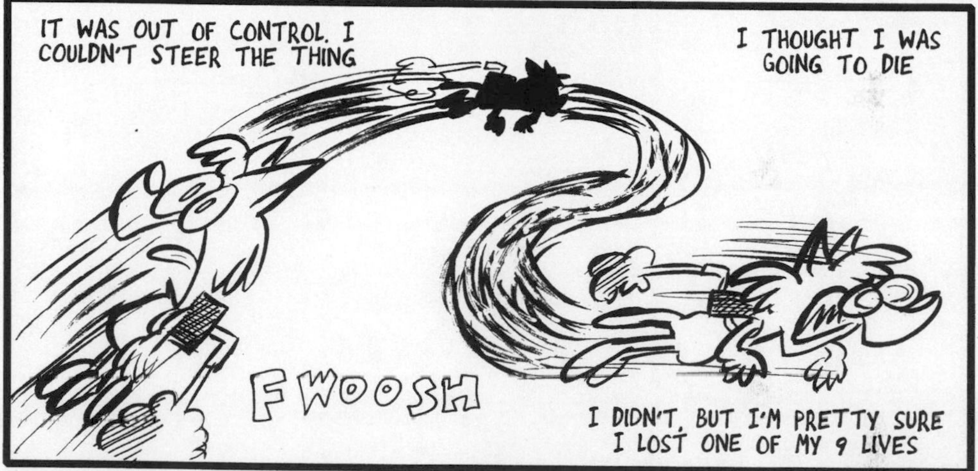
IT WAS OUT OF CONTROL. I COULDN'T STEER THE THING
I THOUGHT I WAS GOING TO DIE
FWOOSH
I DIDN'T, BUT I'M PRETTY SURE I LOST ONE OF MY 9 LIVES

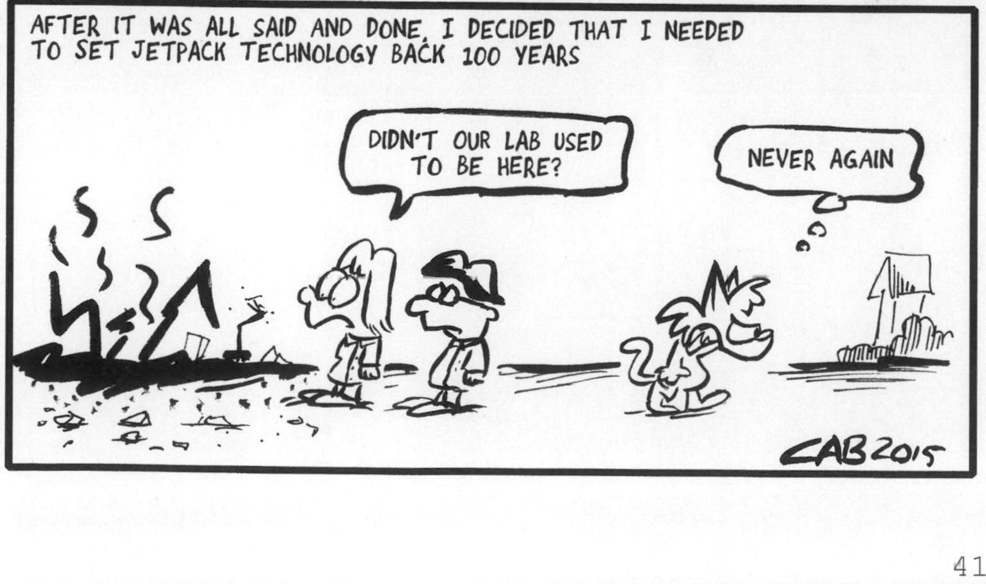
AFTER IT WAS ALL SAID AND DONE, I DECIDED THAT I NEEDED TO SET JETPACK TECHNOLOGY BACK 100 YEARS
DIDN'T OUR LAB USED TO BE HERE?
NEVER AGAIN
CAB 2015

DEAR CAT,

CATS BLINK TO ONE ANOTHER TO SHOW THAT THEY LOVE EACH OTHER. WHAT DO THEY DO WHEN THEY WANT A DIVORCE?

-DISTRESSED CAT

WILL YOU STOP STARING AT ME?

geez
CAB2015
AUGH!
THAT'S IT, I'M LEAVING YOU!
IT ALWAYS WORKS

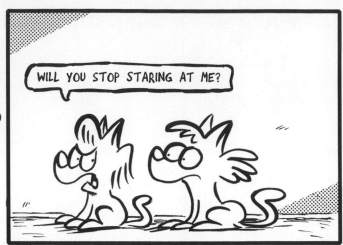

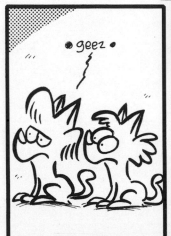

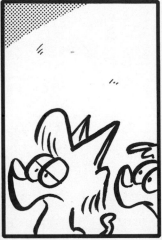

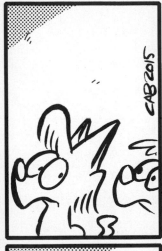

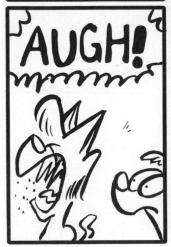

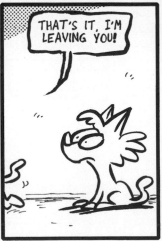

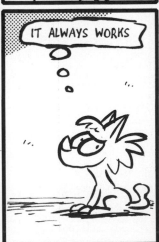

DEAR CAT,

ARE YOU AN INDOOR OR OUTDOOR KIND OF CAT?

-INSIDE OUT

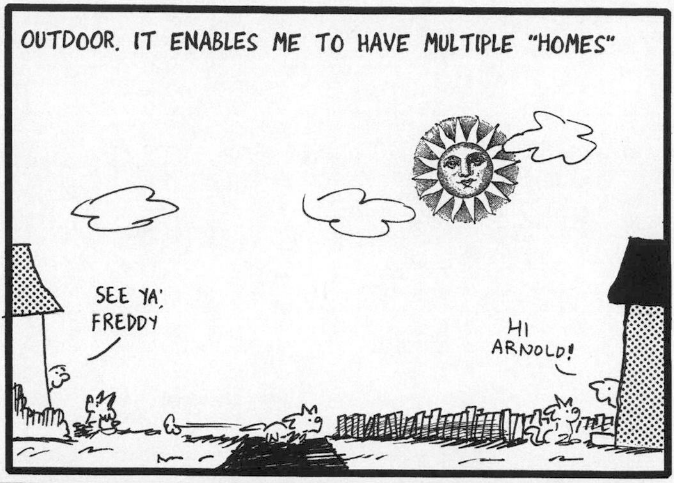
OUTDOOR. IT ENABLES ME TO HAVE MULTIPLE "HOMES"
SEE YA, FREDDY
HI ARNOLD!

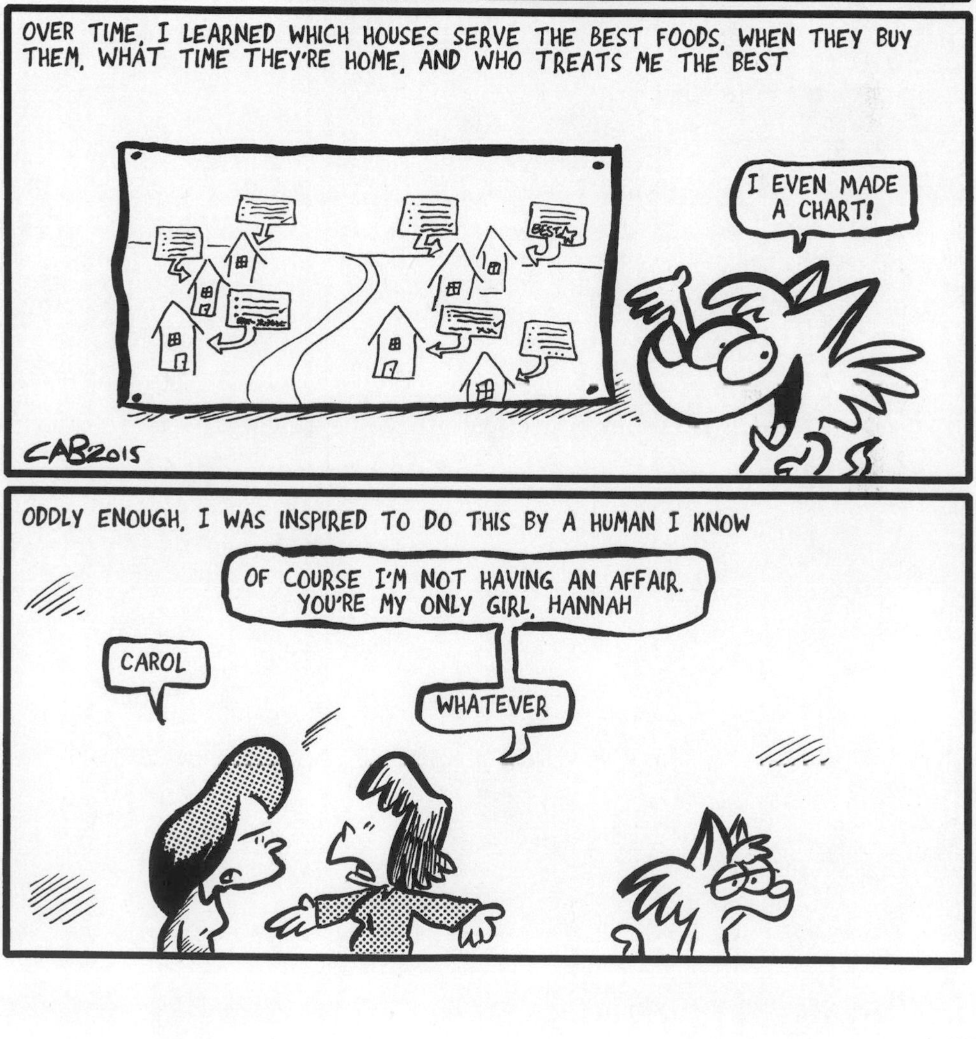
OVER TIME, I LEARNED WHICH HOUSES SERVE THE BEST FOODS, WHEN THEY BUY THEM, WHAT TIME THEY'RE HOME, AND WHO TREATS ME THE BEST
I EVEN MADE A CHART!
CAB2015
ODDLY ENOUGH, I WAS INSPIRED TO DO THIS BY A HUMAN I KNOW
OF COURSE I'M NOT HAVING AN AFFAIR. YOU'RE MY ONLY GIRL, HANNAH
CAROL
WHATEVER

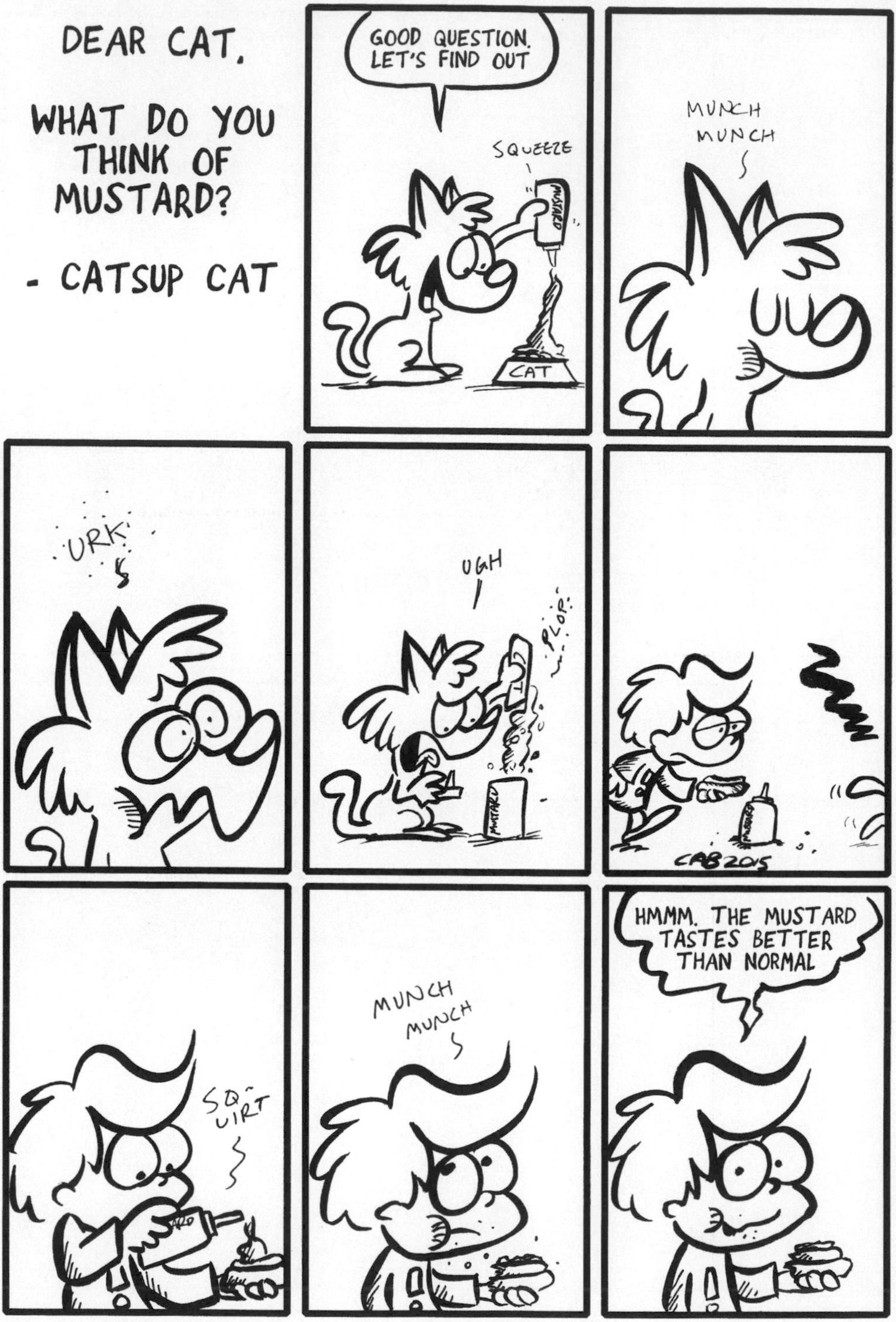
DEAR CAT.
WHAT DO YOU THINK OF MUSTARD?
- CATSUP CAT
GOOD QUESTION. LET'S FIND OUT
SQUEEZE
MUSTARD
CAT
MUNCH MUNCH
URK
UGH
PLOP
CAB2015
SQUIRT
MUNCH MUNCH
HMMM. THE MUSTARD TASTES BETTER THAN NORMAL

DEAR CAT,
HOW CAN YOU BE PROTECTED FROM OTHER CARTOONISTS STEALING YOUR CHARACTERS?
-NOT-SO-KRAZY KAT
OH. THAT'S SOMETHING YOU DON'T HAVE TO WORRY ABOUT
CARTOONISTS ARE AN HONEST BUNCH. THEY WOULD NEVER STOOP SO LOW AS TO STEAL OTHER PEOPLE'S IDEAS
SO IT'S GONNA BE FINE
RIGHT, GUYS?
INDEED, MY FELINE FRIEND
SOMETHING SEEMS OFF ABOUT THIS
CAB 2015
WITH APOLOGIES TO RYAN WEBB, WILL HENRY, STEPHAN PASTIS, JONATHAN LEMON, CHARLES SCHULZ, AND DANA SIMPSON

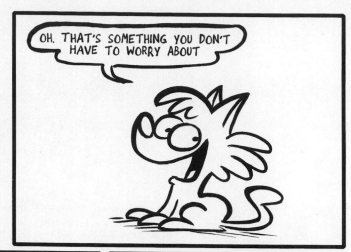

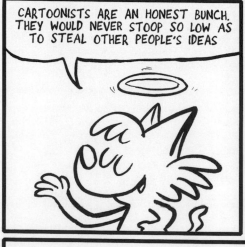

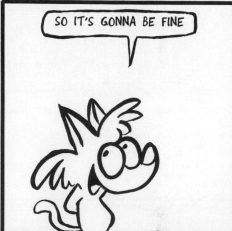

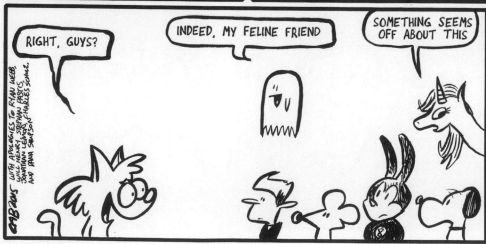

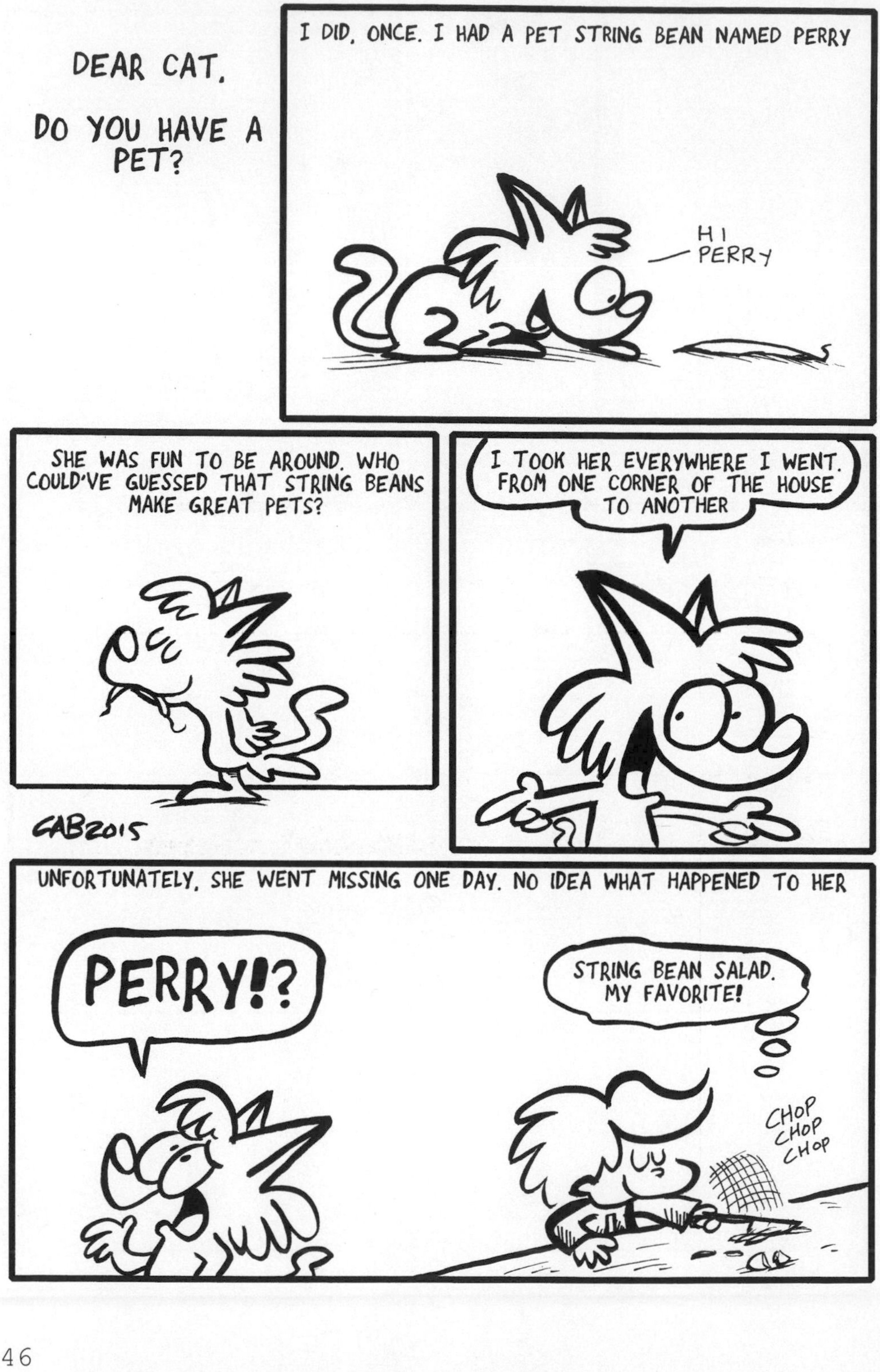
DEAR CAT,
DO YOU HAVE A PET?
I DID, ONCE. I HAD A PET STRING BEAN NAMED PERRY
HI PERRY
SHE WAS FUN TO BE AROUND. WHO COULD'VE GUESSED THAT STRING BEANS MAKE GREAT PETS?
I TOOK HER EVERYWHERE I WENT. FROM ONE CORNER OF THE HOUSE TO ANOTHER
GAB2015
UNFORTUNATELY, SHE WENT MISSING ONE DAY. NO IDEA WHAT HAPPENED TO HER
PERRY!?
STRING BEAN SALAD. MY FAVORITE!
CHOP CHOP CHOP

DEAR CAT,

DO YOU HAVE A FAVORITE CHAIR?

-STOOL PIGEON

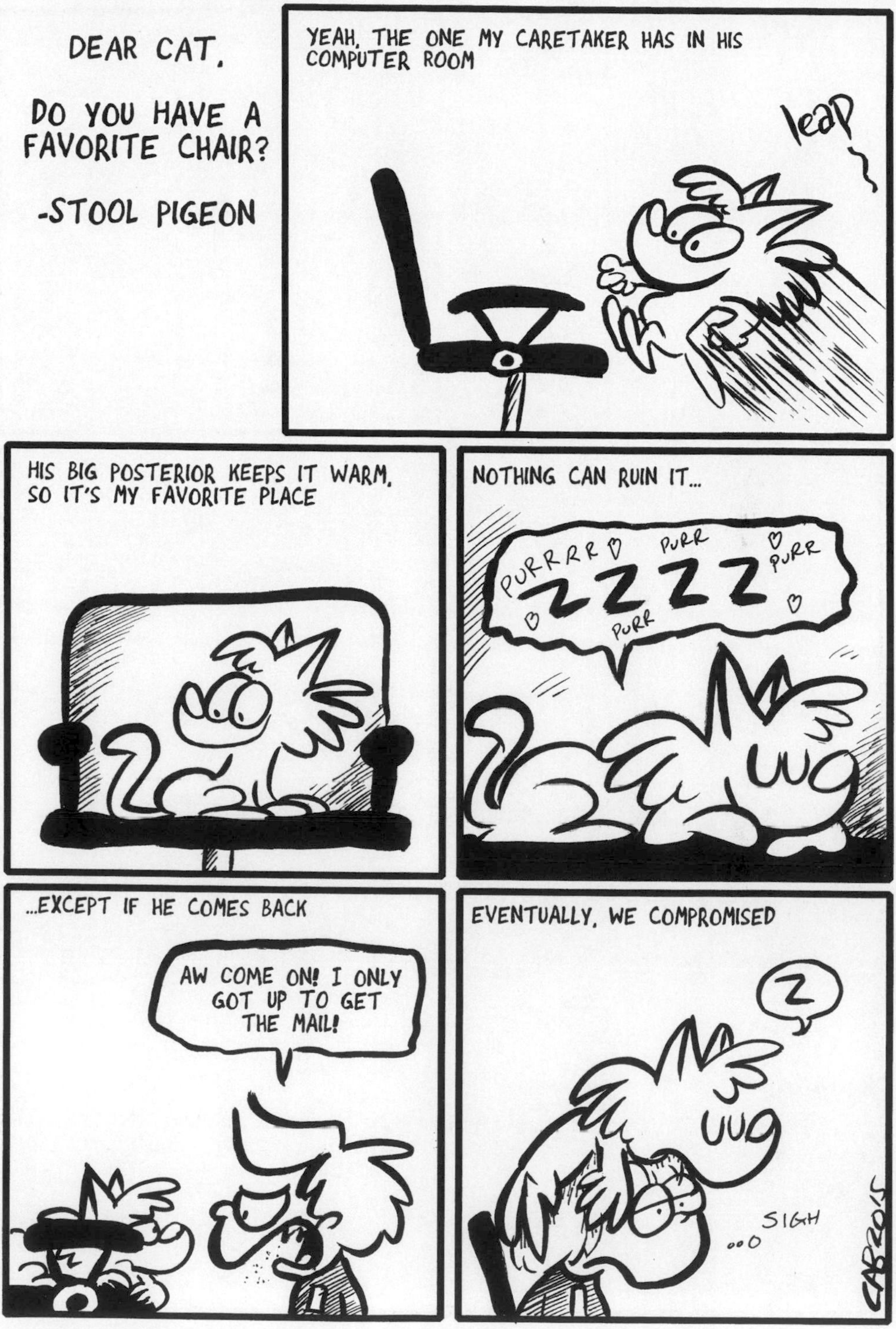
YEAH, THE ONE MY CARETAKER HAS IN HIS COMPUTER ROOM
leap
HIS BIG POSTERIOR KEEPS IT WARM, SO IT'S MY FAVORITE PLACE
NOTHING CAN RUIN IT...
PURRRRR ZZZZ PURR PURR PURR
...EXCEPT IF HE COMES BACK
AW COME ON! I ONLY GOT UP TO GET THE MAIL!
EVENTUALLY, WE COMPROMISED
Z
SIGH

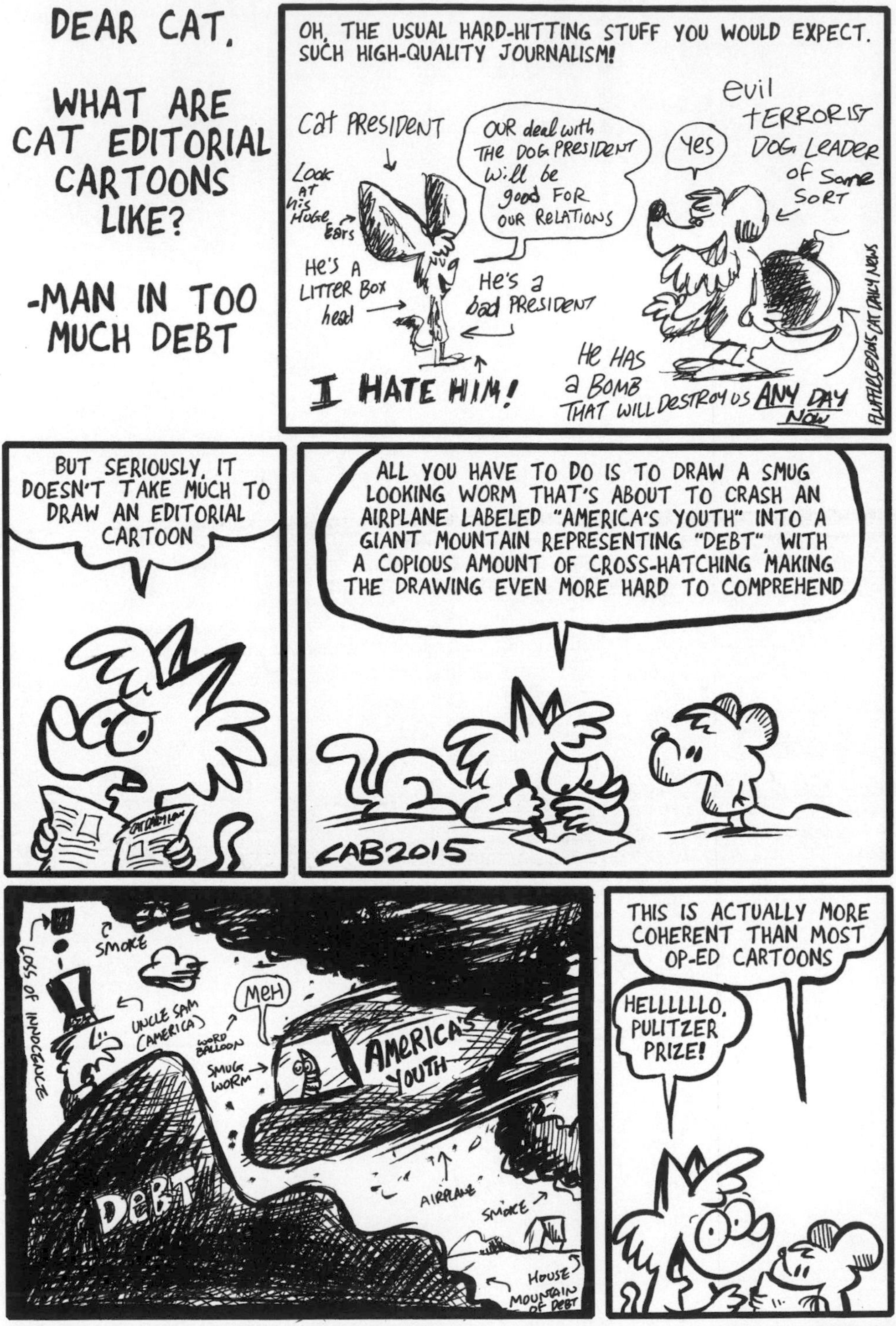
DEAR CAT,
WHAT ARE CAT EDITORIAL CARTOONS LIKE?
-MAN IN TOO MUCH DEBT
OH, THE USUAL HARD-HITTING STUFF YOU WOULD EXPECT. SUCH HIGH-QUALITY JOURNALISM!
Cat PRESIDENT
Look AT his Huge Ears
He's A LITTER Box head
He's a bad PRESIDENT
OUR deal with THE DOG PRESIDENT will be good FOR OUR RELATIONS
I HATE HIM!
Yes
evil TERRORIST DOG LEADER of Some SORT
He HAS a BOMB THAT WILL DESTROY US ANY DAY NOW
BUT SERIOUSLY, IT DOESN'T TAKE MUCH TO DRAW AN EDITORIAL CARTOON
ALL YOU HAVE TO DO IS TO DRAW A SMUG LOOKING WORM THAT'S ABOUT TO CRASH AN AIRPLANE LABELED "AMERICA'S YOUTH" INTO A GIANT MOUNTAIN REPRESENTING "DEBT", WITH A COPIOUS AMOUNT OF CROSS-HATCHING MAKING THE DRAWING EVEN MORE HARD TO COMPREHEND
CAB2015
LOSS OF INNOCENCE
SMOKE
UNCLE SAM (AMERICA)
MEH
WORD BALLOON
SMUG WORM
AMERICA'S YOUTH
DEBT
AIRPLANE
SMOKE
HOUSE
MOUNTAIN OF DEBT
THIS IS ACTUALLY MORE COHERENT THAN MOST OP-ED CARTOONS
HELLLLLLO, PULITZER PRIZE!

DEAR CAT.

WHICH IS BETTER, WAFFLES OR PANCAKES?

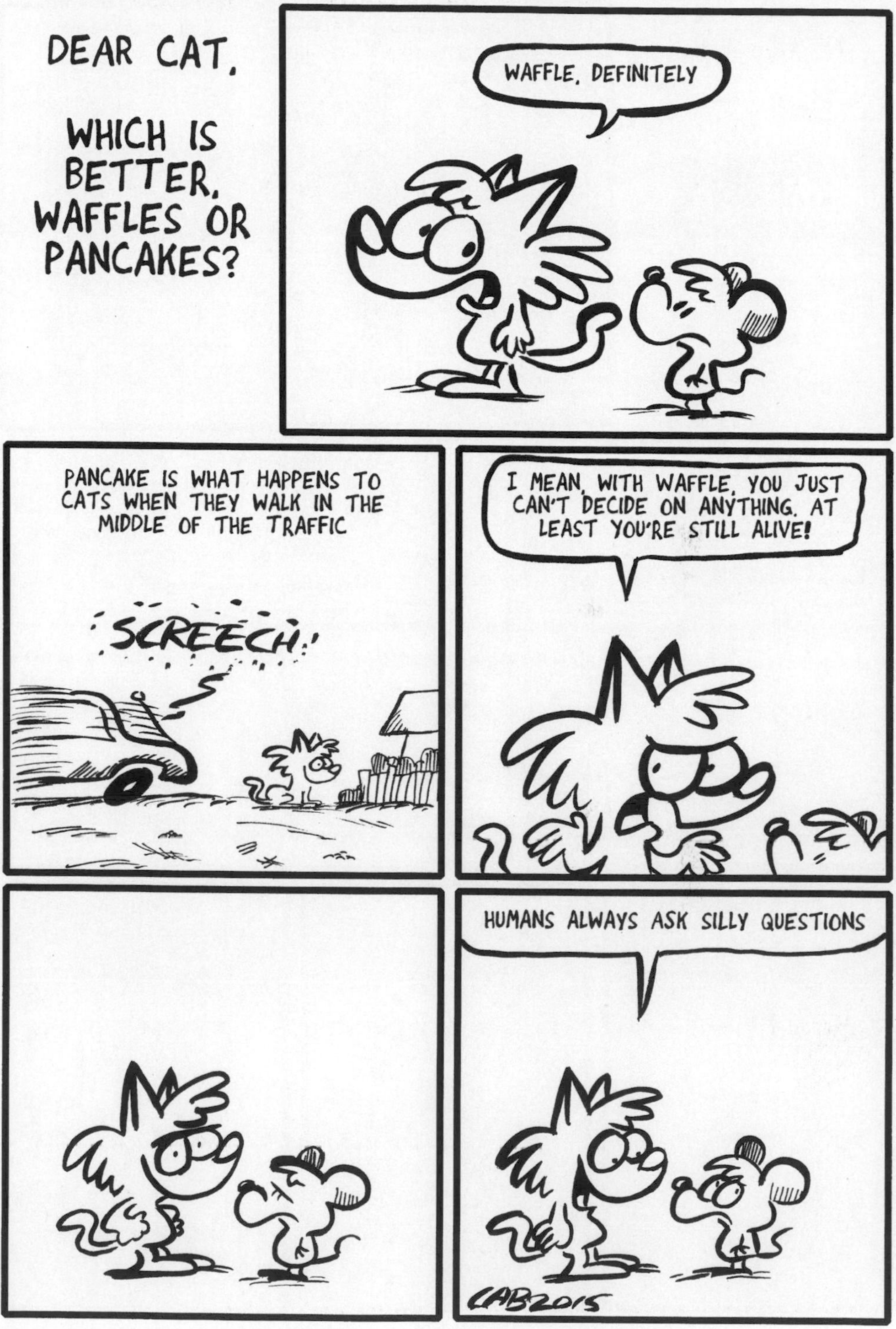
WAFFLE, DEFINITELY
PANCAKE IS WHAT HAPPENS TO CATS WHEN THEY WALK IN THE MIDDLE OF THE TRAFFIC
SCREECH
I MEAN, WITH WAFFLE, YOU JUST CAN'T DECIDE ON ANYTHING. AT LEAST YOU'RE STILL ALIVE!
HUMANS ALWAYS ASK SILLY QUESTIONS
CAB2015

DEAR CAT,

EVER MET A WALKING CATFISH?

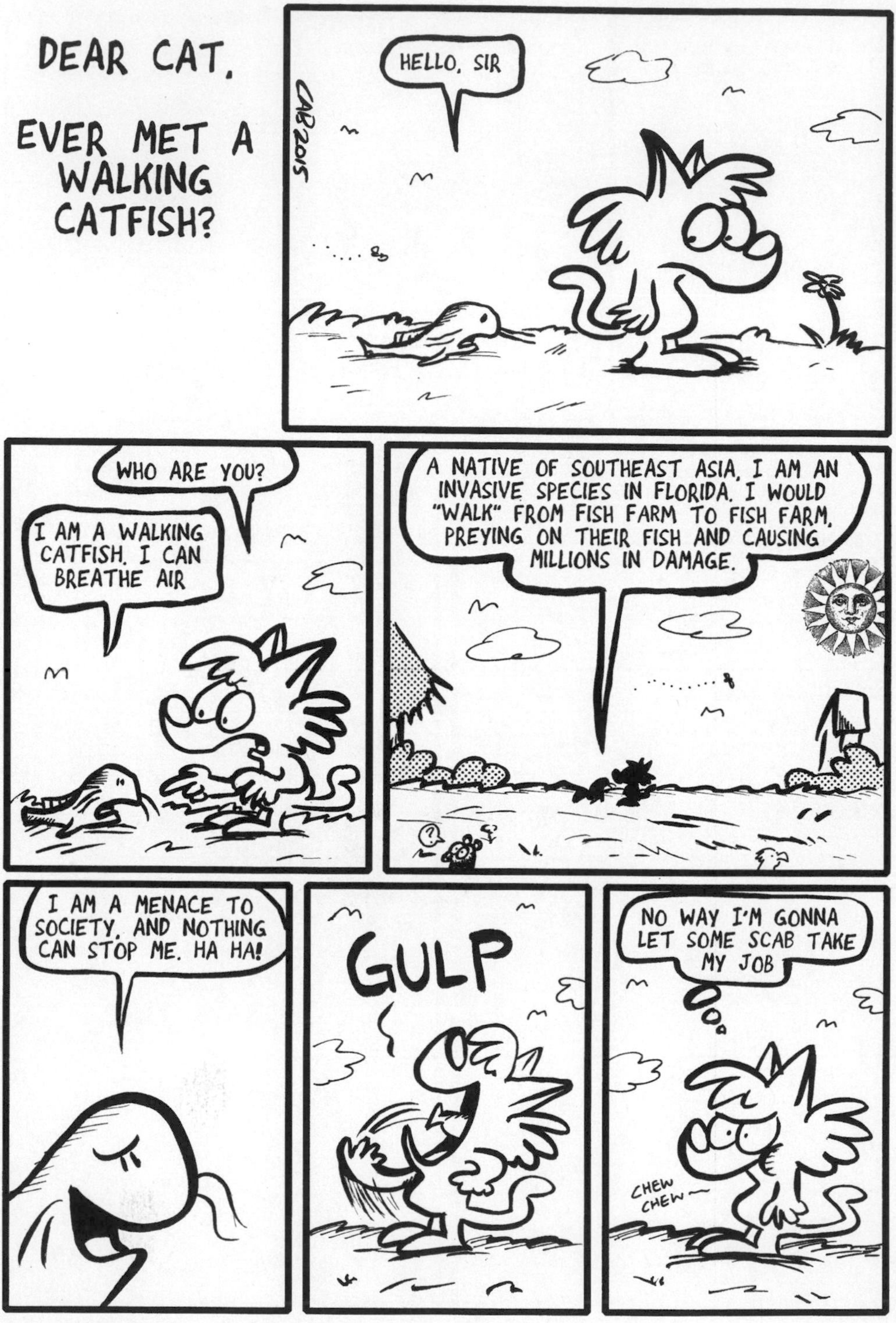
CAB 2015
HELLO, SIR
WHO ARE YOU?
I AM A WALKING CATFISH. I CAN BREATHE AIR
A NATIVE OF SOUTHEAST ASIA, I AM AN INVASIVE SPECIES IN FLORIDA. I WOULD "WALK" FROM FISH FARM TO FISH FARM, PREYING ON THEIR FISH AND CAUSING MILLIONS IN DAMAGE.
I AM A MENACE TO SOCIETY, AND NOTHING CAN STOP ME. HA HA!
GULP
NO WAY I'M GONNA LET SOME SCAB TAKE MY JOB
CHEW CHEW ~

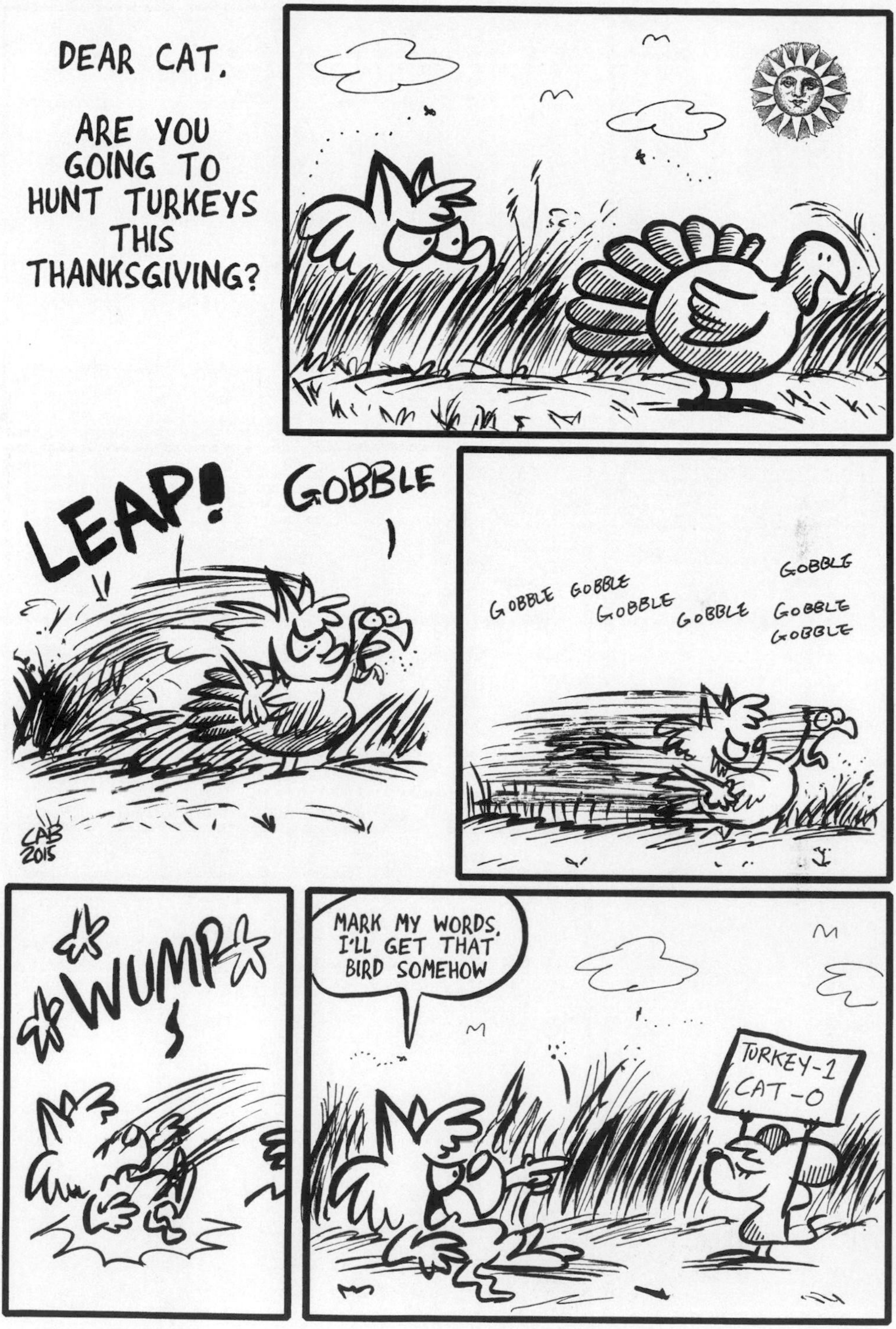
DEAR CAT,
ARE YOU GOING TO HUNT TURKEYS THIS THANKSGIVING?
LEAP!
GOBBLE
CAB 2015
GOBBLE GOBBLE GOBBLE GOBBLE GOBBLE GOBBLE GOBBLE
WUMP
MARK MY WORDS, I'LL GET THAT BIRD SOMEHOW
TURKEY-1 CAT-0

Dear Beneficiary,

kindly contact us back for your payment.

Remain Bless,
Mr.Ben Taka
Western Union

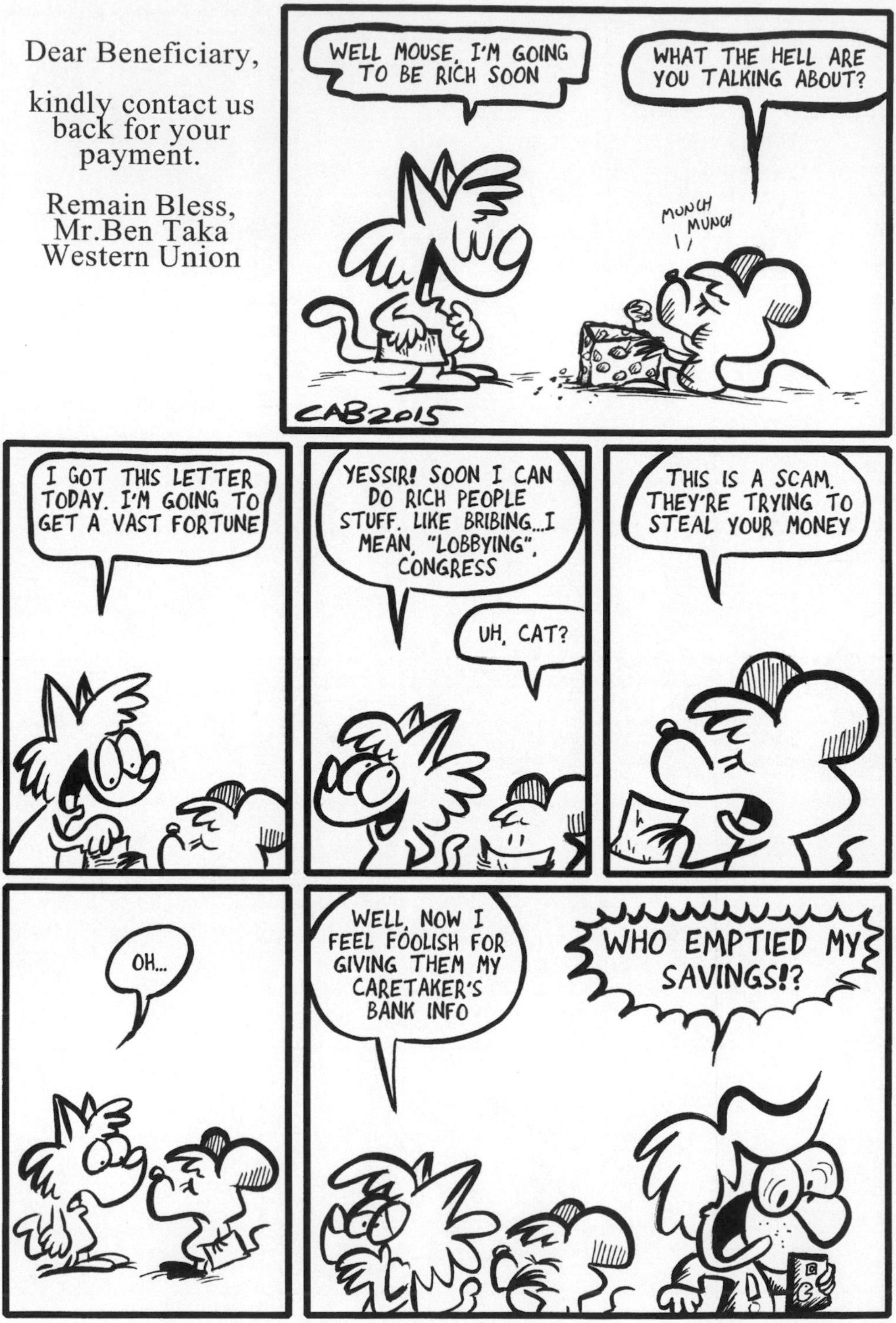
WELL MOUSE, I'M GOING TO BE RICH SOON
WHAT THE HELL ARE YOU TALKING ABOUT?
MUNCH MUNCH
CAB2015
I GOT THIS LETTER TODAY. I'M GOING TO GET A VAST FORTUNE
YESSIR! SOON I CAN DO RICH PEOPLE STUFF. LIKE BRIBING...I MEAN, "LOBBYING", CONGRESS
UH, CAT?
THIS IS A SCAM. THEY'RE TRYING TO STEAL YOUR MONEY
OH...
WELL, NOW I FEEL FOOLISH FOR GIVING THEM MY CARETAKER'S BANK INFO
WHO EMPTIED MY SAVINGS!?

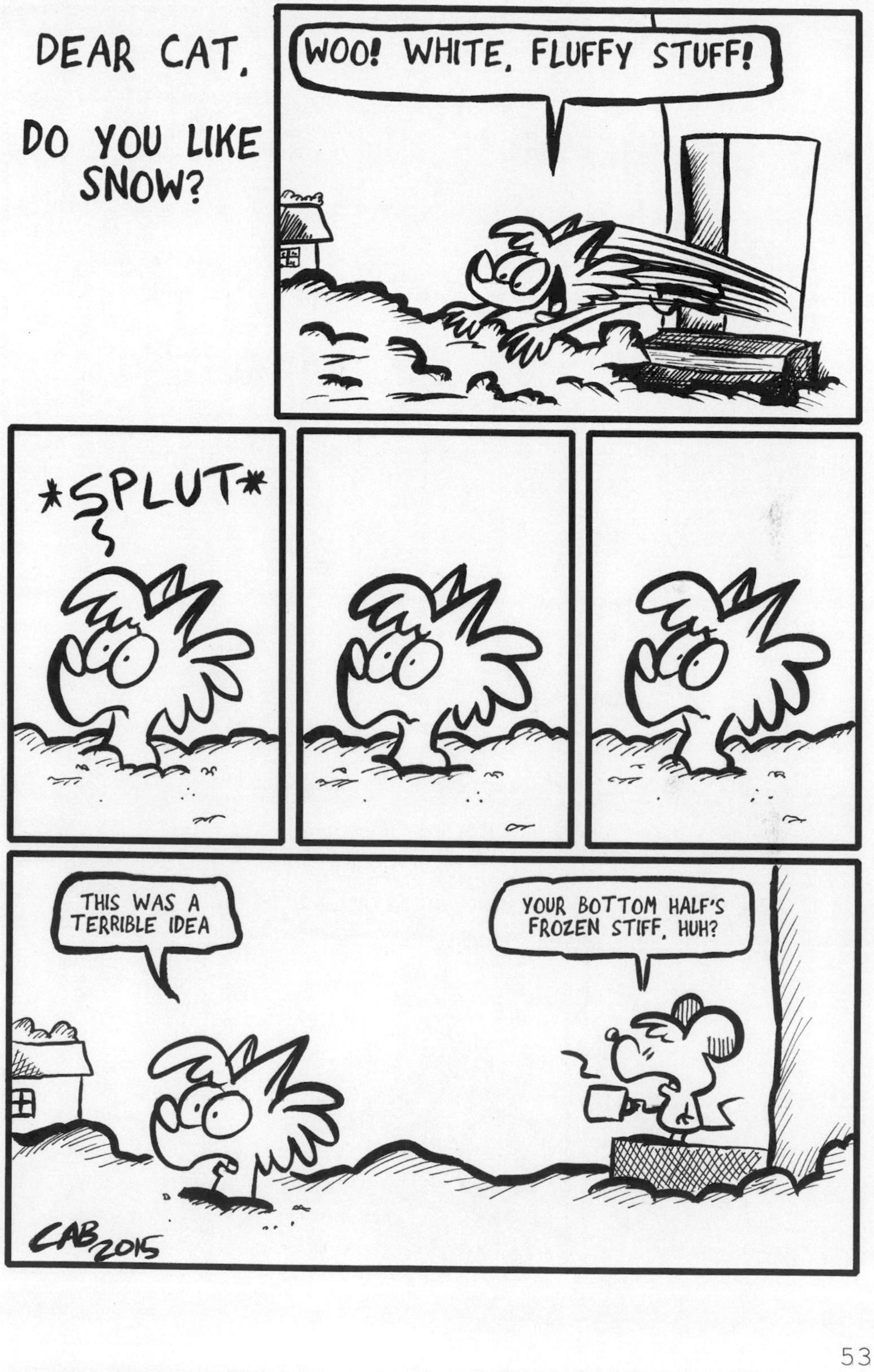
DEAR CAT,
DO YOU LIKE SNOW?
WOO! WHITE, FLUFFY STUFF!
SPLUT
THIS WAS A TERRIBLE IDEA
YOUR BOTTOM HALF'S FROZEN STIFF, HUH?
CAB 2015

DEAR CAT.

ARE YOU PREPARED FOR CHRISTMAS?

- A BASS NAMED RANKIN

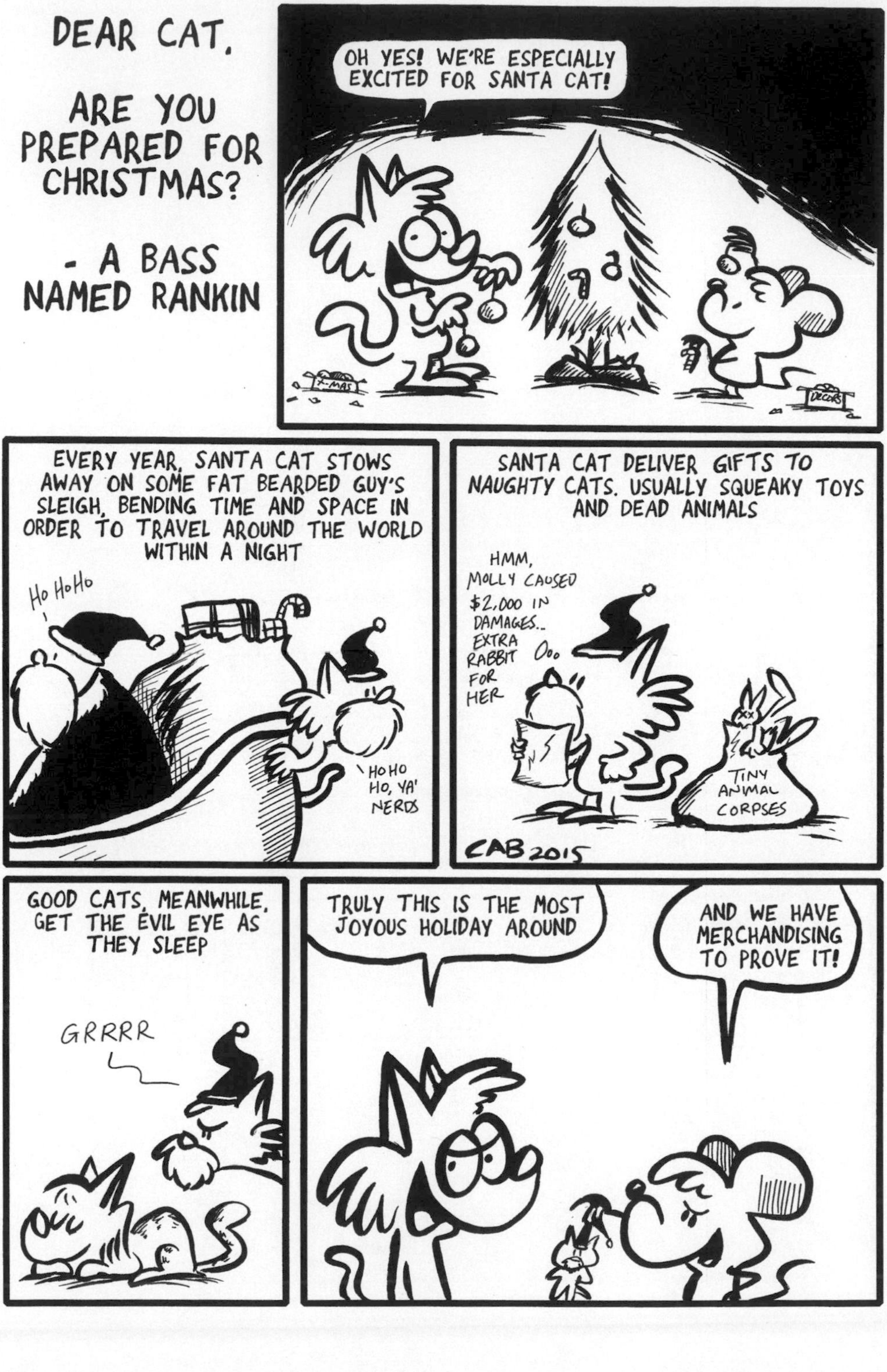

OH YES! WE'RE ESPECIALLY EXCITED FOR SANTA CAT!
X-MAS
DECORS
EVERY YEAR, SANTA CAT STOWS AWAY ON SOME FAT BEARDED GUY'S SLEIGH, BENDING TIME AND SPACE IN ORDER TO TRAVEL AROUND THE WORLD WITHIN A NIGHT
Ho HoHo
HOHO HO, YA' NERDS
SANTA CAT DELIVER GIFTS TO NAUGHTY CATS. USUALLY SQUEAKY TOYS AND DEAD ANIMALS
HMM, MOLLY CAUSED $2,000 IN DAMAGES.. EXTRA RABBIT FOR HER
Ooo
TINY ANIMAL CORPSES
CAB 2015
GOOD CATS, MEANWHILE, GET THE EVIL EYE AS THEY SLEEP
GRRRR
TRULY THIS IS THE MOST JOYOUS HOLIDAY AROUND
AND WE HAVE MERCHANDISING TO PROVE IT!

DEAR CAT,

DO YOU USE THE INTERNET?

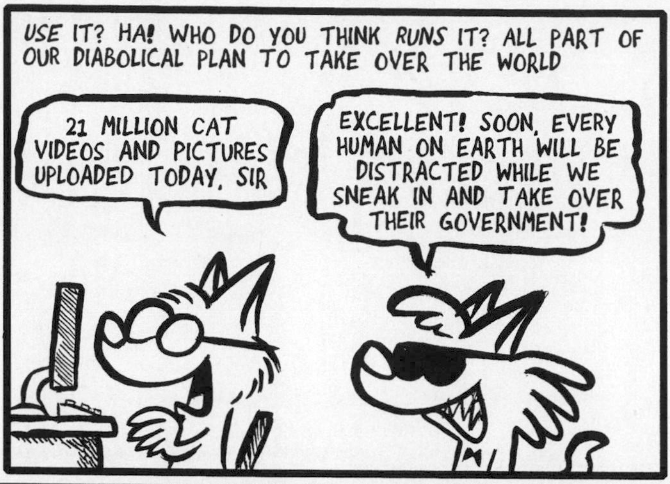
USE IT? HA! WHO DO YOU THINK RUNS IT? ALL PART OF OUR DIABOLICAL PLAN TO TAKE OVER THE WORLD
21 MILLION CAT VIDEOS AND PICTURES UPLOADED TODAY, SIR
EXCELLENT! SOON, EVERY HUMAN ON EARTH WILL BE DISTRACTED WHILE WE SNEAK IN AND TAKE OVER THEIR GOVERNMENT!

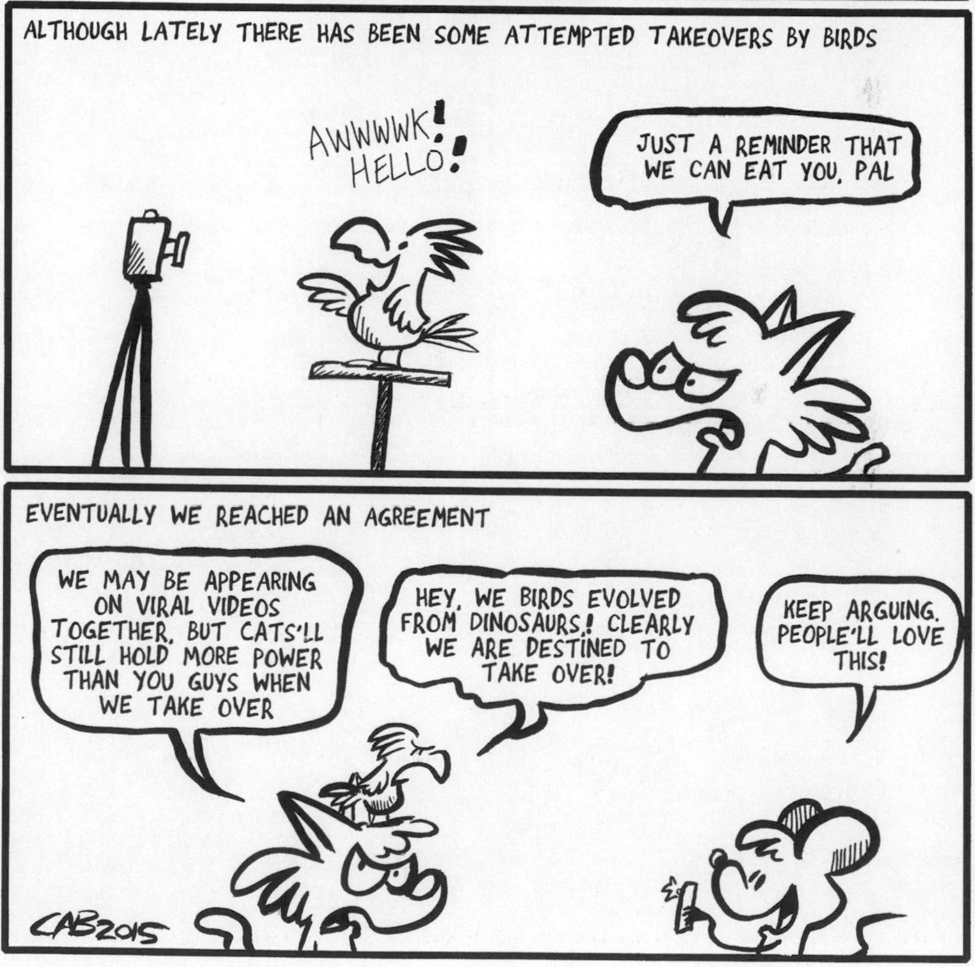
ALTHOUGH LATELY THERE HAS BEEN SOME ATTEMPTED TAKEOVERS BY BIRDS
AWWWWK! HELLO!
JUST A REMINDER THAT WE CAN EAT YOU, PAL
EVENTUALLY WE REACHED AN AGREEMENT
WE MAY BE APPEARING ON VIRAL VIDEOS TOGETHER, BUT CATS'LL STILL HOLD MORE POWER THAN YOU GUYS WHEN WE TAKE OVER
HEY, WE BIRDS EVOLVED FROM DINOSAURS! CLEARLY WE ARE DESTINED TO TAKE OVER!
KEEP ARGUING. PEOPLE'LL LOVE THIS!
CAB2015

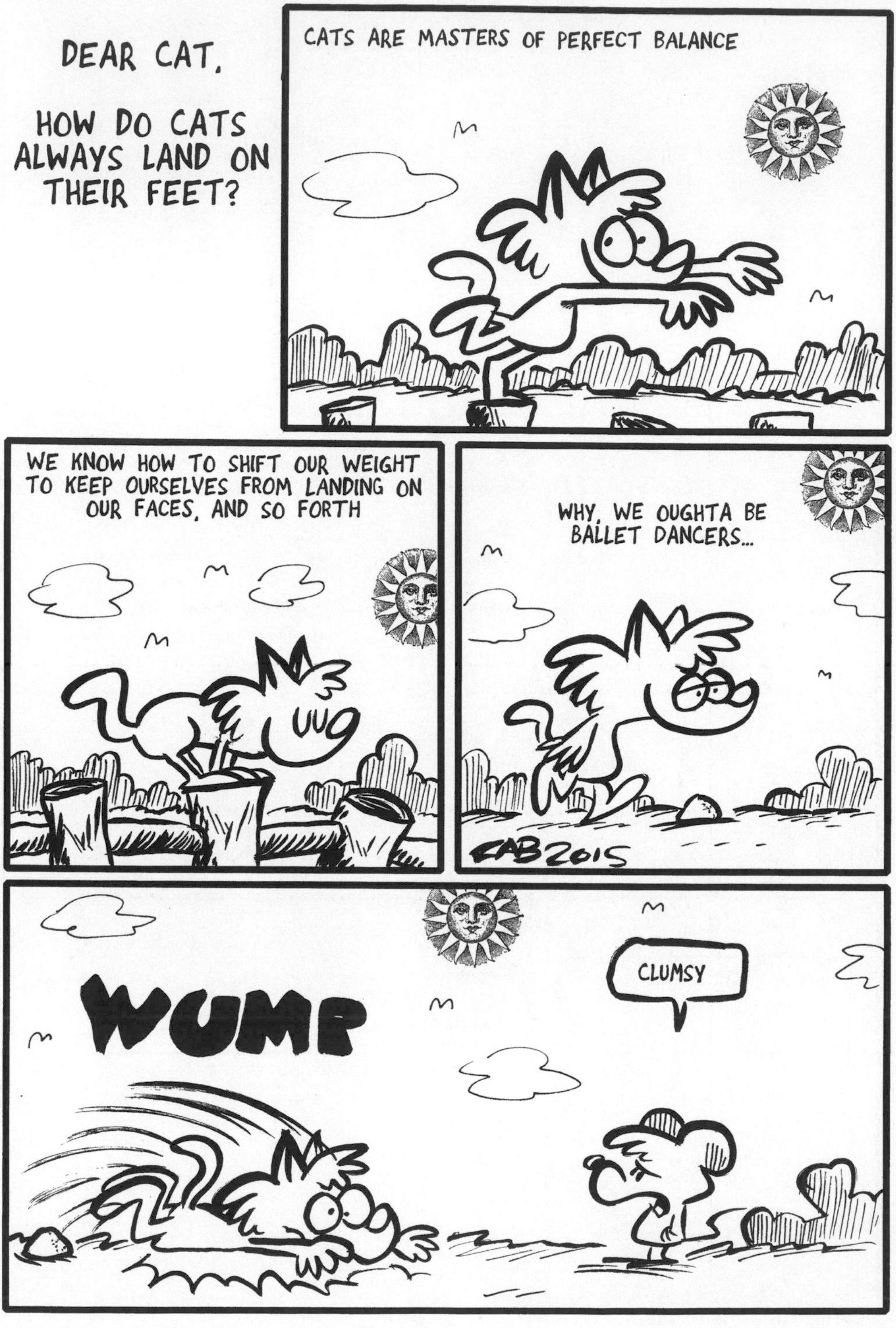
DEAR CAT,
HOW DO CATS ALWAYS LAND ON THEIR FEET?
CATS ARE MASTERS OF PERFECT BALANCE
WE KNOW HOW TO SHIFT OUR WEIGHT TO KEEP OURSELVES FROM LANDING ON OUR FACES, AND SO FORTH
WHY, WE OUGHTA BE BALLET DANCERS...
FAB 2015
WUMP
CLUMSY

DEAR CAT,

DO YOU MAKE ART?

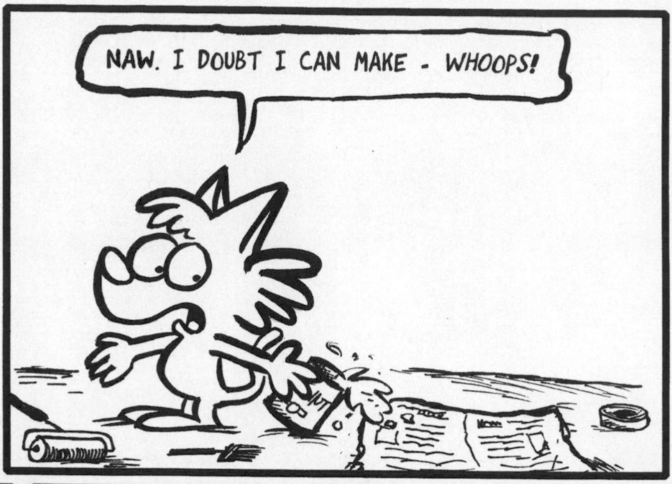
NAW. I DOUBT I CAN MAKE - WHOOPS!

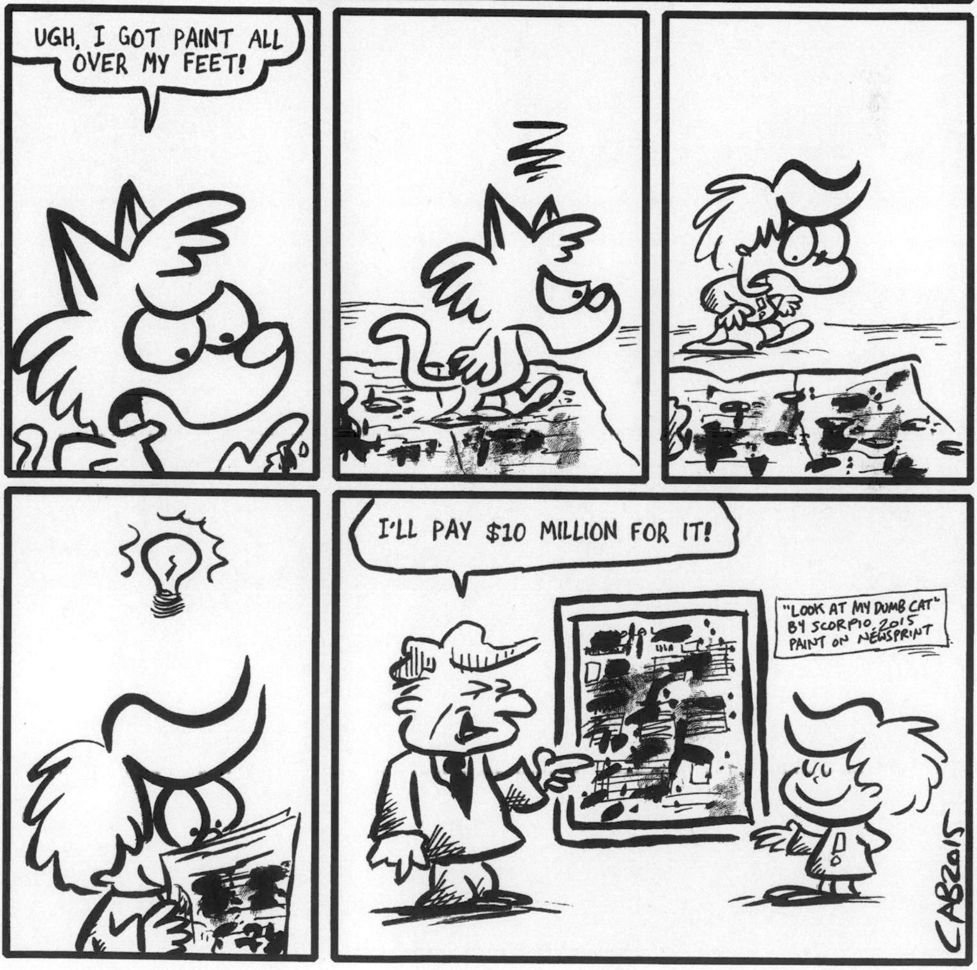
UGH, I GOT PAINT ALL OVER MY FEET!
I'LL PAY $10 MILLION FOR IT!
"LOOK AT MY DUMB CAT"
BY SCORPIO, 2015
PAINT ON NEWSPRINT
CAB2015

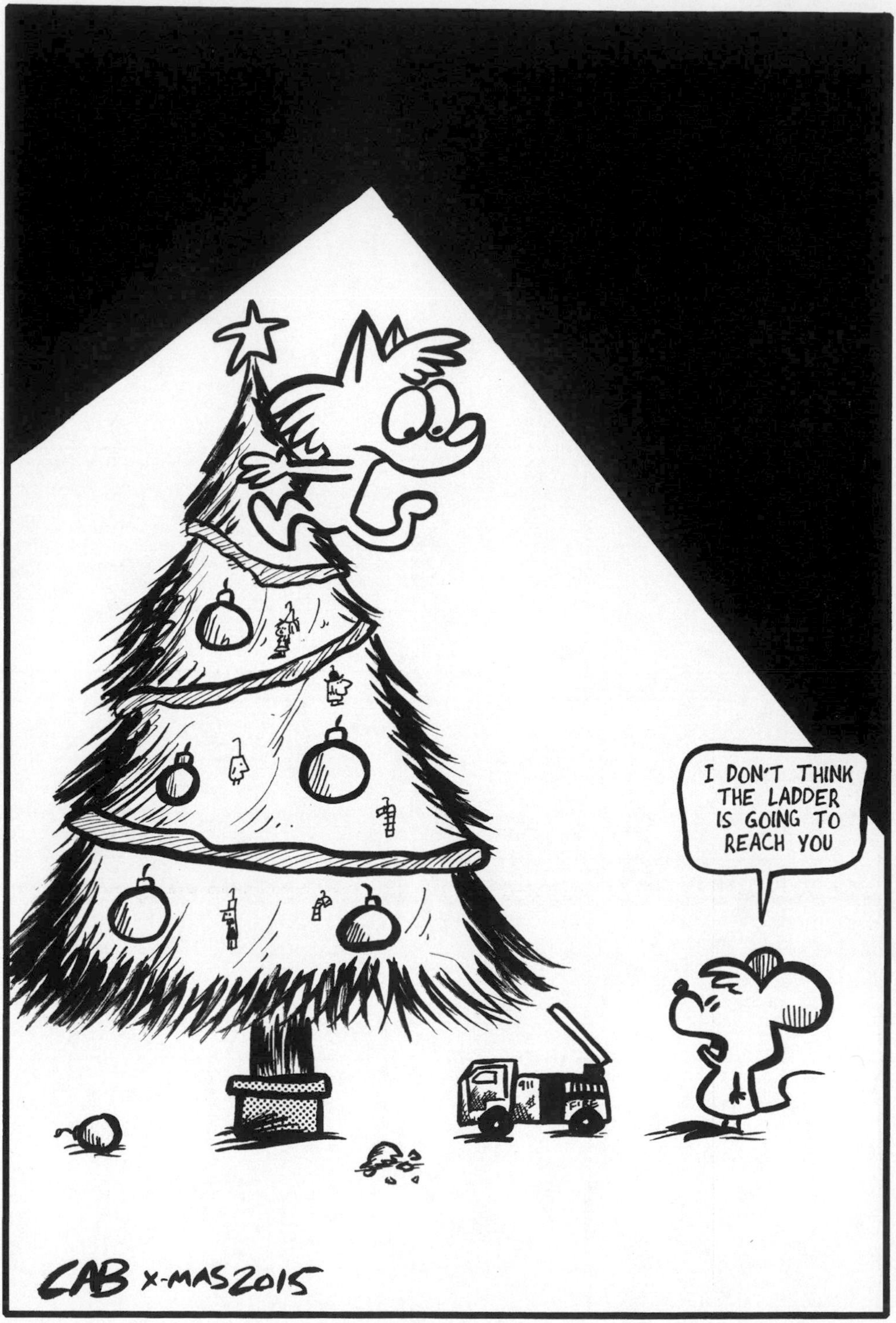
I DON'T THINK THE LADDER IS GOING TO REACH YOU
CAB X-MAS 2015

DEAR CAT,

DO YOU REALLY EXIST OR NOT?

-MR. SHRODINGER

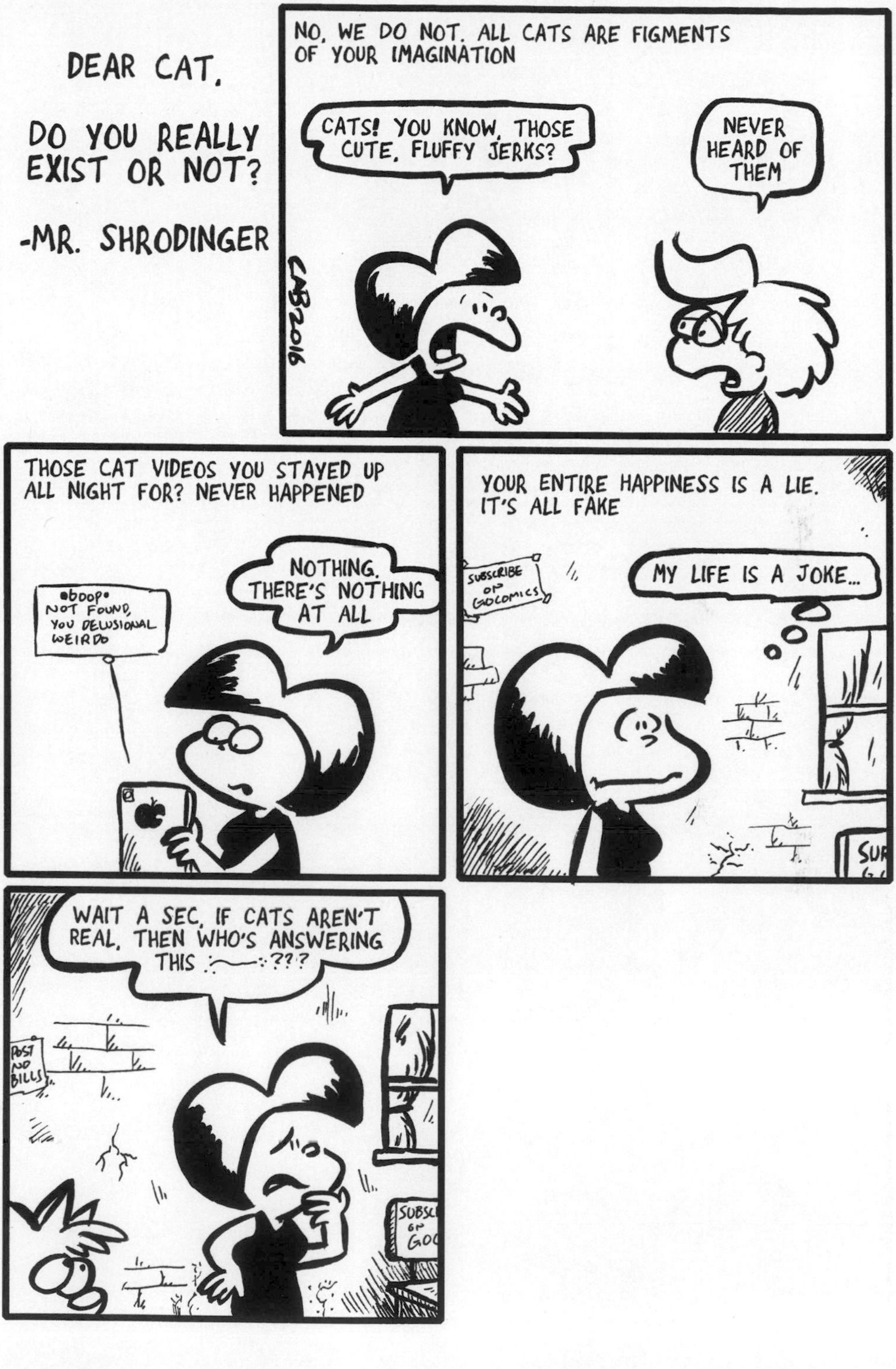
NO, WE DO NOT. ALL CATS ARE FIGMENTS OF YOUR IMAGINATION
CATS! YOU KNOW, THOSE CUTE, FLUFFY JERKS?
NEVER HEARD OF THEM
CAB 2016
THOSE CAT VIDEOS YOU STAYED UP ALL NIGHT FOR? NEVER HAPPENED
NOTHING. THERE'S NOTHING AT ALL
•boop• NOT FOUND, YOU DELUSIONAL WEIRDO
YOUR ENTIRE HAPPINESS IS A LIE. IT'S ALL FAKE
SUBSCRIBE ON GOCOMICS
MY LIFE IS A JOKE...
WAIT A SEC, IF CATS AREN'T REAL, THEN WHO'S ANSWERING THIS ???
POST NO BILLS

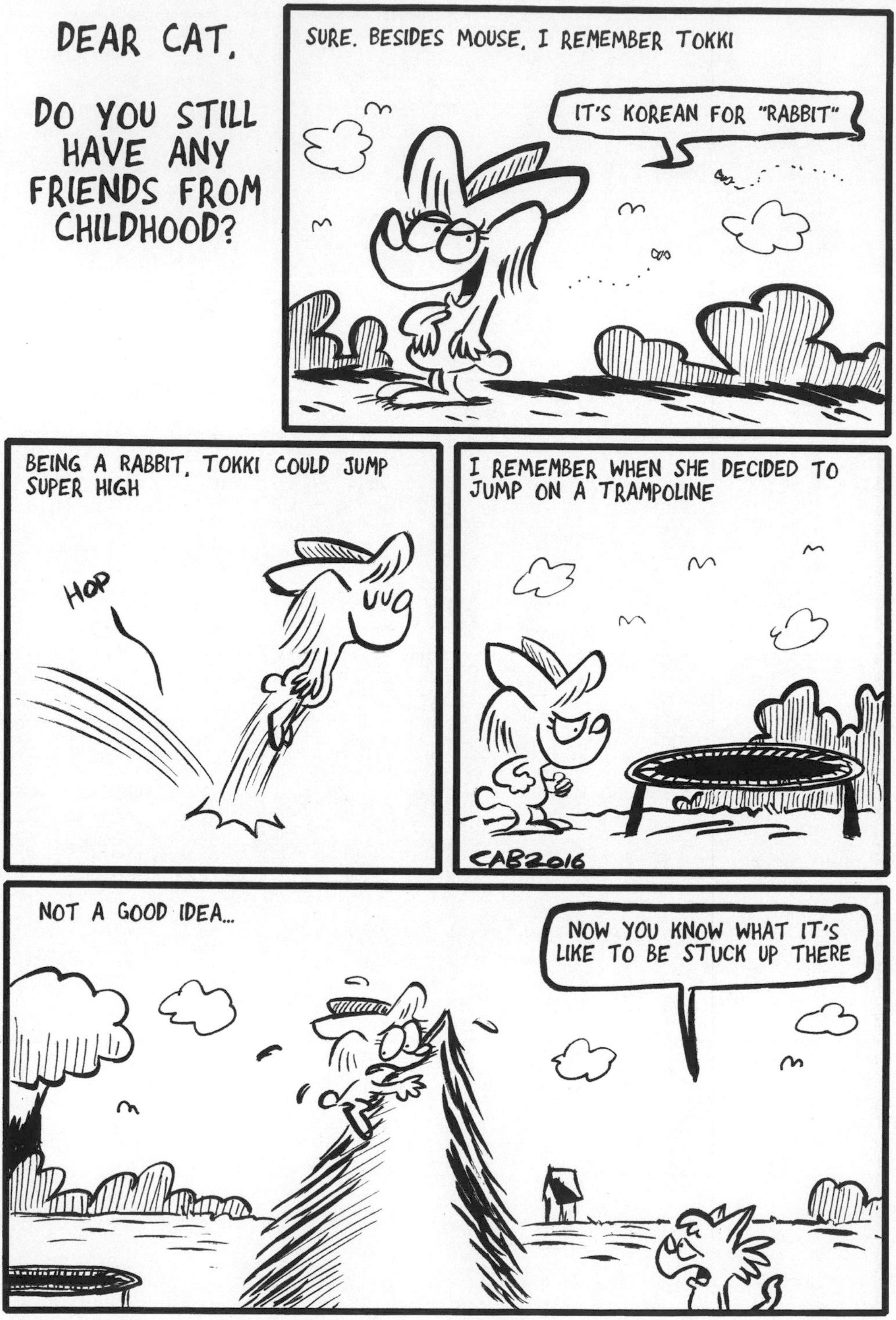
DEAR CAT,
DO YOU STILL HAVE ANY FRIENDS FROM CHILDHOOD?
SURE. BESIDES MOUSE, I REMEMBER TOKKI
IT'S KOREAN FOR "RABBIT"
BEING A RABBIT, TOKKI COULD JUMP SUPER HIGH
HOP
I REMEMBER WHEN SHE DECIDED TO JUMP ON A TRAMPOLINE
CAB2016
NOT A GOOD IDEA...
NOW YOU KNOW WHAT IT'S LIKE TO BE STUCK UP THERE

DEAR CAT,

DOES TOKKI DO ANYTHING *BESIDES* JUMPING ON TRAMPOLINES?

OH ABSOLUTELY! SHE LIKES TO SWING ON TREES, TOO

SHE THINKS SHE'S BEING TARZAN, ALTHOUGH PERSONALLY, I'D SAY SHE'S CLOSER TO GEORGE OF THE JUNGLE

SHE KNEW THE JOB WAS DANGEROUS WHEN SHE TOOK IT

CAB 2016

I MADE THE MISTAKE OF JOINING HER ONCE

THE WORST PART IS, I SAW THIS COMING

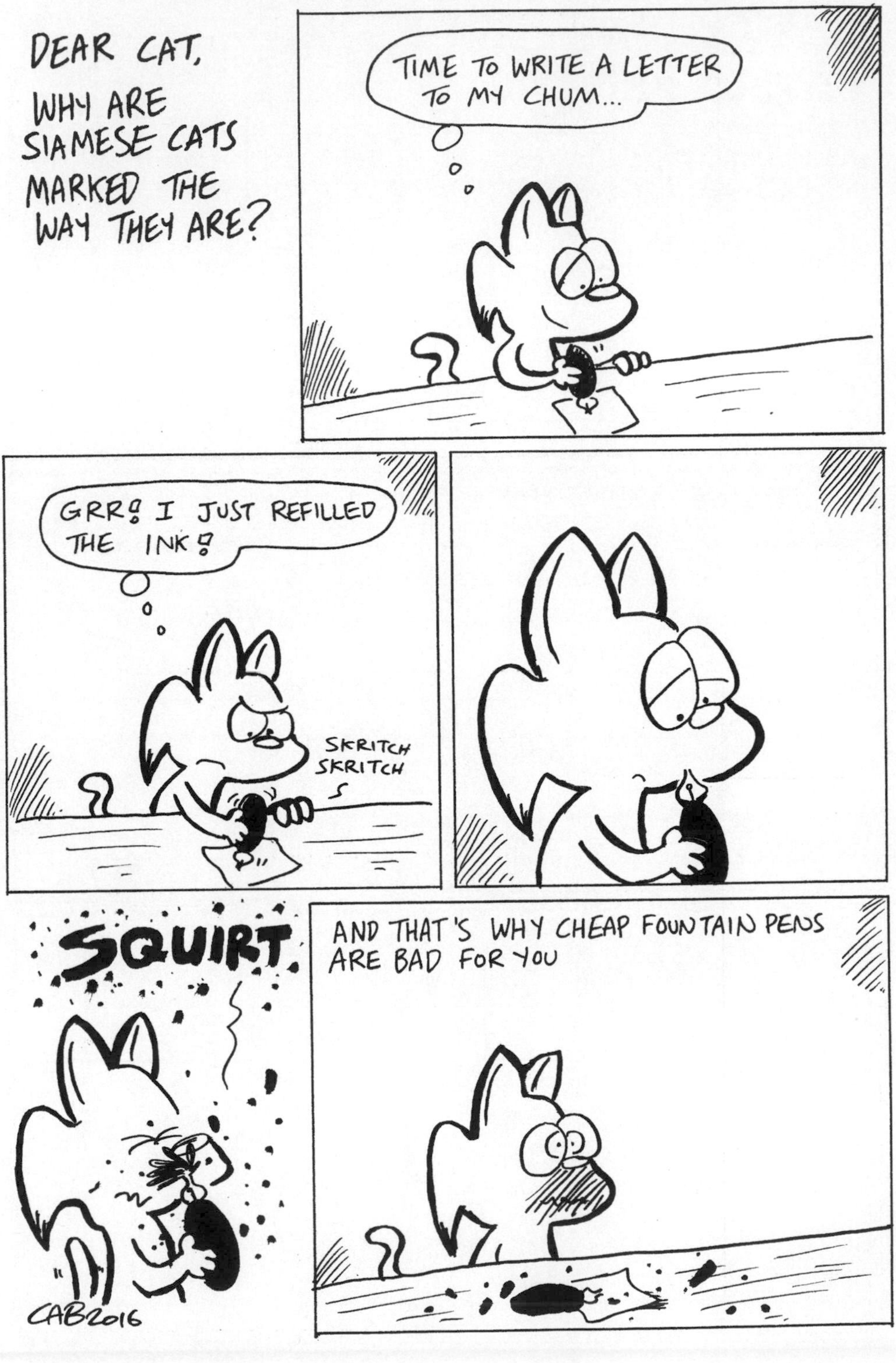
DEAR CAT,
WHY ARE SIAMESE CATS MARKED THE WAY THEY ARE?
TIME TO WRITE A LETTER TO MY CHUM...
GRR! I JUST REFILLED THE INK!
SKRITCH SKRITCH
SQUIRT
CAB2016
AND THAT'S WHY CHEAP FOUNTAIN PENS ARE BAD FOR YOU

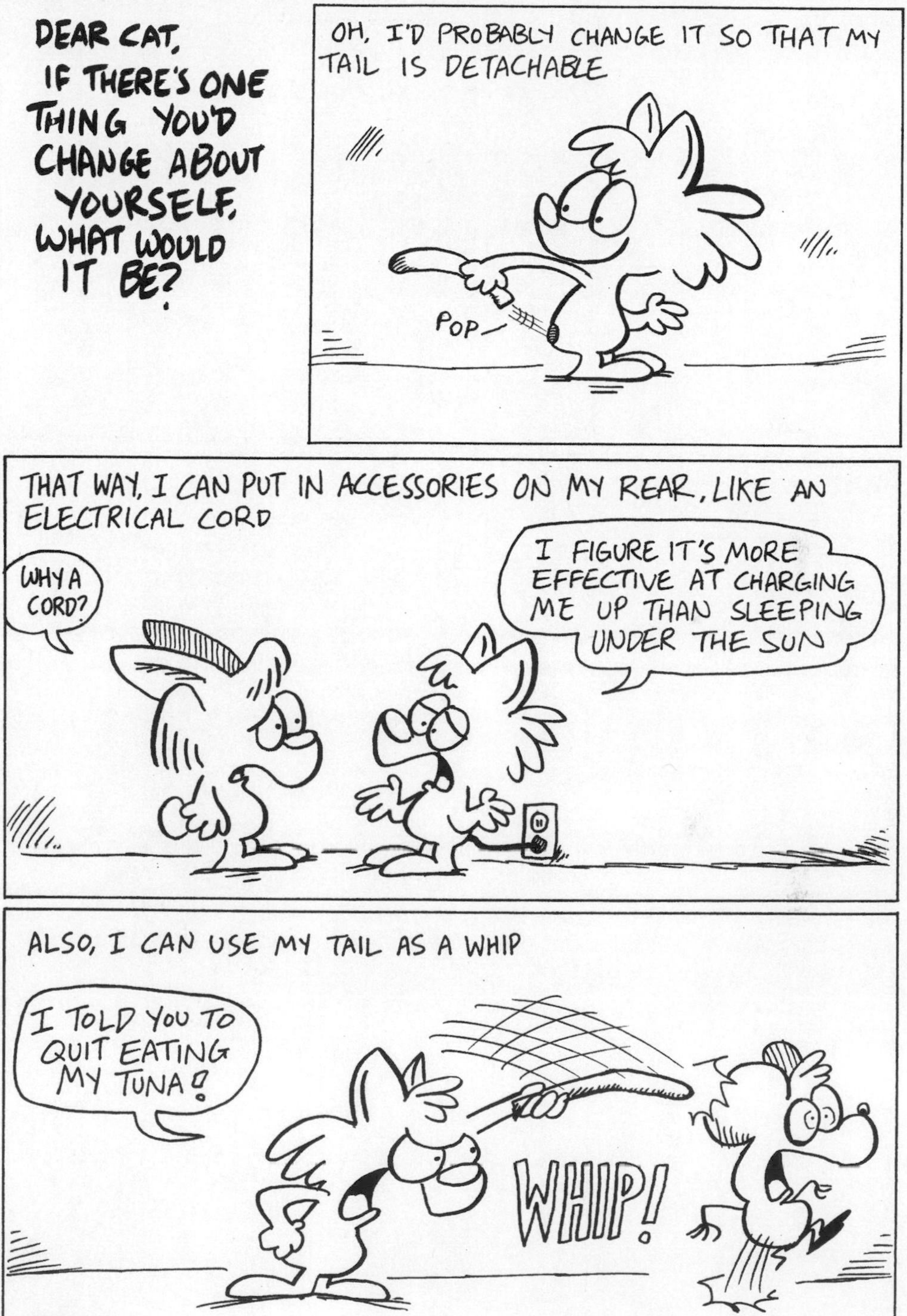
DEAR CAT,
IF THERE'S ONE THING YOU'D CHANGE ABOUT YOURSELF, WHAT WOULD IT BE?
OH, I'D PROBABLY CHANGE IT SO THAT MY TAIL IS DETACHABLE
POP
THAT WAY, I CAN PUT IN ACCESSORIES ON MY REAR, LIKE AN ELECTRICAL CORD
WHY A CORD?
I FIGURE IT'S MORE EFFECTIVE AT CHARGING ME UP THAN SLEEPING UNDER THE SUN
ALSO, I CAN USE MY TAIL AS A WHIP
I TOLD YOU TO QUIT EATING MY TUNA!!
WHIP!
CAB2016

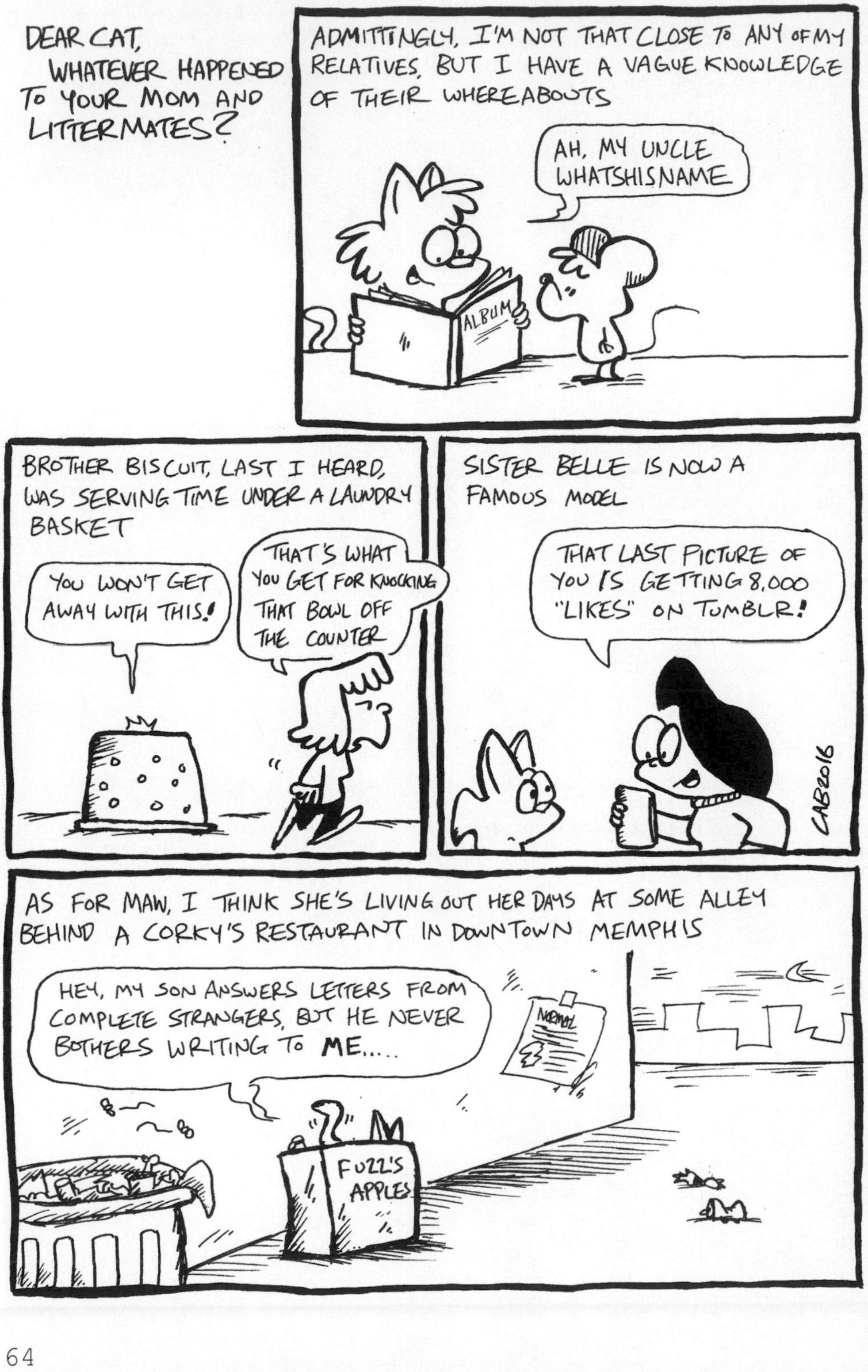
DEAR CAT,
WHATEVER HAPPENED TO YOUR MOM AND LITTERMATES?
ADMITTINGLY, I'M NOT THAT CLOSE TO ANY OF MY RELATIVES, BUT I HAVE A VAGUE KNOWLEDGE OF THEIR WHEREABOUTS
AH, MY UNCLE WHATSHISNAME
ALBUM
BROTHER BISCUIT, LAST I HEARD, WAS SERVING TIME UNDER A LAUNDRY BASKET
YOU WON'T GET AWAY WITH THIS!
THAT'S WHAT YOU GET FOR KNOCKING THAT BOWL OFF THE COUNTER
SISTER BELLE IS NOW A FAMOUS MODEL
THAT LAST PICTURE OF YOU IS GETTING 8,000 "LIKES" ON TUMBLR!
CAB2016
AS FOR MAW, I THINK SHE'S LIVING OUT HER DAYS AT SOME ALLEY BEHIND A CORKY'S RESTAURANT IN DOWNTOWN MEMPHIS
HEY, MY SON ANSWERS LETTERS FROM COMPLETE STRANGERS, BUT HE NEVER BOTHERS WRITING TO ME.....
FUZZ'S APPLES

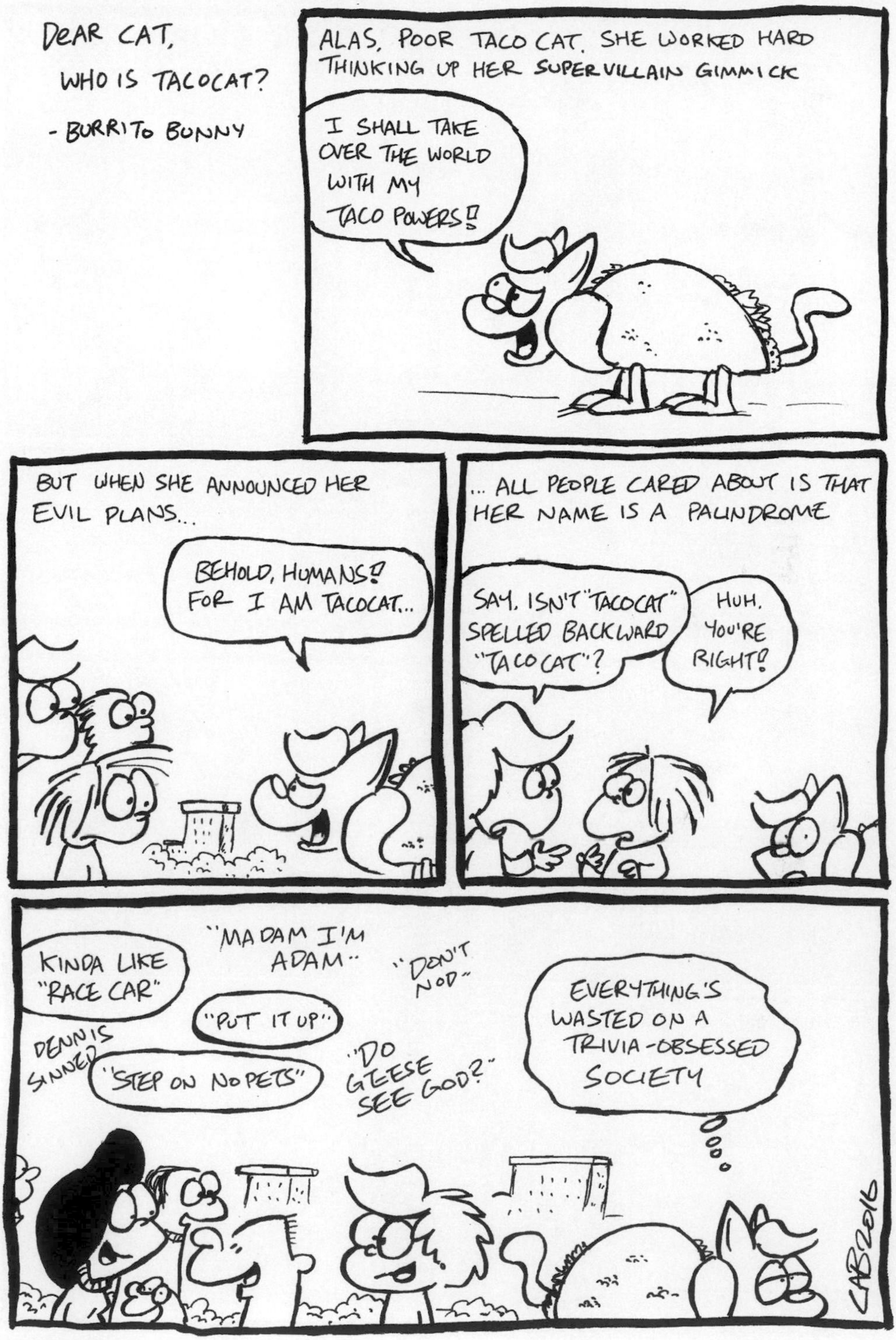
DEAR CAT,
WHO IS TACOCAT?
- BURRITO BUNNY
ALAS, POOR TACO CAT. SHE WORKED HARD THINKING UP HER SUPERVILLAIN GIMMICK
I SHALL TAKE OVER THE WORLD WITH MY TACO POWERS!!
BUT WHEN SHE ANNOUNCED HER EVIL PLANS...
BEHOLD, HUMANS!! FOR I AM TACOCAT...
... ALL PEOPLE CARED ABOUT IS THAT HER NAME IS A PALINDROME
SAY, ISN'T "TACOCAT" SPELLED BACKWARD "TACOCAT"?
HUH. YOU'RE RIGHT!
KINDA LIKE "RACE CAR"
"MADAM I'M ADAM"
"DON'T NOD"
"PUT IT UP"
DENNIS SINNED
"STEP ON NO PETS"
"DO GEESE SEE GOD?"
EVERYTHING'S WASTED ON A TRIVIA-OBSESSED SOCIETY
CAB 2016

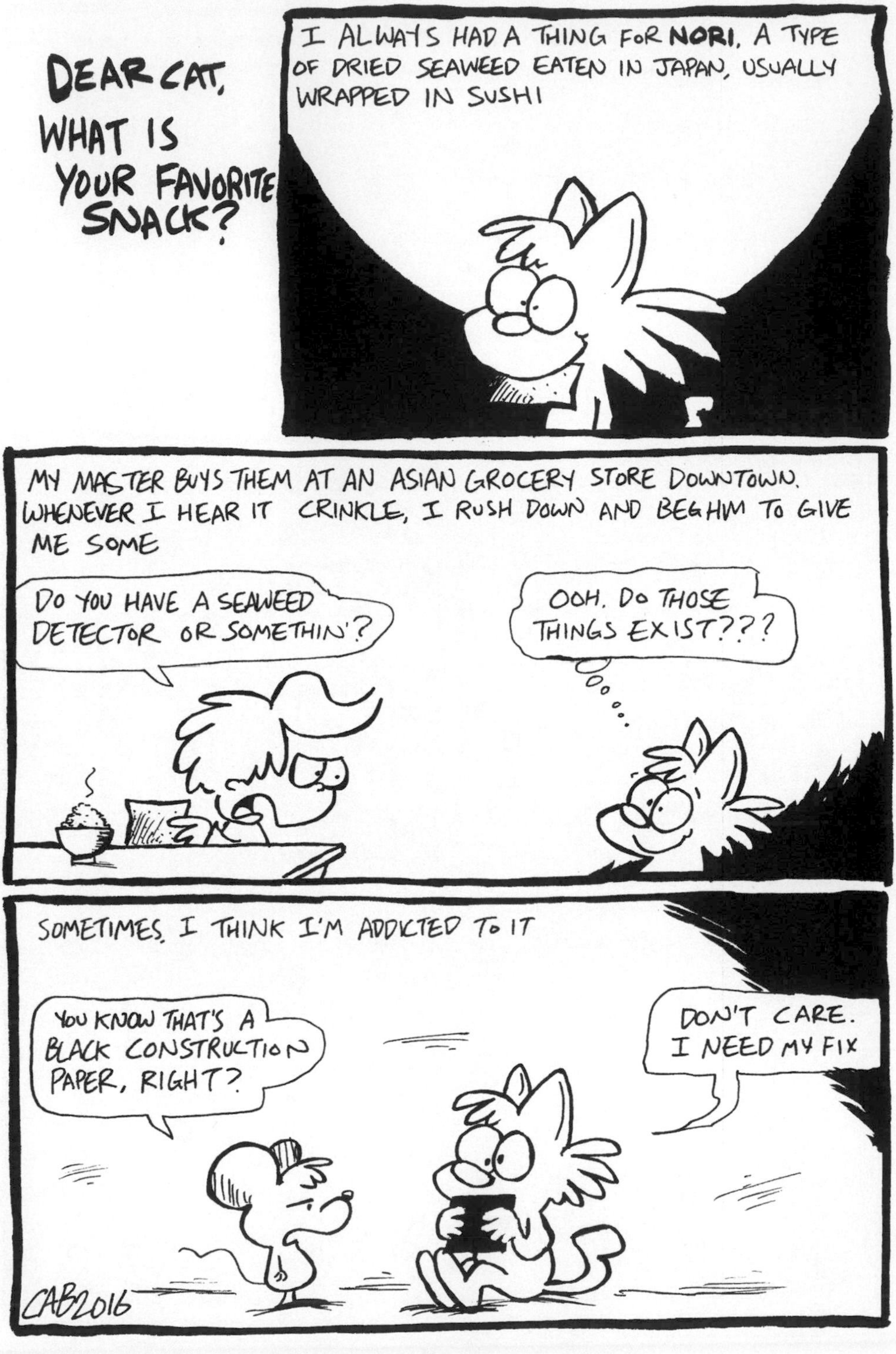
DEAR CAT, WHAT IS YOUR FAVORITE SNACK?
I ALWAYS HAD A THING FOR **NORI**, A TYPE OF DRIED SEAWEED EATEN IN JAPAN, USUALLY WRAPPED IN SUSHI
MY MASTER BUYS THEM AT AN ASIAN GROCERY STORE DOWNTOWN. WHENEVER I HEAR IT CRINKLE, I RUSH DOWN AND BEG HIM TO GIVE ME SOME
DO YOU HAVE A SEAWEED DETECTOR OR SOMETHIN'?
OOH. DO THOSE THINGS EXIST???
SOMETIMES, I THINK I'M ADDICTED TO IT
YOU KNOW THAT'S A BLACK CONSTRUCTION PAPER, RIGHT?
DON'T CARE. I NEED MY FIX
CAB2016

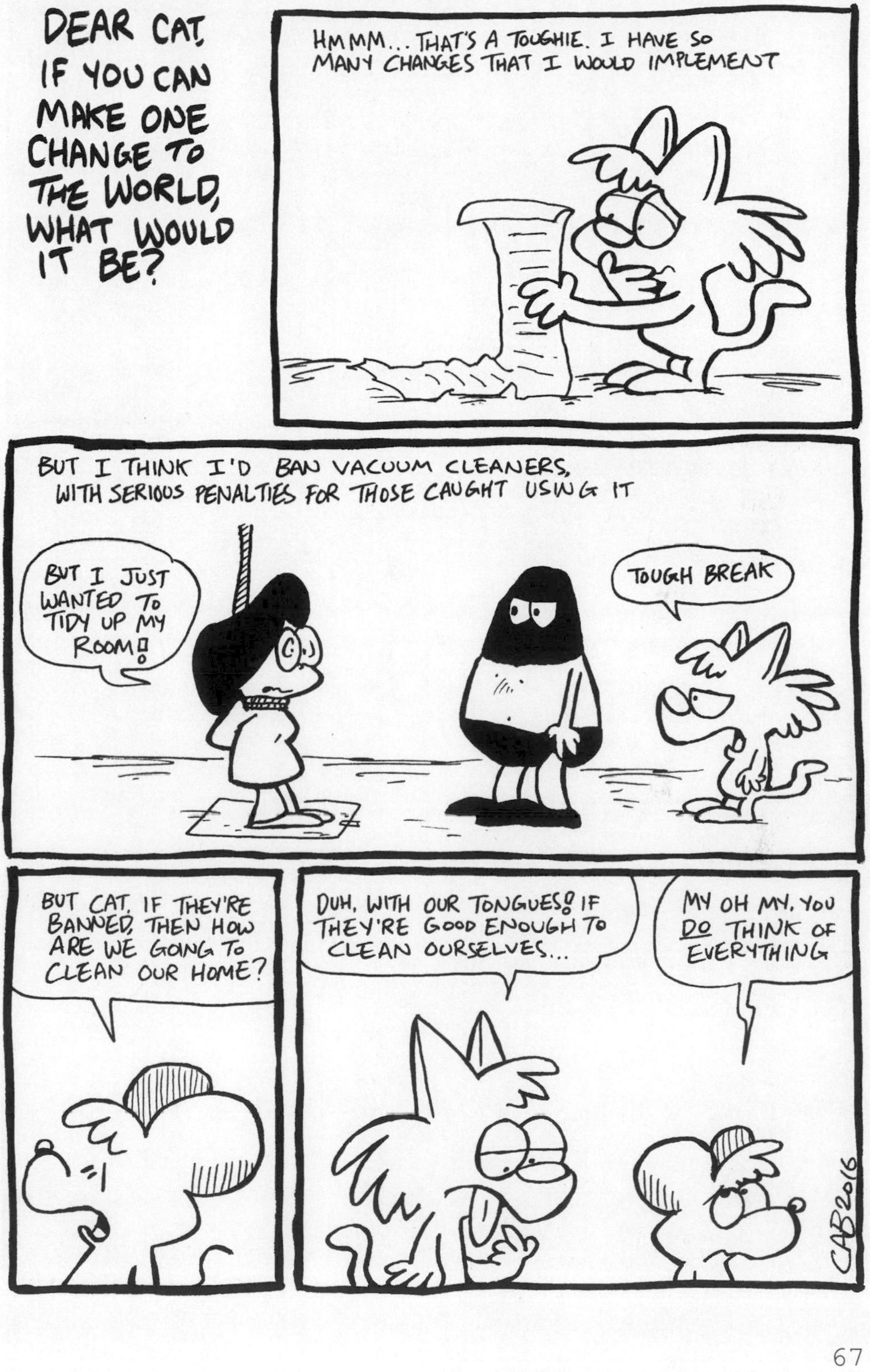
DEAR CAT, IF YOU CAN MAKE ONE CHANGE TO THE WORLD, WHAT WOULD IT BE?
HMMM... THAT'S A TOUGHIE. I HAVE SO MANY CHANGES THAT I WOULD IMPLEMENT
BUT I THINK I'D BAN VACUUM CLEANERS, WITH SERIOUS PENALTIES FOR THOSE CAUGHT USING IT
BUT I JUST WANTED TO TIDY UP MY ROOM!!
TOUGH BREAK
BUT CAT, IF THEY'RE BANNED, THEN HOW ARE WE GOING TO CLEAN OUR HOME?
DUH, WITH OUR TONGUES!! IF THEY'RE GOOD ENOUGH TO CLEAN OURSELVES...
MY OH MY, YOU DO THINK OF EVERYTHING
CAB 2016

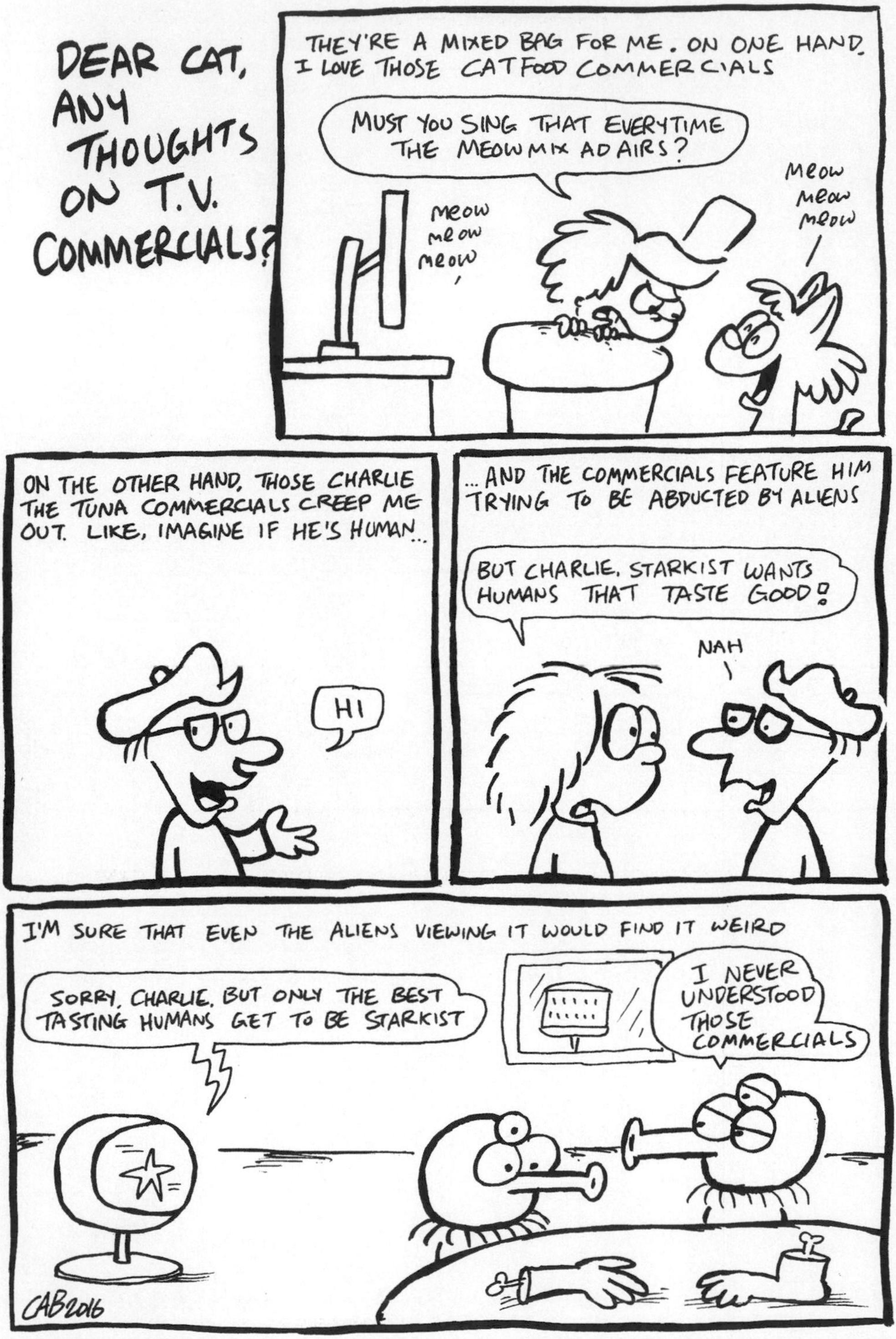
DEAR CAT, ANY THOUGHTS ON T.V. COMMERCIALS?
THEY'RE A MIXED BAG FOR ME. ON ONE HAND, I LOVE THOSE CATFOOD COMMERCIALS
MUST YOU SING THAT EVERYTIME THE MEOWMIX AD AIRS?
MEOW MEOW MEOW
MEOW MEOW MEOW
ON THE OTHER HAND, THOSE CHARLIE THE TUNA COMMERCIALS CREEP ME OUT. LIKE, IMAGINE IF HE'S HUMAN...
HI
...AND THE COMMERCIALS FEATURE HIM TRYING TO BE ABDUCTED BY ALIENS
BUT CHARLIE, STARKIST WANTS HUMANS THAT TASTE GOOD!
NAH
I'M SURE THAT EVEN THE ALIENS VIEWING IT WOULD FIND IT WEIRD
SORRY, CHARLIE, BUT ONLY THE BEST TASTING HUMANS GET TO BE STARKIST
I NEVER UNDERSTOOD THOSE COMMERCIALS
CAB2016

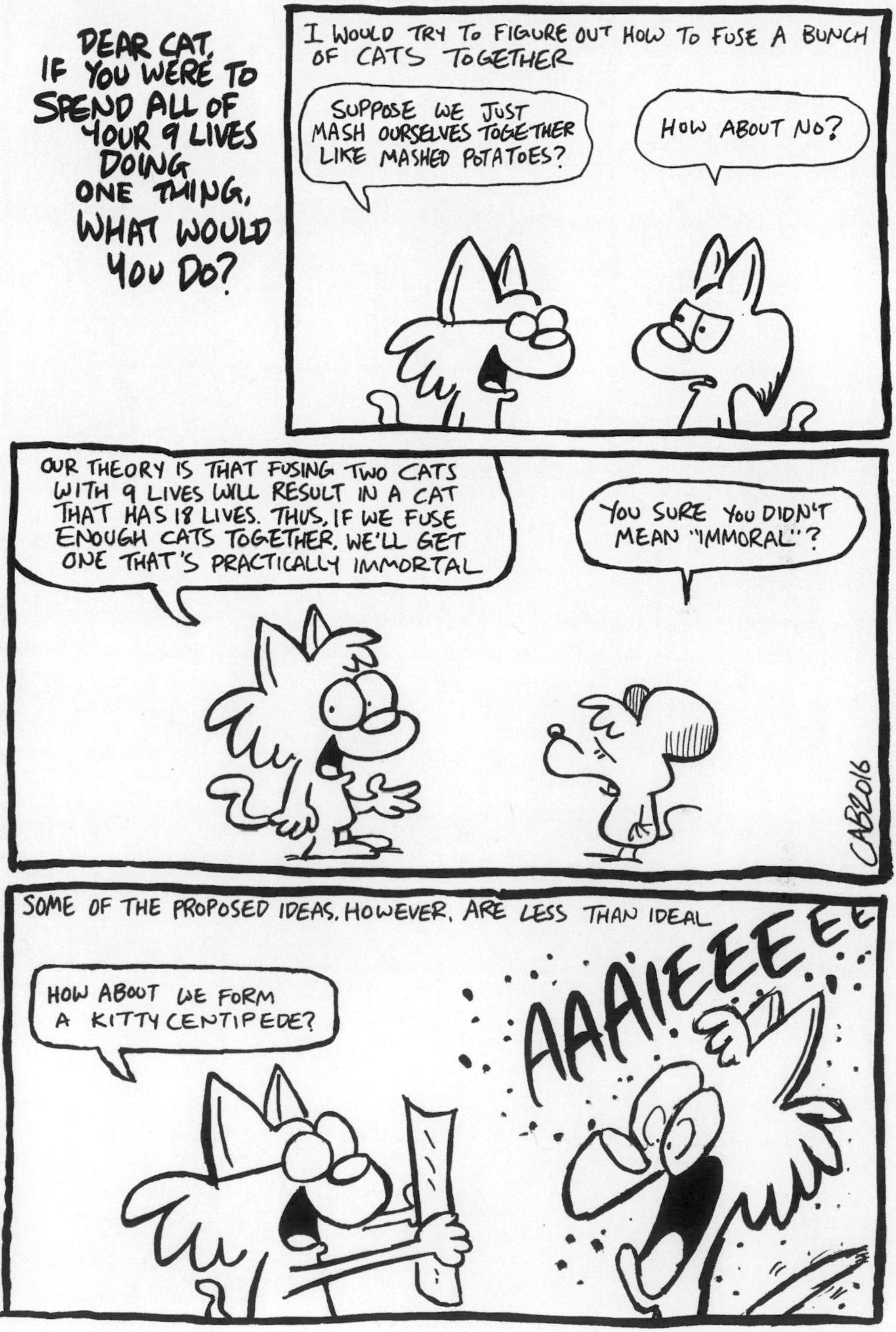
DEAR CAT, IF YOU WERE TO SPEND ALL OF YOUR 9 LIVES DOING ONE THING, WHAT WOULD YOU DO?
I WOULD TRY TO FIGURE OUT HOW TO FUSE A BUNCH OF CATS TOGETHER
SUPPOSE WE JUST MASH OURSELVES TOGETHER LIKE MASHED POTATOES?
HOW ABOUT NO?
OUR THEORY IS THAT FUSING TWO CATS WITH 9 LIVES WILL RESULT IN A CAT THAT HAS 18 LIVES. THUS, IF WE FUSE ENOUGH CATS TOGETHER, WE'LL GET ONE THAT'S PRACTICALLY IMMORTAL
YOU SURE YOU DIDN'T MEAN "IMMORAL"?
CAB2016
SOME OF THE PROPOSED IDEAS, HOWEVER, ARE LESS THAN IDEAL
HOW ABOUT WE FORM A KITTY CENTIPEDE?
AAAIEEEEEE

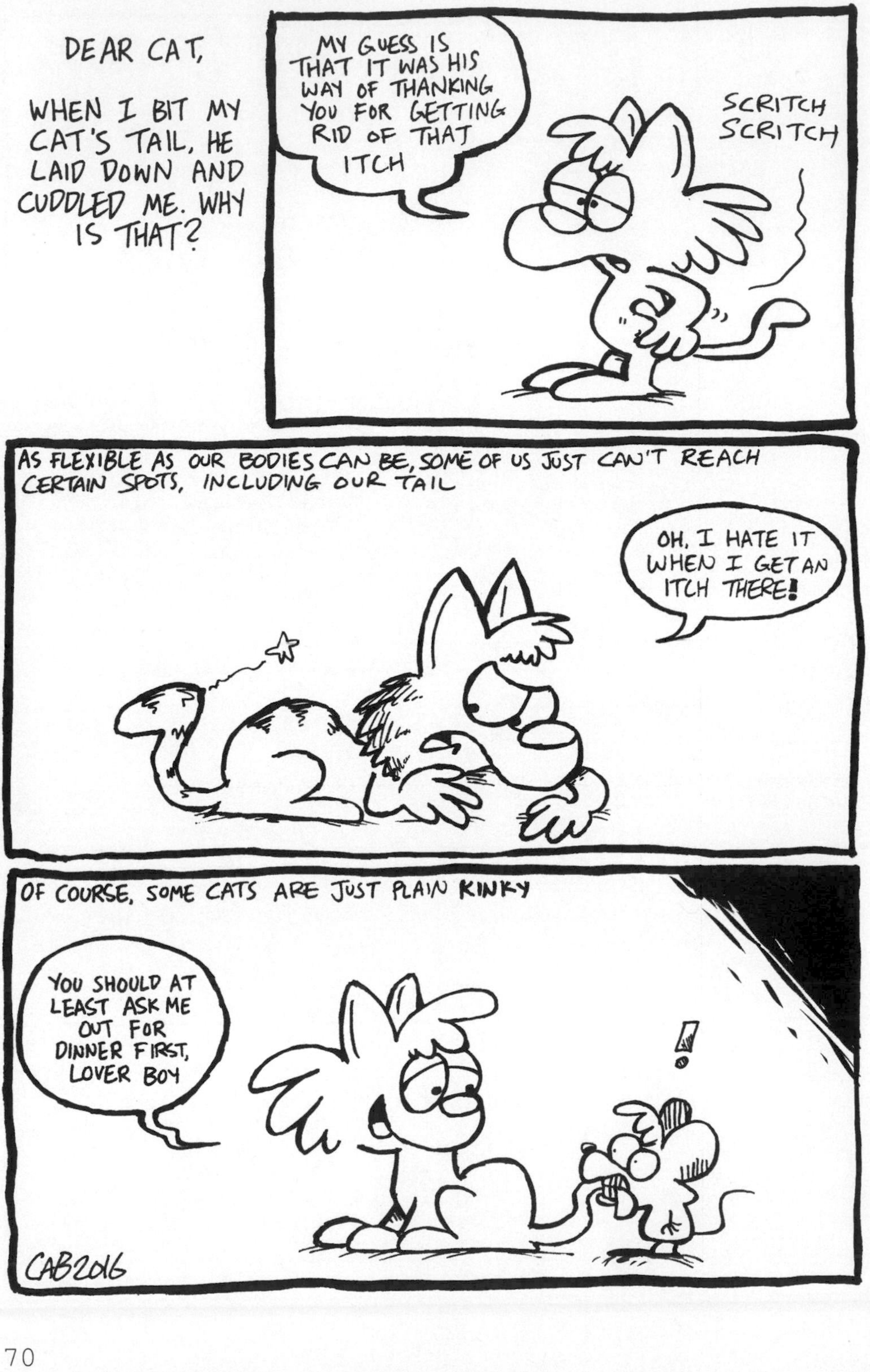
DEAR CAT,
WHEN I BIT MY CAT'S TAIL, HE LAID DOWN AND CUDDLED ME. WHY IS THAT?
MY GUESS IS THAT IT WAS HIS WAY OF THANKING YOU FOR GETTING RID OF THAT ITCH
SCRITCH SCRITCH
AS FLEXIBLE AS OUR BODIES CAN BE, SOME OF US JUST CAN'T REACH CERTAIN SPOTS, INCLUDING OUR TAIL
OH, I HATE IT WHEN I GET AN ITCH THERE!
OF COURSE, SOME CATS ARE JUST PLAIN KINKY
YOU SHOULD AT LEAST ASK ME OUT FOR DINNER FIRST, LOVER BOY
!
CAB2016

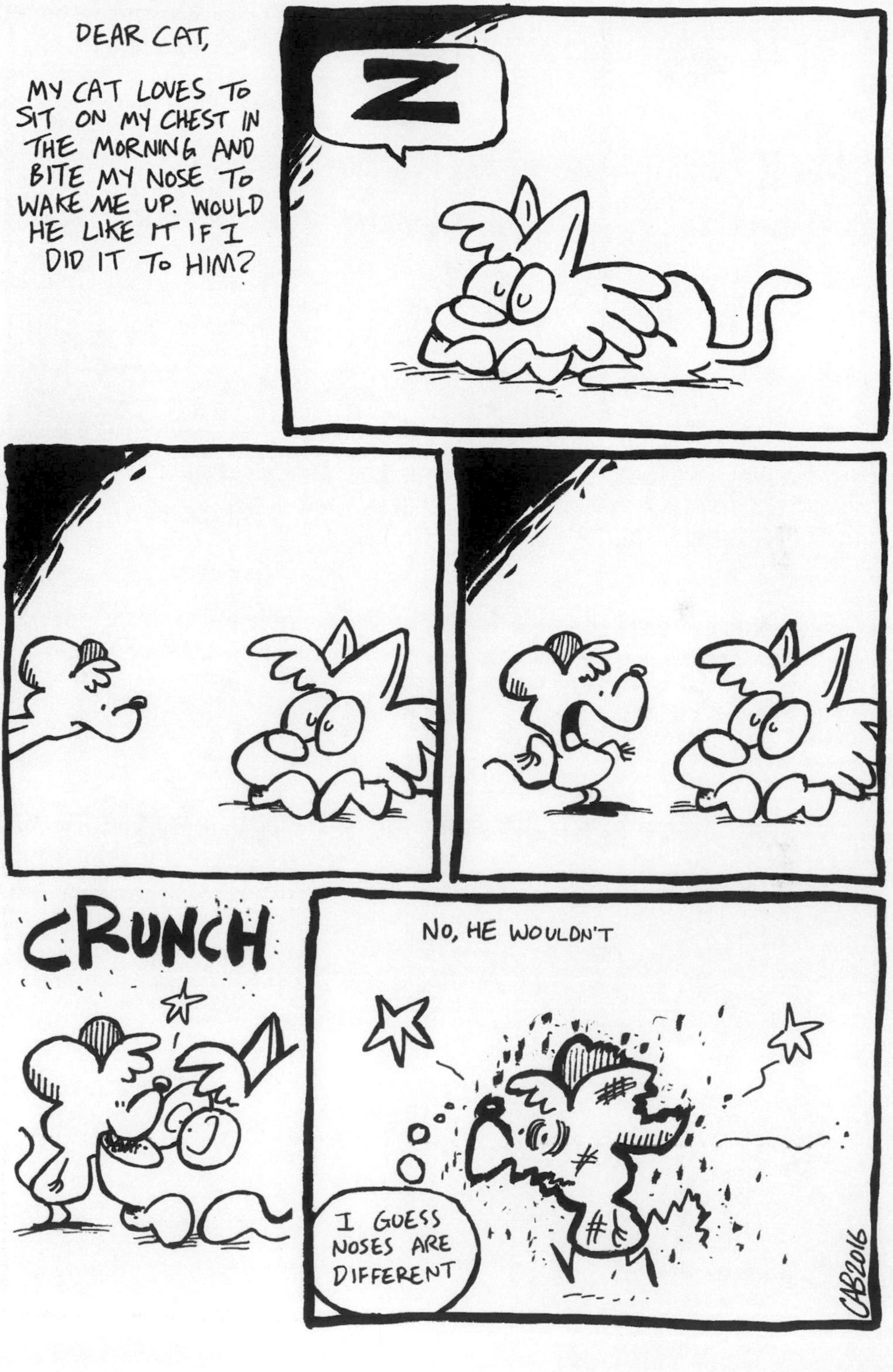
DEAR CAT,
MY CAT LOVES TO SIT ON MY CHEST IN THE MORNING AND BITE MY NOSE TO WAKE ME UP. WOULD HE LIKE IT IF I DID IT TO HIM?
Z
CRUNCH
NO, HE WOULDN'T
I GUESS NOSES ARE DIFFERENT
CAB2016

DEAR CAT, DO YOU FEAR DEATH?

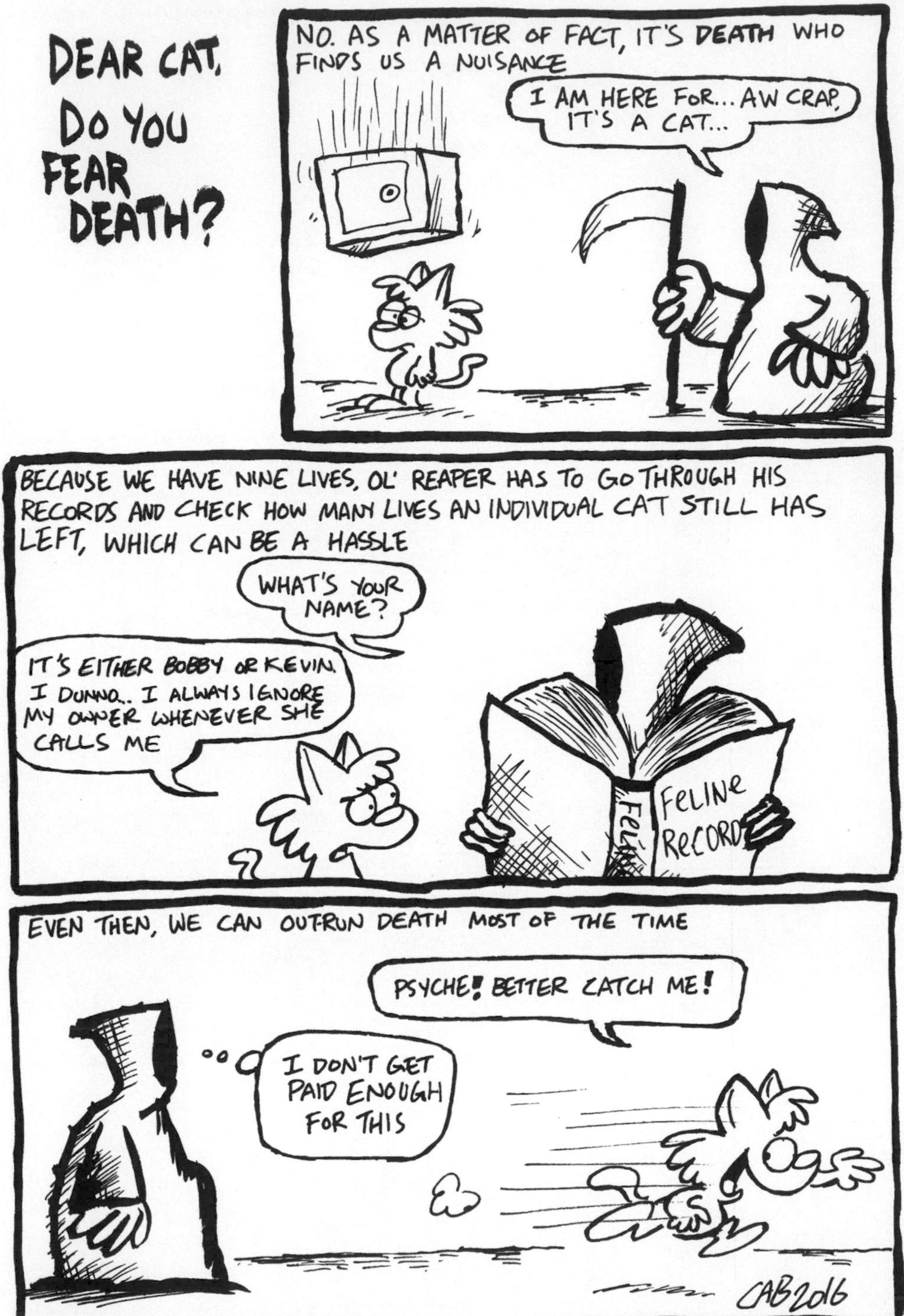
NO. AS A MATTER OF FACT, IT'S DEATH WHO FINDS US A NUISANCE
I AM HERE FOR... AW CRAP, IT'S A CAT...
BECAUSE WE HAVE NINE LIVES, OL' REAPER HAS TO GO THROUGH HIS RECORDS AND CHECK HOW MANY LIVES AN INDIVIDUAL CAT STILL HAS LEFT, WHICH CAN BE A HASSLE
WHAT'S YOUR NAME?
IT'S EITHER BOBBY OR KEVIN. I DUNNO.. I ALWAYS IGNORE MY OWNER WHENEVER SHE CALLS ME
Feline Record
EVEN THEN, WE CAN OUT-RUN DEATH MOST OF THE TIME
PSYCHE! BETTER CATCH ME!
I DON'T GET PAID ENOUGH FOR THIS
CAB 2016

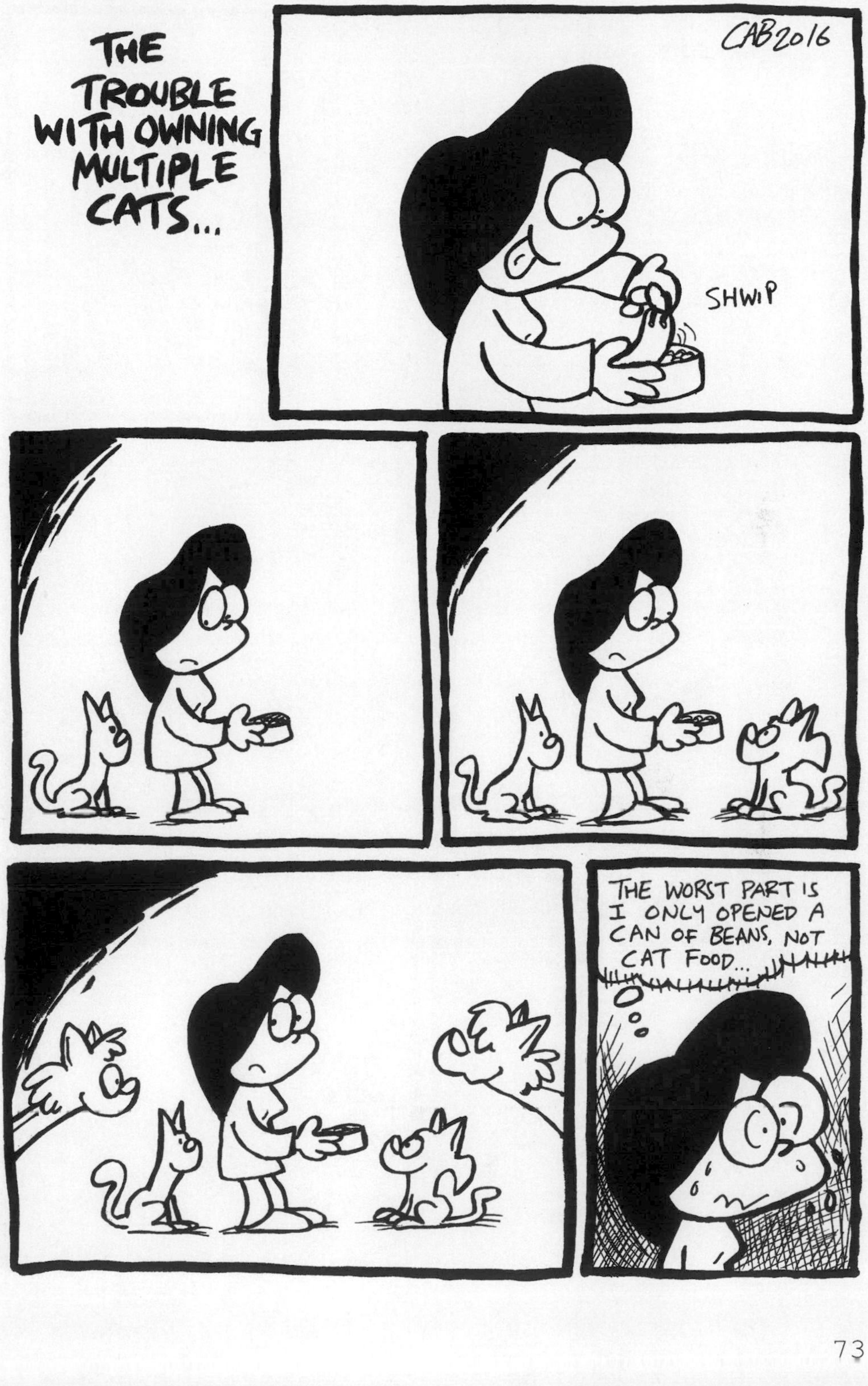
THE TROUBLE WITH OWNING MULTIPLE CATS...
CAB 2016
SHWIP
THE WORST PART IS I ONLY OPENED A CAN OF BEANS, NOT CAT FOOD...

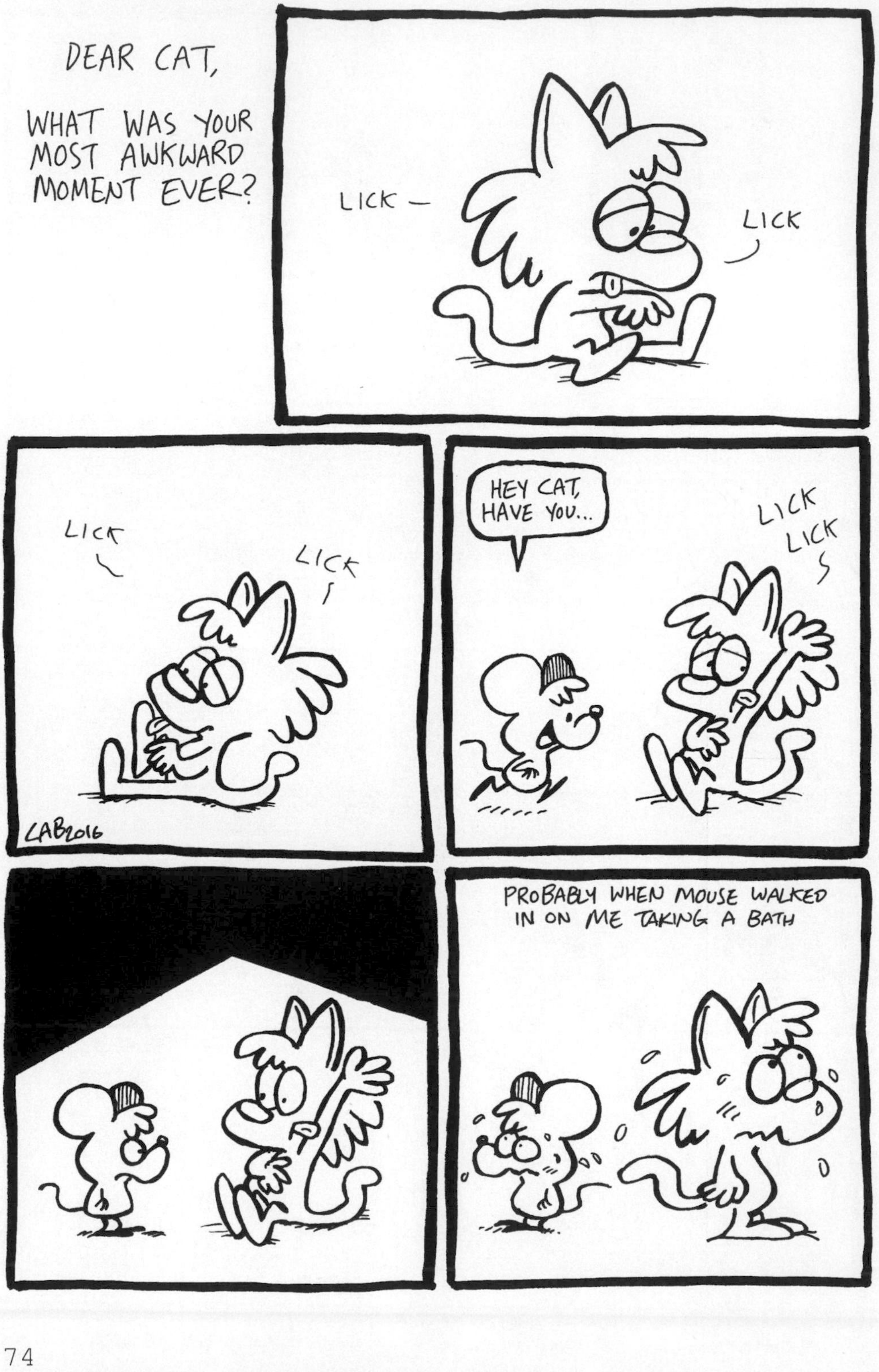
DEAR CAT,
WHAT WAS YOUR MOST AWKWARD MOMENT EVER?
LICK —
LICK
LICK
LICK
CAB2016
HEY CAT, HAVE YOU...
LICK
LICK
PROBABLY WHEN MOUSE WALKED IN ON ME TAKING A BATH

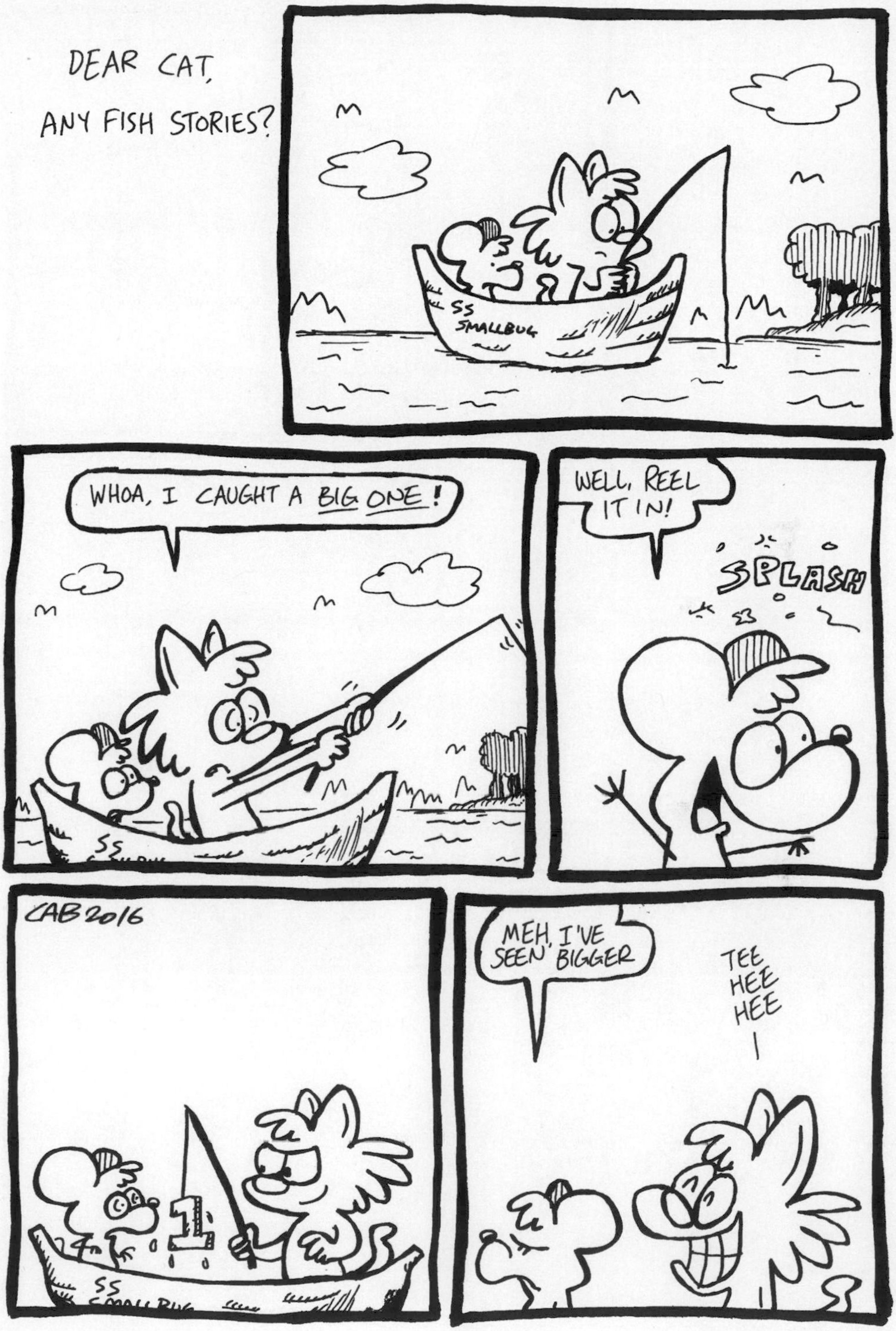
DEAR CAT,
ANY FISH STORIES?
SS SMALLBUG
WHOA, I CAUGHT A BIG ONE!
WELL, REEL IT IN!
SPLASH
CAB 2016
MEH, I'VE SEEN BIGGER
TEE HEE HEE

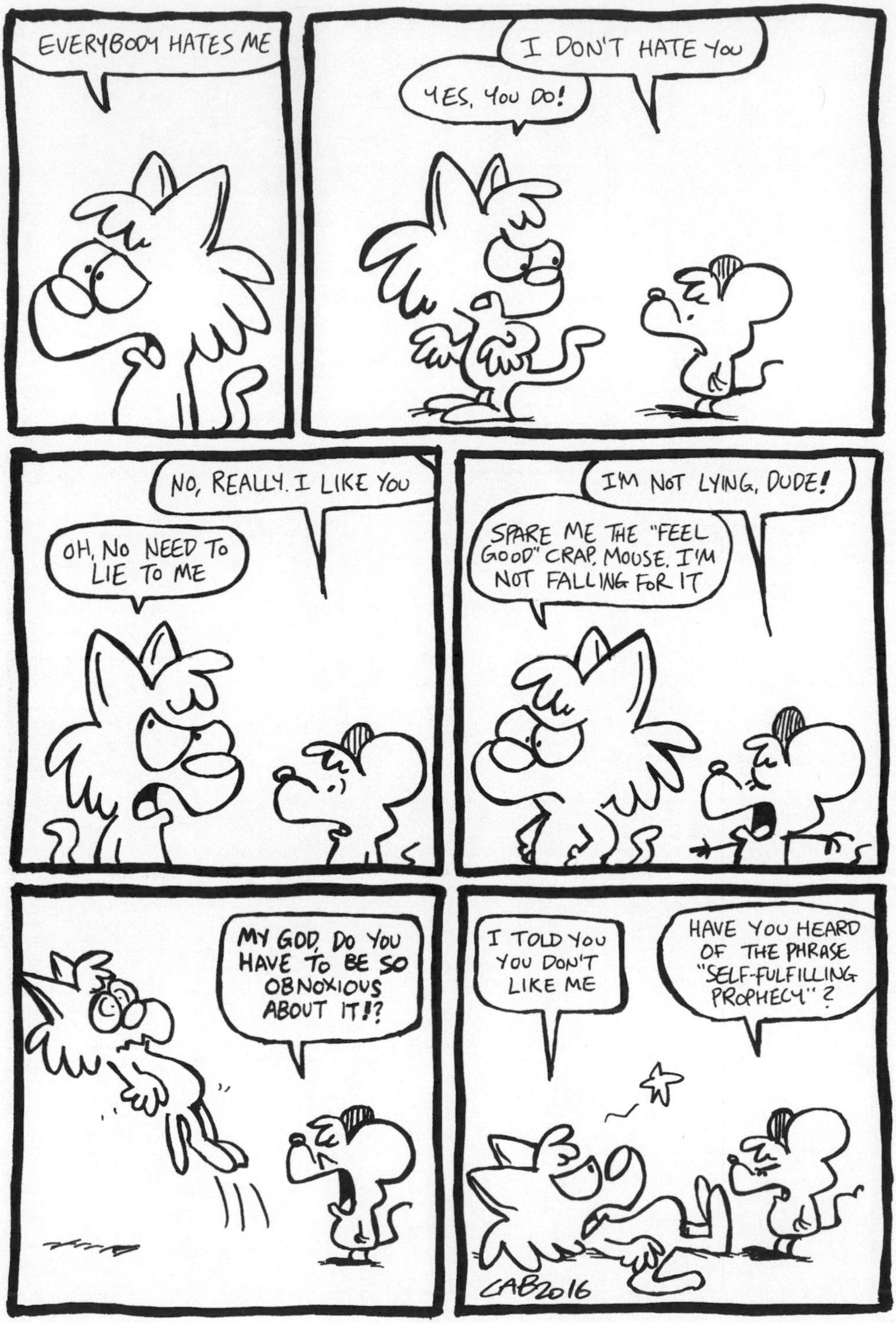
EVERYBODY HATES ME
I DON'T HATE YOU
YES, YOU DO!
NO, REALLY. I LIKE YOU
OH, NO NEED TO LIE TO ME
I'M NOT LYING, DUDE!
SPARE ME THE "FEEL GOOD" CRAP, MOUSE. I'M NOT FALLING FOR IT
MY GOD, DO YOU HAVE TO BE SO OBNOXIOUS ABOUT IT!?
I TOLD YOU YOU DON'T LIKE ME
HAVE YOU HEARD OF THE PHRASE "SELF-FULFILLING PROPHECY"?
CAB2016

DEAR CAT,

IF YOU WERE A **KING**, WHAT COUNTRY WOULD YOU RULE?

OH, THAT'S EASY: JAPAN! FOR STARTERS, THERE'S ALREADY AN ISLAND OVERRUN WITH CATS

田代島
Tashirojima

IT'S A POPULAR TOURIST DESTINATION, TOO!

WE JUST NEED TO GATHER ENOUGH CATS TO TAKE OVER THE MAINLAND...

meow

...PLUS ONE GODZILLA-SIZED CAT, JUST IN CASE...

ALTHOUGH GIVEN JAPAN'S DECLINING BIRTH RATE, THE TAKEOVER WON'T BE MUCH OF A CHALLENGE

THIS IS SOMEWHAT OF A LETDOWN...

CAB2016

DEAR CAT,

HAVE YOU EVER HAD A RUN-IN WITH CURIOSITY?

NOT REALLY, BUT I DID HAVE A DREAM WHERE I WAS STRANDED ON MARS. AT ONE POINT, THE CURIOSITY ROVER ALMOST RAN OVER ME

EEP!

I EVENTUALLY CAUGHT UP WITH THE MARS ROVER AND RODE ON TOP. NOT THAT IT MATTERED. EVEN IN MY DREAM, MARS IS **BORING**

NOT EVEN A McDONALD'S!

I STARTED FOOLING AROUND WITH THE CAMERA

CRIPES, IS THERE **ANYWHERE** IN THE UNIVERSE WHERE WE CAN AVOID CAT PICTURES!?

NASA MISSION CONTROL

CAB 2016

DEAR CAT,

WHY DO YOU LIKE TO HARM LITTLE LIZARDS?

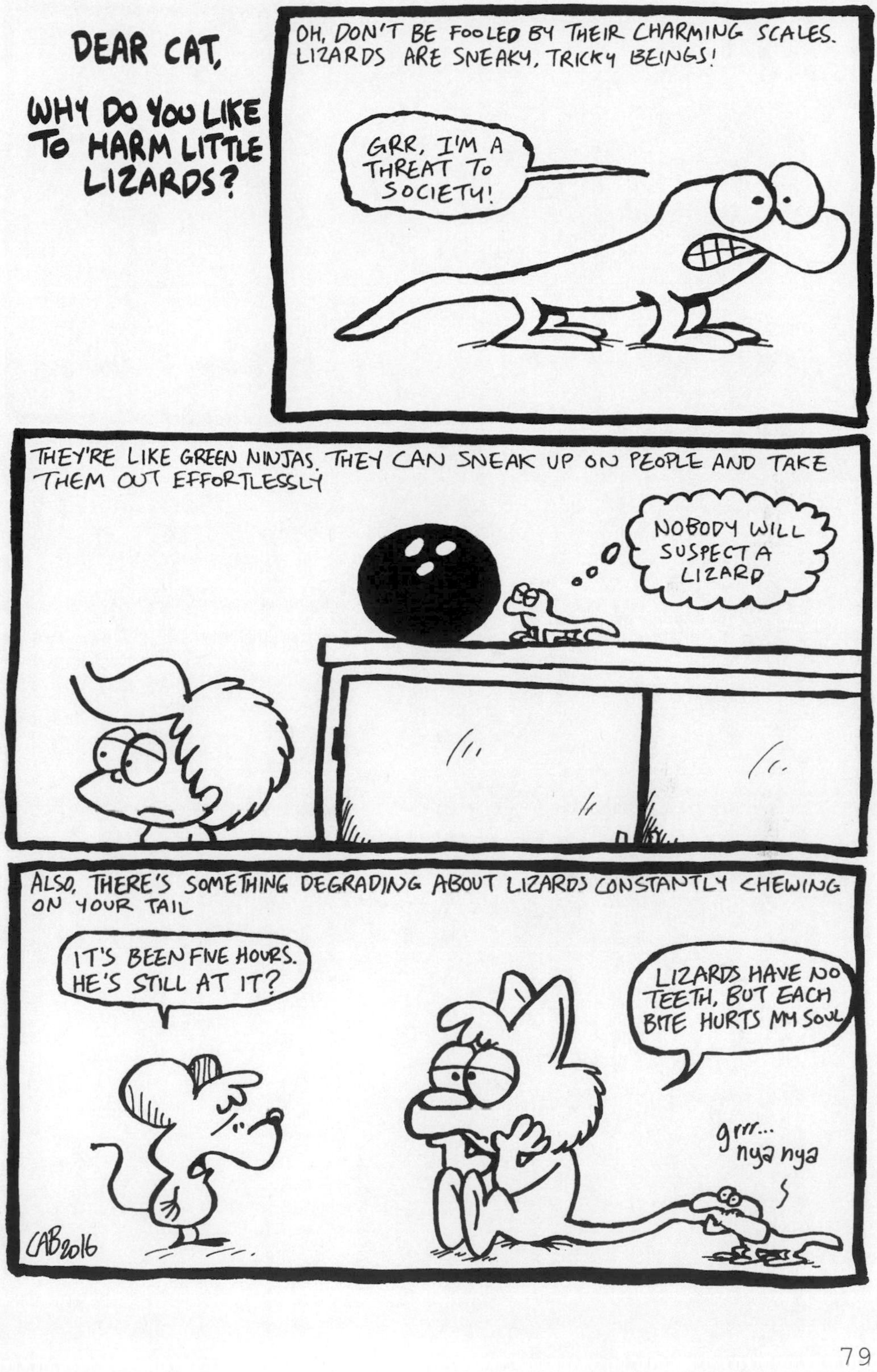
OH, DON'T BE FOOLED BY THEIR CHARMING SCALES. LIZARDS ARE SNEAKY, TRICKY BEINGS!
GRR, I'M A THREAT TO SOCIETY!
THEY'RE LIKE GREEN NINJAS. THEY CAN SNEAK UP ON PEOPLE AND TAKE THEM OUT EFFORTLESSLY
NOBODY WILL SUSPECT A LIZARD
ALSO, THERE'S SOMETHING DEGRADING ABOUT LIZARDS CONSTANTLY CHEWING ON YOUR TAIL
IT'S BEEN FIVE HOURS. HE'S STILL AT IT?
LIZARDS HAVE NO TEETH, BUT EACH BITE HURTS MY SOUL
grrr... nya nya
CAB 2016

DEAR CAT,

DOESN'T LICKING HAIR FEEL WEIRD?

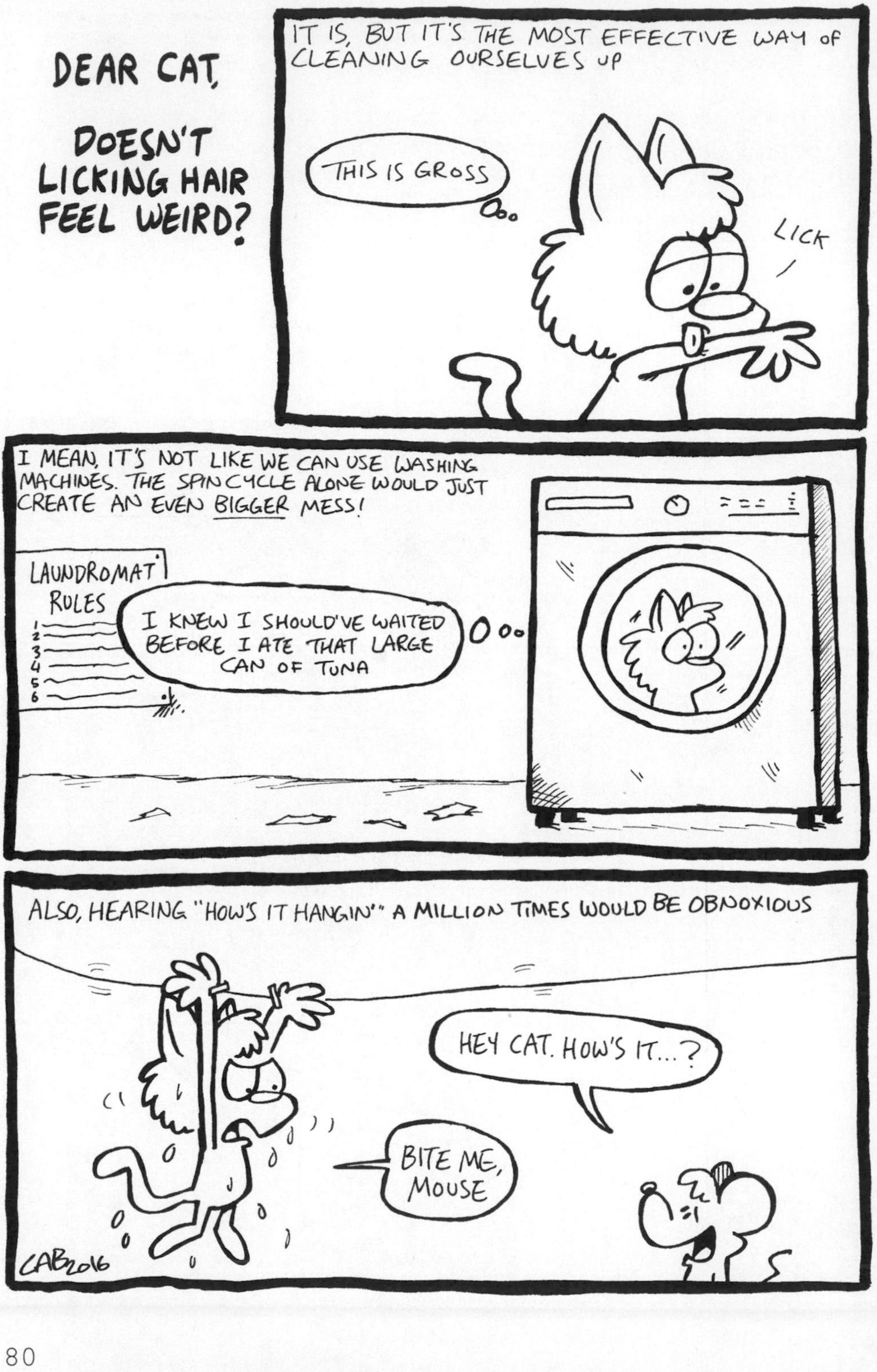

IT IS, BUT IT'S THE MOST EFFECTIVE WAY OF CLEANING OURSELVES UP
THIS IS GROSS
LICK
I MEAN, IT'S NOT LIKE WE CAN USE WASHING MACHINES. THE SPIN CYCLE ALONE WOULD JUST CREATE AN EVEN BIGGER MESS!
LAUNDROMAT RULES
1
2
3
4
5
6
I KNEW I SHOULD'VE WAITED BEFORE I ATE THAT LARGE CAN OF TUNA
ALSO, HEARING "HOW'S IT HANGIN'" A MILLION TIMES WOULD BE OBNOXIOUS
HEY CAT. HOW'S IT...?
BITE ME, MOUSE
CAB2016

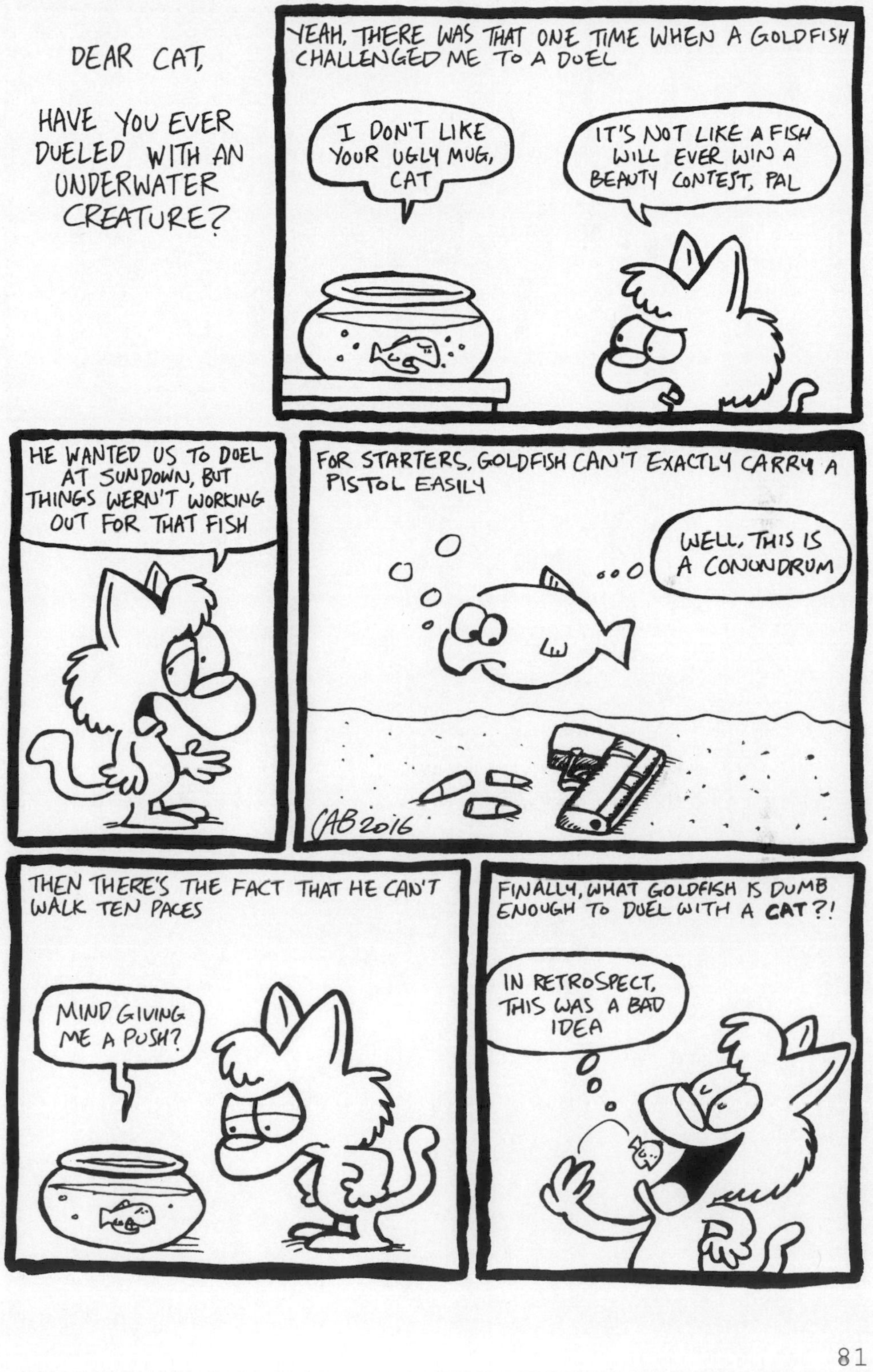
DEAR CAT,
HAVE YOU EVER DUELED WITH AN UNDERWATER CREATURE?
YEAH, THERE WAS THAT ONE TIME WHEN A GOLDFISH CHALLENGED ME TO A DUEL
I DON'T LIKE YOUR UGLY MUG, CAT
IT'S NOT LIKE A FISH WILL EVER WIN A BEAUTY CONTEST, PAL
HE WANTED US TO DUEL AT SUNDOWN, BUT THINGS WERN'T WORKING OUT FOR THAT FISH
FOR STARTERS, GOLDFISH CAN'T EXACTLY CARRY A PISTOL EASILY
WELL, THIS IS A CONUNDRUM
CAB 2016
THEN THERE'S THE FACT THAT HE CAN'T WALK TEN PACES
MIND GIVING ME A PUSH?
FINALLY, WHAT GOLDFISH IS DUMB ENOUGH TO DUEL WITH A CAT?!
IN RETROSPECT, THIS WAS A BAD IDEA

DEAR CAT,

WHY ARE CATS AFRAID OF CUCUMBERS?

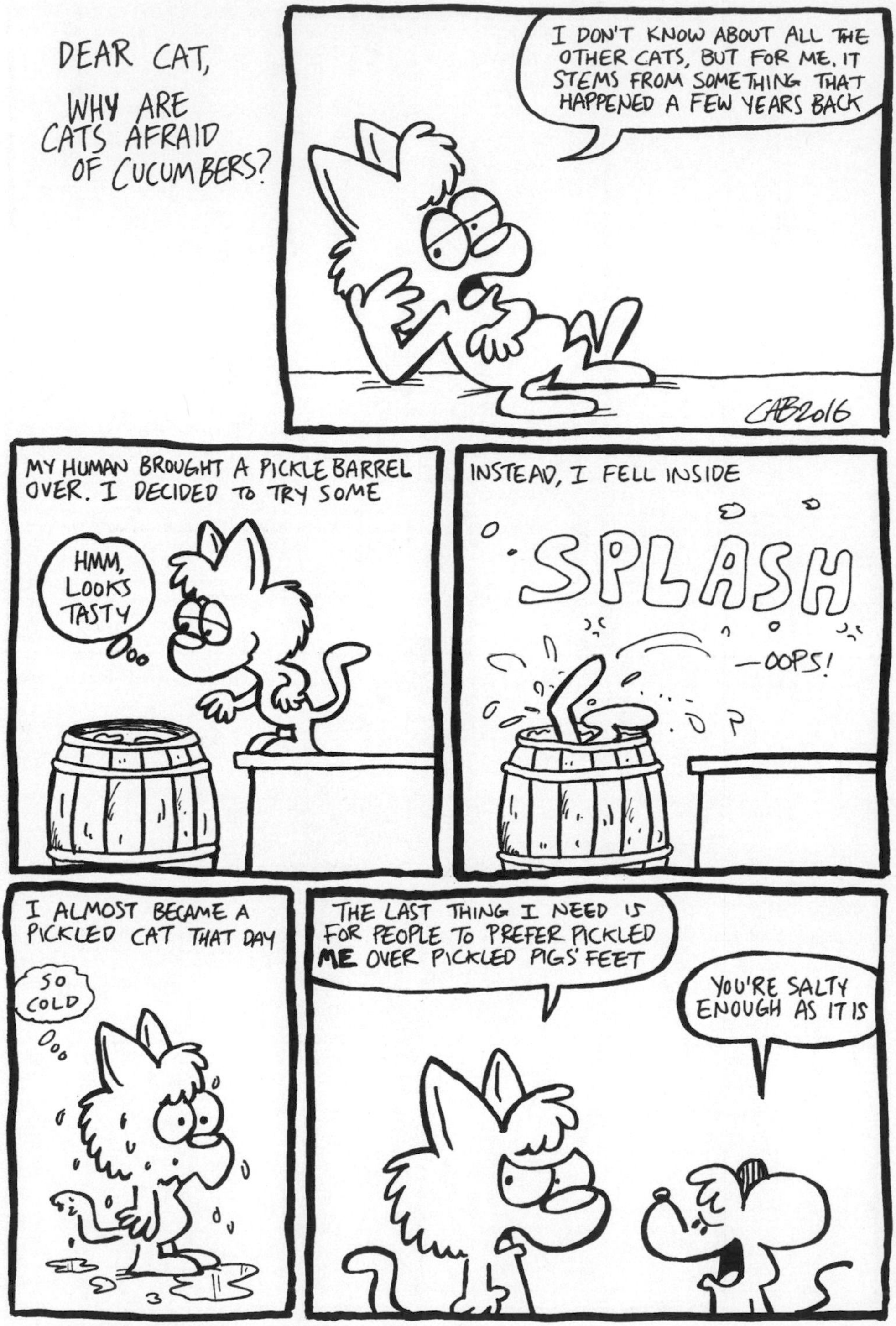
I DON'T KNOW ABOUT ALL THE OTHER CATS, BUT FOR ME, IT STEMS FROM SOMETHING THAT HAPPENED A FEW YEARS BACK
CAB2016
MY HUMAN BROUGHT A PICKLE BARREL OVER. I DECIDED TO TRY SOME
HMM, LOOKS TASTY
INSTEAD, I FELL INSIDE
SPLASH
—OOPS!
I ALMOST BECAME A PICKLED CAT THAT DAY
SO COLD
THE LAST THING I NEED IS FOR PEOPLE TO PREFER PICKLED **ME** OVER PICKLED PIGS' FEET
YOU'RE SALTY ENOUGH AS IT IS

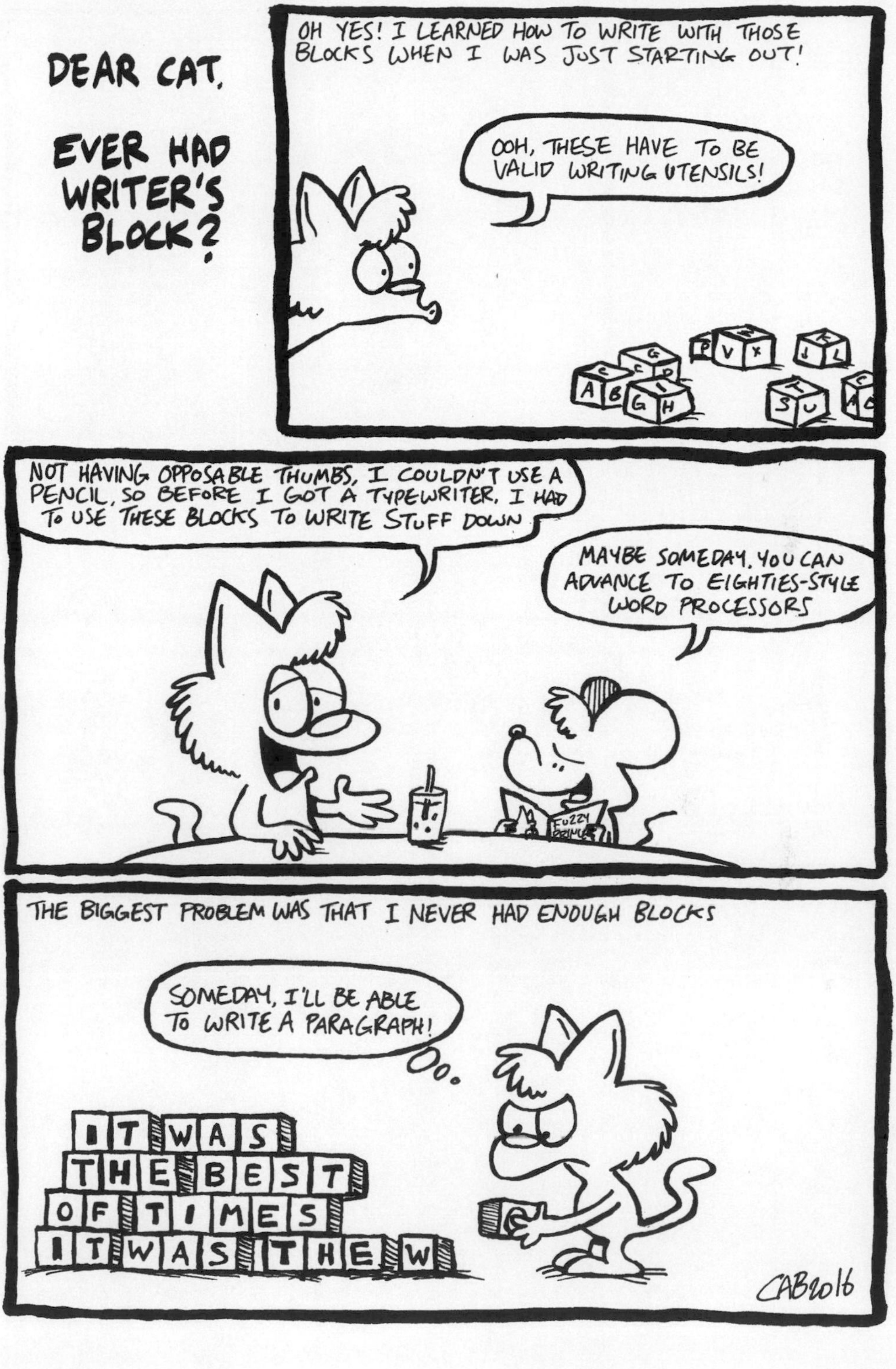
DEAR CAT,
EVER HAD WRITER'S BLOCK?
OH YES! I LEARNED HOW TO WRITE WITH THOSE BLOCKS WHEN I WAS JUST STARTING OUT!
OOH, THESE HAVE TO BE VALID WRITING UTENSILS!
NOT HAVING OPPOSABLE THUMBS, I COULDN'T USE A PENCIL, SO BEFORE I GOT A TYPEWRITER, I HAD TO USE THESE BLOCKS TO WRITE STUFF DOWN.
MAYBE SOMEDAY, YOU CAN ADVANCE TO EIGHTIES-STYLE WORD PROCESSORS
THE BIGGEST PROBLEM WAS THAT I NEVER HAD ENOUGH BLOCKS
SOMEDAY, I'LL BE ABLE TO WRITE A PARAGRAPH!
IT WAS
THE BEST
OF TIMES
IT WAS THE W
CAB2016

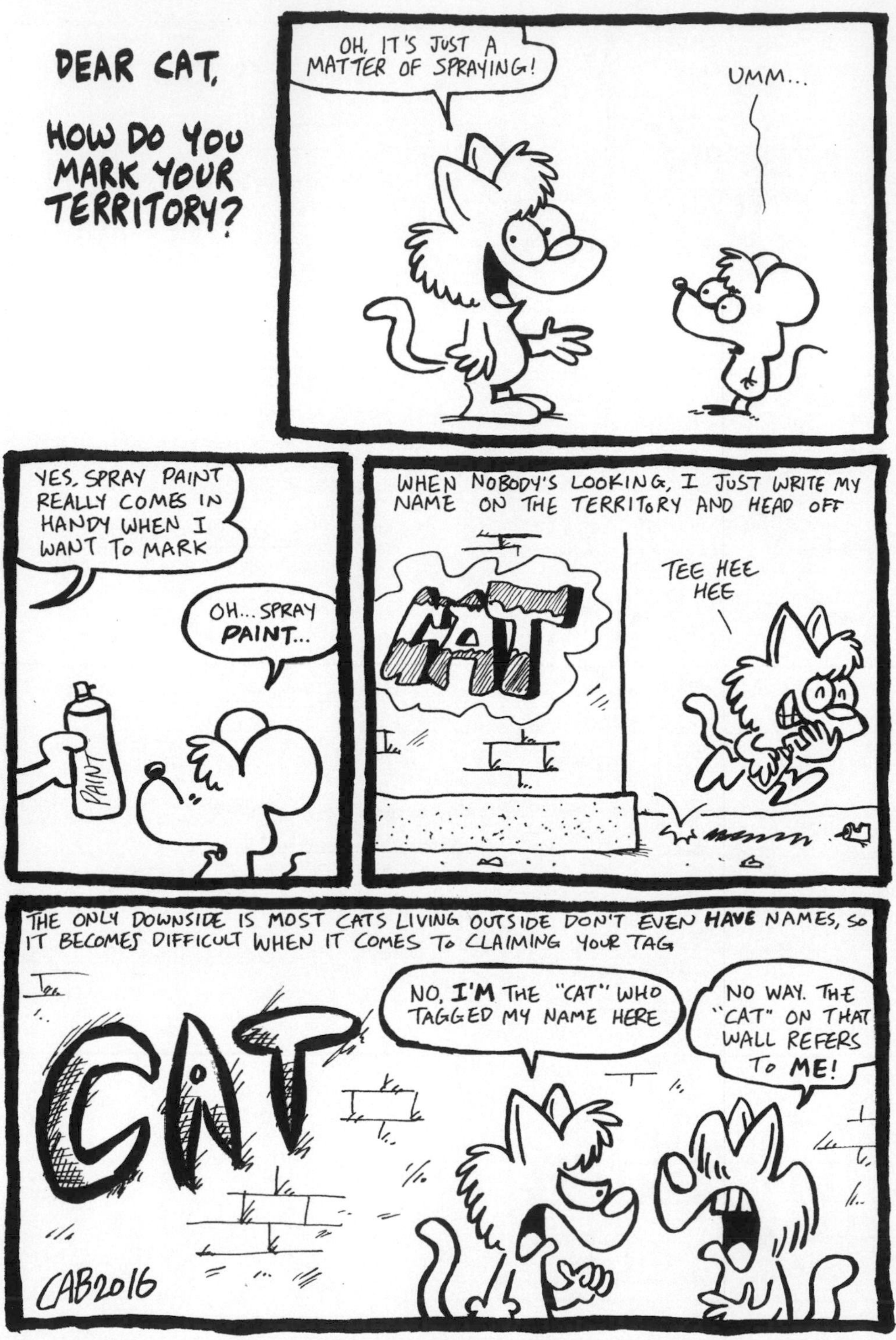
DEAR CAT,
HOW DO YOU MARK YOUR TERRITORY?
OH, IT'S JUST A MATTER OF SPRAYING!
UMM...
YES. SPRAY PAINT REALLY COMES IN HANDY WHEN I WANT TO MARK
OH... SPRAY PAINT...
PAINT
WHEN NOBODY'S LOOKING, I JUST WRITE MY NAME ON THE TERRITORY AND HEAD OFF
CAT
TEE HEE HEE
THE ONLY DOWNSIDE IS MOST CATS LIVING OUTSIDE DON'T EVEN HAVE NAMES, SO IT BECOMES DIFFICULT WHEN IT COMES TO CLAIMING YOUR TAG
CAT
NO, I'M THE "CAT" WHO TAGGED MY NAME HERE
NO WAY. THE "CAT" ON THAT WALL REFERS TO ME!
CAB2016

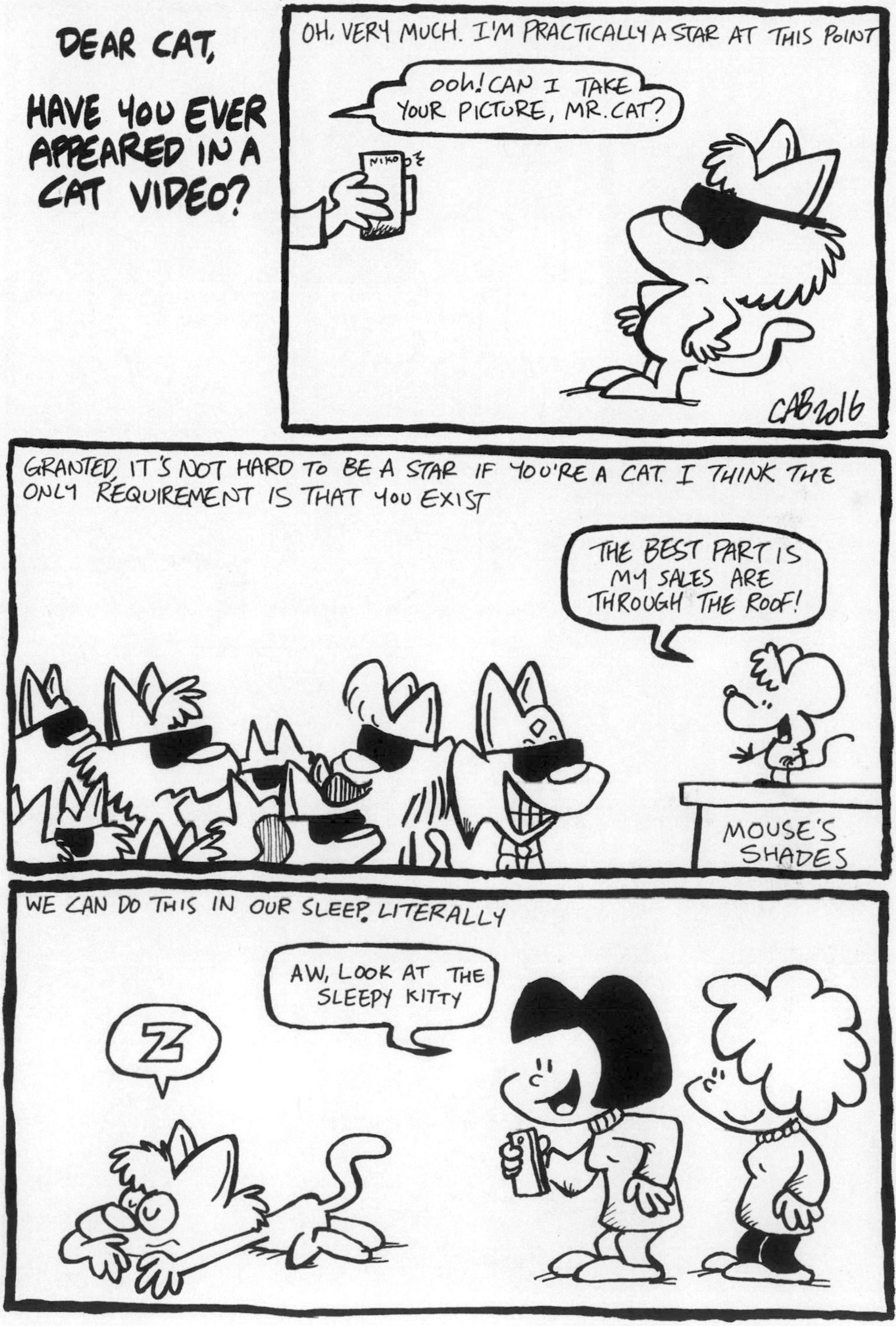
DEAR CAT,
HAVE YOU EVER APPEARED IN A CAT VIDEO?
OH, VERY MUCH. I'M PRACTICALLY A STAR AT THIS POINT
OOH! CAN I TAKE YOUR PICTURE, MR. CAT?
CAB 2016
GRANTED, IT'S NOT HARD TO BE A STAR IF YOU'RE A CAT. I THINK THE ONLY REQUIREMENT IS THAT YOU EXIST
THE BEST PART IS MY SALES ARE THROUGH THE ROOF!
MOUSE'S SHADES
WE CAN DO THIS IN OUR SLEEP. LITERALLY
AW, LOOK AT THE SLEEPY KITTY
Z

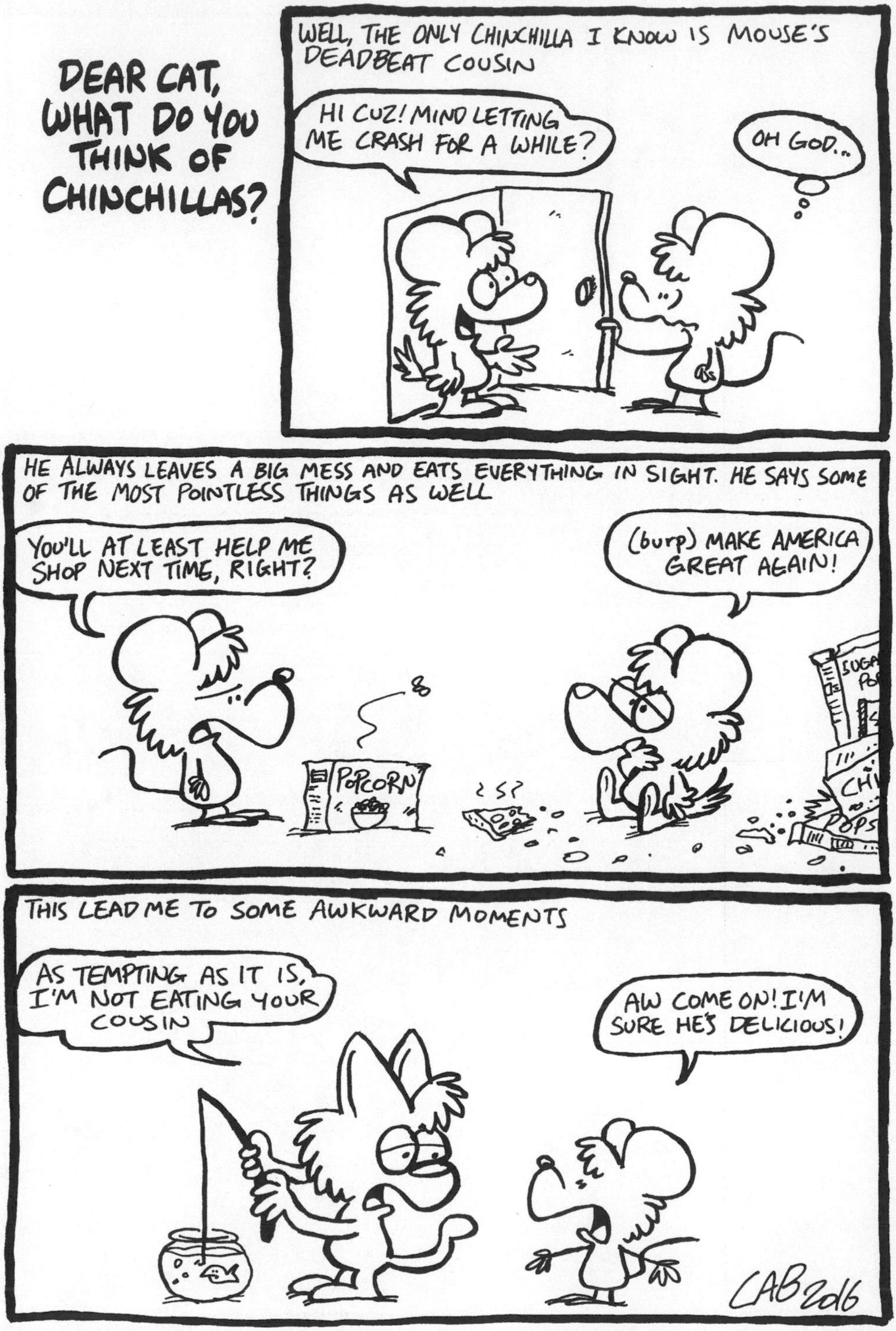
DEAR CAT, WHAT DO YOU THINK OF CHINCHILLAS?
WELL, THE ONLY CHINCHILLA I KNOW IS MOUSE'S DEADBEAT COUSIN
HI CUZ! MIND LETTING ME CRASH FOR A WHILE?
OH GOD...
HE ALWAYS LEAVES A BIG MESS AND EATS EVERYTHING IN SIGHT. HE SAYS SOME OF THE MOST POINTLESS THINGS AS WELL
YOU'LL AT LEAST HELP ME SHOP NEXT TIME, RIGHT?
(burp) MAKE AMERICA GREAT AGAIN!
POPCORN
THIS LEAD ME TO SOME AWKWARD MOMENTS
AS TEMPTING AS IT IS, I'M NOT EATING YOUR COUSIN
AW COME ON! I'M SURE HE'S DELICIOUS!
CAB 2016

DEAR CAT,

DO YOU HAVE A NAME OTHER THAN "CAT"?

YEAH, DOZENS!

WHENEVER I MEET DIFFERENT PEOPLE, THEY GIVE ME DIFFERENT NAMES. IT'S NEVER CONSISTENT

HI MAX!

'SUP, BISCUIT?

HOW ARE YOU, GIZMO?

LOOKIN' FINE, CHAPPY!

CLEVER QUIP

THAT SAID, SOME NAMES ARE BETTER THAN OTHERS

HEY THERE, BOOGER!

I AM SO GOING TO CLAW HIS EYES OUT

DEAR CAT,
DO YOU KNOW PRINCESS KAT?

YEAH, I KNOW HER PRETTY WELL
HMM, WHERE HAVE I SEEN THAT FACE BEFORE?
QUITE FRANKLY, SHE'S A ROYAL PAIN IN THE BUTT
WHIP!
I WISH THAT WAS A HYPERBOLE
YOU'RE JUST JEALOUS BECAUSE I DO HAVE A DETACHABLE TAIL
CAB2016

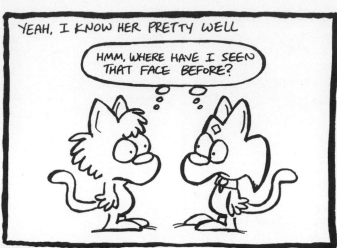

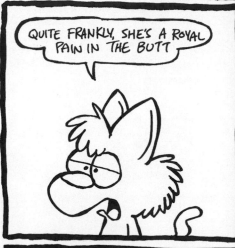

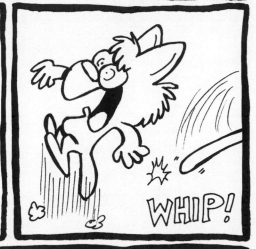

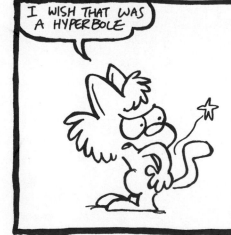

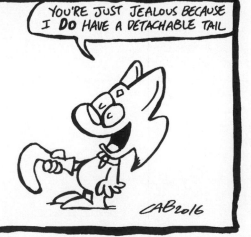

DEAR CAT,

DO YOU WEAR CAT'S PAJAMAS?

SURE, MY FRIEND! IT'S THE BEE'S KNEES, AFTER ALL

MY WHAT?

SERIOUSLY, THOUGH, IT DOESN'T FEEL NECESSARY TO WEAR THEM, GIVEN THAT I HAVE LONG HAIR ALL OVER ME

I LOVE YOUR COAT! WHERE'D YOU GET IT?

MY MOM AND DAD'S DNA

THAT SAID, WITH THE WAY WE SLEEP IN GROUPS, I GUESS I'M TECHNICALLY WEARING OTHER CATS AS PAJAMAS

`NIGHT, PILLOW

HUSH, PAJAMAS

CAB2016

DEAR CAT,

I MADE A JACK-O-LANTERN. WHAT SHOULD I DO WITH THE PUMPKIN GOOP?

WHY, YOU CAN HOLD A GOOP FIGHT!

IT'S A FALL TRADITION!

EACH TEAM WOULD MAKE A PUMPKIN FORT AND THROW A BIG HANDFUL OF GOOP AT EACH OTHER. IT'S ALL FUN AND GAMES!

FLING!

THE BEST PART WOULD BE A FEW MONTHS AFTER, WHEN THE PUMPKINS START TO GROW

THEY'RE SPROUTING AGAIN

GET MY SHOTGUN, IT'S A PUMPKIN INVASION!

DEAR CAT,

DO CATS HAVE ELECTIONS?

WE ONLY ATTEMPTED IT ONCE, WHEN WE THOUGHT OF HAVING A CAT REPRESENT EVERYTHING FELINE TO THE WORLD. WE EVEN NOMINATED TWO CANDIDATES!

VOTE FOR ME!

NO! ME! ME!

VOTE

CAT

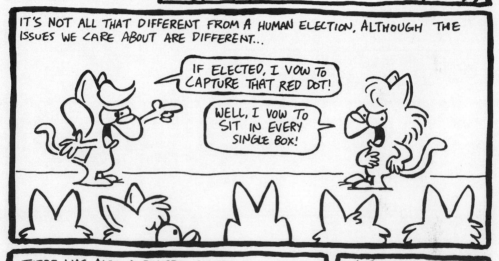

IT'S NOT ALL THAT DIFFERENT FROM A HUMAN ELECTION, ALTHOUGH THE ISSUES WE CARE ABOUT ARE DIFFERENT...

IF ELECTED, I VOW TO CAPTURE THAT RED DOT!

WELL, I VOW TO SIT IN EVERY SINGLE BOX!

THERE WAS ALSO A SCANDAL WHERE ONE OF THE CANDIDATES GOT CAUGHT IN A CATNIP STING

CAB2016

NIP

IN THE END, NEITHER CANDIDATE WON BECAUSE NOBODY BOTHERED TO SHOW UP TO VOTE

VOTE HERE

HUMANS ONLY **WISH** ELECTIONS WOULD GO AWAY

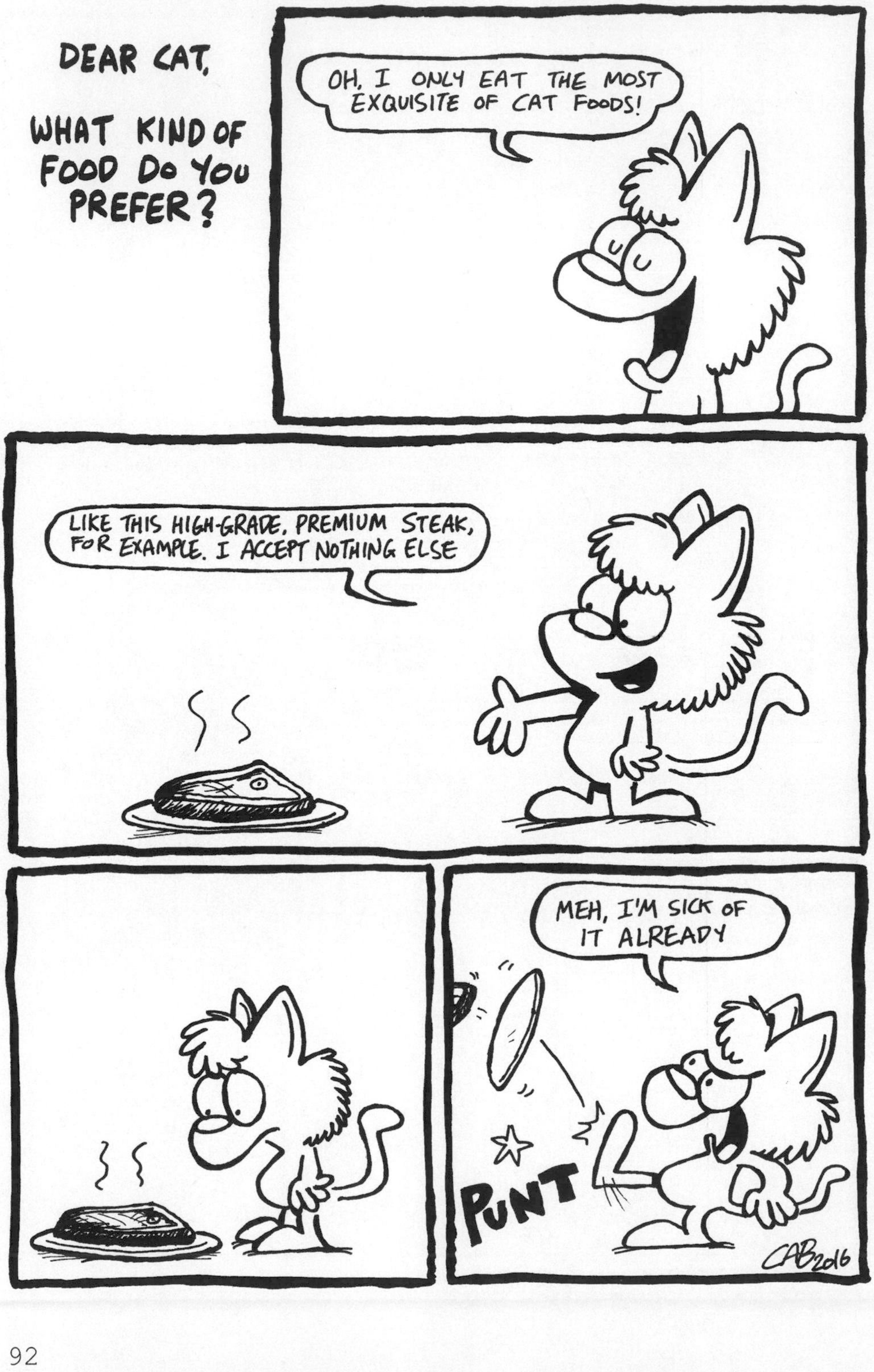
DEAR CAT,
WHAT KIND OF FOOD DO YOU PREFER?
OH, I ONLY EAT THE MOST EXQUISITE OF CAT FOODS!
LIKE THIS HIGH-GRADE, PREMIUM STEAK, FOR EXAMPLE. I ACCEPT NOTHING ELSE
MEH, I'M SICK OF IT ALREADY
PUNT
CAB 2016

DEAR CAT,

WHY ARE CATS AFRAID OF WATER?

I'M SORRY, BUT WATER AND FUR JUST DON'T MIX!
IT'S BAD ENOUGH THAT WE GET SMELLY WHENEVER WE'RE WET, BUT IT'S JUST SO DARN UNCOMFORTABLE GETTING OUR FUR STUCK TO OUR SKIN!
IF MOTHER NATURE WERE A HUMAN, I'D CLAW HER EYES OUT!
ALSO, YOU HAVE TO WATCH OUT FOR THOSE SNEAKY MICE THAT LIKE TO PLAY PRANKS
Z
THIS'LL BE A RIOT!
CAB2016

DEAR CAT,

IS THERE A CAT AIRLINE?

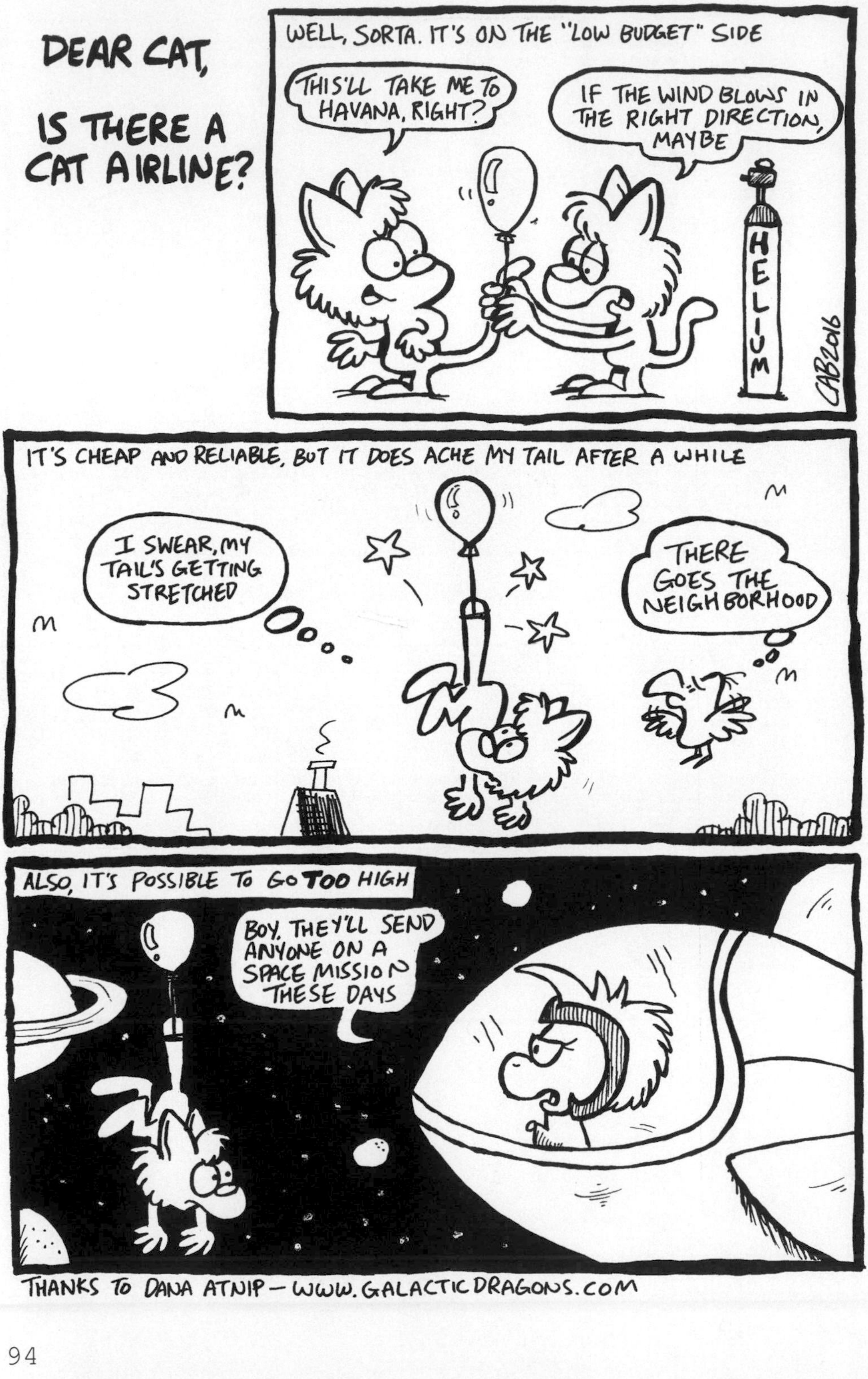
WELL, SORTA. IT'S ON THE "LOW BUDGET" SIDE
THIS'LL TAKE ME TO HAVANA, RIGHT?
IF THE WIND BLOWS IN THE RIGHT DIRECTION, MAYBE
HELIUM
CAB2016
IT'S CHEAP AND RELIABLE, BUT IT DOES ACHE MY TAIL AFTER A WHILE
I SWEAR, MY TAIL'S GETTING STRETCHED
THERE GOES THE NEIGHBORHOOD
ALSO, IT'S POSSIBLE TO GO TOO HIGH
BOY. THEY'LL SEND ANYONE ON A SPACE MISSION THESE DAYS

THANKS TO DANA ATNIP — WWW.GALACTICDRAGONS.COM

DEAR CAT,

DO YOU WRITE LETTERS TO OTHER CATS?

OH ABSOLUTELY! IT'S ALWAYS GOOD TO KEEP IN TOUCH WITH OUR FELINE BROTHERS AND SISTERS

grr...

Hey STUPID! You still owe me $5! Love, CAT

THE ONLY DOWNSIDE IS, MOST CATS DON'T HAVE PHONES OR COMPUTERS, AND MANY DON'T EVEN HAVE A HOME ADDRESS, SO WE HAVE TO TAKE CREATIVE MEASURES TO DELIVER MAIL TO THEM

CAT AIRLINE

NOW DELIVERING MAIL

HELIUM

WHAT CAN I SAY? MY BUSINESS IS GROWING

AND, AS YOU CAN IMAGINE, IT'S NOT UNUSUAL TO HAVE INSTANCES OF CATS READING OTHERS' LETTERS FOR LAUGHS

HAA! LOOKS LIKE THIS CAT OWES MONEY

THANKS FOR GIVING ME THIS SLINGSHOT, NINA! IT'S SO FUN SHOOTING ALL THOSE BALLOONS DOWN!

CAB2016

THANKS TO STEVE OGDEN - WWW.GOCOMICS.COM/MAGNIFICATZ

95

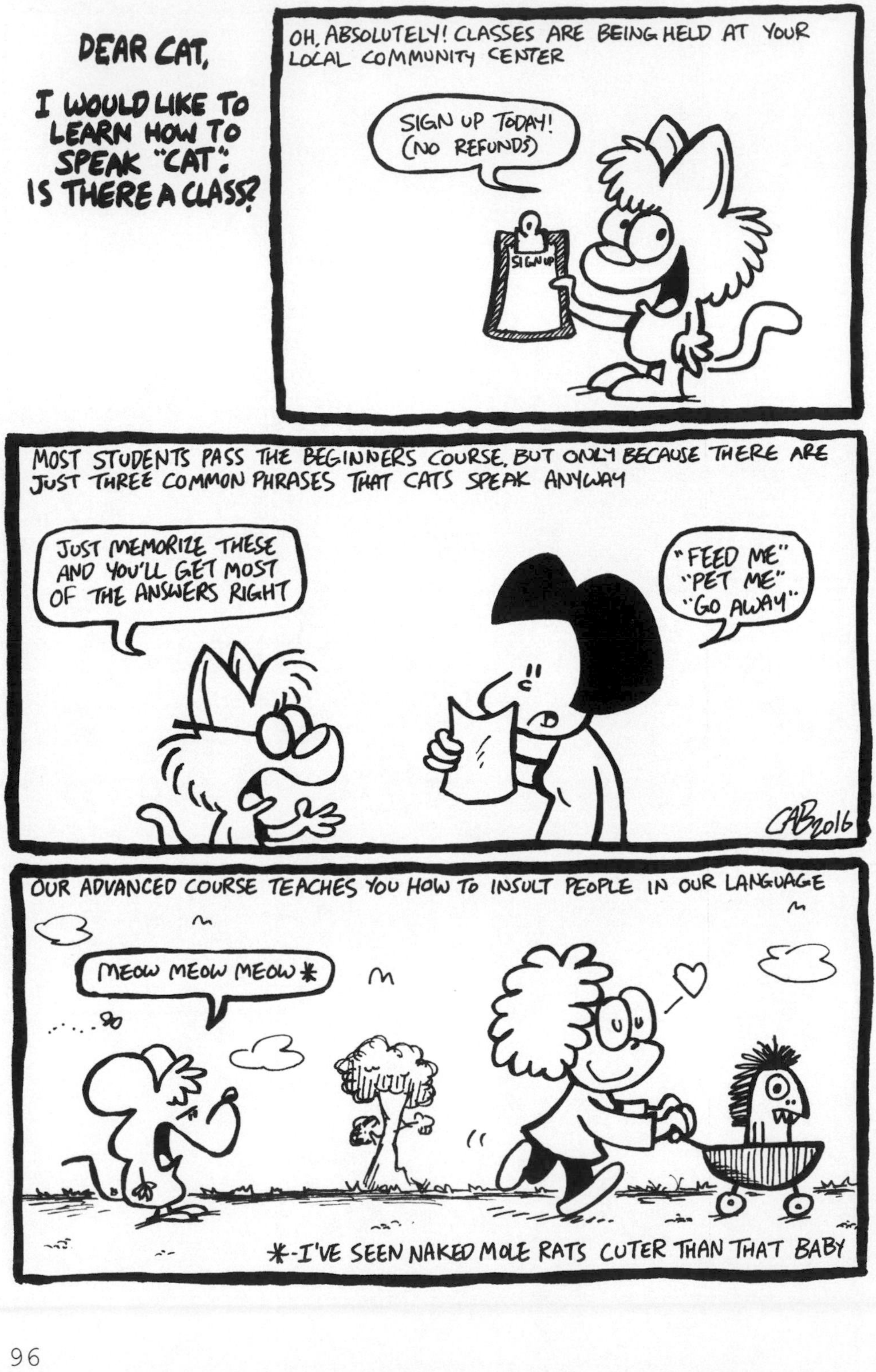
DEAR CAT,
I WOULD LIKE TO LEARN HOW TO SPEAK "CAT". IS THERE A CLASS?
OH, ABSOLUTELY! CLASSES ARE BEING HELD AT YOUR LOCAL COMMUNITY CENTER
SIGN UP TODAY! (NO REFUNDS)
SIGN UP
MOST STUDENTS PASS THE BEGINNERS COURSE, BUT ONLY BECAUSE THERE ARE JUST THREE COMMON PHRASES THAT CATS SPEAK ANYWAY
JUST MEMORIZE THESE AND YOU'LL GET MOST OF THE ANSWERS RIGHT
"FEED ME" "PET ME" "GO AWAY"
CAB 2016
OUR ADVANCED COURSE TEACHES YOU HOW TO INSULT PEOPLE IN OUR LANGUAGE
MEOW MEOW MEOW *
*-I'VE SEEN NAKED MOLE RATS CUTER THAN THAT BABY

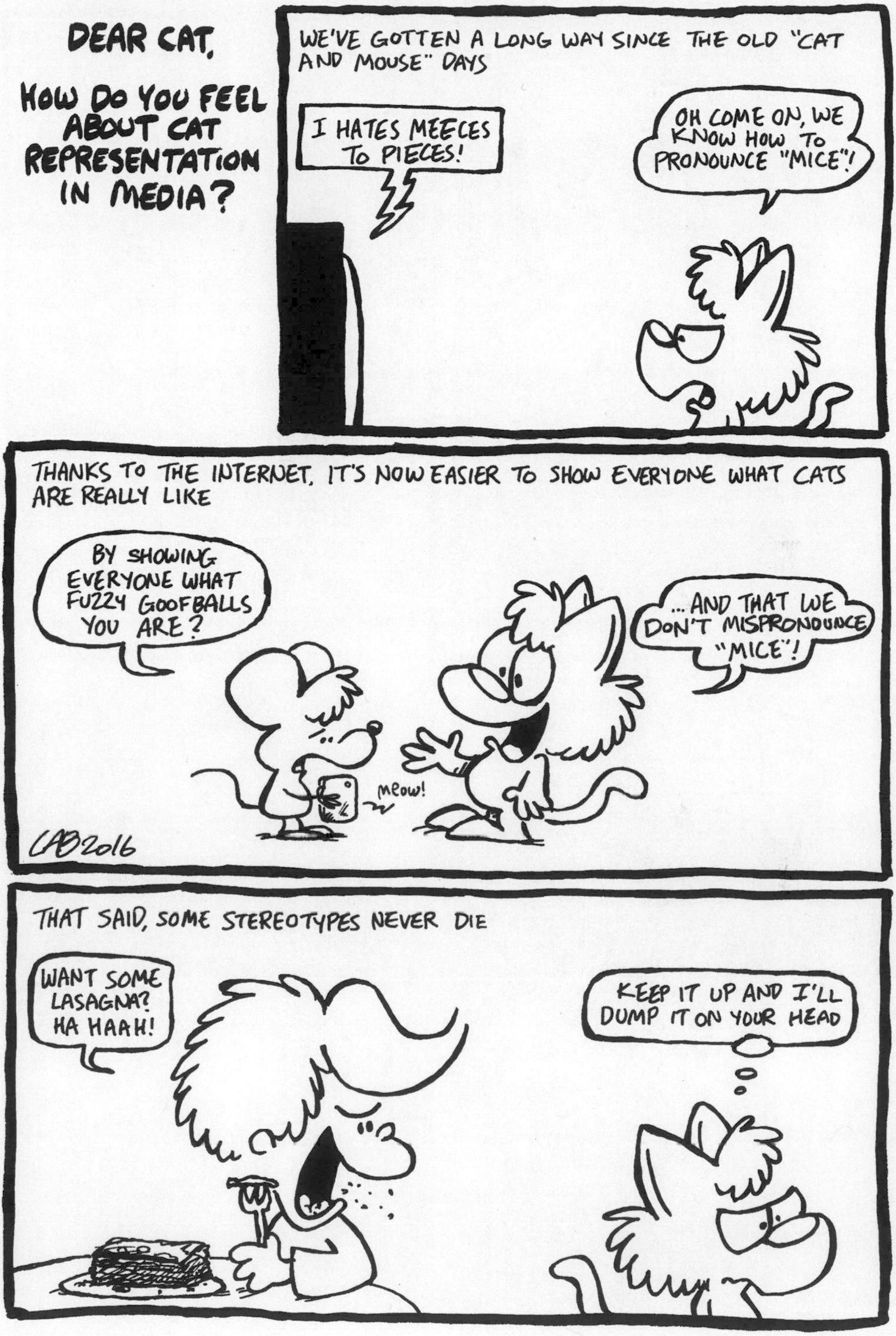
DEAR CAT,
HOW DO YOU FEEL ABOUT CAT REPRESENTATION IN MEDIA?
WE'VE GOTTEN A LONG WAY SINCE THE OLD "CAT AND MOUSE" DAYS
I HATES MEECES TO PIECES!
OH COME ON, WE KNOW HOW TO PRONOUNCE "MICE"!
THANKS TO THE INTERNET, IT'S NOW EASIER TO SHOW EVERYONE WHAT CATS ARE REALLY LIKE
BY SHOWING EVERYONE WHAT FUZZY GOOFBALLS YOU ARE?
...AND THAT WE DON'T MISPRONOUNCE "MICE"!
meow!
CAB 2016
THAT SAID, SOME STEREOTYPES NEVER DIE
WANT SOME LASAGNA? HA HAAH!
KEEP IT UP AND I'LL DUMP IT ON YOUR HEAD

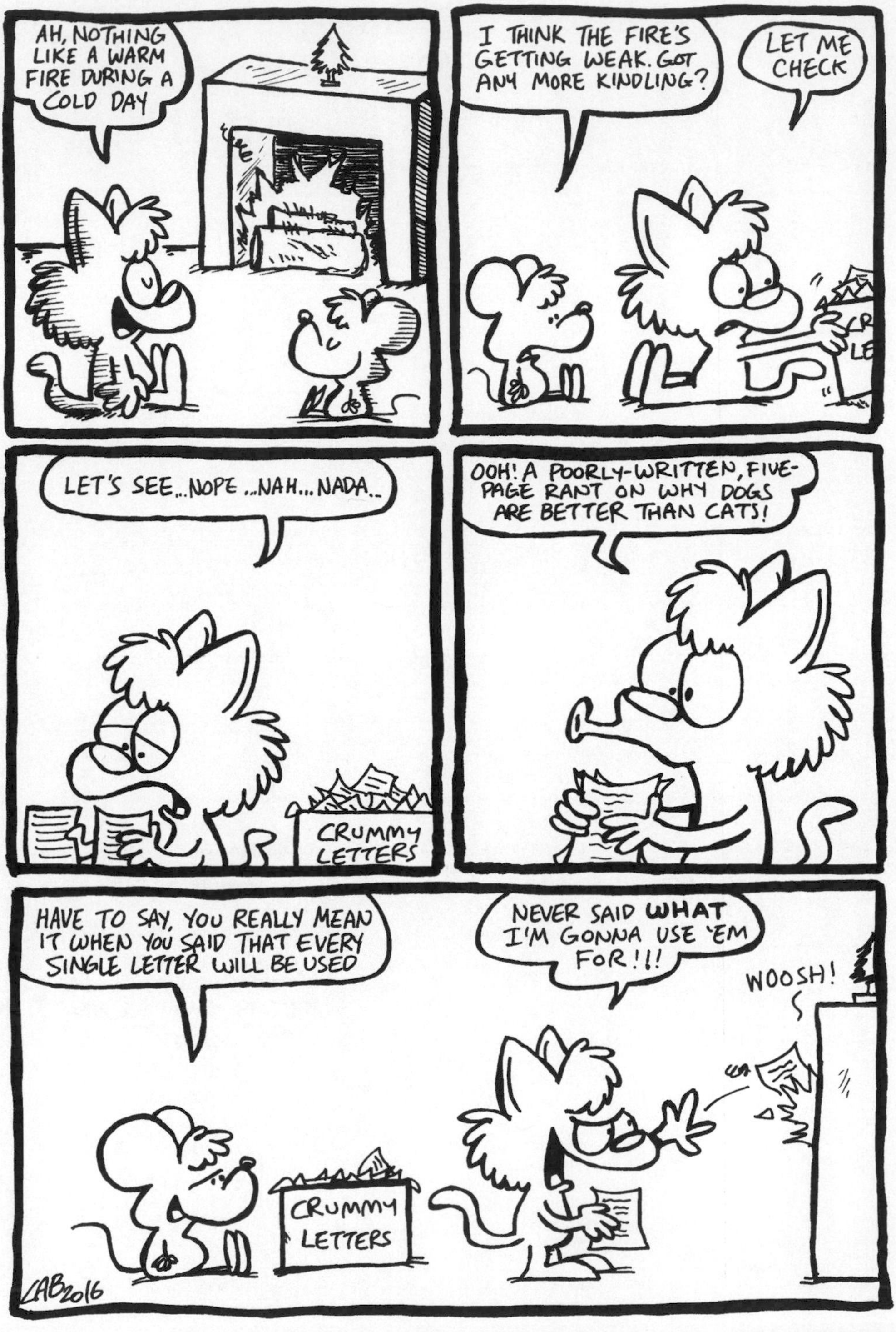
AH, NOTHING LIKE A WARM FIRE DURING A COLD DAY
I THINK THE FIRE'S GETTING WEAK. GOT ANY MORE KINDLING?
LET ME CHECK
LET'S SEE...NOPE...NAH...NADA...
CRUMMY LETTERS
OOH! A POORLY-WRITTEN, FIVE-PAGE RANT ON WHY DOGS ARE BETTER THAN CATS!
HAVE TO SAY, YOU REALLY MEAN IT WHEN YOU SAID THAT EVERY SINGLE LETTER WILL BE USED
NEVER SAID **WHAT** I'M GONNA USE 'EM FOR!!!
WOOSH!
CRUMMY LETTERS
CAB 2016

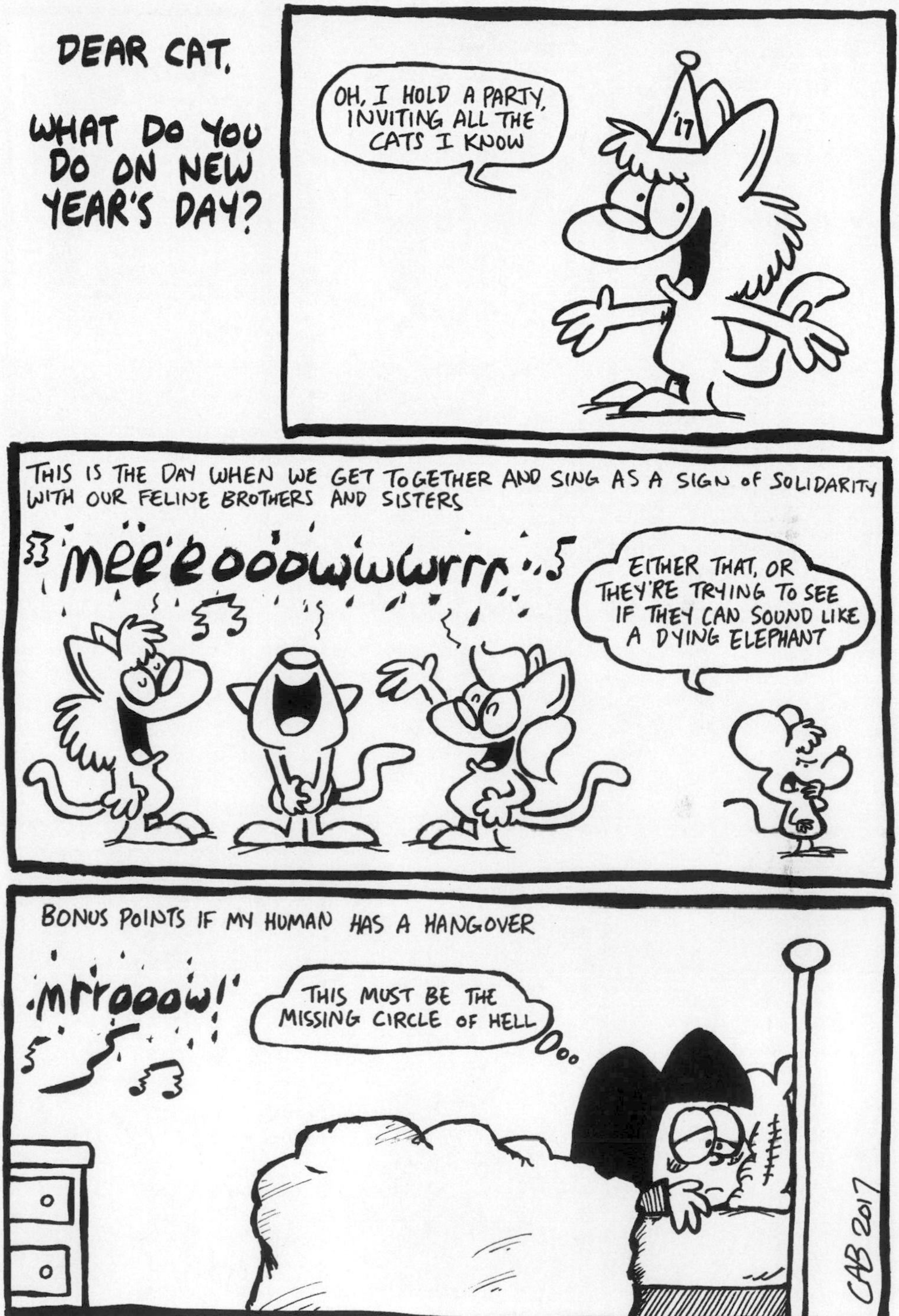

DEAR CAT,
WHAT DO YOU DO ON NEW YEAR'S DAY?
OH, I HOLD A PARTY, INVITING ALL THE CATS I KNOW
'17
THIS IS THE DAY WHEN WE GET TOGETHER AND SING AS A SIGN OF SOLIDARITY WITH OUR FELINE BROTHERS AND SISTERS
meeeooowwwrrr
EITHER THAT, OR THEY'RE TRYING TO SEE IF THEY CAN SOUND LIKE A DYING ELEPHANT
BONUS POINTS IF MY HUMAN HAS A HANGOVER
mrrooow!
THIS MUST BE THE MISSING CIRCLE OF HELL
CAB 2017

DEAR CAT, WHY?

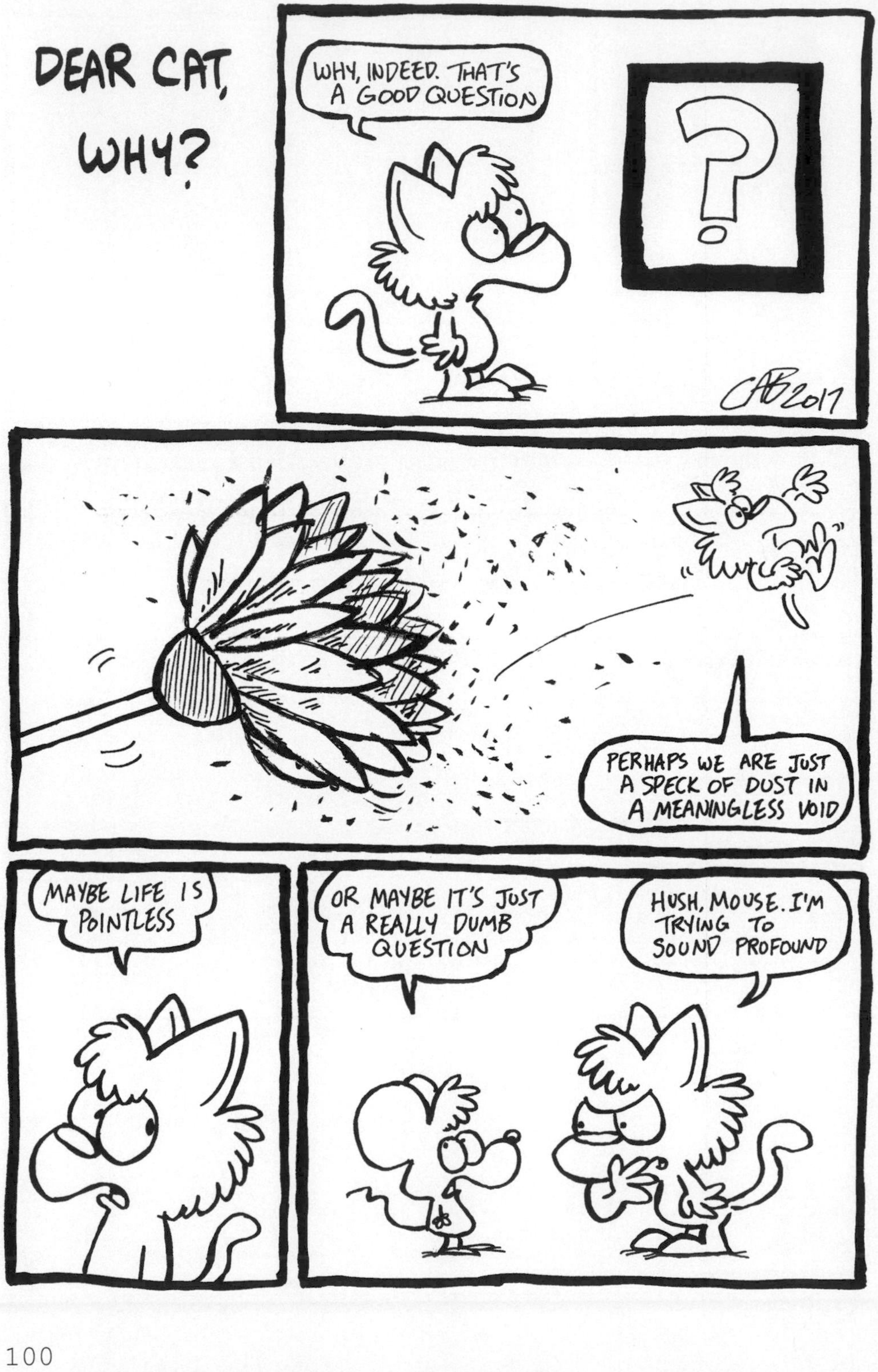
WHY, INDEED. THAT'S A GOOD QUESTION
?
CAB 2017
PERHAPS WE ARE JUST A SPECK OF DUST IN A MEANINGLESS VOID
MAYBE LIFE IS POINTLESS
OR MAYBE IT'S JUST A REALLY DUMB QUESTION
HUSH, MOUSE. I'M TRYING TO SOUND PROFOUND

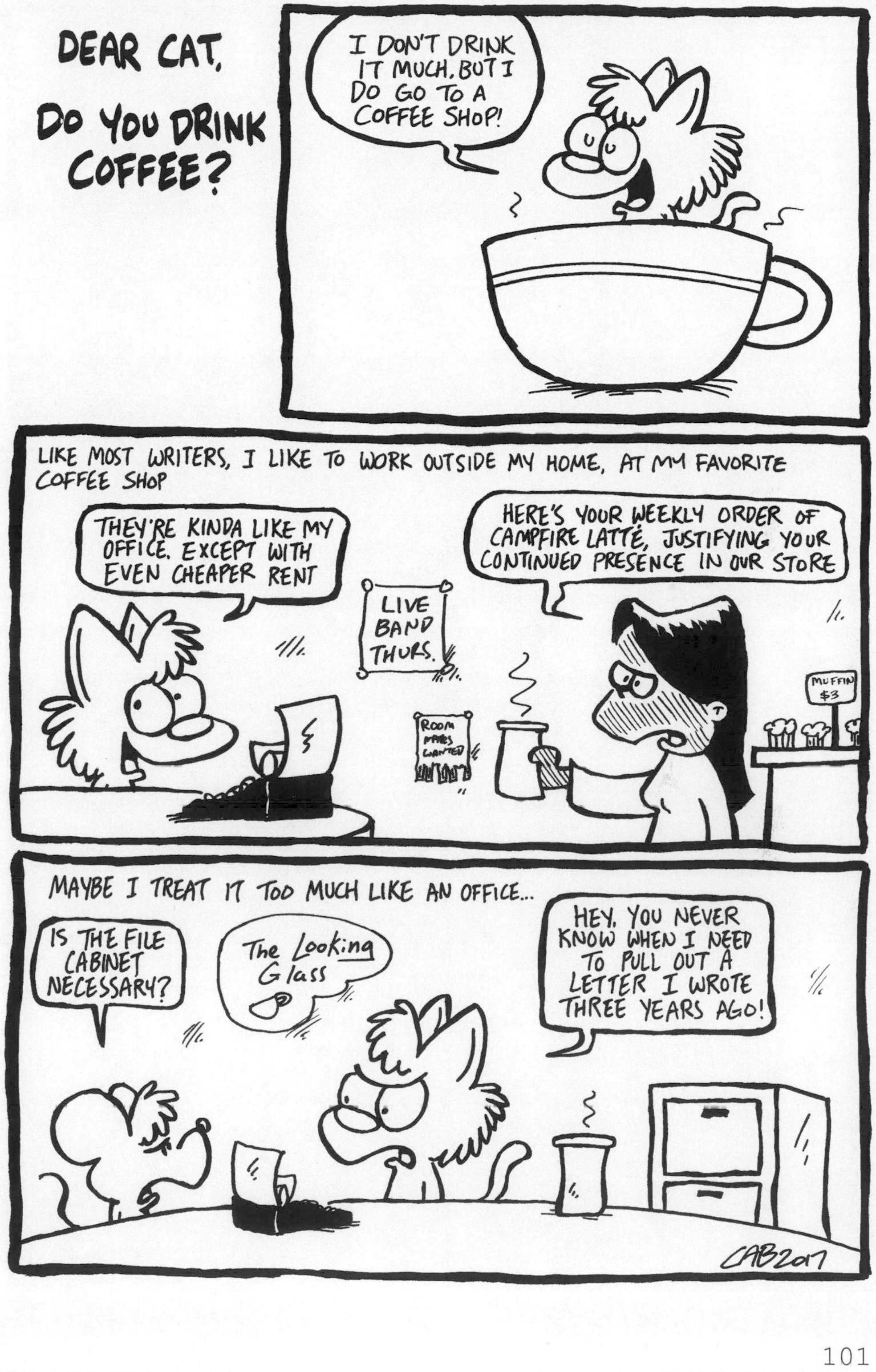
DEAR CAT,
DO YOU DRINK COFFEE?
I DON'T DRINK IT MUCH, BUT I DO GO TO A COFFEE SHOP!
LIKE MOST WRITERS, I LIKE TO WORK OUTSIDE MY HOME, AT MY FAVORITE COFFEE SHOP
THEY'RE KINDA LIKE MY OFFICE. EXCEPT WITH EVEN CHEAPER RENT
HERE'S YOUR WEEKLY ORDER OF CAMPFIRE LATTÉ, JUSTIFYING YOUR CONTINUED PRESENCE IN OUR STORE
LIVE BAND THURS.
ROOM MATES WANTED
MUFFIN $3
MAYBE I TREAT IT TOO MUCH LIKE AN OFFICE...
IS THE FILE CABINET NECESSARY?
The Looking Glass
HEY, YOU NEVER KNOW WHEN I NEED TO PULL OUT A LETTER I WROTE THREE YEARS AGO!
CAB2017

DEAR CAT, DO YOU USE COUPONS?

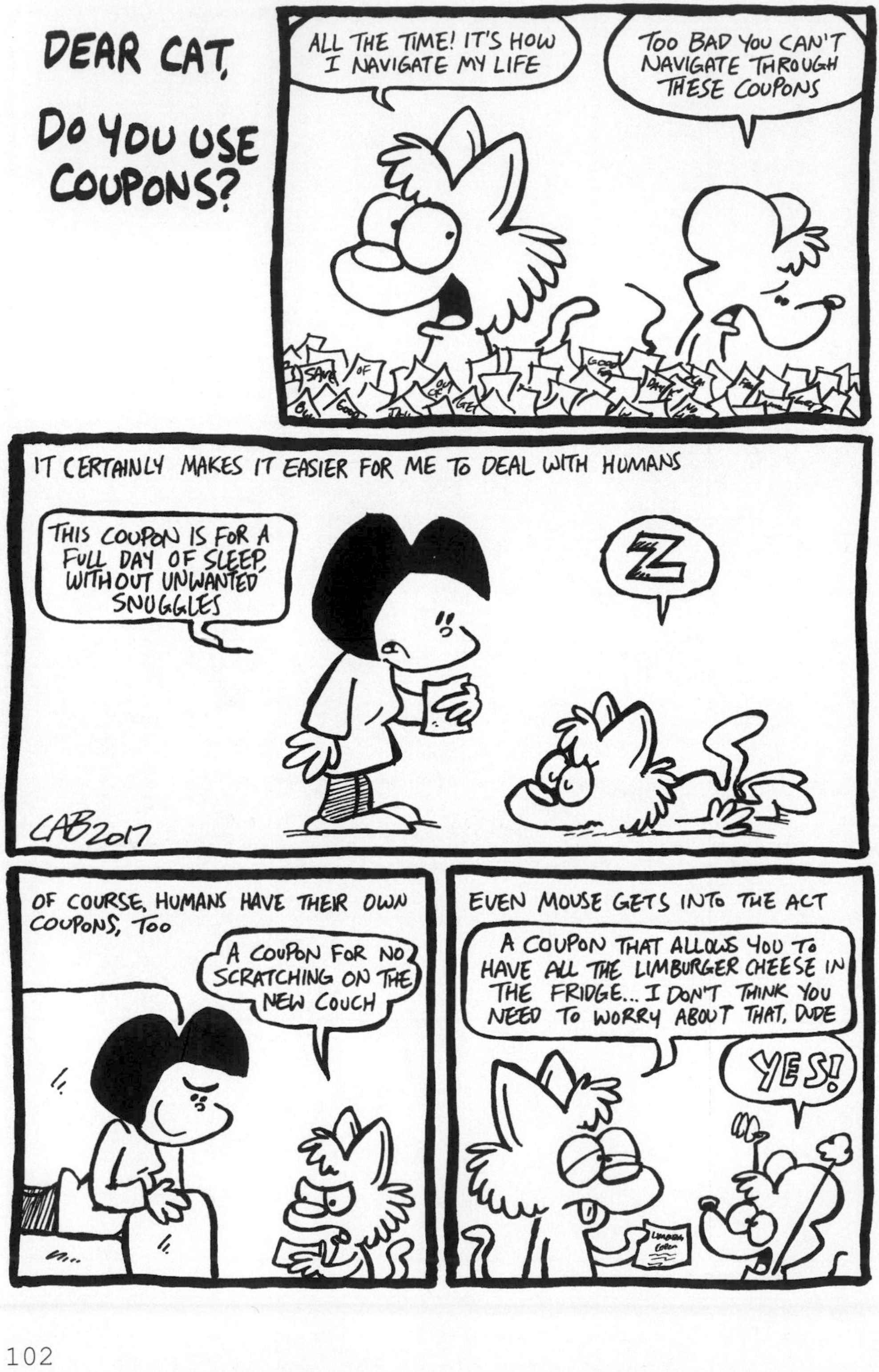

ALL THE TIME! IT'S HOW I NAVIGATE MY LIFE
TOO BAD YOU CAN'T NAVIGATE THROUGH THESE COUPONS
IT CERTAINLY MAKES IT EASIER FOR ME TO DEAL WITH HUMANS
THIS COUPON IS FOR A FULL DAY OF SLEEP, WITHOUT UNWANTED SNUGGLES
Z
CAB 2017
OF COURSE, HUMANS HAVE THEIR OWN COUPONS, TOO
A COUPON FOR NO SCRATCHING ON THE NEW COUCH
EVEN MOUSE GETS INTO THE ACT
A COUPON THAT ALLOWS YOU TO HAVE ALL THE LIMBURGER CHEESE IN THE FRIDGE... I DON'T THINK YOU NEED TO WORRY ABOUT THAT, DUDE
YES!

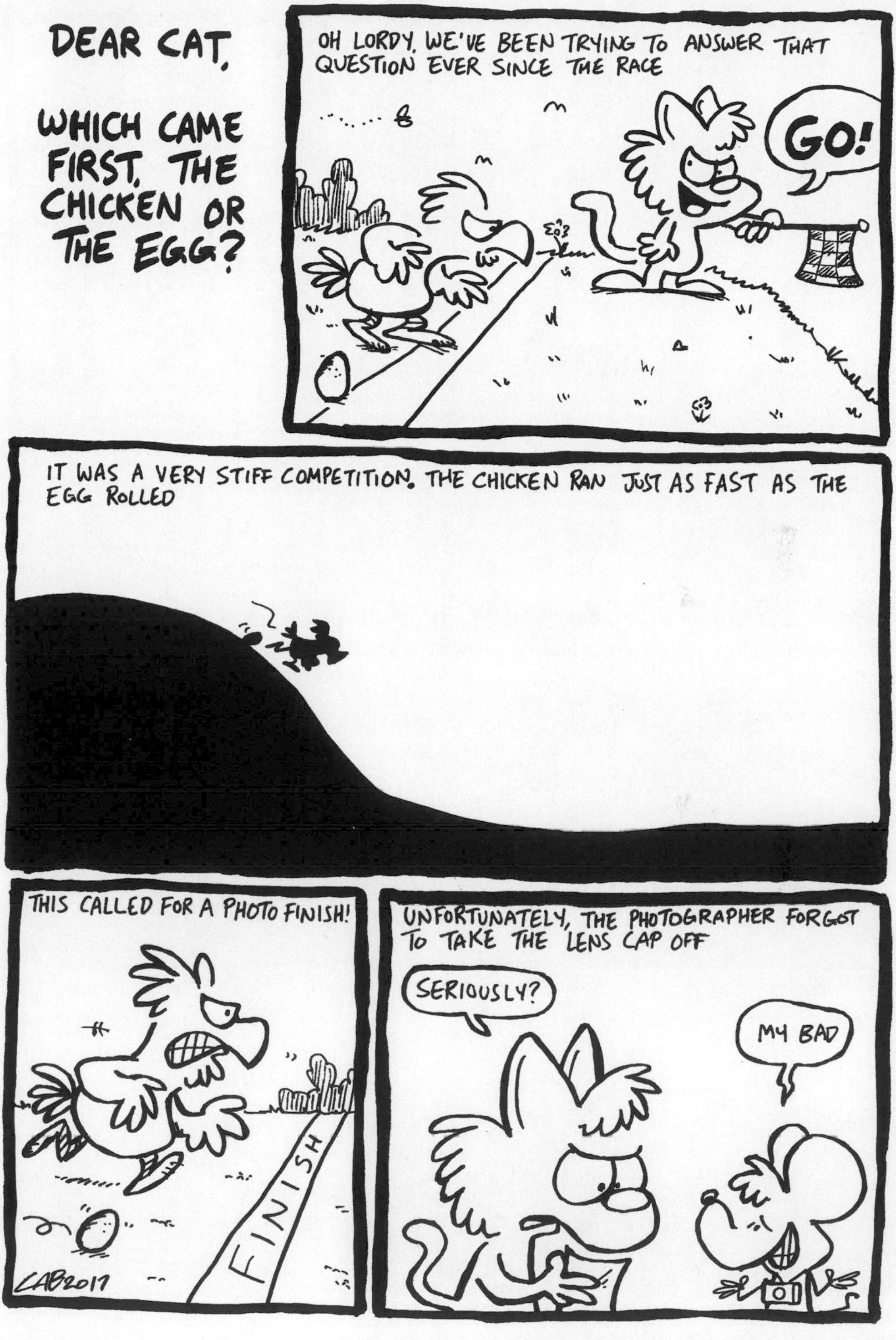
DEAR CAT,
WHICH CAME FIRST, THE CHICKEN OR THE EGG?
OH LORDY. WE'VE BEEN TRYING TO ANSWER THAT QUESTION EVER SINCE THE RACE
GO!
IT WAS A VERY STIFF COMPETITION. THE CHICKEN RAN JUST AS FAST AS THE EGG ROLLED
THIS CALLED FOR A PHOTO FINISH!
FINISH
CAB2017
UNFORTUNATELY, THE PHOTOGRAPHER FORGOT TO TAKE THE LENS CAP OFF
SERIOUSLY?
MY BAD

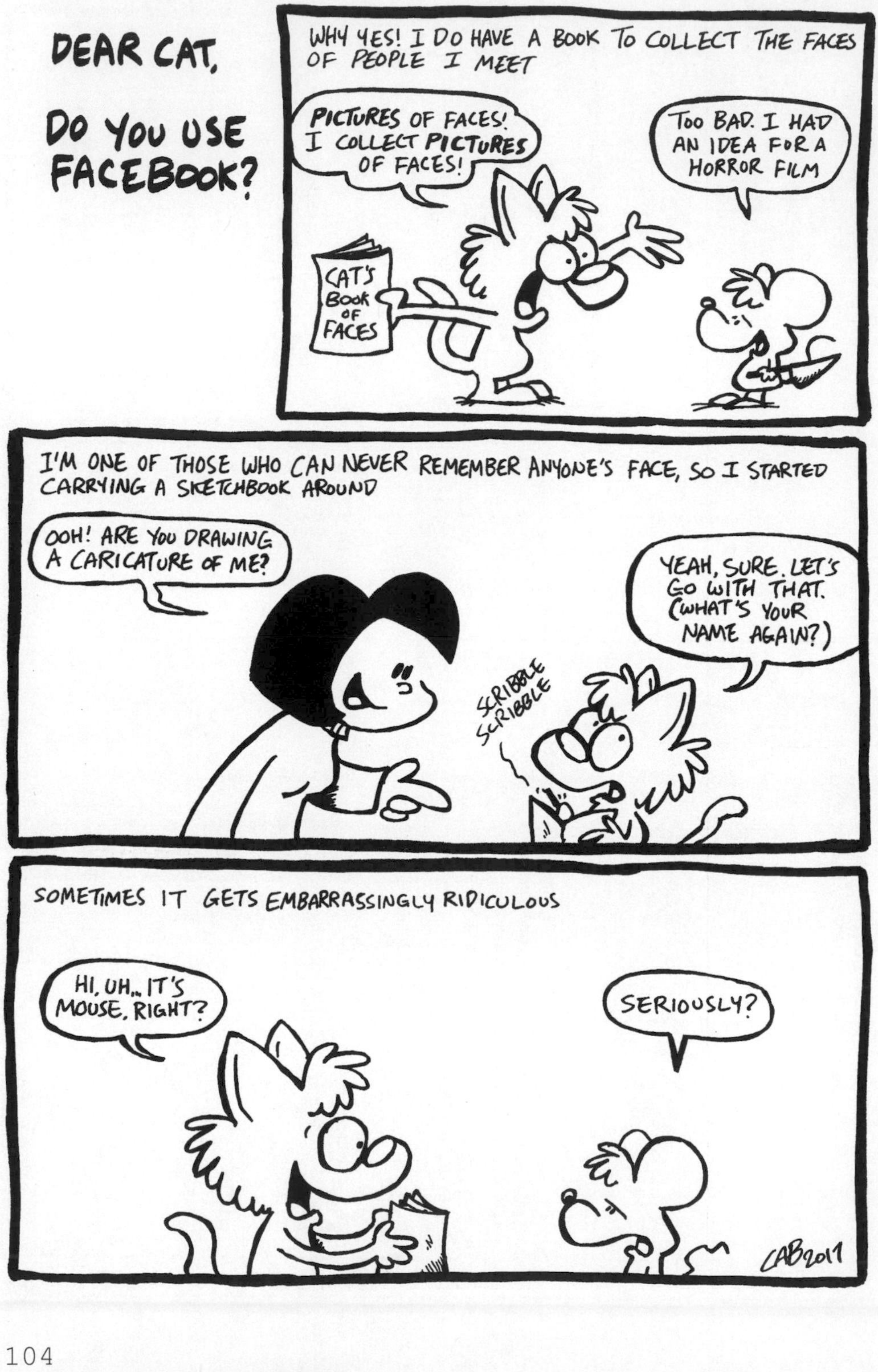
DEAR CAT,
DO YOU USE FACEBOOK?
WHY YES! I DO HAVE A BOOK TO COLLECT THE FACES OF PEOPLE I MEET
PICTURES OF FACES! I COLLECT PICTURES OF FACES!
TOO BAD. I HAD AN IDEA FOR A HORROR FILM
CAT'S BOOK OF FACES
I'M ONE OF THOSE WHO CAN NEVER REMEMBER ANYONE'S FACE, SO I STARTED CARRYING A SKETCHBOOK AROUND
OOH! ARE YOU DRAWING A CARICATURE OF ME?
YEAH, SURE. LET'S GO WITH THAT. (WHAT'S YOUR NAME AGAIN?)
SCRIBBLE SCRIBBLE
SOMETIMES IT GETS EMBARRASSINGLY RIDICULOUS
HI, UH... IT'S MOUSE, RIGHT?
SERIOUSLY?
CAB 2017

**DEAR CAT,
HOW DOES
CATNIP
MAKE YOU
FEEL?**

I STOPPED TAKING CATNIP YEARS AGO FOR A GOOD REASON. THAT STUFF'S STRONG!

I CAN DO ANYTHING!

NIP

I DO REMEMBER FEELING LIKE I WAS FLOATING ON WATER. I HAD NOT A CARE IN THE WORLD!

CAB 2017

THEN I REALIZED SOMETHING...

HEY, CAT!

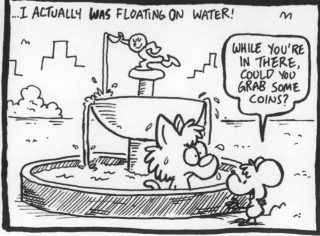

...I ACTUALLY **WAS** FLOATING ON WATER!

WHILE YOU'RE IN THERE, COULD YOU GRAB SOME COINS?

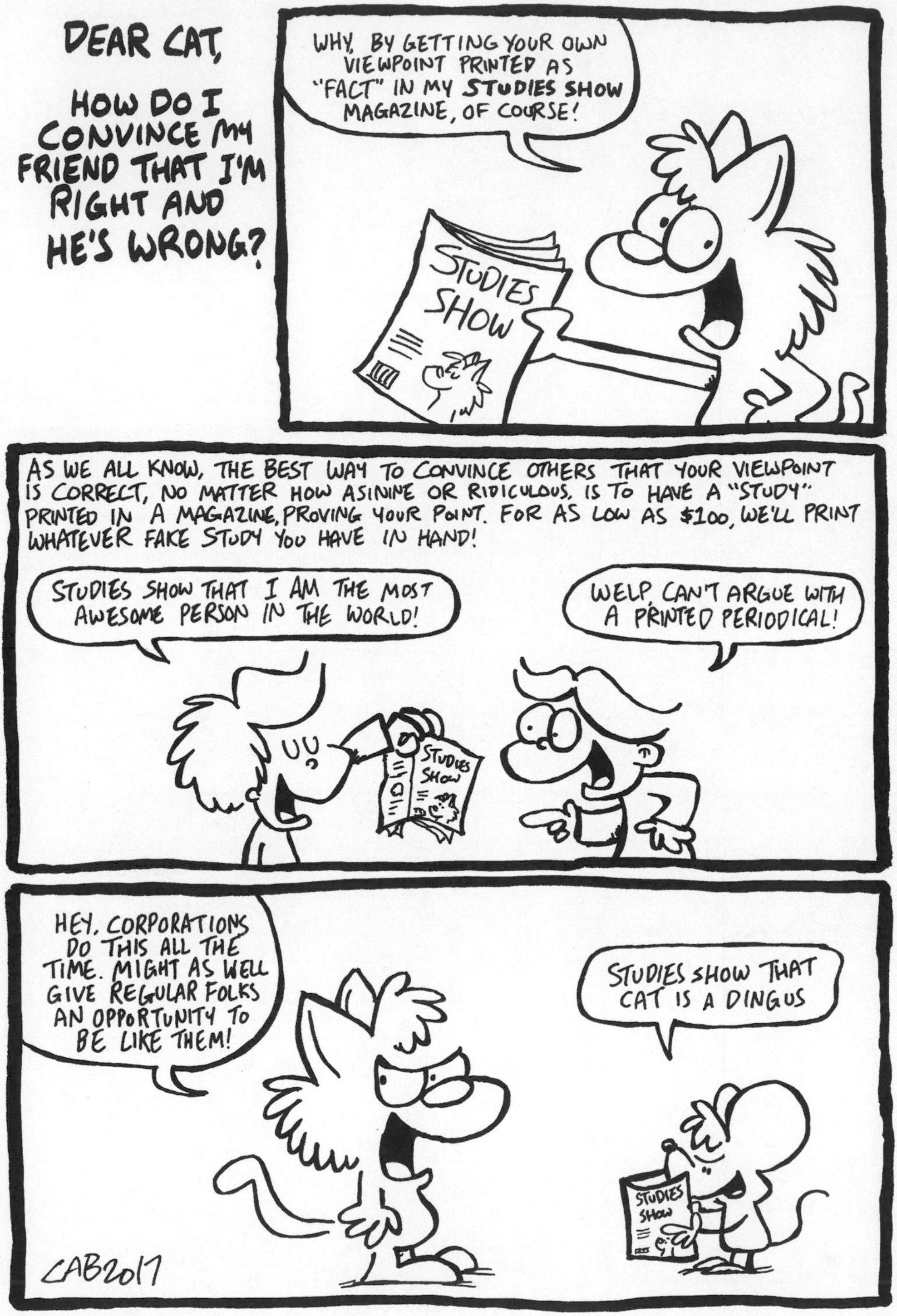
DEAR CAT,
HOW DO I CONVINCE MY FRIEND THAT I'M RIGHT AND HE'S WRONG?
WHY, BY GETTING YOUR OWN VIEWPOINT PRINTED AS "FACT" IN MY STUDIES SHOW MAGAZINE, OF COURSE!
STUDIES SHOW
AS WE ALL KNOW, THE BEST WAY TO CONVINCE OTHERS THAT YOUR VIEWPOINT IS CORRECT, NO MATTER HOW ASININE OR RIDICULOUS, IS TO HAVE A "STUDY" PRINTED IN A MAGAZINE, PROVING YOUR POINT. FOR AS LOW AS $100, WE'LL PRINT WHATEVER FAKE STUDY YOU HAVE IN HAND!
STUDIES SHOW THAT I AM THE MOST AWESOME PERSON IN THE WORLD!
WELP, CAN'T ARGUE WITH A PRINTED PERIODICAL!
STUDIES SHOW
HEY. CORPORATIONS DO THIS ALL THE TIME. MIGHT AS WELL GIVE REGULAR FOLKS AN OPPORTUNITY TO BE LIKE THEM!
STUDIES SHOW THAT CAT IS A DINGUS
STUDIES SHOW
CAB2017

DEAR CAT,
WHAT KIND OF VACATIONS DO CATS GO ON?
WELL, SEEING THAT CATS DO NOTHING MOST OF THE TIME, THE LOGICAL THING IS THAT, FOR OUR VACATION, WE GO TO WORK
TYPE TYPE
I AM SO TEMPTED TO SIT ON THAT KEYBOARD
ACTIVITIES INCLUDE MAKING PRESENTATIONS IN MEETINGS. OF COURSE, NOBODY REALLY PAYS ATTENTION TO THESE THINGS AND ONLY COMES FOR FREE DONUTS
PERA PERA
UGH. COCONUTS
THEN WE PARTAKE IN WATERCOOLER BANTER
I LIKE WATER
FINALLY, TO CAP IT OFF, WE EXECUTE THE WORST OFFICE MANAGER IN THE COMPANY
SO THAT'S WHY NOBODY WANTED TO BE THE BOSS
CAB2017

DEAR CAT,

WHY DO YOU KEEP BUNTING YOUR HEAD ONTO ME?

OH, DON'T MIND ME. I'M JUST PRACTICING FOR THE HEADBUTT COMPETITION, WHERE I CHALLENGE MY ARCH-NEMESIS: GOATS

MARK MY WORDS, I'M GOING TO WIPE YOU OUT SO HARD!

YOU'RE ON!

THOSE GOATS ARE TRICKY BEINGS. THEY NEVER GO DOWN EASILY

YOU CAN DO IT, FRANK!

Grrr!

GO GET 'EM, CAT!

BONK

ALSO, MY HEAD GETS ITCHY SOMETIMES AND THIS IS THE BEST WAY TO SCRATCH IT

AW, HI SWEETIE!

RUB RUB

PURR

OH YEAH, THAT HITS THE SPOT

CAB2017

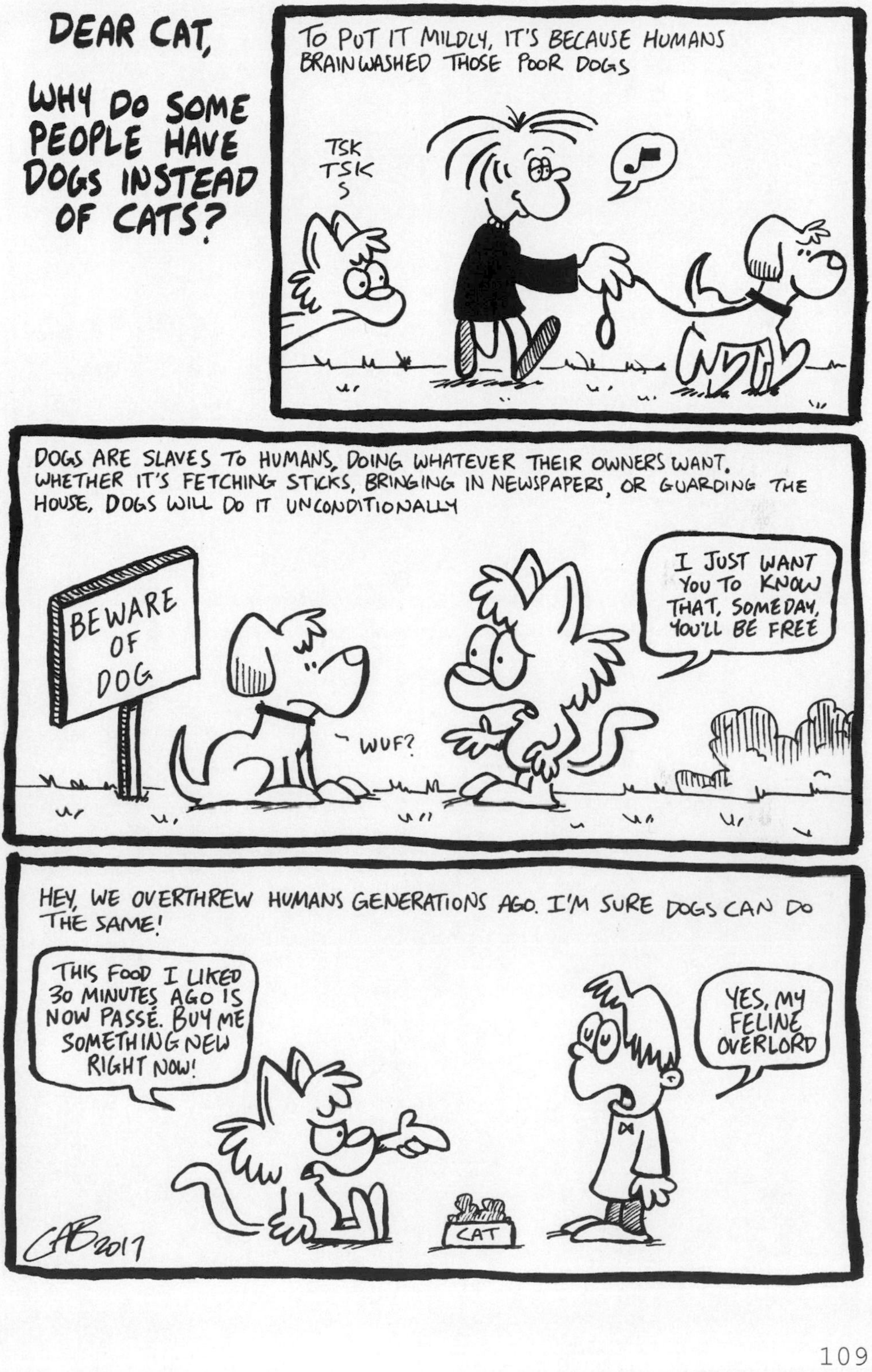
DEAR CAT,
WHY DO SOME PEOPLE HAVE DOGS INSTEAD OF CATS?
TO PUT IT MILDLY, IT'S BECAUSE HUMANS BRAINWASHED THOSE POOR DOGS
TSK TSK S
DOGS ARE SLAVES TO HUMANS, DOING WHATEVER THEIR OWNERS WANT. WHETHER IT'S FETCHING STICKS, BRINGING IN NEWSPAPERS, OR GUARDING THE HOUSE, DOGS WILL DO IT UNCONDITIONALLY
BEWARE OF DOG
WUF?
I JUST WANT YOU TO KNOW THAT, SOMEDAY, YOU'LL BE FREE
HEY, WE OVERTHREW HUMANS GENERATIONS AGO. I'M SURE DOGS CAN DO THE SAME!
THIS FOOD I LIKED 30 MINUTES AGO IS NOW PASSÉ. BUY ME SOMETHING NEW RIGHT NOW!
YES, MY FELINE OVERLORD
CAT
CAB 2017

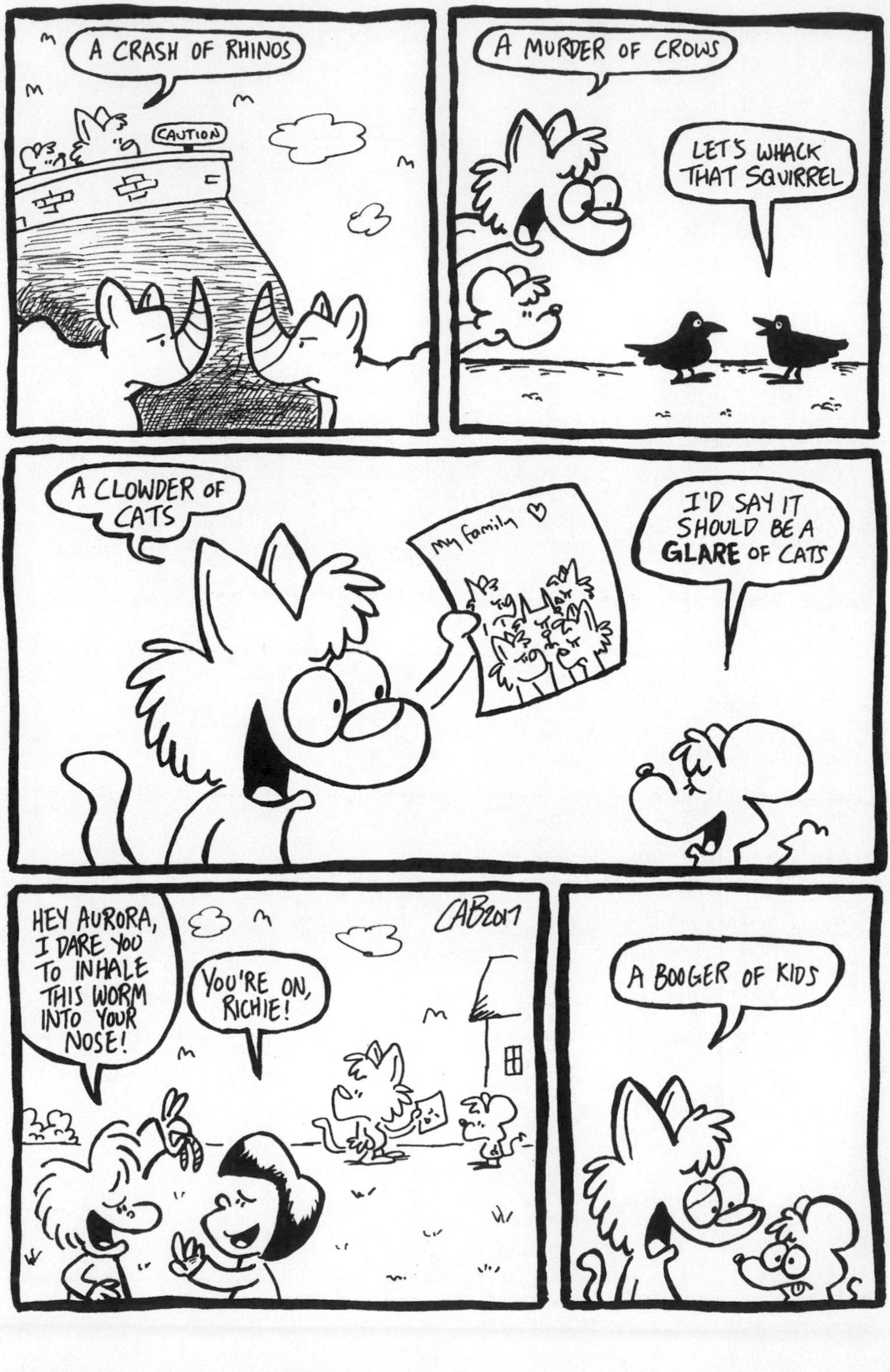
A CRASH OF RHINOS
CAUTION
A MURDER OF CROWS
LET'S WHACK THAT SQUIRREL
A CLOWDER OF CATS
my family
I'D SAY IT SHOULD BE A GLARE OF CATS
HEY AURORA, I DARE YOU TO INHALE THIS WORM INTO YOUR NOSE!
YOU'RE ON, RICHIE!
CAB2017
A BOOGER OF KIDS

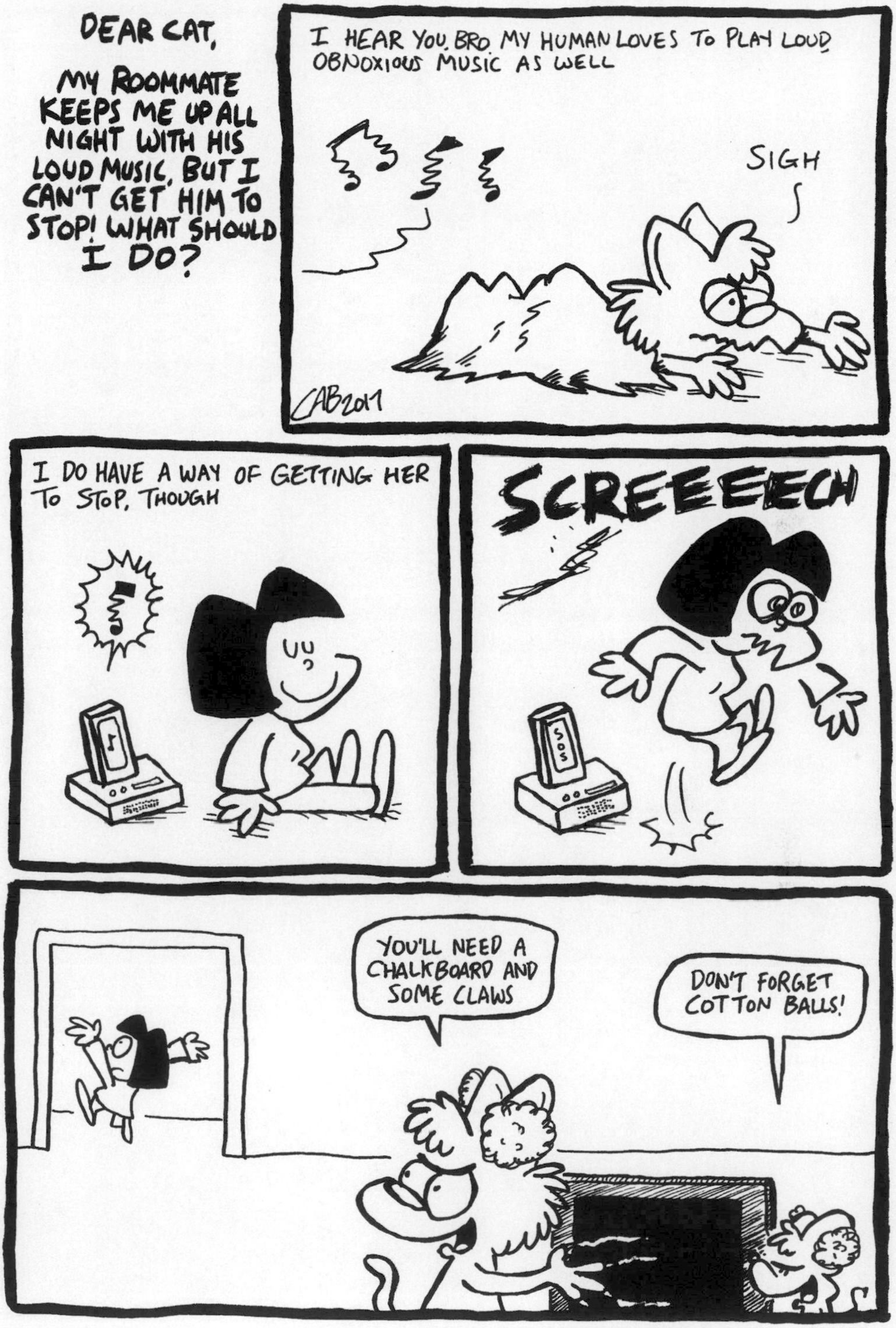
DEAR CAT,
MY ROOMMATE KEEPS ME UP ALL NIGHT WITH HIS LOUD MUSIC, BUT I CAN'T GET HIM TO STOP! WHAT SHOULD I DO?
I HEAR YOU, BRO. MY HUMAN LOVES TO PLAY LOUD OBNOXIOUS MUSIC AS WELL
SIGH
CAB2017
I DO HAVE A WAY OF GETTING HER TO STOP, THOUGH
SCREEEEECH
SOS
YOU'LL NEED A CHALKBOARD AND SOME CLAWS
DON'T FORGET COTTON BALLS!

DEAR CAT,

ARE THERE SEEING-EYE CATS?

OH YES! WHILE EVERYBODY KNOWS WHAT SEEING-EYE DOGS ARE, SEEING-EYE CATS ARE MAKING WAVES IN THE WORLD OF SERVICE ANIMALS. THERE ARE SO MANY ADVANTAGES...

...LIKE BECOMING EXPERT CLIMBERS

(oof) I DON'T THINK I LIKE THIS SHORTCUT TO MY HOUSE

...GETTING EXCERCISE

HEY, WHERE'S THE FIRE!?

...AND, OF COURSE, THE JOY OF BOXES

I DON'T KNOW WHERE WE ARE, BUT THIS IS CALMING

WE ALL NEED A PLACE TO CHILL

CAB 2017

112

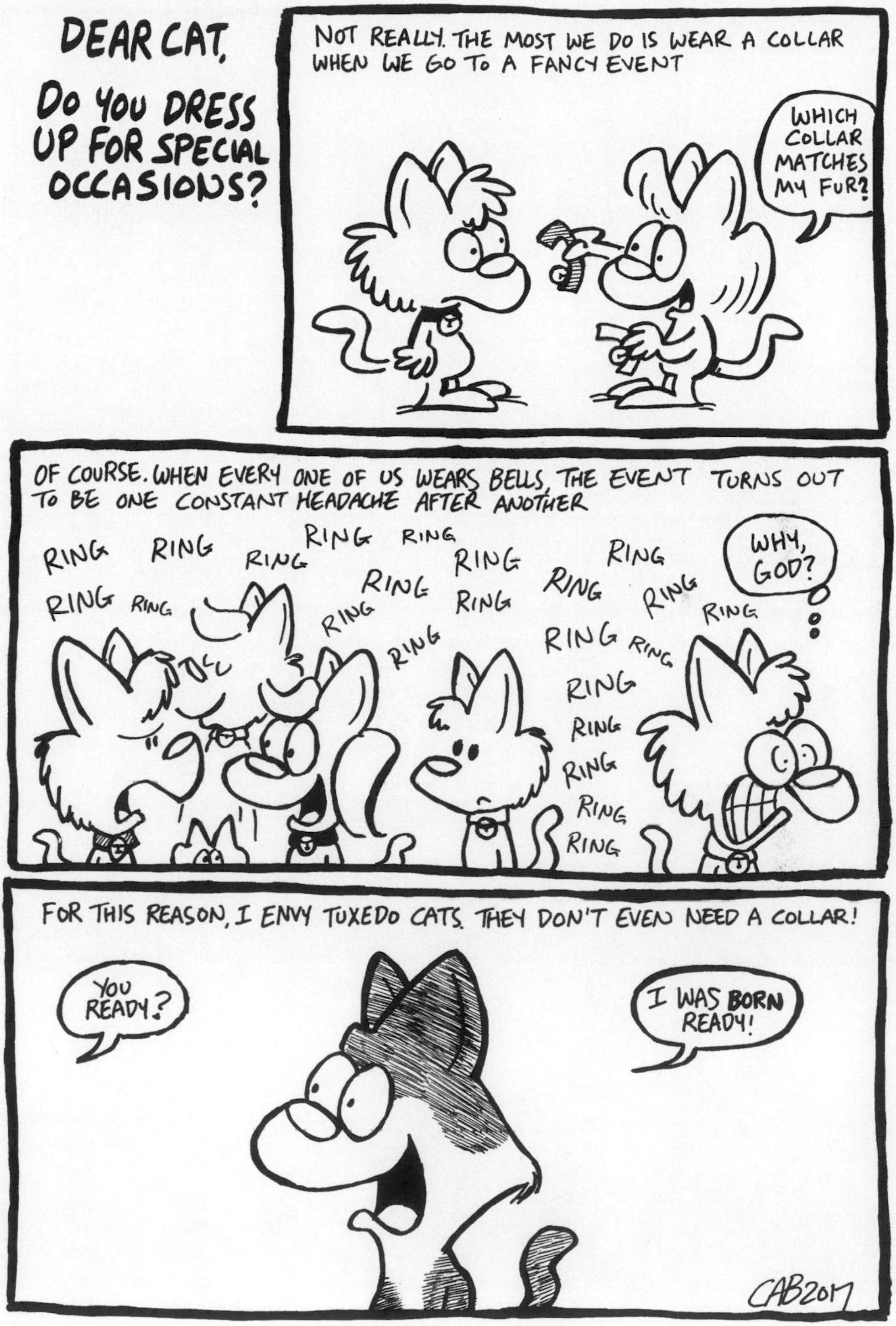
DEAR CAT,
DO YOU DRESS UP FOR SPECIAL OCCASIONS?
NOT REALLY. THE MOST WE DO IS WEAR A COLLAR WHEN WE GO TO A FANCY EVENT
WHICH COLLAR MATCHES MY FUR?
OF COURSE. WHEN EVERY ONE OF US WEARS BELLS, THE EVENT TURNS OUT TO BE ONE CONSTANT HEADACHE AFTER ANOTHER
RING RING RING RING RING RING RING RING
RING RING RING RING RING RING RING RING RING RING RING RING RING RING RING RING
WHY, GOD?
FOR THIS REASON, I ENVY TUXEDO CATS. THEY DON'T EVEN NEED A COLLAR!
YOU READY?
I WAS BORN READY!
CAB2017

DEAR CAT,

MY TEENAGER KEEPS SNEAKING OUT AT NIGHT. HOW DO I STOP HIM?

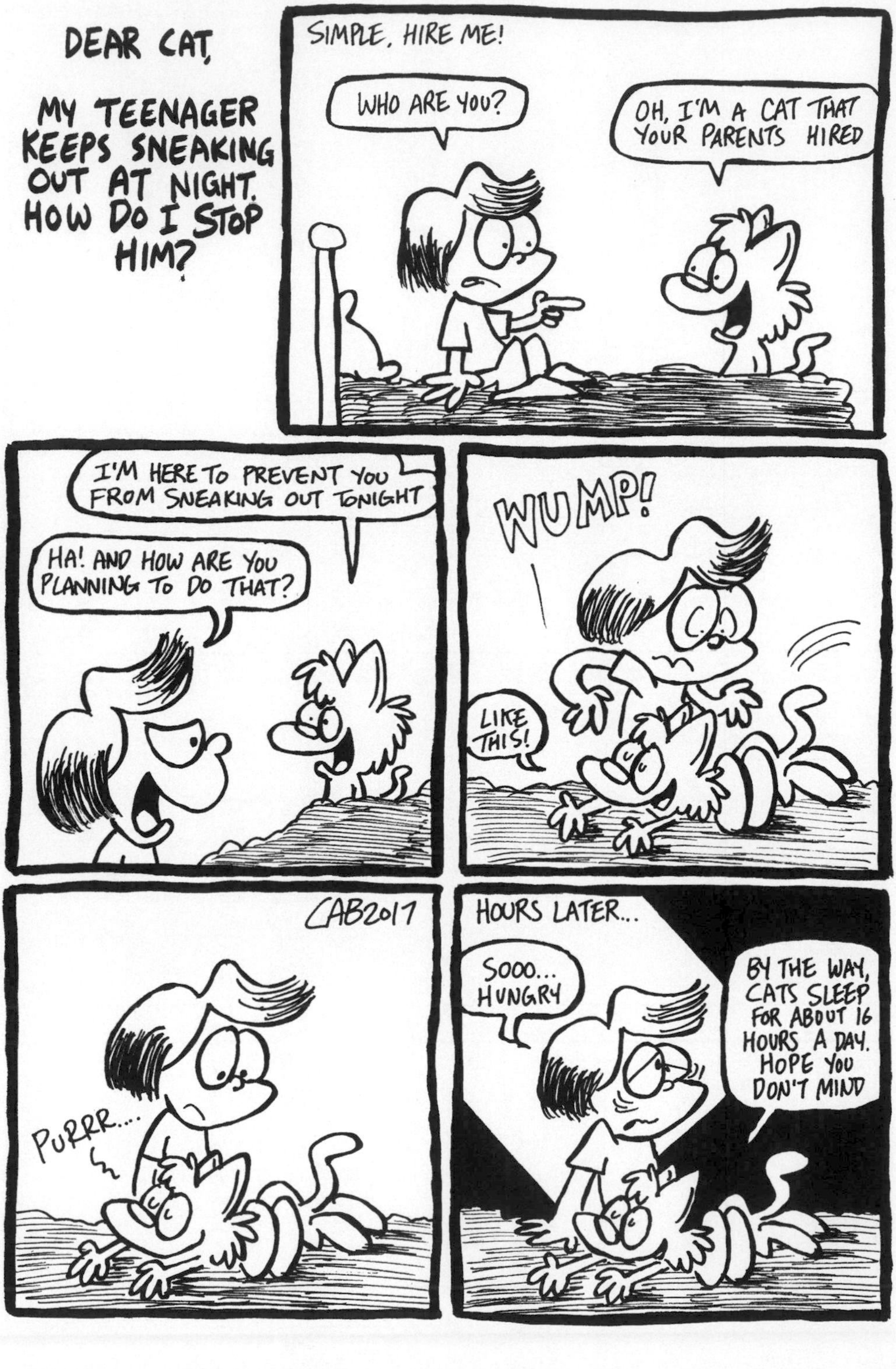
SIMPLE, HIRE ME!
WHO ARE YOU?
OH, I'M A CAT THAT YOUR PARENTS HIRED
I'M HERE TO PREVENT YOU FROM SNEAKING OUT TONIGHT
HA! AND HOW ARE YOU PLANNING TO DO THAT?
WUMP!
LIKE THIS!
CAB2017
PURRR....
HOURS LATER...
SOOO... HUNGRY
BY THE WAY, CATS SLEEP FOR ABOUT 16 HOURS A DAY. HOPE YOU DON'T MIND

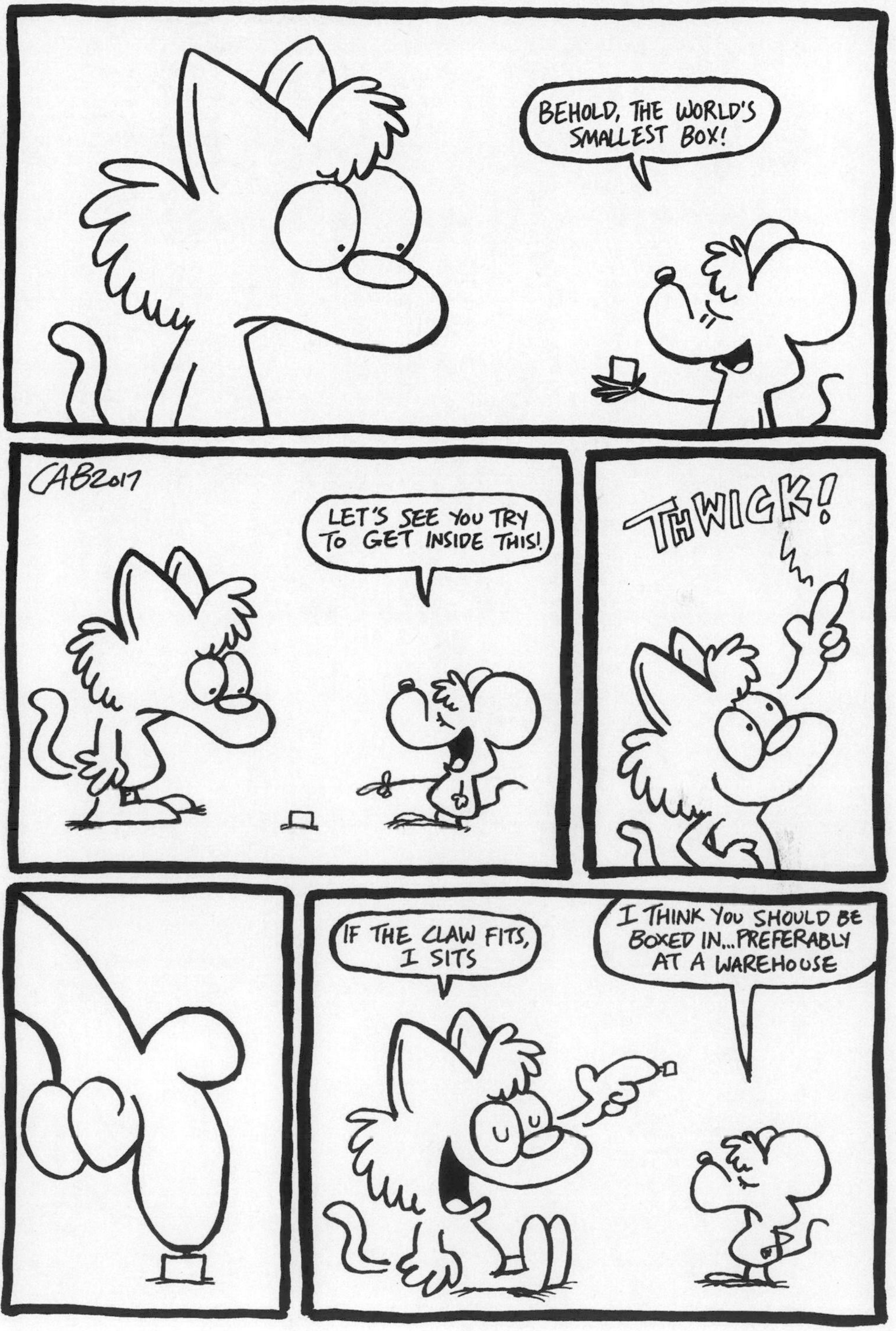
BEHOLD, THE WORLD'S SMALLEST BOX!
CAB2017
LET'S SEE YOU TRY TO GET INSIDE THIS!
THWICK!
IF THE CLAW FITS, I SITS
I THINK YOU SHOULD BE BOXED IN...PREFERABLY AT A WAREHOUSE

DEAR CAT,

THOUGHTS ON DRAGONS?

CATS AND DRAGONS GO HAND IN HAND. WHY, IN ANCIENT CIVILIZATIONS, MANY PEOPLE BELIEVED THAT CATS DESCENDED FROM DRAGONS!

NO THEY DIDN'T!

NUH UH, THIS WEBSITE SAYS SO!

THERE ARE SO MANY SIMILARITIES BETWEEN US. FOR EXAMPLE, WE BOTH HAVE RAZOR-SHARP TEETH

I CAN SNAP THIS TREE IN HALF!

WELL, I CAN SNAP THIS **FISH** IN HALF!

AND WE BOTH HAVE HOARDS

A HOARD OF TREASURE

A HOARD OF PLASTIC BOTTLE CAPS →

CATS DON'T HAVE FIRE BREATH, BUT WE DO HAVE SOMETHING THAT MAKES UP FOR IT

BZZZ

Y'KNOW, CATFOOD BREATH IS THE ULTIMATE WEAPON OF MASS DESTRUCTION

CAB2017

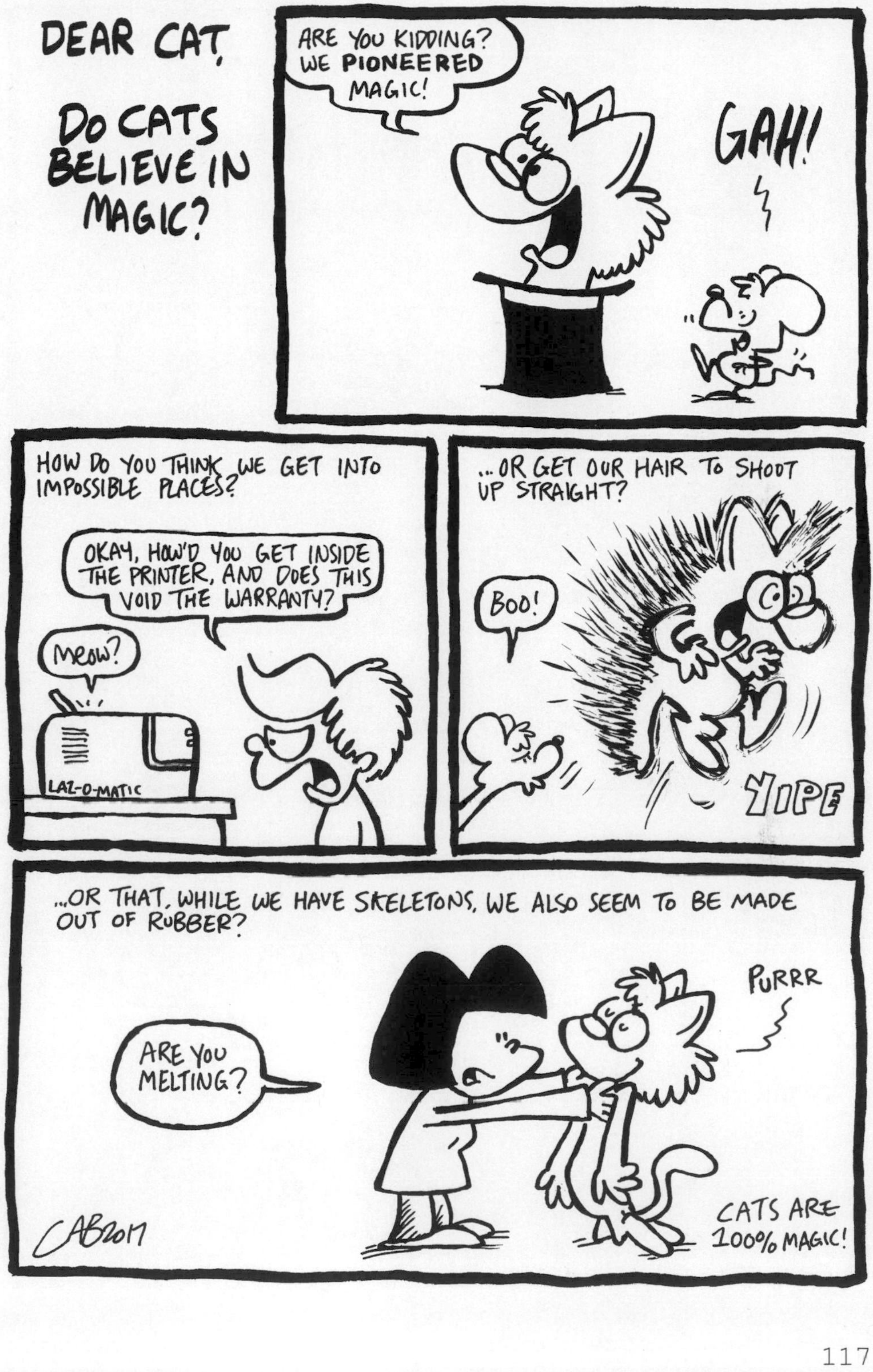
DEAR CAT,
DO CATS BELIEVE IN MAGIC?
ARE YOU KIDDING? WE **PIONEERED** MAGIC!
GAH!
HOW DO YOU THINK WE GET INTO IMPOSSIBLE PLACES?
OKAY, HOW'D YOU GET INSIDE THE PRINTER, AND DOES THIS VOID THE WARRANTY?
MEOW?
LAZ-O-MATIC
...OR GET OUR HAIR TO SHOOT UP STRAIGHT?
BOO!
YIPE
...OR THAT, WHILE WE HAVE SKELETONS, WE ALSO SEEM TO BE MADE OUT OF RUBBER?
ARE YOU MELTING?
PURRR
CATS ARE 100% MAGIC!
CAB2017

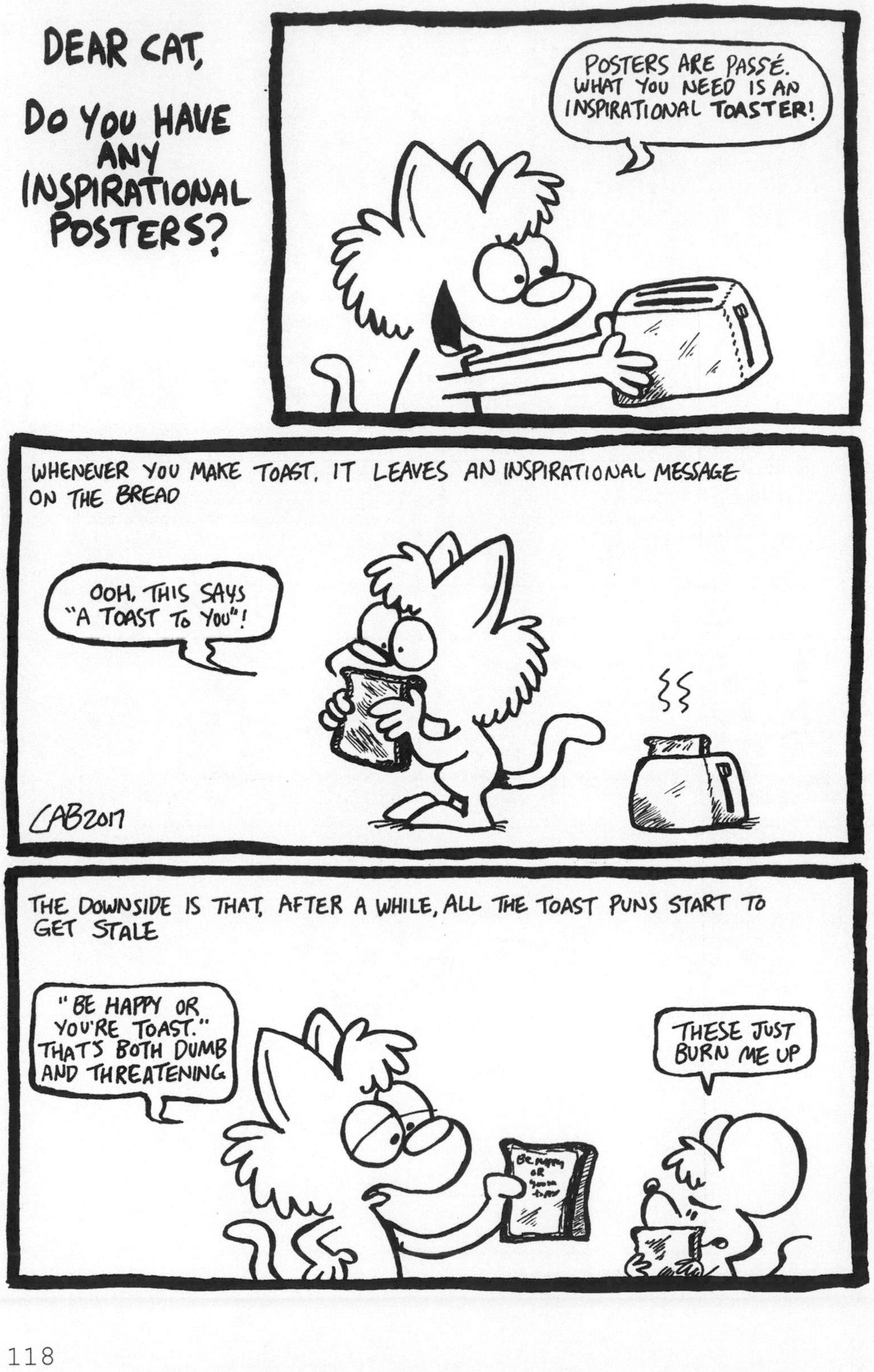
DEAR CAT,
DO YOU HAVE ANY INSPIRATIONAL POSTERS?
POSTERS ARE PASSÉ. WHAT YOU NEED IS AN INSPIRATIONAL TOASTER!
WHENEVER YOU MAKE TOAST, IT LEAVES AN INSPIRATIONAL MESSAGE ON THE BREAD
OOH, THIS SAYS "A TOAST TO YOU"!
CAB2017
THE DOWNSIDE IS THAT, AFTER A WHILE, ALL THE TOAST PUNS START TO GET STALE
"BE HAPPY OR YOU'RE TOAST." THAT'S BOTH DUMB AND THREATENING
THESE JUST BURN ME UP

DEAR CAT,

WHY DOES MY CAT KEEP UNPLUGGING EVERYTHING IN MY HOUSE?

OH, THIS ISN'T BECAUSE YOUR CAT IS BEING A JERK

CATS AREN'T JERKS. HONEST

AND I'M THE STATUE OF LIBERTY

IT'S TO STOP AN ELECTRONIC GHOST FROM HAUNTING YOU!

BWA HA HA! I'M GOING TO SHORT-CIRCUIT YOU DURING YOUR SLEEP!

12:01

CAB 2017

SINCE THEY'RE GHOSTS BASED ON ELECTRICITY, THE ONLY WAY THEY CAN GET IN IS THROUGH POWER CORDS

CURSES! THAT TRICKY FELINE UNPLUGGED THE CPAP MACHINE! I'LL GET HIM FOR THIS!

WHAT TH~?

CPAP

OF COURSE, IF YOUR CAT'S SMART, HE WOULD FIND A FAR MORE PERMANENT SOLUTION TO GET RID OF THE GHOST

NOW THIS IS MORE EFFICIENT!

WRRRRRRRR

THERE'S A POLICE CAR PULLING OVER. MAYBE THEY WANT TO THANK YOU!

DEAR CAT. DO YOU LIKE VACUUM CLEANERS?

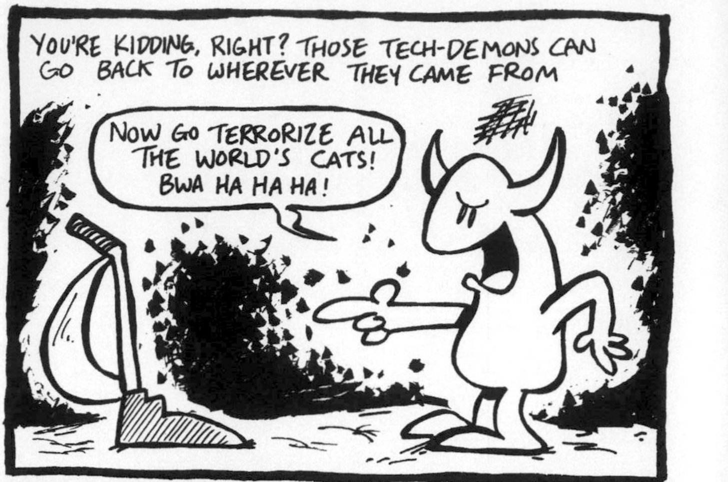
YOU'RE KIDDING, RIGHT? THOSE TECH-DEMONS CAN GO BACK TO WHEREVER THEY CAME FROM
NOW GO TERRORIZE ALL THE WORLD'S CATS! BWA HA HA HA!

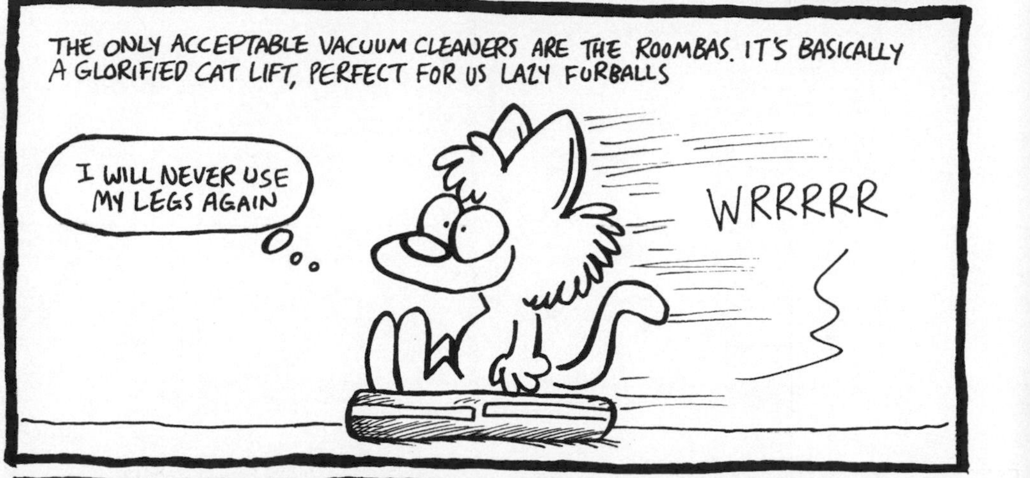
THE ONLY ACCEPTABLE VACUUM CLEANERS ARE THE ROOMBAS. IT'S BASICALLY A GLORIFIED CAT LIFT, PERFECT FOR US LAZY FURBALLS
I WILL NEVER USE MY LEGS AGAIN
WRRRRR

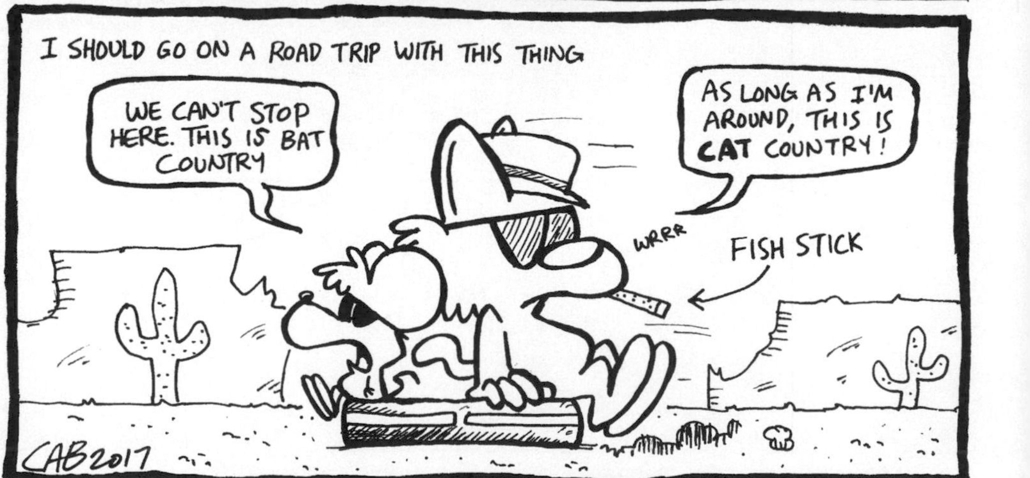
I SHOULD GO ON A ROAD TRIP WITH THIS THING
WE CAN'T STOP HERE. THIS IS BAT COUNTRY
AS LONG AS I'M AROUND, THIS IS CAT COUNTRY!
WRRR
FISH STICK
CAB 2017

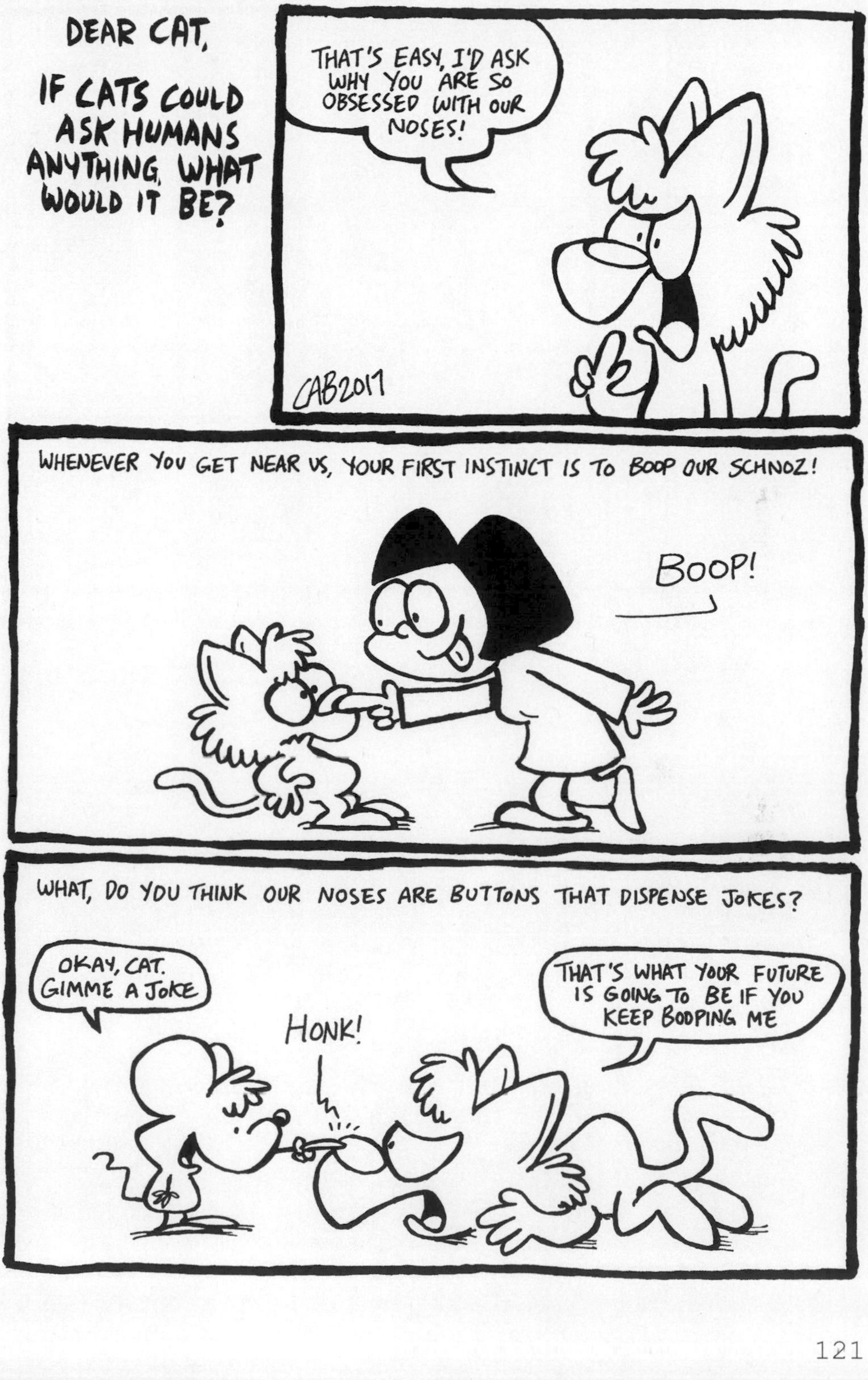
DEAR CAT,
IF CATS COULD ASK HUMANS ANYTHING, WHAT WOULD IT BE?
THAT'S EASY, I'D ASK WHY YOU ARE SO OBSESSED WITH OUR NOSES!
CAB2017
WHENEVER YOU GET NEAR US, YOUR FIRST INSTINCT IS TO BOOP OUR SCHNOZ!
BOOP!
WHAT, DO YOU THINK OUR NOSES ARE BUTTONS THAT DISPENSE JOKES?
OKAY, CAT. GIMME A JOKE
HONK!
THAT'S WHAT YOUR FUTURE IS GOING TO BE IF YOU KEEP BOOPING ME

DEAR CAT,

DO CATS READ COMICS?

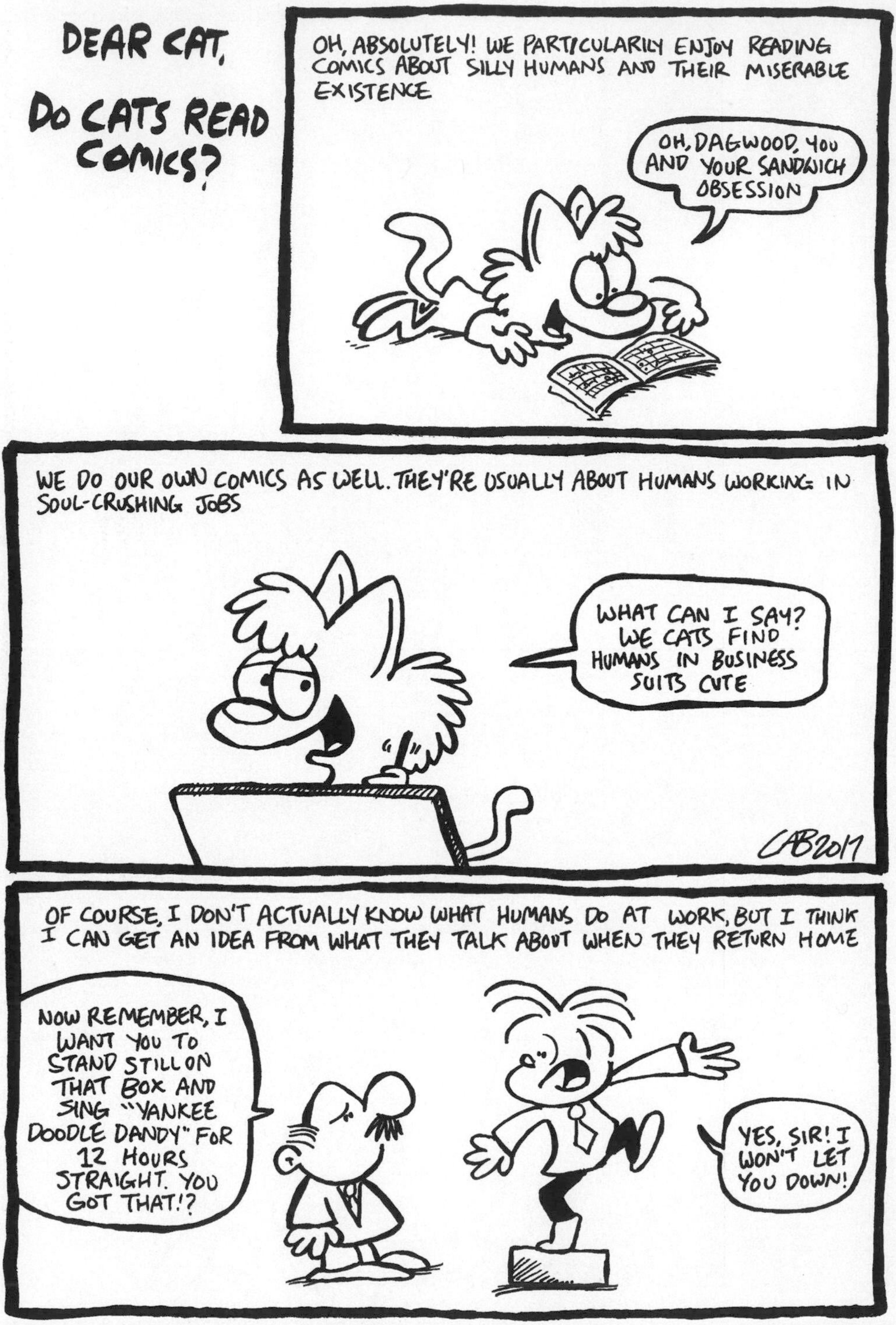

OH, ABSOLUTELY! WE PARTICULARILY ENJOY READING COMICS ABOUT SILLY HUMANS AND THEIR MISERABLE EXISTENCE
OH, DAGWOOD, YOU AND YOUR SANDWICH OBSESSION
WE DO OUR OWN COMICS AS WELL. THEY'RE USUALLY ABOUT HUMANS WORKING IN SOUL-CRUSHING JOBS
WHAT CAN I SAY? WE CATS FIND HUMANS IN BUSINESS SUITS CUTE
CAB2017
OF COURSE, I DON'T ACTUALLY KNOW WHAT HUMANS DO AT WORK, BUT I THINK I CAN GET AN IDEA FROM WHAT THEY TALK ABOUT WHEN THEY RETURN HOME
NOW REMEMBER, I WANT YOU TO STAND STILL ON THAT BOX AND SING "YANKEE DOODLE DANDY" FOR 12 HOURS STRAIGHT. YOU GOT THAT!?
YES, SIR! I WON'T LET YOU DOWN!

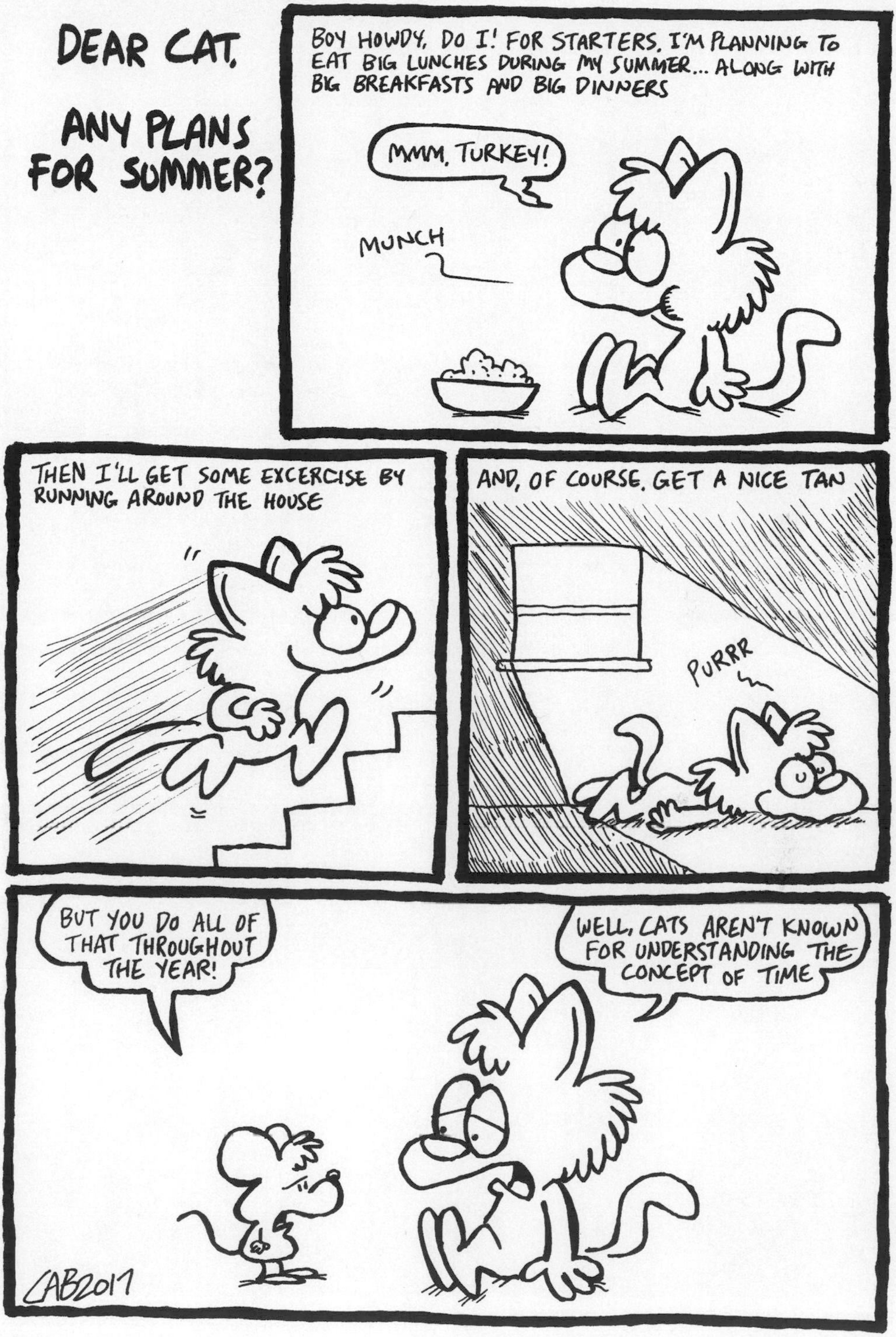
DEAR CAT,
ANY PLANS FOR SUMMER?
BOY HOWDY, DO I! FOR STARTERS, I'M PLANNING TO EAT BIG LUNCHES DURING MY SUMMER... ALONG WITH BIG BREAKFASTS AND BIG DINNERS
MMM, TURKEY!
MUNCH
THEN I'LL GET SOME EXCERCISE BY RUNNING AROUND THE HOUSE
AND, OF COURSE, GET A NICE TAN
PURRR
BUT YOU DO ALL OF THAT THROUGHOUT THE YEAR!
WELL, CATS AREN'T KNOWN FOR UNDERSTANDING THE CONCEPT OF TIME
CAB2017

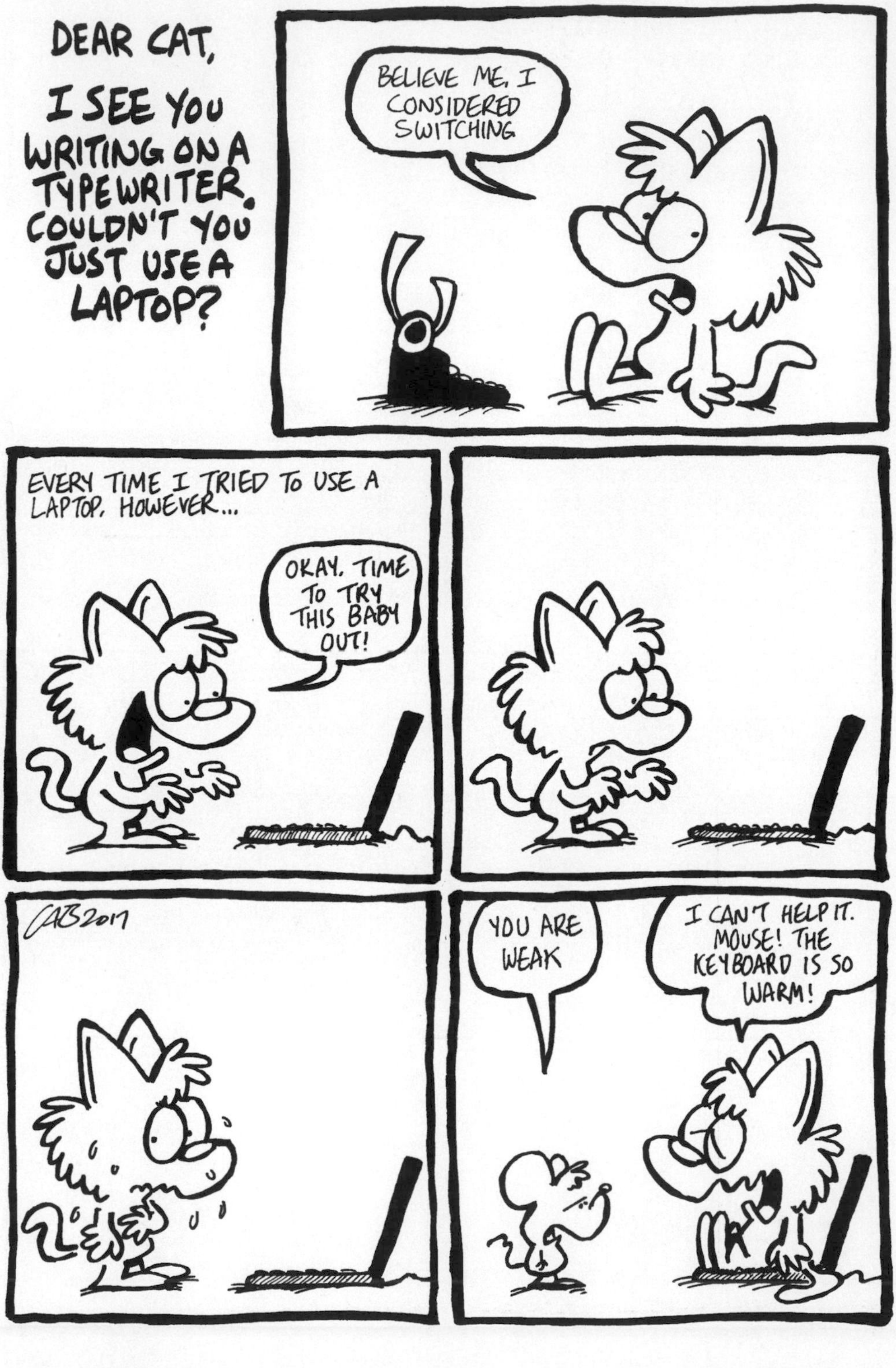
DEAR CAT,
I SEE YOU WRITING ON A TYPEWRITER. COULDN'T YOU JUST USE A LAPTOP?
BELIEVE ME, I CONSIDERED SWITCHING
EVERY TIME I TRIED TO USE A LAPTOP, HOWEVER...
OKAY, TIME TO TRY THIS BABY OUT!
CAB 2017
YOU ARE WEAK
I CAN'T HELP IT, MOUSE! THE KEYBOARD IS SO WARM!

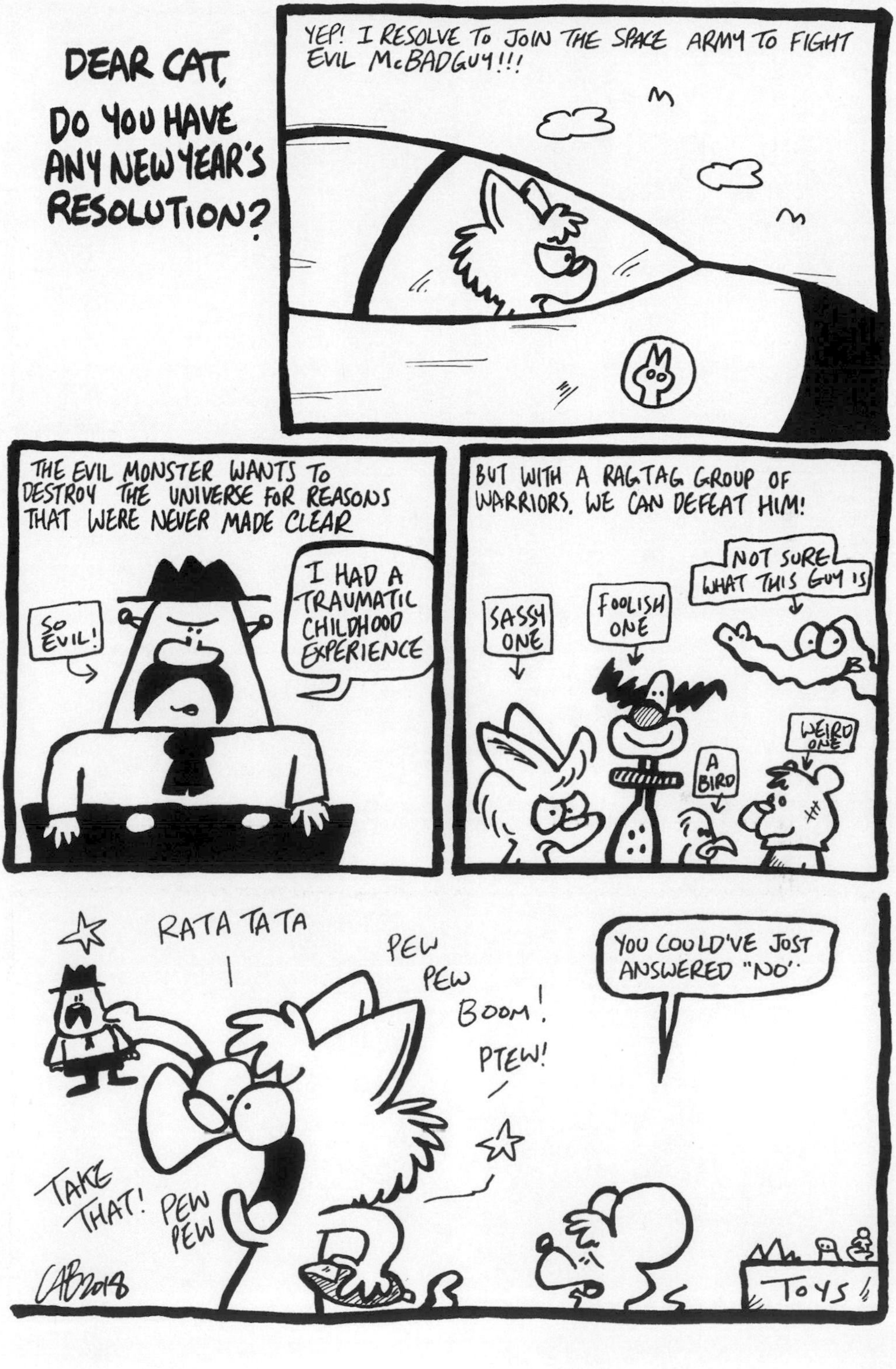
DEAR CAT,
DO YOU HAVE ANY NEW YEAR'S RESOLUTION?
YEP! I RESOLVE TO JOIN THE SPACE ARMY TO FIGHT EVIL McBADGUY!!!
THE EVIL MONSTER WANTS TO DESTROY THE UNIVERSE FOR REASONS THAT WERE NEVER MADE CLEAR
SO EVIL!
I HAD A TRAUMATIC CHILDHOOD EXPERIENCE
BUT WITH A RAGTAG GROUP OF WARRIORS, WE CAN DEFEAT HIM!
SASSY ONE
FOOLISH ONE
NOT SURE WHAT THIS GUY IS
A BIRD
WEIRD ONE
RATA TATA
PEW PEW
BOOM!
PTEW!
TAKE THAT!
PEW PEW
YOU COULD'VE JUST ANSWERED "NO".
TOYS
CAB2018

DEAR CAT,

HOW DO I GET RID OF EMBARASSING MEMORIES?

WHY, YOU JUST NEED TO DRINK MY SPECIAL "FORGET ABOUT IT" MILKSHAKE!

FIRST, GET A BLENDER AND ADD IN EXPIRED MILK, FISH, BROCCOLI, ROTTEN CHEESE, TOMATO JUICE, AND GARLIC

MILK

BLEND EVERYTHING, AND DRINK UP!

THIS WILL GET PEOPLE TO FORGET THEIR EMBARASSING MEMORIES!?

WRRR

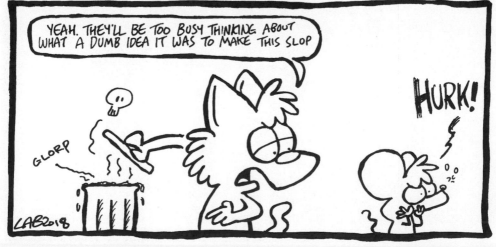

YEAH. THEY'LL BE TOO BUSY THINKING ABOUT WHAT A DUMB IDEA IT WAS TO MAKE THIS SLOP

GLORP

HURK!

LAB2018

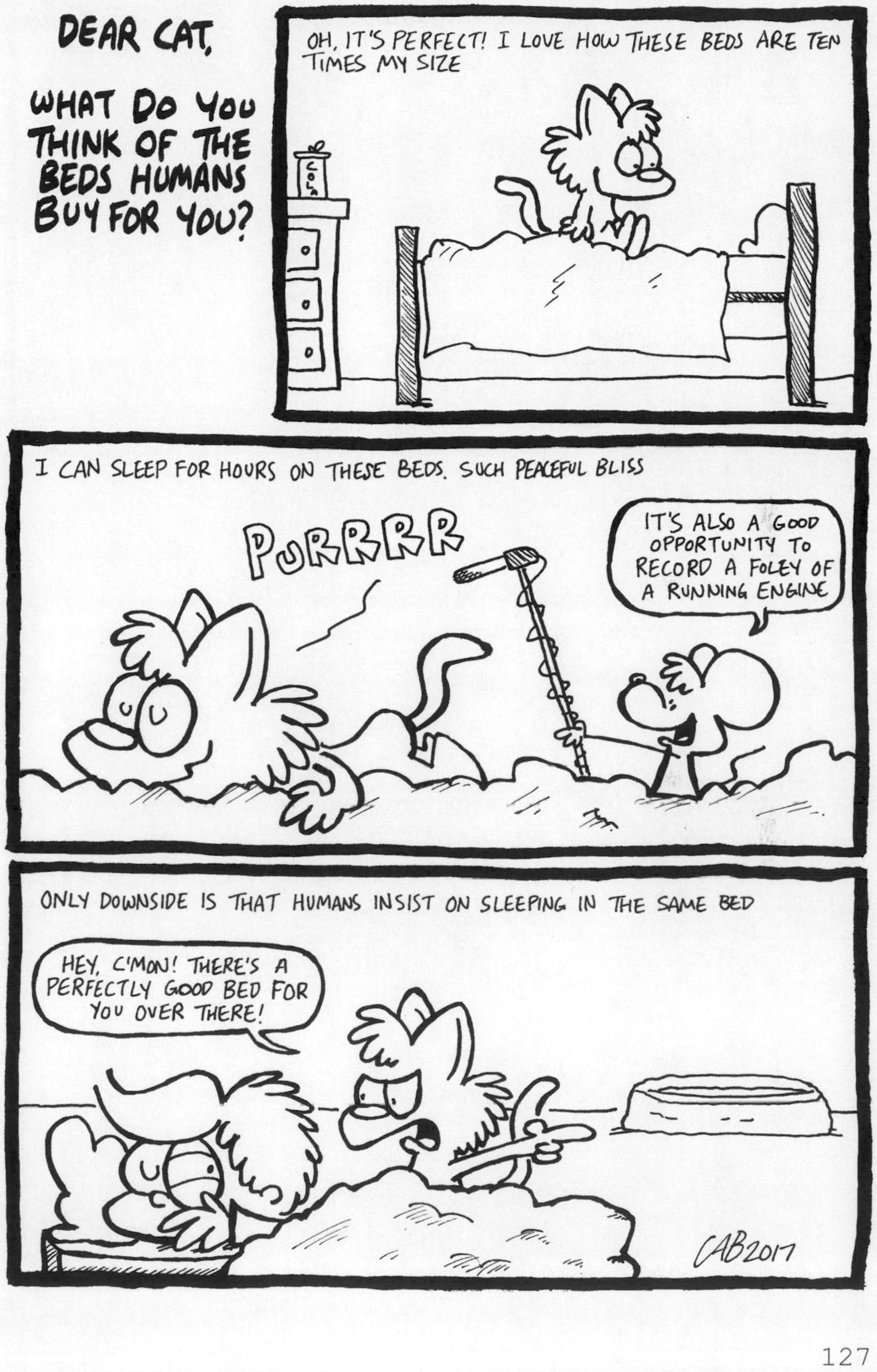
DEAR CAT,
WHAT DO YOU THINK OF THE BEDS HUMANS BUY FOR YOU?
OH, IT'S PERFECT! I LOVE HOW THESE BEDS ARE TEN TIMES MY SIZE
I CAN SLEEP FOR HOURS ON THESE BEDS. SUCH PEACEFUL BLISS
PURRRR
IT'S ALSO A GOOD OPPORTUNITY TO RECORD A FOLEY OF A RUNNING ENGINE
ONLY DOWNSIDE IS THAT HUMANS INSIST ON SLEEPING IN THE SAME BED
HEY, C'MON! THERE'S A PERFECTLY GOOD BED FOR YOU OVER THERE!
CAB 2017

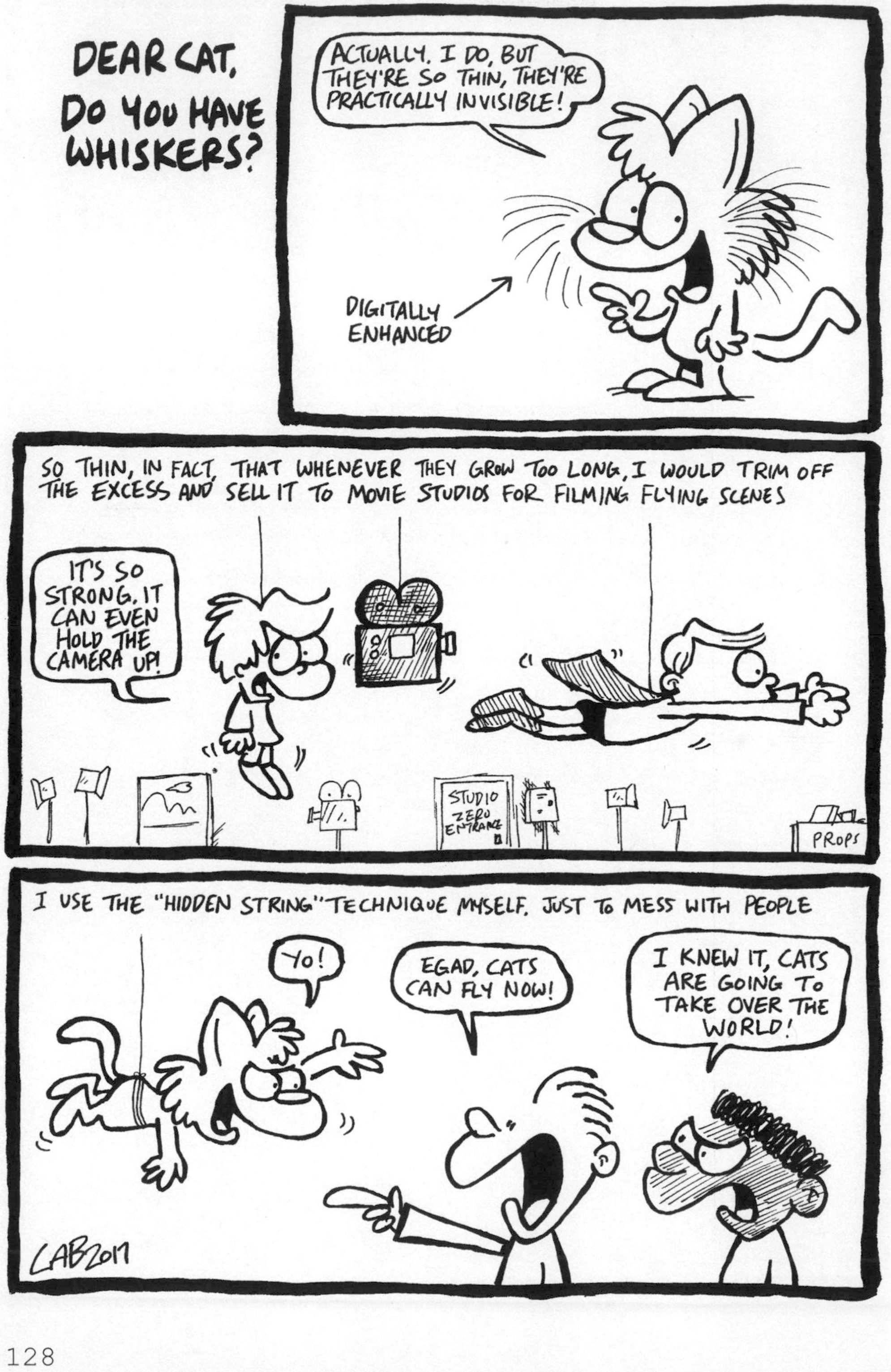
DEAR CAT, DO YOU HAVE WHISKERS?
ACTUALLY, I DO, BUT THEY'RE SO THIN, THEY'RE PRACTICALLY INVISIBLE!
DIGITALLY ENHANCED
SO THIN, IN FACT, THAT WHENEVER THEY GROW TOO LONG, I WOULD TRIM OFF THE EXCESS AND SELL IT TO MOVIE STUDIOS FOR FILMING FLYING SCENES
IT'S SO STRONG, IT CAN EVEN HOLD THE CAMERA UP!
STUDIO ZERO ENTRANCE
PROPS
I USE THE "HIDDEN STRING" TECHNIQUE MYSELF, JUST TO MESS WITH PEOPLE
YO!
EGAD, CATS CAN FLY NOW!
I KNEW IT, CATS ARE GOING TO TAKE OVER THE WORLD!
CAB2017

DEAR CAT,

WHO DO YOU THINK YOU ARE?

THAT'S A GOOD QUESTION

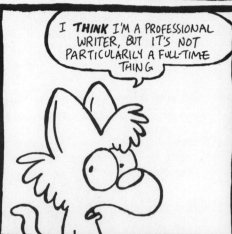

I **THINK** I'M A PROFESSIONAL WRITER, BUT IT'S NOT PARTICULARILY A FULL-TIME THING

I **THINK** I'M SOMEONE'S PET, TOO, BUT *PHHHT!* LIKE I'D LET SOME HUMAN **OWN** ME OR SOMETHING. *HEH*

I **KNOW** I'M A CAT, THOUGH!... BUT WHAT IF I'M ACTUALLY A SPACE ALIEN THAT LOOKS LIKE A CAT, AND I SOMEHOW DIDN'T KNOW THAT?

I THINK YOU'RE CONFUSED

OOH, I CAN GO WITH THAT!

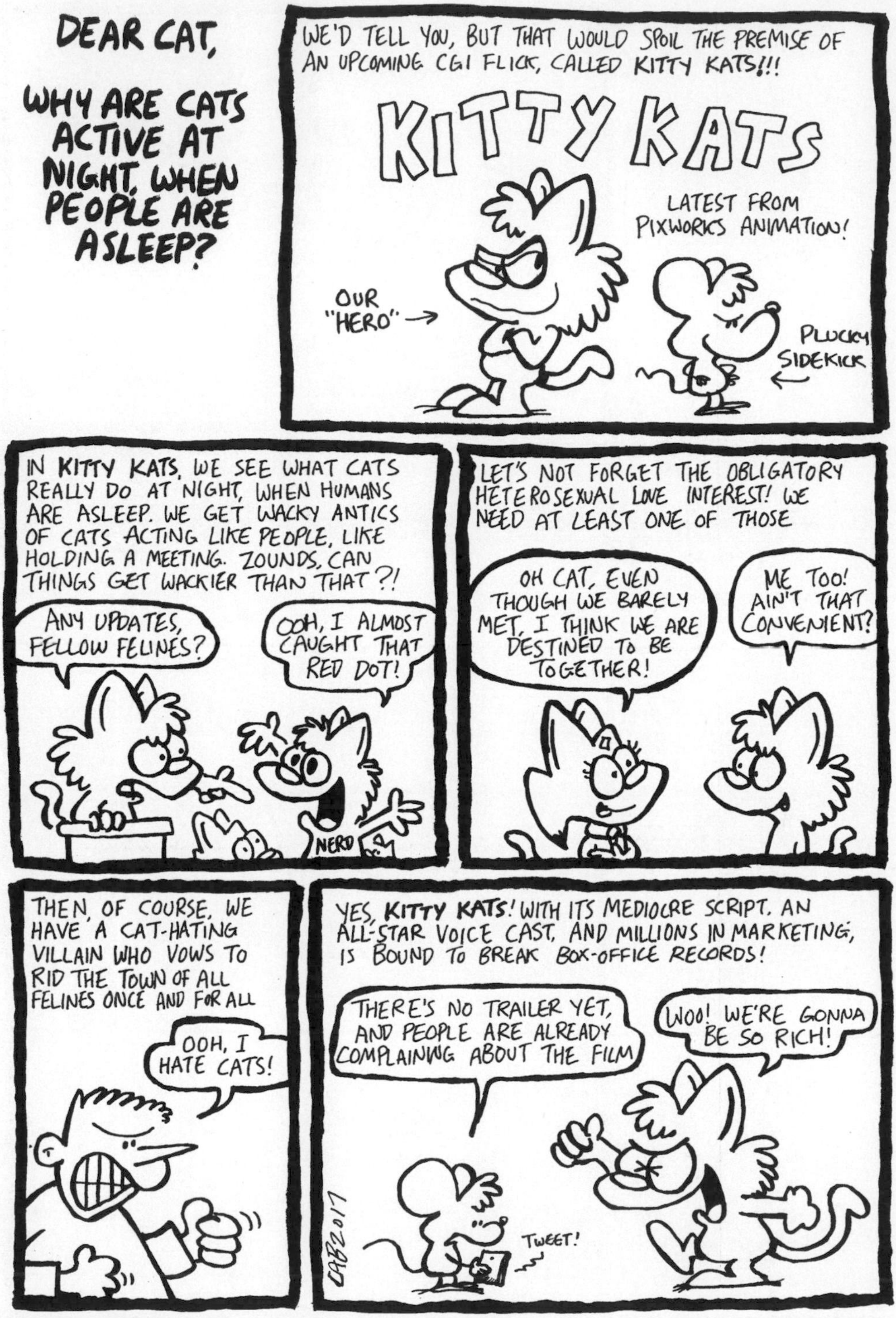
DEAR CAT,
WHY ARE CATS ACTIVE AT NIGHT, WHEN PEOPLE ARE ASLEEP?
WE'D TELL YOU, BUT THAT WOULD SPOIL THE PREMISE OF AN UPCOMING CGI FLICK, CALLED KITTY KATS!!!
KITTY KATS
LATEST FROM PIXWORKS ANIMATION!
OUR "HERO"
PLUCKY SIDEKICK
IN KITTY KATS, WE SEE WHAT CATS REALLY DO AT NIGHT, WHEN HUMANS ARE ASLEEP. WE GET WACKY ANTICS OF CATS ACTING LIKE PEOPLE, LIKE HOLDING A MEETING. ZOUNDS, CAN THINGS GET WACKIER THAN THAT?!
ANY UPDATES, FELLOW FELINES?
OOH, I ALMOST CAUGHT THAT RED DOT!
NERD
LET'S NOT FORGET THE OBLIGATORY HETEROSEXUAL LOVE INTEREST! WE NEED AT LEAST ONE OF THOSE
OH CAT, EVEN THOUGH WE BARELY MET, I THINK WE ARE DESTINED TO BE TOGETHER!
ME TOO! AIN'T THAT CONVENIENT?
THEN, OF COURSE, WE HAVE A CAT-HATING VILLAIN WHO VOWS TO RID THE TOWN OF ALL FELINES ONCE AND FOR ALL
OOH, I HATE CATS!
YES, KITTY KATS! WITH ITS MEDIOCRE SCRIPT, AN ALL-STAR VOICE CAST, AND MILLIONS IN MARKETING, IS BOUND TO BREAK BOX-OFFICE RECORDS!
THERE'S NO TRAILER YET, AND PEOPLE ARE ALREADY COMPLAINING ABOUT THE FILM
WOO! WE'RE GONNA BE SO RICH!
TWEET!
CAB2017

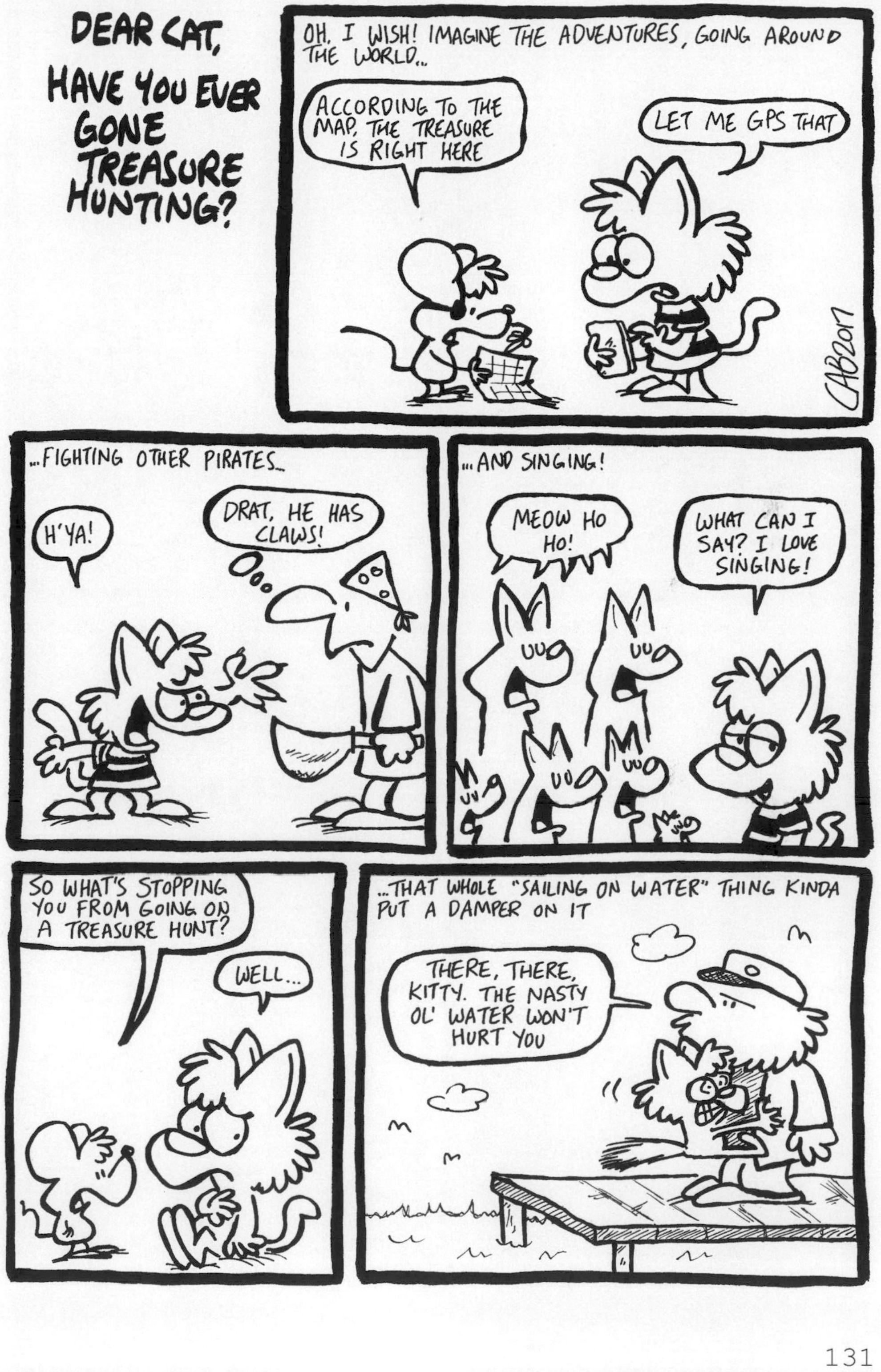
DEAR CAT,
HAVE YOU EVER GONE TREASURE HUNTING?
OH, I WISH! IMAGINE THE ADVENTURES, GOING AROUND THE WORLD...
ACCORDING TO THE MAP, THE TREASURE IS RIGHT HERE
LET ME GPS THAT
CAB2017
...FIGHTING OTHER PIRATES...
H'YA!
DRAT, HE HAS CLAWS!
...AND SINGING!
MEOW HO HO!
WHAT CAN I SAY? I LOVE SINGING!
SO WHAT'S STOPPING YOU FROM GOING ON A TREASURE HUNT?
WELL...
...THAT WHOLE "SAILING ON WATER" THING KINDA PUT A DAMPER ON IT
THERE, THERE, KITTY. THE NASTY OL' WATER WON'T HURT YOU

DEAR CAT, PILLOW FORTS OR BOX FORTS?

WHY SETTLE ON ONE OR THE OTHER WHEN YOU CAN HAVE BOTH? A PILLOW FORT INSIDE A BOX FORT!
IT'S LIKE TURDUCKEN!
DUDE, NO!
WITH ME SANDWICHED BETWEEN PILLOWS INSIDE A BOX, I HAVE THE ULTIMATE PROTECTION!
YES, THIS IS THE...WAIT... I THINK I'M STUCK!
PERHAPS I DID NOT THINK THIS THROUGH
CAB 2017

DEAR CAT,

DO YOU WATCH ANIME?

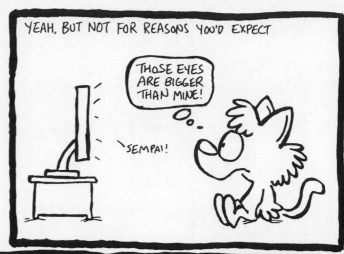

YEAH, BUT NOT FOR REASONS YOU'D EXPECT

THOSE EYES ARE BIGGER THAN MINE!

SEMPAI!

YES, EYES. US CATS WATCH ANIME IN ORDER TO FIGURE OUT HOW TO GET OUR EYES TO BE AS BIG AS THEIR CHARACTERS

NOT THE FIRST TIME CARTOONS INFLUENCED HOW OUR EYES LOOK. SIMILAR THING HAPPENED BACK IN THE 1930s

I EVEN HEAR THAT A CERTAIN PRINCESS IS GETTING INTO THE ACT!

DO YOU THINK THIS WILL GET ME TAKEN SERIOUSLY?

MUST...KEEP... STRAIGHT FACE

Snerk!

CAB2017 WITH THANKS TO CHRIS "COCO" TENEYCK

133

DEAR CAT,

WHY DO HUMANS THINK CATS CAN'T SING?

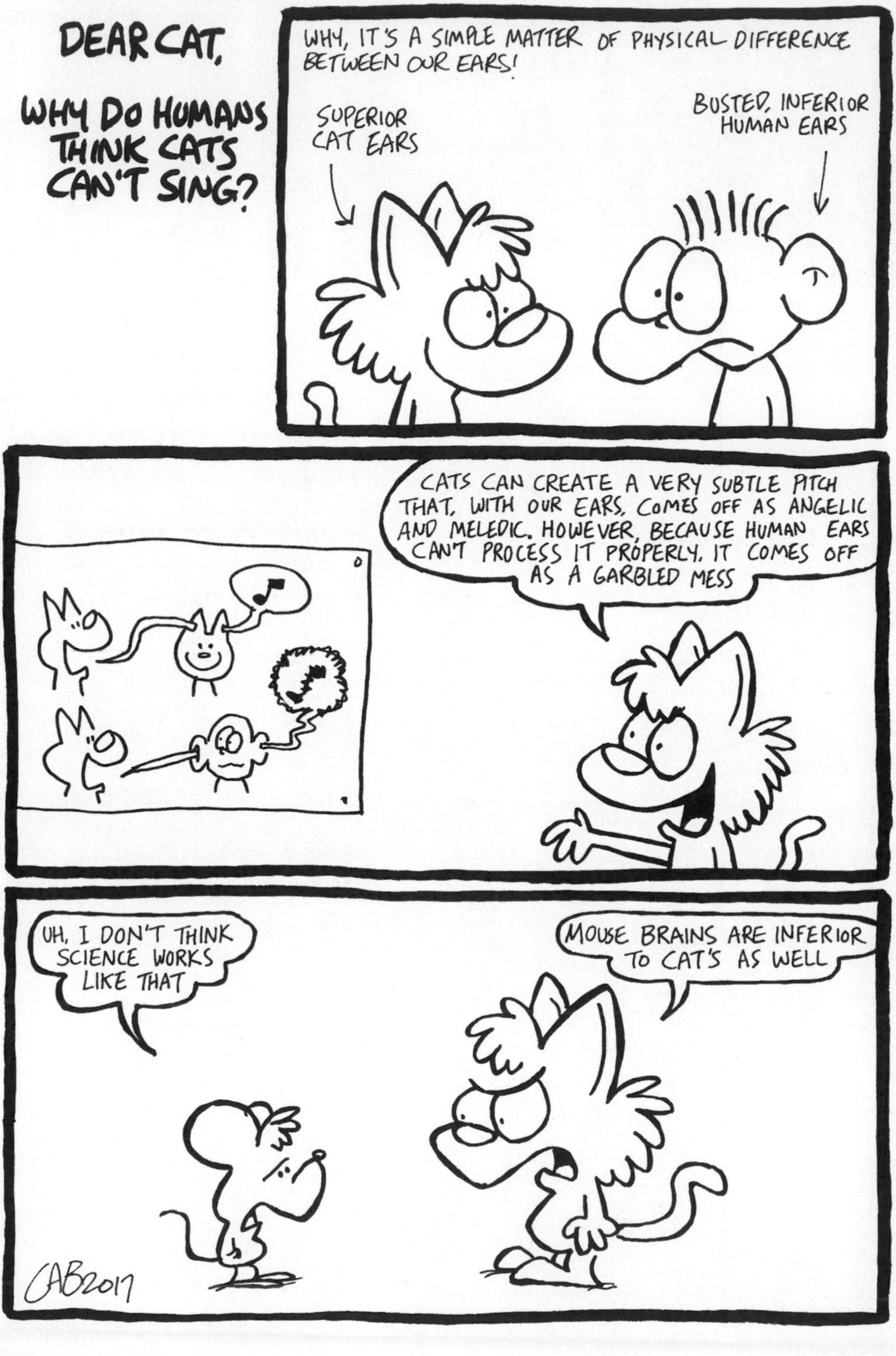
WHY, IT'S A SIMPLE MATTER OF PHYSICAL DIFFERENCE BETWEEN OUR EARS!
SUPERIOR CAT EARS
BUSTED, INFERIOR HUMAN EARS
CATS CAN CREATE A VERY SUBTLE PITCH THAT, WITH OUR EARS, COMES OFF AS ANGELIC AND MELEDIC. HOWEVER, BECAUSE HUMAN EARS CAN'T PROCESS IT PROPERLY, IT COMES OFF AS A GARBLED MESS
UH, I DON'T THINK SCIENCE WORKS LIKE THAT
MOUSE BRAINS ARE INFERIOR TO CAT'S AS WELL
CAB2017

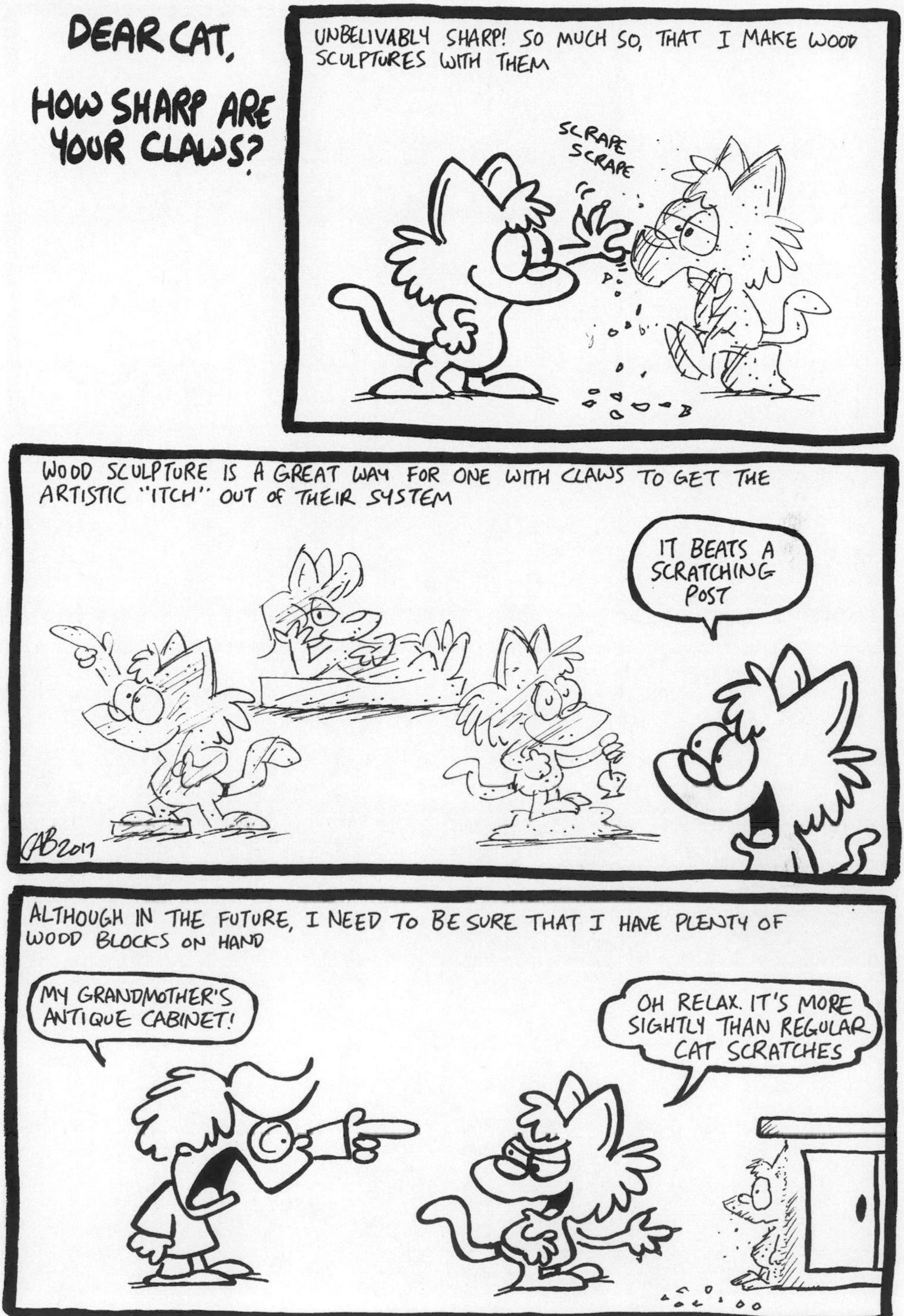
DEAR CAT,
HOW SHARP ARE YOUR CLAWS?
UNBELIVABLY SHARP! SO MUCH SO, THAT I MAKE WOOD SCULPTURES WITH THEM
SCRAPE SCRAPE
WOOD SCULPTURE IS A GREAT WAY FOR ONE WITH CLAWS TO GET THE ARTISTIC "ITCH" OUT OF THEIR SYSTEM
IT BEATS A SCRATCHING POST
CAB 2017
ALTHOUGH IN THE FUTURE, I NEED TO BE SURE THAT I HAVE PLENTY OF WOOD BLOCKS ON HAND
MY GRANDMOTHER'S ANTIQUE CABINET!
OH RELAX. IT'S MORE SIGHTLY THAN REGULAR CAT SCRATCHES

DEAR CAT,

ARE CATS PSYCHIC?

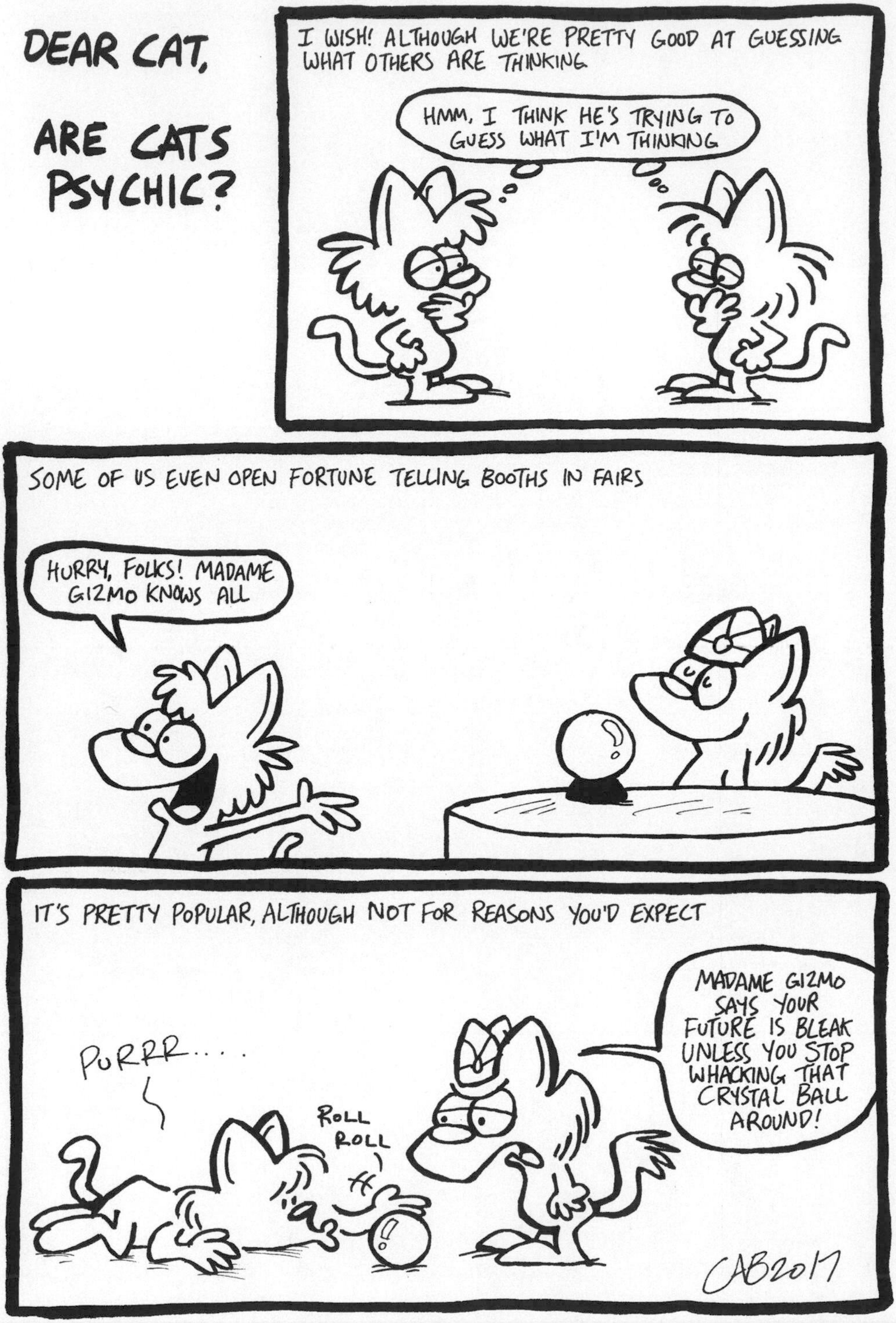
I WISH! ALTHOUGH WE'RE PRETTY GOOD AT GUESSING WHAT OTHERS ARE THINKING
HMM, I THINK HE'S TRYING TO GUESS WHAT I'M THINKING
SOME OF US EVEN OPEN FORTUNE TELLING BOOTHS IN FAIRS
HURRY, FOLKS! MADAME GIZMO KNOWS ALL
IT'S PRETTY POPULAR, ALTHOUGH NOT FOR REASONS YOU'D EXPECT
PURRR....
ROLL ROLL
MADAME GIZMO SAYS YOUR FUTURE IS BLEAK UNLESS YOU STOP WHACKING THAT CRYSTAL BALL AROUND!
CAB2017

DEAR CAT,

WOULD YOU BATHE IN JELLO?

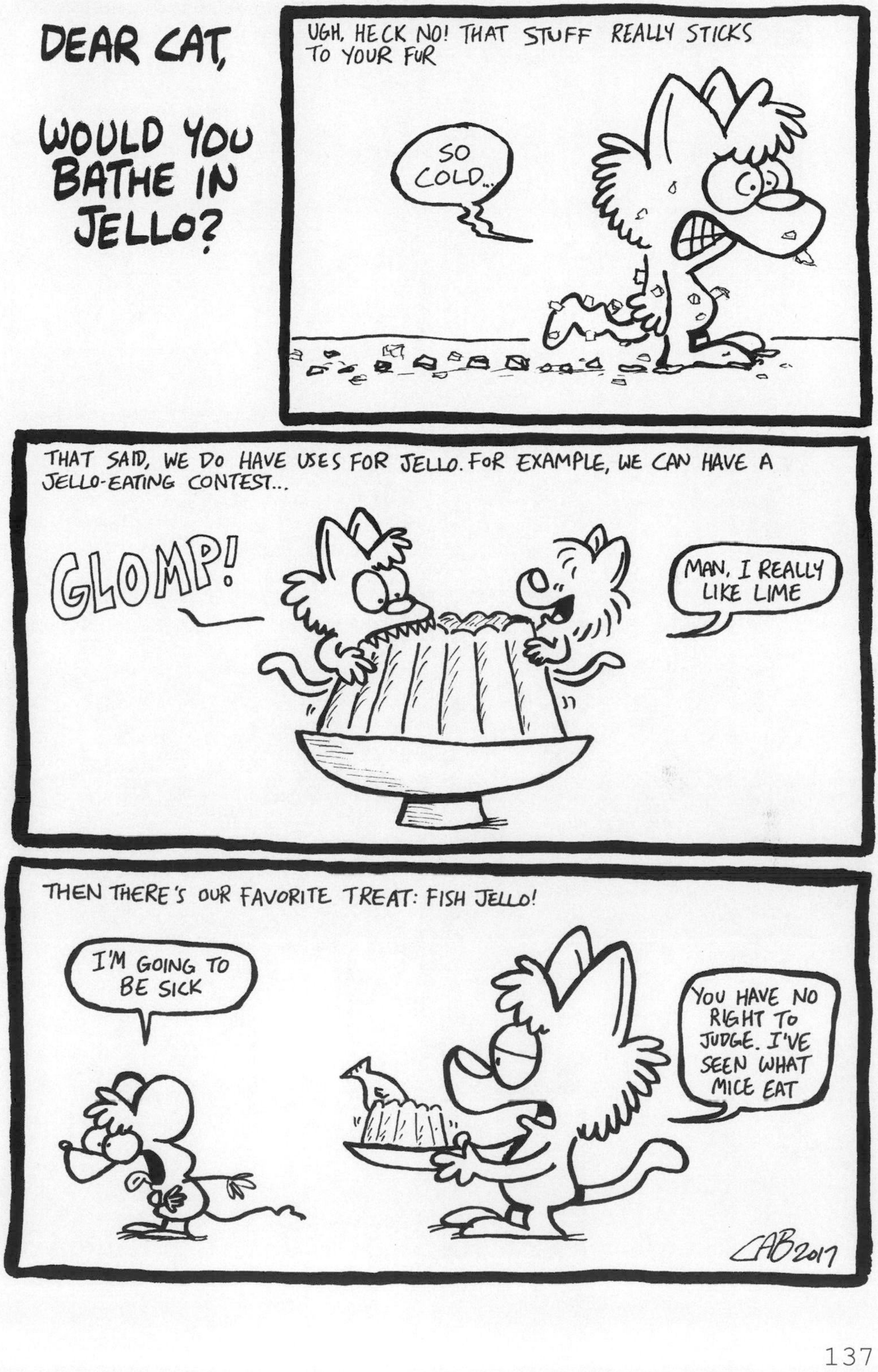
UGH, HECK NO! THAT STUFF REALLY STICKS TO YOUR FUR
SO COLD...
THAT SAID, WE DO HAVE USES FOR JELLO. FOR EXAMPLE, WE CAN HAVE A JELLO-EATING CONTEST...
GLOMP!
MAN, I REALLY LIKE LIME
THEN THERE'S OUR FAVORITE TREAT: FISH JELLO!
I'M GOING TO BE SICK
YOU HAVE NO RIGHT TO JUDGE. I'VE SEEN WHAT MICE EAT
CAB 2017

DEAR CAT,

WHAT IS THE MEANING OF LIFE?

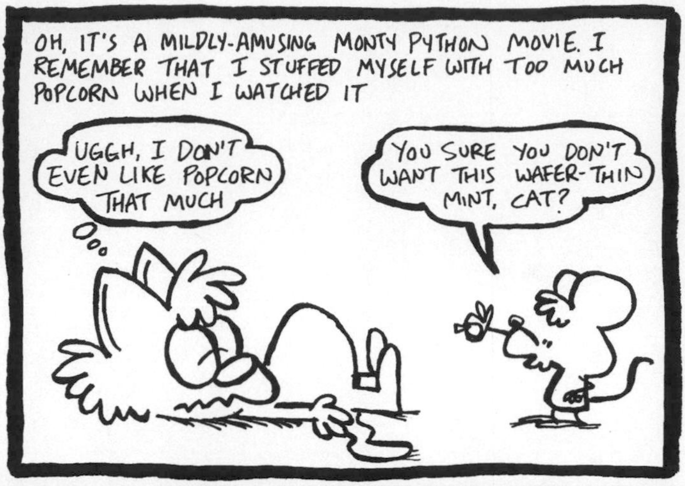

OH, IT'S A MILDLY-AMUSING MONTY PYTHON MOVIE. I REMEMBER THAT I STUFFED MYSELF WITH TOO MUCH POPCORN WHEN I WATCHED IT
UGGH, I DON'T EVEN LIKE POPCORN THAT MUCH
YOU SURE YOU DON'T WANT THIS WAFER-THIN MINT, CAT?

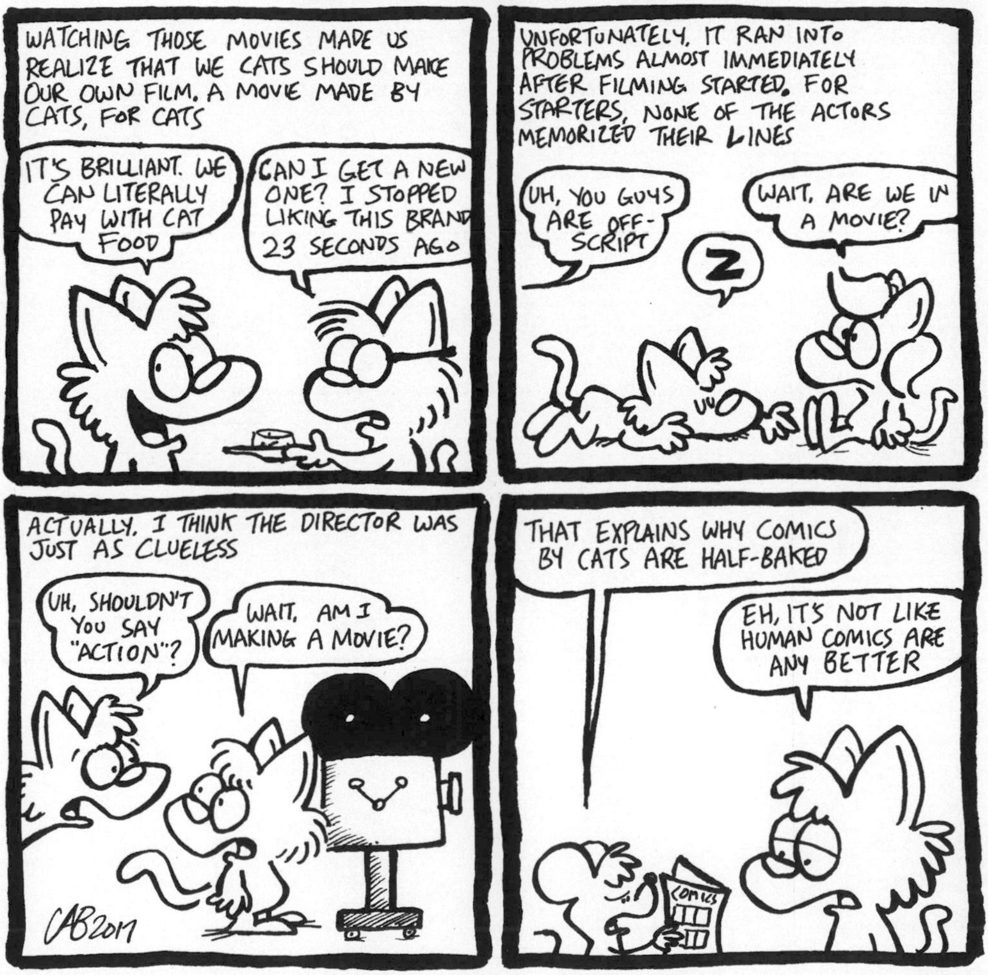

WATCHING THOSE MOVIES MADE US REALIZE THAT WE CATS SHOULD MAKE OUR OWN FILM. A MOVIE MADE BY CATS, FOR CATS
IT'S BRILLIANT. WE CAN LITERALLY PAY WITH CAT FOOD
CAN I GET A NEW ONE? I STOPPED LIKING THIS BRAND 23 SECONDS AGO
UNFORTUNATELY, IT RAN INTO PROBLEMS ALMOST IMMEDIATELY AFTER FILMING STARTED. FOR STARTERS, NONE OF THE ACTORS MEMORIZED THEIR LINES
UH, YOU GUYS ARE OFF-SCRIPT
Z
WAIT, ARE WE IN A MOVIE?
ACTUALLY, I THINK THE DIRECTOR WAS JUST AS CLUELESS
UH, SHOULDN'T YOU SAY "ACTION"?
WAIT, AM I MAKING A MOVIE?
CAB2017
THAT EXPLAINS WHY COMICS BY CATS ARE HALF-BAKED
EH, IT'S NOT LIKE HUMAN COMICS ARE ANY BETTER
COMICS

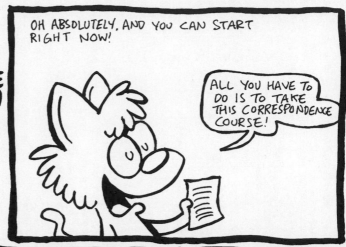

DEAR CAT,
IS IT TRUE THAT EVERYONE WANTS TO BE A CAT?
OH ABSOLUTELY. AND YOU CAN START RIGHT NOW!
ALL YOU HAVE TO DO IS TO TAKE THIS CORRESPONDENCE COURSE!
FIRST, YOU HAVE TO TAKE A 3-DAY SERIES ON HOW TO BE A PICKY EATER, THEN YOU HAVE A 3-WEEK LESSON ON THE ART OF SLEEPING ON BOOKS, KEYBOARDS, OR WHATEVER THE HUMAN IS PAYING ATTENTION TO, THEN....
ALL THIS TO BECOME A CAT!?
FORGET IT. I'M JUST GOING TO TAKE A NAP INSTEAD
CONGRATULATIONS, YOU'RE A CAT NOW
YOU'RE A CAT
GIVING UP A TASK TO TAKE A NAP IS THE MOST CAT THING ANYONE CAN DO
SO EVERYONE'S A CAT, THEN
CAB 2017

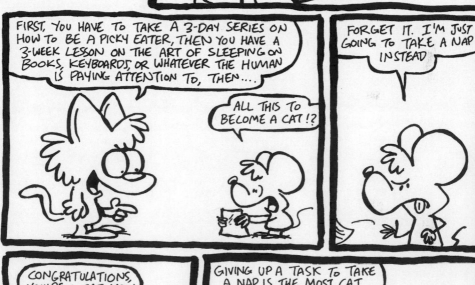

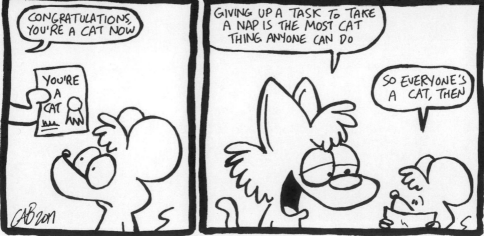

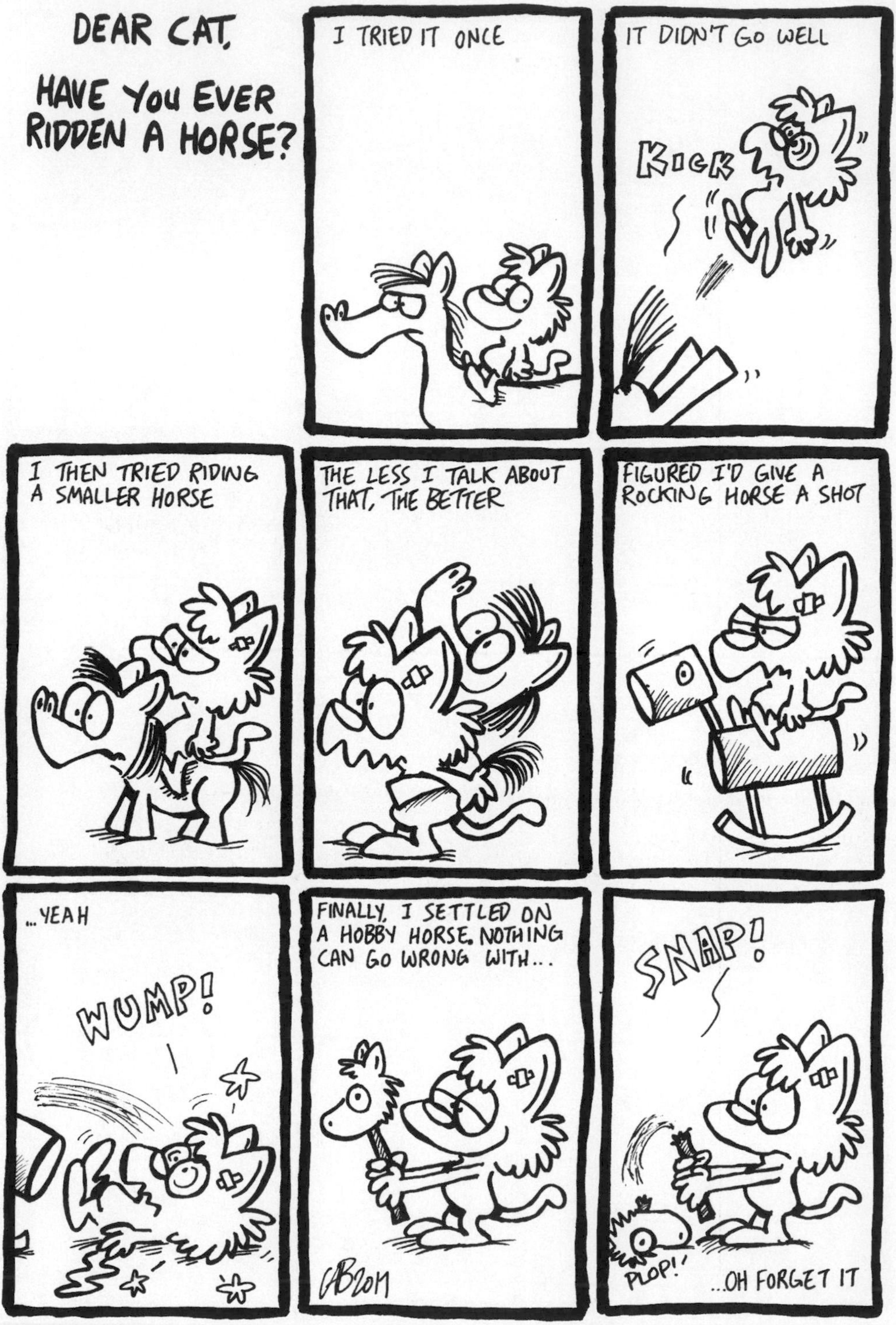
DEAR CAT,
HAVE YOU EVER RIDDEN A HORSE?
I TRIED IT ONCE
IT DIDN'T GO WELL
KICK
I THEN TRIED RIDING A SMALLER HORSE
THE LESS I TALK ABOUT THAT, THE BETTER
FIGURED I'D GIVE A ROCKING HORSE A SHOT
...YEAH
WUMP!
FINALLY, I SETTLED ON A HOBBY HORSE. NOTHING CAN GO WRONG WITH...
SNAP!
PLOP!
...OH FORGET IT

DEAR CAT,

DO YOU KNOW WHICH CAT CLIMBED HIGHEST IN A TREE?

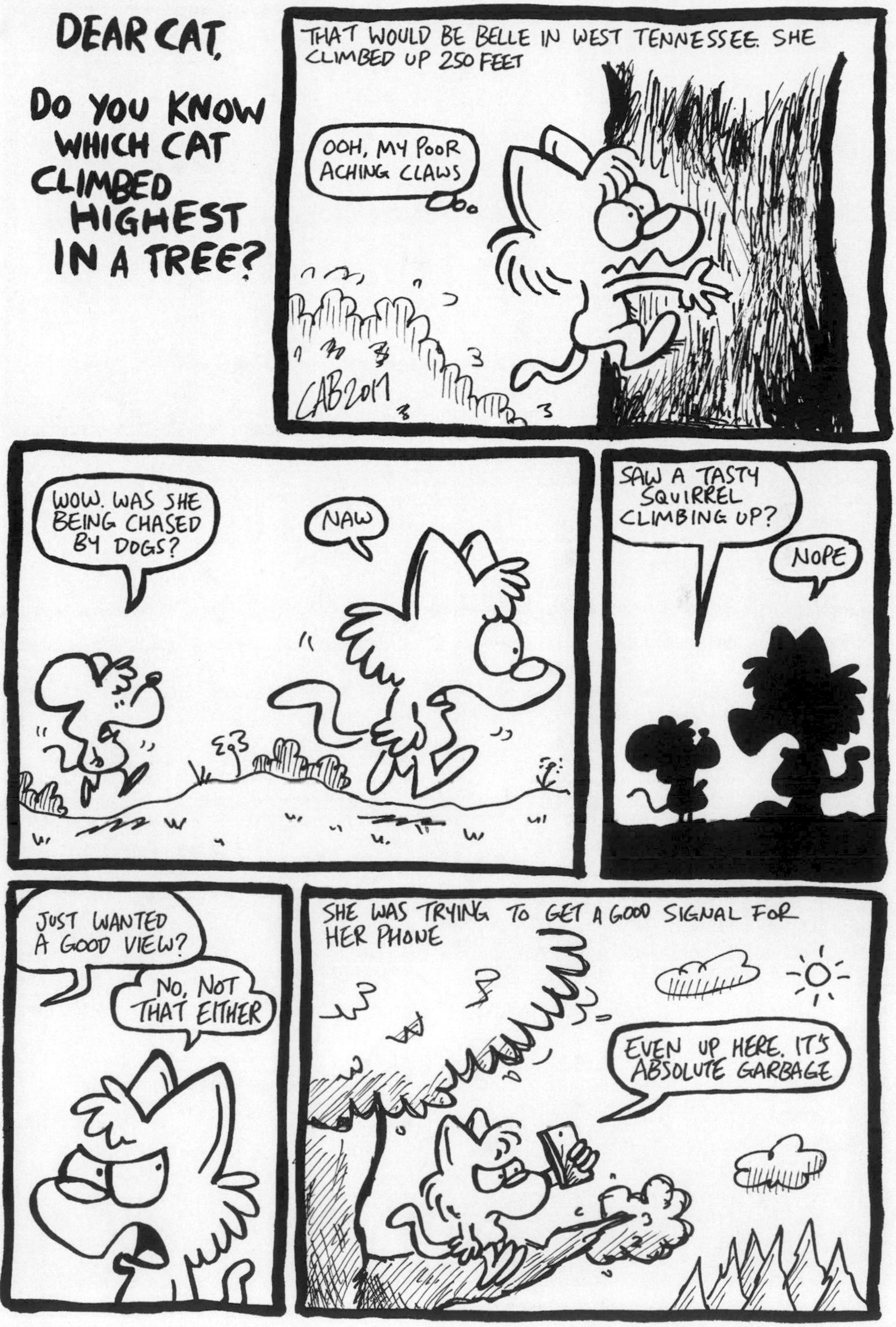
THAT WOULD BE BELLE IN WEST TENNESSEE. SHE CLIMBED UP 250 FEET
OOH, MY POOR ACHING CLAWS
CAB 2017
WOW. WAS SHE BEING CHASED BY DOGS?
NAW
SAW A TASTY SQUIRREL CLIMBING UP?
NOPE
JUST WANTED A GOOD VIEW?
NO, NOT THAT EITHER
SHE WAS TRYING TO GET A GOOD SIGNAL FOR HER PHONE
EVEN UP HERE. IT'S ABSOLUTE GARBAGE

DEAR CAT,

IF YOU COULD BE BIG OR SMALL, WHICH WOULD YOU CHOOSE?

OH, I WOULD BE SMALL, LIKE MOUSE!

REALLY? HOW COME?

WELL, FOR STARTERS, THE AMOUNT OF MISCHIEF I CAN CAUSE IS GOING TO INCREASE GREATLY

OH GOD, THEIR CLAWS ARE EVEN MORE POINTY WHEN THEY'RE SMALL

MROW

ALSO, ME BEING SMALL MEANS THAT FOOD WILL BE LARGER IN PROPORTION

I'M IN HEAVEN

WELL, IF I COULD, I WOULD BE AS BIG AS YOU!

REALLY? WHAT WOULD YOU DO?

OH, THIS AND THAT

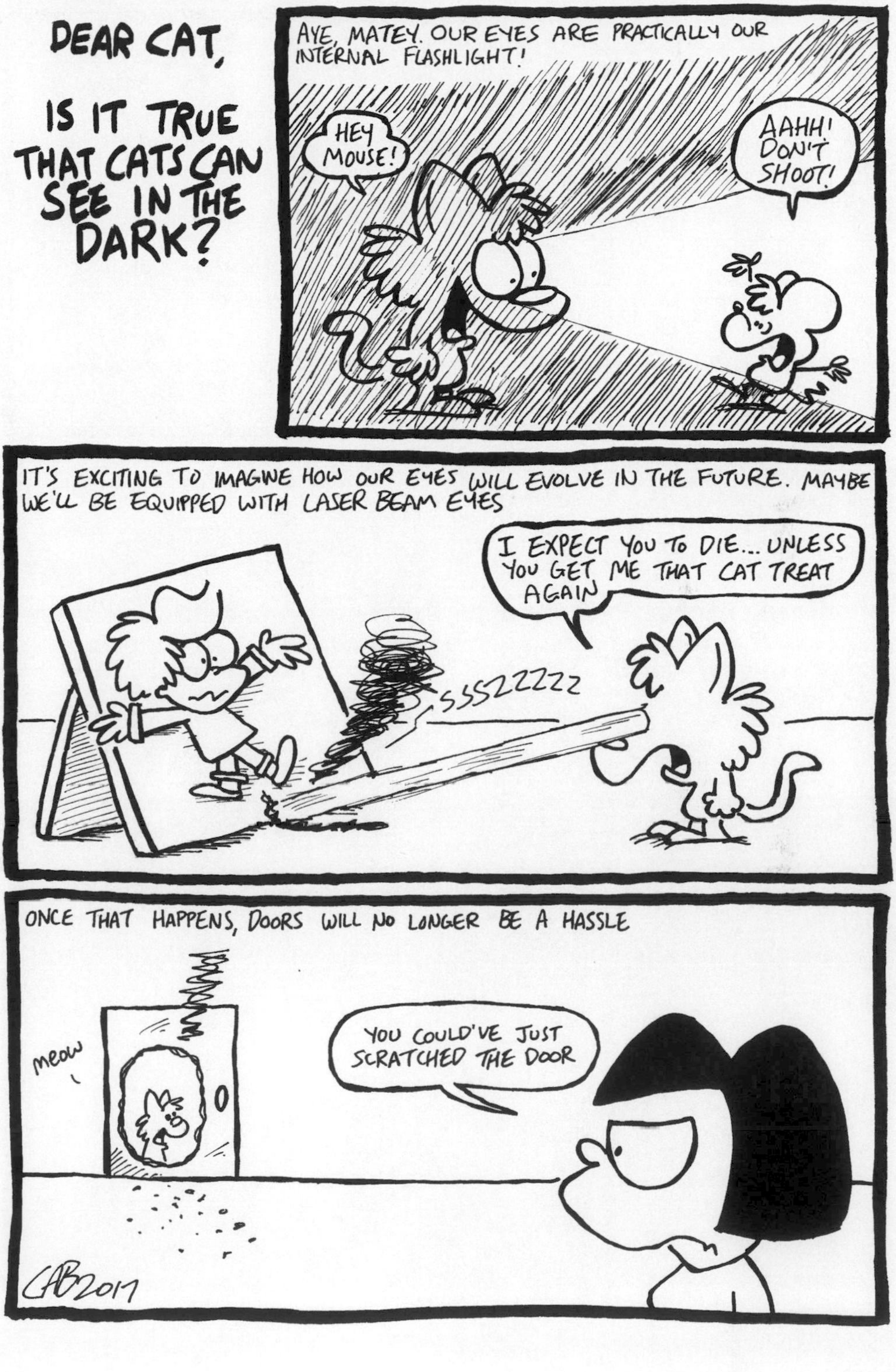
DEAR CAT,
IS IT TRUE THAT CATS CAN SEE IN THE DARK?
AYE, MATEY. OUR EYES ARE PRACTICALLY OUR INTERNAL FLASHLIGHT!
HEY MOUSE!
AAHH! DON'T SHOOT!
IT'S EXCITING TO IMAGINE HOW OUR EYES WILL EVOLVE IN THE FUTURE. MAYBE WE'LL BE EQUIPPED WITH LASER BEAM EYES
I EXPECT YOU TO DIE... UNLESS YOU GET ME THAT CAT TREAT AGAIN
SSSZZZZZ
ONCE THAT HAPPENS, DOORS WILL NO LONGER BE A HASSLE
meow
YOU COULD'VE JUST SCRATCHED THE DOOR
CAB2017

DEAR CAT

HAS A CAT EVER CAUSED A WORLD CRISIS?

OH LORDY, A FEW YEARS BACK A CAT NAMED HAROLD CAUSED A MASSIVE PANIC WHEN HE ACCIDENTLY HACKED INTO THE GOVERNMENT SERVERS AND DELETED EVERYTHING BY SITTING ON A KEYBOARD

HAROLD, YOU COLLAPSED ALL THE WORLD'S GOVERNMENTS!!!

OOPS

THINGS GOT ROUGH AFTER THE PROBLEM SPREAD. BANKS WERE WIPED OUT, THE ECONOMY WENT CAPUT, IMPORTANT DATA DESTROYED... IT WAS CHAOS

AAHHH

AAIEEE!

BOOM

WOW, THOSE WHO SAID CATS WOULD RUIN EVERYTHING WERN'T KIDDING

AS YOU CAN IMAGINE, ALL THE COMMENTATORS WANTED HIS HEAD

WE MUST STOP THESE FUZZY TERRORISTS!

CAB2017

ON THE OTHER HAND, THOUGH, HE DID GET SOME OPPORTUNITIES

"ANONYMOUS" IS OFFERING YOU A JOB

PHHT, HOW CAN I FOLLOW UP IF THEY WON'T TELL ME THE NAME?

DEAR CAT,

MY CAT KEEPS COLLECTING PLASTIC BOTTLE CAPS. WHAT'S UP WITH THAT?

MY FRIEND, PLASTIC CAPS ARE A VALUABLE RESOURCE FOR US CATS! WE USE IT AS A CURRENCY
I'LL GIVE YOU TWO CAPS FOR THAT DEAD HAMSTER
SOLD!
CAT THINGS
WE ALSO USE THEM AS PUCKS WHEN PLAYING CAT HOCKEY
WACK
AND OL' BECK HITS IT! CAN IT GET PAST THE GOALIE?
CAB 2017
WE ALSO GIVE IT OUT TO KITTENS DURING HALLOWEEN
HERE YOU GO, KIDDIES!
WHOA. TWO CAPS AND A DEAD BIRD!
BETTER THAN THE HOUSES THAT GIVE OUT CANDIES. ICK!

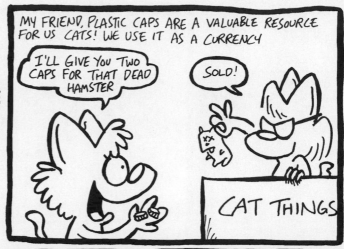

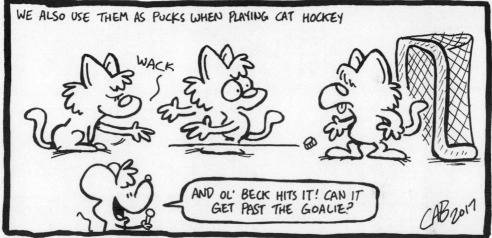

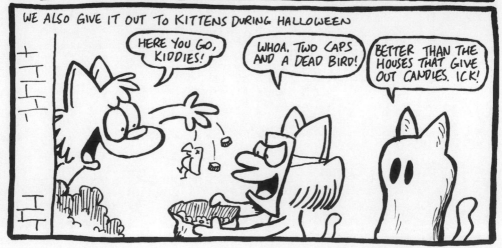

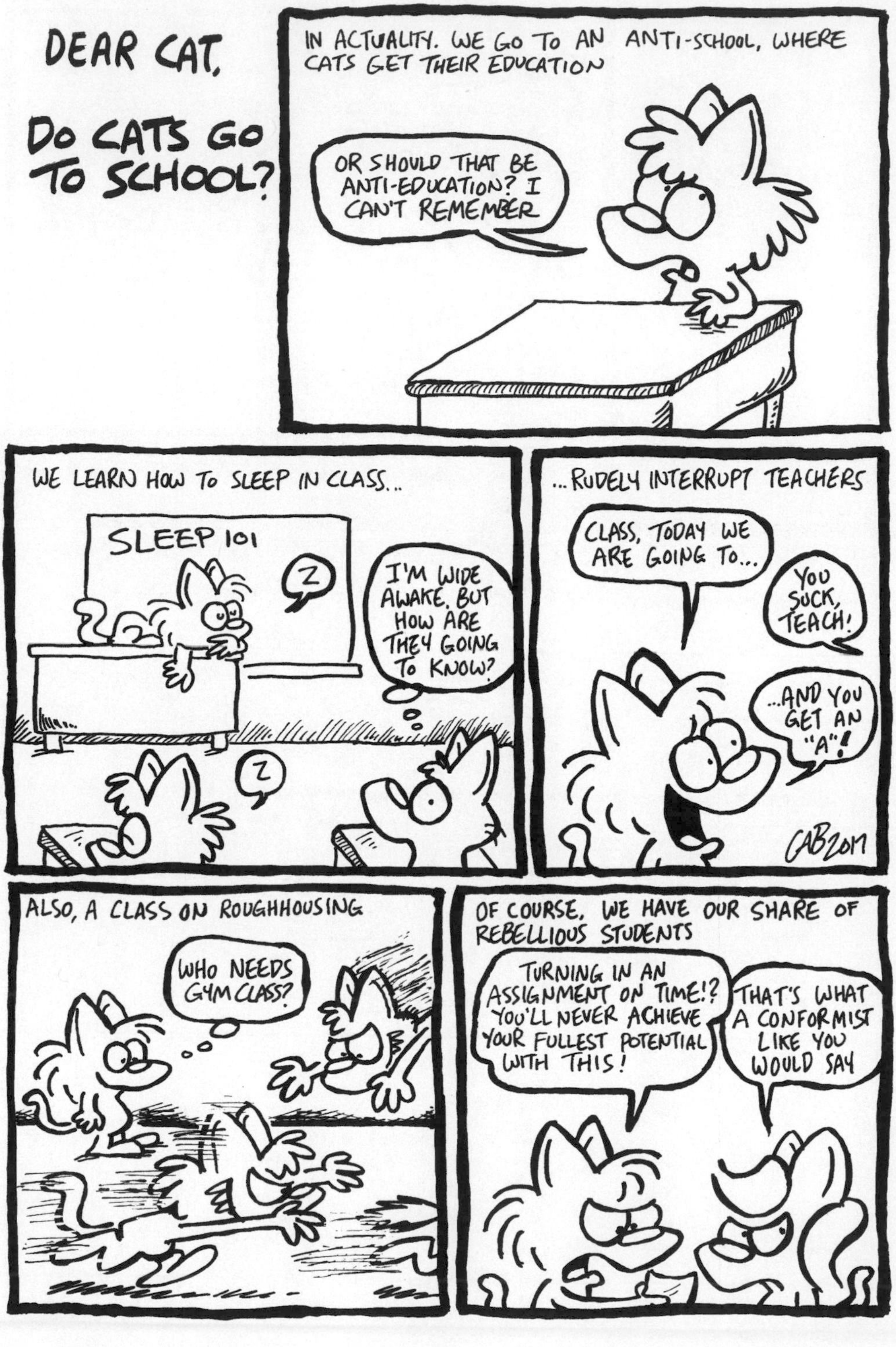
DEAR CAT,
DO CATS GO TO SCHOOL?
IN ACTUALITY, WE GO TO AN ANTI-SCHOOL, WHERE CATS GET THEIR EDUCATION
OR SHOULD THAT BE ANTI-EDUCATION? I CAN'T REMEMBER
WE LEARN HOW TO SLEEP IN CLASS...
SLEEP 101
Z
I'M WIDE AWAKE, BUT HOW ARE THEY GOING TO KNOW?
Z
...RUDELY INTERRUPT TEACHERS
CLASS, TODAY WE ARE GOING TO...
YOU SUCK, TEACH!
...AND YOU GET AN "A"!
CAB 2017
ALSO, A CLASS ON ROUGHHOUSING
WHO NEEDS GYM CLASS?
OF COURSE, WE HAVE OUR SHARE OF REBELLIOUS STUDENTS
TURNING IN AN ASSIGNMENT ON TIME!? YOU'LL NEVER ACHIEVE YOUR FULLEST POTENTIAL WITH THIS!
THAT'S WHAT A CONFORMIST LIKE YOU WOULD SAY

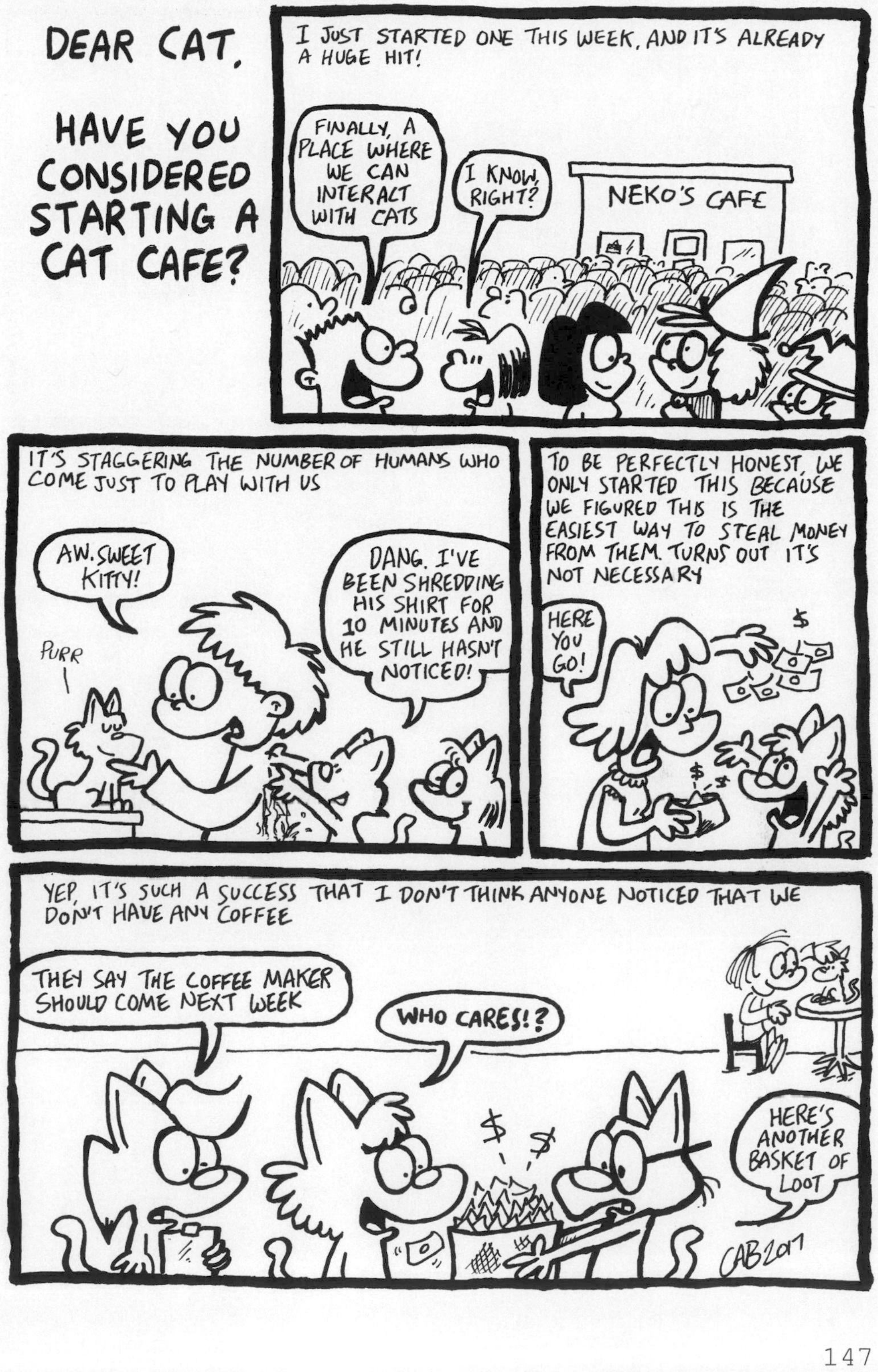
DEAR CAT,
HAVE YOU CONSIDERED STARTING A CAT CAFE?
I JUST STARTED ONE THIS WEEK, AND IT'S ALREADY A HUGE HIT!
FINALLY, A PLACE WHERE WE CAN INTERACT WITH CATS
I KNOW, RIGHT?
NEKO'S CAFE
IT'S STAGGERING THE NUMBER OF HUMANS WHO COME JUST TO PLAY WITH US
AW. SWEET KITTY!
PURR
DANG. I'VE BEEN SHREDDING HIS SHIRT FOR 10 MINUTES AND HE STILL HASN'T NOTICED!
TO BE PERFECTLY HONEST, WE ONLY STARTED THIS BECAUSE WE FIGURED THIS IS THE EASIEST WAY TO STEAL MONEY FROM THEM. TURNS OUT IT'S NOT NECESSARY
HERE YOU GO!
YEP, IT'S SUCH A SUCCESS THAT I DON'T THINK ANYONE NOTICED THAT WE DON'T HAVE ANY COFFEE
THEY SAY THE COFFEE MAKER SHOULD COME NEXT WEEK
WHO CARES!?
HERE'S ANOTHER BASKET OF LOOT
CAB 2017

DEAR CAT,

WHAT DO YOU DO WHEN THERE'S A BLACKOUT?

OH, BLACKOUTS ARE THE BEST! THAT'S WHEN WE GET TO RULE THE HOUSE!

FELLOW FELINES, TONIGHT IS OUR NIGHT!

WE CAN DO ALL SORTS OF STUFF, SUCH AS TRIPPING PEOPLE BLINDLY SEARCHING FOR A FLASHLIGHT

I KNOW I LEFT IT HERE... OOPS!

TRIP!

Hee Hee Hee

ALSO, IT ALLOWS US TO DO THINGS WITHOUT HUMANS SEEING US

NOT OFTEN DO WE GET TO PLAY POKER WHEN PEOPLE ARE AROUND

WISH I COULD SEE THE CARDS BETTER

BLACK CATS IN PARTICULAR TAKE ADVANTAGE OF THE DARKNESS TO BE ALL NINJA, ALTHOUGH SOME MAY GO TOO FAR WITH THIS

WHERE DO YOU EVEN FIND SHURIKENS?!

YOU CAN FIND ANYTHING ON eBAY!

GAB2017

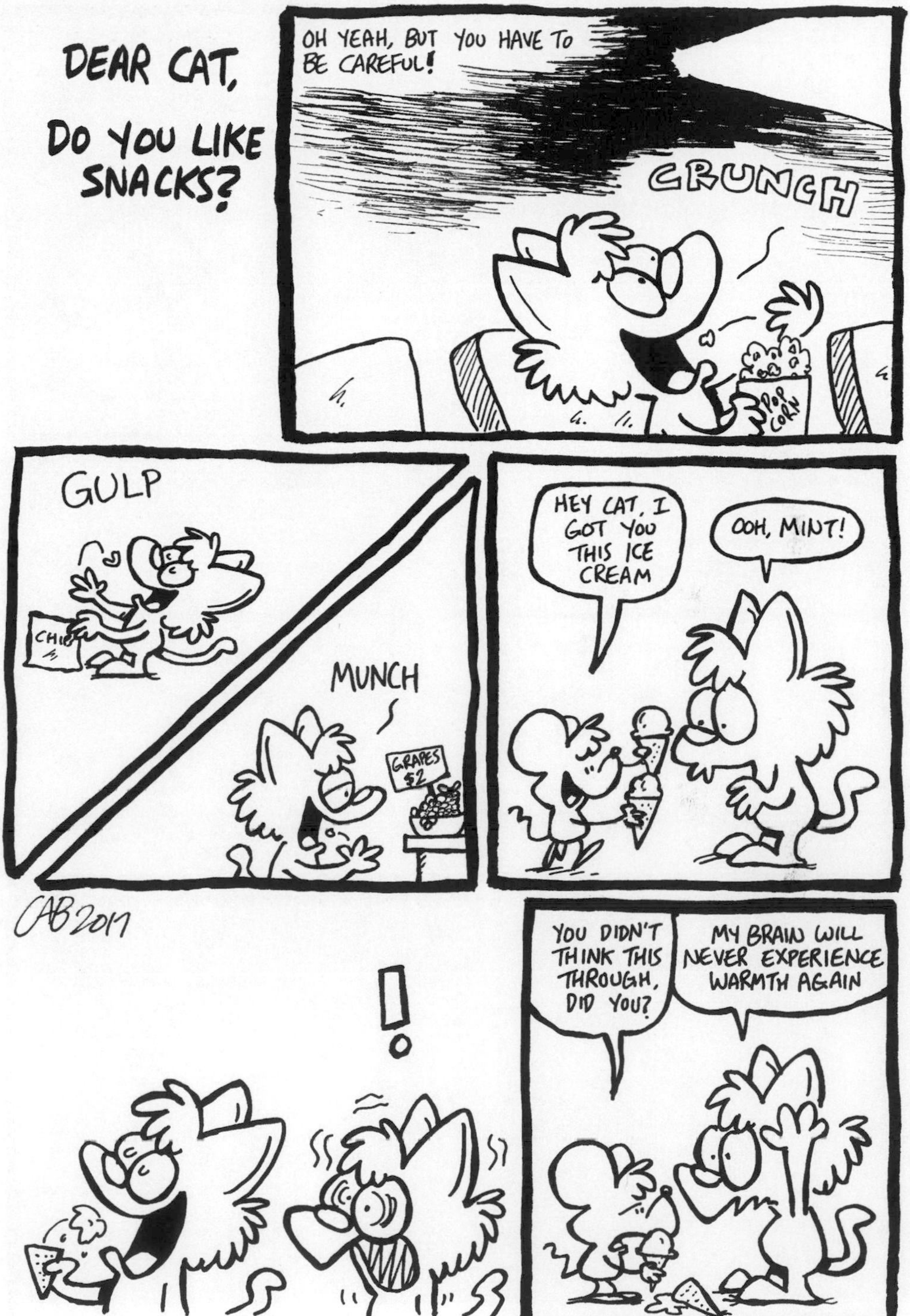
DEAR CAT,
DO YOU LIKE SNACKS?
OH YEAH, BUT YOU HAVE TO BE CAREFUL!
CRUNCH
POP CORN
GULP
MUNCH
GRAPES $2
HEY CAT, I GOT YOU THIS ICE CREAM
OOH, MINT!
CAB 2017
!
YOU DIDN'T THINK THIS THROUGH, DID YOU?
MY BRAIN WILL NEVER EXPERIENCE WARMTH AGAIN

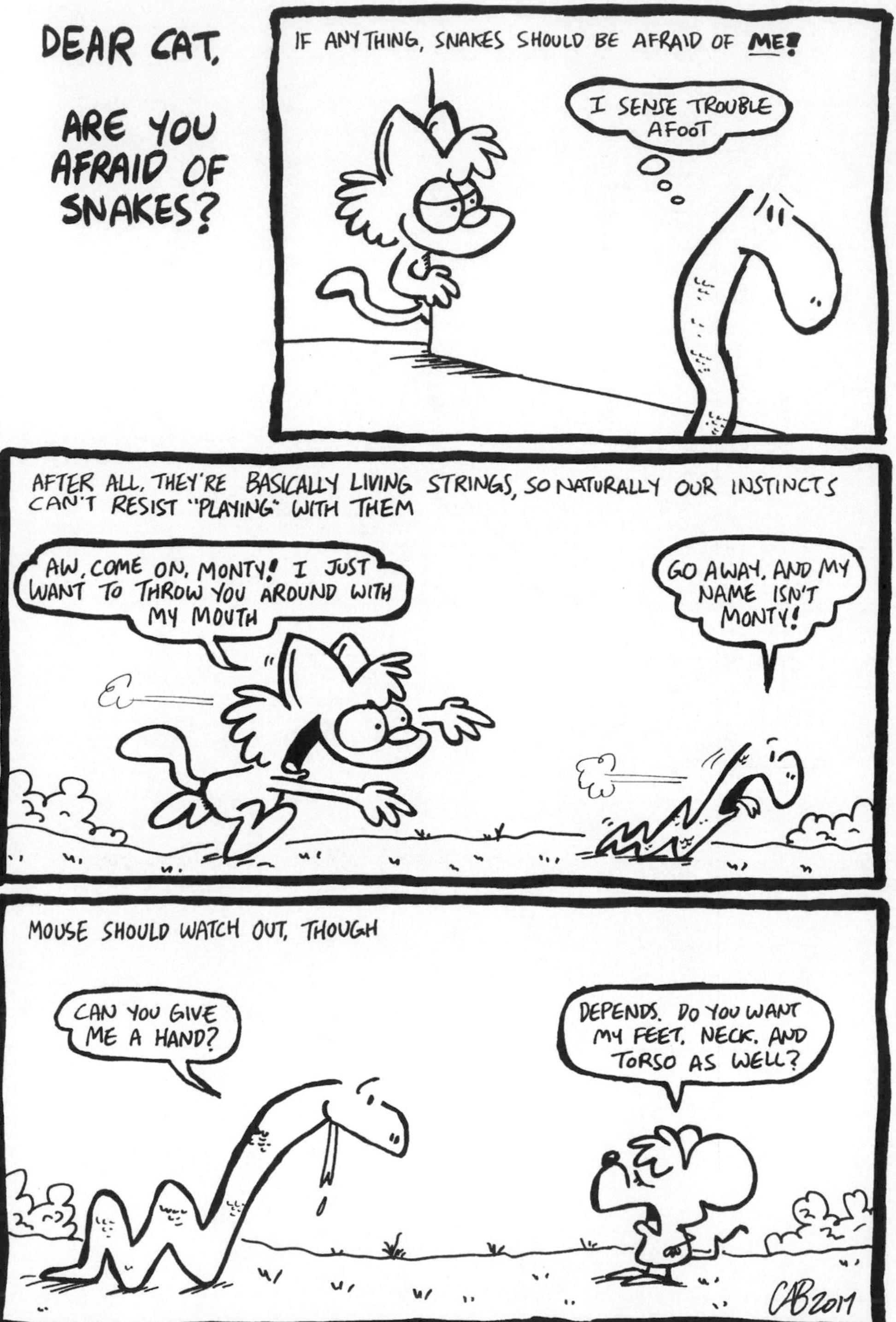
DEAR CAT,
ARE YOU AFRAID OF SNAKES?
IF ANYTHING, SNAKES SHOULD BE AFRAID OF ME!
I SENSE TROUBLE AFOOT
AFTER ALL, THEY'RE BASICALLY LIVING STRINGS, SO NATURALLY OUR INSTINCTS CAN'T RESIST "PLAYING" WITH THEM
AW, COME ON, MONTY! I JUST WANT TO THROW YOU AROUND WITH MY MOUTH
GO AWAY. AND MY NAME ISN'T MONTY!
MOUSE SHOULD WATCH OUT, THOUGH
CAN YOU GIVE ME A HAND?
DEPENDS. DO YOU WANT MY FEET, NECK, AND TORSO AS WELL?
CAB 2011

DEAR CAT,

WHAT DO YOU DO WHEN YOUR OWNER GETS A COLD?

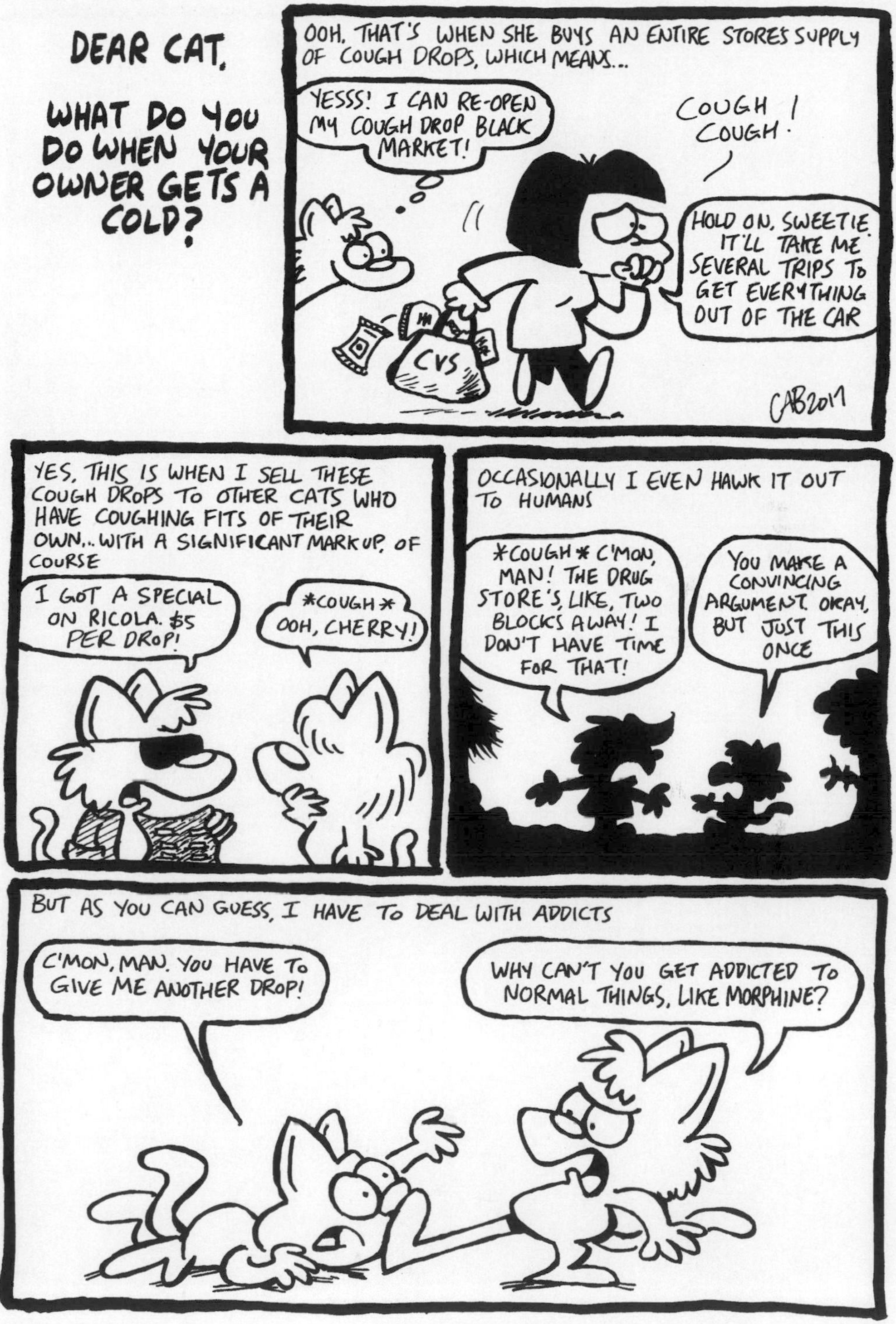
OOH, THAT'S WHEN SHE BUYS AN ENTIRE STORE'S SUPPLY OF COUGH DROPS, WHICH MEANS...
YESSS! I CAN RE-OPEN MY COUGH DROP BLACK MARKET!
COUGH! COUGH!
HOLD ON, SWEETIE. IT'LL TAKE ME SEVERAL TRIPS TO GET EVERYTHING OUT OF THE CAR
CVS
CAB2017
YES, THIS IS WHEN I SELL THESE COUGH DROPS TO OTHER CATS WHO HAVE COUGHING FITS OF THEIR OWN... WITH A SIGNIFICANT MARKUP, OF COURSE
I GOT A SPECIAL ON RICOLA. $5 PER DROP!
COUGH OOH, CHERRY!
OCCASIONALLY I EVEN HAWK IT OUT TO HUMANS
COUGH C'MON, MAN! THE DRUG STORE'S, LIKE, TWO BLOCKS AWAY! I DON'T HAVE TIME FOR THAT!
YOU MAKE A CONVINCING ARGUMENT. OKAY, BUT JUST THIS ONCE
BUT AS YOU CAN GUESS, I HAVE TO DEAL WITH ADDICTS
C'MON, MAN. YOU HAVE TO GIVE ME ANOTHER DROP!
WHY CAN'T YOU GET ADDICTED TO NORMAL THINGS, LIKE MORPHINE?

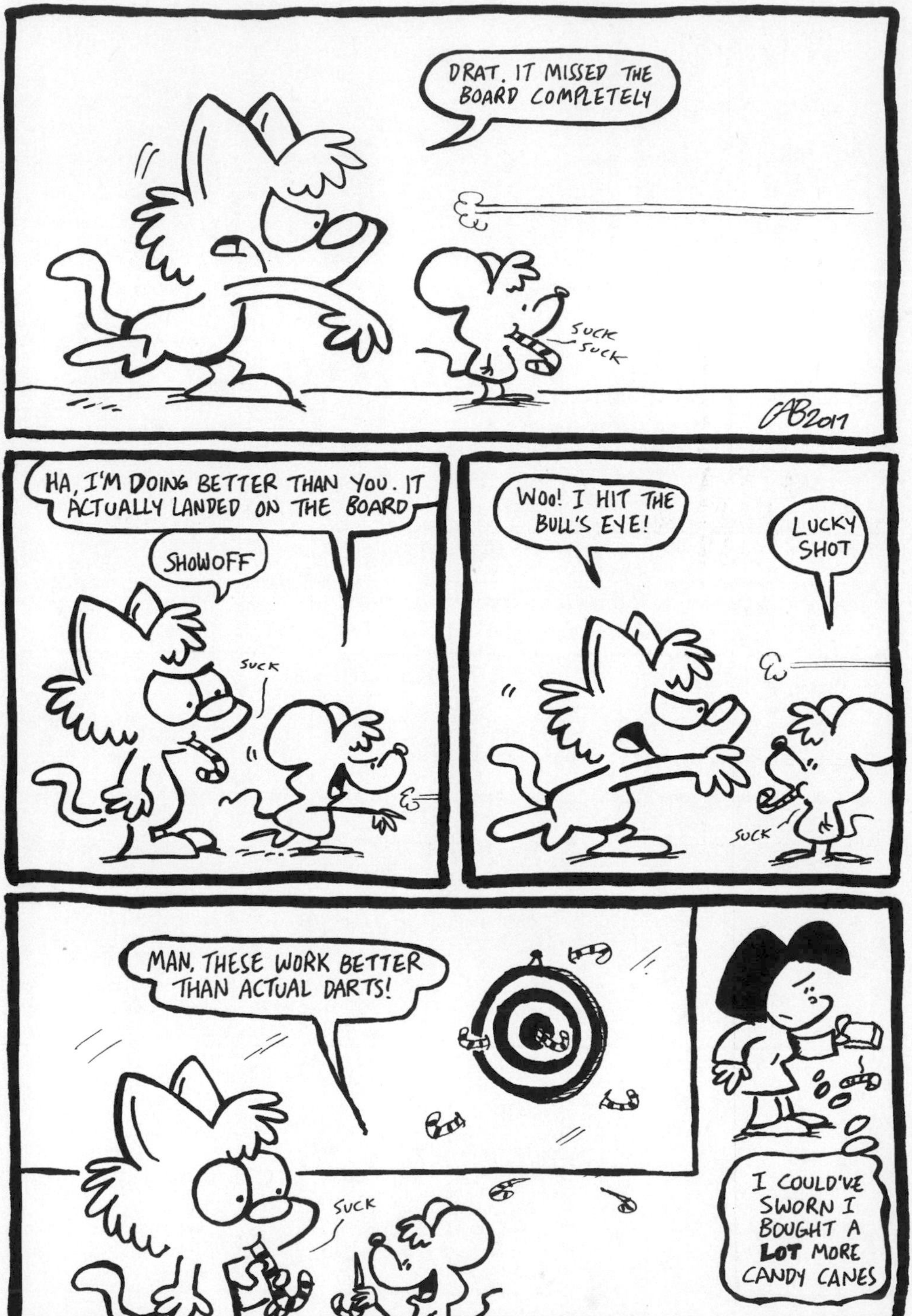
DRAT. IT MISSED THE BOARD COMPLETELY
SUCK SUCK
AB2017
HA, I'M DOING BETTER THAN YOU. IT ACTUALLY LANDED ON THE BOARD
SHOWOFF
SUCK
WOO! I HIT THE BULL'S EYE!
LUCKY SHOT
SUCK
MAN, THESE WORK BETTER THAN ACTUAL DARTS!
SUCK
I COULD'VE SWORN I BOUGHT A **LOT** MORE CANDY CANES

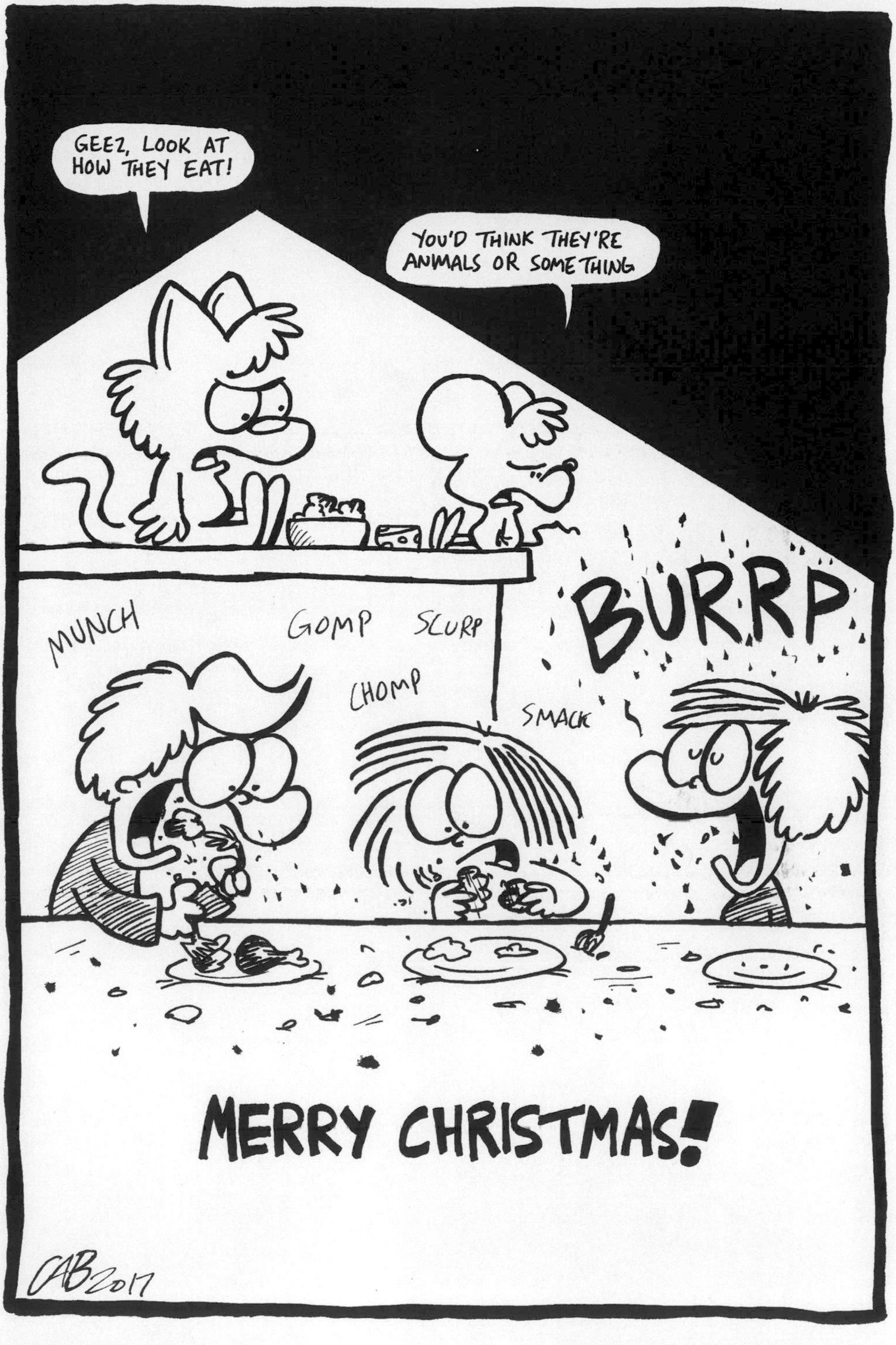
GEEZ, LOOK AT HOW THEY EAT!
YOU'D THINK THEY'RE ANIMALS OR SOMETHING
MUNCH
GOMP
SLURP
CHOMP
SMACK
BURRP
MERRY CHRISTMAS!
CAB 2017

DEAR CAT,

FINAL THOUGHTS FOR 2017?

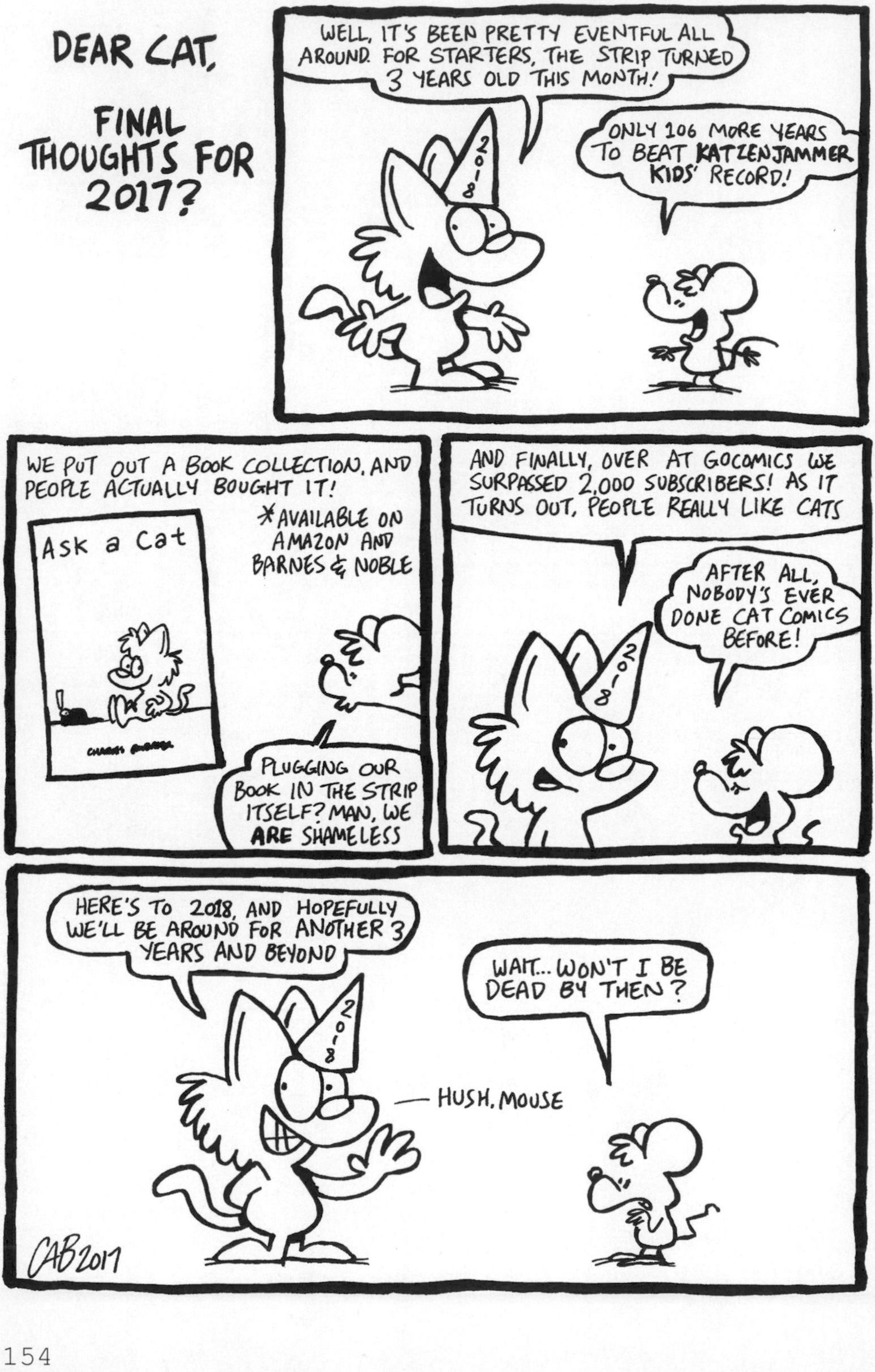

WELL, IT'S BEEN PRETTY EVENTFUL ALL AROUND. FOR STARTERS, THE STRIP TURNED 3 YEARS OLD THIS MONTH!
2018
ONLY 106 MORE YEARS TO BEAT KATZENJAMMER KIDS' RECORD!
WE PUT OUT A BOOK COLLECTION, AND PEOPLE ACTUALLY BOUGHT IT!
Ask a Cat
*AVAILABLE ON AMAZON AND BARNES & NOBLE
PLUGGING OUR BOOK IN THE STRIP ITSELF? MAN, WE **ARE** SHAMELESS
AND FINALLY, OVER AT GOCOMICS WE SURPASSED 2,000 SUBSCRIBERS! AS IT TURNS OUT, PEOPLE REALLY LIKE CATS
AFTER ALL, NOBODY'S EVER DONE CAT COMICS BEFORE!
2018
HERE'S TO 2018, AND HOPEFULLY WE'LL BE AROUND FOR ANOTHER 3 YEARS AND BEYOND
WAIT... WON'T I BE DEAD BY THEN?
2018
— HUSH, MOUSE
CAB 2017

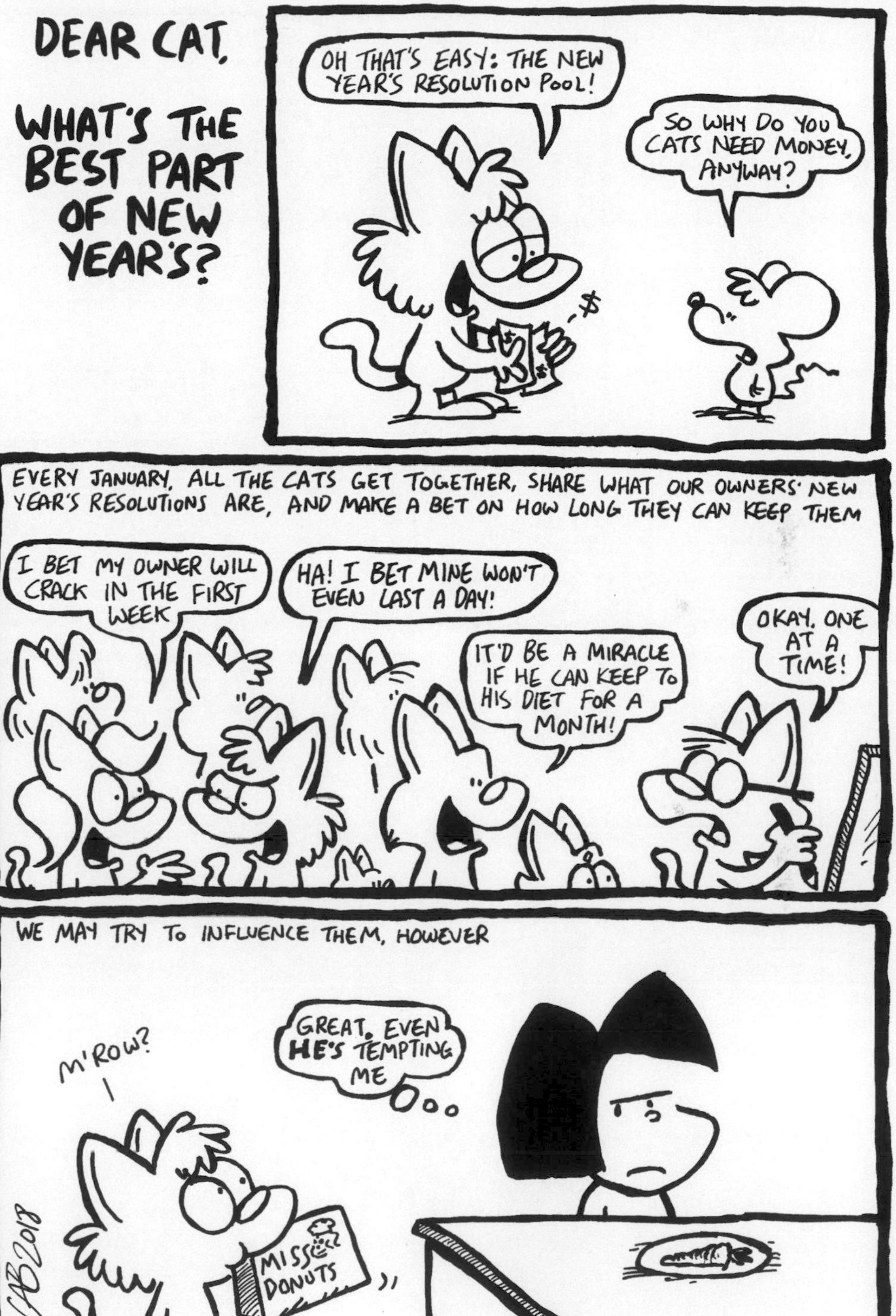
DEAR CAT,
WHAT'S THE BEST PART OF NEW YEAR'S?
OH THAT'S EASY: THE NEW YEAR'S RESOLUTION POOL!
SO WHY DO YOU CATS NEED MONEY, ANYWAY?
EVERY JANUARY, ALL THE CATS GET TOGETHER, SHARE WHAT OUR OWNERS' NEW YEAR'S RESOLUTIONS ARE, AND MAKE A BET ON HOW LONG THEY CAN KEEP THEM
I BET MY OWNER WILL CRACK IN THE FIRST WEEK
HA! I BET MINE WON'T EVEN LAST A DAY!
IT'D BE A MIRACLE IF HE CAN KEEP TO HIS DIET FOR A MONTH!
OKAY, ONE AT A TIME!
WE MAY TRY TO INFLUENCE THEM, HOWEVER
M'ROW?
GREAT, EVEN **HE'S** TEMPTING ME
MISS DONUTS
CAB 2018

DEAR CAT,

WHY DOES MY CAT RUB UP ON ME WHENEVER I'M ON THE PHONE?

OH, THAT'S NOTHING. MORE THAN A REALLY ELABORATE FORM OF SNOOPING, MY FRIEND!

YOU ARE NOT GOING TO BELIEVE WHAT MR. GLYNN WAS WEARING AT WORK TODAY, MARL!

OH, THIS IS GOSSIP GOLD

PURRR

OH SURE, PEOPLE ALWAYS SNOOP ON ONE ANOTHER WHENEVER THEY TALK TO SOMEONE ON THE PHONE, BUT WHAT THEY FAIL TO REALIZE IS THAT THE MOST INCONSPICUOUS WAY OF DOING THIS IS TO GET REALLY ANNOYINGLY CLOSE!

SO ANYWAY, THINGS ARE ~ WOOPS! SORRY, MY CAT'S BEING WEIRDLY LOVEY-DOVEY AGAIN

I COULD BLACKMAIL YOU RIGHT NOW, YA' KNOW

PURRRR

SO, HAS THE N.S.A. OFFERED YOU A JOB YET?

MULTIPLE TIMES, BUT I'M NOT BIG ON THIS WHOLE "JOB" THING

CAB 2018

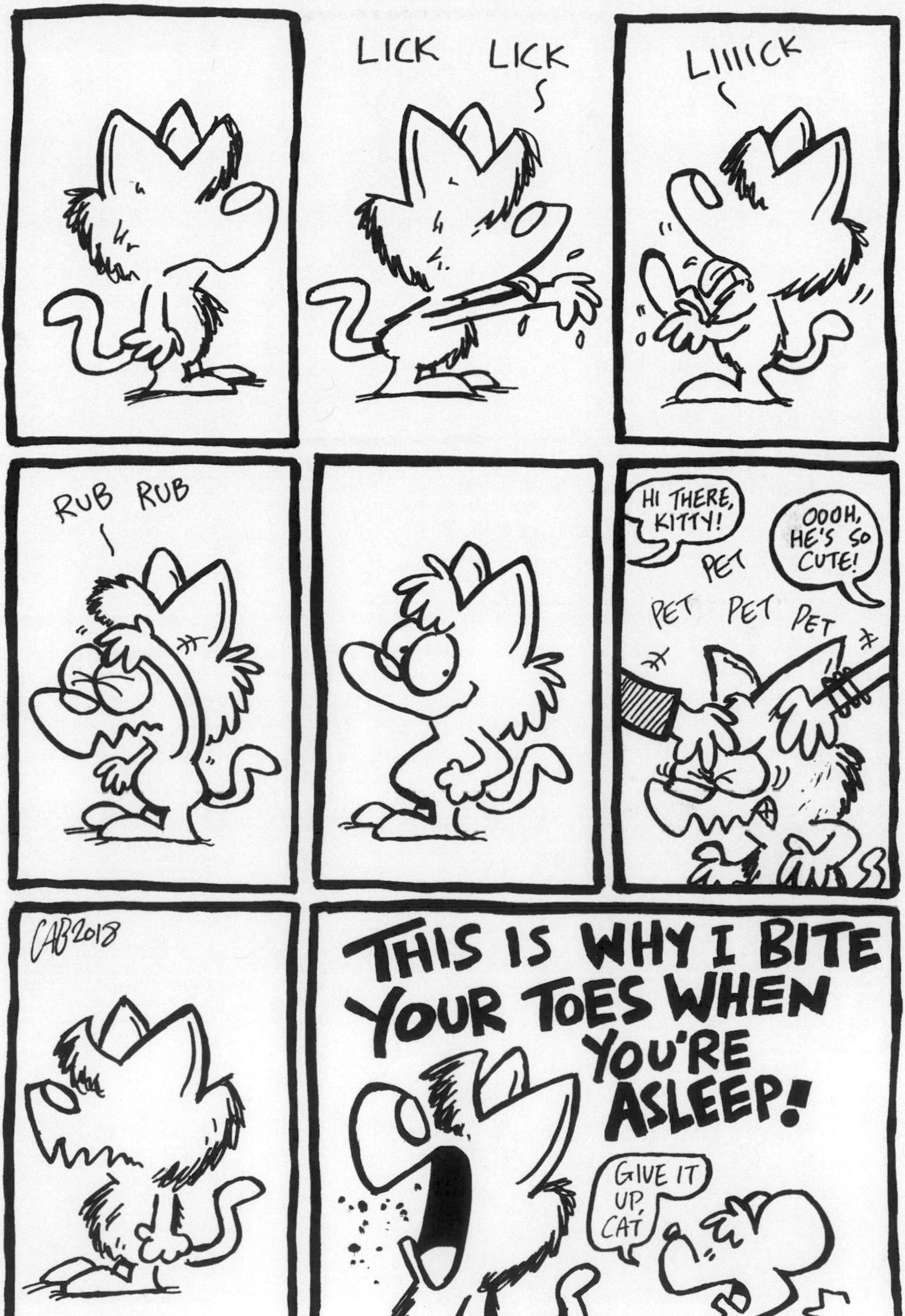
LICK LICK
LIIIICK
RUB RUB
HI THERE, KITTY!
OOOH, HE'S SO CUTE!
PET PET PET PET
CAB 2018
THIS IS WHY I BITE YOUR TOES WHEN YOU'RE ASLEEP!
GIVE IT UP, CAT

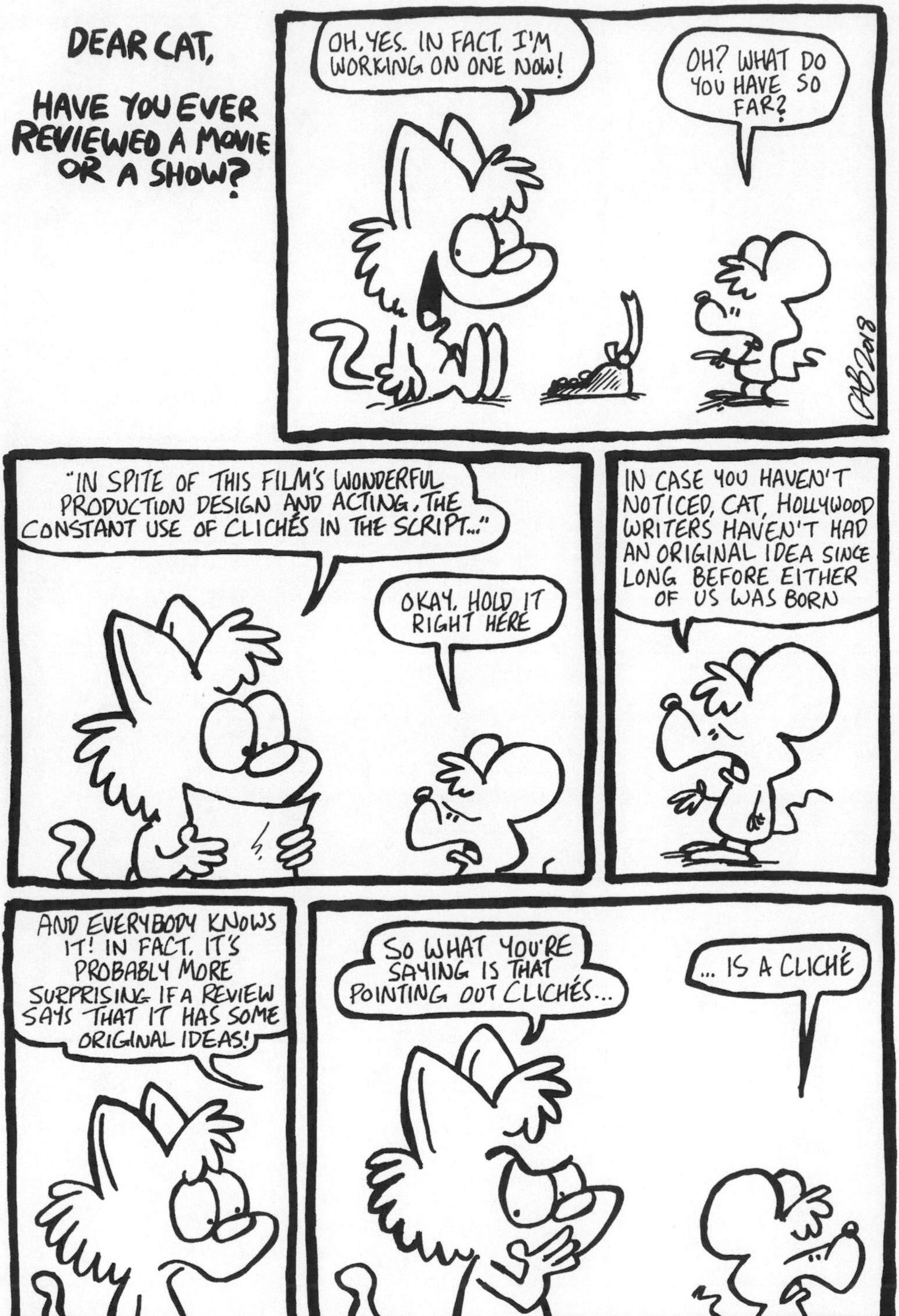
DEAR CAT,
HAVE YOU EVER REVIEWED A MOVIE OR A SHOW?
OH, YES. IN FACT, I'M WORKING ON ONE NOW!
OH? WHAT DO YOU HAVE SO FAR?
CAB 2018
"IN SPITE OF THIS FILM'S WONDERFUL PRODUCTION DESIGN AND ACTING, THE CONSTANT USE OF CLICHÉS IN THE SCRIPT..."
OKAY. HOLD IT RIGHT HERE
IN CASE YOU HAVEN'T NOTICED, CAT, HOLLYWOOD WRITERS HAVEN'T HAD AN ORIGINAL IDEA SINCE LONG BEFORE EITHER OF US WAS BORN
AND EVERYBODY KNOWS IT! IN FACT, IT'S PROBABLY MORE SURPRISING IF A REVIEW SAYS THAT IT HAS SOME ORIGINAL IDEAS!
SO WHAT YOU'RE SAYING IS THAT POINTING OUT CLICHÉS...
... IS A CLICHÉ

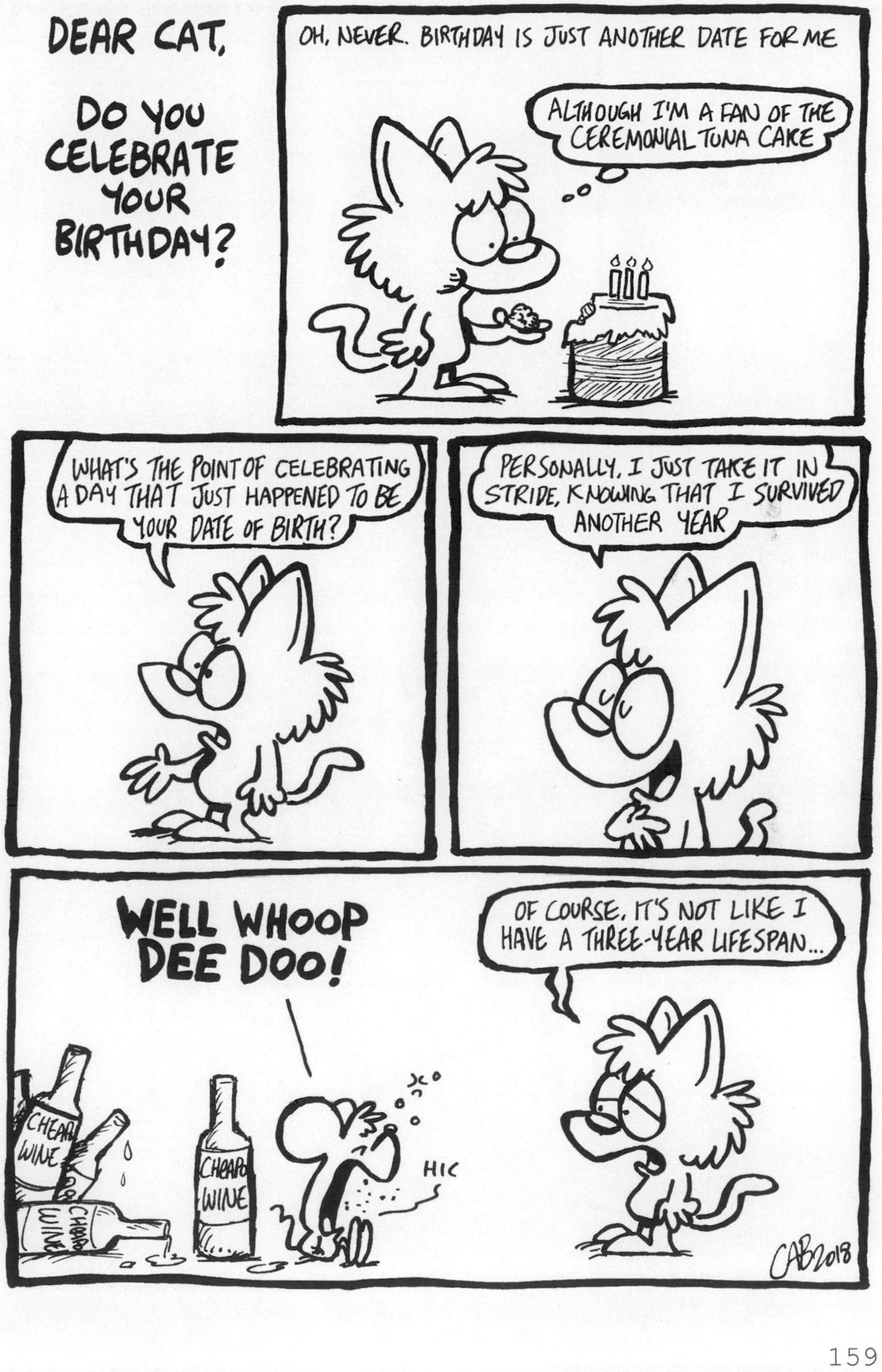
DEAR CAT,
DO YOU CELEBRATE YOUR BIRTHDAY?
OH, NEVER. BIRTHDAY IS JUST ANOTHER DATE FOR ME
ALTHOUGH I'M A FAN OF THE CEREMONIAL TUNA CAKE
WHAT'S THE POINT OF CELEBRATING A DAY THAT JUST HAPPENED TO BE YOUR DATE OF BIRTH?
PERSONALLY, I JUST TAKE IT IN STRIDE, KNOWING THAT I SURVIVED ANOTHER YEAR
WELL WHOOP DEE DOO!
CHEAP WINE
CHEAP WINE
CHEAP WINE
HIC
OF COURSE, IT'S NOT LIKE I HAVE A THREE-YEAR LIFESPAN...
CAB 2018

DEAR CAT,

WHAT DO YOU THINK OF RACCOONS?

OODH, I CAN'T STAND RACCOONS!

YOU'RE JUST JEALOUS, CAT

RUBBISH

WHERE DO I START, THAT THEY STEAL FOOD THAT DOESN'T BELONG TO THEM?

MMM, CHEWY

WANT ME TO CLAW YOUR EYES OUT?

CAT

OR THAT THEY BITE YOU FOR THE HECK OF IT?

I'M IN SUCH EXCRUCIATING PAIN RIGHT NOW

SHALL I GO ON ABOUT HOW THEY KEEP KNOCKING THINGS OVER?

KICK!

BWA HA HA

BUT YOU DO ALL OF THAT YOURSELF, CAT!

EXACTLY! RACCOONS ARE NOTHING MORE THAN BOOTLEG CATS!

CAB 2018

160

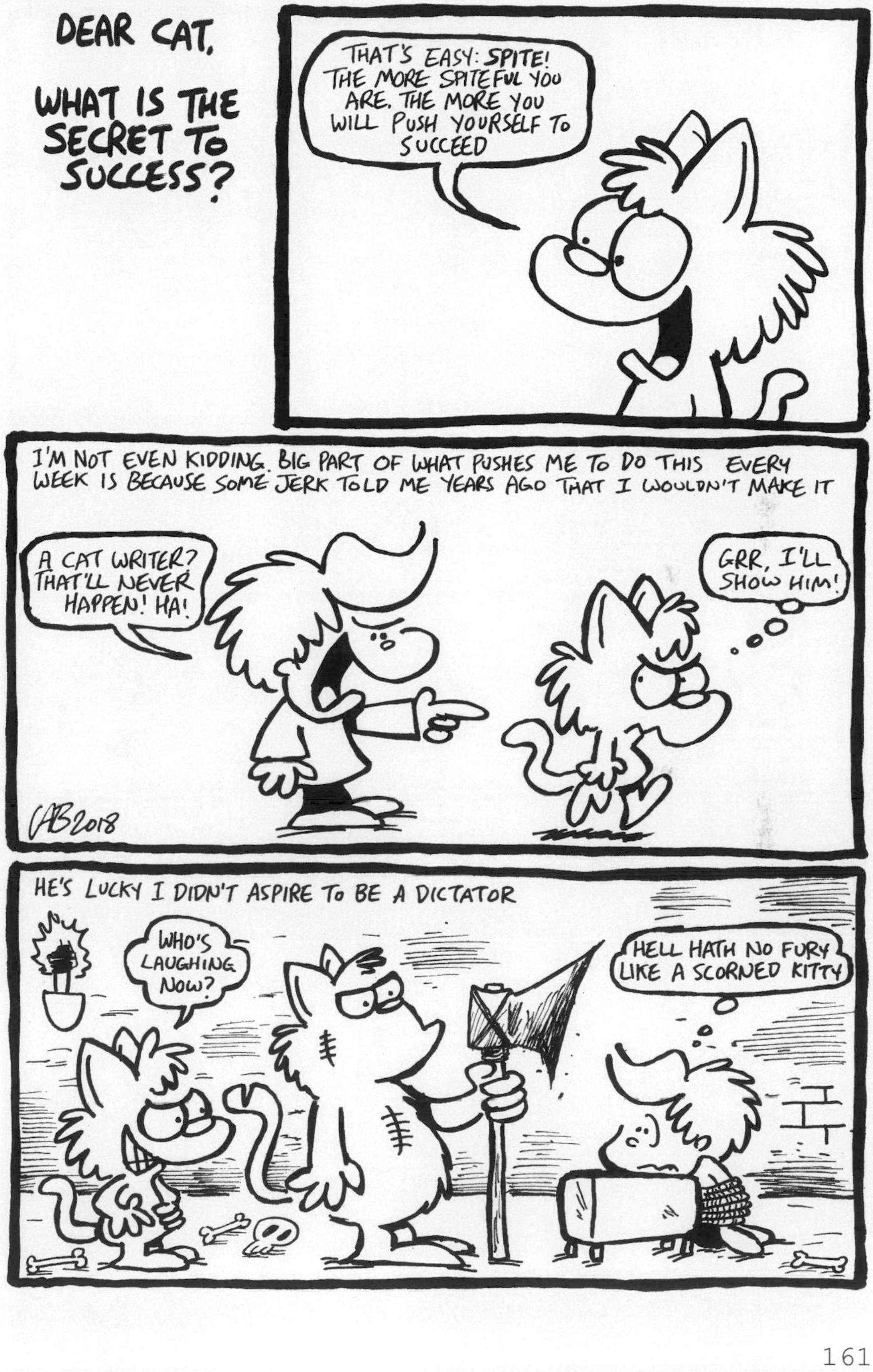
DEAR CAT,
WHAT IS THE SECRET TO SUCCESS?
THAT'S EASY: SPITE! THE MORE SPITEFUL YOU ARE, THE MORE YOU WILL PUSH YOURSELF TO SUCCEED
I'M NOT EVEN KIDDING. BIG PART OF WHAT PUSHES ME TO DO THIS EVERY WEEK IS BECAUSE SOME JERK TOLD ME YEARS AGO THAT I WOULDN'T MAKE IT
A CAT WRITER? THAT'LL NEVER HAPPEN! HA!
GRR, I'LL SHOW HIM!
CAB 2018
HE'S LUCKY I DIDN'T ASPIRE TO BE A DICTATOR
WHO'S LAUGHING NOW?
HELL HATH NO FURY LIKE A SCORNED KITTY

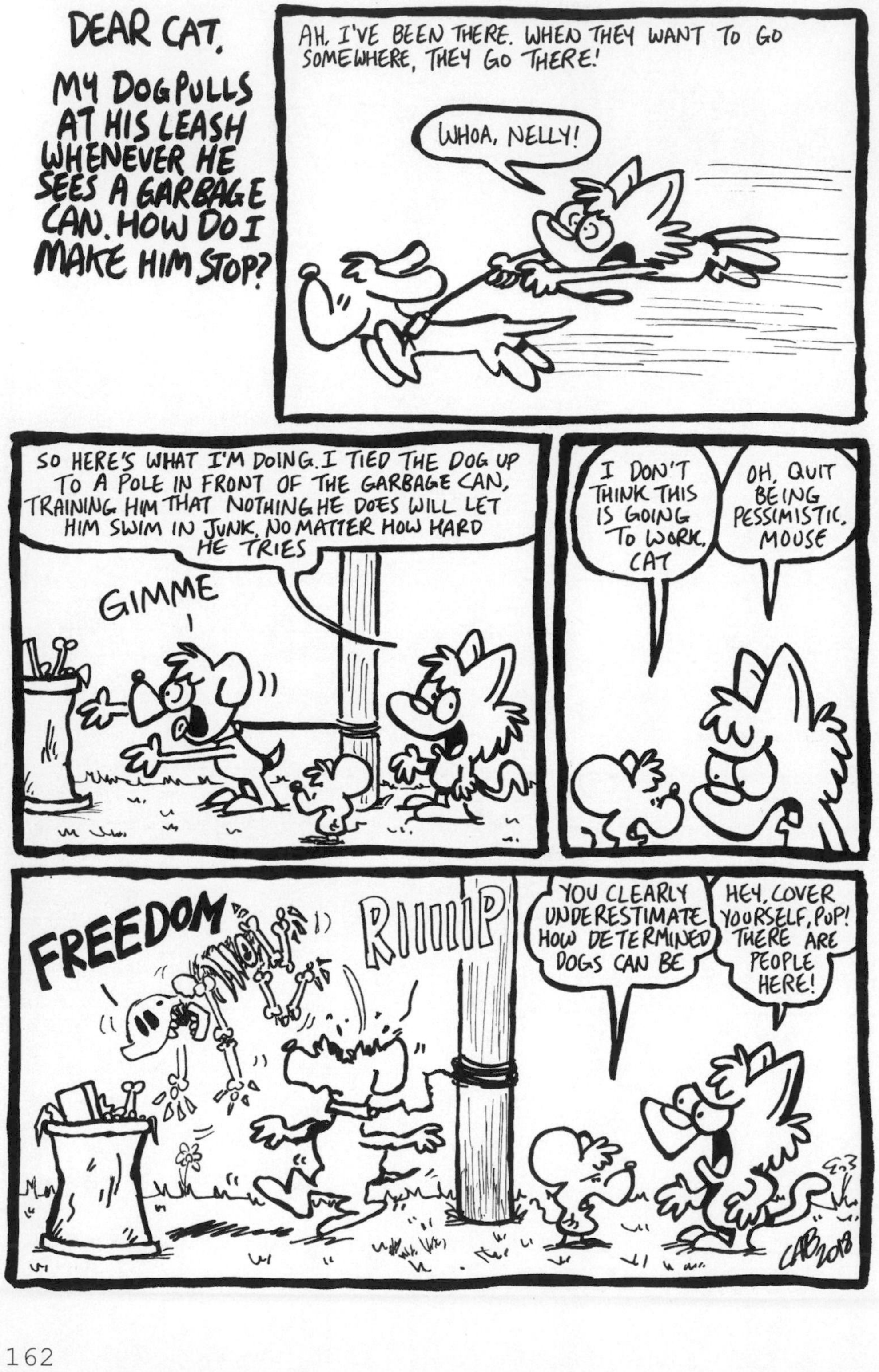
DEAR CAT,
MY DOG PULLS AT HIS LEASH WHENEVER HE SEES A GARBAGE CAN. HOW DO I MAKE HIM STOP?
AH, I'VE BEEN THERE. WHEN THEY WANT TO GO SOMEWHERE, THEY GO THERE!
WHOA, NELLY!
SO HERE'S WHAT I'M DOING. I TIED THE DOG UP TO A POLE IN FRONT OF THE GARBAGE CAN, TRAINING HIM THAT NOTHING HE DOES WILL LET HIM SWIM IN JUNK, NO MATTER HOW HARD HE TRIES
GIMME
I DON'T THINK THIS IS GOING TO WORK, CAT
OH, QUIT BEING PESSIMISTIC, MOUSE
FREEDOM
RIIIIIP
YOU CLEARLY UNDERESTIMATE HOW DETERMINED DOGS CAN BE
HEY, COVER YOURSELF, PUP! THERE ARE PEOPLE HERE!
CAB 2018

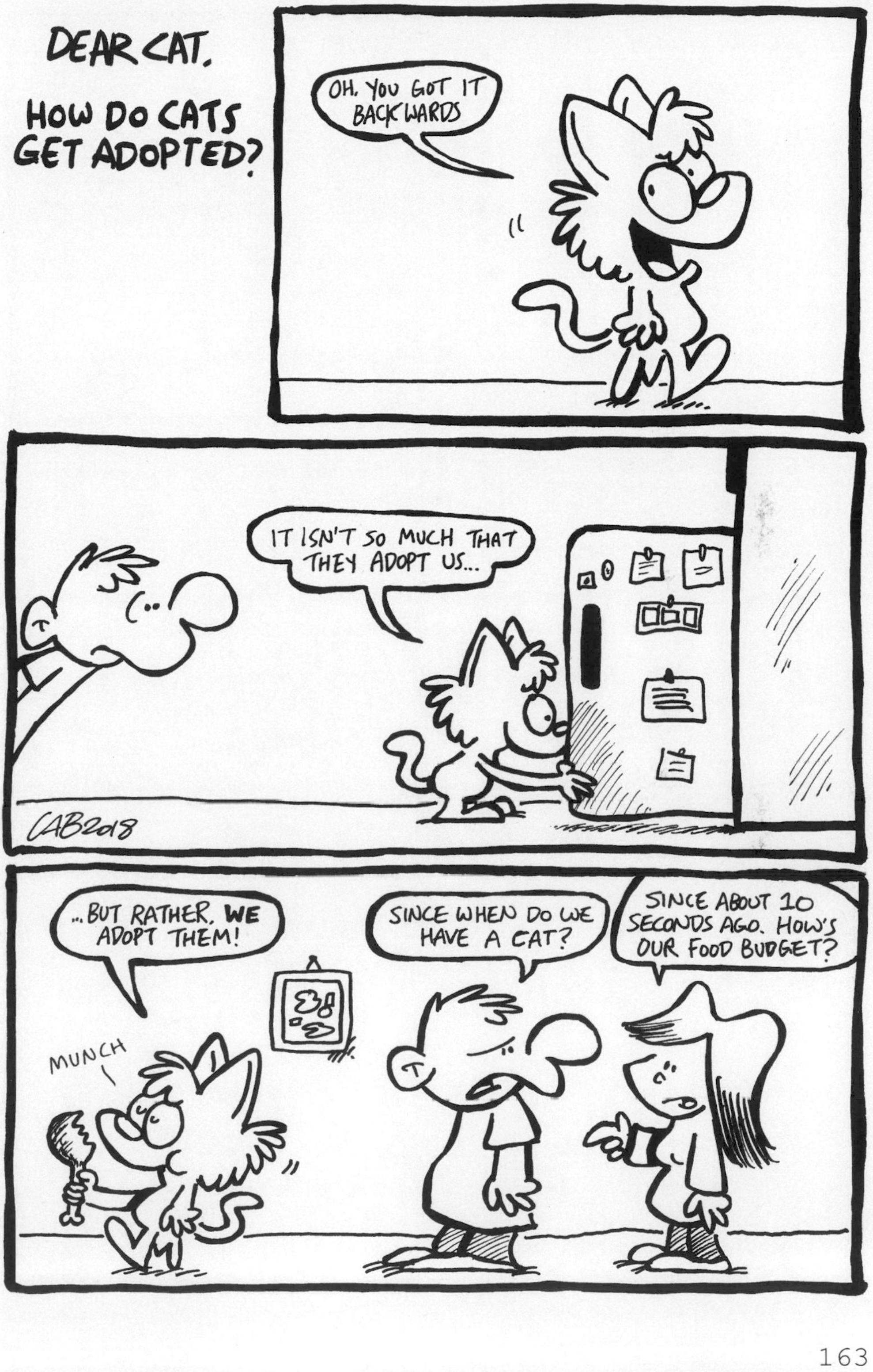
DEAR CAT,
HOW DO CATS GET ADOPTED?
OH, YOU GOT IT BACKWARDS
IT ISN'T SO MUCH THAT THEY ADOPT US...
CAB2018
...BUT RATHER, **WE** ADOPT THEM!
MUNCH
SINCE WHEN DO WE HAVE A CAT?
SINCE ABOUT 10 SECONDS AGO. HOW'S OUR FOOD BUDGET?

DEAR CAT,

WHERE HAVE YOU BEEN?!

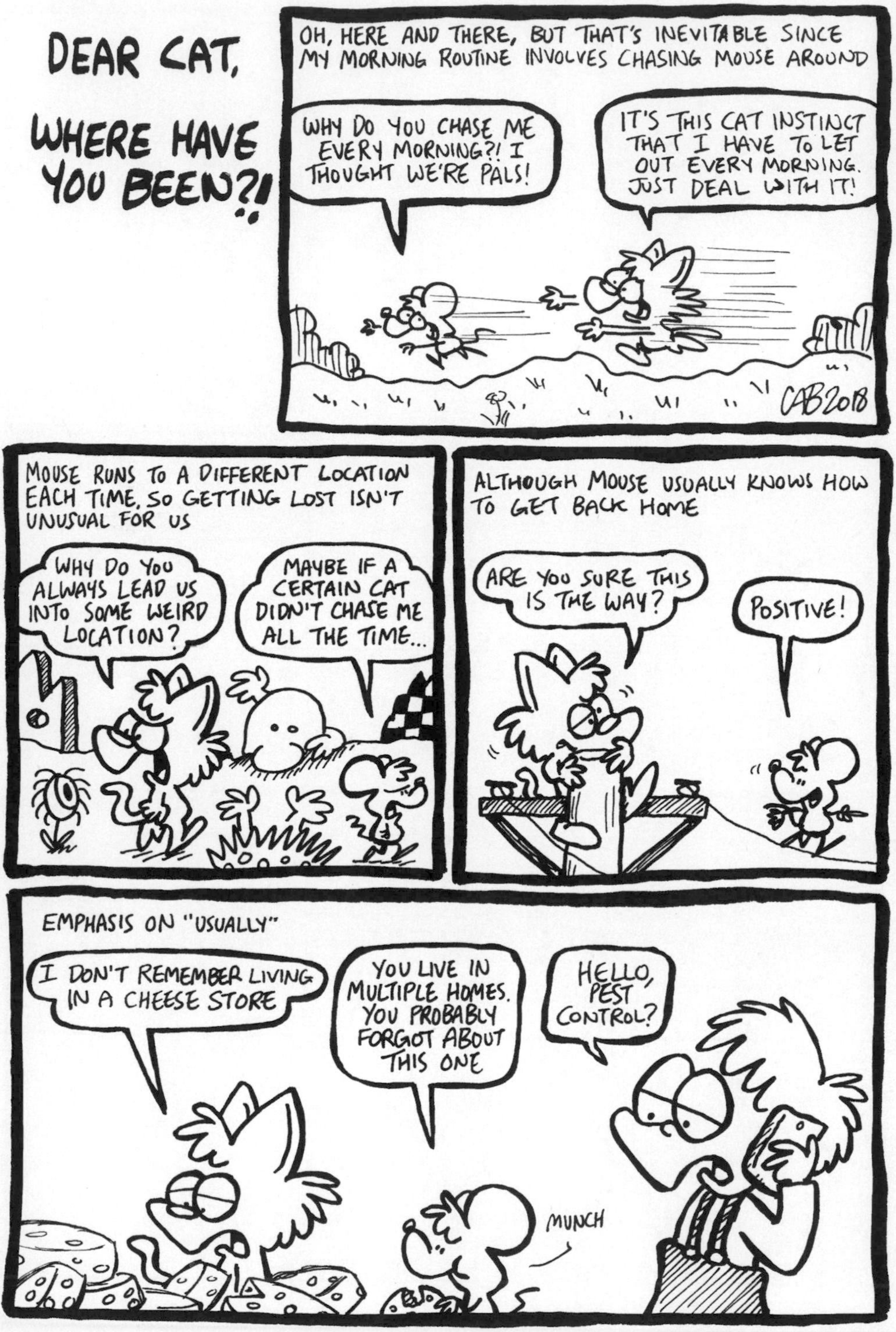
OH, HERE AND THERE, BUT THAT'S INEVITABLE SINCE MY MORNING ROUTINE INVOLVES CHASING MOUSE AROUND
WHY DO YOU CHASE ME EVERY MORNING?! I THOUGHT WE'RE PALS!
IT'S THIS CAT INSTINCT THAT I HAVE TO LET OUT EVERY MORNING. JUST DEAL WITH IT!
CAB2018
MOUSE RUNS TO A DIFFERENT LOCATION EACH TIME, SO GETTING LOST ISN'T UNUSUAL FOR US
WHY DO YOU ALWAYS LEAD US INTO SOME WEIRD LOCATION?
MAYBE IF A CERTAIN CAT DIDN'T CHASE ME ALL THE TIME...
ALTHOUGH MOUSE USUALLY KNOWS HOW TO GET BACK HOME
ARE YOU SURE THIS IS THE WAY?
POSITIVE!
EMPHASIS ON "USUALLY"
I DON'T REMEMBER LIVING IN A CHEESE STORE
YOU LIVE IN MULTIPLE HOMES. YOU PROBABLY FORGOT ABOUT THIS ONE
HELLO, PEST CONTROL?
MUNCH

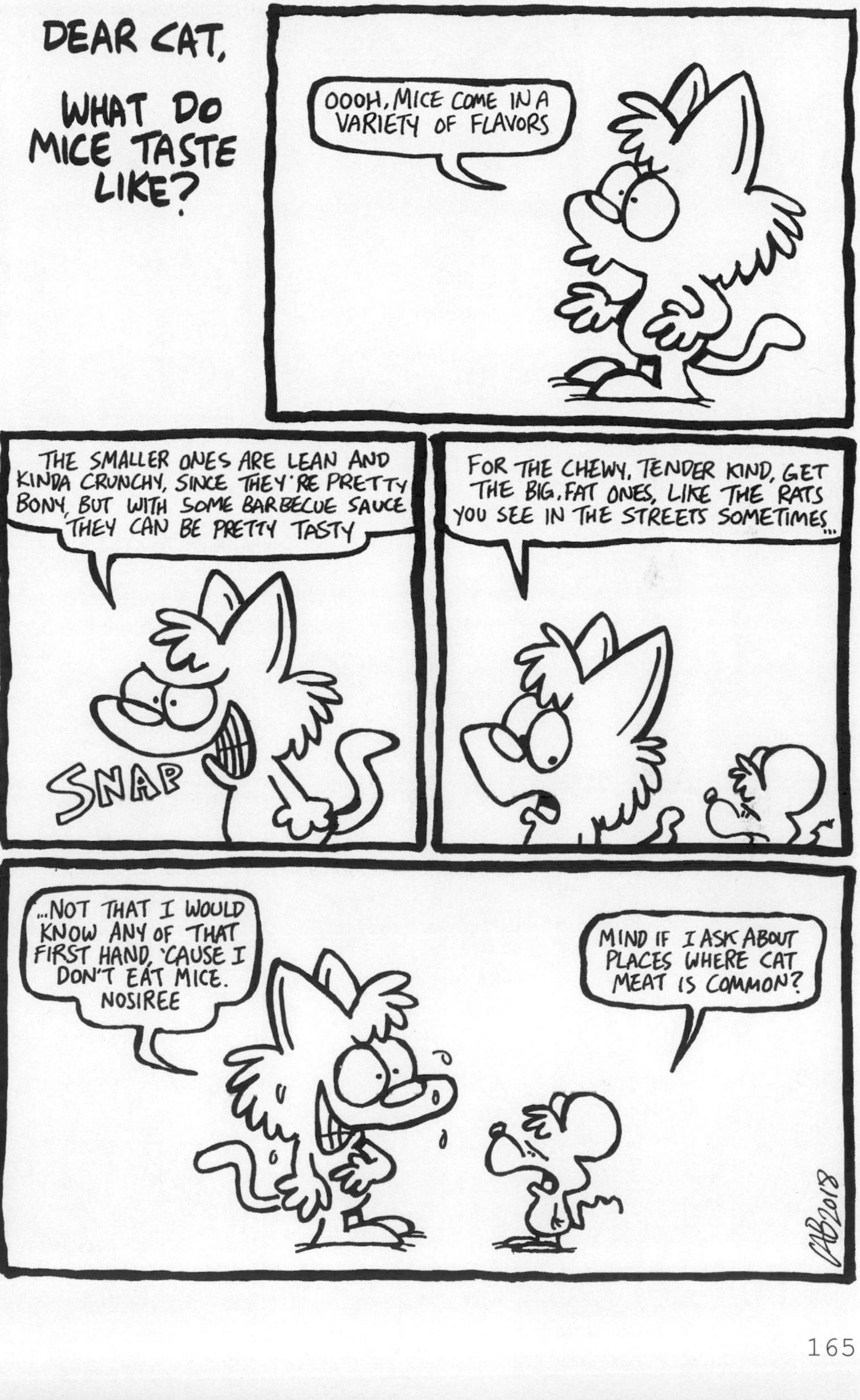
DEAR CAT,
WHAT DO MICE TASTE LIKE?
OOOH, MICE COME IN A VARIETY OF FLAVORS
THE SMALLER ONES ARE LEAN AND KINDA CRUNCHY, SINCE THEY'RE PRETTY BONY, BUT WITH SOME BARBECUE SAUCE THEY CAN BE PRETTY TASTY
SNAP
FOR THE CHEWY, TENDER KIND, GET THE BIG, FAT ONES, LIKE THE RATS YOU SEE IN THE STREETS SOMETIMES...
...NOT THAT I WOULD KNOW ANY OF THAT FIRST HAND, 'CAUSE I DON'T EAT MICE. NOSIREE
MIND IF I ASK ABOUT PLACES WHERE CAT MEAT IS COMMON?
CAB 2018

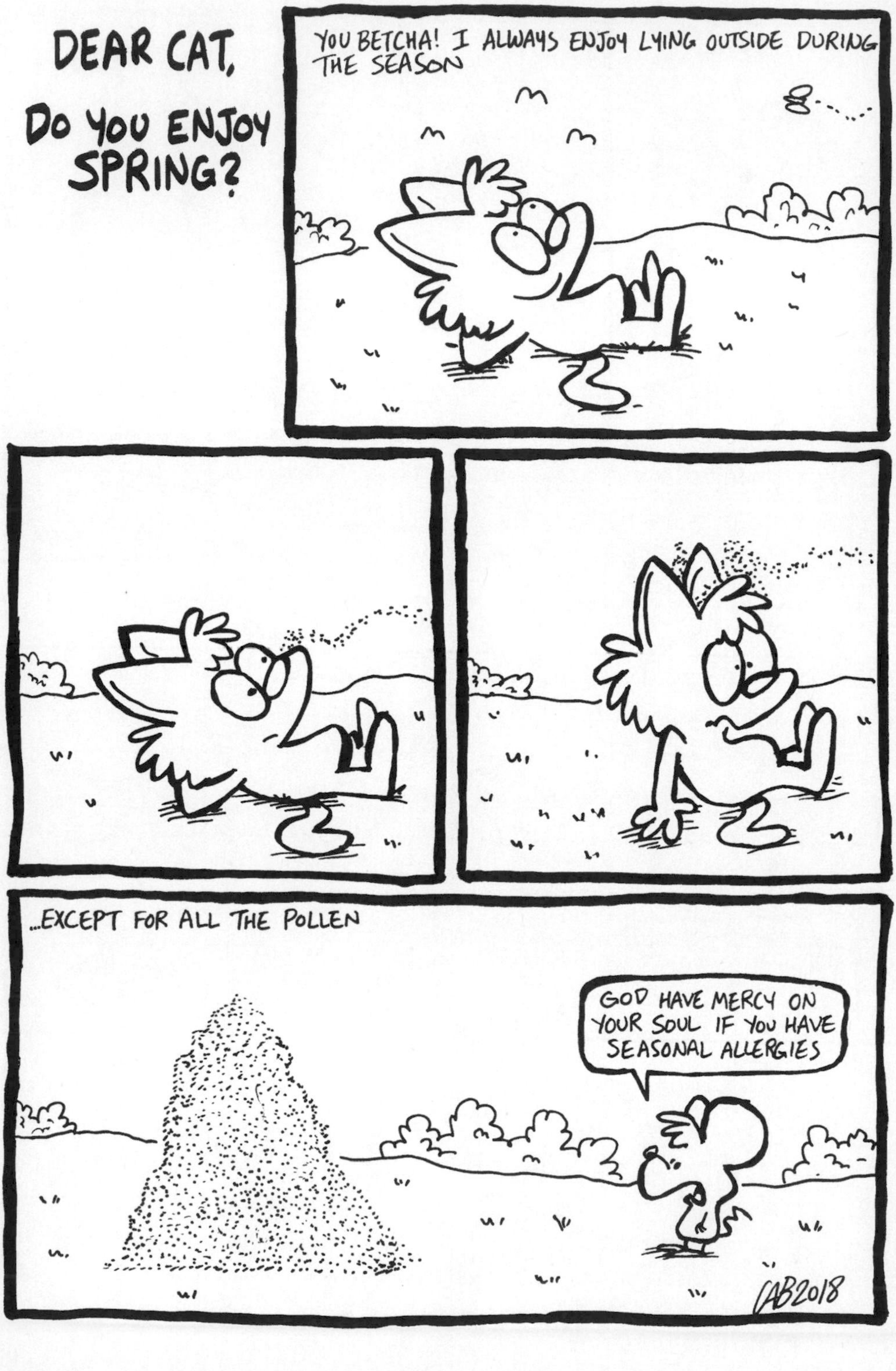
DEAR CAT,
DO YOU ENJOY SPRING?
YOU BETCHA! I ALWAYS ENJOY LYING OUTSIDE DURING THE SEASON
...EXCEPT FOR ALL THE POLLEN
GOD HAVE MERCY ON YOUR SOUL IF YOU HAVE SEASONAL ALLERGIES
CAB2018

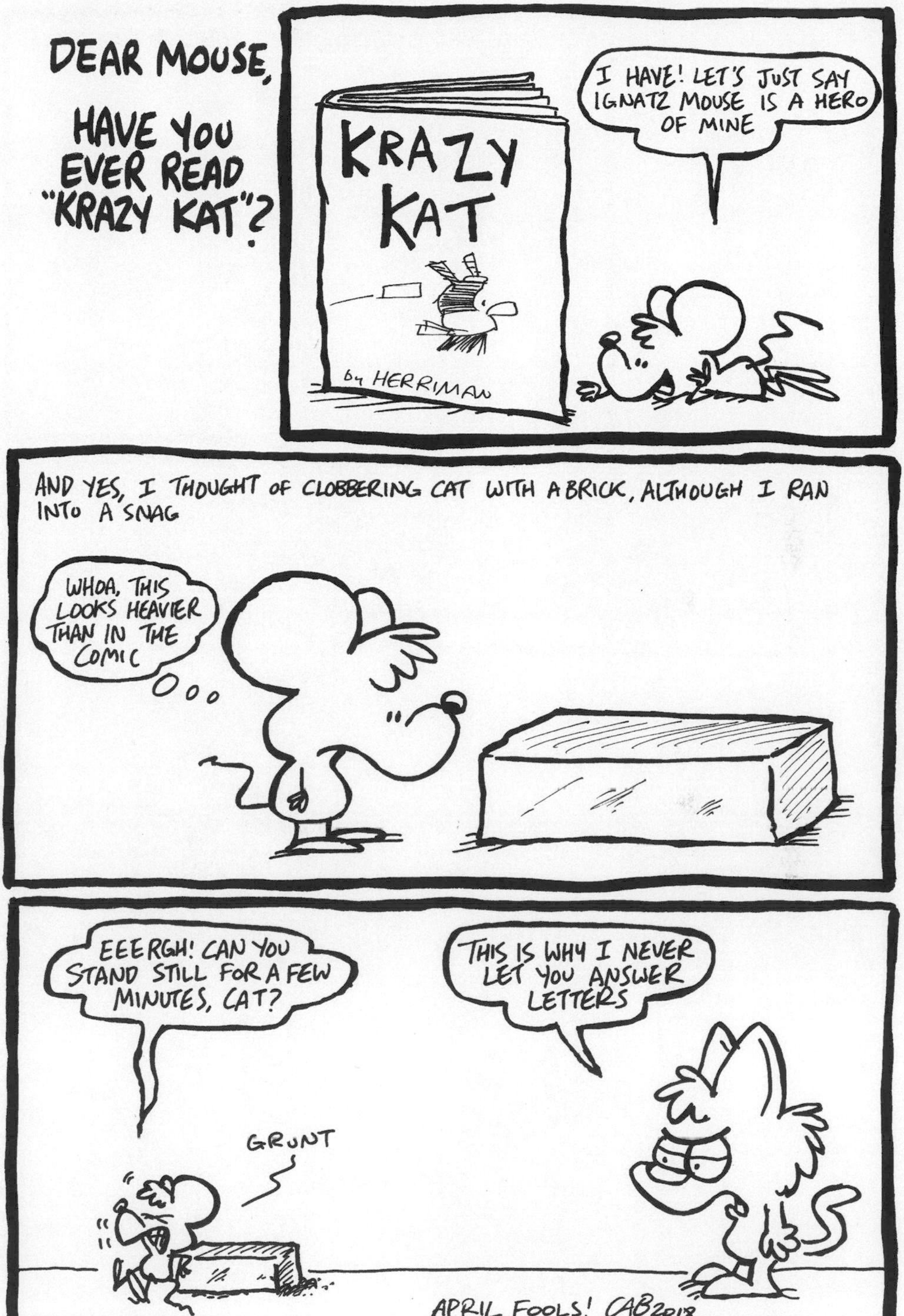
DEAR MOUSE,
HAVE YOU EVER READ "KRAZY KAT"?
KRAZY KAT
by HERRIMAN
I HAVE! LET'S JUST SAY IGNATZ MOUSE IS A HERO OF MINE
AND YES, I THOUGHT OF CLOBBERING CAT WITH A BRICK, ALTHOUGH I RAN INTO A SNAG
WHOA, THIS LOOKS HEAVIER THAN IN THE COMIC
EEERGH! CAN YOU STAND STILL FOR A FEW MINUTES, CAT?
THIS IS WHY I NEVER LET YOU ANSWER LETTERS
GRUNT
APRIL FOOLS! CAB 2018

DEAR CAT,

DO YOU HAVE YOUR OWN LINE OF FASHION?

WE DO, ACTUALLY! WE'VE ALL HAD THEM SINCE BIRTH

WHAT CAN I SAY? WE'RE BORN PERFECT

OF COURSE, WE CAN'T ACTUALLY SELL OUR FUR, ALTHOUGH THAT DOESN'T STOP CERTAIN (ahem) INDIVIDUALS FROM TRYING TO BUY FROM US

MISS de VIL'S ON THE PHONE AGAIN, WANTING TO TALK ABOUT SOME "BUSINESS VENTURE"

UGH. WHY CAN'T SHE BOTHER SOME DOGS OR WHATEVER?

HOWEVER, WE DO HAVE WORKAROUNDS FOR THOSE WHO WANT TO LOOK FABULOUS

THERE'S A REASON WHY I DON'T KEEP MY DARK CLOTHES AROUND

WHY NOT? THOSE TEND TO WORK BEST WITH MY "FUR TRANSFER"

LAB2018

DEAR CAT, ARE CROWS SMART?

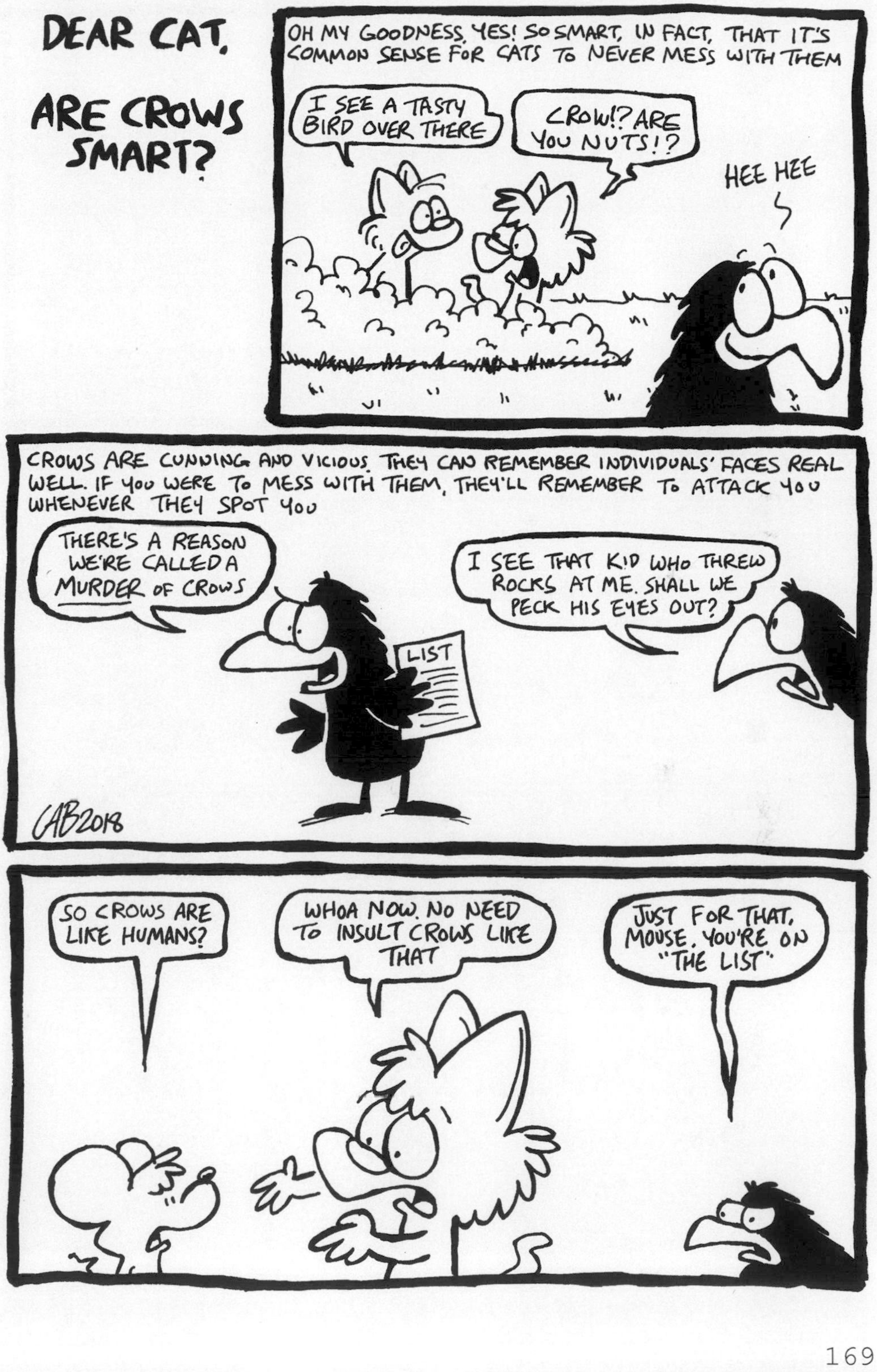
OH MY GOODNESS, YES! SO SMART, IN FACT, THAT IT'S COMMON SENSE FOR CATS TO NEVER MESS WITH THEM
I SEE A TASTY BIRD OVER THERE
CROW!? ARE YOU NUTS!?
HEE HEE
CROWS ARE CUNNING AND VICIOUS. THEY CAN REMEMBER INDIVIDUALS' FACES REAL WELL. IF YOU WERE TO MESS WITH THEM, THEY'LL REMEMBER TO ATTACK YOU WHENEVER THEY SPOT YOU
THERE'S A REASON WE'RE CALLED A MURDER OF CROWS
LIST
I SEE THAT KID WHO THREW ROCKS AT ME. SHALL WE PECK HIS EYES OUT?
CAB 2018
SO CROWS ARE LIKE HUMANS?
WHOA NOW. NO NEED TO INSULT CROWS LIKE THAT
JUST FOR THAT, MOUSE, YOU'RE ON "THE LIST"

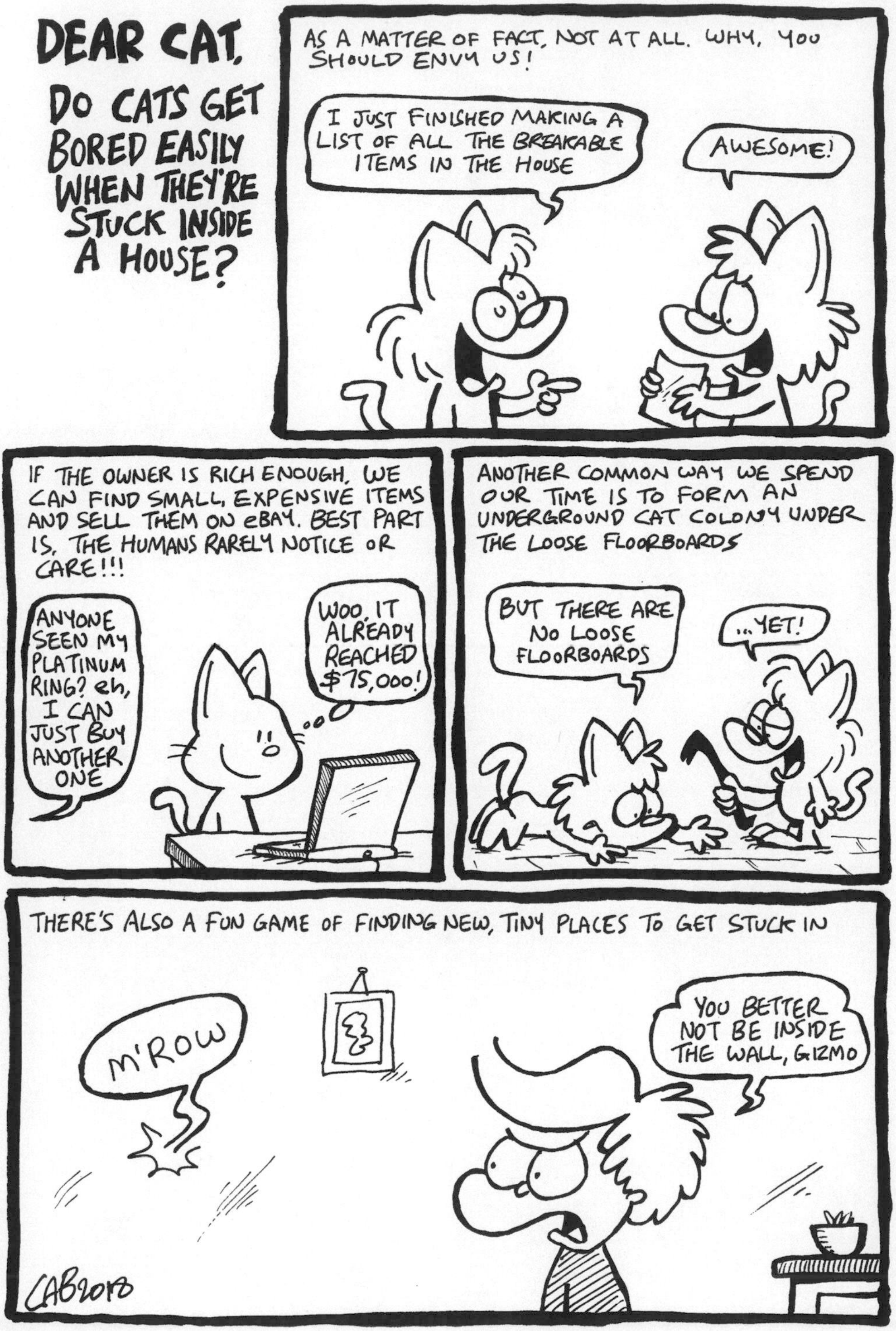
DEAR CAT,
DO CATS GET BORED EASILY WHEN THEY'RE STUCK INSIDE A HOUSE?
AS A MATTER OF FACT, NOT AT ALL. WHY, YOU SHOULD ENVY US!
I JUST FINISHED MAKING A LIST OF ALL THE BREAKABLE ITEMS IN THE HOUSE
AWESOME!
IF THE OWNER IS RICH ENOUGH, WE CAN FIND SMALL, EXPENSIVE ITEMS AND SELL THEM ON eBAY. BEST PART IS, THE HUMANS RARELY NOTICE OR CARE!!!
ANYONE SEEN MY PLATINUM RING? eh, I CAN JUST BUY ANOTHER ONE
WOO, IT ALREADY REACHED $75,000!
ANOTHER COMMON WAY WE SPEND OUR TIME IS TO FORM AN UNDERGROUND CAT COLONY UNDER THE LOOSE FLOORBOARDS
BUT THERE ARE NO LOOSE FLOORBOARDS
...YET!
THERE'S ALSO A FUN GAME OF FINDING NEW, TINY PLACES TO GET STUCK IN
M'ROW
YOU BETTER NOT BE INSIDE THE WALL, GIZMO
CAB2018

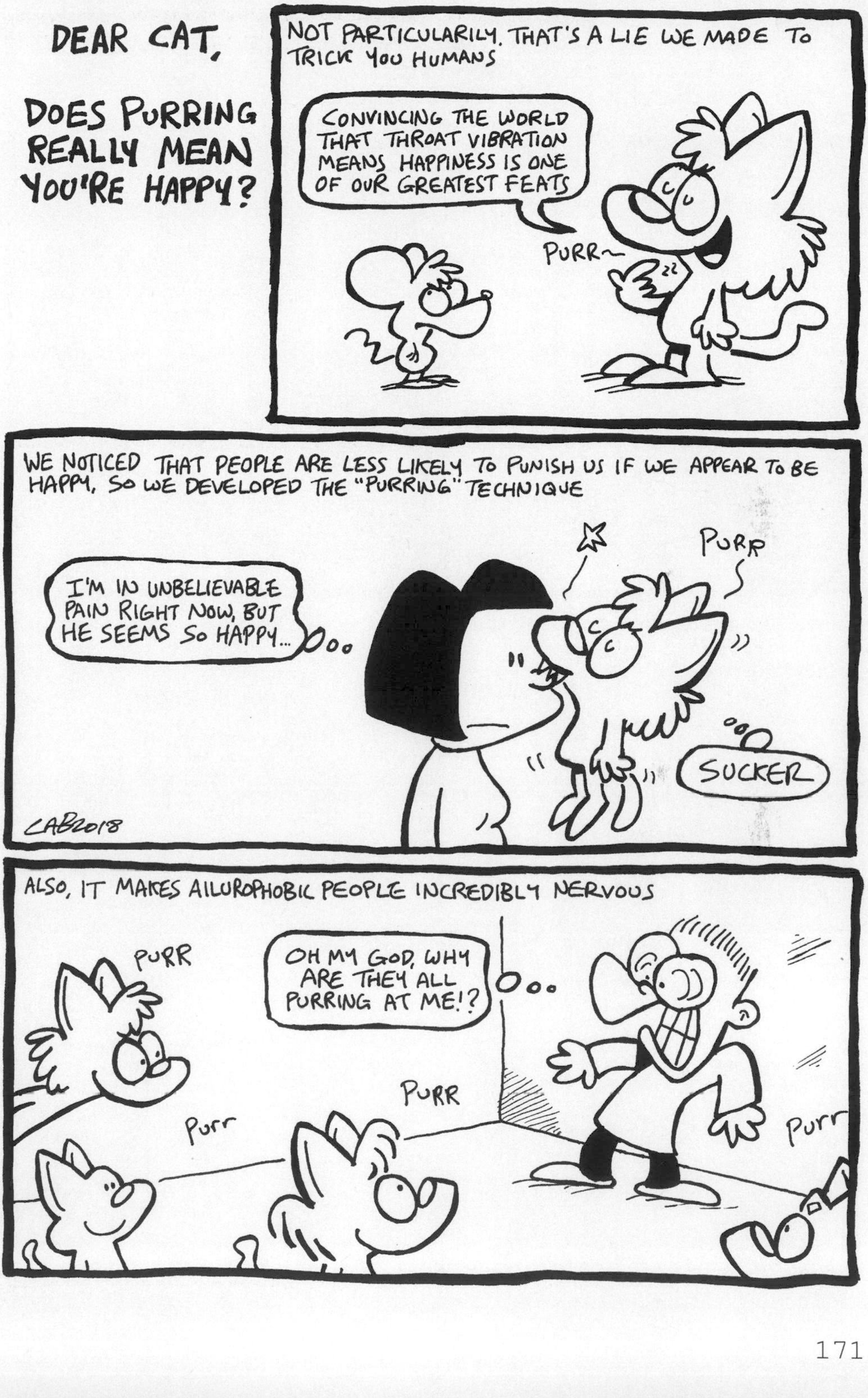
DEAR CAT,
DOES PURRING REALLY MEAN YOU'RE HAPPY?
NOT PARTICULARILY. THAT'S A LIE WE MADE TO TRICK YOU HUMANS
CONVINCING THE WORLD THAT THROAT VIBRATION MEANS HAPPINESS IS ONE OF OUR GREATEST FEATS
PURR~
WE NOTICED THAT PEOPLE ARE LESS LIKELY TO PUNISH US IF WE APPEAR TO BE HAPPY, SO WE DEVELOPED THE "PURRING" TECHNIQUE
PURR
I'M IN UNBELIEVABLE PAIN RIGHT NOW, BUT HE SEEMS SO HAPPY...
SUCKER
CAB2018
ALSO, IT MAKES AILUROPHOBIC PEOPLE INCREDIBLY NERVOUS
PURR
OH MY GOD, WHY ARE THEY ALL PURRING AT ME!?
PURR
Purr
Purr

DEAR CAT,

MY CAT SHEDS SO MUCH HAIR, YOU CAN MAKE ANOTHER CAT OUT OF IT. WHAT SHOULD I DO?

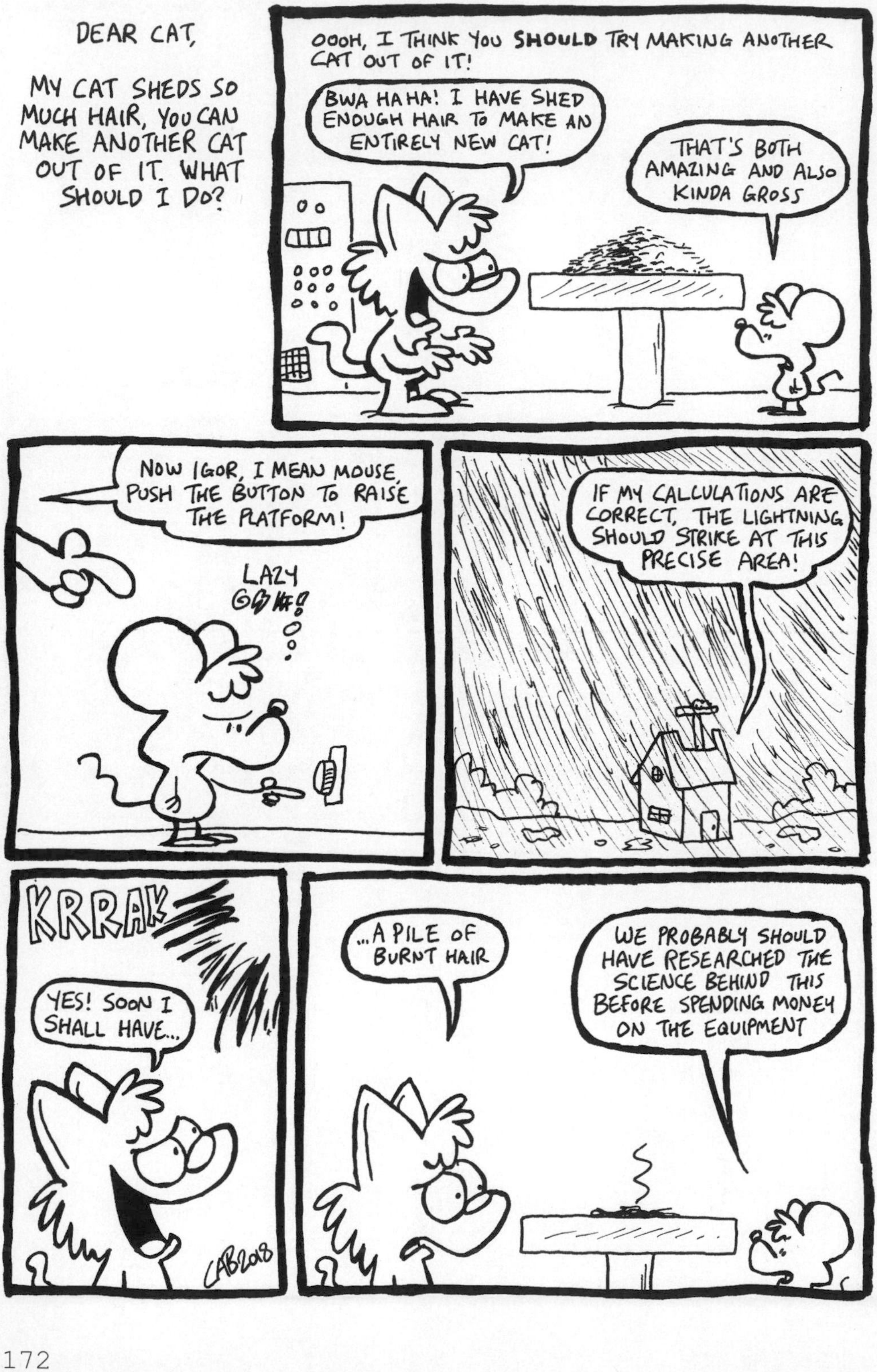

OOOH, I THINK YOU **SHOULD** TRY MAKING ANOTHER CAT OUT OF IT!
BWA HA HA! I HAVE SHED ENOUGH HAIR TO MAKE AN ENTIRELY NEW CAT!
THAT'S BOTH AMAZING AND ALSO KINDA GROSS
NOW IGOR, I MEAN MOUSE, PUSH THE BUTTON TO RAISE THE PLATFORM!
LAZY
IF MY CALCULATIONS ARE CORRECT, THE LIGHTNING SHOULD STRIKE AT THIS PRECISE AREA!
KRRAK
YES! SOON I SHALL HAVE...
CAB2018
...A PILE OF BURNT HAIR
WE PROBABLY SHOULD HAVE RESEARCHED THE SCIENCE BEHIND THIS BEFORE SPENDING MONEY ON THE EQUIPMENT

DEAR CAT,

DO YOU WORRY THAT YOU'RE ADDICTED TO SCRATCHING THINGS?

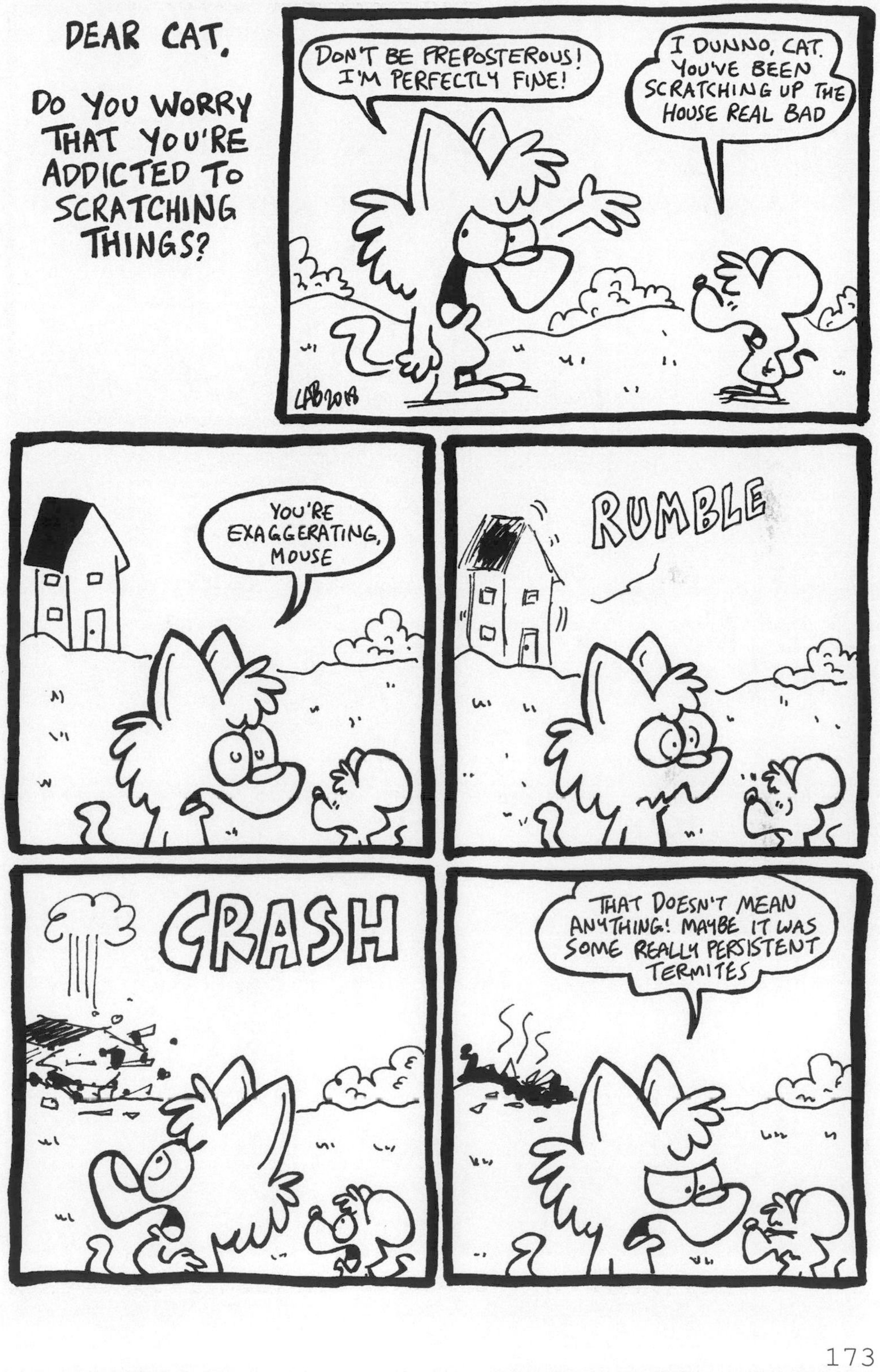
DON'T BE PREPOSTEROUS! I'M PERFECTLY FINE!
I DUNNO, CAT. YOU'VE BEEN SCRATCHING UP THE HOUSE REAL BAD
YOU'RE EXAGGERATING, MOUSE
RUMBLE
CRASH
THAT DOESN'T MEAN ANYTHING! MAYBE IT WAS SOME REALLY PERSISTENT TERMITES

DEAR CAT,

ARE FOXES REALLY THAT CLEVER?

OH, THEY ABSOLUTELY ARE, AND FOR A VERY GOOD REASON

FOXES MIMIC CATS!

COPY CATS, IF YOU WILL (GEDDIT?)

SERIOUSLY, THEY TRY TO LOOK LIKE US!

LARGE EARS

BOOPY NOSE

FLUFFY TAIL

WEIRD, ADORABLE FACE THAT'S A CROSS BETWEEN A CAT AND A DOG

AND THEY KNOW HOW TO INDULGE HUMAN'S FASCINATION WITH "CUTE"

AW, I'M SO GOING TO SHARE THIS ON BUZZTWIT!

SQUEAK

LAB 2018

I HATE THEM

AT LEAST YOU DON'T HAVE CHICKEN FARMERS SHOOTING AT YOU

DEAR CAT,

DO YOU LIKE TO SWIM IN A POOL?

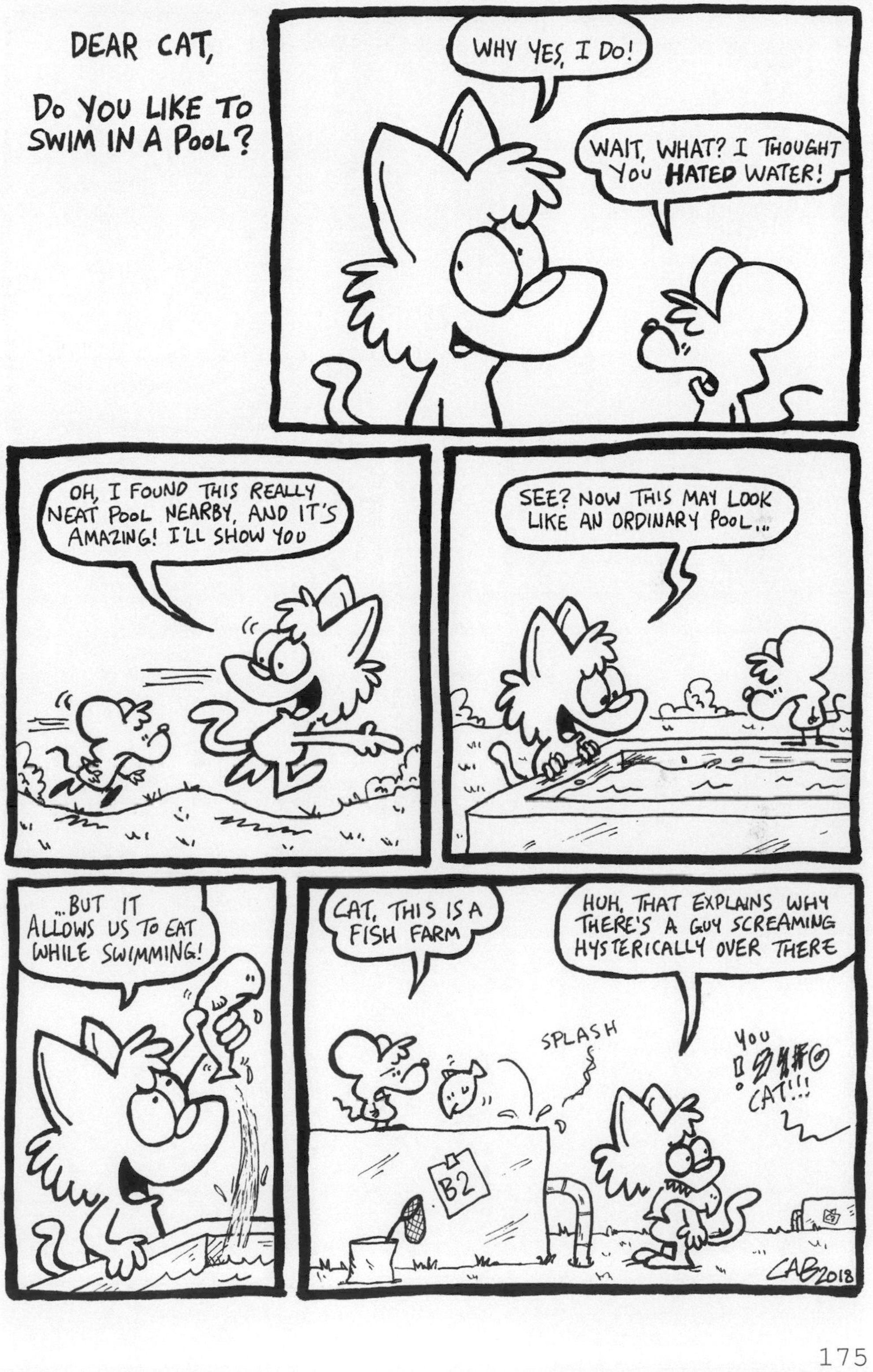
WHY YES, I DO!
WAIT, WHAT? I THOUGHT YOU **HATED** WATER!
OH, I FOUND THIS REALLY NEAT POOL NEARBY, AND IT'S AMAZING! I'LL SHOW YOU
SEE? NOW THIS MAY LOOK LIKE AN ORDINARY POOL...
...BUT IT ALLOWS US TO EAT WHILE SWIMMING!
CAT, THIS IS A FISH FARM
HUH, THAT EXPLAINS WHY THERE'S A GUY SCREAMING HYSTERICALLY OVER THERE
SPLASH
YOU
CAT!!!
B2
CAB 2018

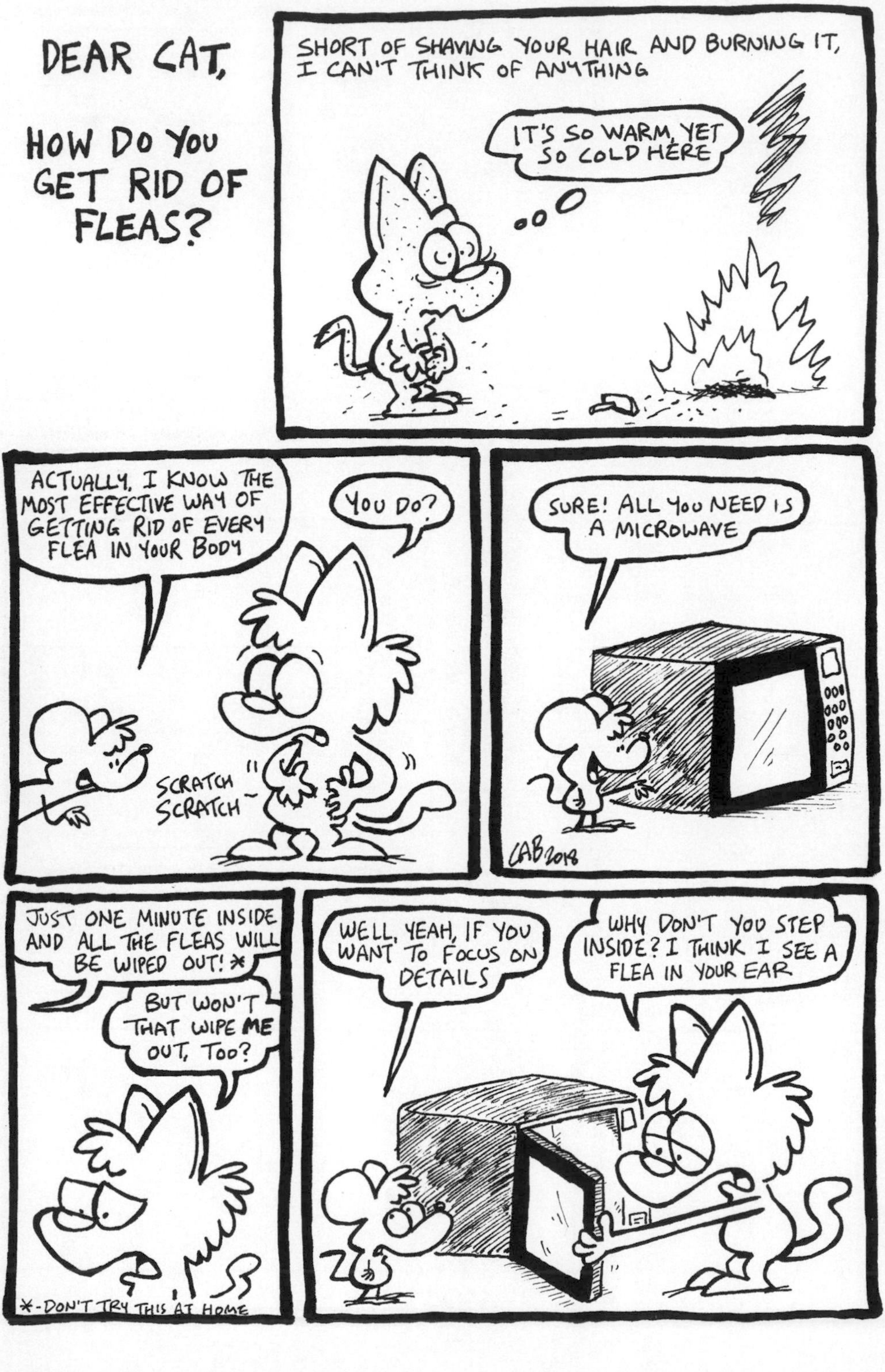
DEAR CAT,
HOW DO YOU GET RID OF FLEAS?
SHORT OF SHAVING YOUR HAIR AND BURNING IT, I CAN'T THINK OF ANYTHING
IT'S SO WARM, YET SO COLD HERE
ACTUALLY, I KNOW THE MOST EFFECTIVE WAY OF GETTING RID OF EVERY FLEA IN YOUR BODY
YOU DO?
SCRATCH SCRATCH
SURE! ALL YOU NEED IS A MICROWAVE
CAB 2018
JUST ONE MINUTE INSIDE AND ALL THE FLEAS WILL BE WIPED OUT! *
BUT WON'T THAT WIPE ME OUT, TOO?
*-DON'T TRY THIS AT HOME
WELL, YEAH, IF YOU WANT TO FOCUS ON DETAILS
WHY DON'T YOU STEP INSIDE? I THINK I SEE A FLEA IN YOUR EAR

THE FLEA PROBLEM, CONTINUED

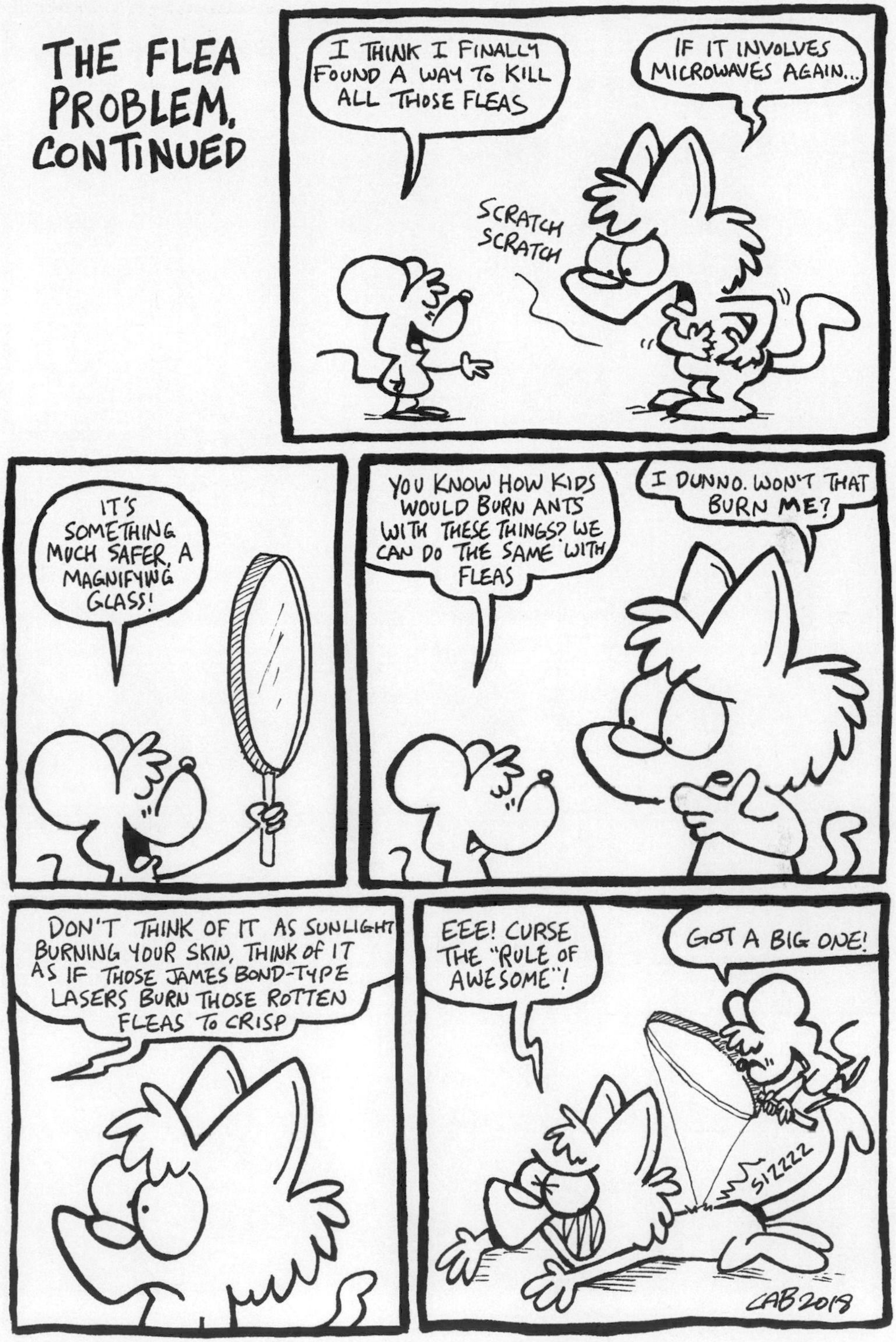
I THINK I FINALLY FOUND A WAY TO KILL ALL THOSE FLEAS
IF IT INVOLVES MICROWAVES AGAIN...
SCRATCH SCRATCH
IT'S SOMETHING MUCH SAFER, A MAGNIFYING GLASS!
YOU KNOW HOW KIDS WOULD BURN ANTS WITH THESE THINGS? WE CAN DO THE SAME WITH FLEAS
I DUNNO. WON'T THAT BURN ME?
DON'T THINK OF IT AS SUNLIGHT BURNING YOUR SKIN, THINK OF IT AS IF THOSE JAMES BOND-TYPE LASERS BURN THOSE ROTTEN FLEAS TO CRISP
EEE! CURSE THE "RULE OF AWESOME"!
GOT A BIG ONE!
SIZZZZ
CAB 2018

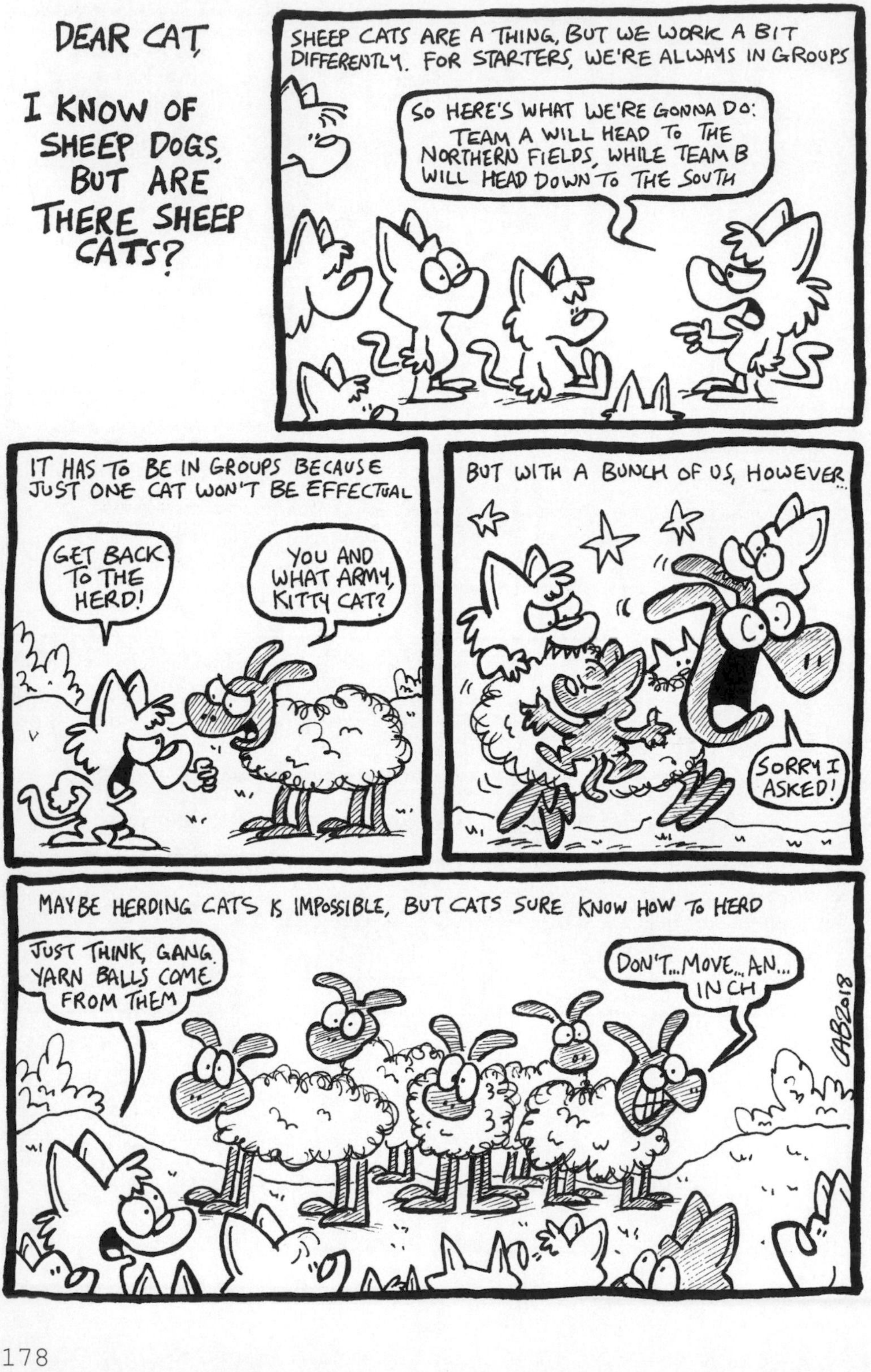
DEAR CAT,
I KNOW OF SHEEP DOGS, BUT ARE THERE SHEEP CATS?
SHEEP CATS ARE A THING, BUT WE WORK A BIT DIFFERENTLY. FOR STARTERS, WE'RE ALWAYS IN GROUPS
SO HERE'S WHAT WE'RE GONNA DO: TEAM A WILL HEAD TO THE NORTHERN FIELDS, WHILE TEAM B WILL HEAD DOWN TO THE SOUTH
IT HAS TO BE IN GROUPS BECAUSE JUST ONE CAT WON'T BE EFFECTUAL
GET BACK TO THE HERD!
YOU AND WHAT ARMY, KITTY CAT?
BUT WITH A BUNCH OF US, HOWEVER...
SORRY I ASKED!
MAYBE HERDING CATS IS IMPOSSIBLE, BUT CATS SURE KNOW HOW TO HERD
JUST THINK, GANG. YARN BALLS COME FROM THEM
DON'T... MOVE... AN... INCH
CAB 2018

DEAR CAT,
WHY DO YOU KEEP STEALING MY SOCKS?
I SHOULD BE ASKING WHY YOU KEEP STEALING MY SOCKS!
I MEAN, WHY WOULD YOU HUMANS NEED A TAIL COZY ANYWAY?
UH, CAT?
SOCKS ARE DESIGNED FOR PEOPLE'S FEET, NOT CAT'S TAILS
OH GROSS, HUMAN FEET WERE INSIDE THESE THINGS!?! BLARGH!
AW COME ON, I'VE SEEN YOU STEP ON WORSE THINGS
CAB2018
MAYBE SO, BUT AT LEAST WE LICK OUR TOES CLEAN REGULARILY!
OH YEAH, MUCH MORE SANITARY

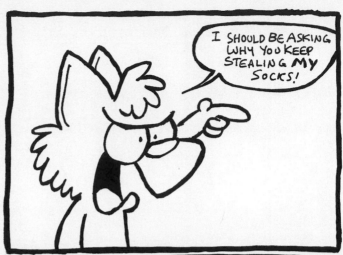

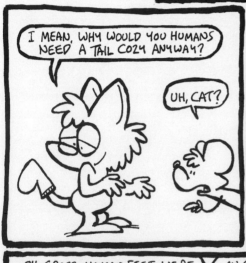

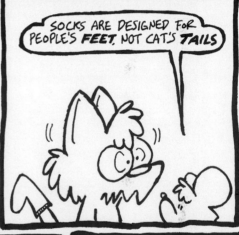

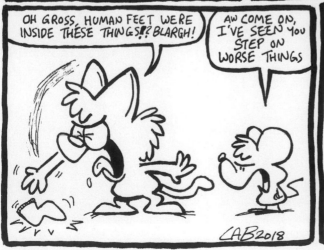

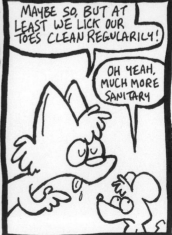

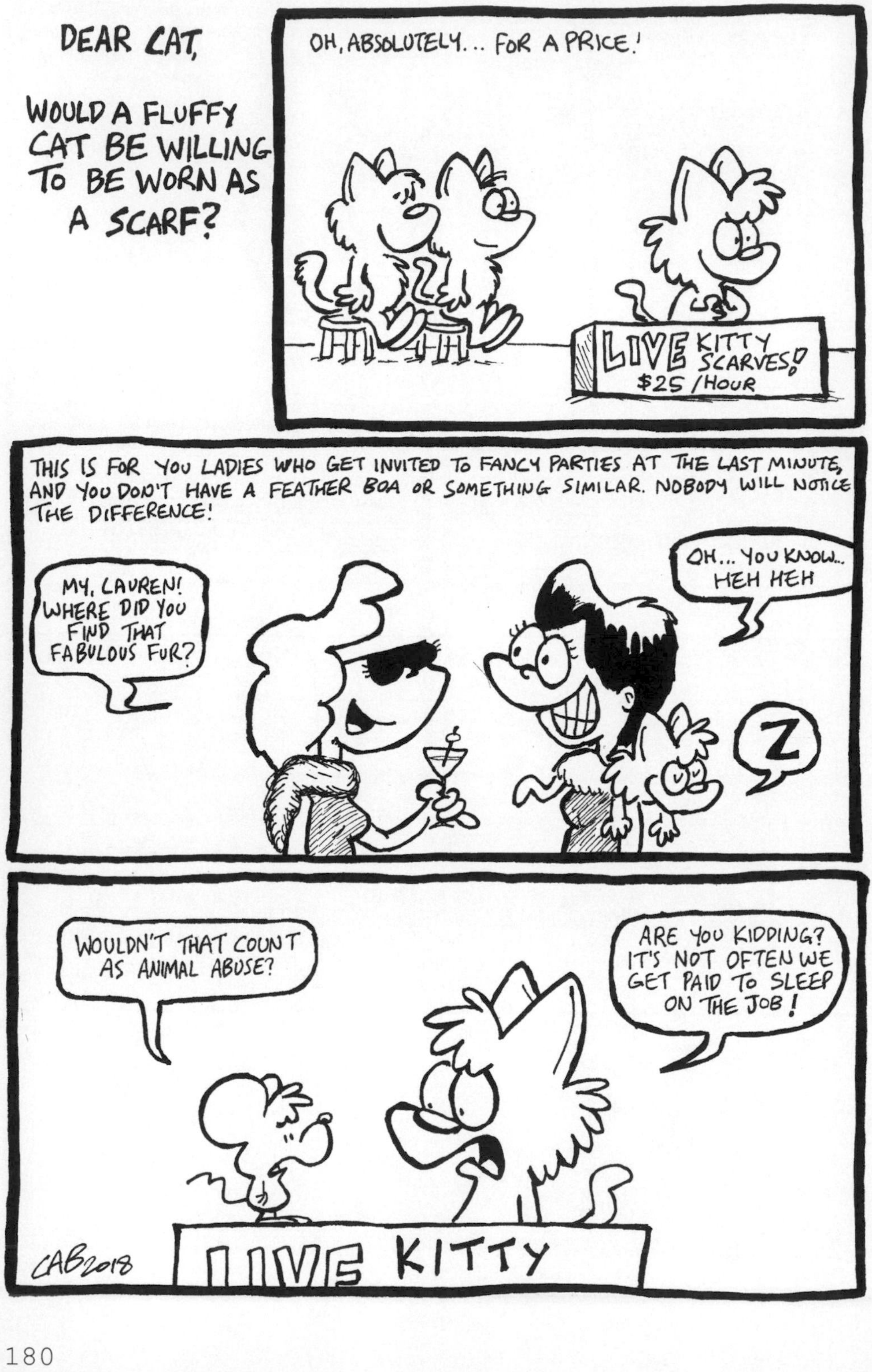
DEAR CAT,
WOULD A FLUFFY CAT BE WILLING TO BE WORN AS A SCARF?
OH, ABSOLUTELY... FOR A PRICE!
LIVE KITTY SCARVES! $25 /HOUR
THIS IS FOR YOU LADIES WHO GET INVITED TO FANCY PARTIES AT THE LAST MINUTE, AND YOU DON'T HAVE A FEATHER BOA OR SOMETHING SIMILAR. NOBODY WILL NOTICE THE DIFFERENCE!
MY, LAUREN! WHERE DID YOU FIND THAT FABULOUS FUR?
OH... YOU KNOW... HEH HEH
Z
WOULDN'T THAT COUNT AS ANIMAL ABUSE?
ARE YOU KIDDING? IT'S NOT OFTEN WE GET PAID TO SLEEP ON THE JOB!
LIVE KITTY
CAB 2018

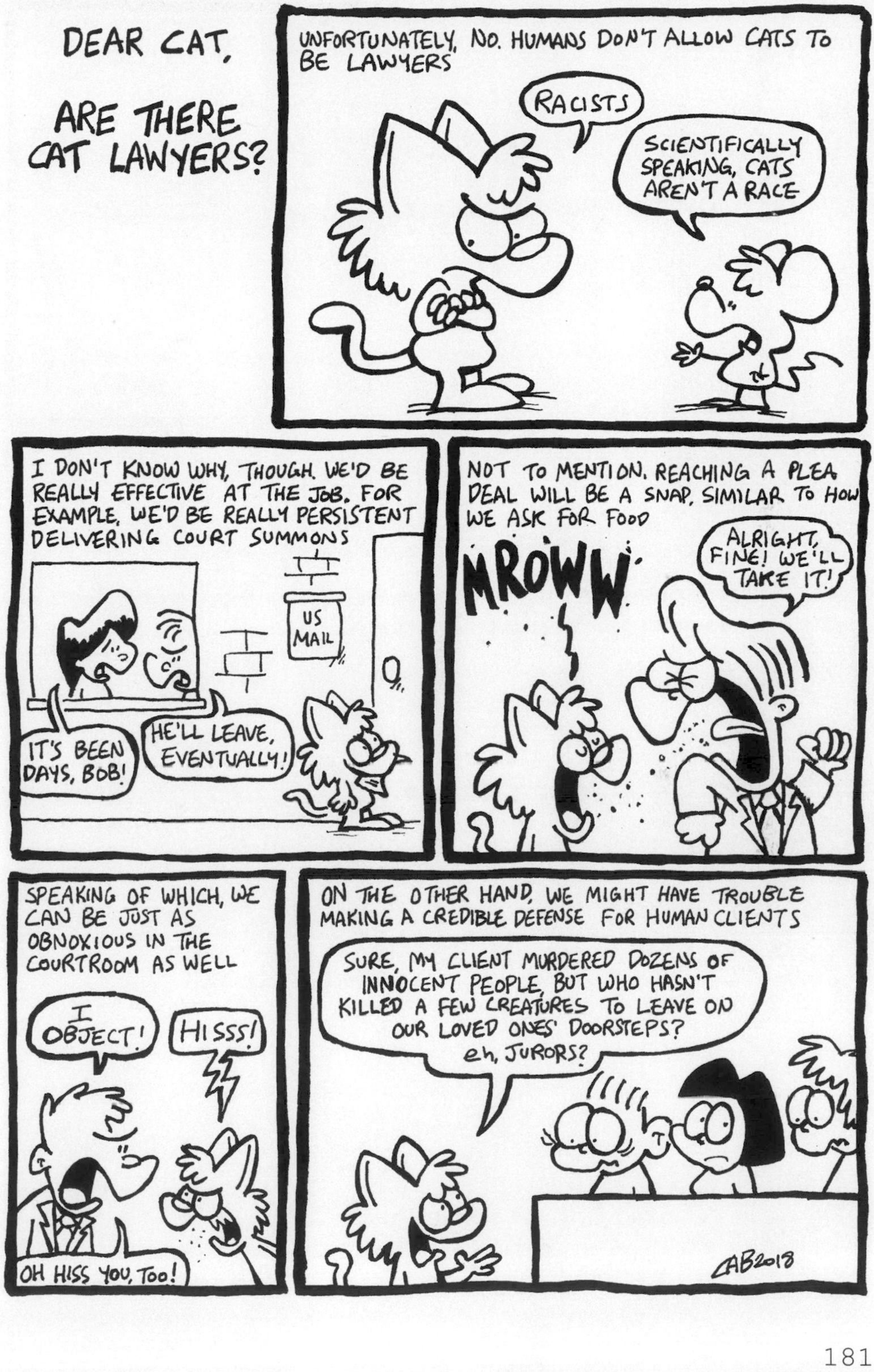

DEAR CAT,
ARE THERE CAT LAWYERS?
UNFORTUNATELY, NO. HUMANS DON'T ALLOW CATS TO BE LAWYERS
RACISTS
SCIENTIFICALLY SPEAKING, CATS AREN'T A RACE
I DON'T KNOW WHY, THOUGH. WE'D BE REALLY EFFECTIVE AT THE JOB. FOR EXAMPLE, WE'D BE REALLY PERSISTENT DELIVERING COURT SUMMONS
US MAIL
IT'S BEEN DAYS, BOB!
HE'LL LEAVE, EVENTUALLY!
NOT TO MENTION, REACHING A PLEA DEAL WILL BE A SNAP, SIMILAR TO HOW WE ASK FOR FOOD
MROWW
ALRIGHT, FINE! WE'LL TAKE IT!
SPEAKING OF WHICH, WE CAN BE JUST AS OBNOXIOUS IN THE COURTROOM AS WELL
I OBJECT!
HISSS!
OH HISS YOU, TOO!
ON THE OTHER HAND, WE MIGHT HAVE TROUBLE MAKING A CREDIBLE DEFENSE FOR HUMAN CLIENTS
SURE, MY CLIENT MURDERED DOZENS OF INNOCENT PEOPLE, BUT WHO HASN'T KILLED A FEW CREATURES TO LEAVE ON OUR LOVED ONES' DOORSTEPS? eh, JURORS?
CAB2018

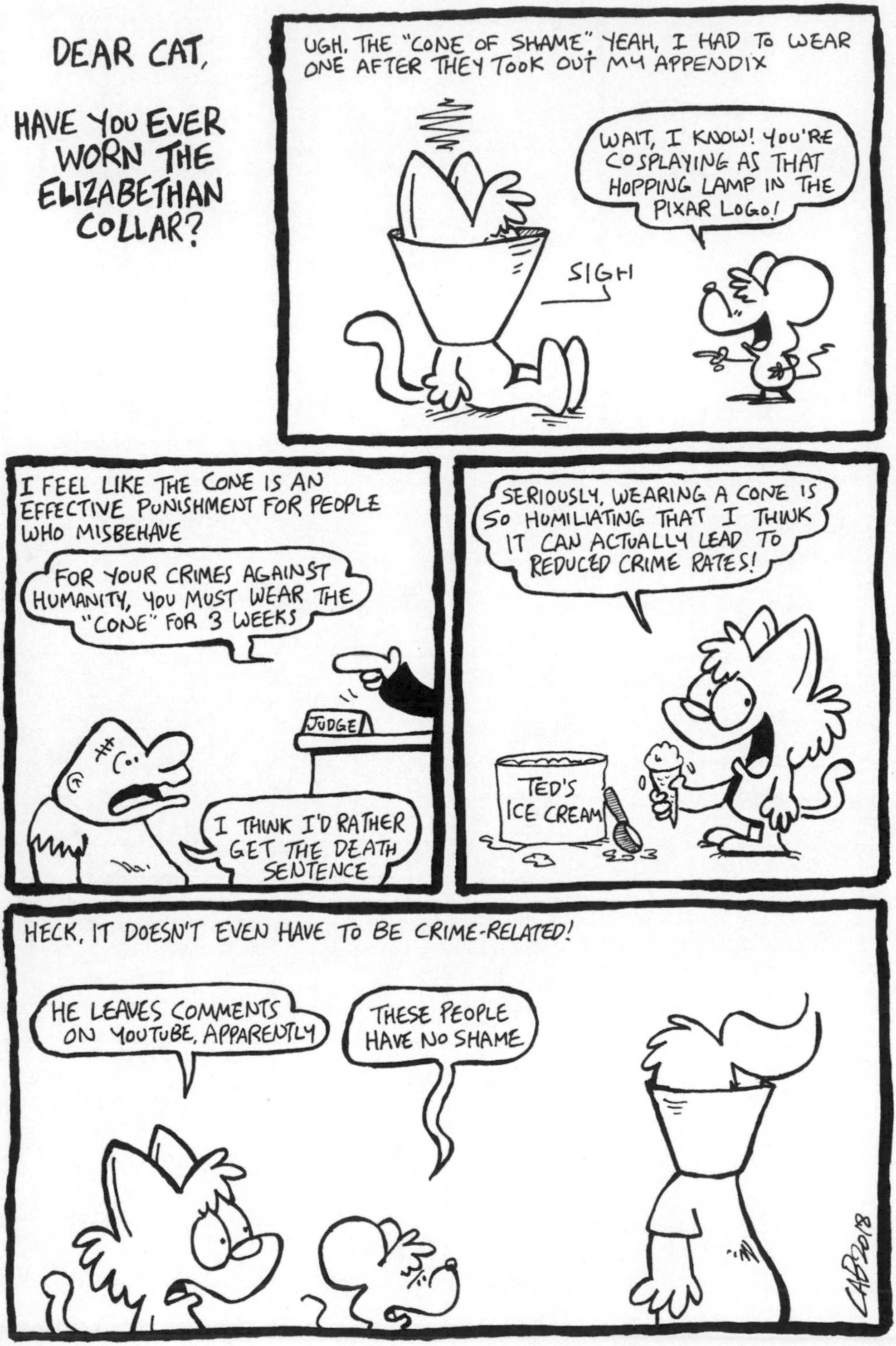

DEAR CAT,
HAVE YOU EVER WORN THE ELIZABETHAN COLLAR?
UGH. THE "CONE OF SHAME". YEAH, I HAD TO WEAR ONE AFTER THEY TOOK OUT MY APPENDIX
WAIT, I KNOW! YOU'RE COSPLAYING AS THAT HOPPING LAMP IN THE PIXAR LOGO!
SIGH
I FEEL LIKE THE CONE IS AN EFFECTIVE PUNISHMENT FOR PEOPLE WHO MISBEHAVE
FOR YOUR CRIMES AGAINST HUMANITY, YOU MUST WEAR THE "CONE" FOR 3 WEEKS
JUDGE
I THINK I'D RATHER GET THE DEATH SENTENCE
SERIOUSLY, WEARING A CONE IS SO HUMILIATING THAT I THINK IT CAN ACTUALLY LEAD TO REDUCED CRIME RATES!
TED'S ICE CREAM
HECK, IT DOESN'T EVEN HAVE TO BE CRIME-RELATED!
HE LEAVES COMMENTS ON YOUTUBE, APPARENTLY
THESE PEOPLE HAVE NO SHAME

DEAR CAT

WHAT WOULD HELL BE LIKE FOR A CAT?

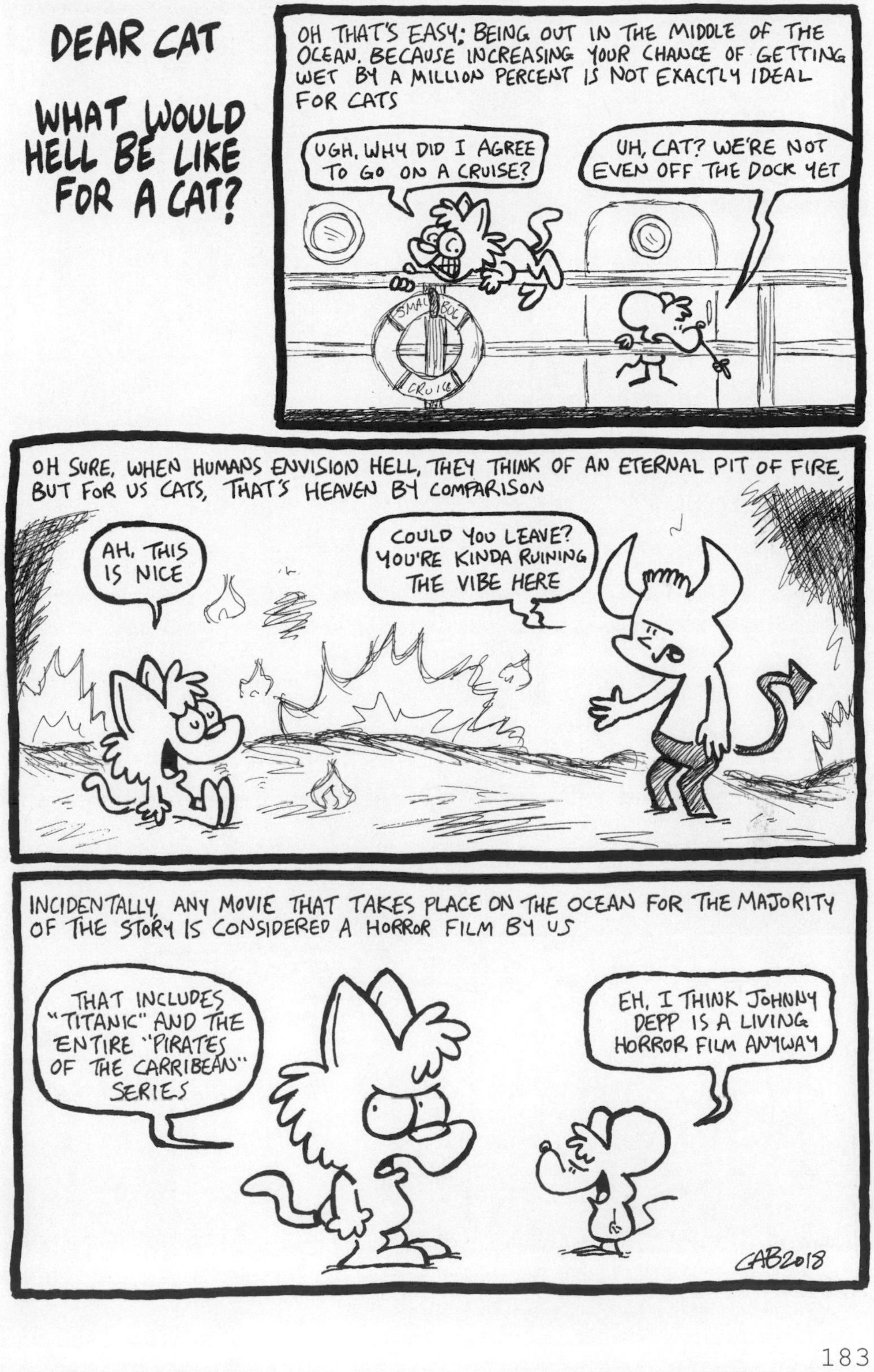
OH THAT'S EASY: BEING OUT IN THE MIDDLE OF THE OCEAN. BECAUSE INCREASING YOUR CHANCE OF GETTING WET BY A MILLION PERCENT IS NOT EXACTLY IDEAL FOR CATS
UGH. WHY DID I AGREE TO GO ON A CRUISE?
UH, CAT? WE'RE NOT EVEN OFF THE DOCK YET
CRUISE
OH SURE, WHEN HUMANS ENVISION HELL, THEY THINK OF AN ETERNAL PIT OF FIRE, BUT FOR US CATS, THAT'S HEAVEN BY COMPARISON
AH, THIS IS NICE
COULD YOU LEAVE? YOU'RE KINDA RUINING THE VIBE HERE
INCIDENTALLY, ANY MOVIE THAT TAKES PLACE ON THE OCEAN FOR THE MAJORITY OF THE STORY IS CONSIDERED A HORROR FILM BY US
THAT INCLUDES "TITANIC" AND THE ENTIRE "PIRATES OF THE CARRIBEAN" SERIES
EH, I THINK JOHNNY DEPP IS A LIVING HORROR FILM ANYWAY
CAB2018

DEAR CAT, HOW WOULD YOU RUN A RESTAURANT?

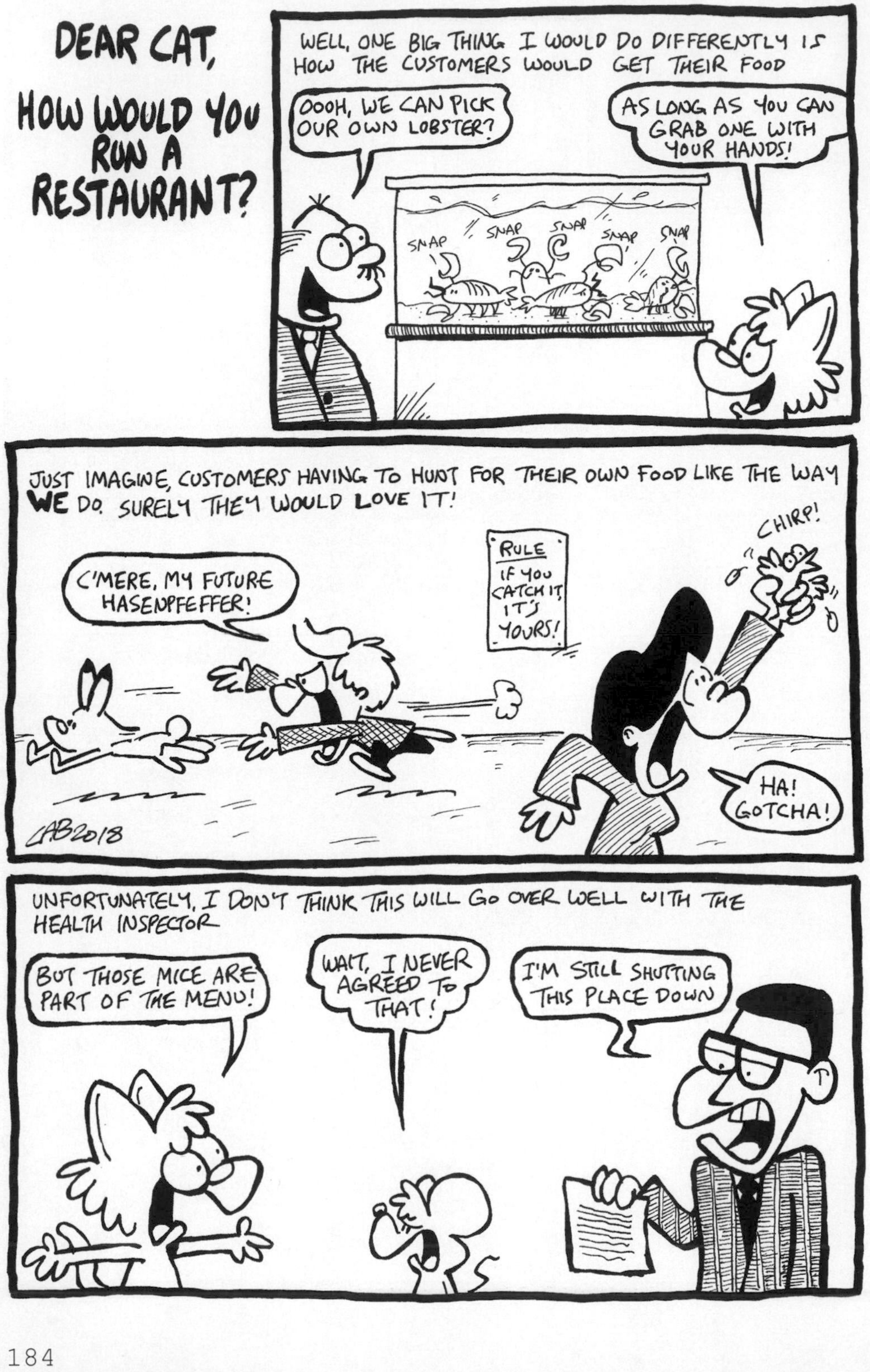
WELL, ONE BIG THING I WOULD DO DIFFERENTLY IS HOW THE CUSTOMERS WOULD GET THEIR FOOD
OOOH, WE CAN PICK OUR OWN LOBSTER?
AS LONG AS YOU CAN GRAB ONE WITH YOUR HANDS!
SNAP
SNAP
SNAP
SNAP
SNAP
JUST IMAGINE, CUSTOMERS HAVING TO HUNT FOR THEIR OWN FOOD LIKE THE WAY WE DO. SURELY THEY WOULD LOVE IT!
C'MERE, MY FUTURE HASENPFEFFER!
RULE IF YOU CATCH IT, IT'S YOURS!
CHIRP!
HA! GOTCHA!
CAB2018
UNFORTUNATELY, I DON'T THINK THIS WILL GO OVER WELL WITH THE HEALTH INSPECTOR
BUT THOSE MICE ARE PART OF THE MENU!
WAIT, I NEVER AGREED TO THAT!
I'M STILL SHUTTING THIS PLACE DOWN

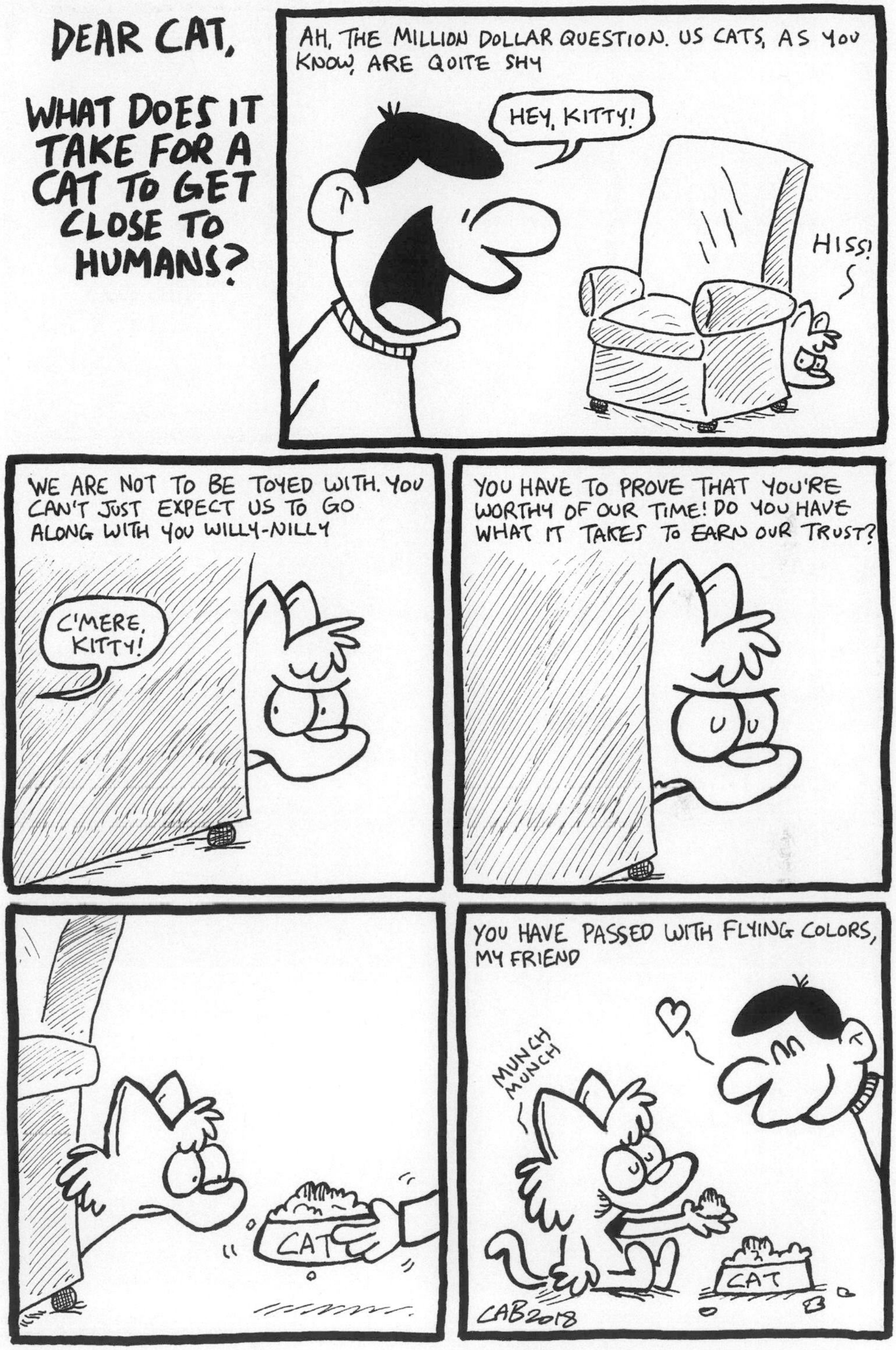
DEAR CAT,
WHAT DOES IT TAKE FOR A CAT TO GET CLOSE TO HUMANS?
AH, THE MILLION DOLLAR QUESTION. US CATS, AS YOU KNOW, ARE QUITE SHY
HEY, KITTY!
HISS!
WE ARE NOT TO BE TOYED WITH. YOU CAN'T JUST EXPECT US TO GO ALONG WITH YOU WILLY-NILLY
C'MERE, KITTY!
YOU HAVE TO PROVE THAT YOU'RE WORTHY OF OUR TIME! DO YOU HAVE WHAT IT TAKES TO EARN OUR TRUST?
CAT
YOU HAVE PASSED WITH FLYING COLORS, MY FRIEND
MUNCH MUNCH
CAT
CAB2018

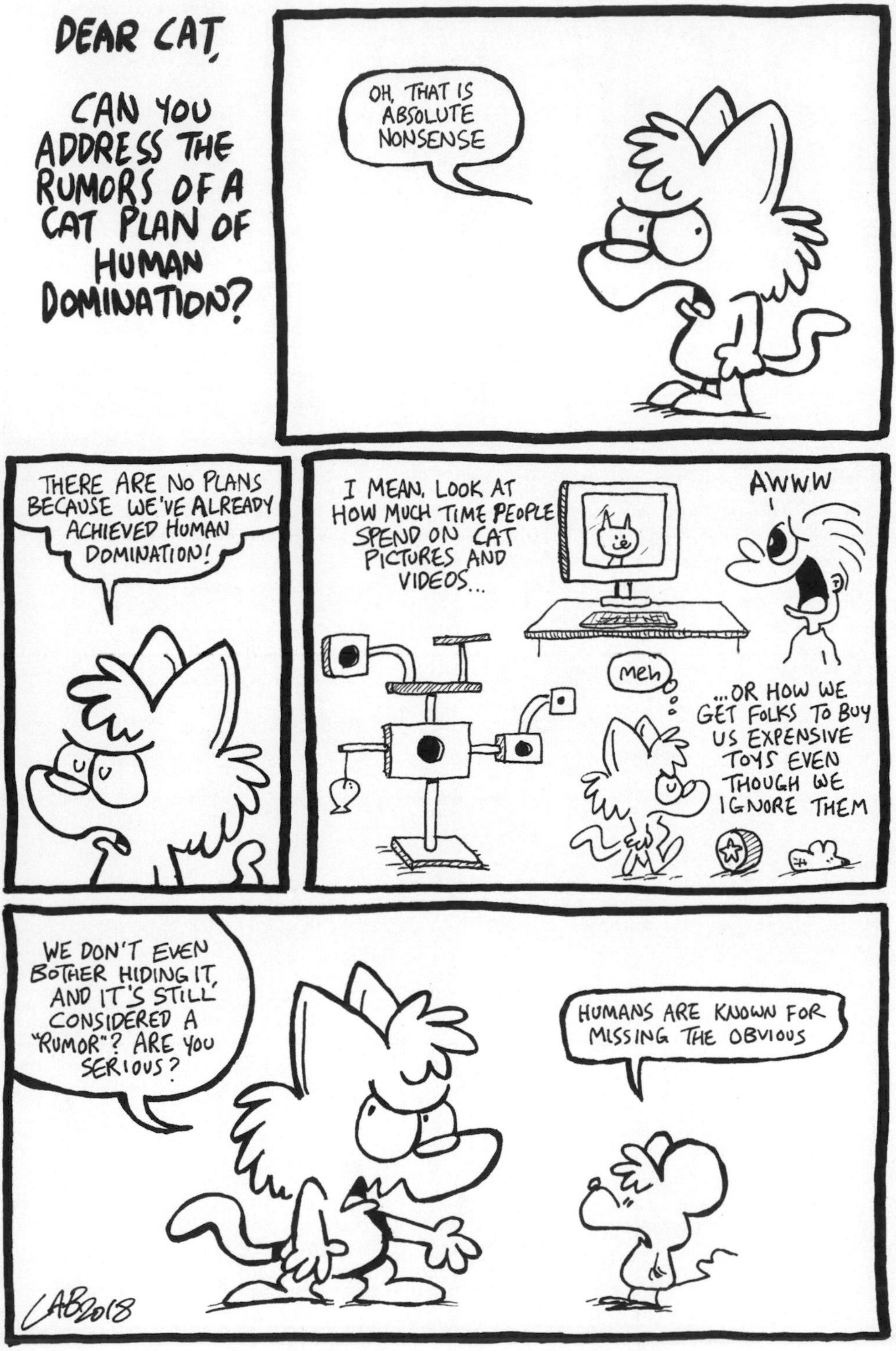
DEAR CAT,
CAN YOU ADDRESS THE RUMORS OF A CAT PLAN OF HUMAN DOMINATION?
OH, THAT IS ABSOLUTE NONSENSE
THERE ARE NO PLANS BECAUSE WE'VE ALREADY ACHIEVED HUMAN DOMINATION!
I MEAN, LOOK AT HOW MUCH TIME PEOPLE SPEND ON CAT PICTURES AND VIDEOS...
AWWW
meh
...OR HOW WE GET FOLKS TO BUY US EXPENSIVE TOYS EVEN THOUGH WE IGNORE THEM
WE DON'T EVEN BOTHER HIDING IT, AND IT'S STILL CONSIDERED A "RUMOR"? ARE YOU SERIOUS?
HUMANS ARE KNOWN FOR MISSING THE OBVIOUS
LAB2018

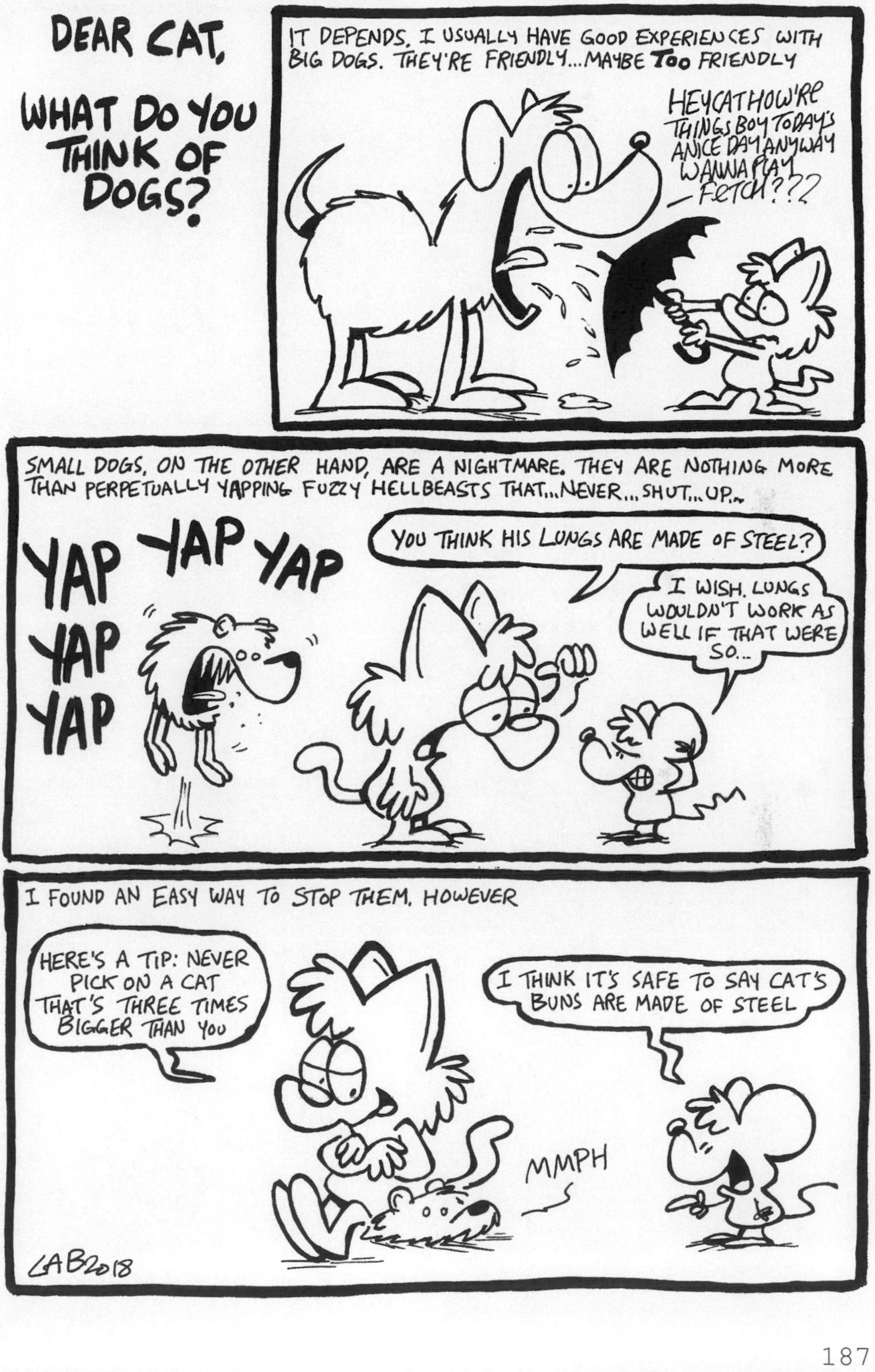
DEAR CAT,
WHAT DO YOU THINK OF DOGS?
IT DEPENDS. I USUALLY HAVE GOOD EXPERIENCES WITH BIG DOGS. THEY'RE FRIENDLY... MAYBE TOO FRIENDLY
HEYCATHOW'RE THINGSBOYTODAY'S ANICEDAYANYWAY WANNAPLAY FETCH???
SMALL DOGS, ON THE OTHER HAND, ARE A NIGHTMARE. THEY ARE NOTHING MORE THAN PERPETUALLY YAPPING FUZZY HELLBEASTS THAT... NEVER... SHUT... UP...
YAP YAP YAP YAP YAP
YOU THINK HIS LUNGS ARE MADE OF STEEL?
I WISH. LUNGS WOULDN'T WORK AS WELL IF THAT WERE SO...
I FOUND AN EASY WAY TO STOP THEM, HOWEVER
HERE'S A TIP: NEVER PICK ON A CAT THAT'S THREE TIMES BIGGER THAN YOU
I THINK IT'S SAFE TO SAY CAT'S BUNS ARE MADE OF STEEL
MMPH
LAB2018

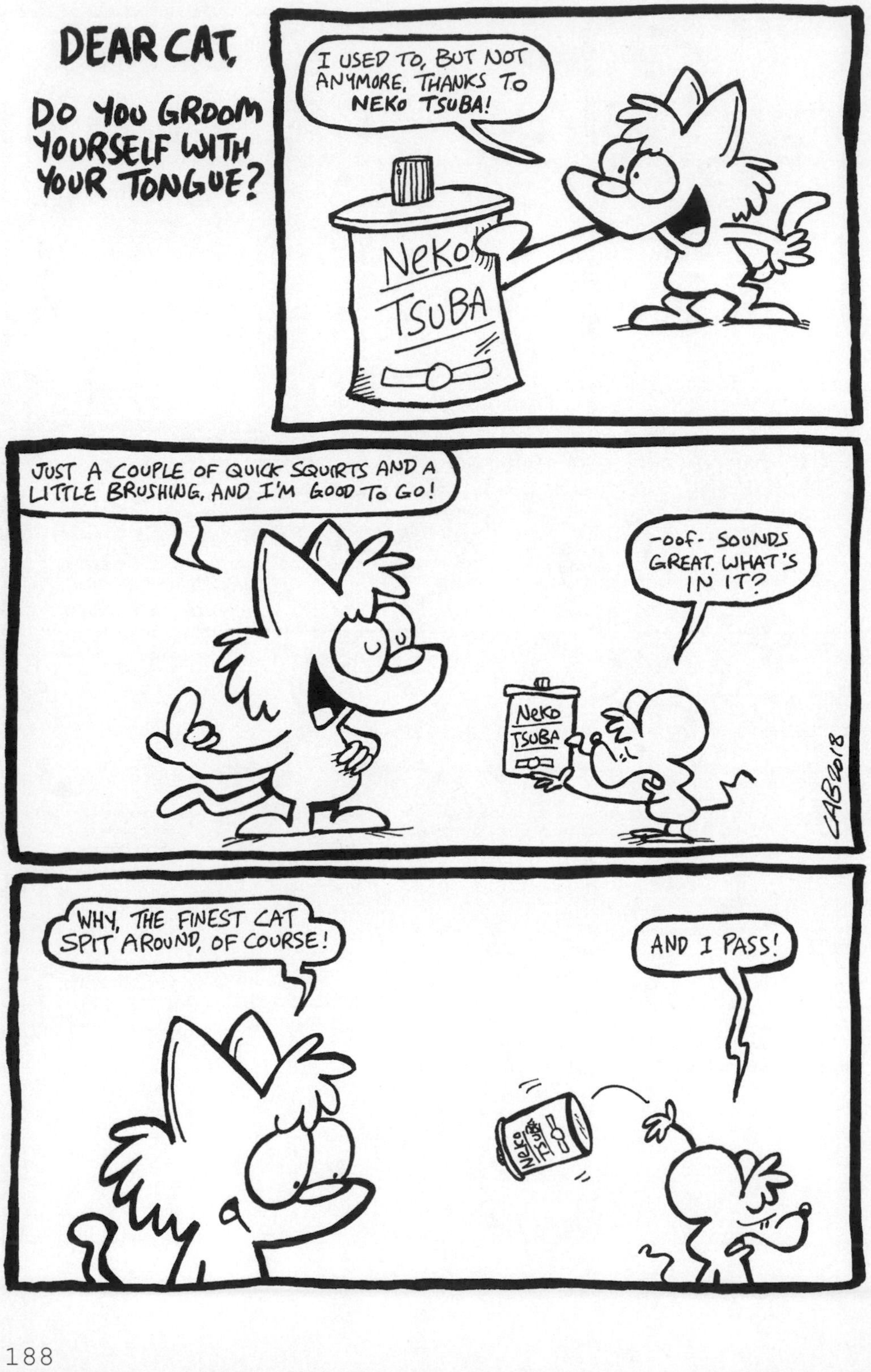
DEAR CAT,
DO YOU GROOM YOURSELF WITH YOUR TONGUE?
I USED TO, BUT NOT ANYMORE, THANKS TO NEKO TSUBA!
NEKO TSUBA
JUST A COUPLE OF QUICK SQUIRTS AND A LITTLE BRUSHING, AND I'M GOOD TO GO!
-oof- SOUNDS GREAT. WHAT'S IN IT?
NEKO TSUBA
CAB2018
WHY, THE FINEST CAT SPIT AROUND, OF COURSE!
AND I PASS!
NEKO TSUBA

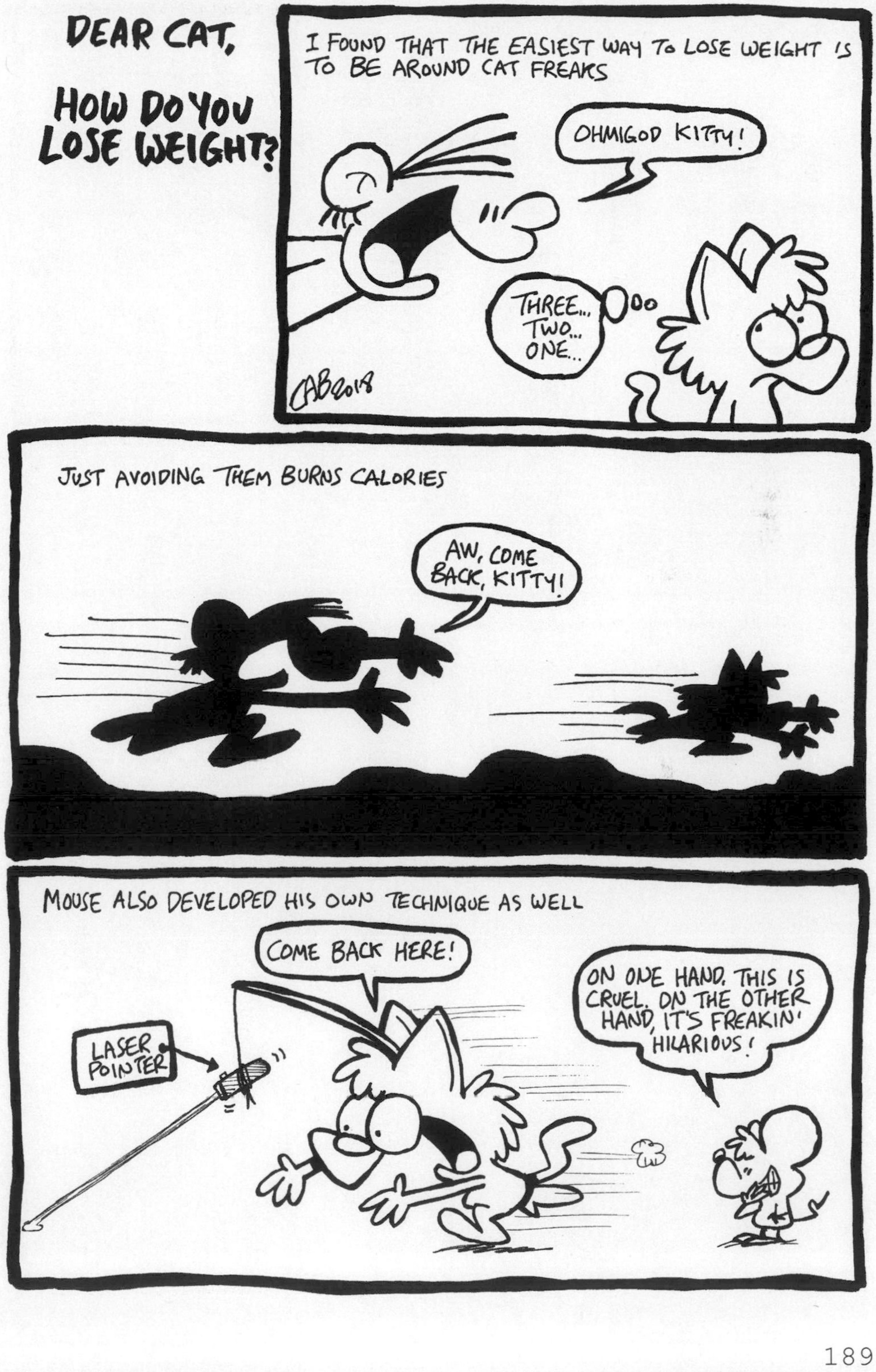
DEAR CAT,
HOW DO YOU LOSE WEIGHT?
I FOUND THAT THE EASIEST WAY TO LOSE WEIGHT IS TO BE AROUND CAT FREAKS
OHMIGOD KITTY!
THREE... TWO... ONE...
CAB 2018
JUST AVOIDING THEM BURNS CALORIES
AW, COME BACK, KITTY!
MOUSE ALSO DEVELOPED HIS OWN TECHNIQUE AS WELL
COME BACK HERE!
LASER POINTER
ON ONE HAND, THIS IS CRUEL. ON THE OTHER HAND, IT'S FREAKIN' HILARIOUS!

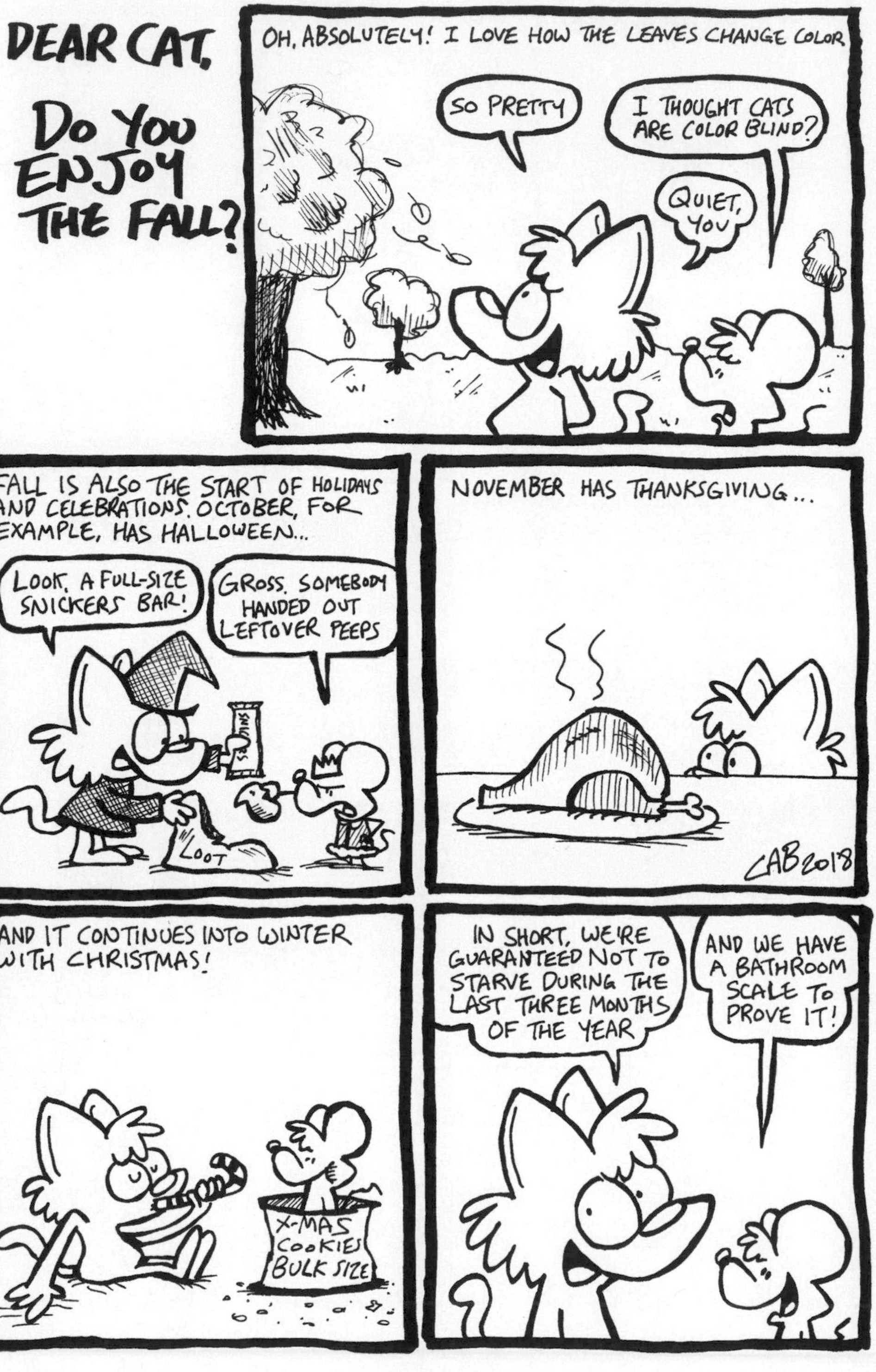
DEAR CAT,
DO YOU ENJOY THE FALL?
OH, ABSOLUTELY! I LOVE HOW THE LEAVES CHANGE COLOR
SO PRETTY
I THOUGHT CATS ARE COLOR BLIND?
QUIET, YOU
FALL IS ALSO THE START OF HOLIDAYS AND CELEBRATIONS. OCTOBER, FOR EXAMPLE, HAS HALLOWEEN...
LOOK, A FULL-SIZE SNICKERS BAR!
GROSS. SOMEBODY HANDED OUT LEFTOVER PEEPS
LOOT
NOVEMBER HAS THANKSGIVING...
CAB 2018
AND IT CONTINUES INTO WINTER WITH CHRISTMAS!
X-MAS COOKIES BULK SIZE
IN SHORT, WE'RE GUARANTEED NOT TO STARVE DURING THE LAST THREE MONTHS OF THE YEAR
AND WE HAVE A BATHROOM SCALE TO PROVE IT!

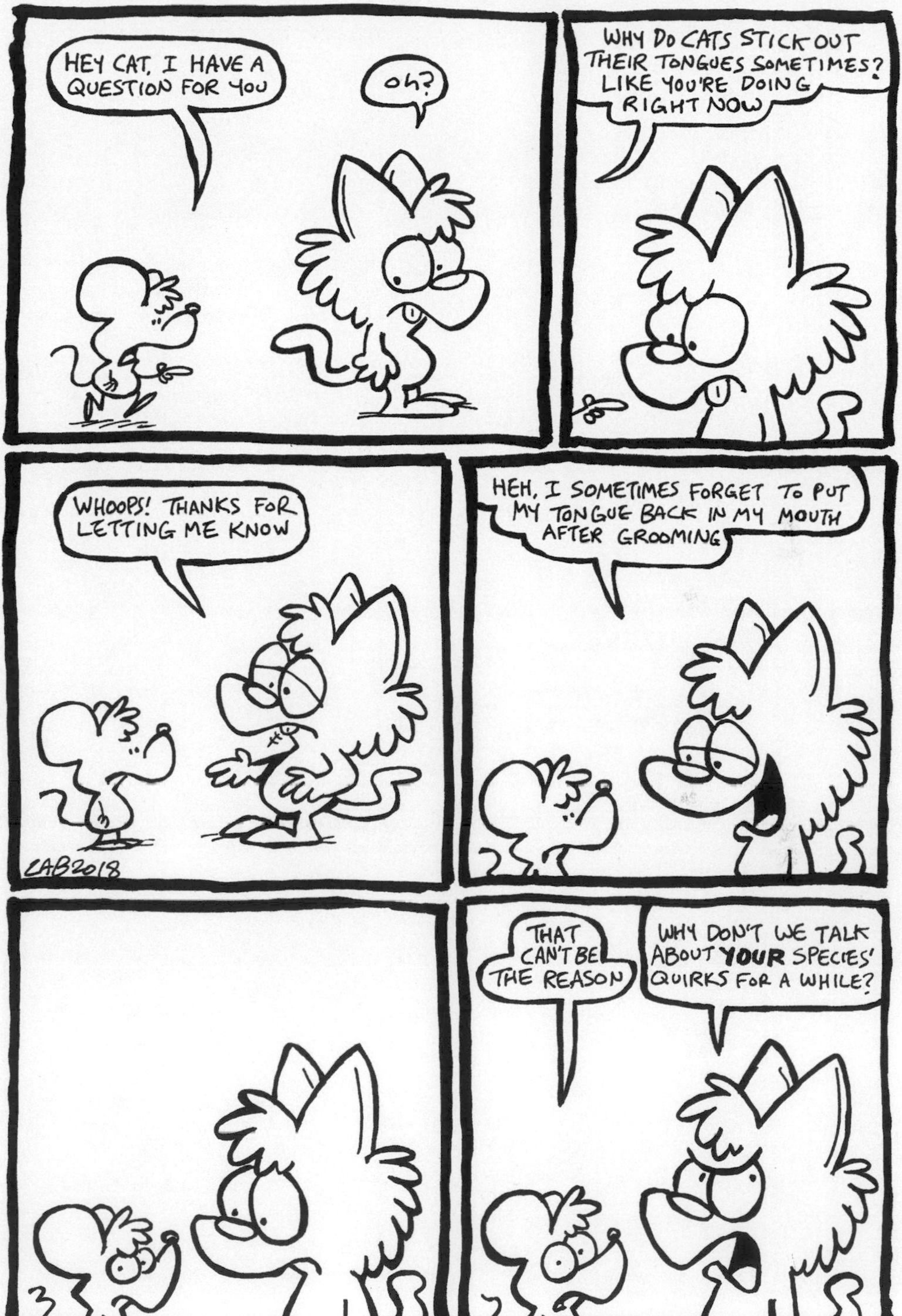
HEY CAT, I HAVE A QUESTION FOR YOU
OH?
WHY DO CATS STICK OUT THEIR TONGUES SOMETIMES? LIKE YOU'RE DOING RIGHT NOW
WHOOPS! THANKS FOR LETTING ME KNOW
CAB2018
HEH, I SOMETIMES FORGET TO PUT MY TONGUE BACK IN MY MOUTH AFTER GROOMING
THAT CAN'T BE THE REASON
WHY DON'T WE TALK ABOUT **YOUR** SPECIES' QUIRKS FOR A WHILE?

DEAR CAT,

ARE THERE CAT HAZARDS IN THE FALL SEASON?

NOT THAT I CAN THINK OF. FALL IS PRETTY SAFE

THERE ARE NO HAZARDOUS WEATHER CONDITIONS, NO EXTREME HEAT... IT'S PERFECT!

WRR

OKAY, WE **DO** HAVE TO WATCH OUT FOR THE MOWERS

WRR

CAB 2018

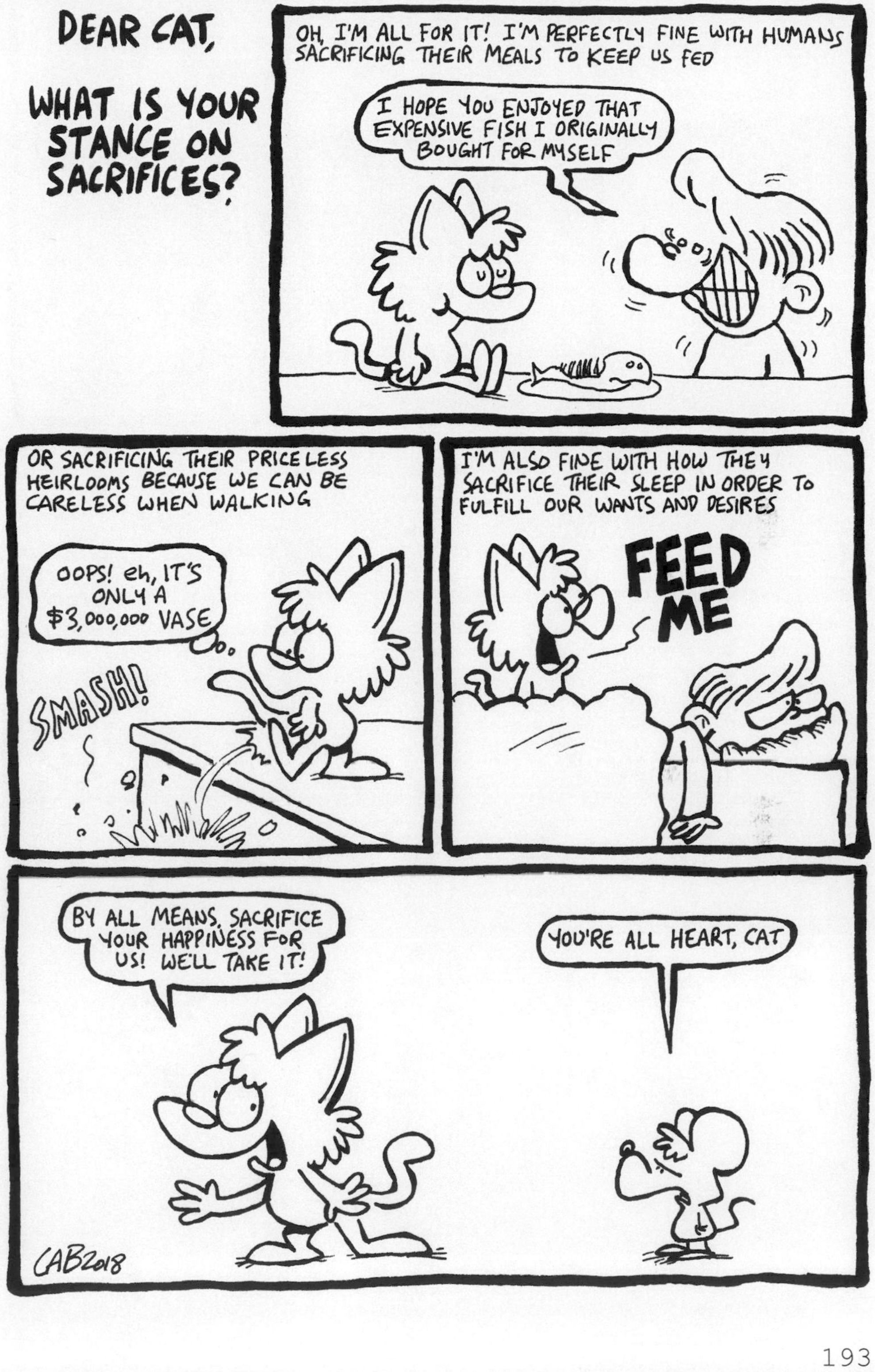
DEAR CAT,
WHAT IS YOUR STANCE ON SACRIFICES?
OH, I'M ALL FOR IT! I'M PERFECTLY FINE WITH HUMANS SACRIFICING THEIR MEALS TO KEEP US FED
I HOPE YOU ENJOYED THAT EXPENSIVE FISH I ORIGINALLY BOUGHT FOR MYSELF
OR SACRIFICING THEIR PRICELESS HEIRLOOMS BECAUSE WE CAN BE CARELESS WHEN WALKING
OOPS! eh, IT'S ONLY A $3,000,000 VASE
SMASH!
I'M ALSO FINE WITH HOW THEY SACRIFICE THEIR SLEEP IN ORDER TO FULFILL OUR WANTS AND DESIRES
FEED ME
BY ALL MEANS, SACRIFICE YOUR HAPPINESS FOR US! WE'LL TAKE IT!
YOU'RE ALL HEART, CAT
CAB2018

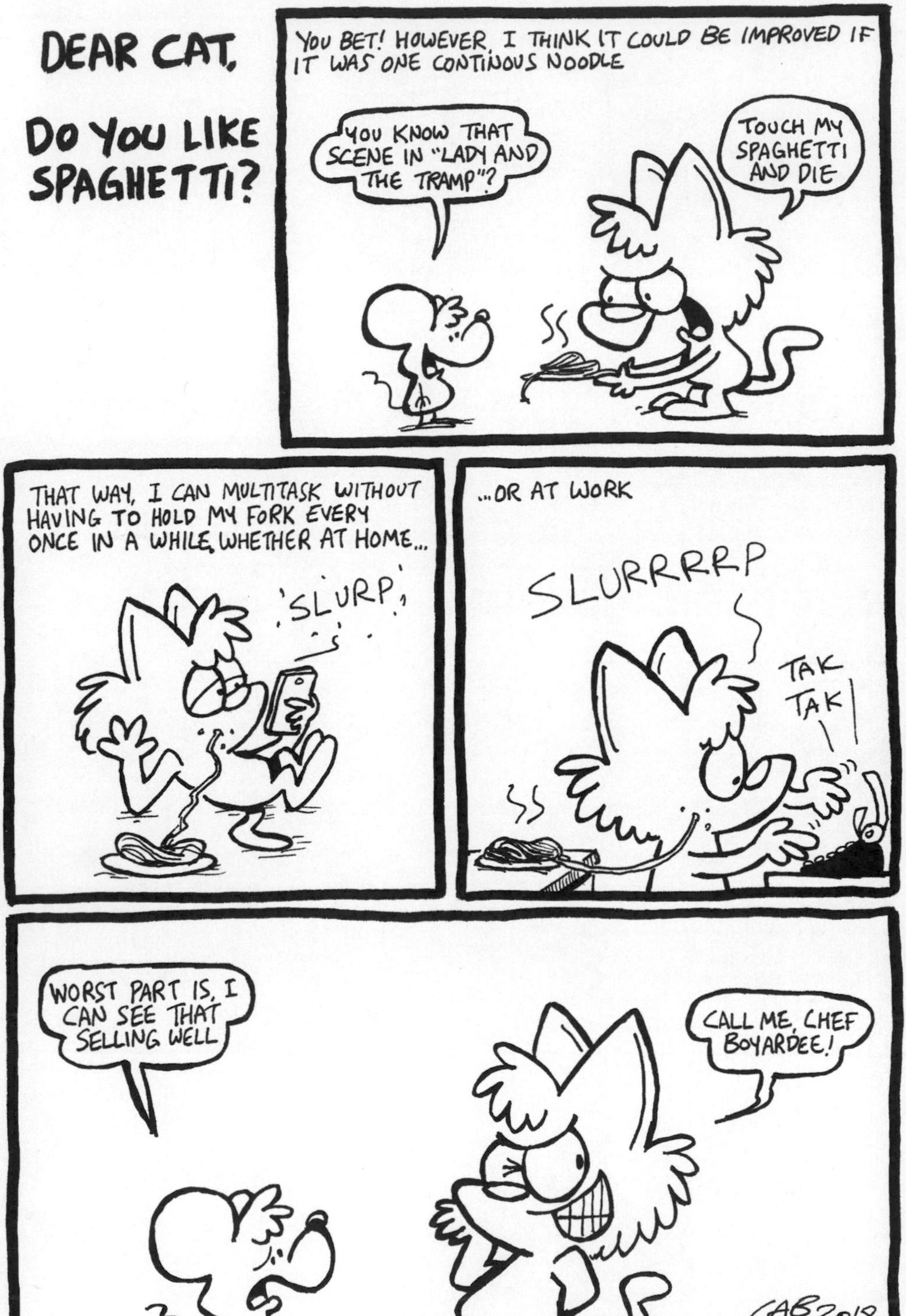
DEAR CAT,
DO YOU LIKE SPAGHETTI?
YOU BET! HOWEVER, I THINK IT COULD BE IMPROVED IF IT WAS ONE CONTINOUS NOODLE
YOU KNOW THAT SCENE IN "LADY AND THE TRAMP"?
TOUCH MY SPAGHETTI AND DIE
THAT WAY, I CAN MULTITASK WITHOUT HAVING TO HOLD MY FORK EVERY ONCE IN A WHILE, WHETHER AT HOME...
SLURP
...OR AT WORK
SLURRRRP
TAK TAK
WORST PART IS, I CAN SEE THAT SELLING WELL
CALL ME, CHEF BOYARDEE!
GAB 2018

DEAR CAT.
WHAT ARE THE SIGNS THAT YOU'RE GETTING OLD?
WELL, IT DEPENDS ON WHO YOU ASK. TAKE HUMANS, FOR EXAMPLE
DEAR LORD. THERE ARE PEOPLE BORN IN 2000 WHO CAN LEGALLY BUY TOBACCO
WOW. "THE POWERPUFF GIRLS" CAME OUT 20 YEARS AGO!
EARL'S Convenience shop
FOR US CATS, THERE ARE A FEW SIGNS. LIKE INTERACTIVE LASER POINTERS *
MAN, I REMEMBER WHEN HUMANS HAD TO MANUALLY WAVE THE POINTER AROUND BY HAND
*- ACTUAL DEVICE
THEN THERE ARE CAT VIDEOS
AW, WHAT A CUTE KITTY!
BACK IN MY DAY, HUMANS HAD TO ADMIRE CATS IN PERSON
M'ROW
LET IT GO, GRAMPS
IF YOU THINK THAT'S RIDICULOUS, YOU SHOULD LOOK AT MOUSE
I'M OLD. I REMEMBER WATCHING "BLACK PANTHER" WHEN IT CAME OUT
IT ONLY CAME OUT 8 MONTHS AGO
THAT'S NEARLY 1/3 OF MY LIFESPAN!
CAB 2018

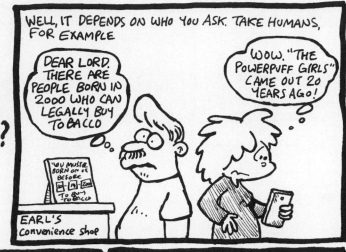

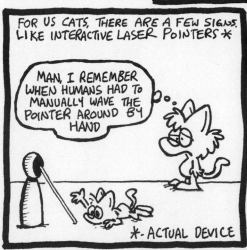

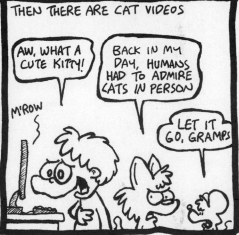

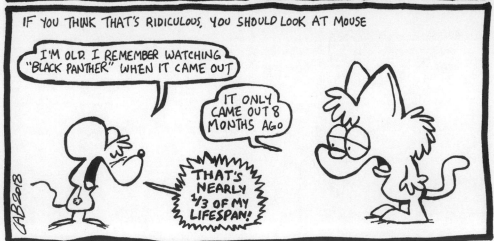

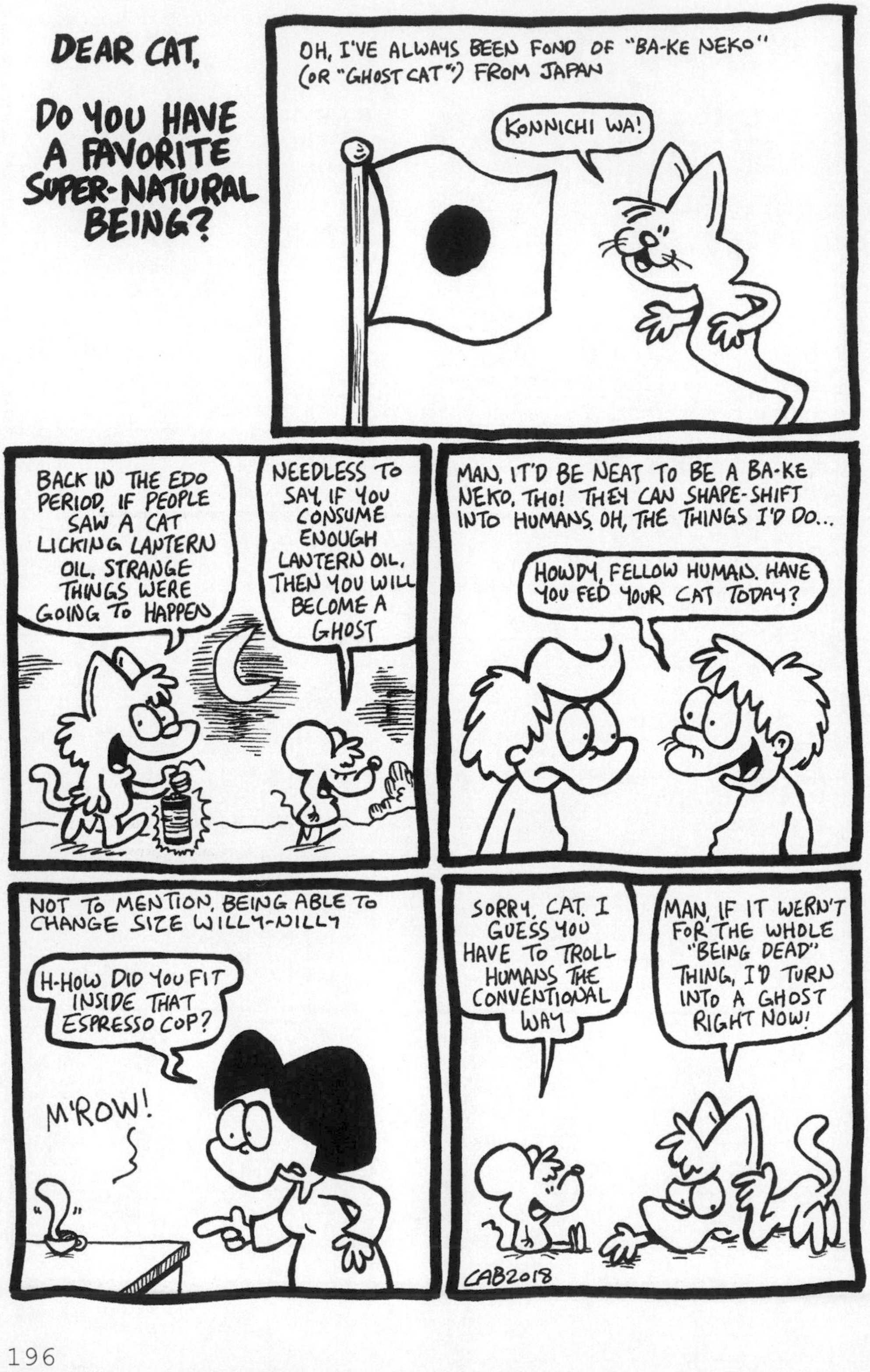
DEAR CAT,
DO YOU HAVE A FAVORITE SUPER-NATURAL BEING?
OH, I'VE ALWAYS BEEN FOND OF "BA-KE NEKO" (OR "GHOST CAT") FROM JAPAN
KONNICHI WA!
BACK IN THE EDO PERIOD, IF PEOPLE SAW A CAT LICKING LANTERN OIL, STRANGE THINGS WERE GOING TO HAPPEN
NEEDLESS TO SAY, IF YOU CONSUME ENOUGH LANTERN OIL, THEN YOU WILL BECOME A GHOST
MAN, IT'D BE NEAT TO BE A BA-KE NEKO, THO! THEY CAN SHAPE-SHIFT INTO HUMANS. OH, THE THINGS I'D DO...
HOWDY, FELLOW HUMAN. HAVE YOU FED YOUR CAT TODAY?
NOT TO MENTION, BEING ABLE TO CHANGE SIZE WILLY-NILLY
H-HOW DID YOU FIT INSIDE THAT ESPRESSO CUP?
M'ROW!
SORRY, CAT. I GUESS YOU HAVE TO TROLL HUMANS THE CONVENTIONAL WAY
MAN, IF IT WERN'T FOR THE WHOLE "BEING DEAD" THING, I'D TURN INTO A GHOST RIGHT NOW!
CAB2018

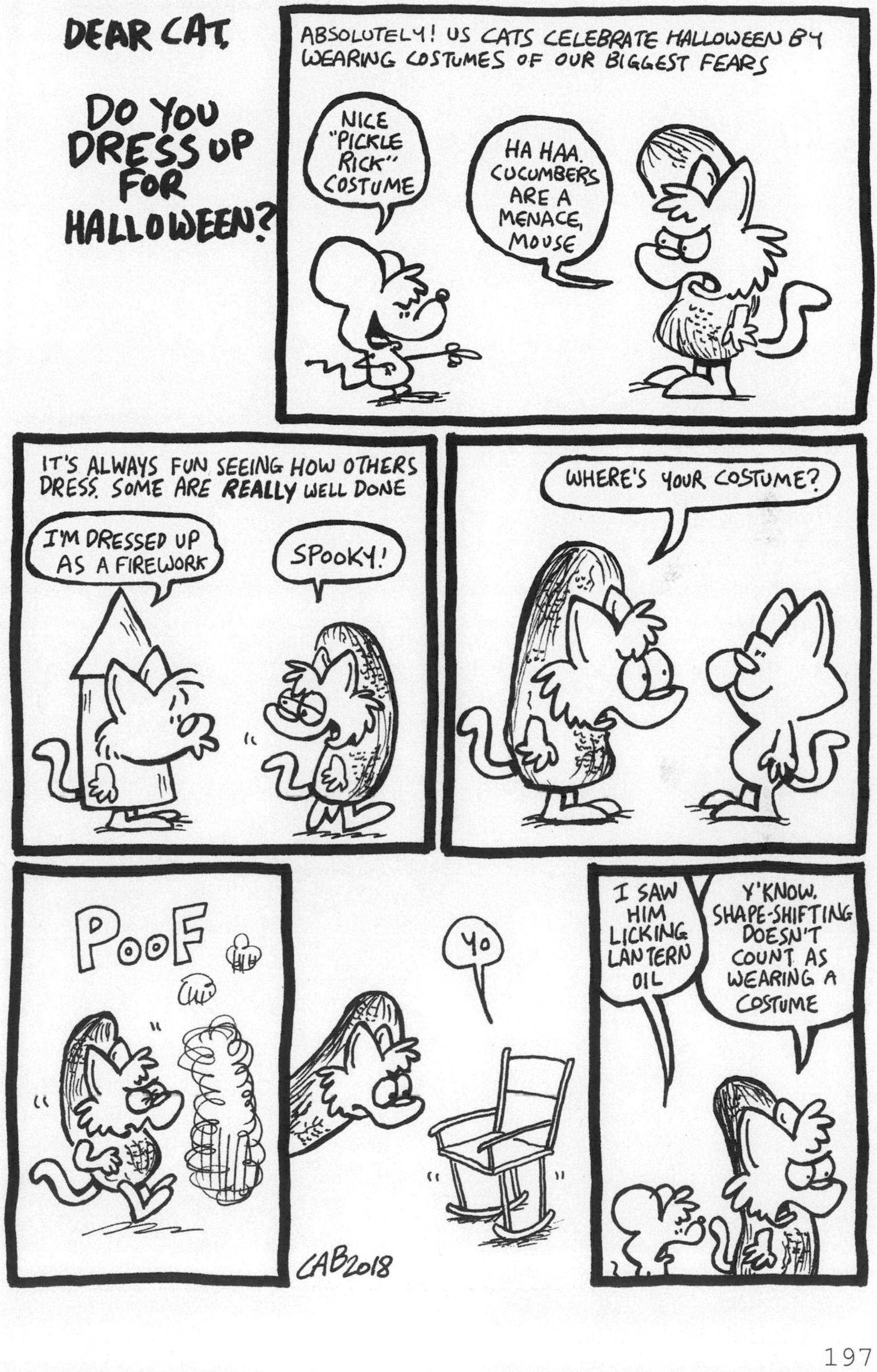
DEAR CAT,
DO YOU DRESS UP FOR HALLOWEEN?
ABSOLUTELY! US CATS CELEBRATE HALLOWEEN BY WEARING COSTUMES OF OUR BIGGEST FEARS
NICE "PICKLE RICK" COSTUME
HA HAA. CUCUMBERS ARE A MENACE, MOUSE
IT'S ALWAYS FUN SEEING HOW OTHERS DRESS. SOME ARE **REALLY** WELL DONE
I'M DRESSED UP AS A FIREWORK
SPOOKY!
WHERE'S YOUR COSTUME?
POOF
YO
I SAW HIM LICKING LANTERN OIL
Y'KNOW. SHAPE-SHIFTING DOESN'T COUNT AS WEARING A COSTUME
CAB 2018

DEAR CAT,

HOW DO YOU SAVE ON TRAVEL?

THERE ARE MANY WAYS! PEOPLE ALWAYS COMPLAIN ABOUT THE COST OF TRAVEL, BUT FOLLOW MY ADVICE AND YOU SHOULD SAVE BIG!

FOR ONLY $53 WE'LL CATAPULT YOU TO THE DIRECTION OF YOUR DESTINATION

CATAPULT CHEAP TRAVEL

FOR STARTERS, TRY MAILING YOURSELF! A PRIORITY POSTAGE RATE IS STILL A LOT CHEAPER THAN EVEN THE CHEAPEST PLANE TICKETS

AND I HAVE MORE LEG ROOM, TOO

TO: TOKYO

YOU CAN ALSO TRY BEFRIENDING A GIANT BIRD AS WELL

BANG

JUST BE CAREFUL TO AVOID HUNTING SEASON

POW

BLAST

IF NONE OF THAT WORKS, MAY I SUGGEST STOWING AWAY INSIDE SOMEONE'S LUGGAGE?

THERE'S A $25 FEE FOR LUGGAGE CHECK-IN

SUCKER...

CAB 2018

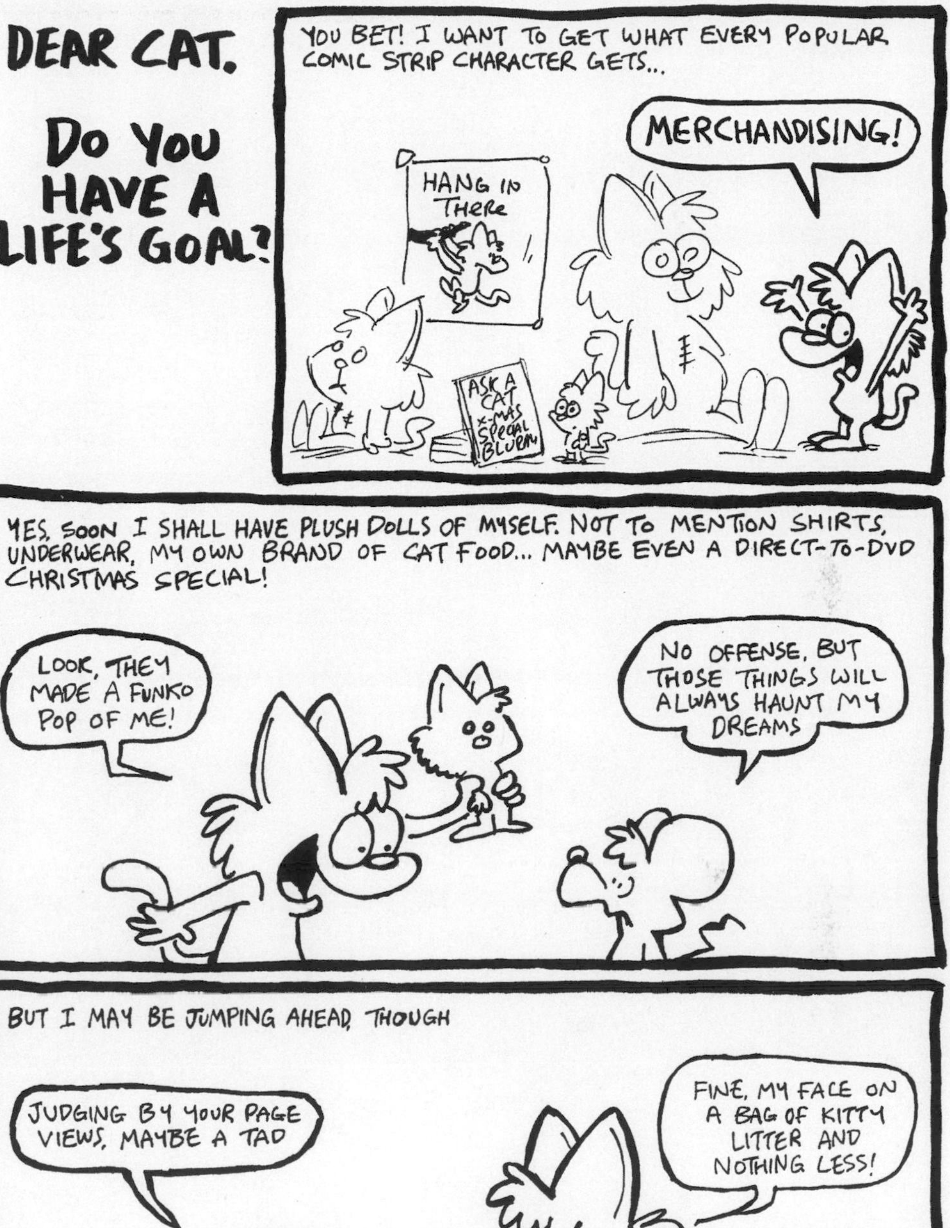
DEAR CAT.
DO YOU HAVE A LIFE'S GOAL?
YOU BET! I WANT TO GET WHAT EVERY POPULAR COMIC STRIP CHARACTER GETS...
MERCHANDISING!
HANG IN THERE
ASK A CAT X-MAS SPECIAL BLU-RAY
YES, SOON I SHALL HAVE PLUSH DOLLS OF MYSELF. NOT TO MENTION SHIRTS, UNDERWEAR, MY OWN BRAND OF CAT FOOD... MAYBE EVEN A DIRECT-TO-DVD CHRISTMAS SPECIAL!
LOOK, THEY MADE A FUNKO POP OF ME!
NO OFFENSE, BUT THOSE THINGS WILL ALWAYS HAUNT MY DREAMS
BUT I MAY BE JUMPING AHEAD, THOUGH
JUDGING BY YOUR PAGE VIEWS, MAYBE A TAD
FINE, MY FACE ON A BAG OF KITTY LITTER AND NOTHING LESS!
CAB 2018

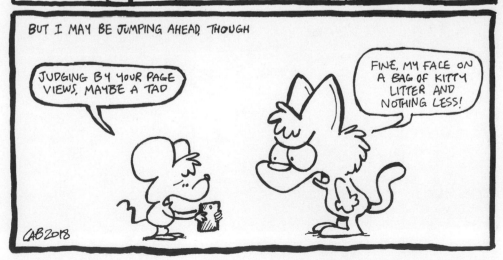

DEAR CAT,

HOW DO I GET RID OF MY HEADACHE?

AH, THE DREADED HEADACHE. WE'VE ALL BEEN THERE

I THOUGHT CATS HATED WATER

YOU GOTTA DO WHAT YOU GOTTA DO

THE STANDARD ASPIRIN IS ALWAYS A GOOD CHOICE

ASPIRIN

YOU CAN ALSO DO SOMETHING THAT MAKES YOU FORGET YOUR HEADACHE

WELL (HUFF) IT WORKS!

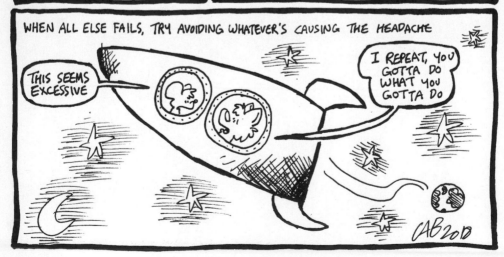

WHEN ALL ELSE FAILS, TRY AVOIDING WHATEVER'S CAUSING THE HEADACHE

THIS SEEMS EXCESSIVE

I REPEAT, YOU GOTTA DO WHAT YOU GOTTA DO

CAB 2010

DEAR CAT,

WHAT KIND OF CHRISTMAS TREE DO YOU ENJOY CLIMBING?

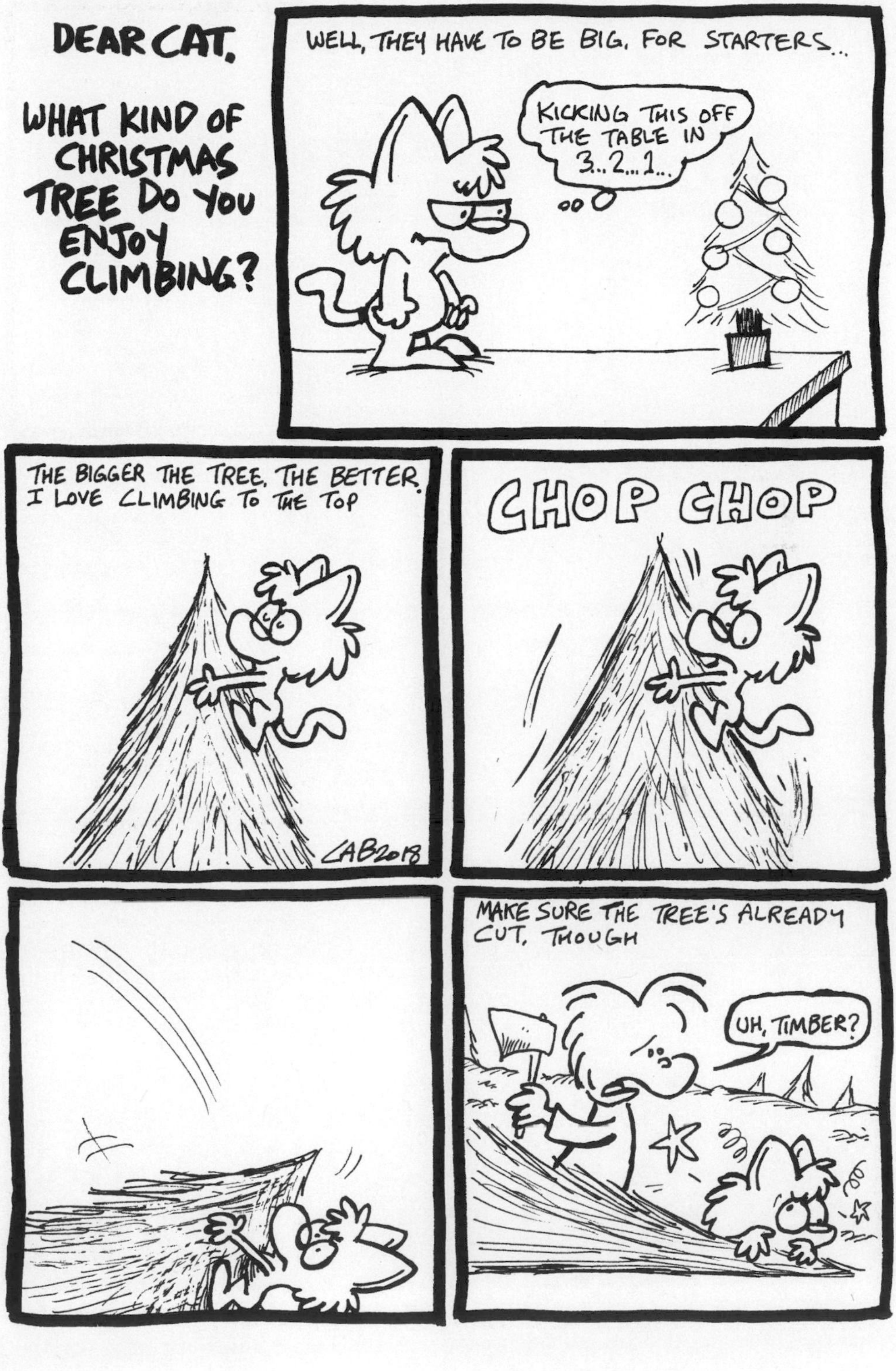
WELL, THEY HAVE TO BE BIG, FOR STARTERS...
KICKING THIS OFF THE TABLE IN 3...2...1...
THE BIGGER THE TREE, THE BETTER. I LOVE CLIMBING TO THE TOP
CAB2018
CHOP CHOP
MAKE SURE THE TREE'S ALREADY CUT, THOUGH
UH, TIMBER?

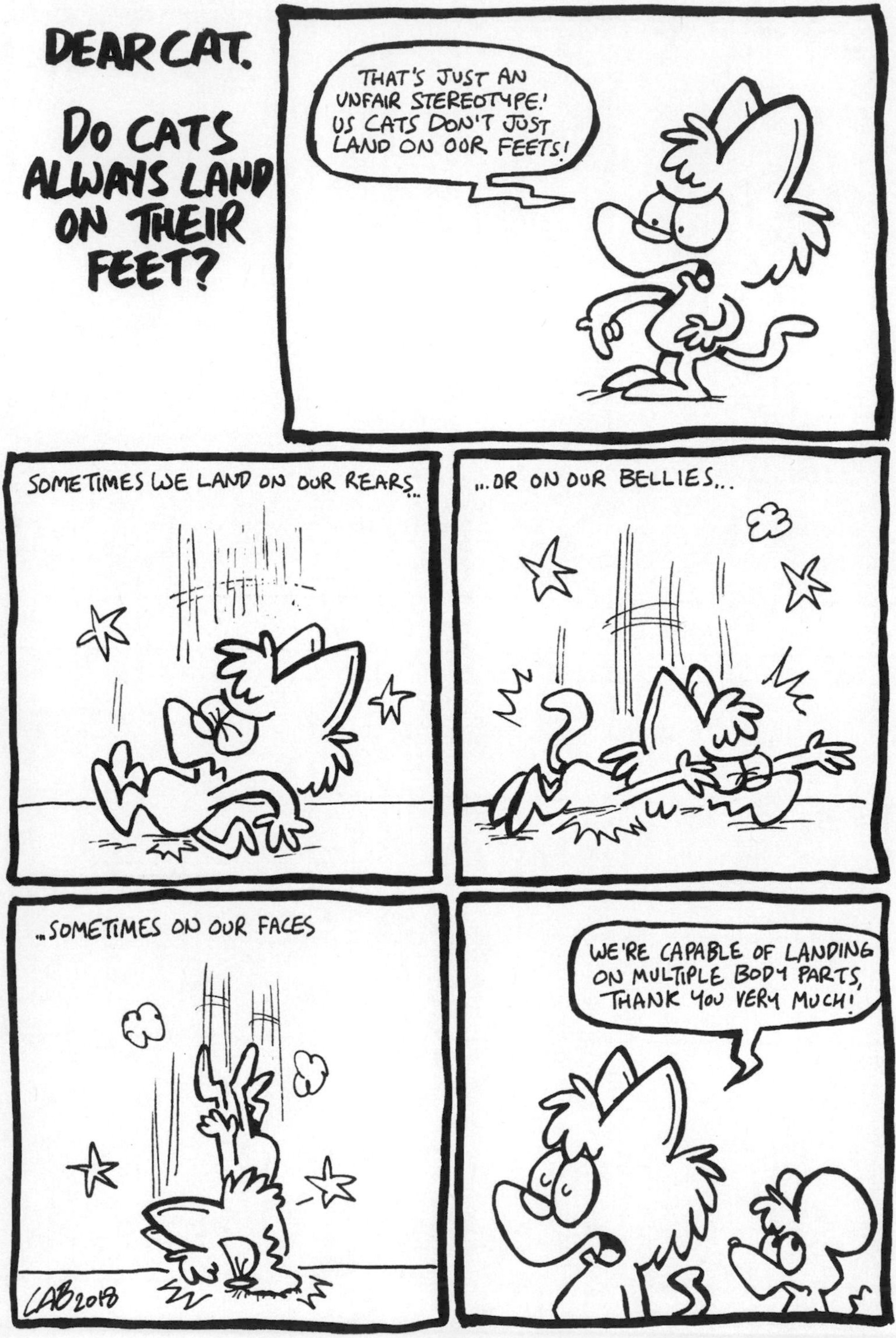
DEAR CAT.
DO CATS ALWAYS LAND ON THEIR FEET?
THAT'S JUST AN UNFAIR STEREOTYPE! US CATS DON'T JUST LAND ON OUR FEETS!
SOMETIMES WE LAND ON OUR REARS...
...OR ON OUR BELLIES...
..SOMETIMES ON OUR FACES
WE'RE CAPABLE OF LANDING ON MULTIPLE BODY PARTS, THANK YOU VERY MUCH!
LAB 2018

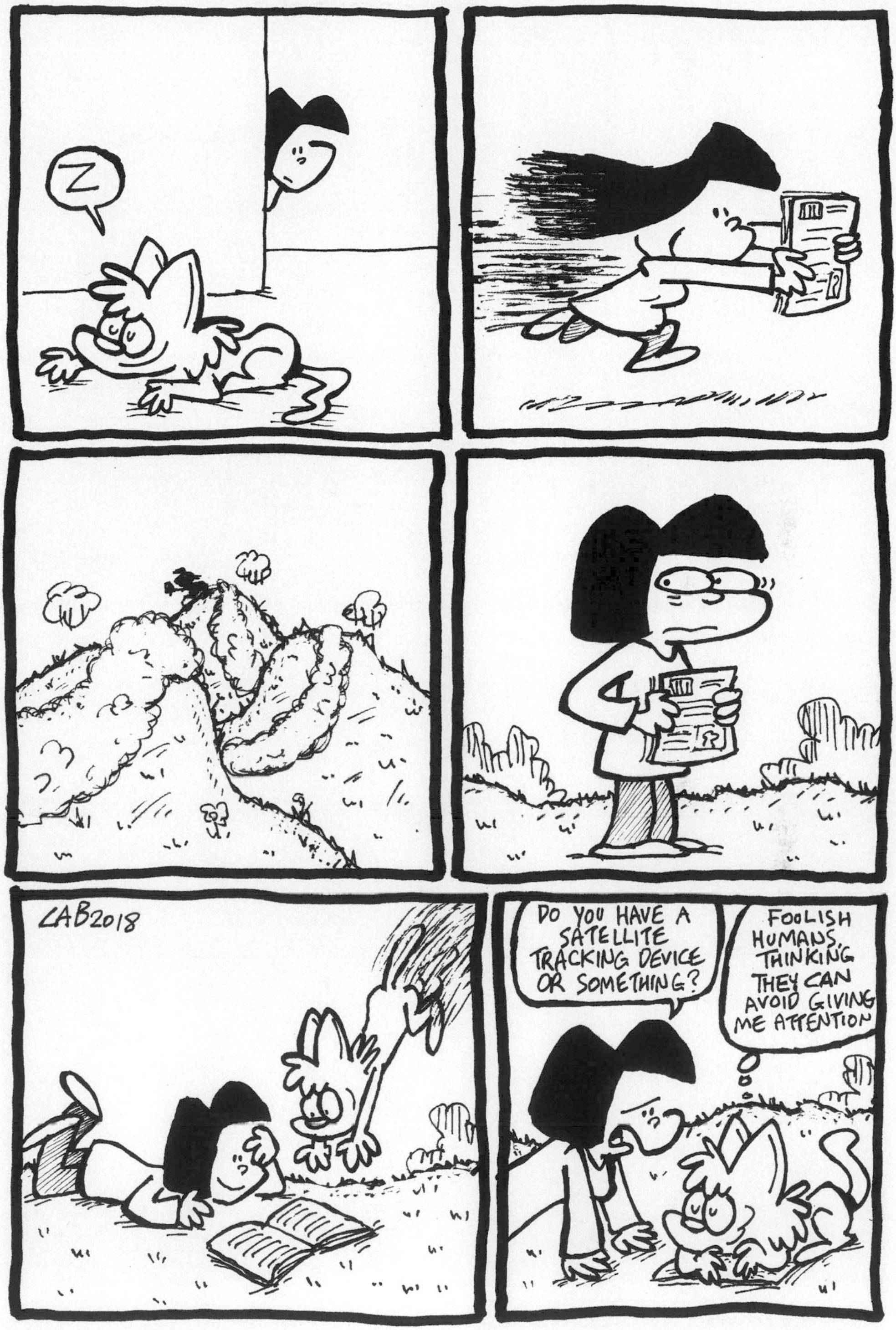
Z
CAB2018
DO YOU HAVE A SATELLITE TRACKING DEVICE OR SOMETHING?
FOOLISH HUMANS, THINKING THEY CAN AVOID GIVING ME ATTENTION

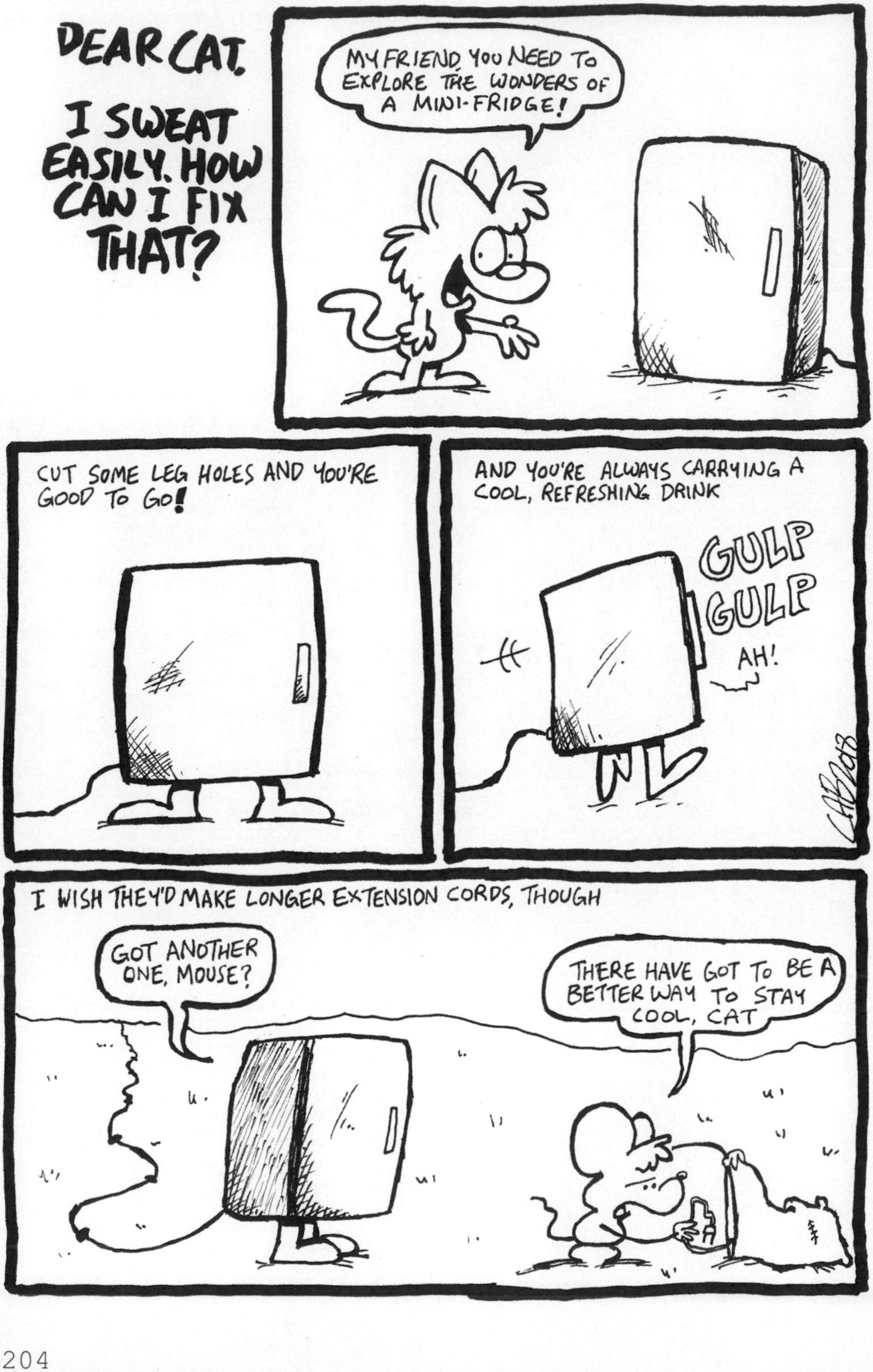
DEAR CAT.
I SWEAT EASILY. HOW CAN I FIX THAT?
MY FRIEND, YOU NEED TO EXPLORE THE WONDERS OF A MINI-FRIDGE!
CUT SOME LEG HOLES AND YOU'RE GOOD TO GO!
AND YOU'RE ALWAYS CARRYING A COOL, REFRESHING DRINK
GULP
GULP
AH!
I WISH THEY'D MAKE LONGER EXTENSION CORDS, THOUGH
GOT ANOTHER ONE, MOUSE?
THERE HAVE GOT TO BE A BETTER WAY TO STAY COOL, CAT

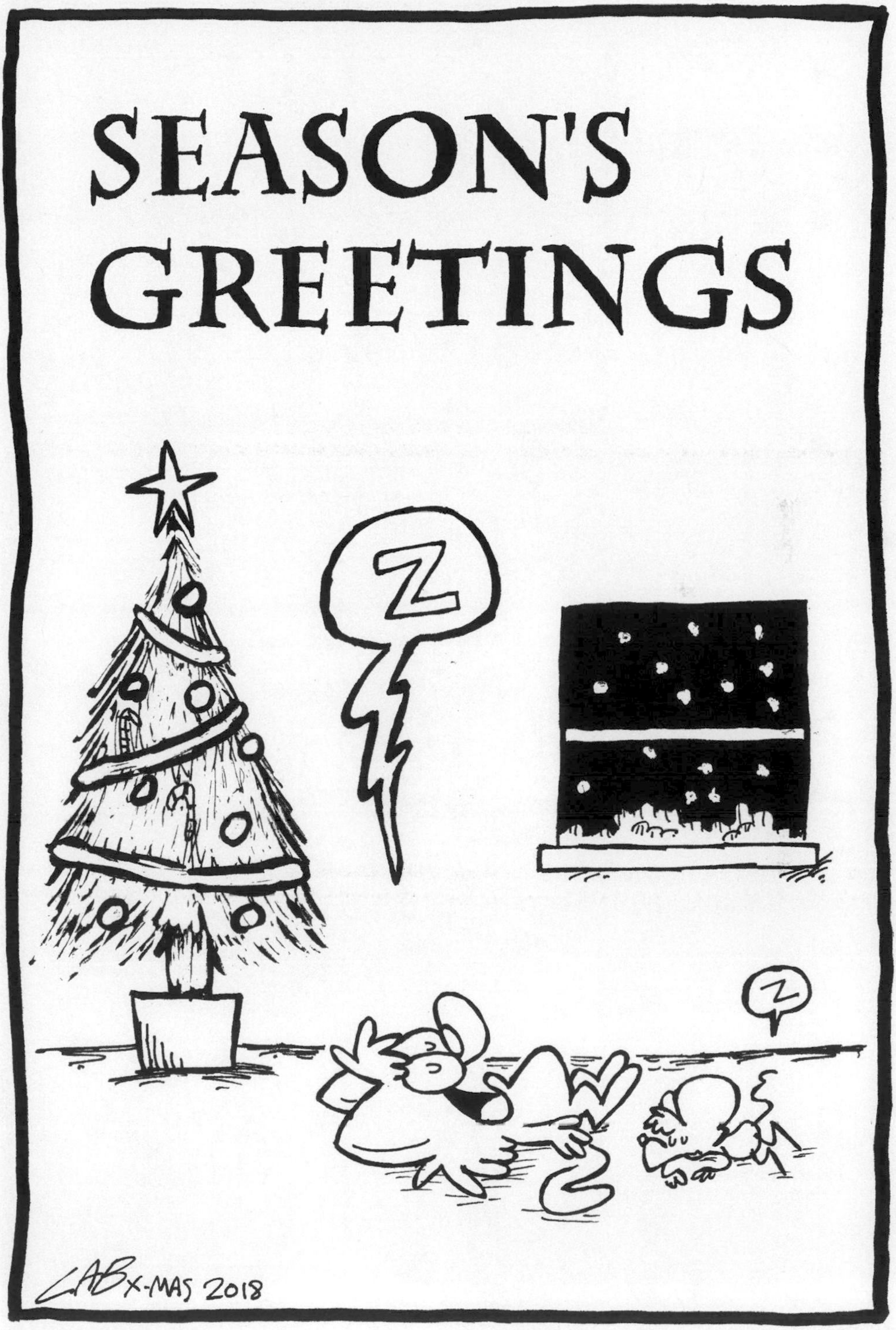
SEASON'S GREETINGS
Z
Z
CAB X-MAS 2018

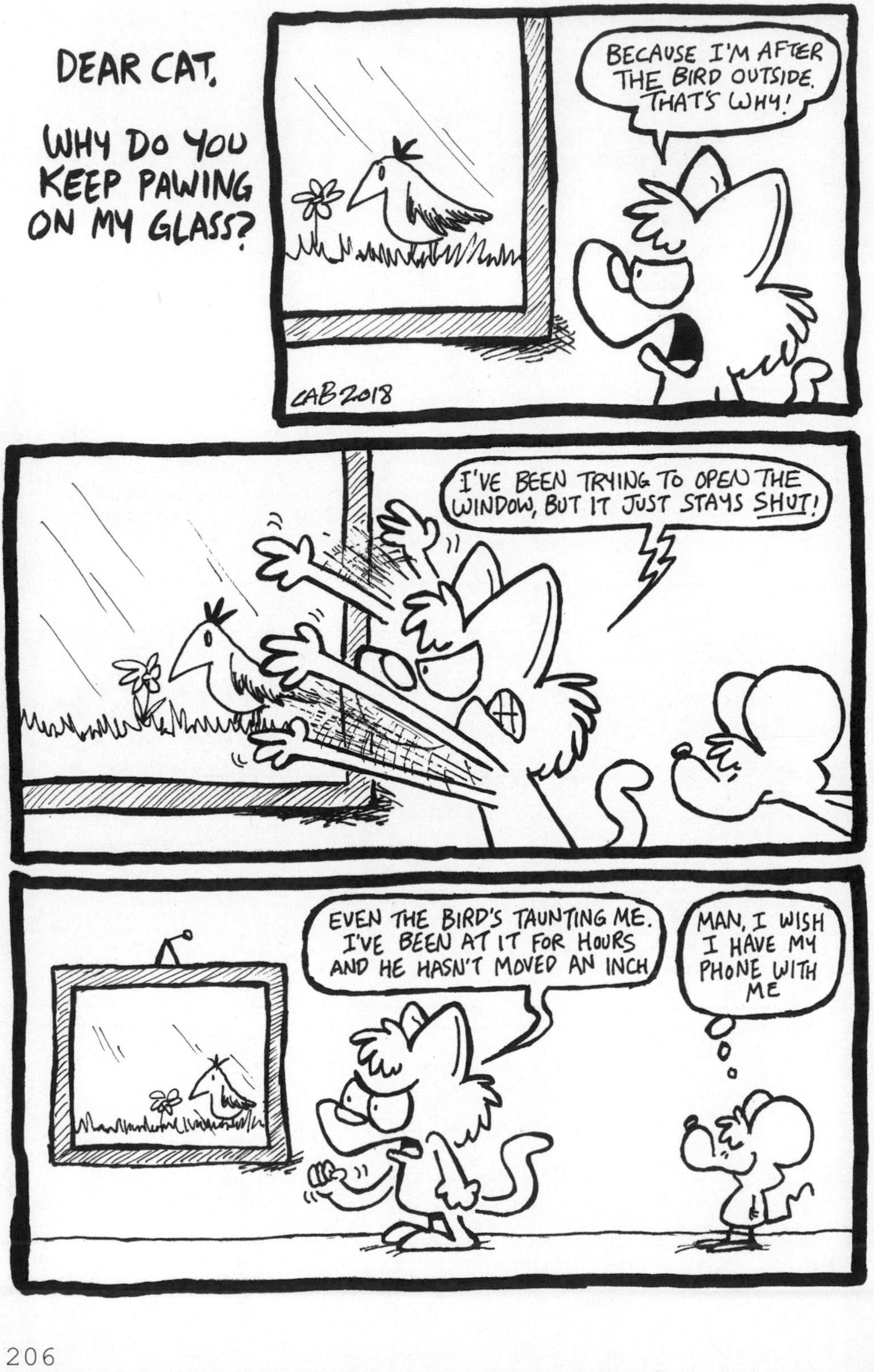
DEAR CAT.
WHY DO YOU KEEP PAWING ON MY GLASS?
BECAUSE I'M AFTER THE BIRD OUTSIDE. THAT'S WHY!
CAB 2018
I'VE BEEN TRYING TO OPEN THE WINDOW, BUT IT JUST STAYS SHUT!
EVEN THE BIRD'S TAUNTING ME. I'VE BEEN AT IT FOR HOURS AND HE HASN'T MOVED AN INCH
MAN, I WISH I HAVE MY PHONE WITH ME

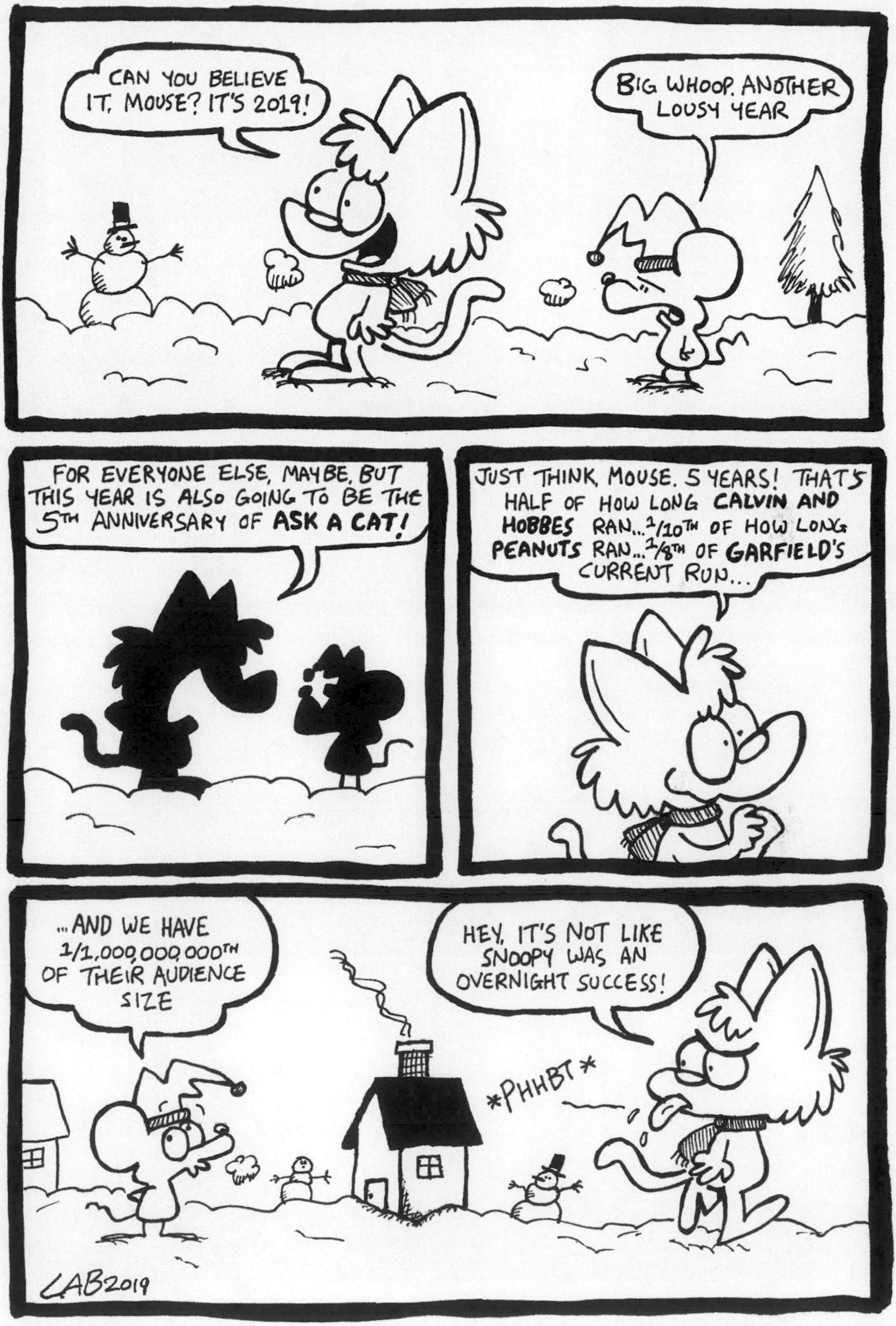
CAN YOU BELIEVE IT, MOUSE? IT'S 2019!
BIG WHOOP. ANOTHER LOUSY YEAR
FOR EVERYONE ELSE, MAYBE. BUT THIS YEAR IS ALSO GOING TO BE THE 5TH ANNIVERSARY OF ASK A CAT!
JUST THINK, MOUSE. 5 YEARS! THAT'S HALF OF HOW LONG CALVIN AND HOBBES RAN... 1/10TH OF HOW LONG PEANUTS RAN... 1/8TH OF GARFIELD'S CURRENT RUN...
...AND WE HAVE 1/1,000,000,000TH OF THEIR AUDIENCE SIZE
HEY, IT'S NOT LIKE SNOOPY WAS AN OVERNIGHT SUCCESS!
PHHBT
LAB 2019

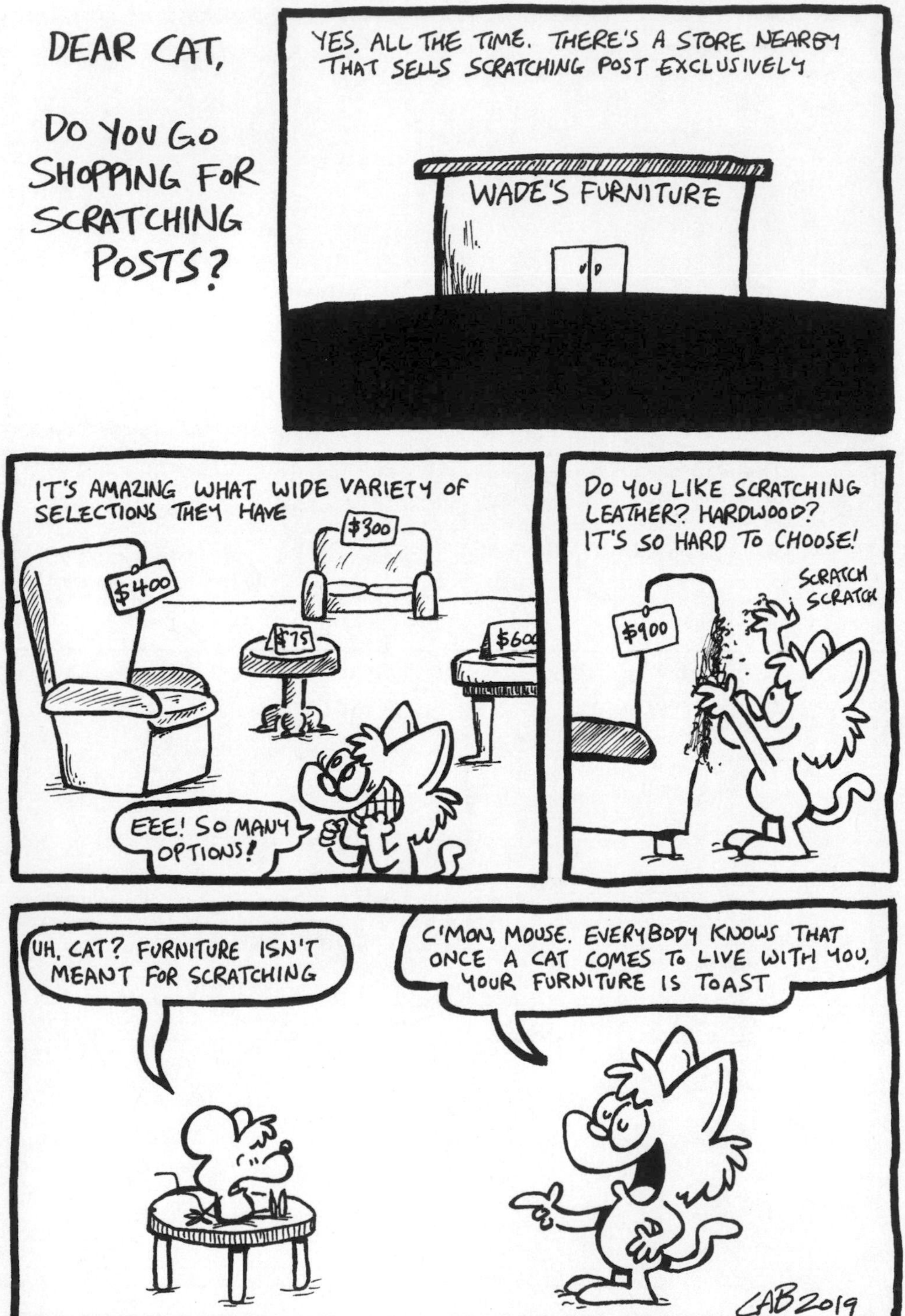
DEAR CAT,
DO YOU GO SHOPPING FOR SCRATCHING POSTS?
YES, ALL THE TIME. THERE'S A STORE NEARBY THAT SELLS SCRATCHING POST EXCLUSIVELY
WADE'S FURNITURE
IT'S AMAZING WHAT WIDE VARIETY OF SELECTIONS THEY HAVE
$300
$400
$75
$600
EEE! SO MANY OPTIONS!
DO YOU LIKE SCRATCHING LEATHER? HARDWOOD? IT'S SO HARD TO CHOOSE!
SCRATCH SCRATCH
$900
UH, CAT? FURNITURE ISN'T MEANT FOR SCRATCHING
C'MON, MOUSE. EVERYBODY KNOWS THAT ONCE A CAT COMES TO LIVE WITH YOU, YOUR FURNITURE IS TOAST
CAB 2019

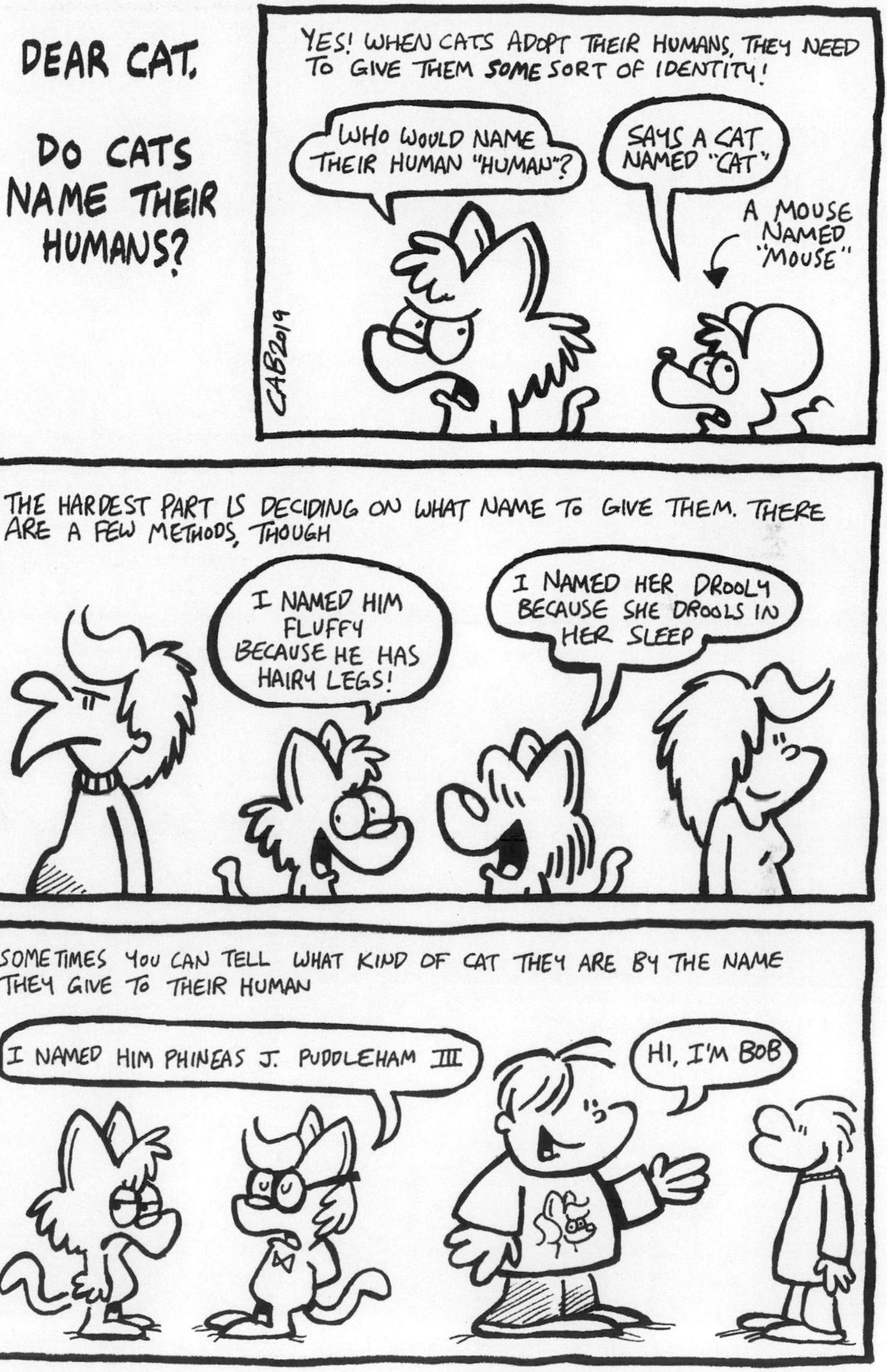
DEAR CAT,
DO CATS NAME THEIR HUMANS?
YES! WHEN CATS ADOPT THEIR HUMANS, THEY NEED TO GIVE THEM SOME SORT OF IDENTITY!
WHO WOULD NAME THEIR HUMAN "HUMAN"?
SAYS A CAT NAMED "CAT"
A MOUSE NAMED "MOUSE"
CAB2019
THE HARDEST PART IS DECIDING ON WHAT NAME TO GIVE THEM. THERE ARE A FEW METHODS, THOUGH
I NAMED HIM FLUFFY BECAUSE HE HAS HAIRY LEGS!
I NAMED HER DROOLY BECAUSE SHE DROOLS IN HER SLEEP
SOMETIMES YOU CAN TELL WHAT KIND OF CAT THEY ARE BY THE NAME THEY GIVE TO THEIR HUMAN
I NAMED HIM PHINEAS J. PUDDLEHAM III
HI, I'M BOB

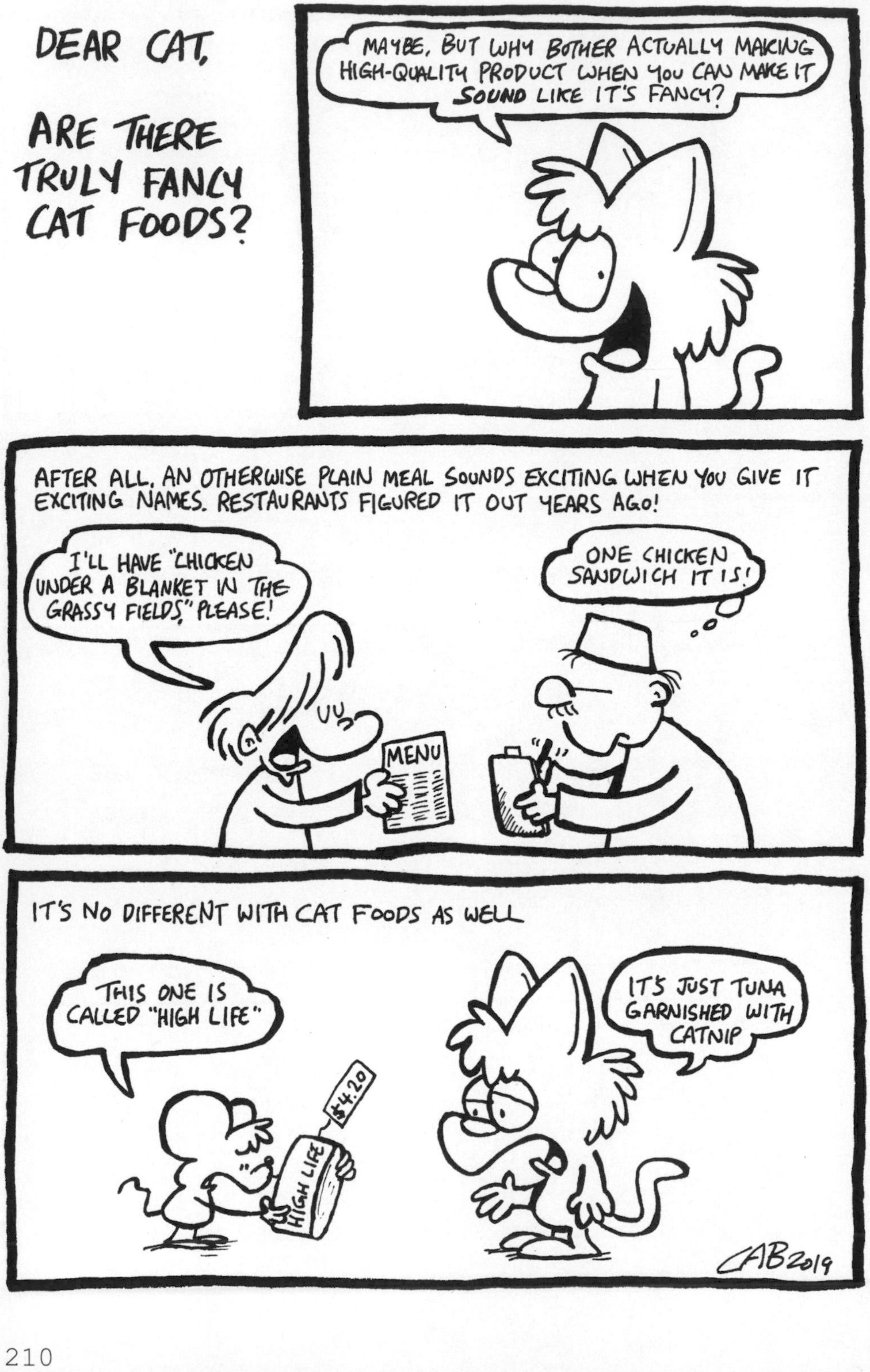
DEAR CAT,
ARE THERE TRULY FANCY CAT FOODS?
MAYBE, BUT WHY BOTHER ACTUALLY MAKING HIGH-QUALITY PRODUCT WHEN YOU CAN MAKE IT SOUND LIKE IT'S FANCY?
AFTER ALL, AN OTHERWISE PLAIN MEAL SOUNDS EXCITING WHEN YOU GIVE IT EXCITING NAMES. RESTAURANTS FIGURED IT OUT YEARS AGO!
I'LL HAVE "CHICKEN UNDER A BLANKET IN THE GRASSY FIELDS," PLEASE!
MENU
ONE CHICKEN SANDWICH IT IS!
IT'S NO DIFFERENT WITH CAT FOODS AS WELL
THIS ONE IS CALLED "HIGH LIFE"
$4.20
HIGH LIFE
IT'S JUST TUNA GARNISHED WITH CATNIP
CAB 2019

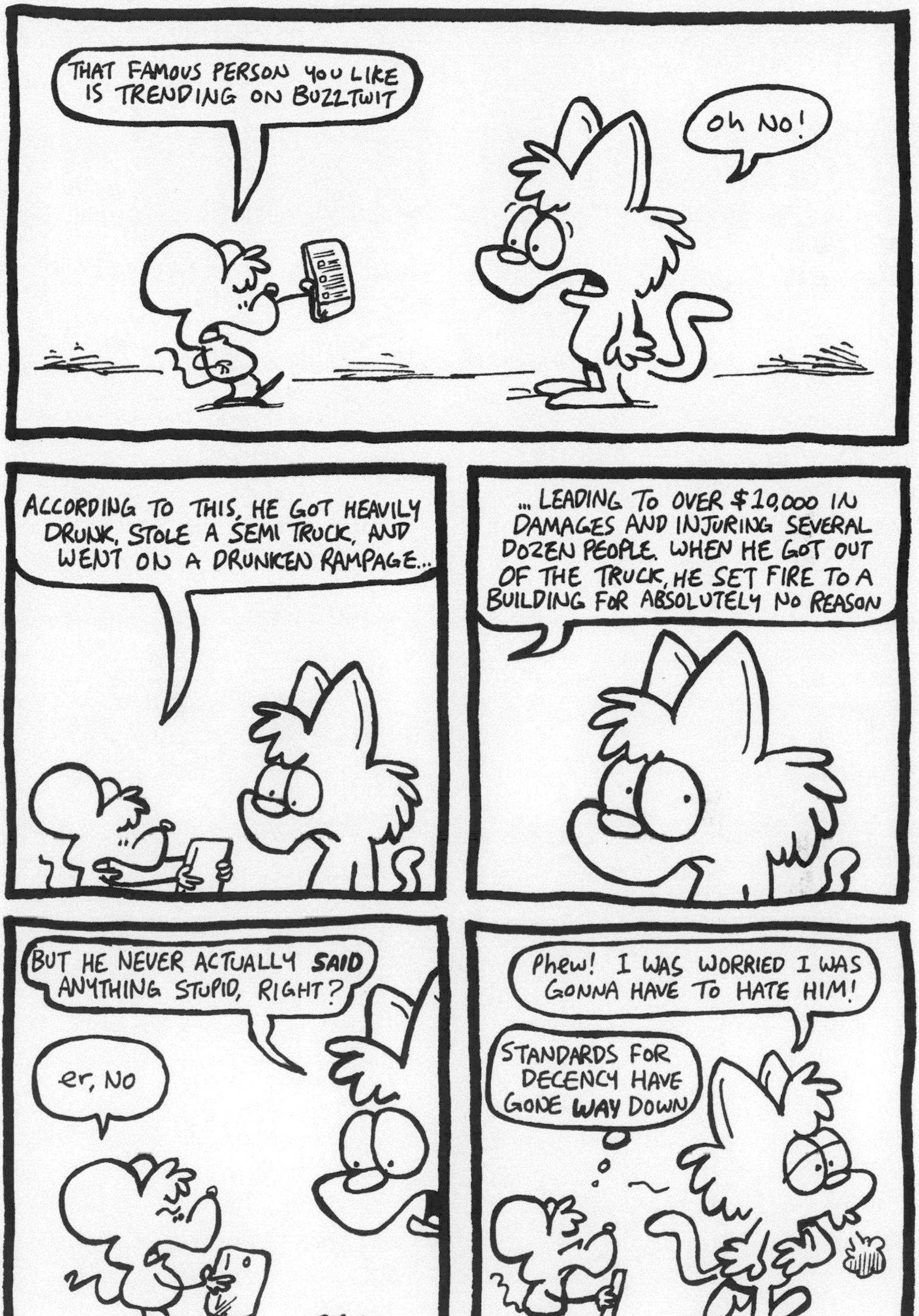
THAT FAMOUS PERSON YOU LIKE IS TRENDING ON BUZZTWIT
Oh NO!
ACCORDING TO THIS, HE GOT HEAVILY DRUNK, STOLE A SEMI TRUCK, AND WENT ON A DRUNKEN RAMPAGE...
... LEADING TO OVER $10,000 IN DAMAGES AND INJURING SEVERAL DOZEN PEOPLE. WHEN HE GOT OUT OF THE TRUCK, HE SET FIRE TO A BUILDING FOR ABSOLUTELY NO REASON
BUT HE NEVER ACTUALLY SAID ANYTHING STUPID, RIGHT?
er, NO
CAB2019
Phew! I WAS WORRIED I WAS GONNA HAVE TO HATE HIM!
STANDARDS FOR DECENCY HAVE GONE WAY DOWN

DEAR CAT.

WHAT SPELLS WOULD YOU CAST IF YOU GOT A MAGIC WAND?

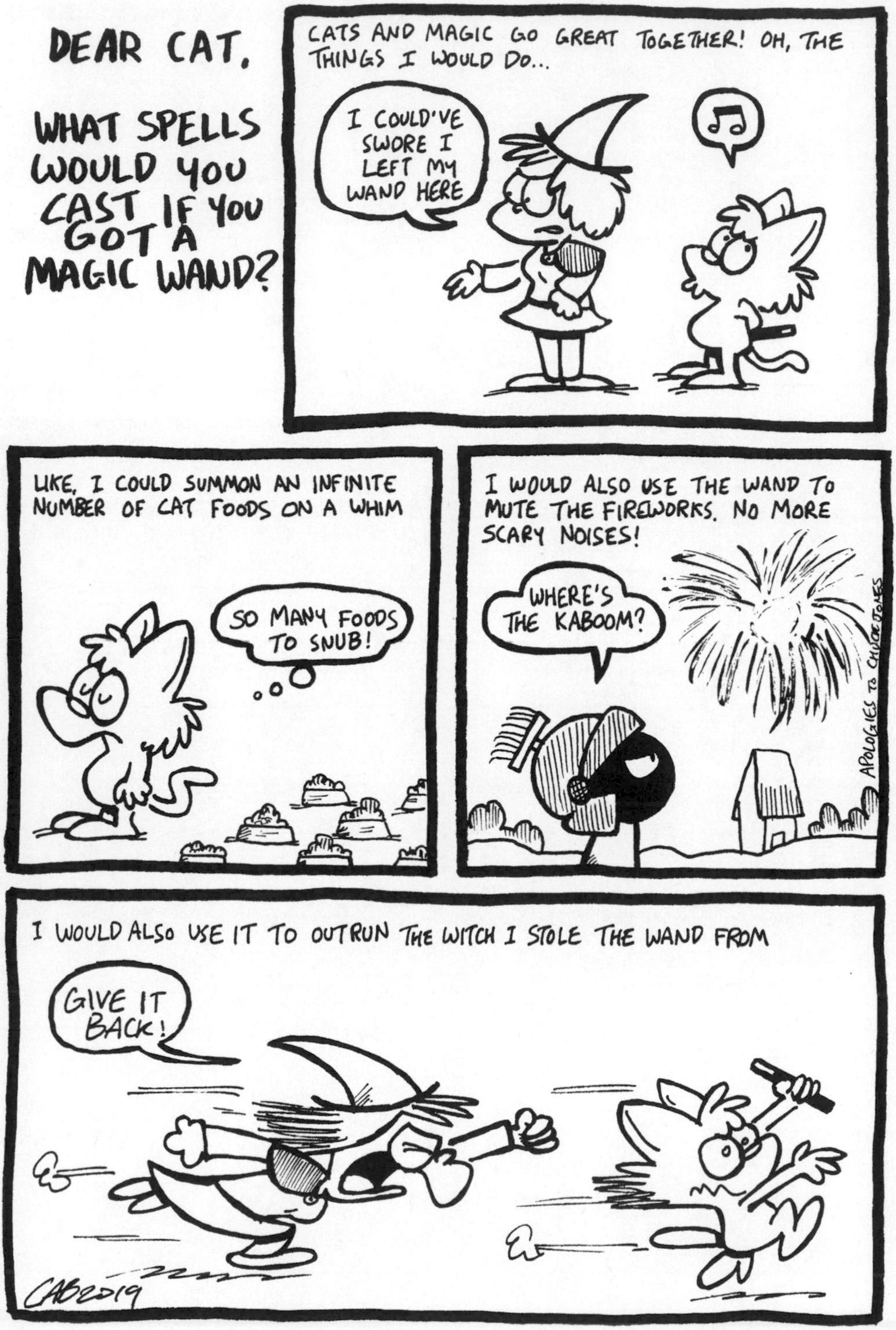
CATS AND MAGIC GO GREAT TOGETHER! OH, THE THINGS I WOULD DO...
I COULD'VE SWORE I LEFT MY WAND HERE
♫
LIKE, I COULD SUMMON AN INFINITE NUMBER OF CAT FOODS ON A WHIM
SO MANY FOODS TO SNUB!
I WOULD ALSO USE THE WAND TO MUTE THE FIREWORKS. NO MORE SCARY NOISES!
WHERE'S THE KABOOM?
APOLOGIES TO CHUCK JONES
I WOULD ALSO USE IT TO OUTRUN THE WITCH I STOLE THE WAND FROM
GIVE IT BACK!
CAB2019

DEAR CAT,

WOULD YOU DATE A MERMAID?

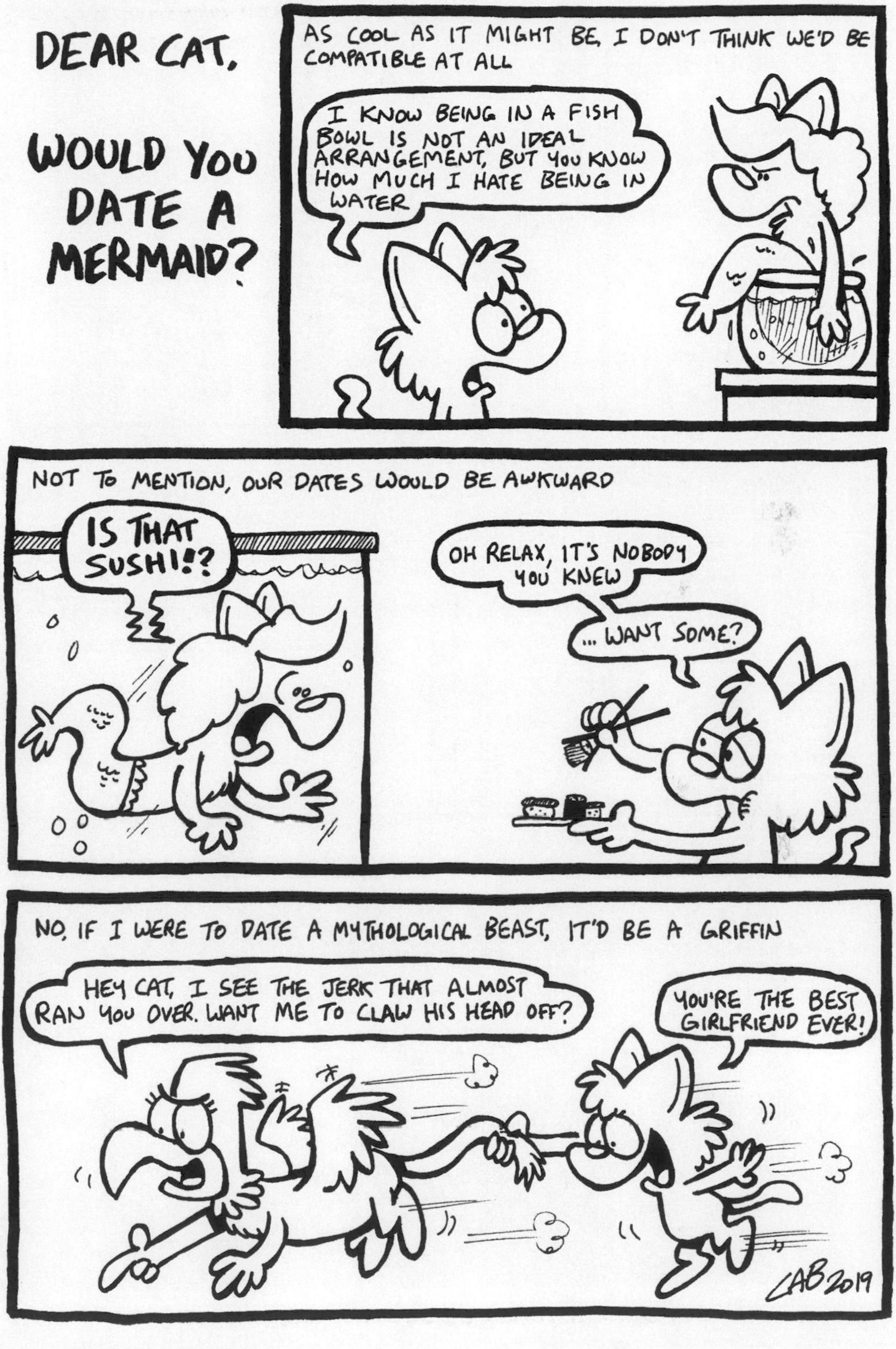

AS COOL AS IT MIGHT BE, I DON'T THINK WE'D BE COMPATIBLE AT ALL
I KNOW BEING IN A FISH BOWL IS NOT AN IDEAL ARRANGEMENT, BUT YOU KNOW HOW MUCH I HATE BEING IN WATER
NOT TO MENTION, OUR DATES WOULD BE AWKWARD
IS THAT SUSHI!?
OH RELAX, IT'S NOBODY YOU KNEW
... WANT SOME?
NO, IF I WERE TO DATE A MYTHOLOGICAL BEAST, IT'D BE A GRIFFIN
HEY CAT, I SEE THE JERK THAT ALMOST RAN YOU OVER. WANT ME TO CLAW HIS HEAD OFF?
YOU'RE THE BEST GIRLFRIEND EVER!
CAB 2019

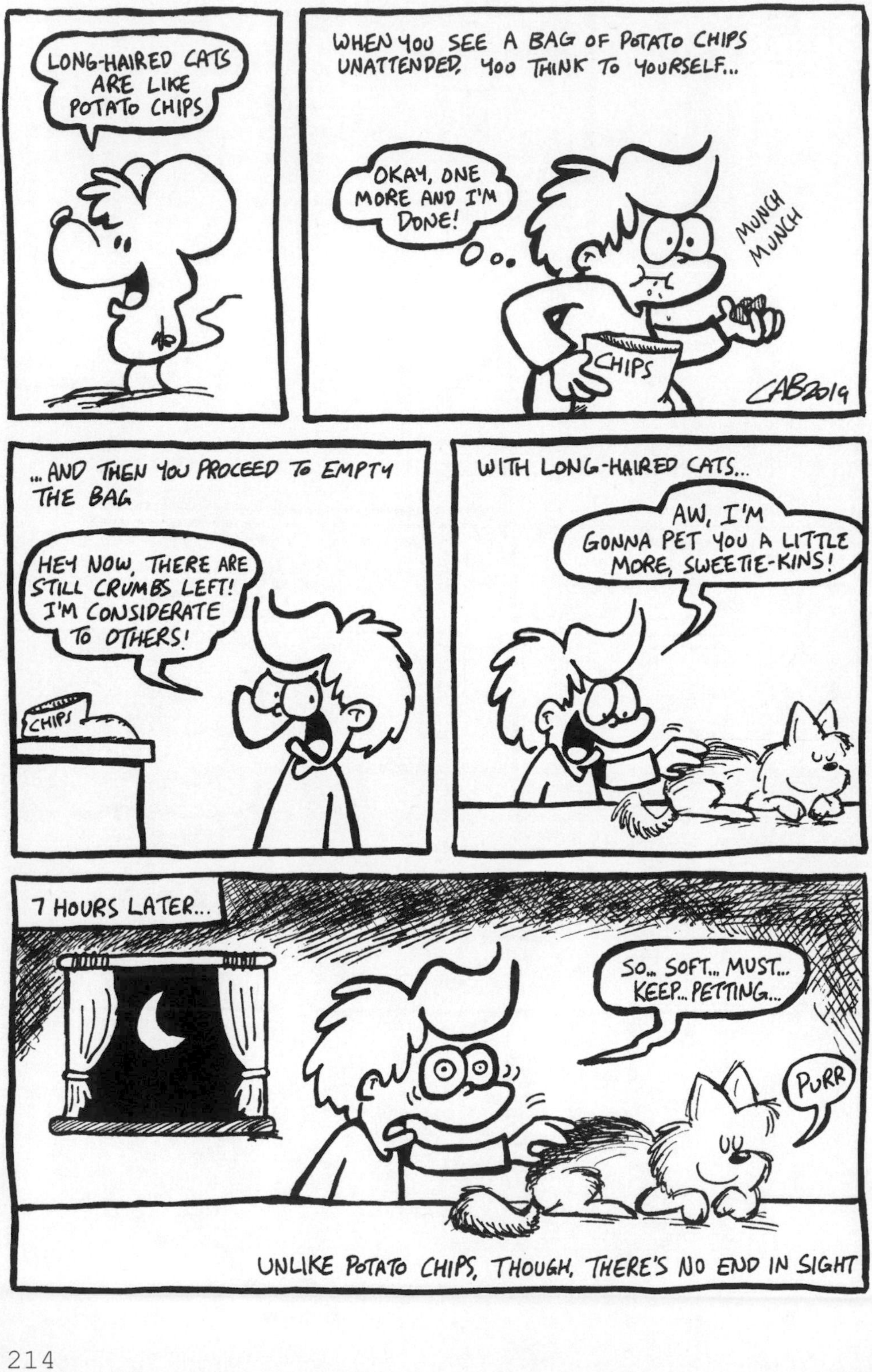
LONG-HAIRED CATS ARE LIKE POTATO CHIPS
WHEN YOU SEE A BAG OF POTATO CHIPS UNATTENDED, YOU THINK TO YOURSELF...
OKAY, ONE MORE AND I'M DONE!
MUNCH MUNCH
CHIPS
CAB2019
...AND THEN YOU PROCEED TO EMPTY THE BAG
HEY NOW, THERE ARE STILL CRUMBS LEFT! I'M CONSIDERATE TO OTHERS!
CHIPS
WITH LONG-HAIRED CATS...
AW, I'M GONNA PET YOU A LITTLE MORE, SWEETIE-KINS!
7 HOURS LATER...
SO... SOFT... MUST... KEEP... PETTING...
PURR
UNLIKE POTATO CHIPS, THOUGH, THERE'S NO END IN SIGHT

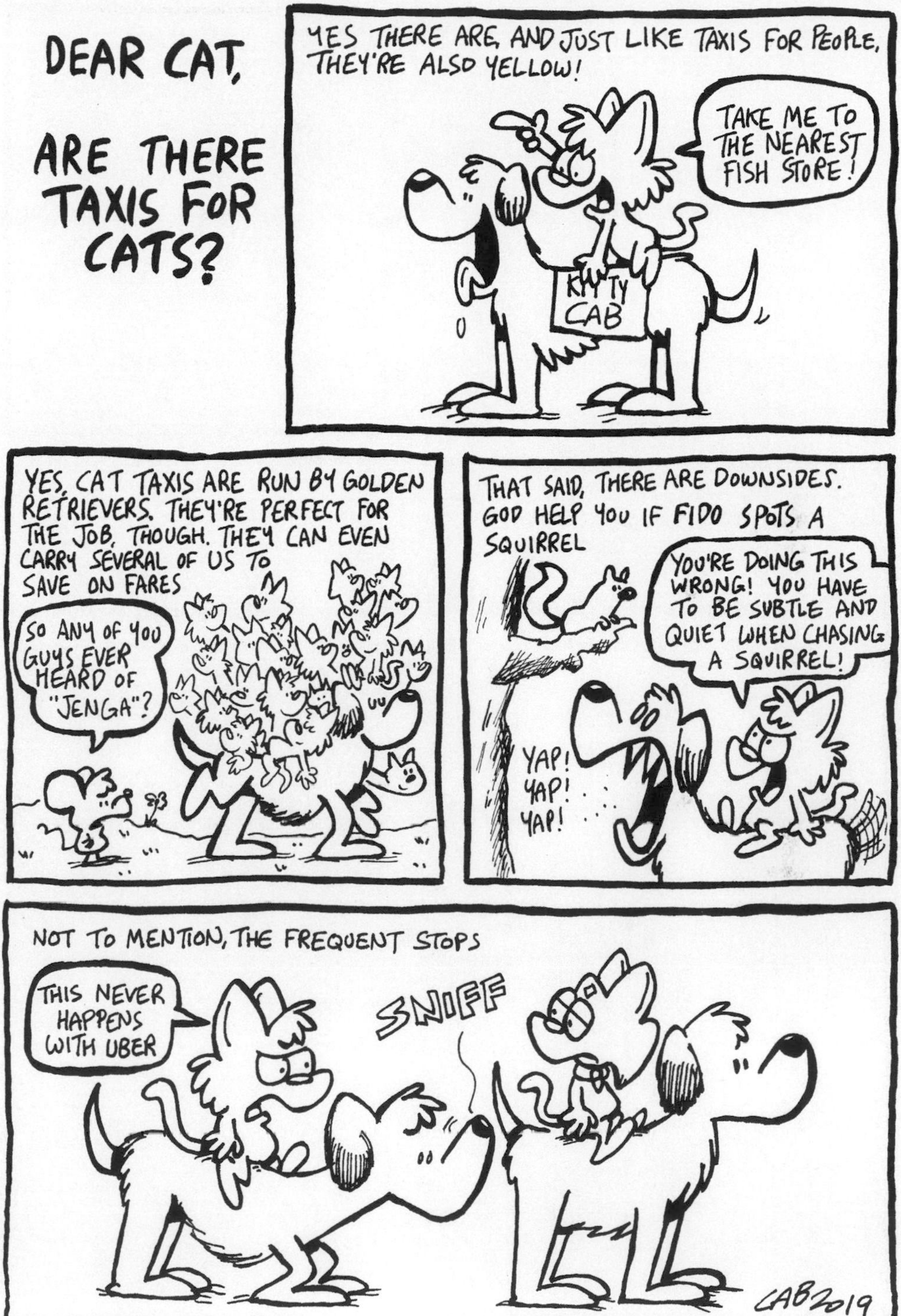
DEAR CAT,
ARE THERE TAXIS FOR CATS?
YES THERE ARE, AND JUST LIKE TAXIS FOR PEOPLE, THEY'RE ALSO YELLOW!
TAKE ME TO THE NEAREST FISH STORE!
KITTY CAB
YES, CAT TAXIS ARE RUN BY GOLDEN RETRIEVERS. THEY'RE PERFECT FOR THE JOB, THOUGH. THEY CAN EVEN CARRY SEVERAL OF US TO SAVE ON FARES
SO ANY OF YOU GUYS EVER HEARD OF "JENGA"?
THAT SAID, THERE ARE DOWNSIDES. GOD HELP YOU IF FIDO SPOTS A SQUIRREL
YOU'RE DOING THIS WRONG! YOU HAVE TO BE SUBTLE AND QUIET WHEN CHASING A SQUIRREL!
YAP! YAP! YAP!
NOT TO MENTION, THE FREQUENT STOPS
THIS NEVER HAPPENS WITH UBER
SNIFF
CAB 2019

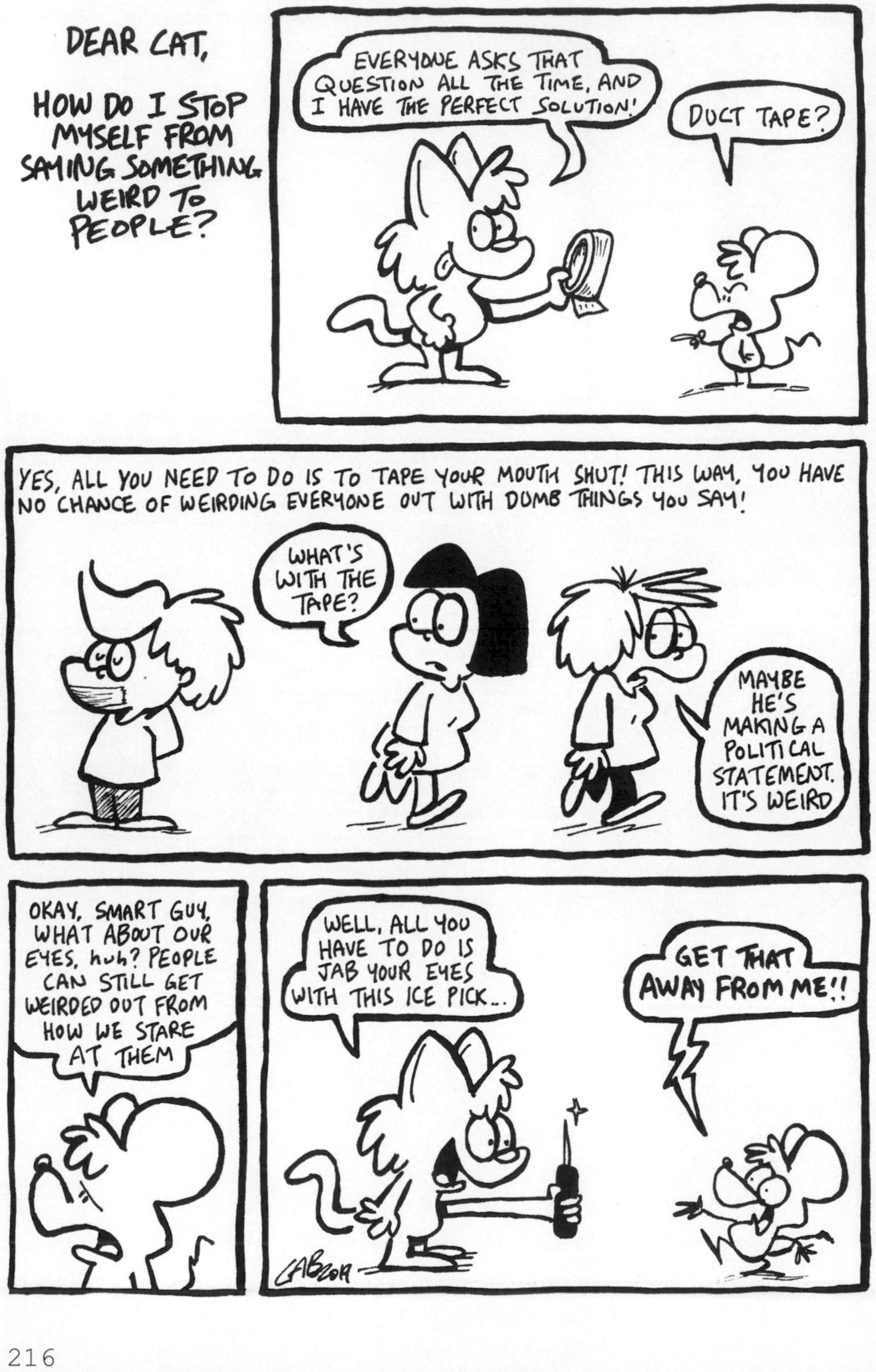
DEAR CAT,
HOW DO I STOP MYSELF FROM SAYING SOMETHING WEIRD TO PEOPLE?
EVERYONE ASKS THAT QUESTION ALL THE TIME, AND I HAVE THE PERFECT SOLUTION!
DUCT TAPE?
YES, ALL YOU NEED TO DO IS TO TAPE YOUR MOUTH SHUT! THIS WAY, YOU HAVE NO CHANCE OF WEIRDING EVERYONE OUT WITH DUMB THINGS YOU SAY!
WHAT'S WITH THE TAPE?
MAYBE HE'S MAKING A POLITICAL STATEMENT. IT'S WEIRD
OKAY, SMART GUY, WHAT ABOUT OUR EYES, huh? PEOPLE CAN STILL GET WEIRDED OUT FROM HOW WE STARE AT THEM
WELL, ALL YOU HAVE TO DO IS JAB YOUR EYES WITH THIS ICE PICK...
GET THAT AWAY FROM ME!!

DEAR CAT,

DO YOU LIKE SPRING?

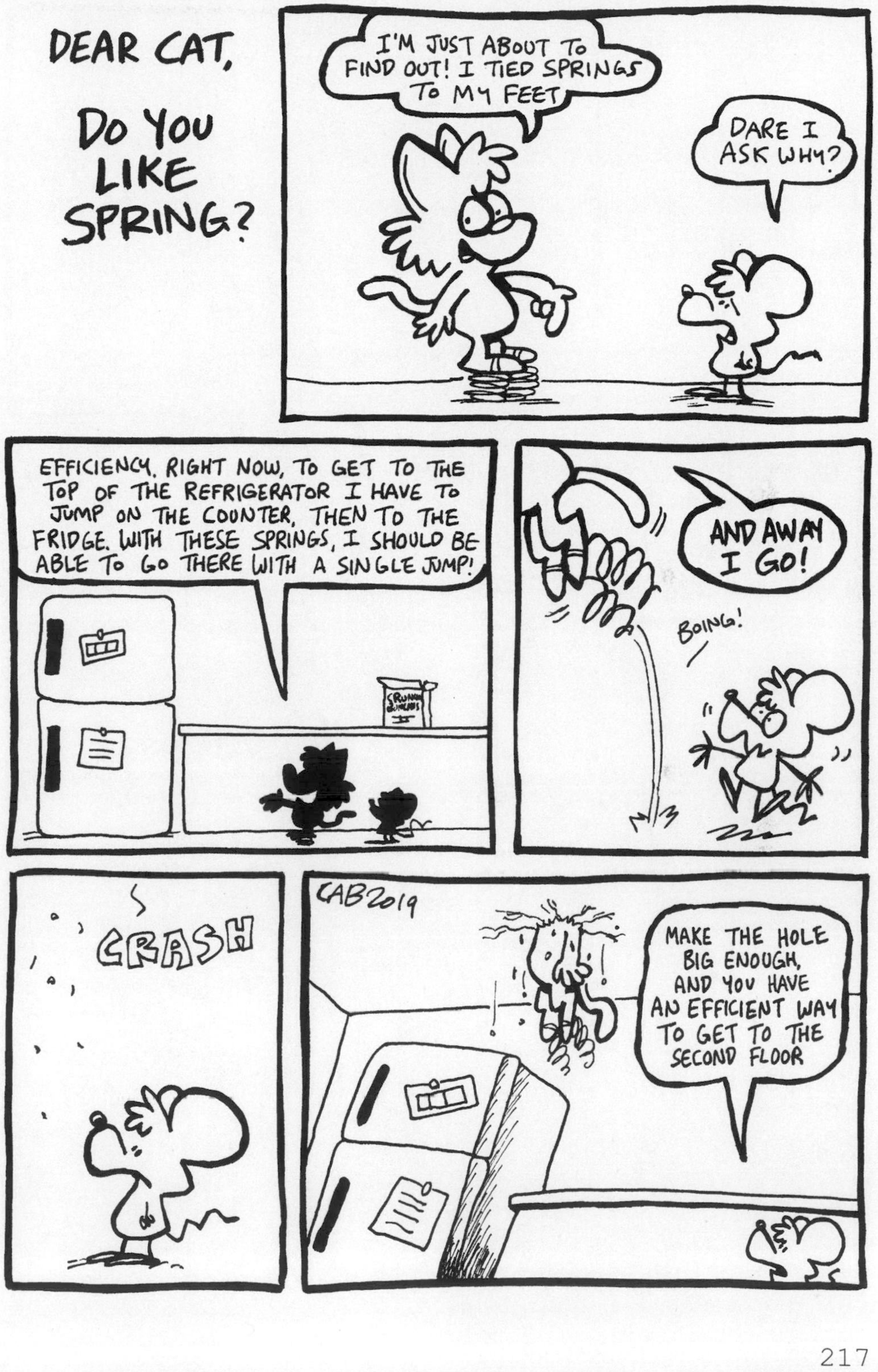

I'M JUST ABOUT TO FIND OUT! I TIED SPRINGS TO MY FEET
DARE I ASK WHY?
EFFICIENCY. RIGHT NOW, TO GET TO THE TOP OF THE REFRIGERATOR I HAVE TO JUMP ON THE COUNTER, THEN TO THE FRIDGE. WITH THESE SPRINGS, I SHOULD BE ABLE TO GO THERE WITH A SINGLE JUMP!
AND AWAY I GO!
BOING!
CRASH
CAB2019
MAKE THE HOLE BIG ENOUGH, AND YOU HAVE AN EFFICIENT WAY TO GET TO THE SECOND FLOOR

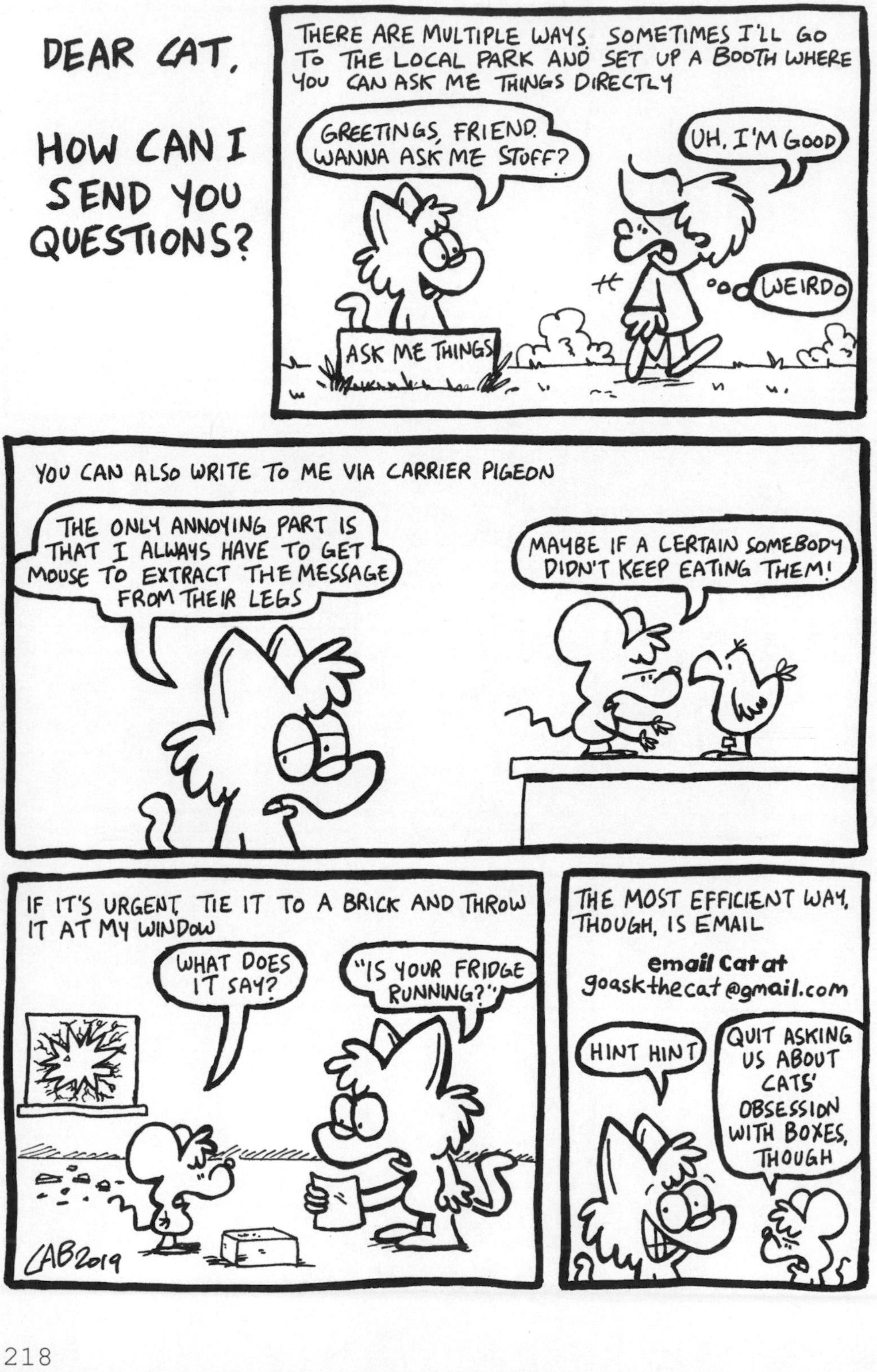
DEAR CAT,
HOW CAN I SEND YOU QUESTIONS?
THERE ARE MULTIPLE WAYS. SOMETIMES I'LL GO TO THE LOCAL PARK AND SET UP A BOOTH WHERE YOU CAN ASK ME THINGS DIRECTLY
GREETINGS, FRIEND. WANNA ASK ME STUFF?
ASK ME THINGS
UH, I'M GOOD
WEIRDO
YOU CAN ALSO WRITE TO ME VIA CARRIER PIGEON
THE ONLY ANNOYING PART IS THAT I ALWAYS HAVE TO GET MOUSE TO EXTRACT THE MESSAGE FROM THEIR LEGS
MAYBE IF A CERTAIN SOMEBODY DIDN'T KEEP EATING THEM!
IF IT'S URGENT, TIE IT TO A BRICK AND THROW IT AT MY WINDOW
WHAT DOES IT SAY?
"IS YOUR FRIDGE RUNNING?"
CAB 2019
THE MOST EFFICIENT WAY, THOUGH, IS EMAIL
email Cat at
goaskthecat@gmail.com
HINT HINT
QUIT ASKING US ABOUT CATS' OBSESSION WITH BOXES, THOUGH

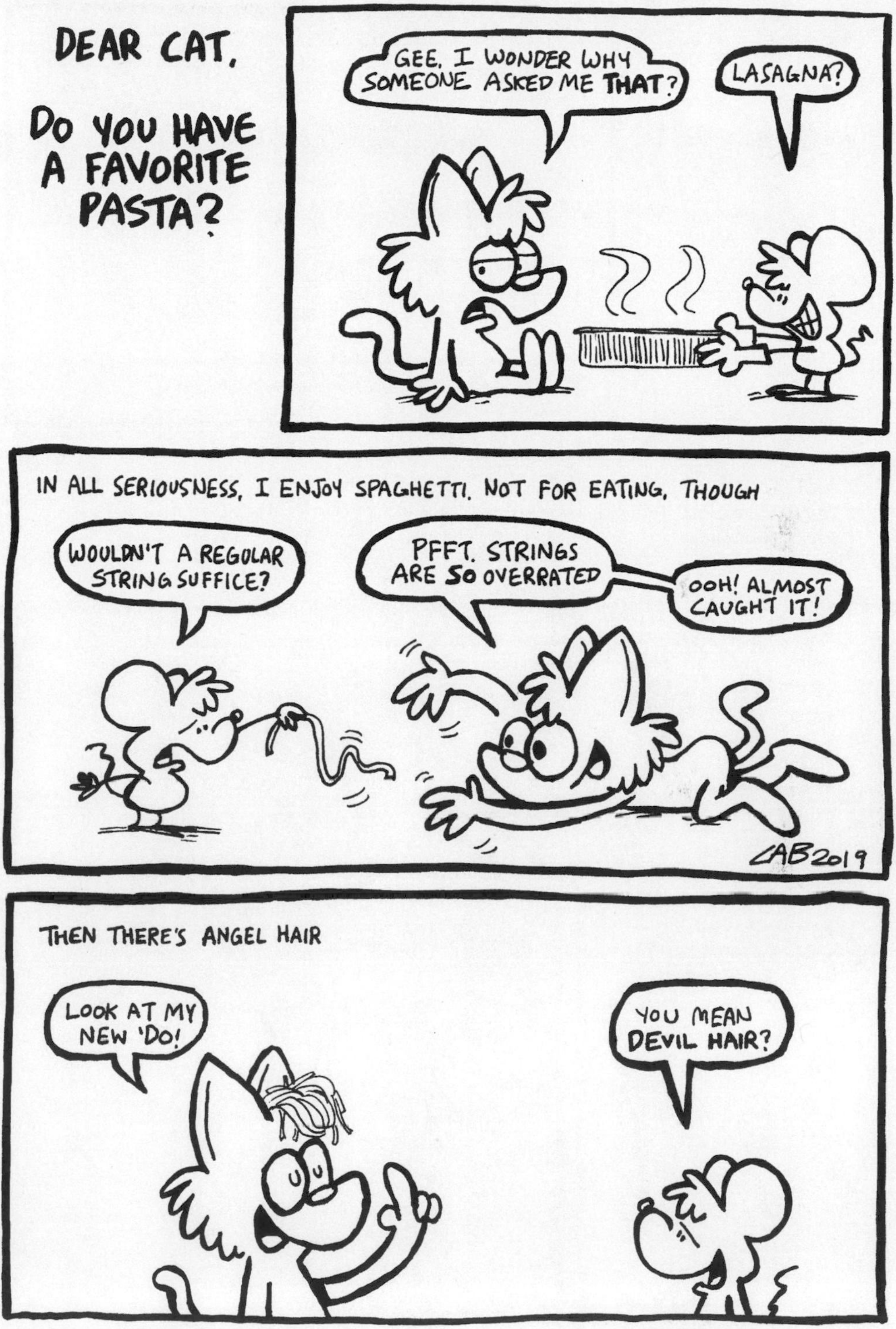
DEAR CAT,
DO YOU HAVE A FAVORITE PASTA?
GEE, I WONDER WHY SOMEONE ASKED ME THAT?
LASAGNA?
IN ALL SERIOUSNESS, I ENJOY SPAGHETTI. NOT FOR EATING, THOUGH
WOULDN'T A REGULAR STRING SUFFICE?
PFFT. STRINGS ARE SO OVERRATED
OOH! ALMOST CAUGHT IT!
CAB 2019
THEN THERE'S ANGEL HAIR
LOOK AT MY NEW 'DO!
YOU MEAN DEVIL HAIR?

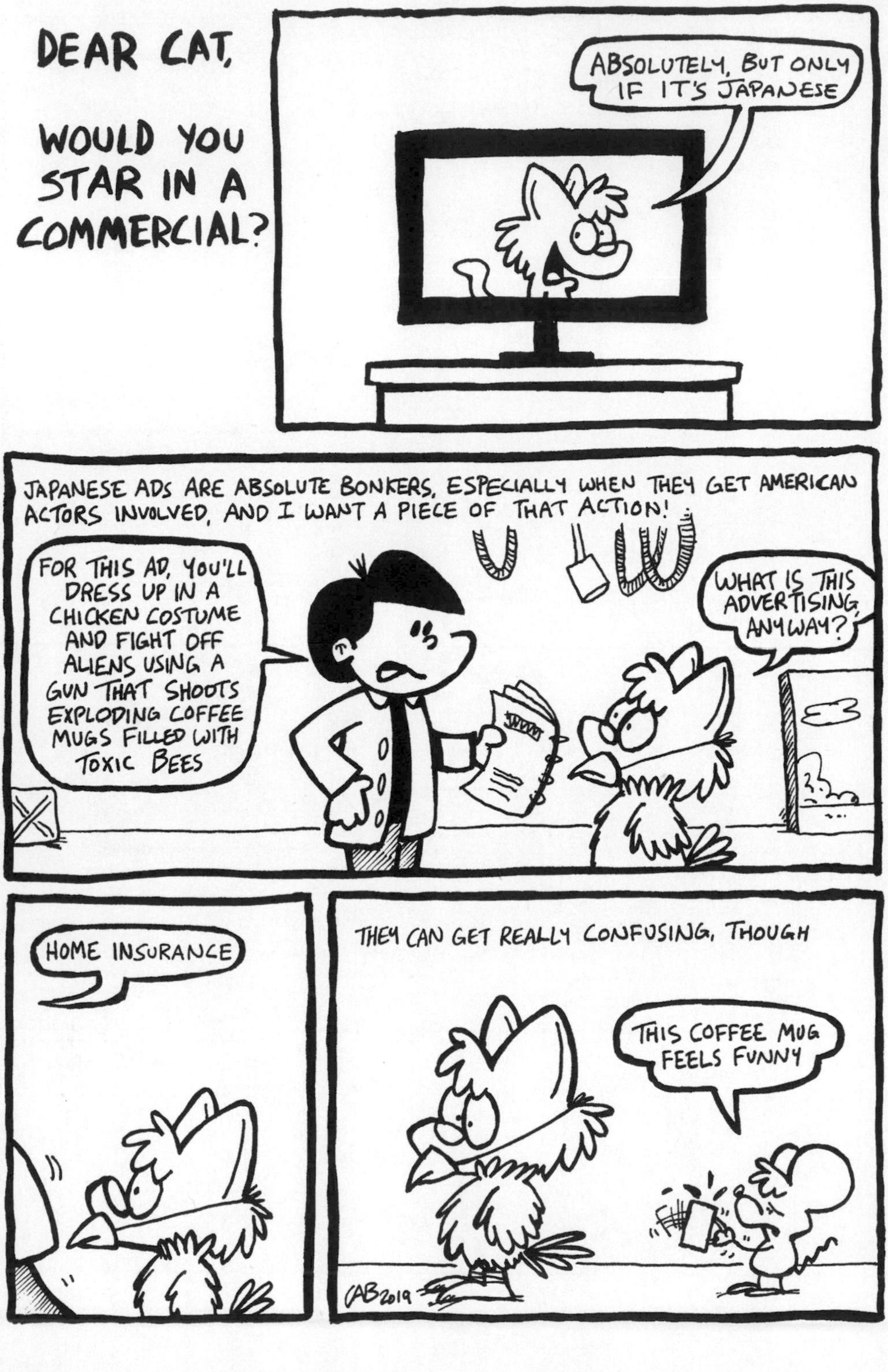

DEAR CAT,
WOULD YOU STAR IN A COMMERCIAL?
ABSOLUTELY, BUT ONLY IF IT'S JAPANESE
JAPANESE ADS ARE ABSOLUTE BONKERS, ESPECIALLY WHEN THEY GET AMERICAN ACTORS INVOLVED, AND I WANT A PIECE OF THAT ACTION!
FOR THIS AD, YOU'LL DRESS UP IN A CHICKEN COSTUME AND FIGHT OFF ALIENS USING A GUN THAT SHOOTS EXPLODING COFFEE MUGS FILLED WITH TOXIC BEES
WHAT IS THIS ADVERTISING, ANYWAY?
HOME INSURANCE
THEY CAN GET REALLY CONFUSING, THOUGH
THIS COFFEE MUG FEELS FUNNY
CAB 2019

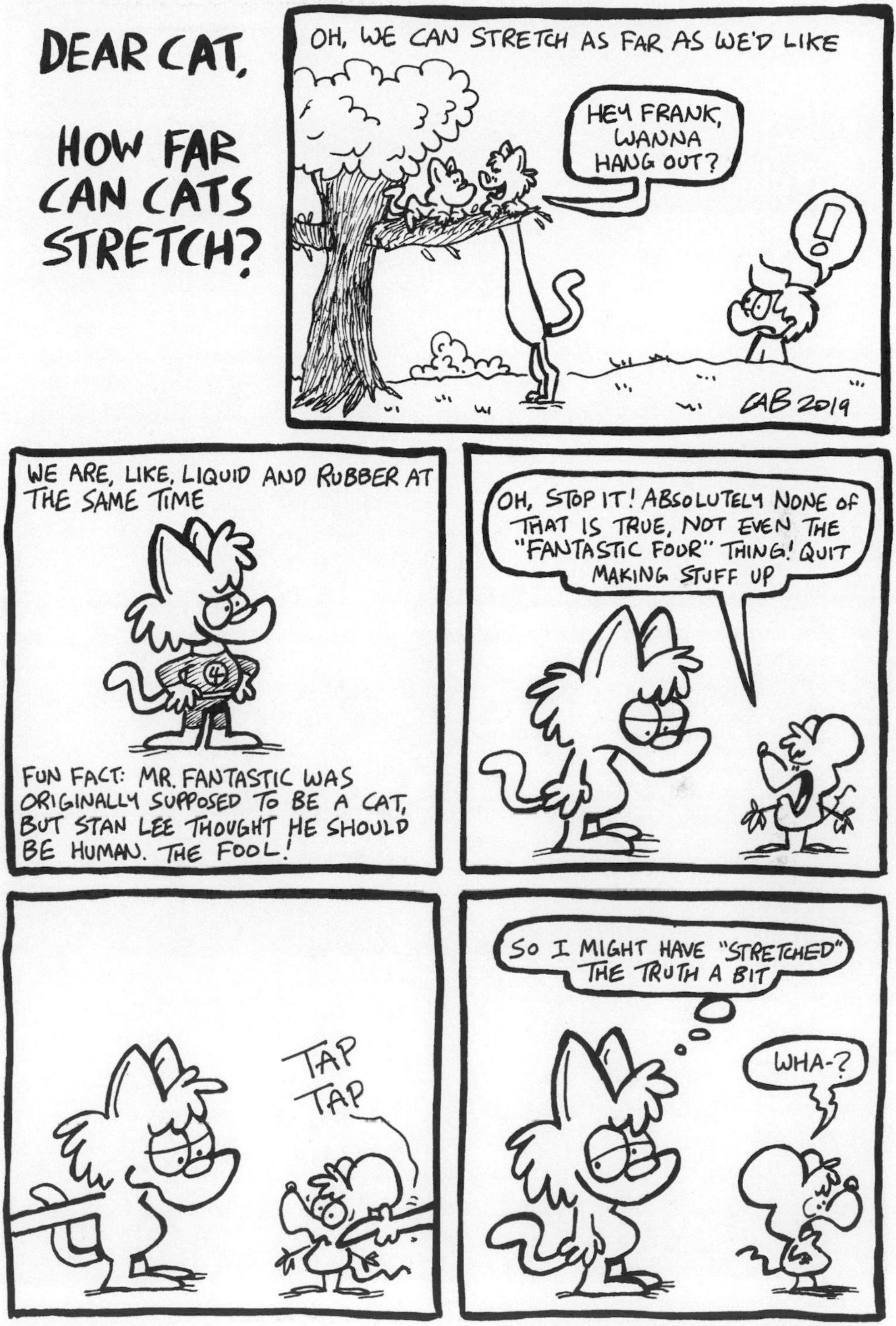
DEAR CAT,
HOW FAR CAN CATS STRETCH?
OH, WE CAN STRETCH AS FAR AS WE'D LIKE
HEY FRANK, WANNA HANG OUT?
!
CAB 2019
WE ARE, LIKE, LIQUID AND RUBBER AT THE SAME TIME
4
FUN FACT: MR. FANTASTIC WAS ORIGINALLY SUPPOSED TO BE A CAT, BUT STAN LEE THOUGHT HE SHOULD BE HUMAN. THE FOOL!
OH, STOP IT! ABSOLUTELY NONE OF THAT IS TRUE, NOT EVEN THE "FANTASTIC FOUR" THING! QUIT MAKING STUFF UP
TAP TAP
SO I MIGHT HAVE "STRETCHED" THE TRUTH A BIT
WHA-?

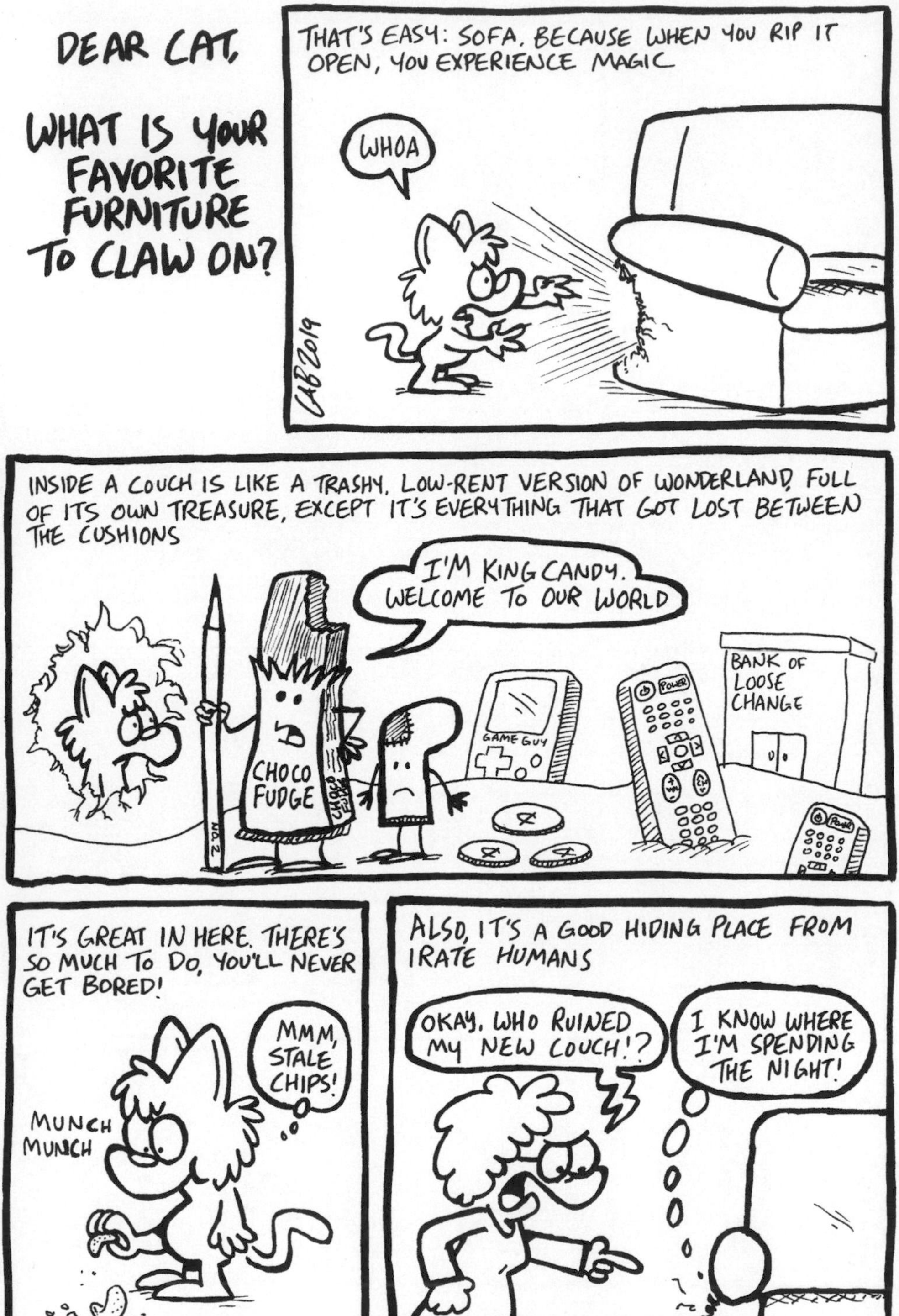
DEAR CAT,
WHAT IS YOUR FAVORITE FURNITURE TO CLAW ON?
THAT'S EASY: SOFA, BECAUSE WHEN YOU RIP IT OPEN, YOU EXPERIENCE MAGIC
WHOA
CAB 2019
INSIDE A COUCH IS LIKE A TRASHY, LOW-RENT VERSION OF WONDERLAND, FULL OF ITS OWN TREASURE, EXCEPT IT'S EVERYTHING THAT GOT LOST BETWEEN THE CUSHIONS
I'M KING CANDY. WELCOME TO OUR WORLD
CHOCO FUDGE
GAME GUY
POWER
BANK OF LOOSE CHANGE
IT'S GREAT IN HERE. THERE'S SO MUCH TO DO, YOU'LL NEVER GET BORED!
MUNCH MUNCH
MMM, STALE CHIPS!
ALSO, IT'S A GOOD HIDING PLACE FROM IRATE HUMANS
OKAY. WHO RUINED MY NEW COUCH!?
I KNOW WHERE I'M SPENDING THE NIGHT!

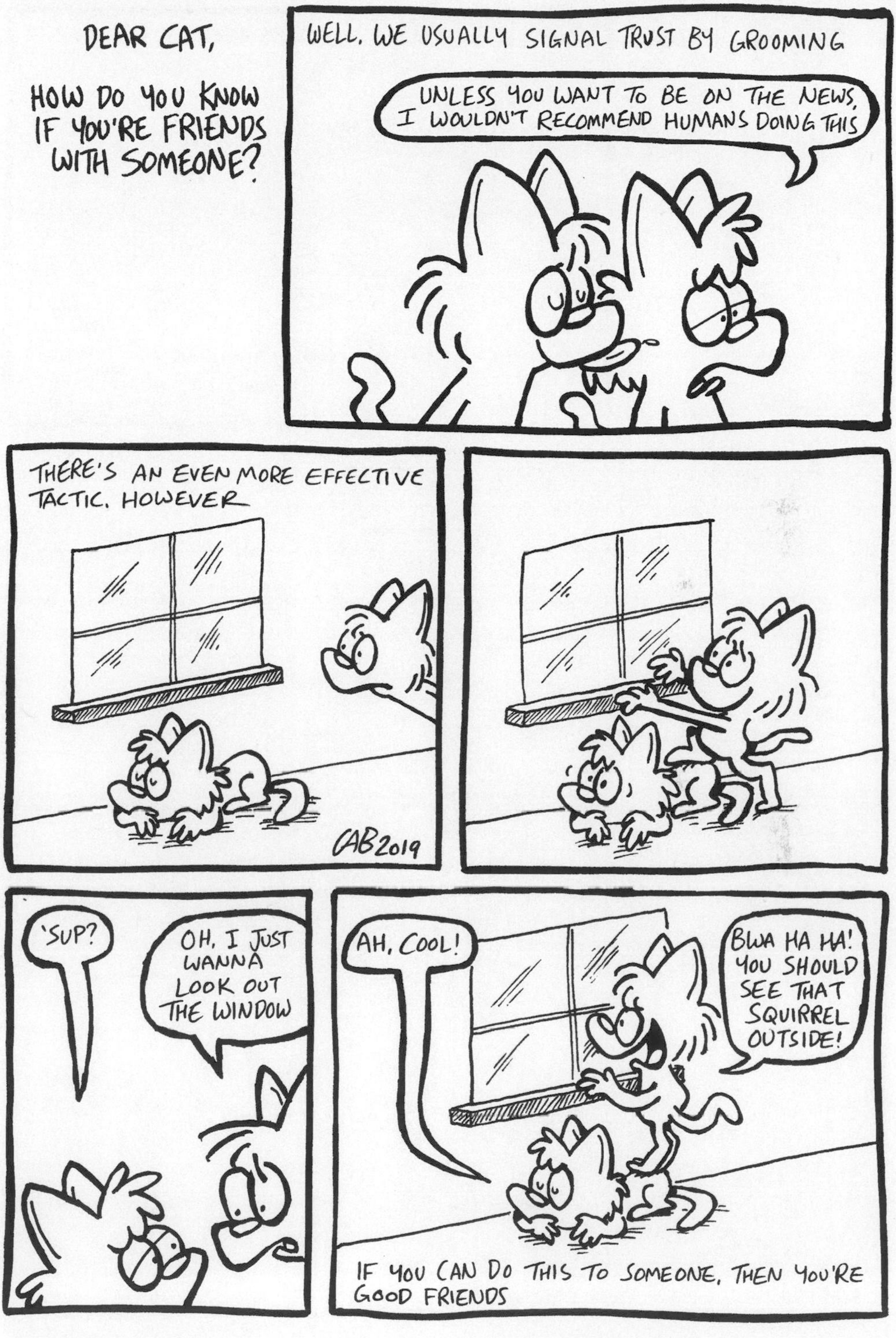
DEAR CAT,
HOW DO YOU KNOW IF YOU'RE FRIENDS WITH SOMEONE?
WELL, WE USUALLY SIGNAL TRUST BY GROOMING
UNLESS YOU WANT TO BE ON THE NEWS, I WOULDN'T RECOMMEND HUMANS DOING THIS
THERE'S AN EVEN MORE EFFECTIVE TACTIC, HOWEVER
CAB 2019
'SUP?
OH, I JUST WANNA LOOK OUT THE WINDOW
AH, COOL!
BWA HA HA! YOU SHOULD SEE THAT SQUIRREL OUTSIDE!
IF YOU CAN DO THIS TO SOMEONE, THEN YOU'RE GOOD FRIENDS

DEAR CAT,

ARE THERE CATS THAT ARE YOUR ENEMIES?

OH YES, BOO FROM NEXT DOOR. HOW I DESPISE HIM!

GRR...

HE COMMITTED THE UNFORGIVABLE CRIME OF "BEING IN MY TERRITORY". FOR THAT, HE MUST SUFFER

☰ – CAT'S TERRITORY

O – NOT CAT'S TERRITORY

WHAT TH-? THIS ENCOMPASSES THE ENTIRE WORLD!

NOT TRUE! I HAVE NO STAKE IN THE TERRITORIES CIRCLED ON THE MAP

CAB2019

IN FACT, BOO CAN MOVE INTO THOSE PLACES IF HE LIKES. HONEST

THOSE ARE ALL THE VETS IN THE WORLD, HUH?

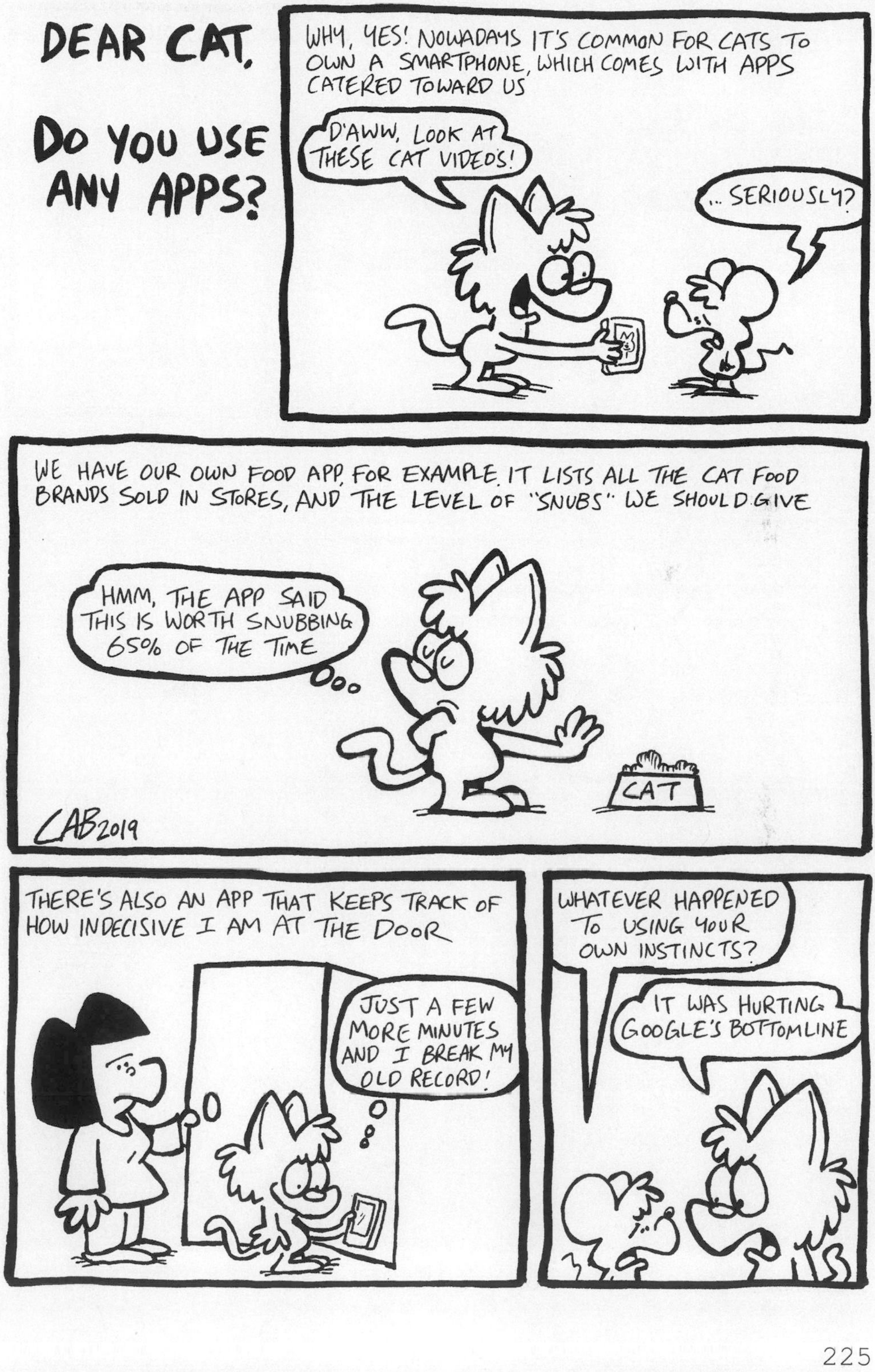
DEAR CAT, DO YOU USE ANY APPS?
WHY, YES! NOWADAYS IT'S COMMON FOR CATS TO OWN A SMARTPHONE, WHICH COMES WITH APPS CATERED TOWARD US
D'AWW, LOOK AT THESE CAT VIDEOS!
... SERIOUSLY?
WE HAVE OUR OWN FOOD APP, FOR EXAMPLE. IT LISTS ALL THE CAT FOOD BRANDS SOLD IN STORES, AND THE LEVEL OF "SNUBS" WE SHOULD GIVE
HMM, THE APP SAID THIS IS WORTH SNUBBING 65% OF THE TIME
CAT
CAB 2019
THERE'S ALSO AN APP THAT KEEPS TRACK OF HOW INDECISIVE I AM AT THE DOOR
JUST A FEW MORE MINUTES AND I BREAK MY OLD RECORD!
WHATEVER HAPPENED TO USING YOUR OWN INSTINCTS?
IT WAS HURTING GOOGLE'S BOTTOMLINE

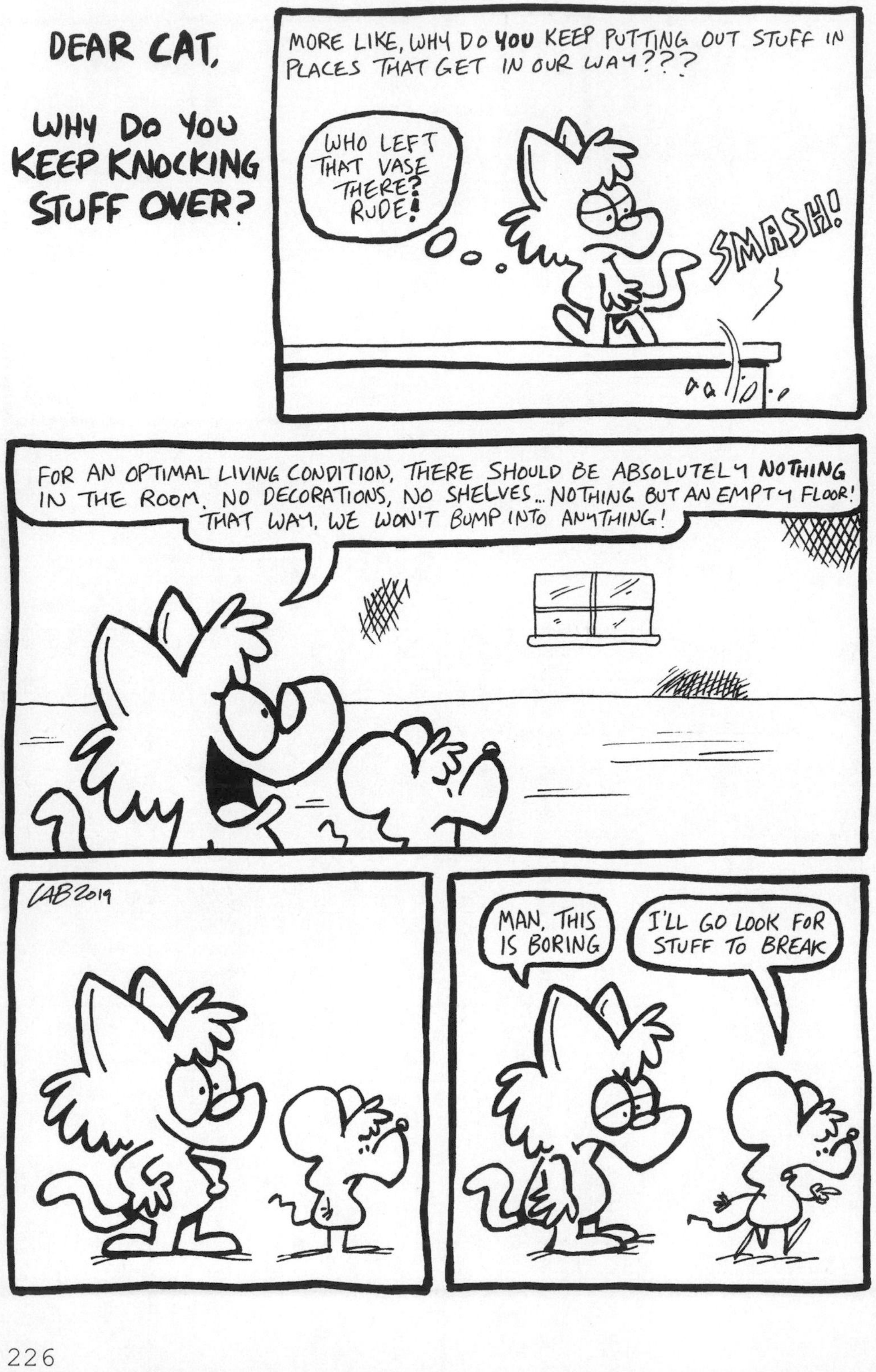
DEAR CAT,
WHY DO YOU KEEP KNOCKING STUFF OVER?
MORE LIKE, WHY DO **YOU** KEEP PUTTING OUT STUFF IN PLACES THAT GET IN OUR WAY???
WHO LEFT THAT VASE THERE? RUDE!
SMASH!
FOR AN OPTIMAL LIVING CONDITION, THERE SHOULD BE ABSOLUTELY **NOTHING** IN THE ROOM. NO DECORATIONS, NO SHELVES... NOTHING BUT AN EMPTY FLOOR! THAT WAY, WE WON'T BUMP INTO ANYTHING!
LAB 2019
MAN, THIS IS BORING
I'LL GO LOOK FOR STUFF TO BREAK

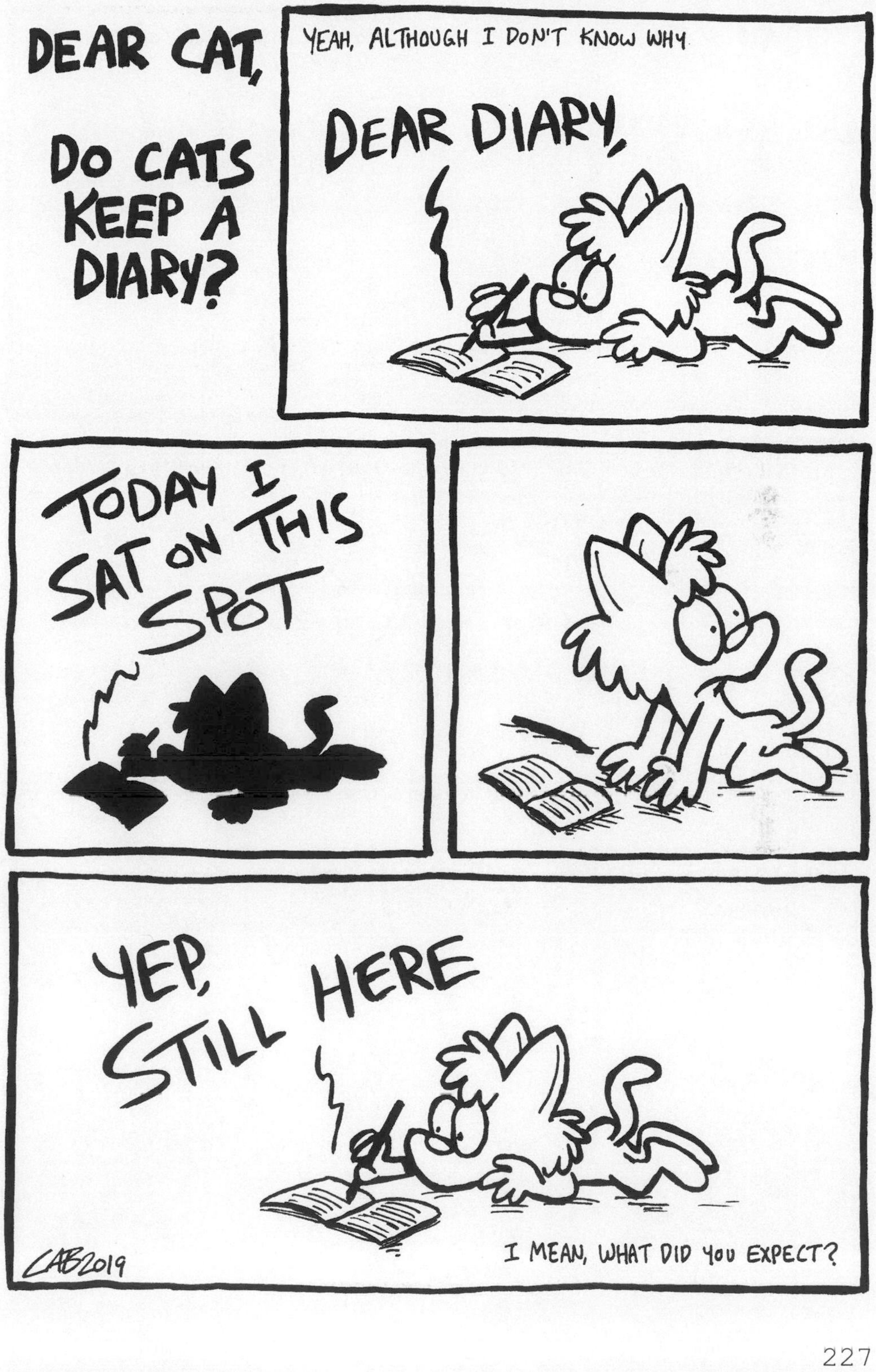
DEAR CAT,
DO CATS KEEP A DIARY?
YEAH, ALTHOUGH I DON'T KNOW WHY
DEAR DIARY,
TODAY I SAT ON THIS SPOT
YEP, STILL HERE
I MEAN, WHAT DID YOU EXPECT?
CAB2019

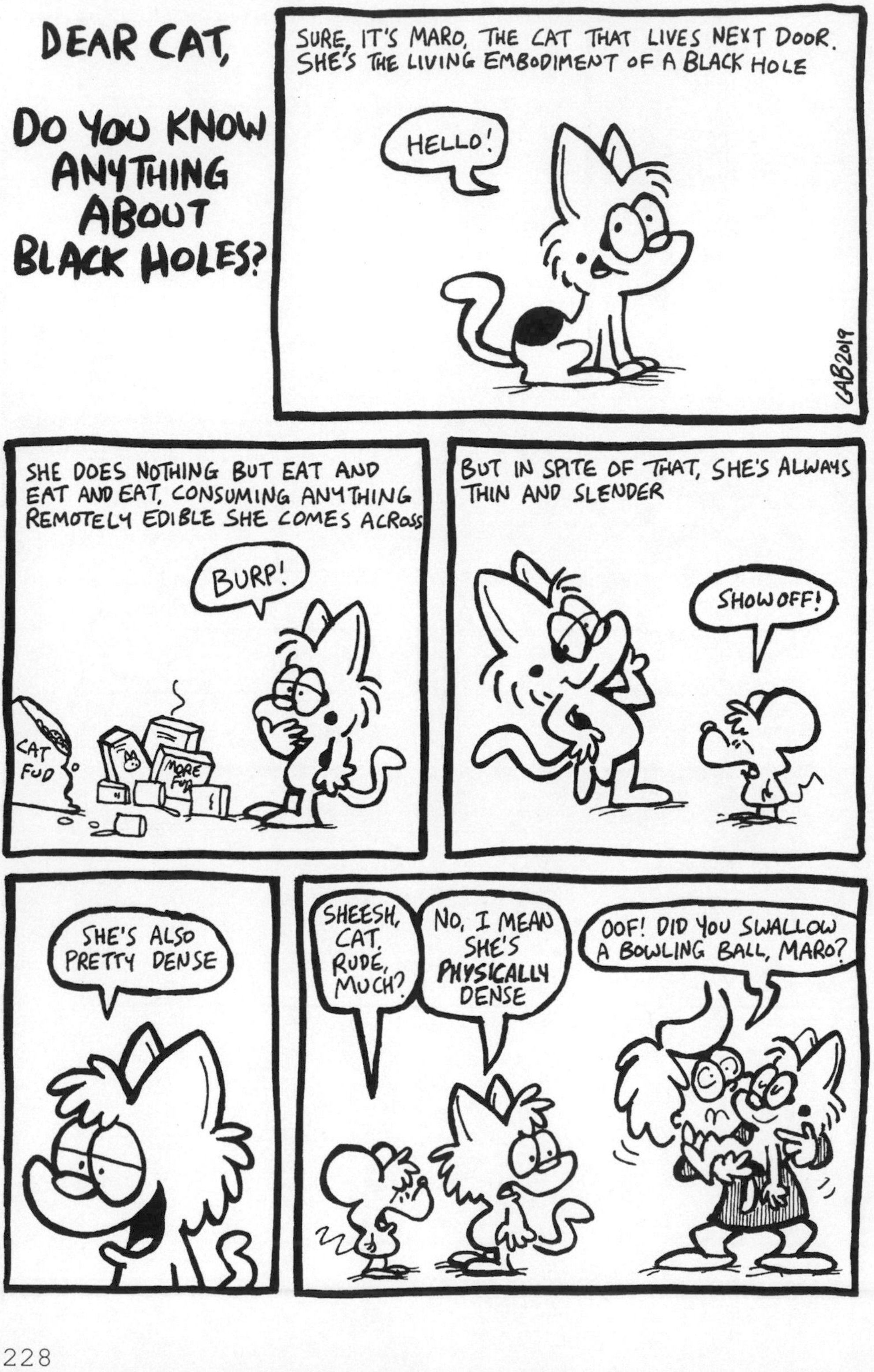
DEAR CAT,
DO YOU KNOW ANYTHING ABOUT BLACK HOLES?
SURE, IT'S MARO, THE CAT THAT LIVES NEXT DOOR. SHE'S THE LIVING EMBODIMENT OF A BLACK HOLE
HELLO!
CAB2019
SHE DOES NOTHING BUT EAT AND EAT AND EAT, CONSUMING ANYTHING REMOTELY EDIBLE SHE COMES ACROSS
BURP!
CAT FUD
MORE FUD
BUT IN SPITE OF THAT, SHE'S ALWAYS THIN AND SLENDER
SHOWOFF!
SHE'S ALSO PRETTY DENSE
SHEESH, CAT, RUDE, MUCH?
NO, I MEAN SHE'S PHYSICALLY DENSE
OOF! DID YOU SWALLOW A BOWLING BALL, MARO?

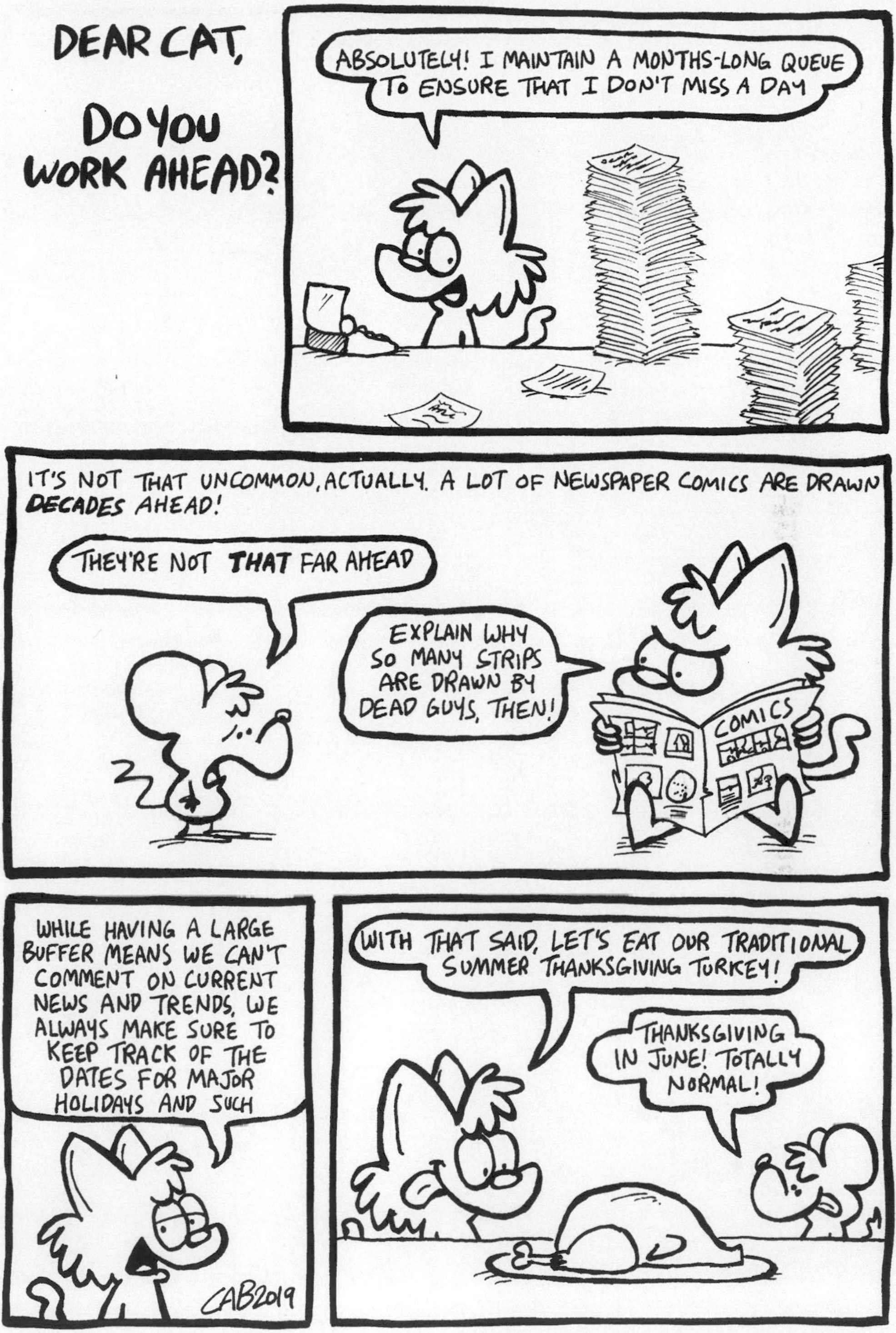
DEAR CAT,
DO YOU WORK AHEAD?
ABSOLUTELY! I MAINTAIN A MONTHS-LONG QUEUE TO ENSURE THAT I DON'T MISS A DAY
IT'S NOT THAT UNCOMMON, ACTUALLY. A LOT OF NEWSPAPER COMICS ARE DRAWN DECADES AHEAD!
THEY'RE NOT THAT FAR AHEAD
EXPLAIN WHY SO MANY STRIPS ARE DRAWN BY DEAD GUYS, THEN!
COMICS
WHILE HAVING A LARGE BUFFER MEANS WE CAN'T COMMENT ON CURRENT NEWS AND TRENDS, WE ALWAYS MAKE SURE TO KEEP TRACK OF THE DATES FOR MAJOR HOLIDAYS AND SUCH
CAB2019
WITH THAT SAID, LET'S EAT OUR TRADITIONAL SUMMER THANKSGIVING TURKEY!
THANKSGIVING IN JUNE! TOTALLY NORMAL!

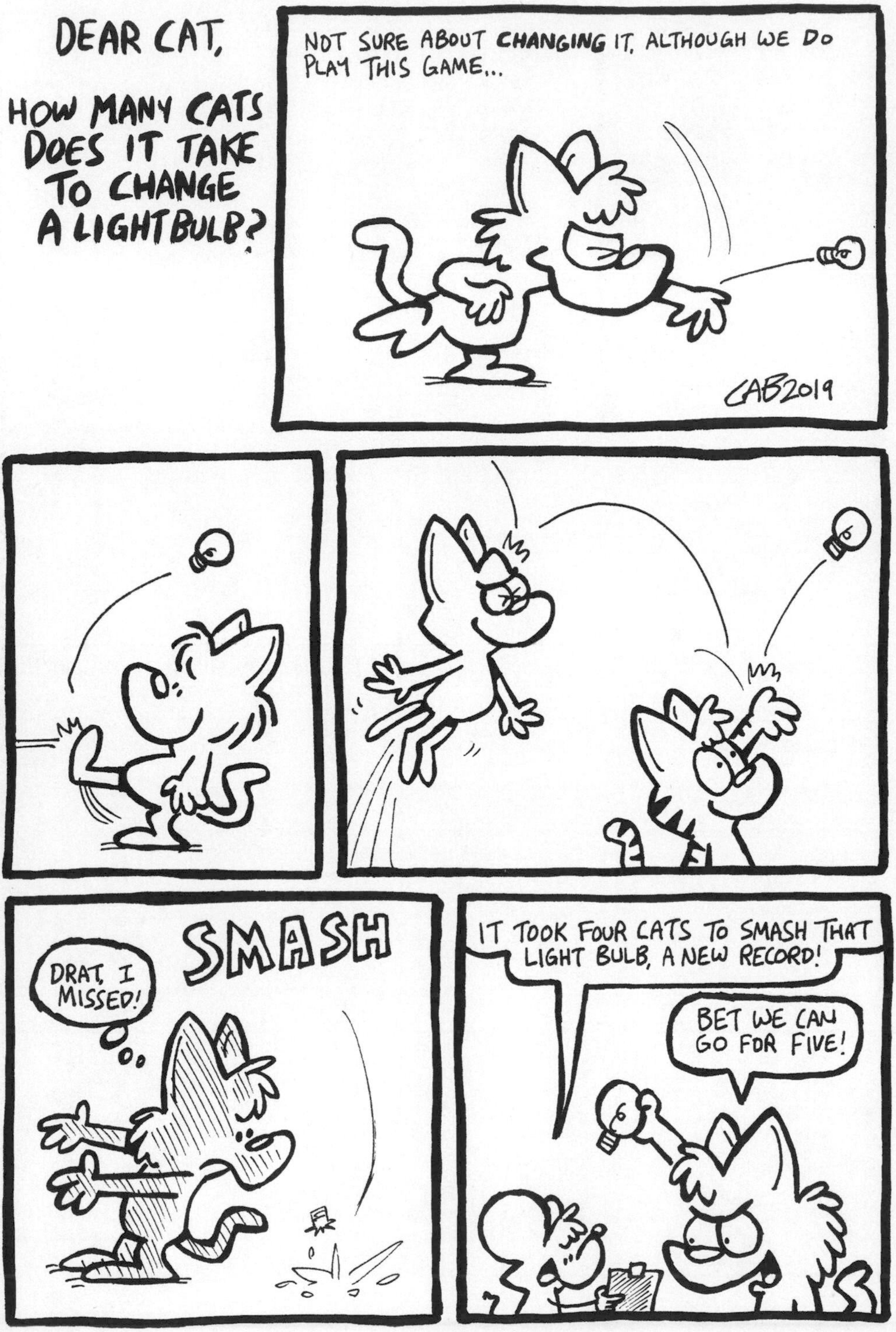
DEAR CAT,
HOW MANY CATS DOES IT TAKE TO CHANGE A LIGHTBULB?
NOT SURE ABOUT **CHANGING** IT, ALTHOUGH WE DO PLAY THIS GAME...
CAB2019
DRAT, I MISSED!
SMASH
IT TOOK FOUR CATS TO SMASH THAT LIGHT BULB, A NEW RECORD!
BET WE CAN GO FOR FIVE!

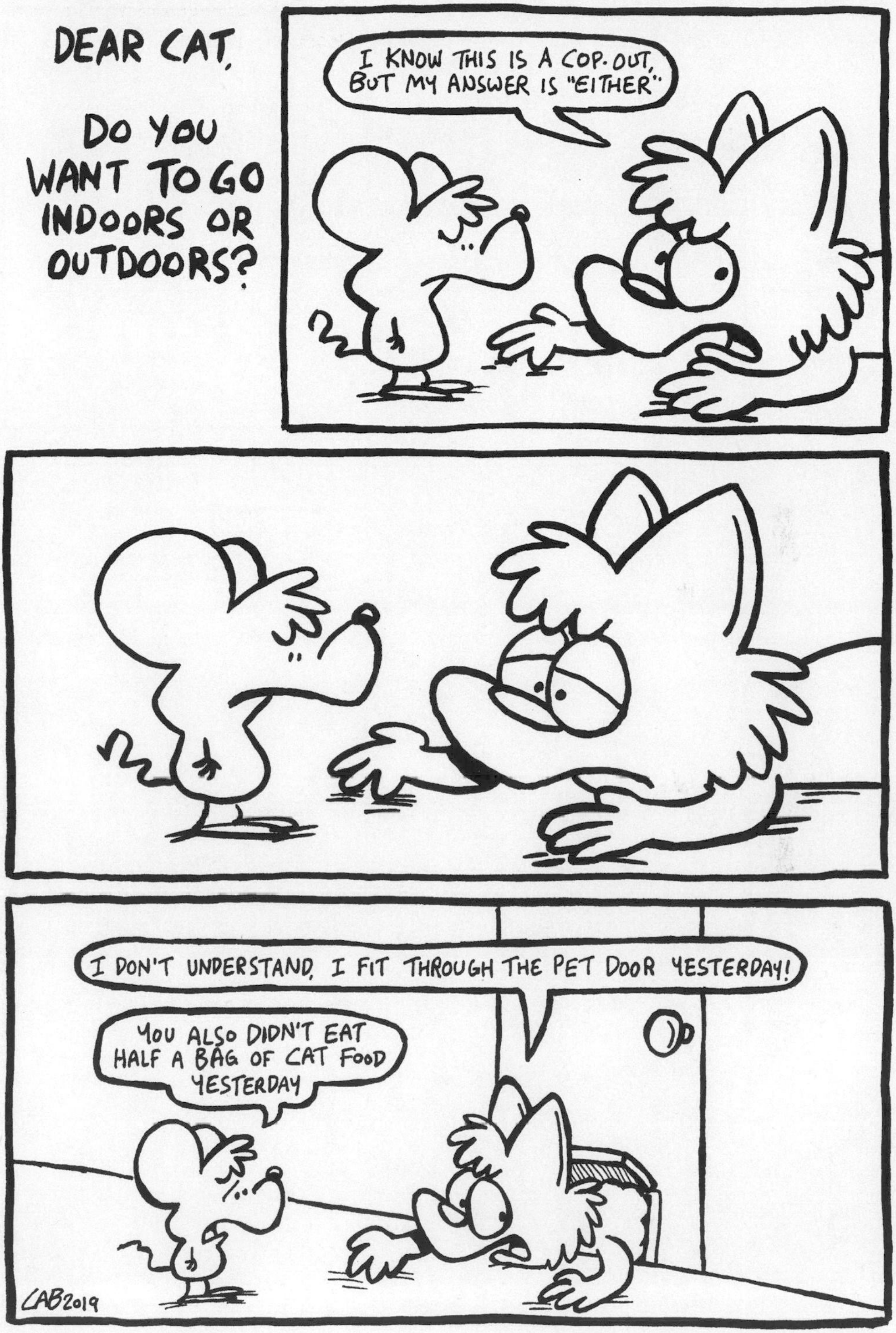
DEAR CAT,
DO YOU WANT TO GO INDOORS OR OUTDOORS?
I KNOW THIS IS A COP-OUT, BUT MY ANSWER IS "EITHER"
I DON'T UNDERSTAND, I FIT THROUGH THE PET DOOR YESTERDAY!
YOU ALSO DIDN'T EAT HALF A BAG OF CAT FOOD YESTERDAY
CAB2019

DEAR CAT,

WOULD YOU LIKE TO BE A GIANT?

BEING A GIANT **DOES** PRESENT SOME ADVANTAGES

HEY YA' DOG

I WASN'T BARKING AT YOU! HONEST!

NOT TO MENTION, IT WOULD PROVIDE THE COMMUNITY WITH A NEW ENERGY SOURCE

I RECHARGED MY PHONE WITH HIS STATIC ELECTRICITY!

THE ONLY DOWNSIDE IS, KIDS WOULD USE ME AS A HIDING SPOT FOR THE GAME OF "HIDE AND SEEK"

I FOUND YOU, JEFF!

AND I THOUGHT FLEAS WERE ANNOYING!

CAB 2019

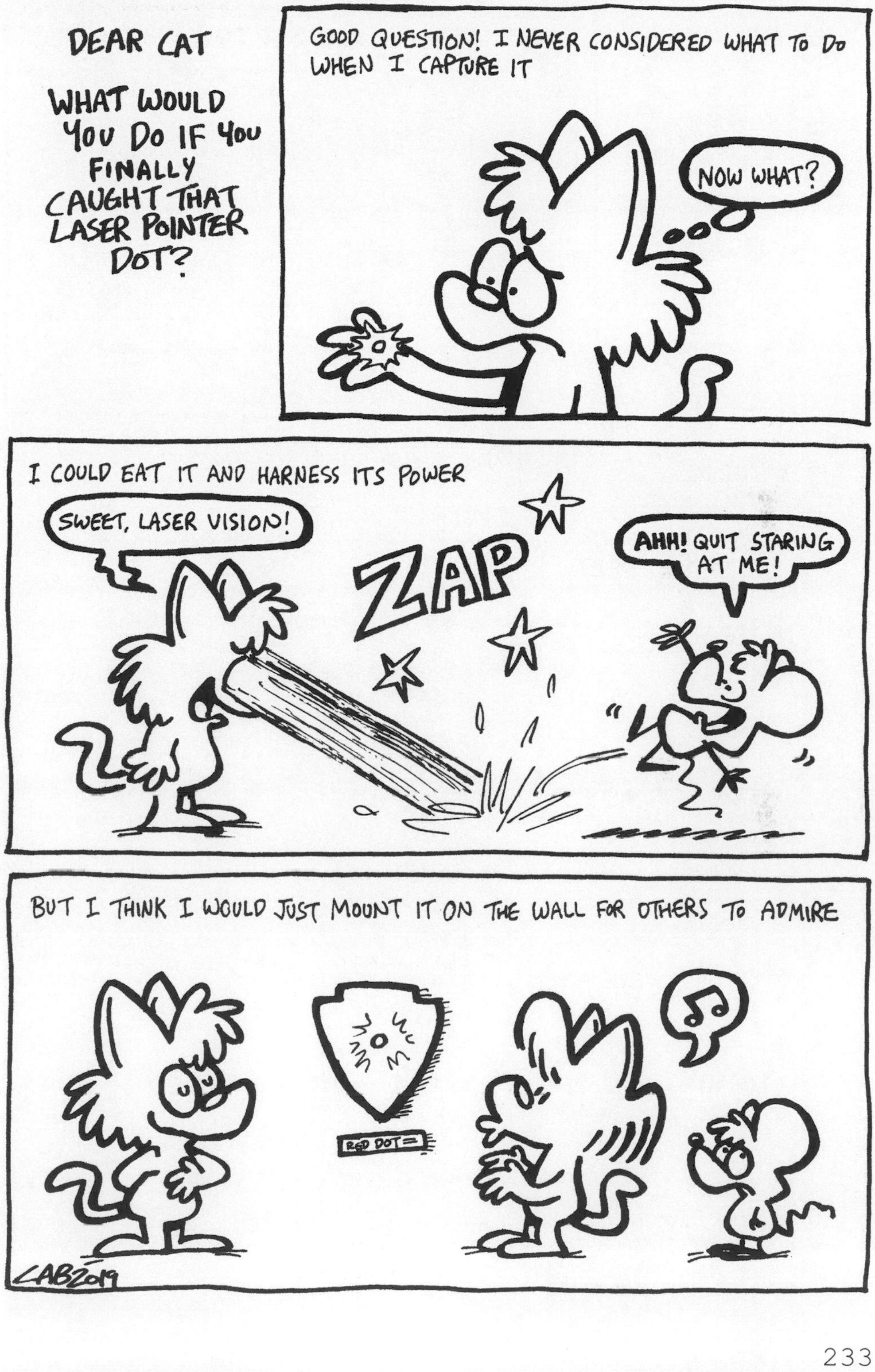
DEAR CAT
WHAT WOULD YOU DO IF YOU FINALLY CAUGHT THAT LASER POINTER DOT?
GOOD QUESTION! I NEVER CONSIDERED WHAT TO DO WHEN I CAPTURE IT
NOW WHAT?
I COULD EAT IT AND HARNESS ITS POWER
SWEET, LASER VISION!
ZAP
AHH! QUIT STARING AT ME!
BUT I THINK I WOULD JUST MOUNT IT ON THE WALL FOR OTHERS TO ADMIRE
RED DOT
CAB2019

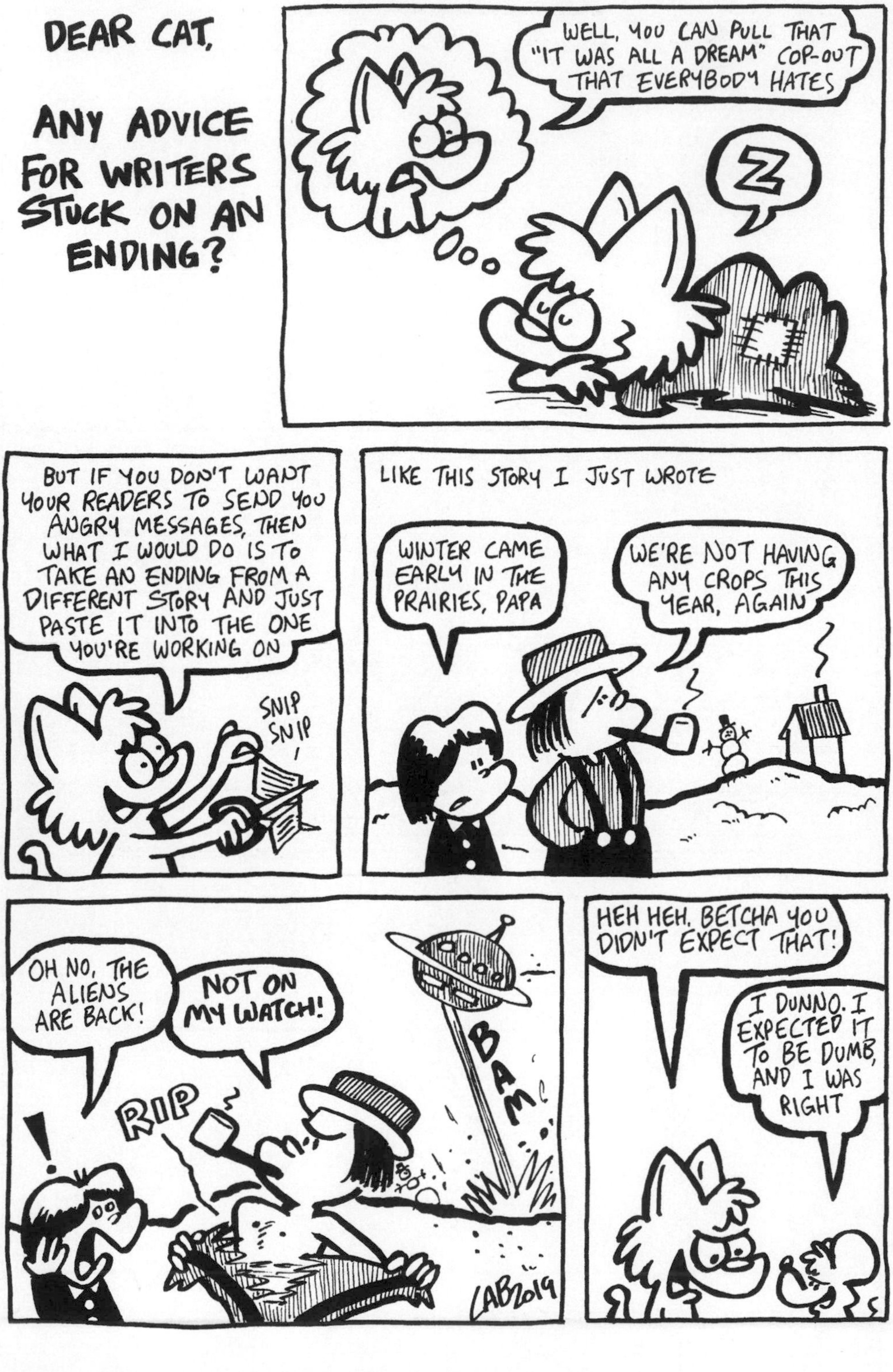
DEAR CAT,
ANY ADVICE FOR WRITERS STUCK ON AN ENDING?
WELL, YOU CAN PULL THAT "IT WAS ALL A DREAM" COP-OUT THAT EVERYBODY HATES
Z
BUT IF YOU DON'T WANT YOUR READERS TO SEND YOU ANGRY MESSAGES, THEN WHAT I WOULD DO IS TO TAKE AN ENDING FROM A DIFFERENT STORY AND JUST PASTE IT INTO THE ONE YOU'RE WORKING ON
SNIP SNIP
LIKE THIS STORY I JUST WROTE
WINTER CAME EARLY IN THE PRAIRIES, PAPA
WE'RE NOT HAVING ANY CROPS THIS YEAR, AGAIN
OH NO, THE ALIENS ARE BACK!
NOT ON MY WATCH!
RIP
BAM
LAB2019
HEH HEH. BETCHA YOU DIDN'T EXPECT THAT!
I DUNNO. I EXPECTED IT TO BE DUMB, AND I WAS RIGHT

DEAR CAT,

DO CATS THINK HUMANS ARE OVERGROWN CATS?

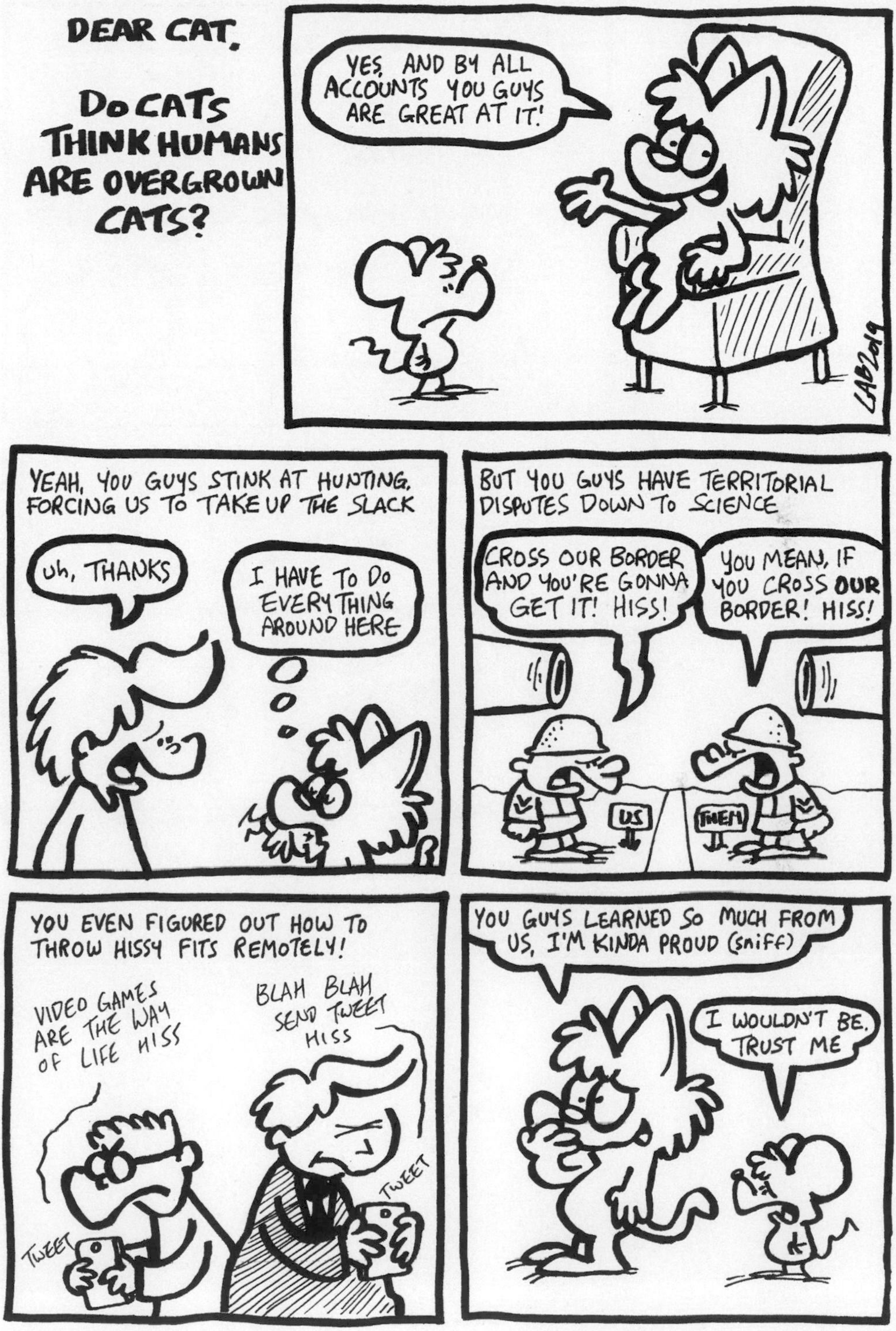
YES, AND BY ALL ACCOUNTS YOU GUYS ARE GREAT AT IT!
LAB2019
YEAH, YOU GUYS STINK AT HUNTING, FORCING US TO TAKE UP THE SLACK
uh, THANKS
I HAVE TO DO EVERYTHING AROUND HERE
BUT YOU GUYS HAVE TERRITORIAL DISPUTES DOWN TO SCIENCE
CROSS OUR BORDER AND YOU'RE GONNA GET IT! HISS!
YOU MEAN, IF YOU CROSS OUR BORDER! HISS!
US
THEM
YOU EVEN FIGURED OUT HOW TO THROW HISSY FITS REMOTELY!
VIDEO GAMES ARE THE WAY OF LIFE HISS
BLAH BLAH SEND TWEET HISS
TWEET
TWEET
YOU GUYS LEARNED SO MUCH FROM US, I'M KINDA PROUD (sniff)
I WOULDN'T BE. TRUST ME

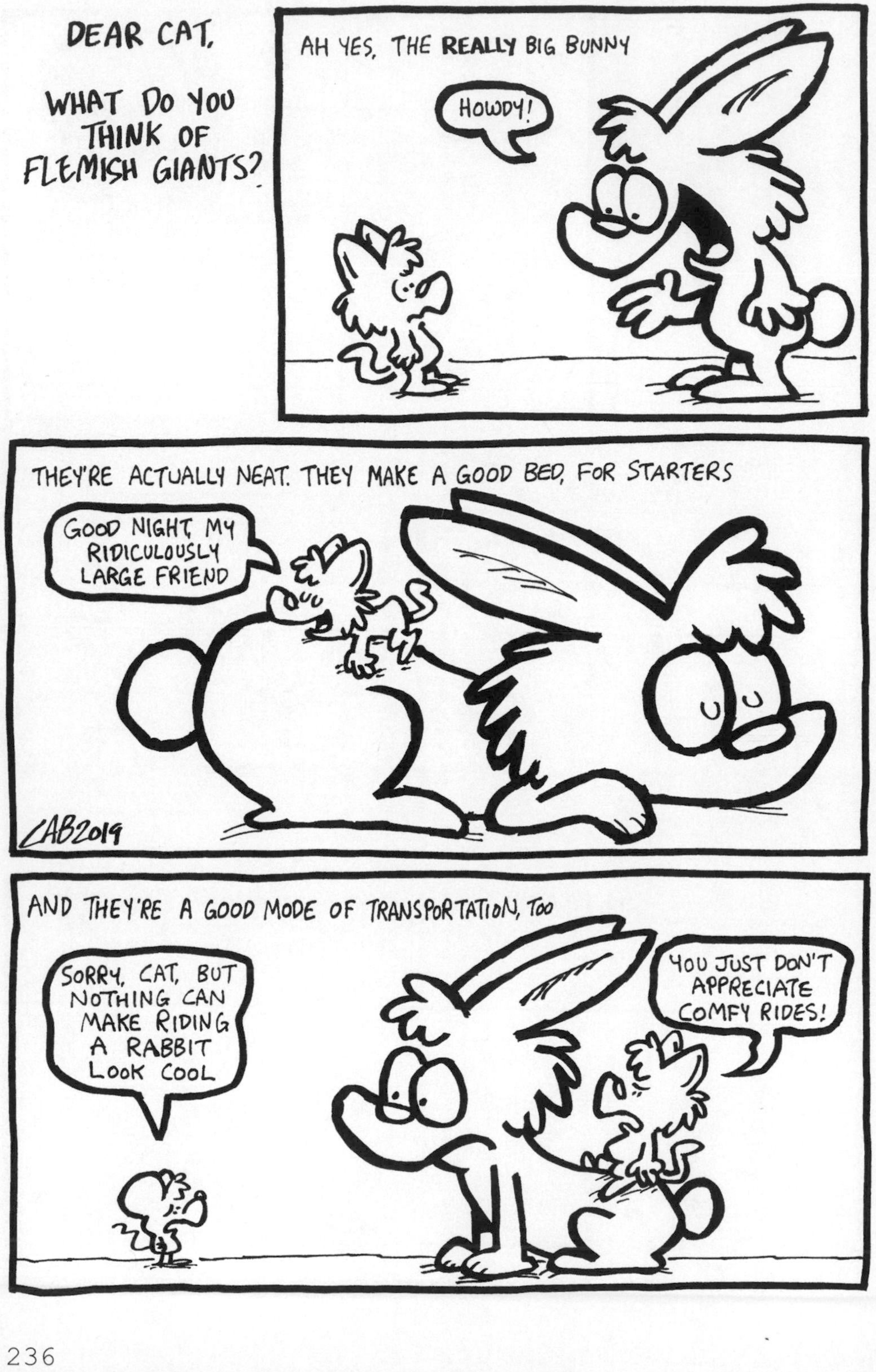
DEAR CAT,
WHAT DO YOU THINK OF FLEMISH GIANTS?
AH YES, THE **REALLY** BIG BUNNY
HOWDY!
THEY'RE ACTUALLY NEAT. THEY MAKE A GOOD BED, FOR STARTERS
GOOD NIGHT, MY RIDICULOUSLY LARGE FRIEND
CAB2019
AND THEY'RE A GOOD MODE OF TRANSPORTATION, TOO
SORRY, CAT, BUT NOTHING CAN MAKE RIDING A RABBIT LOOK COOL
YOU JUST DON'T APPRECIATE COMFY RIDES!

DEAR CAT,

HOW COME YOU NO LONGER LIKE THE FOOD FROM LAST WEEK?

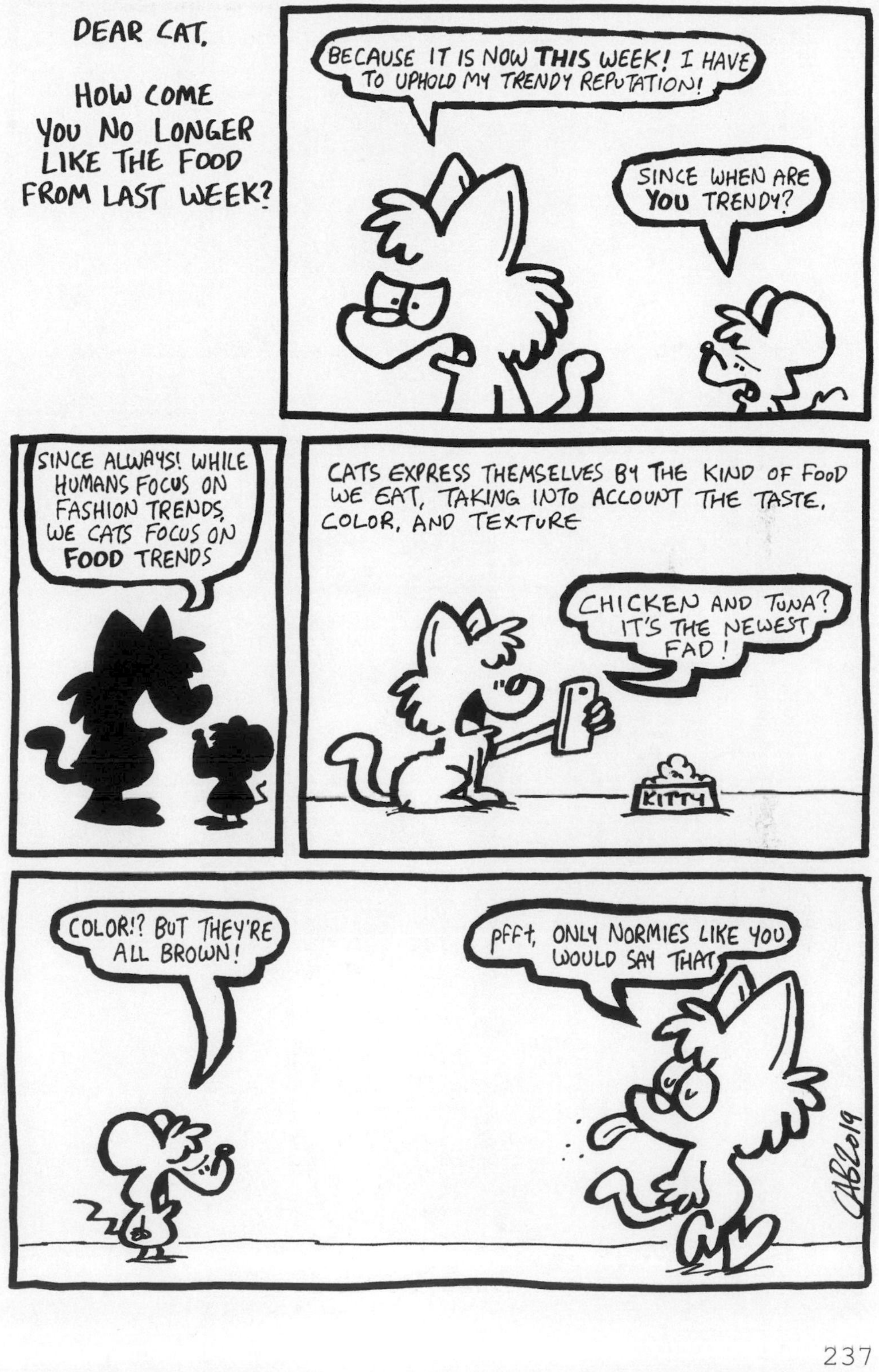

BECAUSE IT IS NOW **THIS** WEEK! I HAVE TO UPHOLD MY TRENDY REPUTATION!
SINCE WHEN ARE **YOU** TRENDY?
SINCE ALWAYS! WHILE HUMANS FOCUS ON FASHION TRENDS, WE CATS FOCUS ON **FOOD** TRENDS
CATS EXPRESS THEMSELVES BY THE KIND OF FOOD WE EAT, TAKING INTO ACCOUNT THE TASTE, COLOR, AND TEXTURE
CHICKEN AND TUNA? IT'S THE NEWEST FAD!
KITTY
COLOR!? BUT THEY'RE ALL BROWN!
pfft, ONLY NORMIES LIKE YOU WOULD SAY THAT
CABCo2019

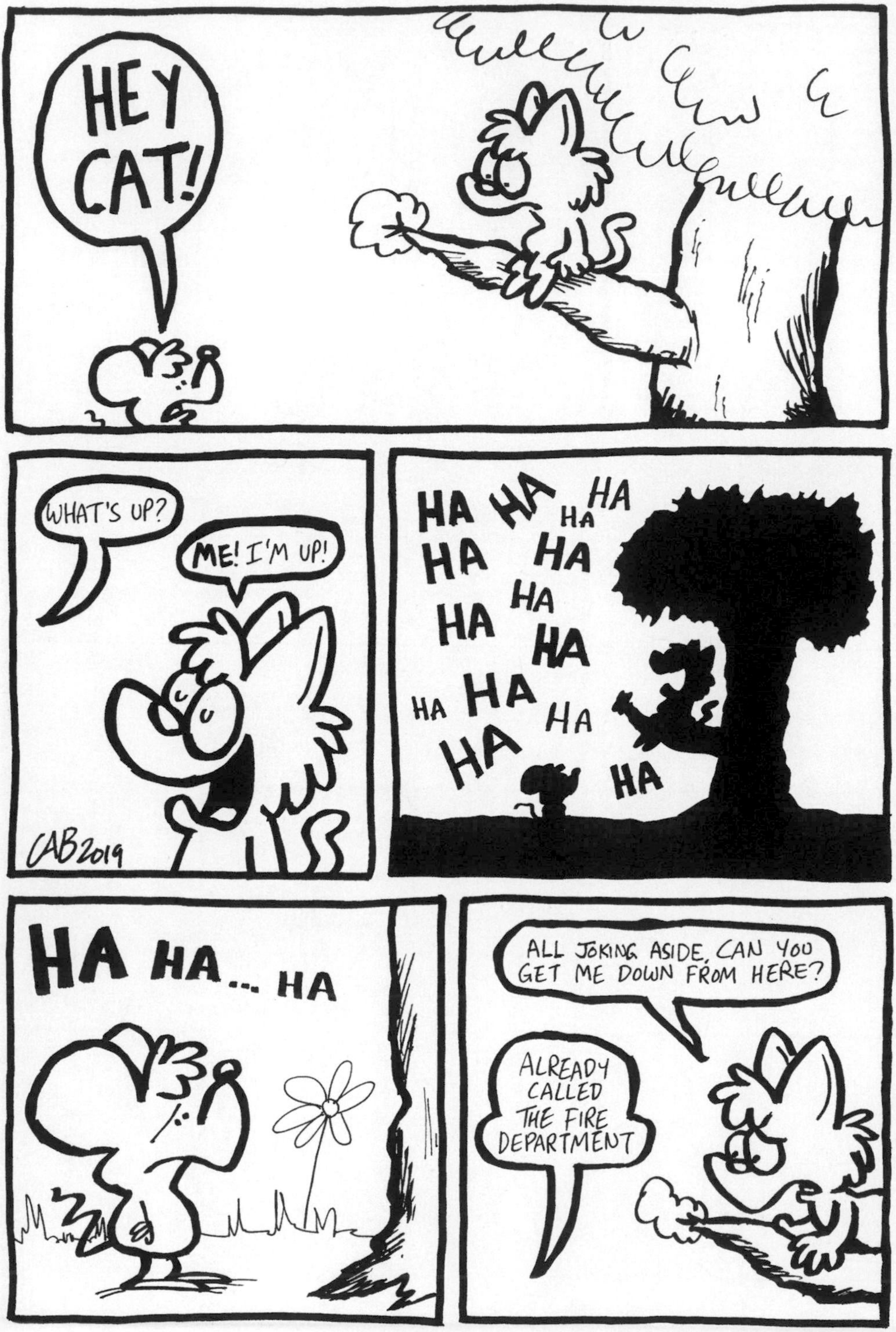
HEY CAT!
WHAT'S UP?
ME! I'M UP!
HA HA HA HA HA HA HA HA HA HA HA HA HA HA HA HA
HA HA... HA
ALL JOKING ASIDE, CAN YOU GET ME DOWN FROM HERE?
ALREADY CALLED THE FIRE DEPARTMENT
CAB 2019

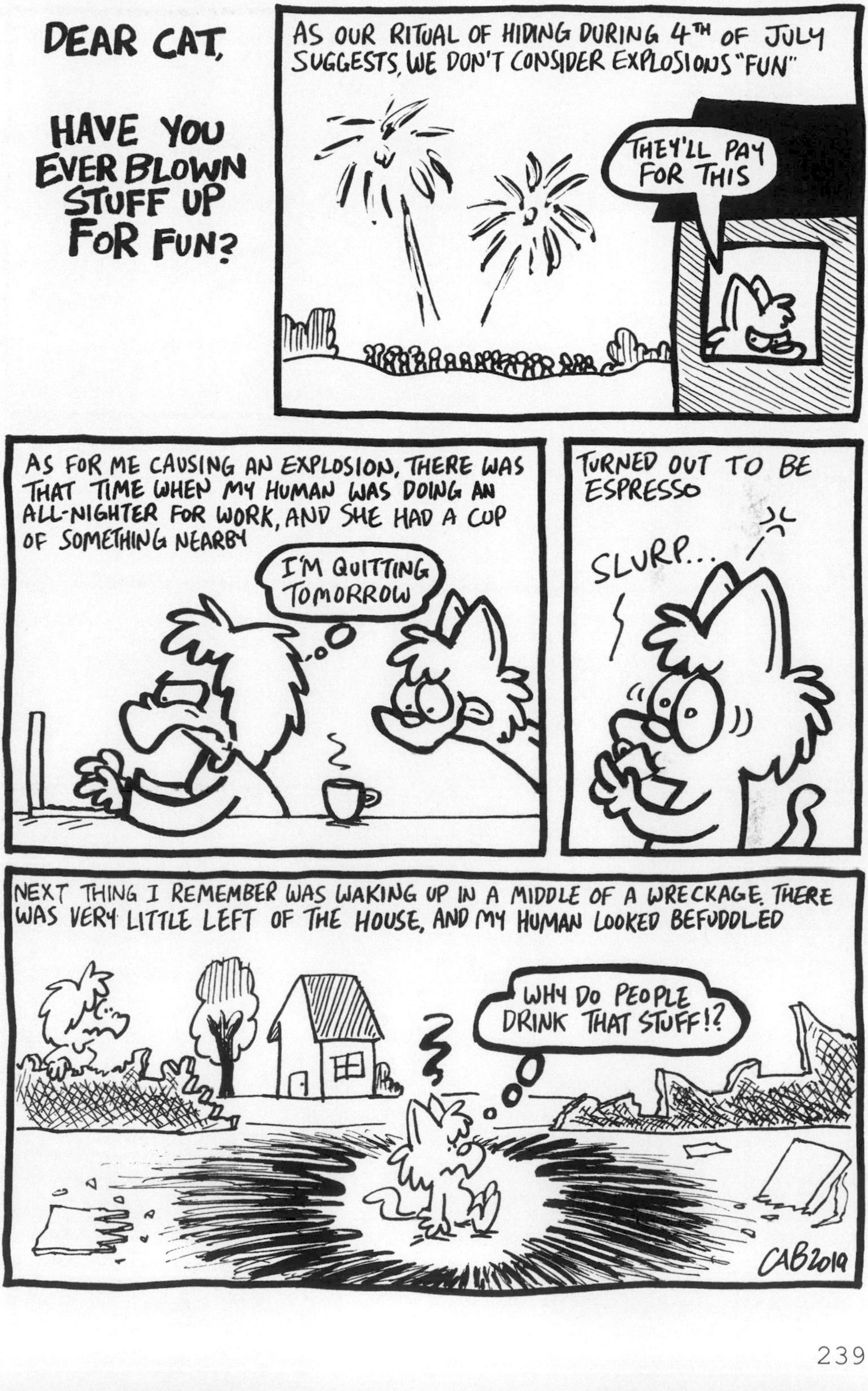
DEAR CAT,
HAVE YOU EVER BLOWN STUFF UP FOR FUN?
AS OUR RITUAL OF HIDING DURING 4TH OF JULY SUGGESTS, WE DON'T CONSIDER EXPLOSIONS "FUN"
THEY'LL PAY FOR THIS
AS FOR ME CAUSING AN EXPLOSION, THERE WAS THAT TIME WHEN MY HUMAN WAS DOING AN ALL-NIGHTER FOR WORK, AND SHE HAD A CUP OF SOMETHING NEARBY
I'M QUITTING TOMORROW
TURNED OUT TO BE ESPRESSO
SLURP...
NEXT THING I REMEMBER WAS WAKING UP IN A MIDDLE OF A WRECKAGE. THERE WAS VERY LITTLE LEFT OF THE HOUSE, AND MY HUMAN LOOKED BEFUDDLED
WHY DO PEOPLE DRINK THAT STUFF!?
CAB2019

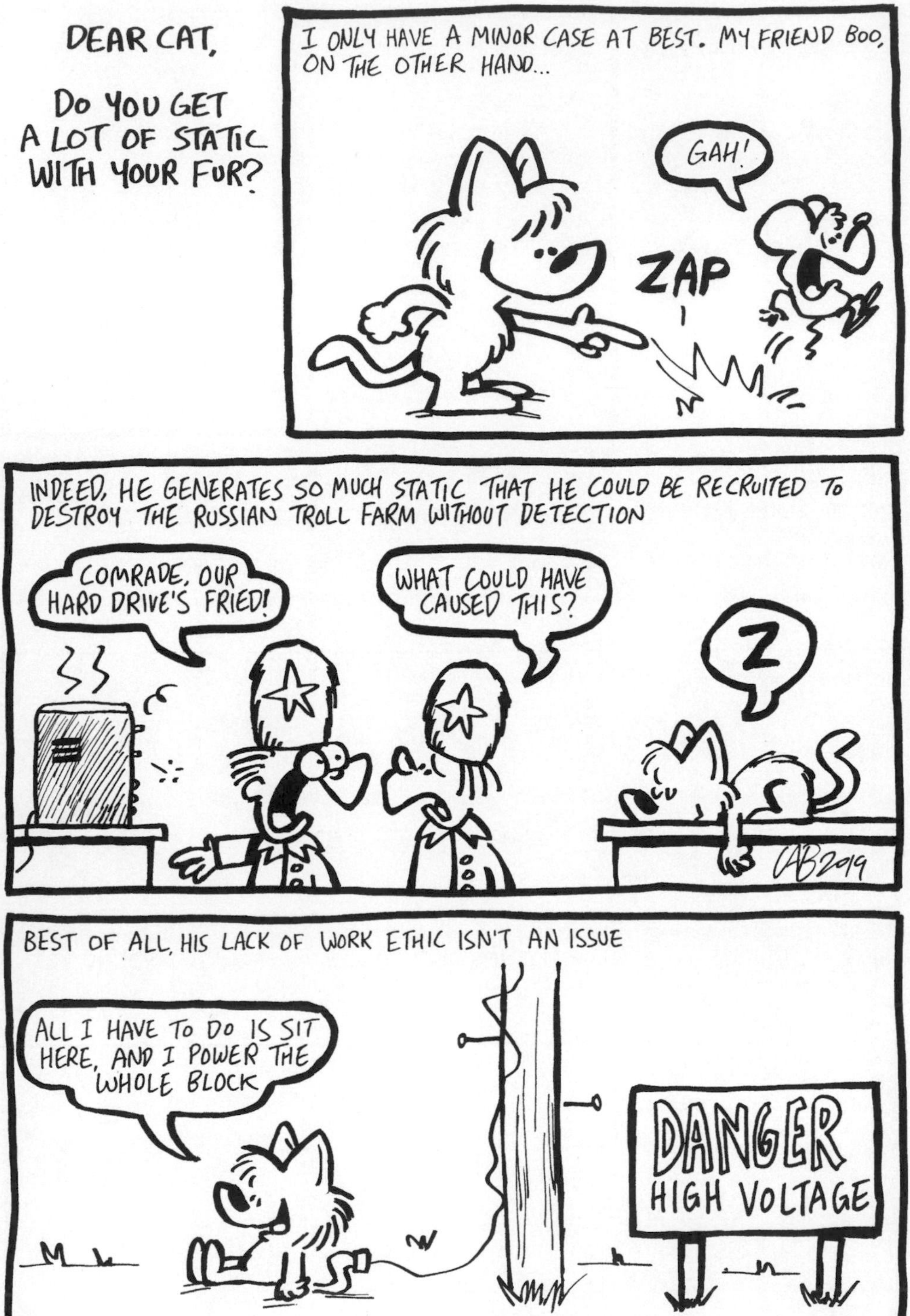
DEAR CAT,
DO YOU GET A LOT OF STATIC WITH YOUR FUR?
I ONLY HAVE A MINOR CASE AT BEST. MY FRIEND BOO, ON THE OTHER HAND...
GAH!
ZAP
INDEED, HE GENERATES SO MUCH STATIC THAT HE COULD BE RECRUITED TO DESTROY THE RUSSIAN TROLL FARM WITHOUT DETECTION
COMRADE, OUR HARD DRIVE'S FRIED!
WHAT COULD HAVE CAUSED THIS?
Z
CAB 2019
BEST OF ALL, HIS LACK OF WORK ETHIC ISN'T AN ISSUE
ALL I HAVE TO DO IS SIT HERE, AND I POWER THE WHOLE BLOCK
DANGER
HIGH VOLTAGE

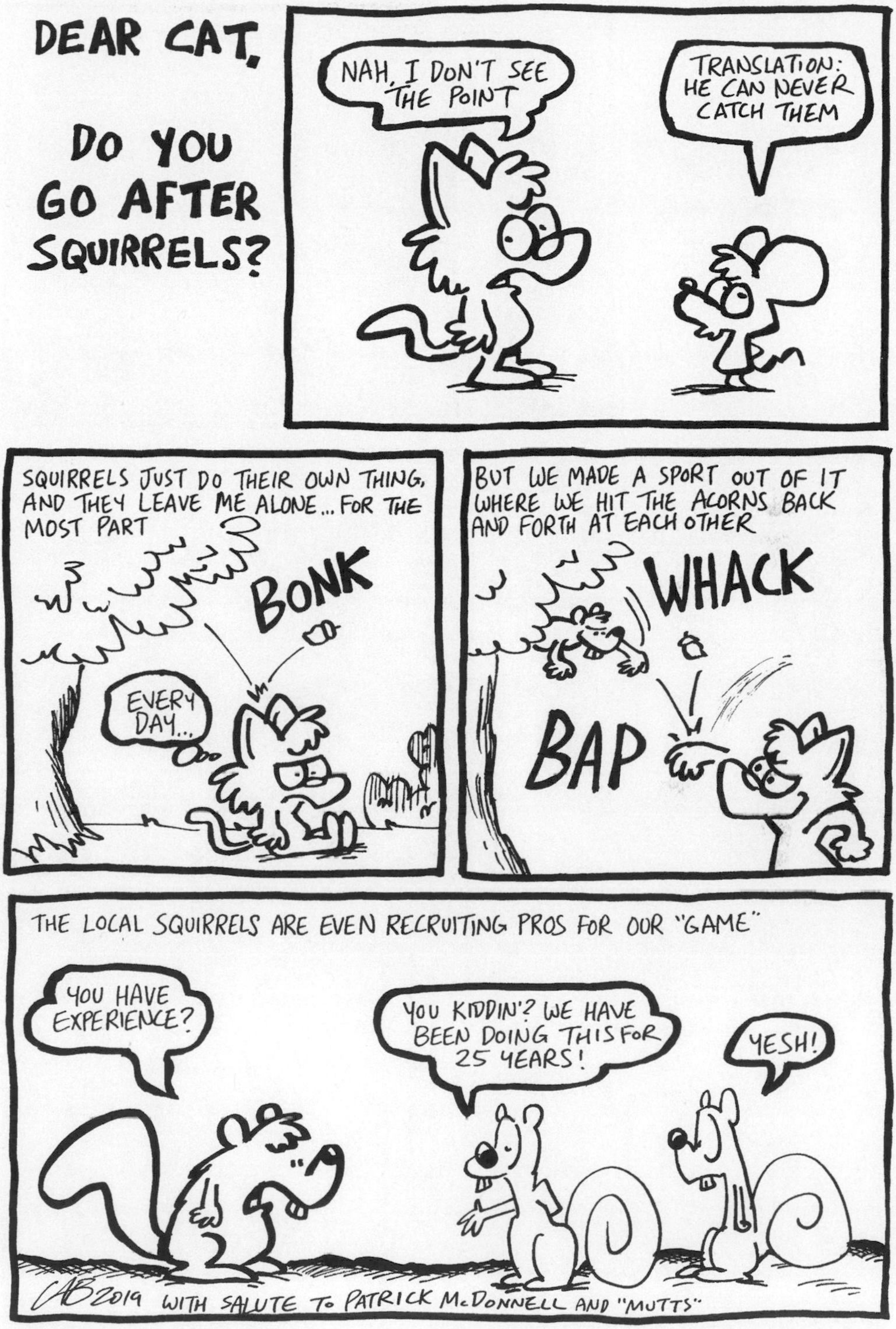
DEAR CAT,
DO YOU GO AFTER SQUIRRELS?
NAH, I DON'T SEE THE POINT
TRANSLATION: HE CAN NEVER CATCH THEM
SQUIRRELS JUST DO THEIR OWN THING, AND THEY LEAVE ME ALONE... FOR THE MOST PART
BONK
EVERY DAY...
BUT WE MADE A SPORT OUT OF IT WHERE WE HIT THE ACORNS BACK AND FORTH AT EACH OTHER
WHACK
BAP
THE LOCAL SQUIRRELS ARE EVEN RECRUITING PROS FOR OUR "GAME"
YOU HAVE EXPERIENCE?
YOU KIDDIN'? WE HAVE BEEN DOING THIS FOR 25 YEARS!
YESH!
CAB 2019 WITH SALUTE TO PATRICK McDONNELL AND "MUTTS"

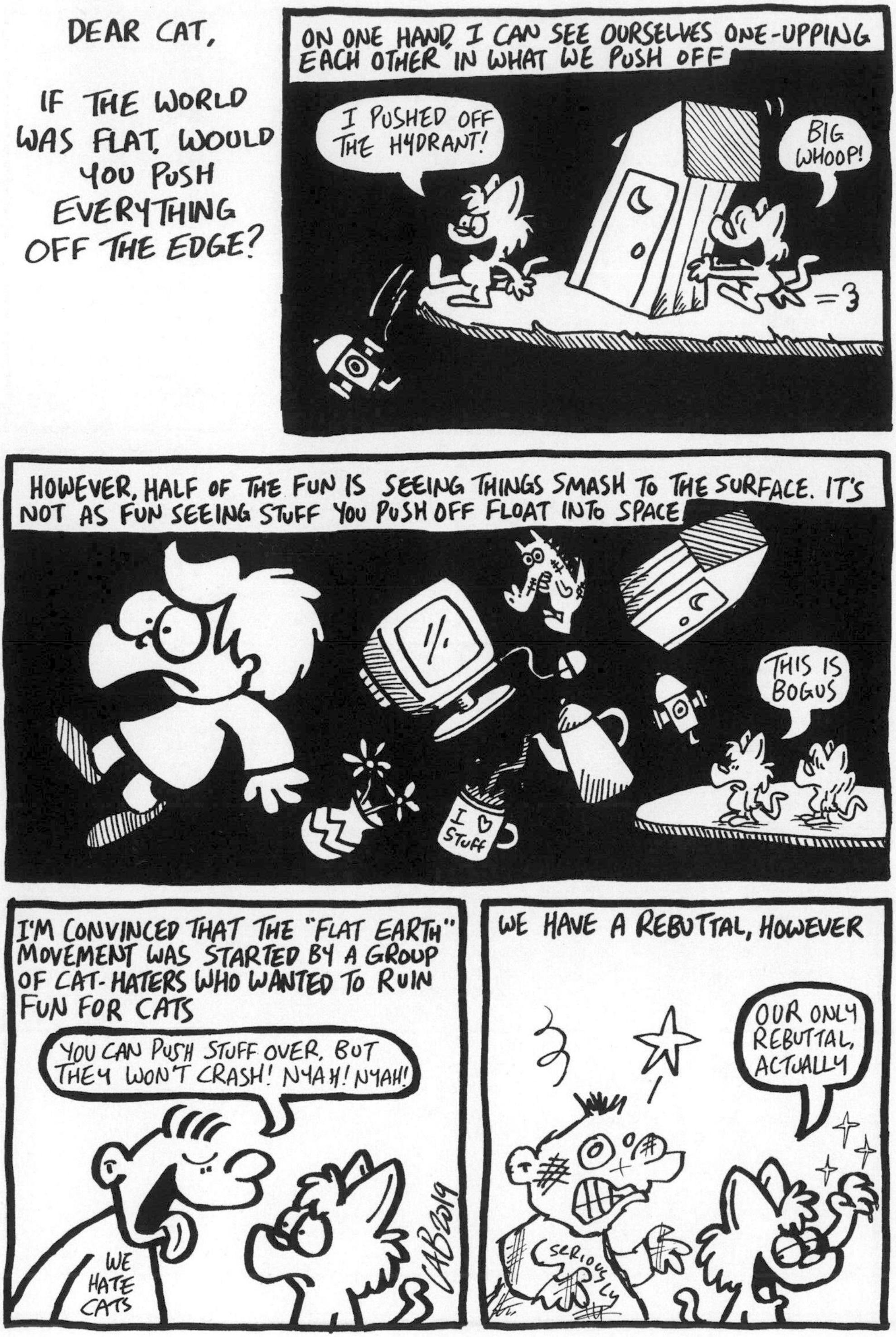
DEAR CAT,
IF THE WORLD WAS FLAT, WOULD YOU PUSH EVERYTHING OFF THE EDGE?
ON ONE HAND, I CAN SEE OURSELVES ONE-UPPING EACH OTHER IN WHAT WE PUSH OFF
I PUSHED OFF THE HYDRANT!
BIG WHOOP!
HOWEVER, HALF OF THE FUN IS SEEING THINGS SMASH TO THE SURFACE. IT'S NOT AS FUN SEEING STUFF YOU PUSH OFF FLOAT INTO SPACE
I ♡ STUFF
THIS IS BOGUS
I'M CONVINCED THAT THE "FLAT EARTH" MOVEMENT WAS STARTED BY A GROUP OF CAT-HATERS WHO WANTED TO RUIN FUN FOR CATS
YOU CAN PUSH STUFF OVER, BUT THEY WON'T CRASH! NYAH! NYAH!
WE HATE CATS
CAB2019
WE HAVE A REBUTTAL, HOWEVER
OUR ONLY REBUTTAL, ACTUALLY
SERIOUSLY

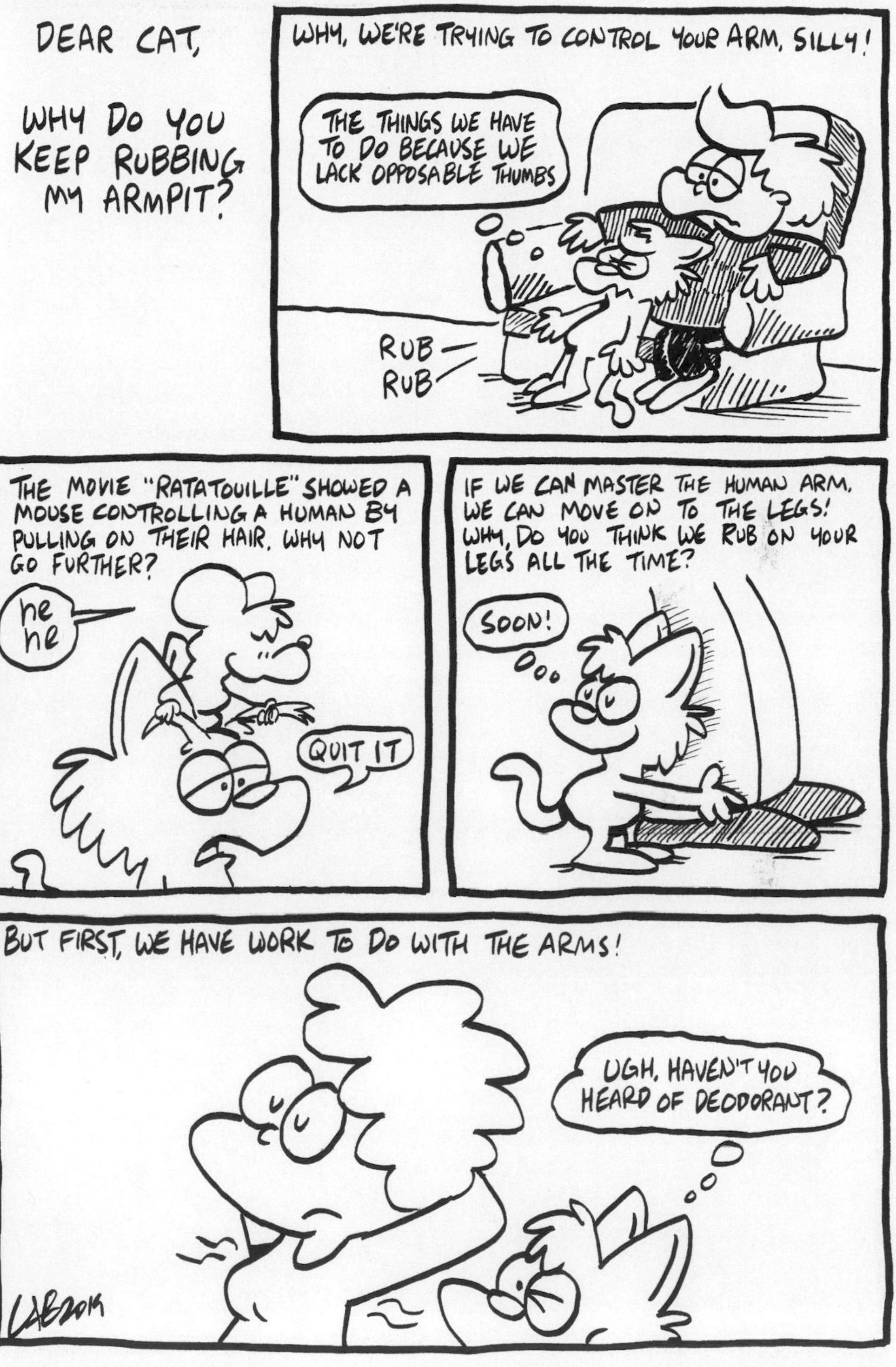
DEAR CAT,
WHY DO YOU KEEP RUBBING MY ARMPIT?
WHY, WE'RE TRYING TO CONTROL YOUR ARM, SILLY!
THE THINGS WE HAVE TO DO BECAUSE WE LACK OPPOSABLE THUMBS
RUB
RUB
THE MOVIE "RATATOUILLE" SHOWED A MOUSE CONTROLLING A HUMAN BY PULLING ON THEIR HAIR. WHY NOT GO FURTHER?
he he
QUIT IT
IF WE CAN MASTER THE HUMAN ARM, WE CAN MOVE ON TO THE LEGS! WHY, DO YOU THINK WE RUB ON YOUR LEGS ALL THE TIME?
SOON!
BUT FIRST, WE HAVE WORK TO DO WITH THE ARMS!
UGH, HAVEN'T YOU HEARD OF DEODORANT?
LAB2014

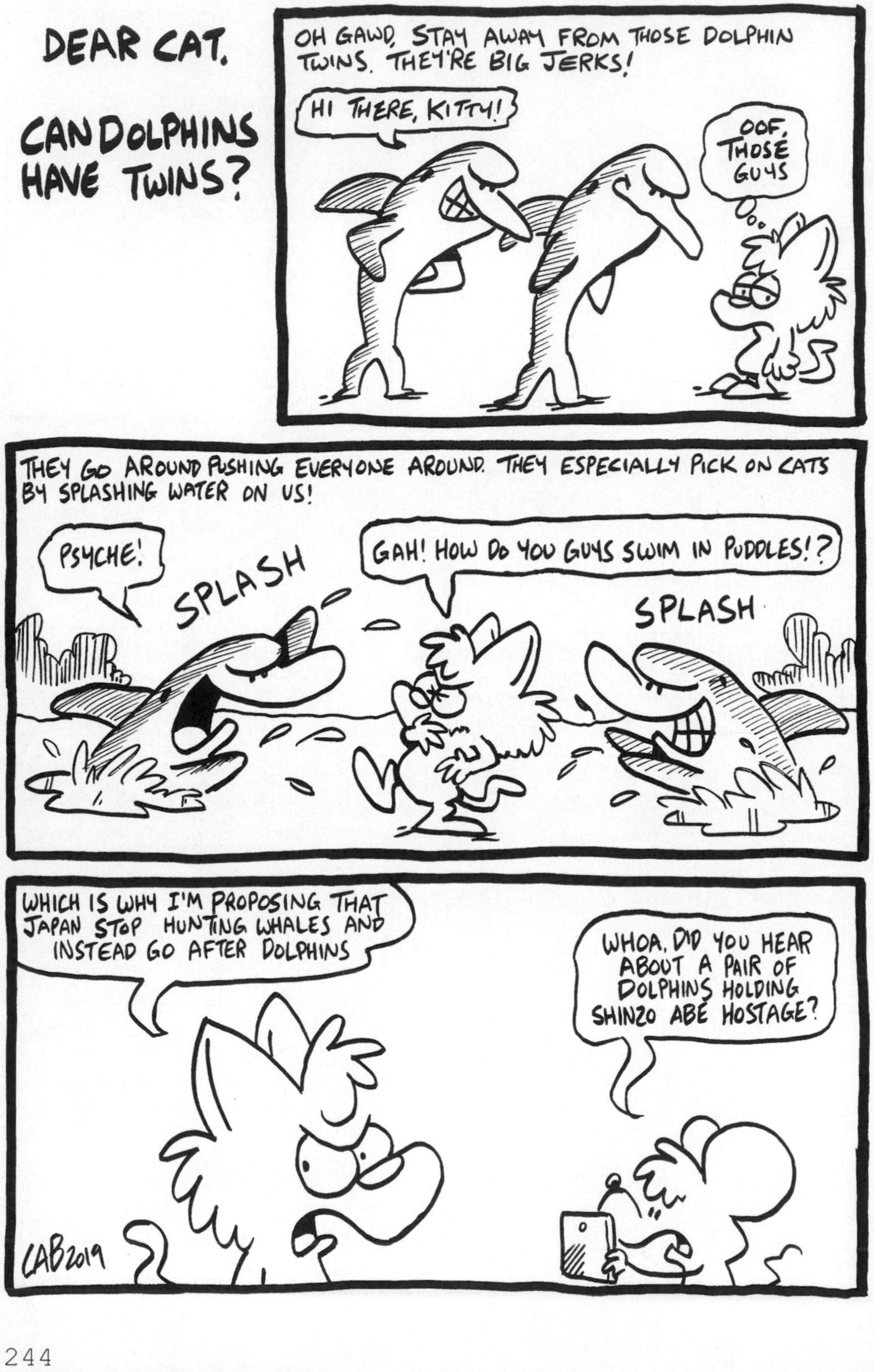
DEAR CAT.
CAN DOLPHINS HAVE TWINS?
OH GAWD, STAY AWAY FROM THOSE DOLPHIN TWINS. THEY'RE BIG JERKS!
HI THERE, KITTY!
OOF, THOSE GUYS
THEY GO AROUND PUSHING EVERYONE AROUND. THEY ESPECIALLY PICK ON CATS BY SPLASHING WATER ON US!
PSYCHE!
SPLASH
GAH! HOW DO YOU GUYS SWIM IN PUDDLES!?
SPLASH
WHICH IS WHY I'M PROPOSING THAT JAPAN STOP HUNTING WHALES AND INSTEAD GO AFTER DOLPHINS
WHOA. DID YOU HEAR ABOUT A PAIR OF DOLPHINS HOLDING SHINZO ABE HOSTAGE?
CAB2019

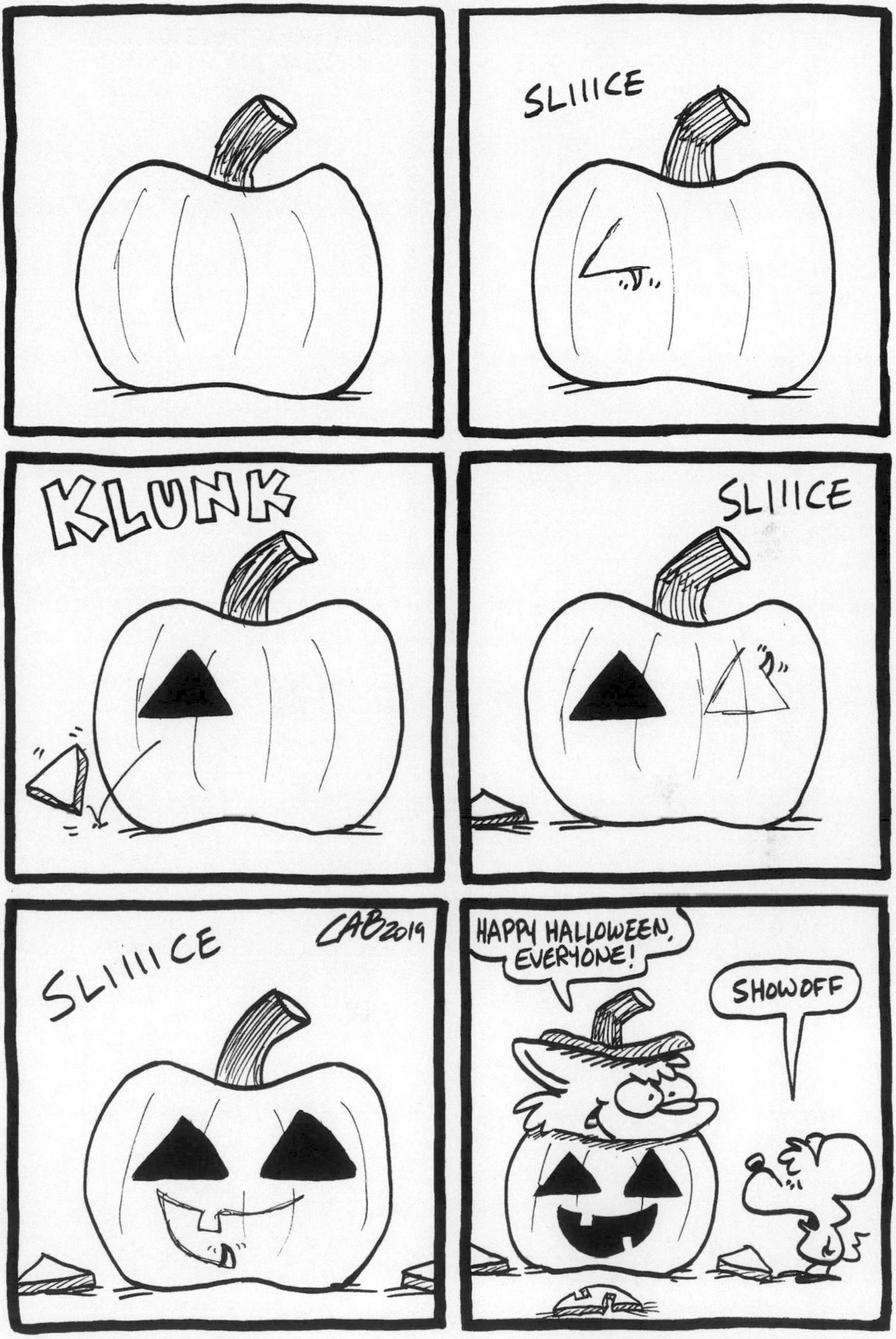
SLIIICE
KLUNK
SLIIICE
SLIIIICE
CAB 2019
HAPPY HALLOWEEN, EVERYONE!
SHOWOFF

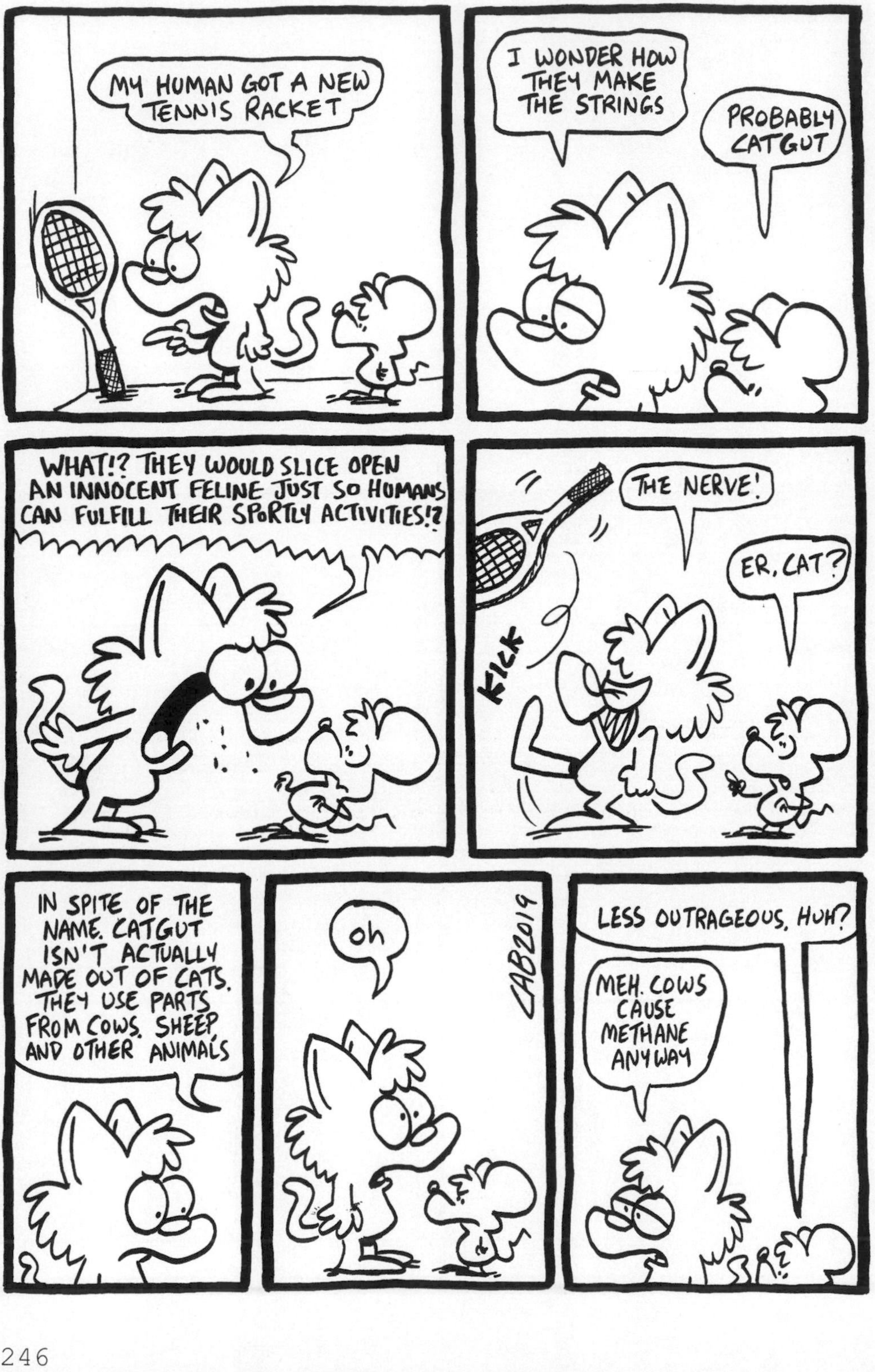
MY HUMAN GOT A NEW TENNIS RACKET
I WONDER HOW THEY MAKE THE STRINGS
PROBABLY CATGUT
WHAT!? THEY WOULD SLICE OPEN AN INNOCENT FELINE JUST SO HUMANS CAN FULFILL THEIR SPORTLY ACTIVITIES!?
THE NERVE!
KICK
ER, CAT?
IN SPITE OF THE NAME, CATGUT ISN'T ACTUALLY MADE OUT OF CATS. THEY USE PARTS FROM COWS, SHEEP AND OTHER ANIMALS
oh
CAB2019
LESS OUTRAGEOUS, HUH?
MEH. COWS CAUSE METHANE ANYWAY

DEAR CAT, I GOT A ROCK

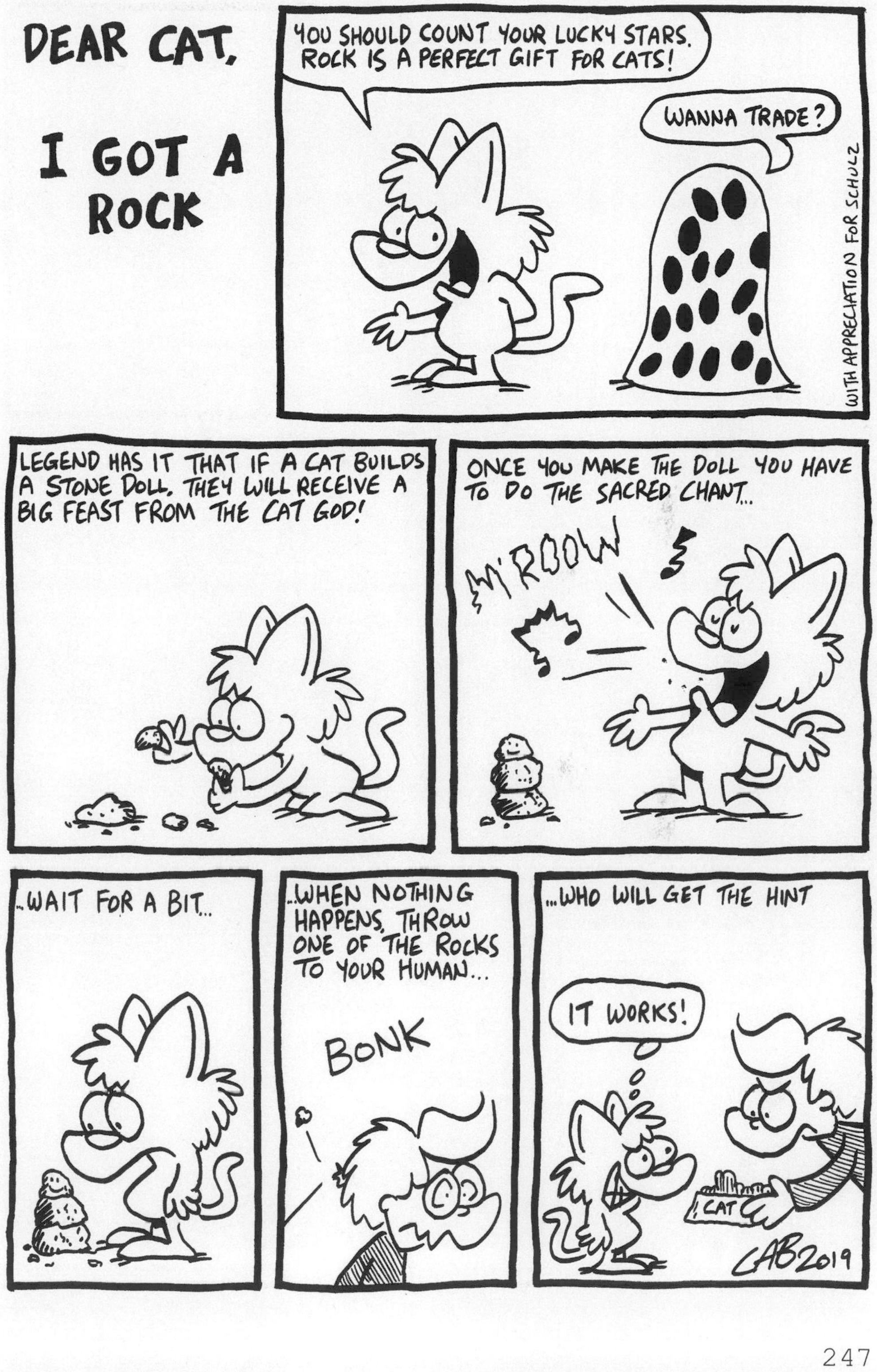

YOU SHOULD COUNT YOUR LUCKY STARS. ROCK IS A PERFECT GIFT FOR CATS!
WANNA TRADE?
WITH APPRECIATION FOR SCHULZ
LEGEND HAS IT THAT IF A CAT BUILDS A STONE DOLL, THEY WILL RECEIVE A BIG FEAST FROM THE CAT GOD!
ONCE YOU MAKE THE DOLL YOU HAVE TO DO THE SACRED CHANT...
M'ROOW
...WAIT FOR A BIT...
...WHEN NOTHING HAPPENS, THROW ONE OF THE ROCKS TO YOUR HUMAN...
BONK
...WHO WILL GET THE HINT
IT WORKS!
CAT
CAB 2019

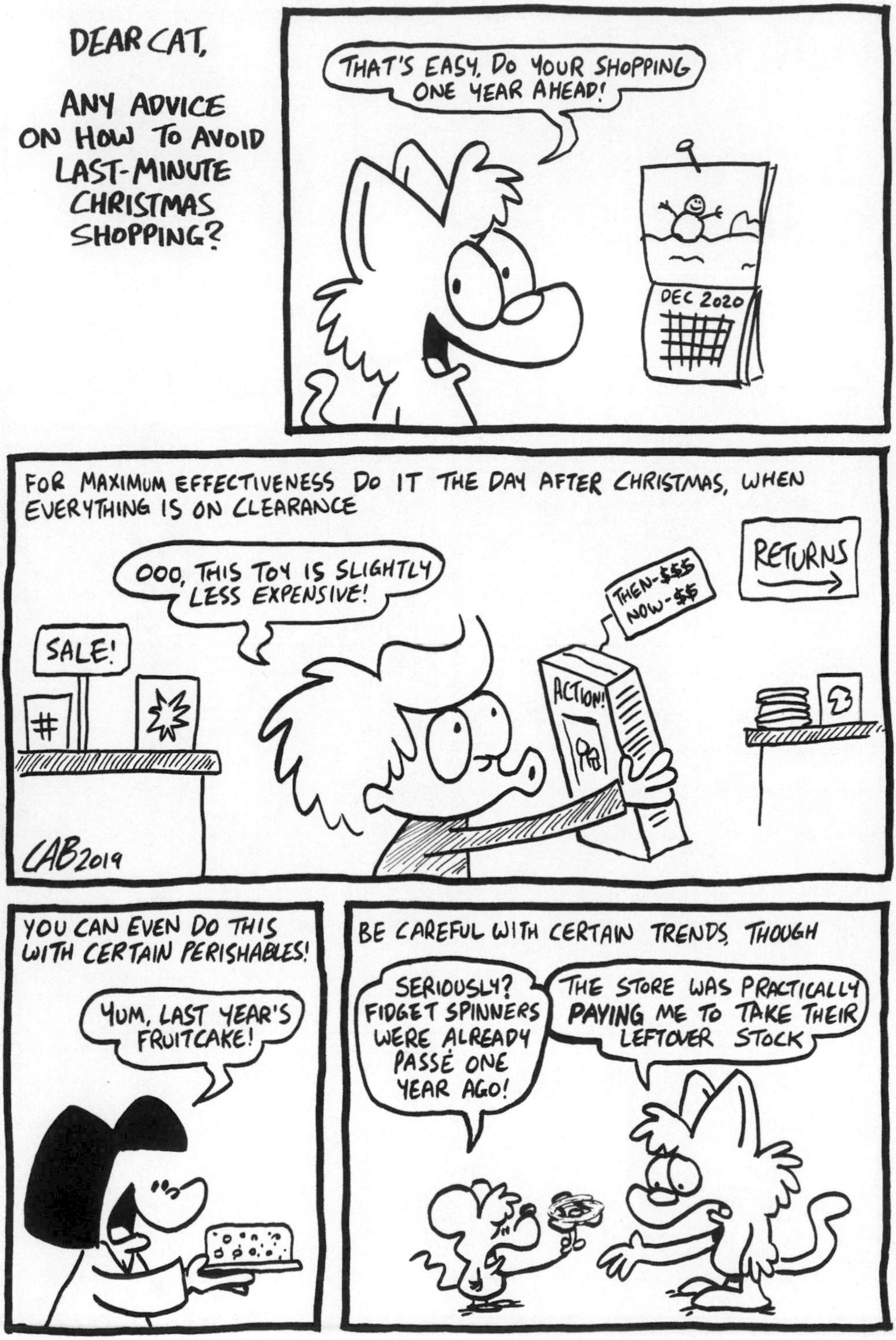
DEAR CAT,
ANY ADVICE ON HOW TO AVOID LAST-MINUTE CHRISTMAS SHOPPING?
THAT'S EASY. DO YOUR SHOPPING ONE YEAR AHEAD!
DEC 2020
FOR MAXIMUM EFFECTIVENESS DO IT THE DAY AFTER CHRISTMAS, WHEN EVERYTHING IS ON CLEARANCE
OOO, THIS TOY IS SLIGHTLY LESS EXPENSIVE!
THEN-$$$
NOW-$$
RETURNS
SALE!
ACTION!
CAB2019
YOU CAN EVEN DO THIS WITH CERTAIN PERISHABLES!
YUM, LAST YEAR'S FRUITCAKE!
BE CAREFUL WITH CERTAIN TRENDS, THOUGH
SERIOUSLY? FIDGET SPINNERS WERE ALREADY PASSÉ ONE YEAR AGO!
THE STORE WAS PRACTICALLY PAYING ME TO TAKE THEIR LEFTOVER STOCK

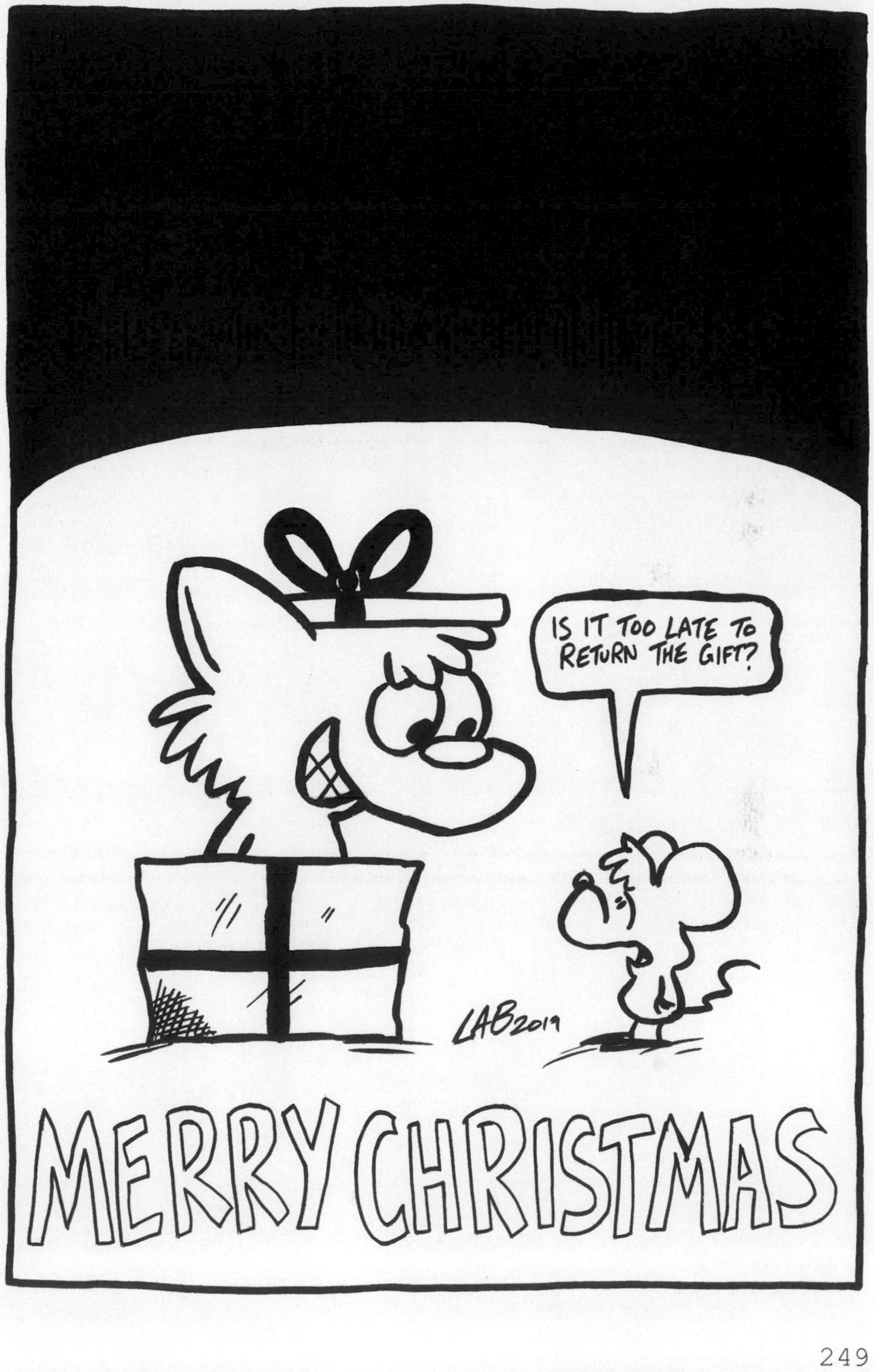
IS IT TOO LATE TO RETURN THE GIFT?
LAB2019
MERRY CHRISTMAS

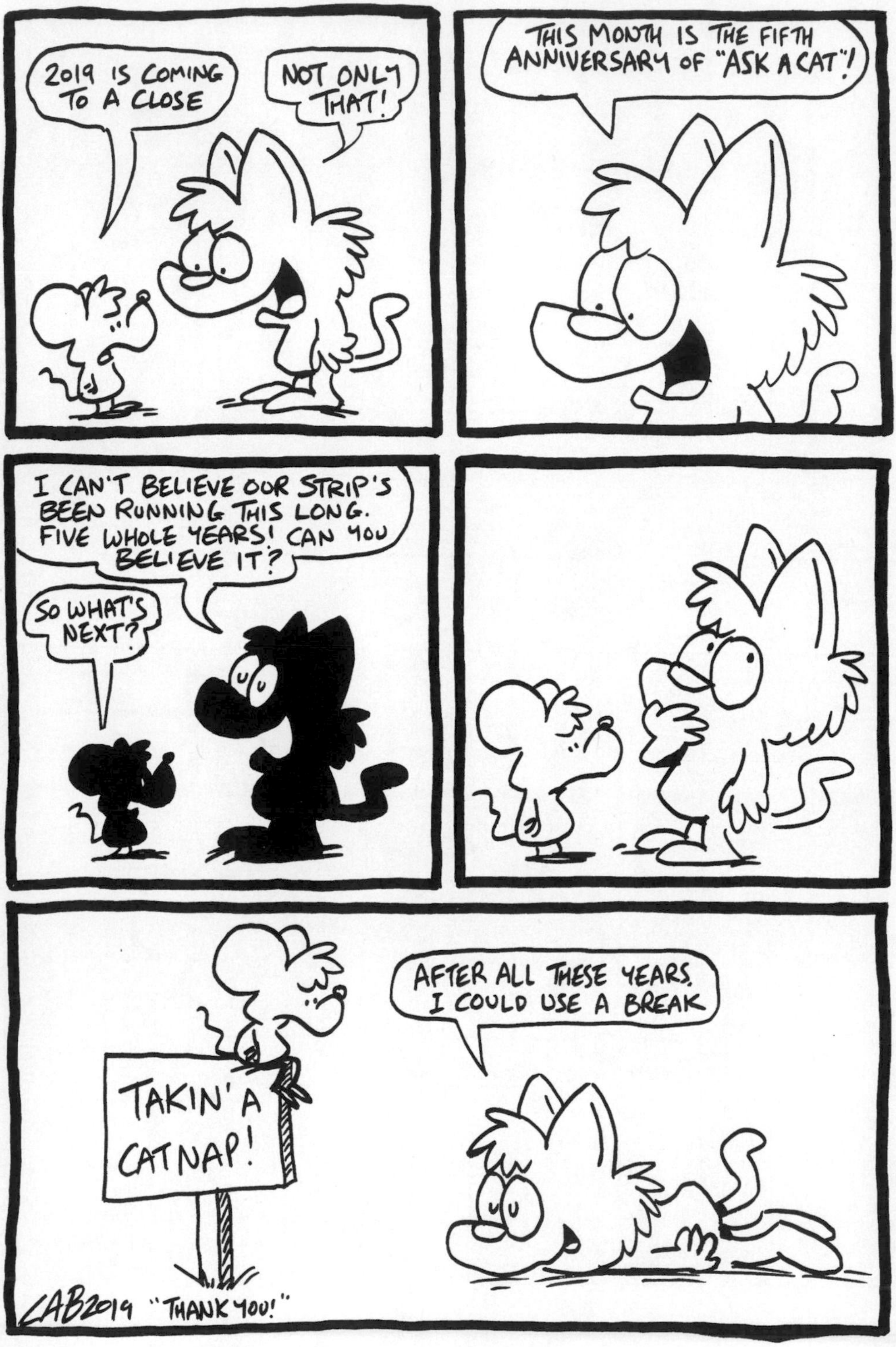
2019 IS COMING TO A CLOSE
NOT ONLY THAT!
THIS MONTH IS THE FIFTH ANNIVERSARY OF "ASK A CAT"!
I CAN'T BELIEVE OUR STRIP'S BEEN RUNNING THIS LONG. FIVE WHOLE YEARS! CAN YOU BELIEVE IT?
SO WHAT'S NEXT?
AFTER ALL THESE YEARS, I COULD USE A BREAK
TAKIN' A CATNAP!
CAB2019 "THANK YOU!"

OTHER COMICS

A selection of one-shot comics I have done over the years.

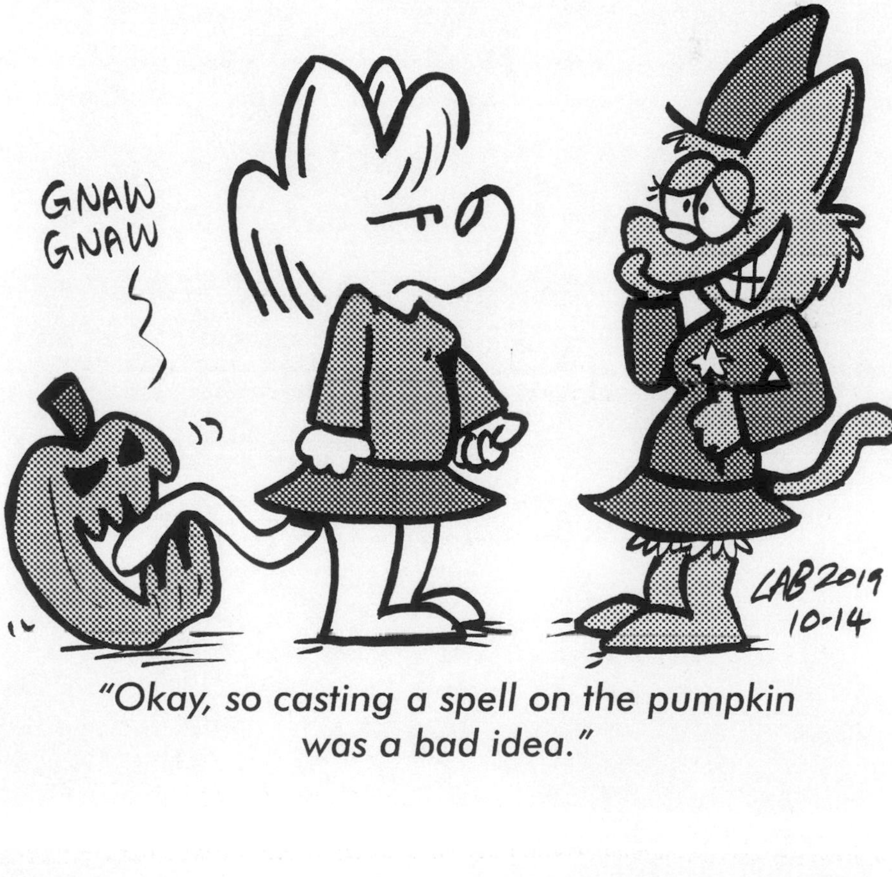
GNAW
GNAW
LAB 2019
10-14

"Okay, so casting a spell on the pumpkin was a bad idea."

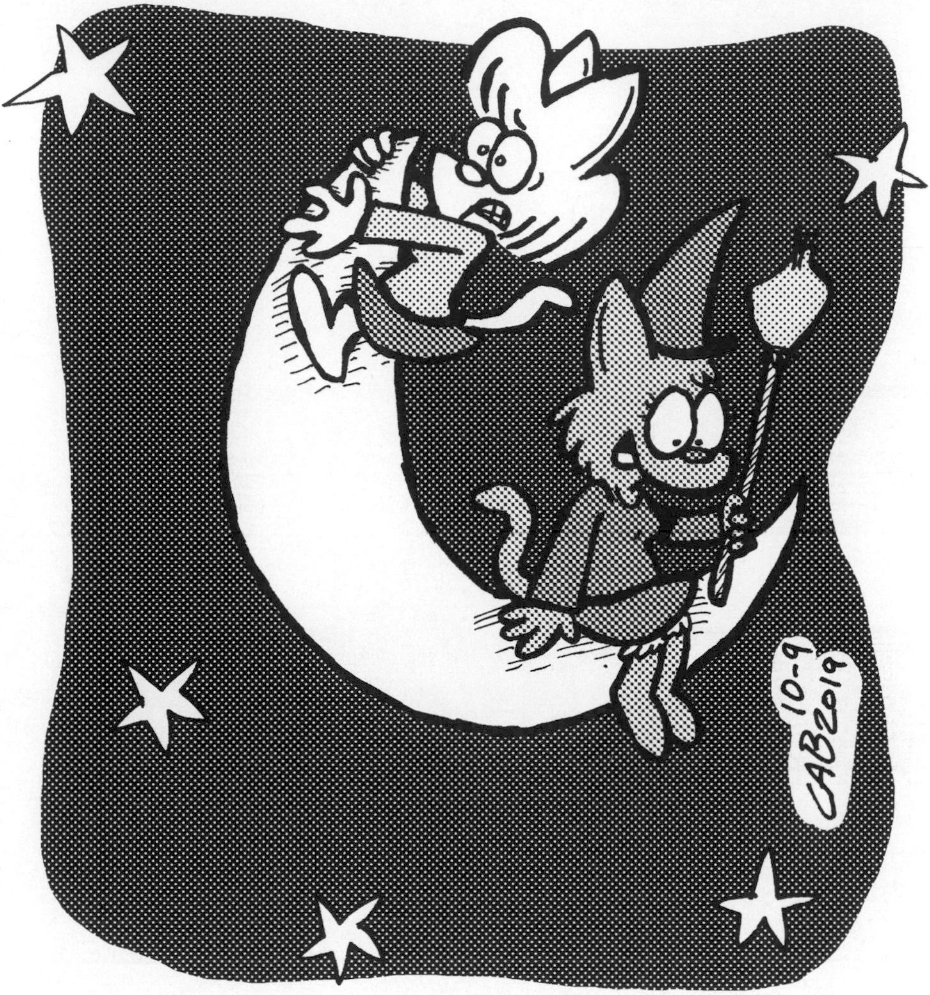
10-9
CAB2019

"Isn't the night view great!?"

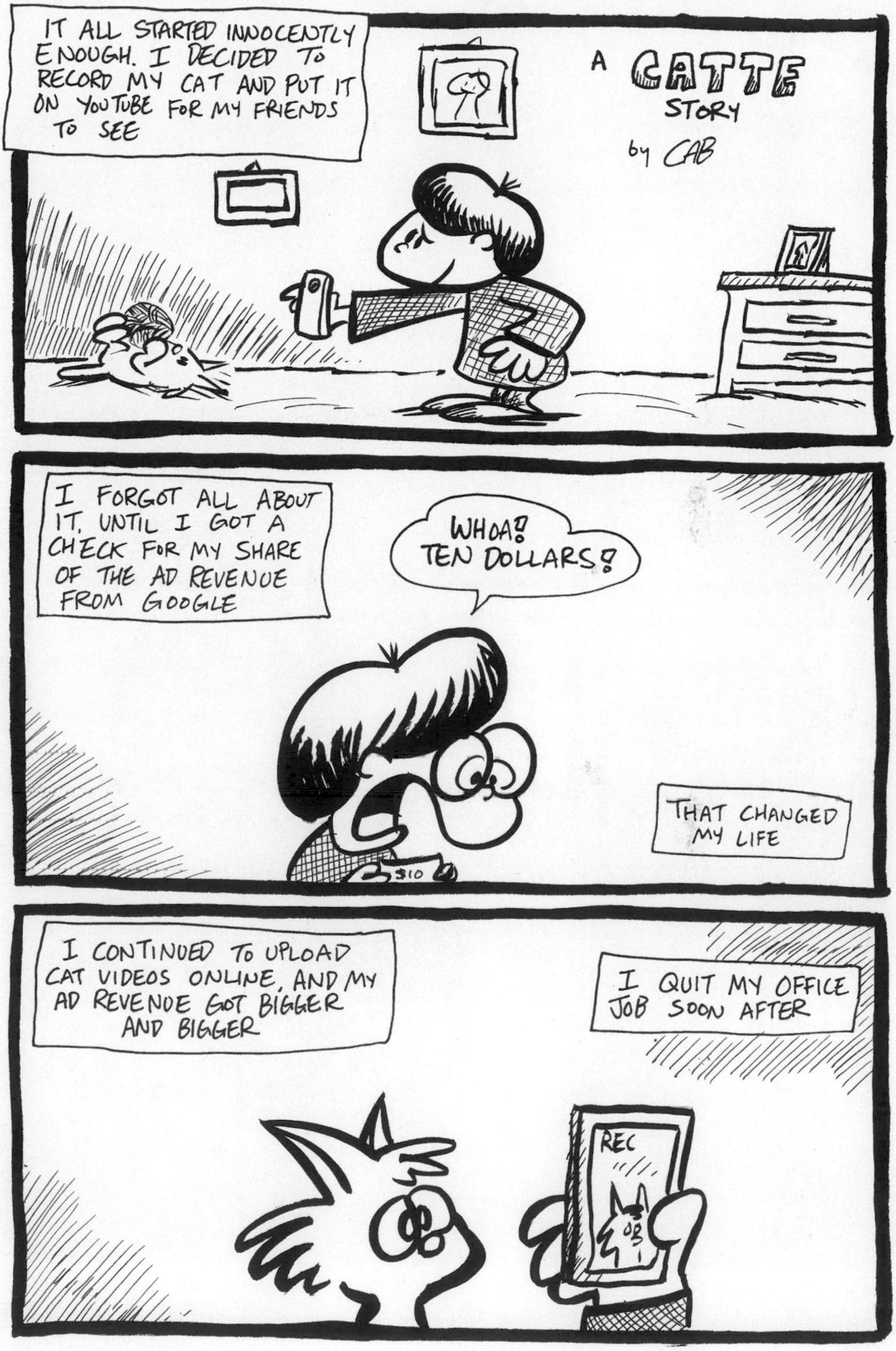
IT ALL STARTED INNOCENTLY ENOUGH. I DECIDED TO RECORD MY CAT AND PUT IT ON YOUTUBE FOR MY FRIENDS TO SEE
A CATTE STORY
by CAB
I FORGOT ALL ABOUT IT, UNTIL I GOT A CHECK FOR MY SHARE OF THE AD REVENUE FROM GOOGLE
WHOA!! TEN DOLLARS!!
THAT CHANGED MY LIFE
$10
I CONTINUED TO UPLOAD CAT VIDEOS ONLINE, AND MY AD REVENUE GOT BIGGER AND BIGGER
I QUIT MY OFFICE JOB SOON AFTER
REC

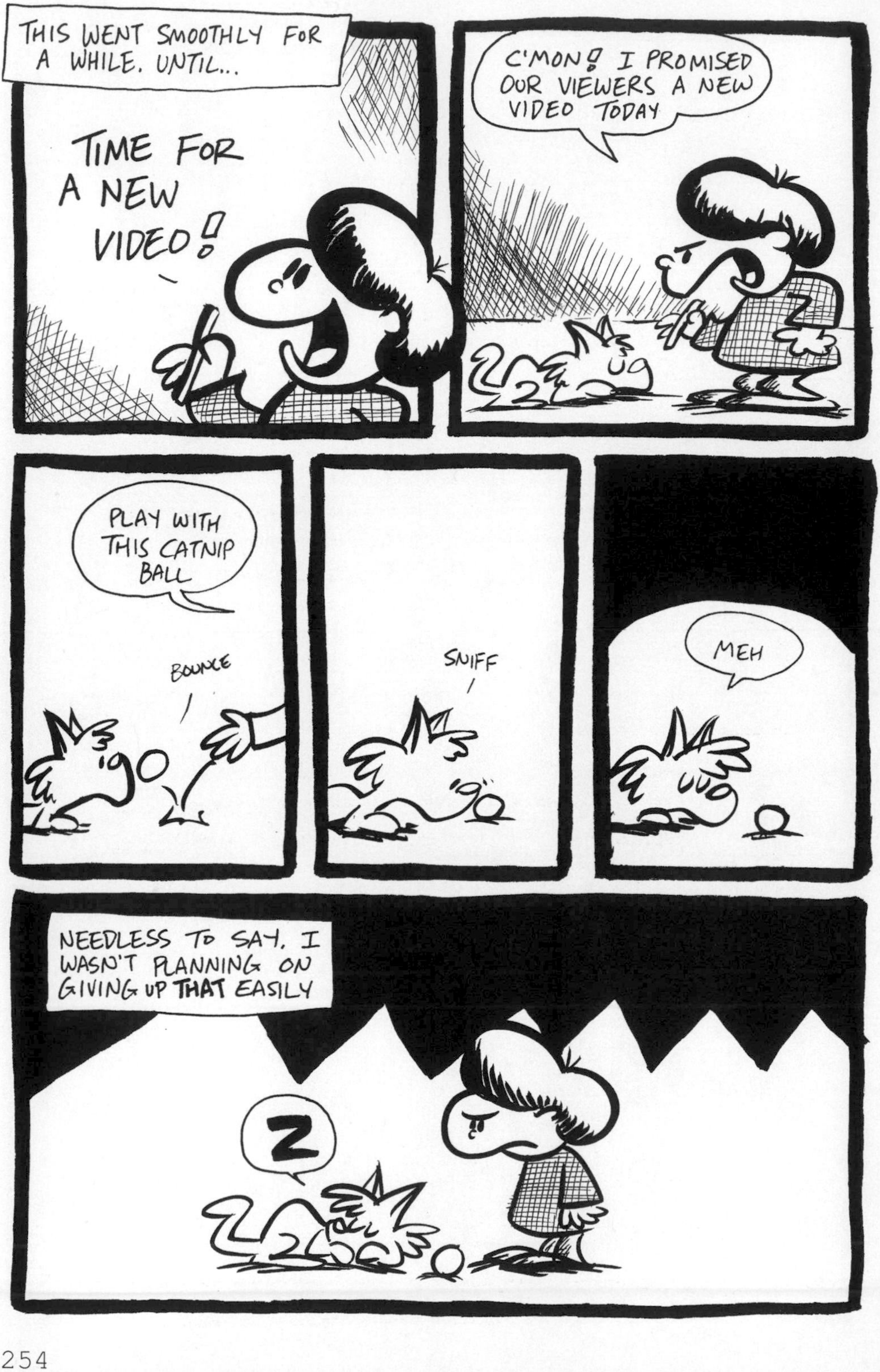

THIS WENT SMOOTHLY FOR A WHILE. UNTIL...
TIME FOR A NEW VIDEO!!
C'MON!! I PROMISED OUR VIEWERS A NEW VIDEO TODAY
PLAY WITH THIS CATNIP BALL
BOUNCE
SNIFF
MEH
NEEDLESS TO SAY, I WASN'T PLANNING ON GIVING UP **THAT** EASILY
Z

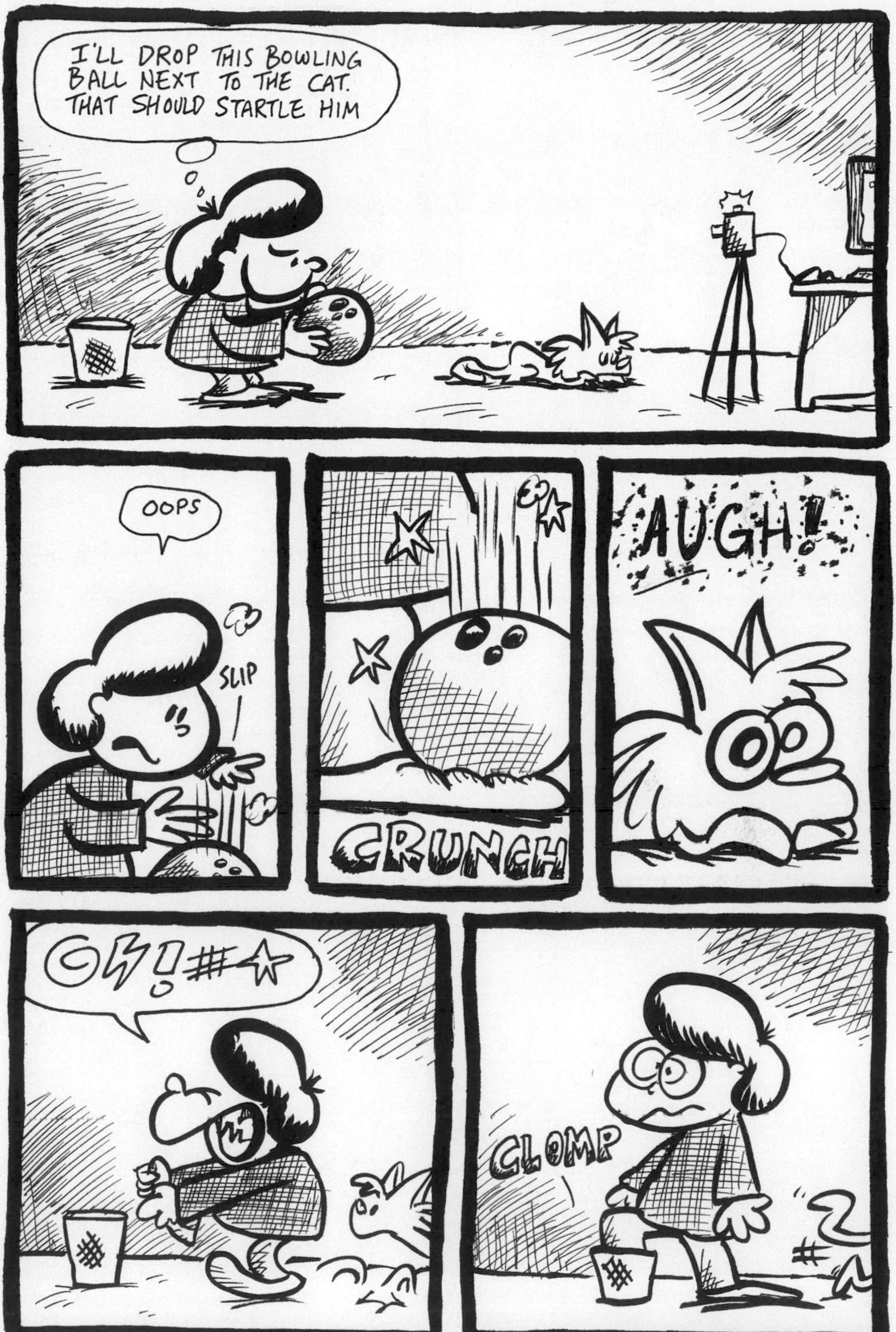
I'LL DROP THIS BOWLING BALL NEXT TO THE CAT. THAT SHOULD STARTLE HIM
OOPS
SLIP
CRUNCH
AUGH!
CLOMP

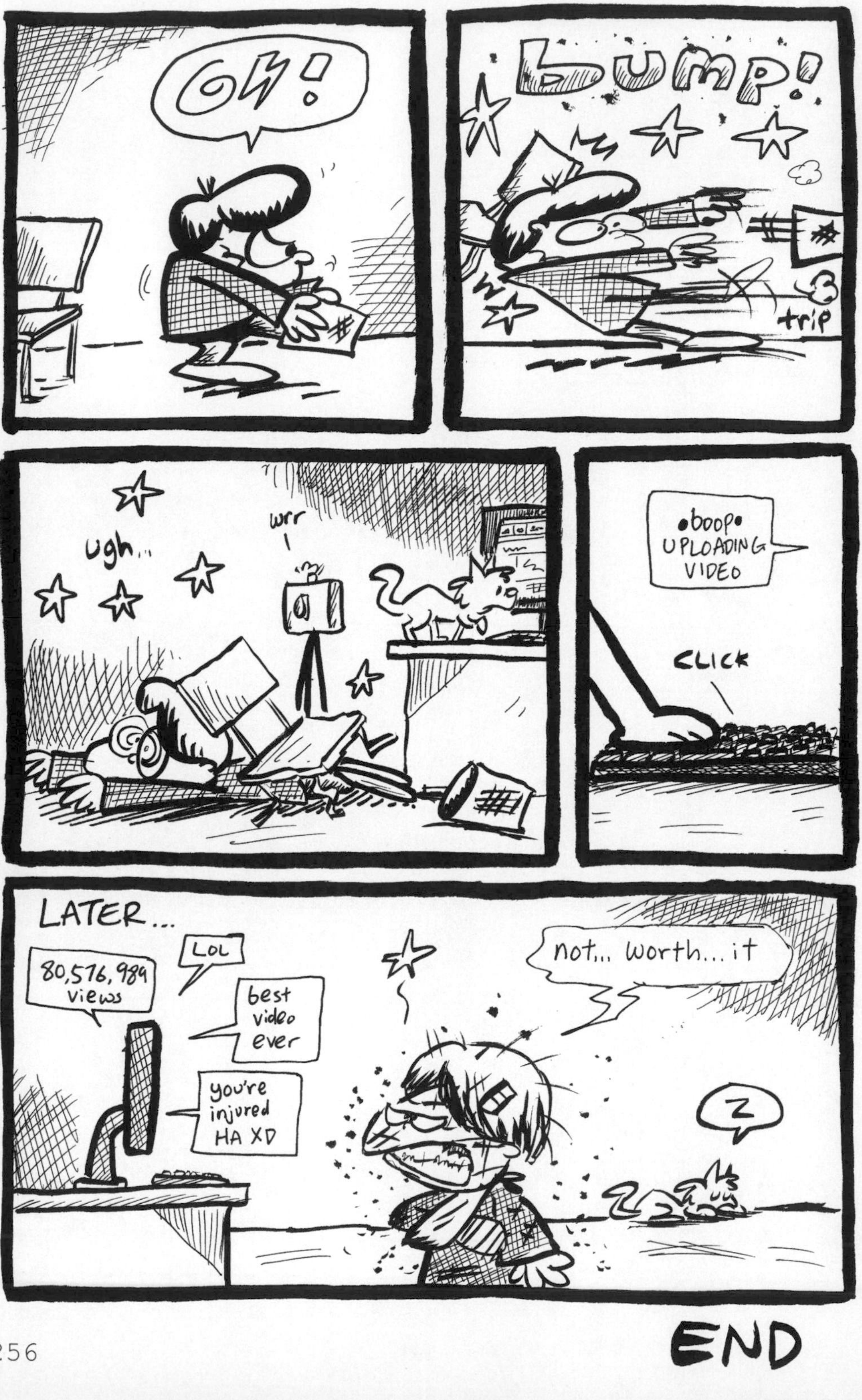
Oh!
bump!
trip
ugh...
wrr
•boop•
UPLOADING
VIDEO
CLICK
LATER...
80,576,989
views
LOL
best
video
ever
you're
injured
HA XD
not... worth... it
z
END

THE GHOST CAT

by CAB

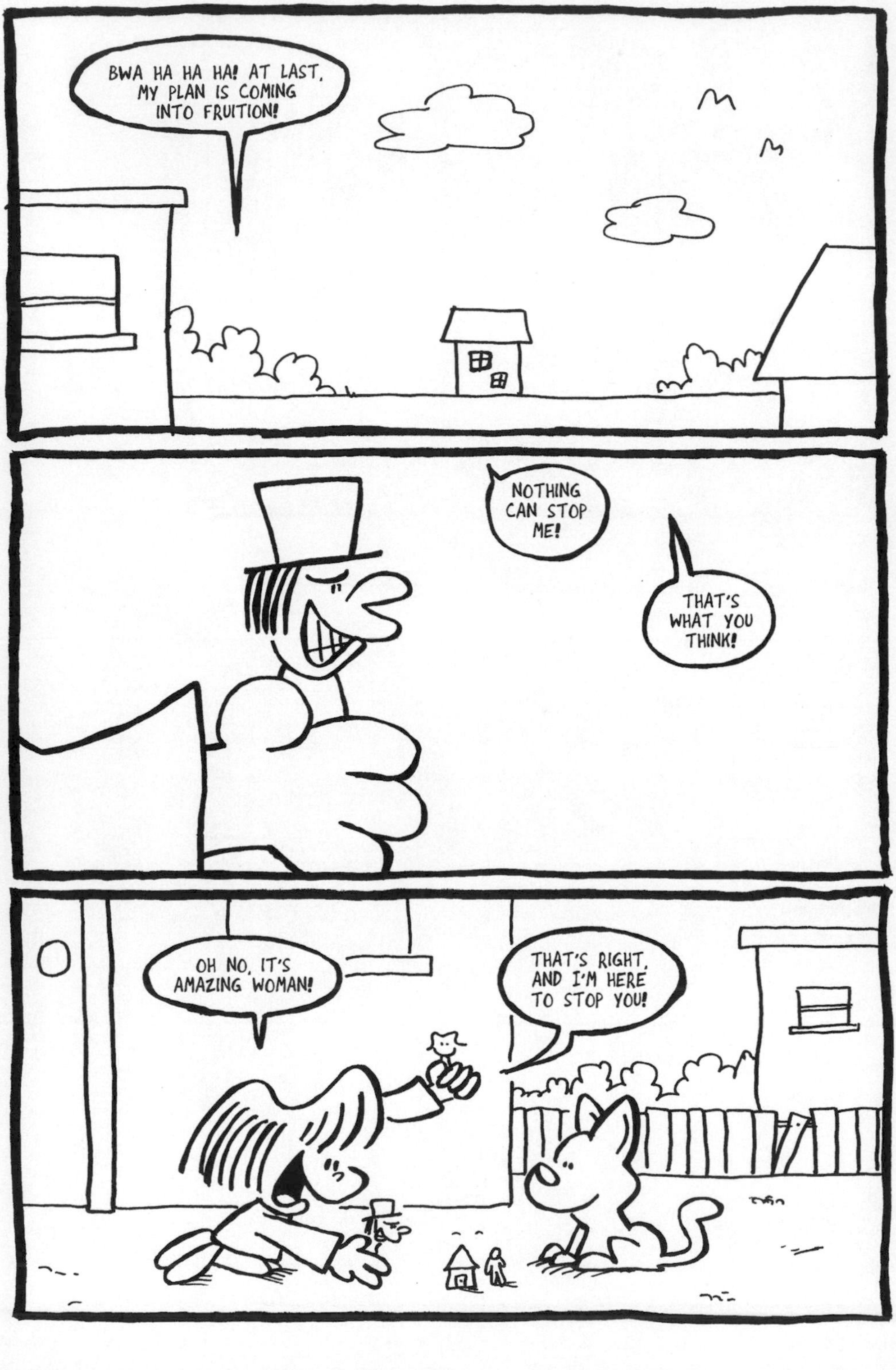
BWA HA HA HA! AT LAST, MY PLAN IS COMING INTO FRUITION!
NOTHING CAN STOP ME!
THAT'S WHAT YOU THINK!
OH NO, IT'S AMAZING WOMAN!
THAT'S RIGHT, AND I'M HERE TO STOP YOU!

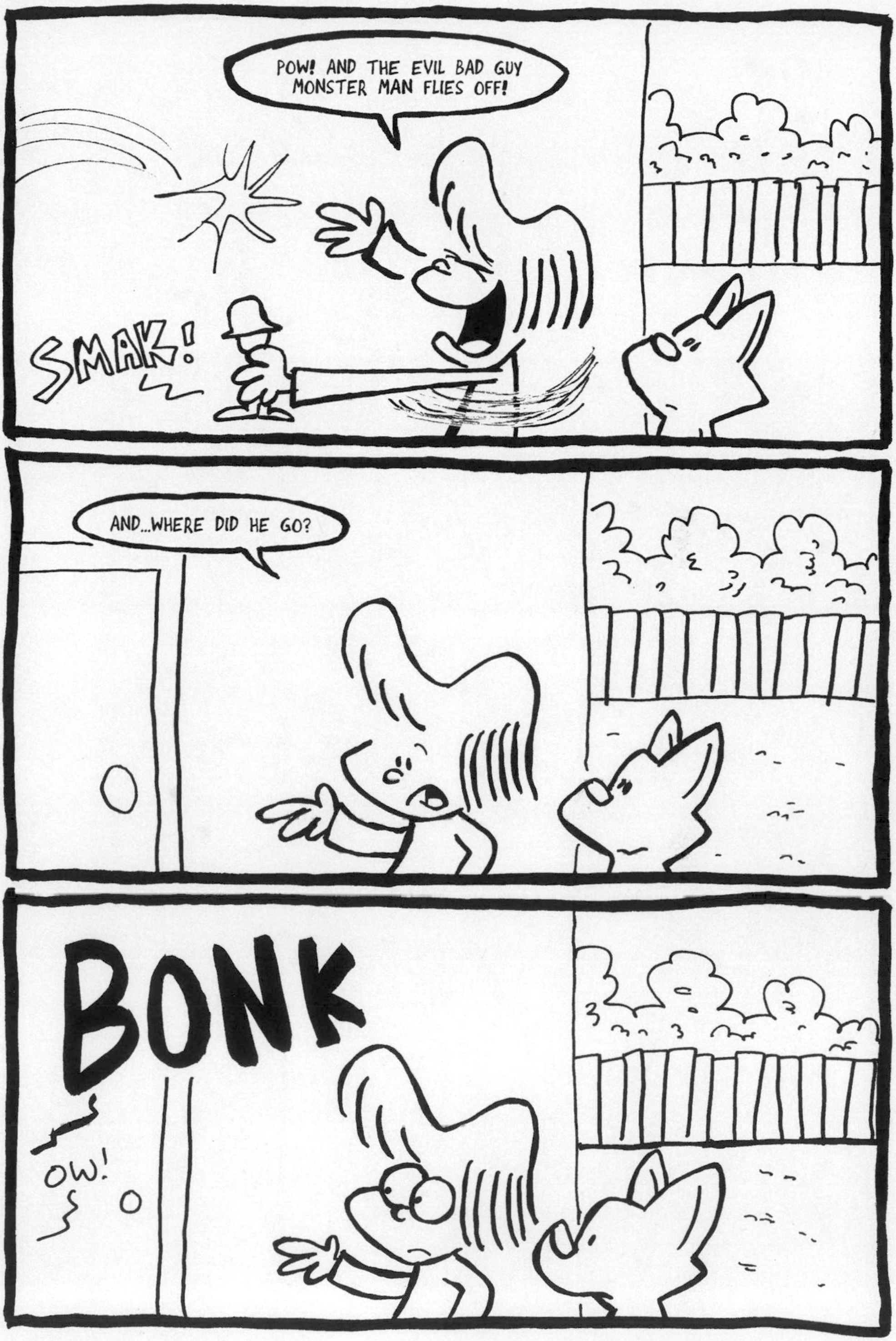
POW! AND THE EVIL BAD GUY MONSTER MAN FLIES OFF!
SMAK!
AND...WHERE DID HE GO?
BONK
OW!

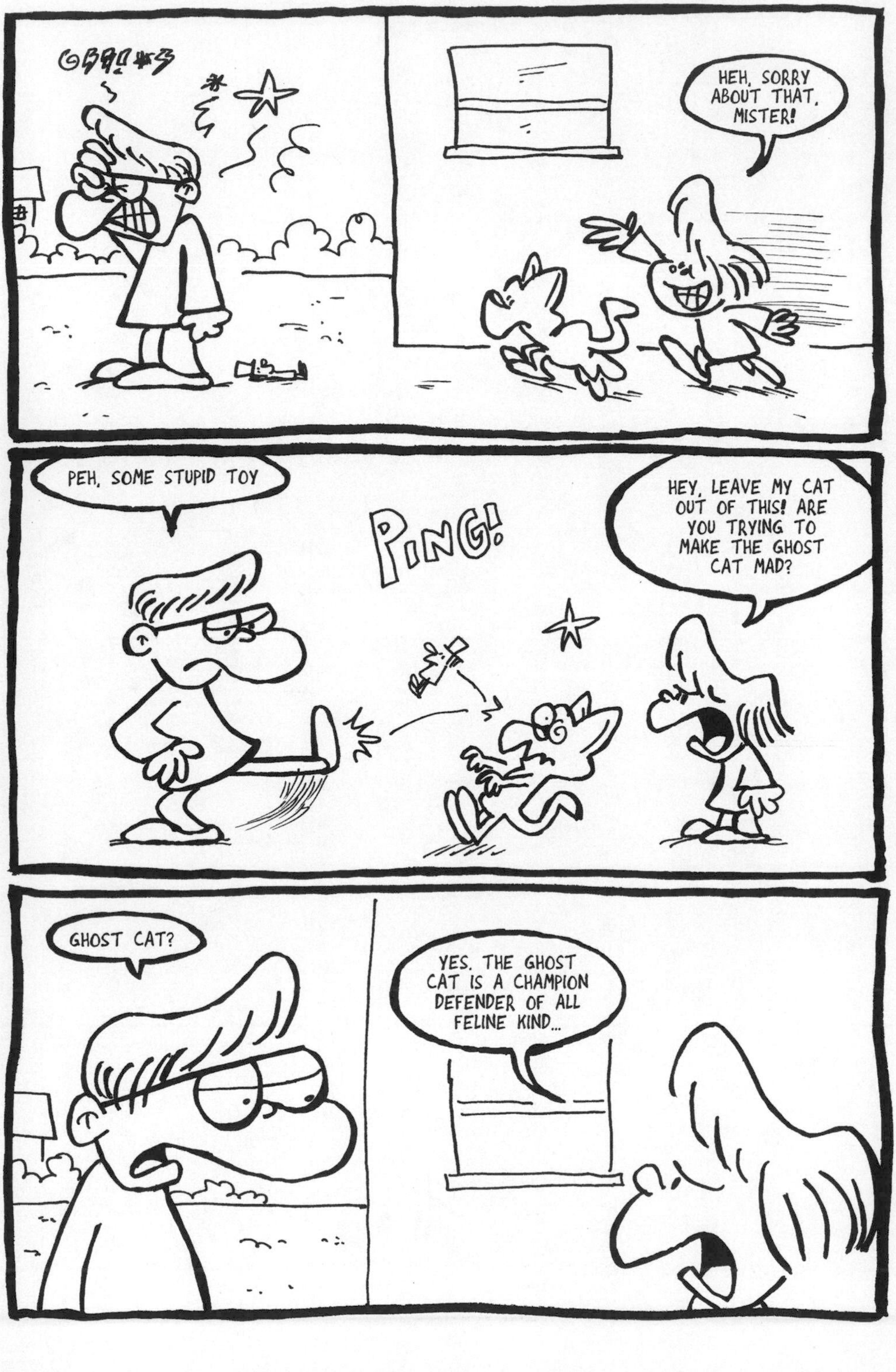
HEH, SORRY ABOUT THAT, MISTER!
PEH, SOME STUPID TOY
PING!
HEY, LEAVE MY CAT OUT OF THIS! ARE YOU TRYING TO MAKE THE GHOST CAT MAD?
GHOST CAT?
YES. THE GHOST CAT IS A CHAMPION DEFENDER OF ALL FELINE KIND...

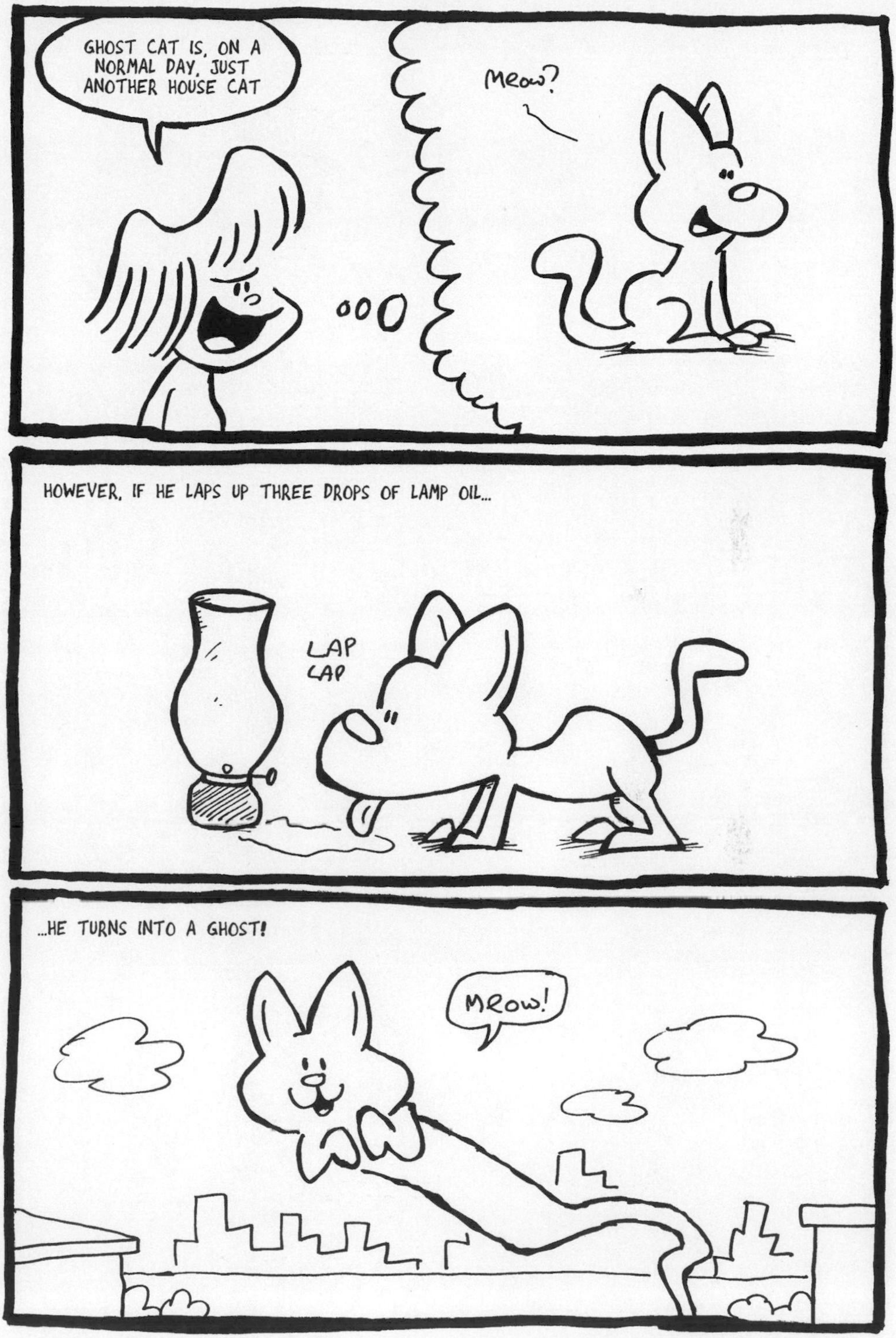
GHOST CAT IS, ON A NORMAL DAY, JUST ANOTHER HOUSE CAT
MEOW?
OOO
HOWEVER, IF HE LAPS UP THREE DROPS OF LAMP OIL...
LAP LAP
...HE TURNS INTO A GHOST!
MEOW!

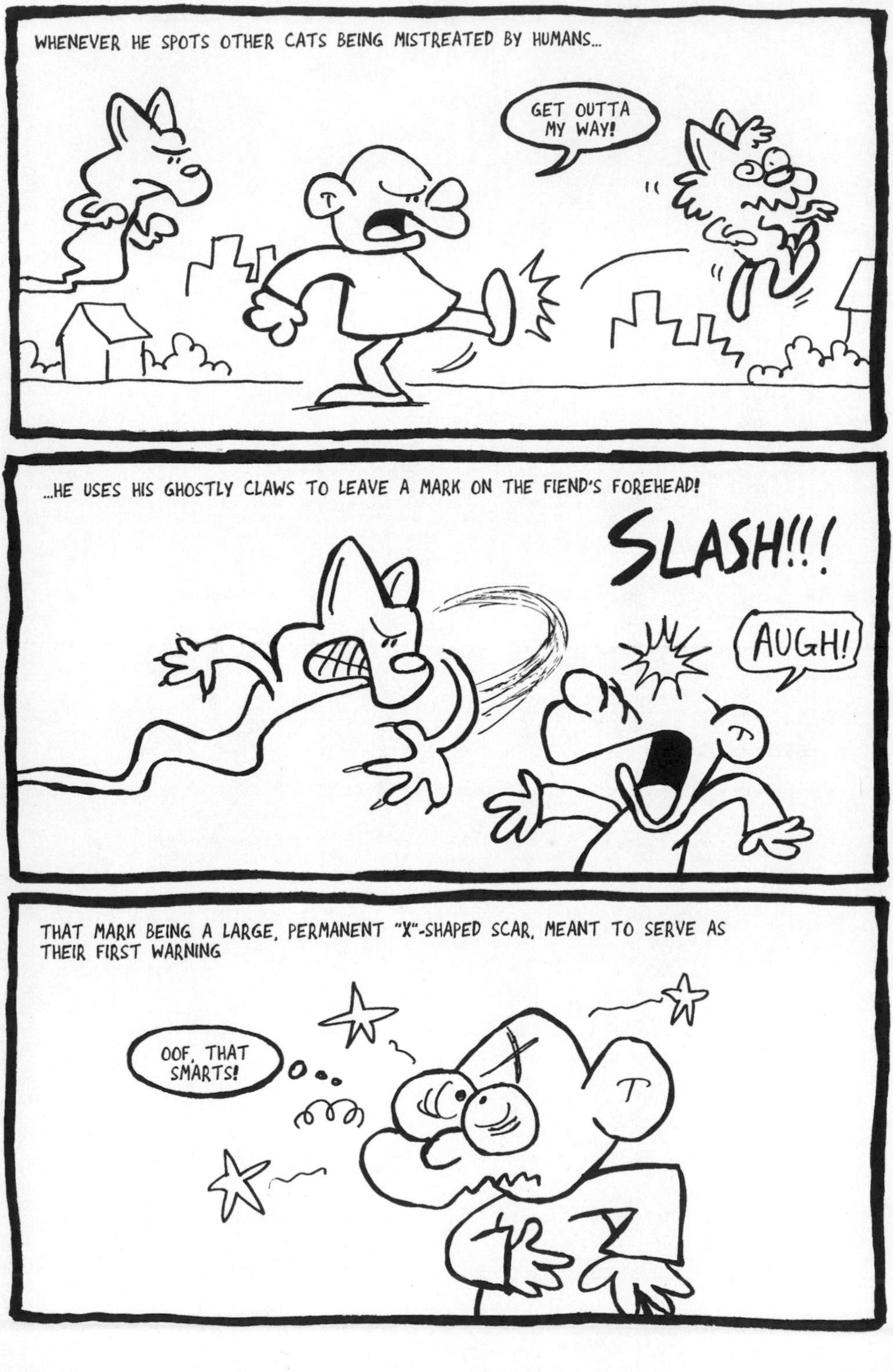
WHENEVER HE SPOTS OTHER CATS BEING MISTREATED BY HUMANS...
GET OUTTA MY WAY!
...HE USES HIS GHOSTLY CLAWS TO LEAVE A MARK ON THE FIEND'S FOREHEAD!
SLASH!!!
AUGH!
THAT MARK BEING A LARGE, PERMANENT "X"-SHAPED SCAR, MEANT TO SERVE AS THEIR FIRST WARNING
OOF, THAT SMARTS!

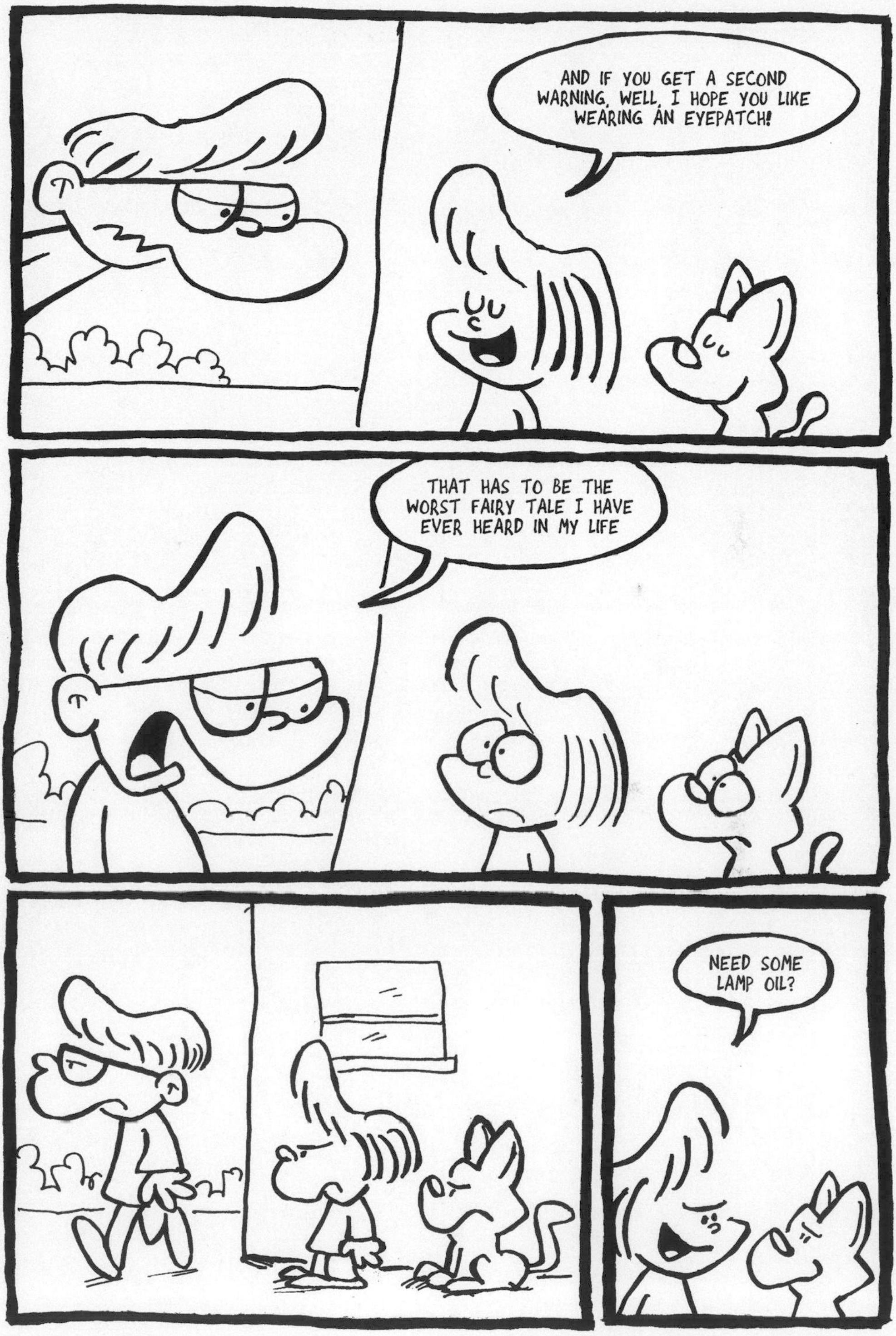
AND IF YOU GET A SECOND WARNING, WELL, I HOPE YOU LIKE WEARING AN EYEPATCH!
THAT HAS TO BE THE WORST FAIRY TALE I HAVE EVER HEARD IN MY LIFE
NEED SOME LAMP OIL?

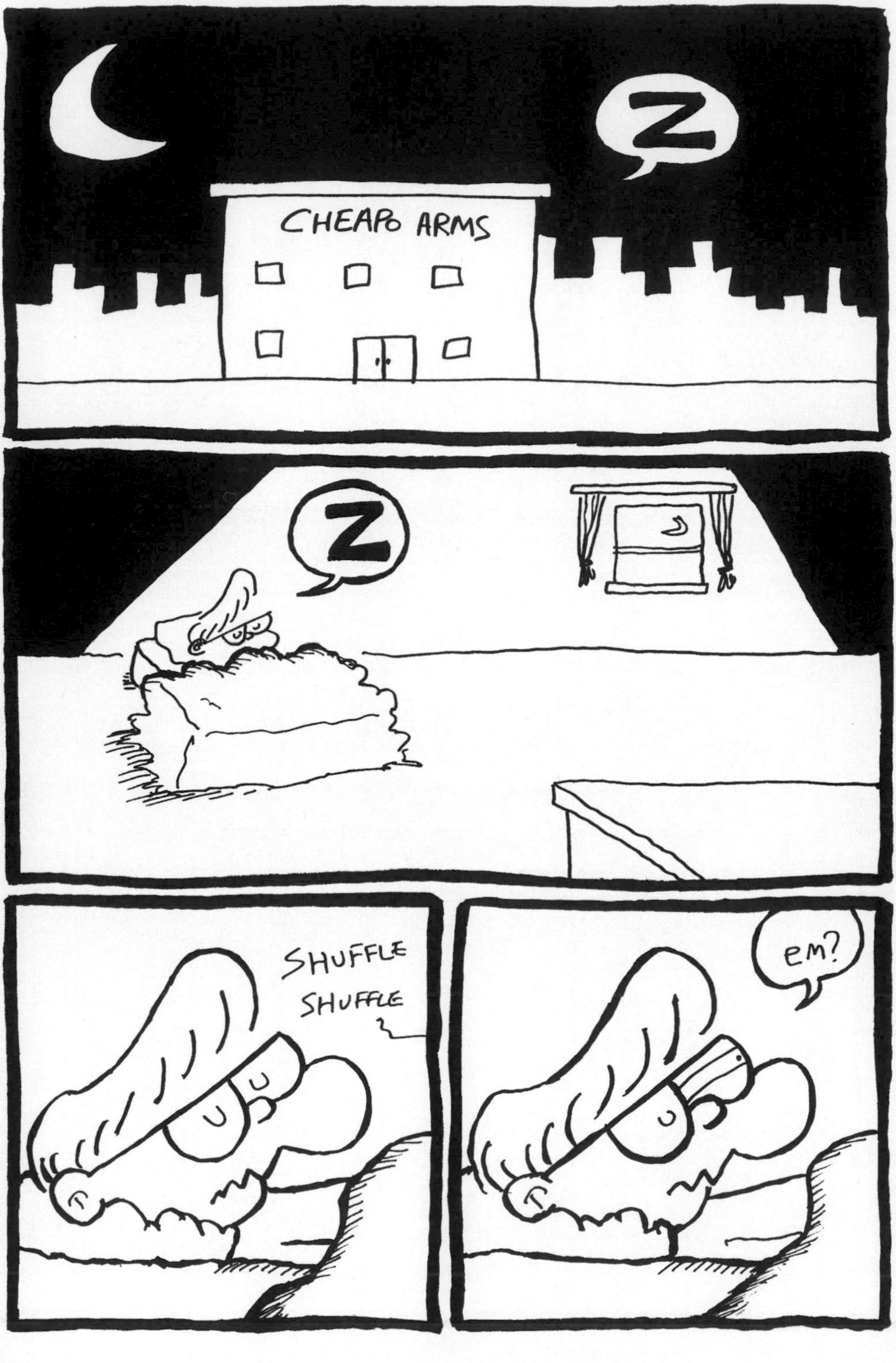
Z
CHEAPO ARMS
Z
SHUFFLE
SHUFFLE
em?

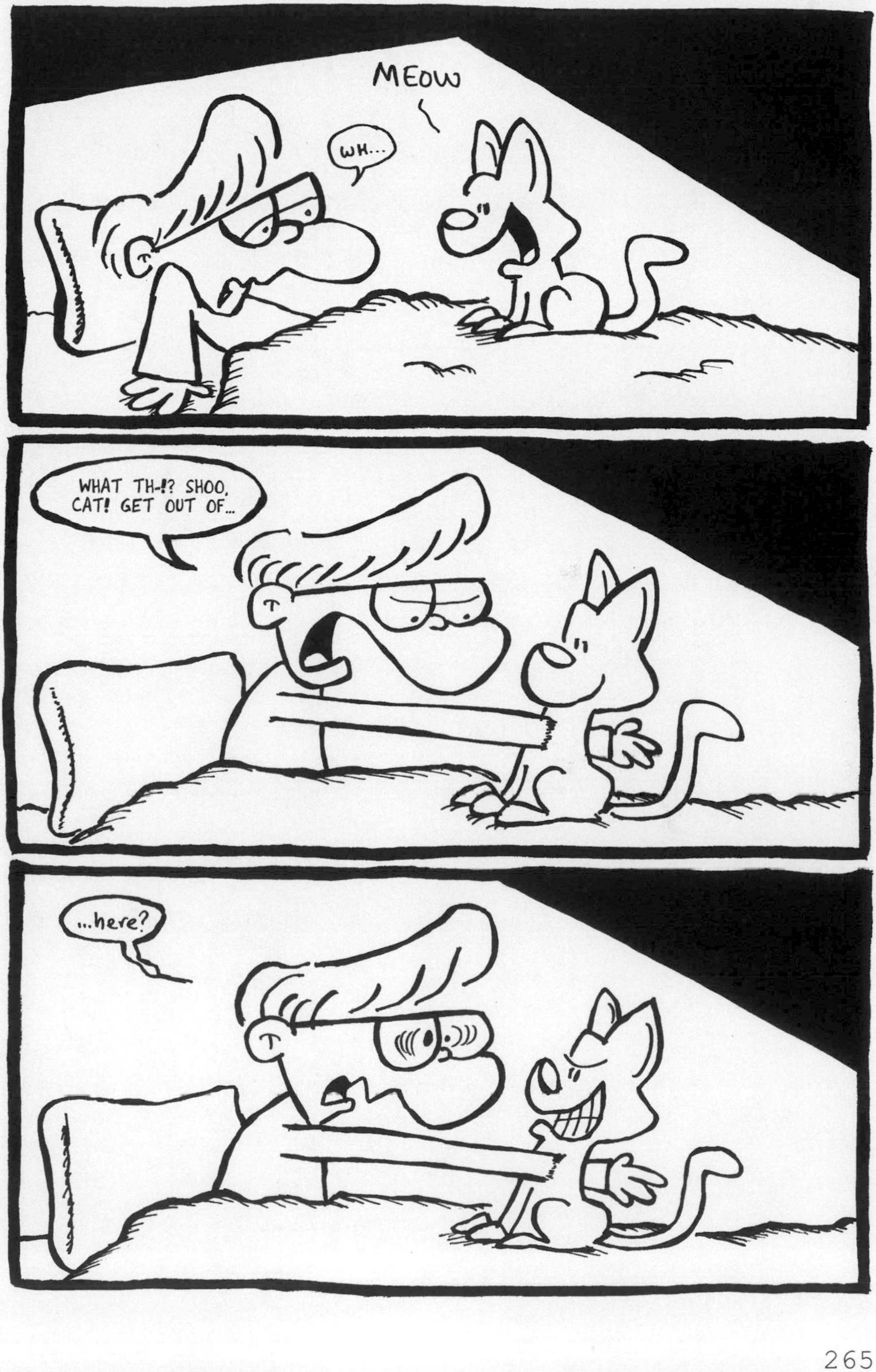
MEOW
WH...
WHAT TH-!? SHOO, CAT! GET OUT OF...
...here?

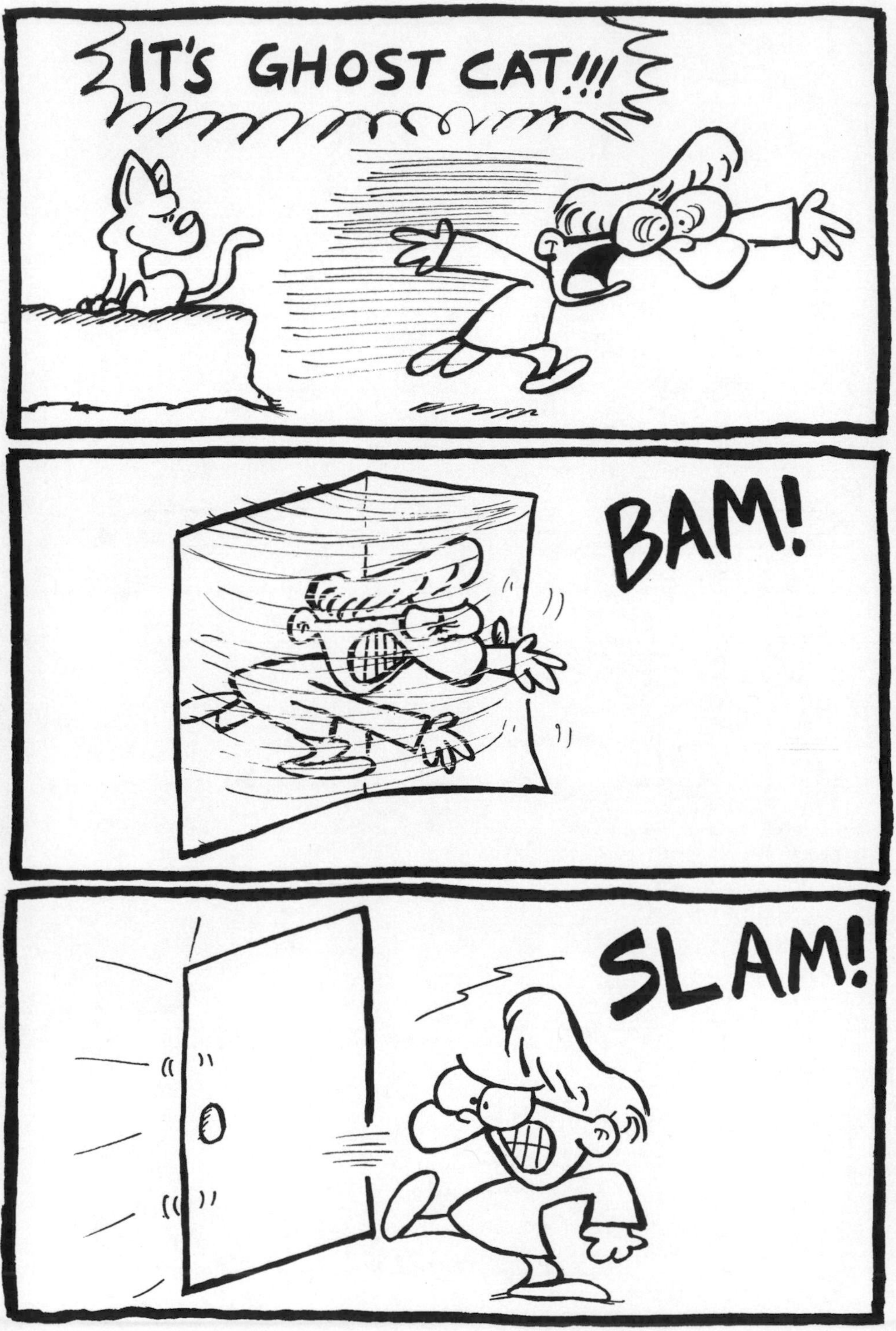
IT'S GHOST CAT!!!
BAM!
SLAM!

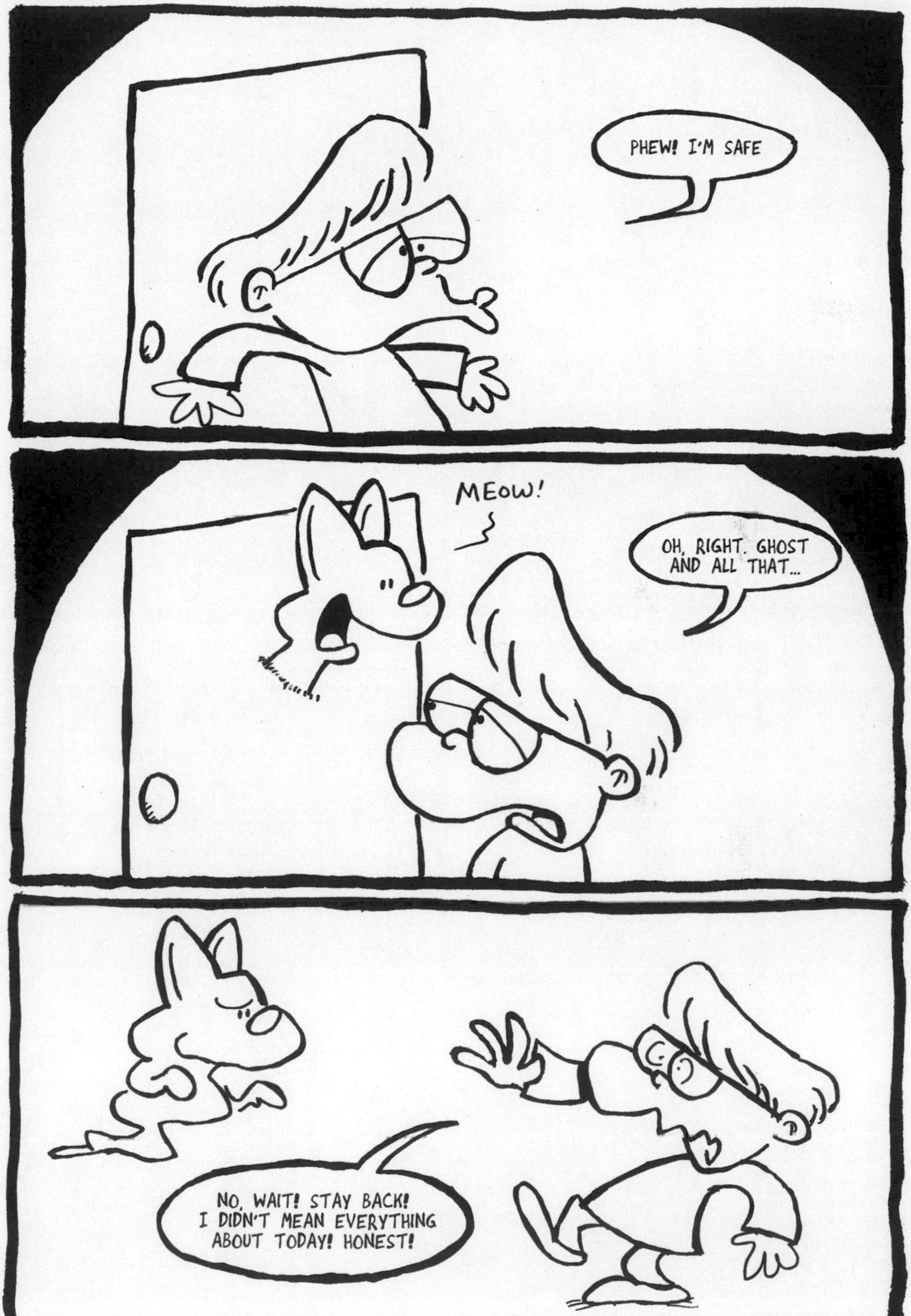
PHEW! I'M SAFE
MEOW!
OH, RIGHT. GHOST AND ALL THAT...
NO, WAIT! STAY BACK! I DIDN'T MEAN EVERYTHING ABOUT TODAY! HONEST!

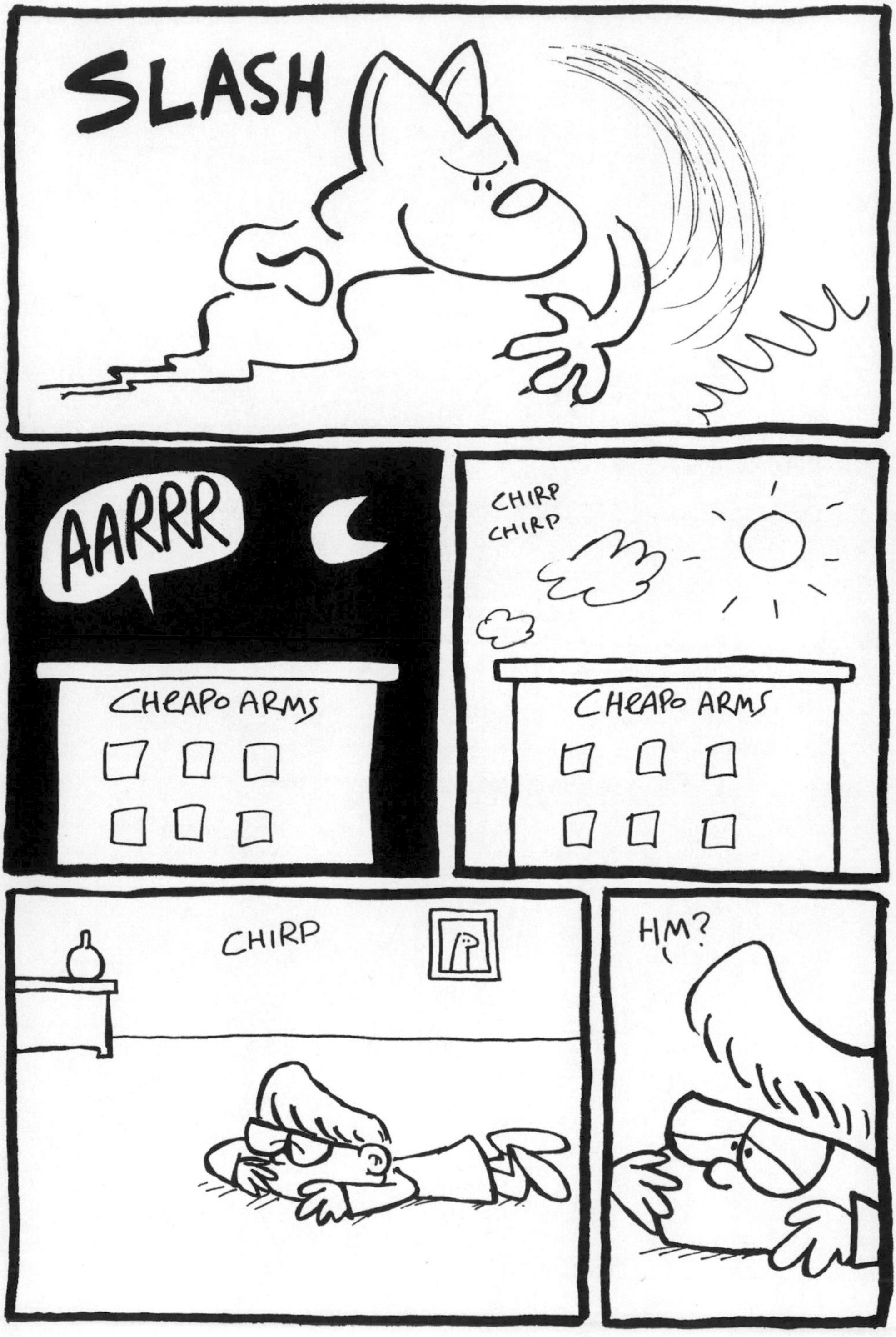
SLASH
AARRR
CHEAPO ARMS
CHIRP
CHIRP
CHEAPO ARMS
CHIRP
HM?

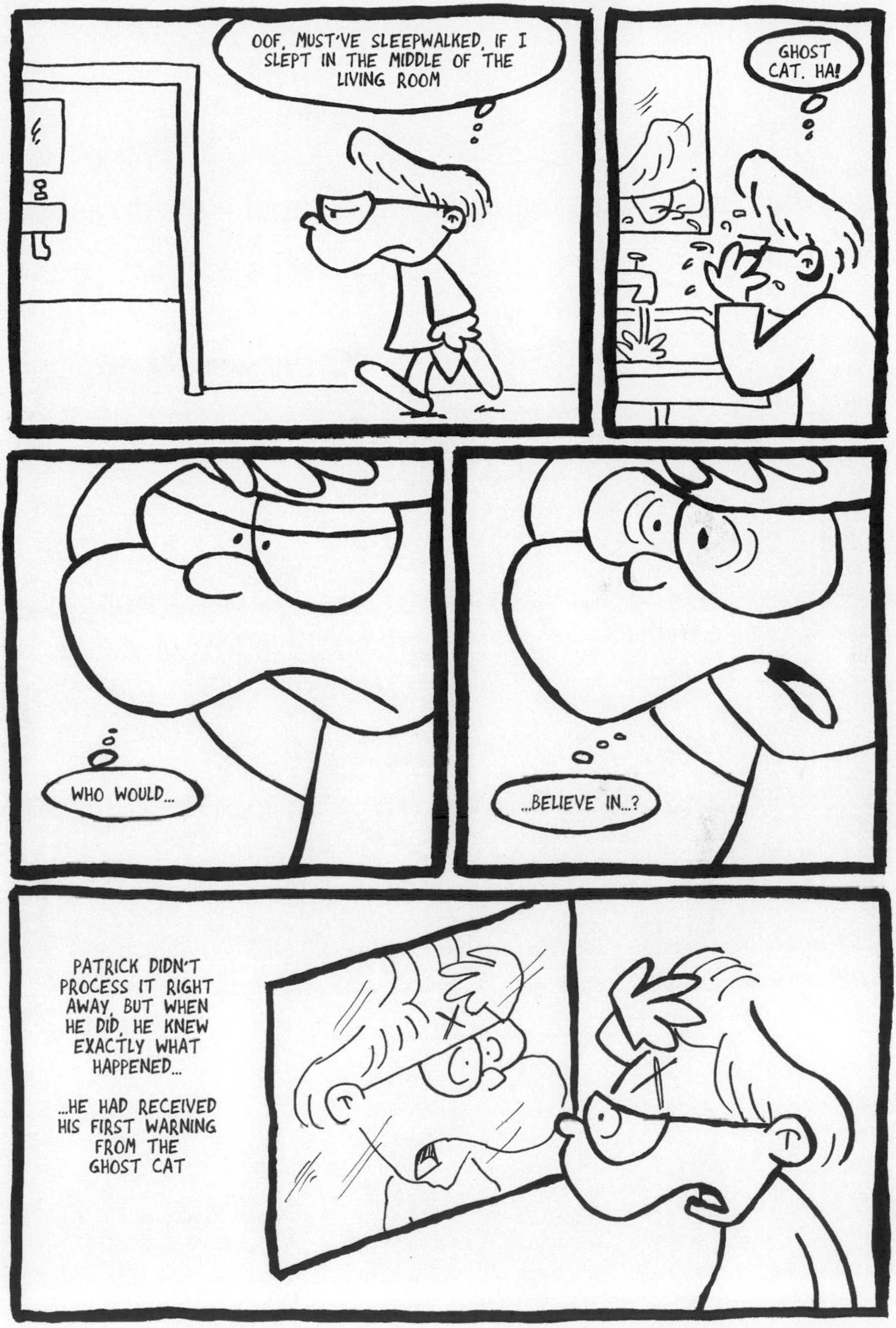
OOF, MUST'VE SLEEPWALKED, IF I SLEPT IN THE MIDDLE OF THE LIVING ROOM
GHOST CAT. HA!
WHO WOULD...
...BELIEVE IN...?
PATRICK DIDN'T PROCESS IT RIGHT AWAY, BUT WHEN HE DID, HE KNEW EXACTLY WHAT HAPPENED...
...HE HAD RECEIVED HIS FIRST WARNING FROM THE GHOST CAT

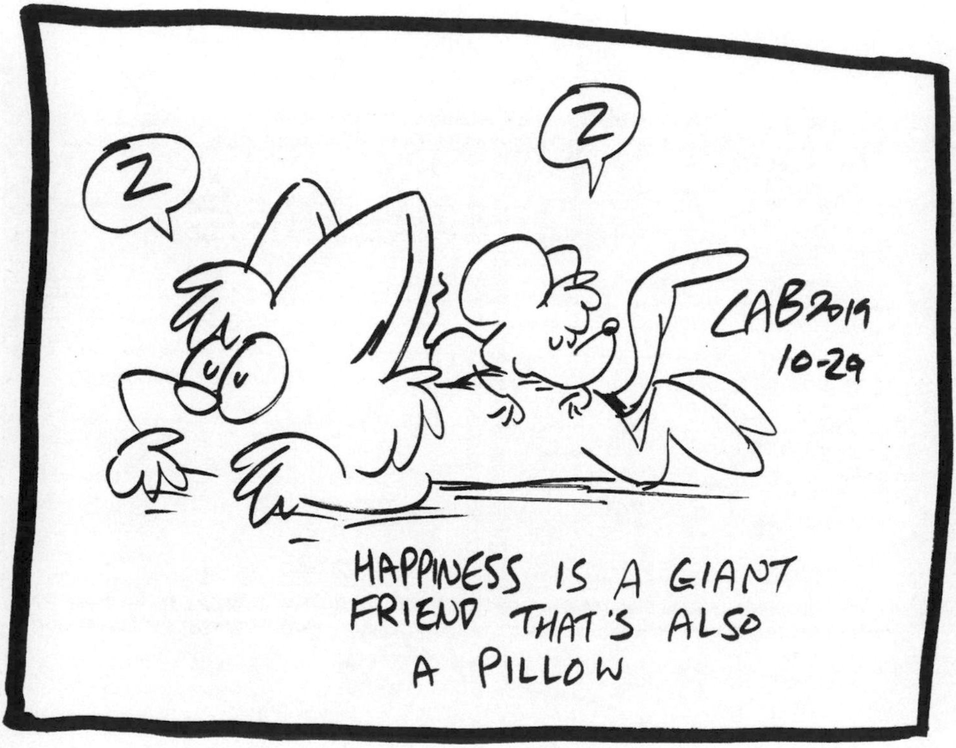
Z
Z
CAB2019
10-29
HAPPINESS IS A GIANT FRIEND THAT'S ALSO A PILLOW

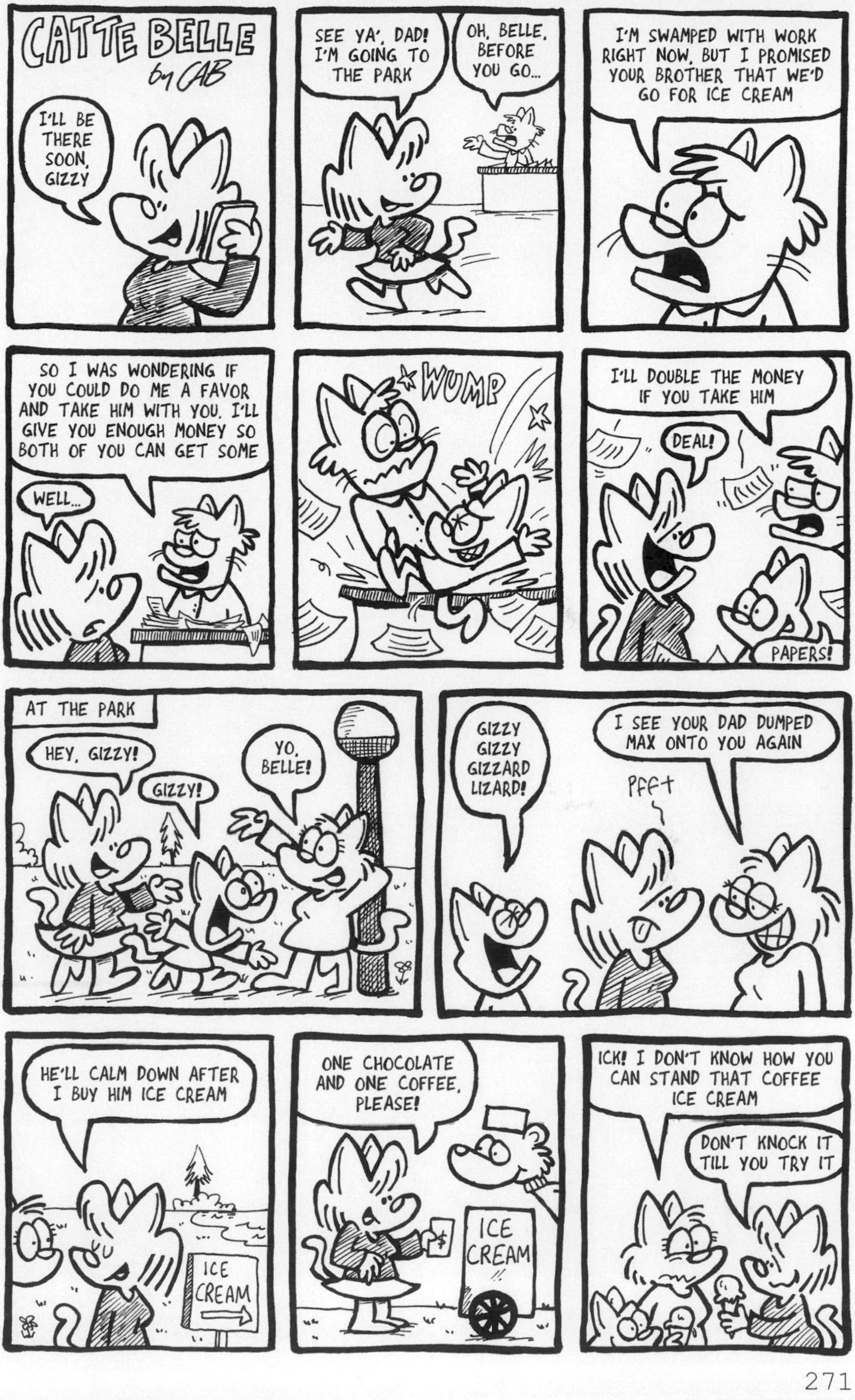
CATTE BELLE
by CAB
I'LL BE THERE SOON, GIZZY
SEE YA', DAD! I'M GOING TO THE PARK
OH, BELLE, BEFORE YOU GO...
I'M SWAMPED WITH WORK RIGHT NOW, BUT I PROMISED YOUR BROTHER THAT WE'D GO FOR ICE CREAM
SO I WAS WONDERING IF YOU COULD DO ME A FAVOR AND TAKE HIM WITH YOU. I'LL GIVE YOU ENOUGH MONEY SO BOTH OF YOU CAN GET SOME
WELL...
WUMP
I'LL DOUBLE THE MONEY IF YOU TAKE HIM
DEAL!
PAPERS!
AT THE PARK
HEY, GIZZY!
GIZZY!
YO, BELLE!
GIZZY GIZZY GIZZARD LIZARD!
I SEE YOUR DAD DUMPED MAX ONTO YOU AGAIN
PFFT
HE'LL CALM DOWN AFTER I BUY HIM ICE CREAM
ICE CREAM
ONE CHOCOLATE AND ONE COFFEE, PLEASE!
ICE CREAM
ICK! I DON'T KNOW HOW YOU CAN STAND THAT COFFEE ICE CREAM
DON'T KNOCK IT TILL YOU TRY IT

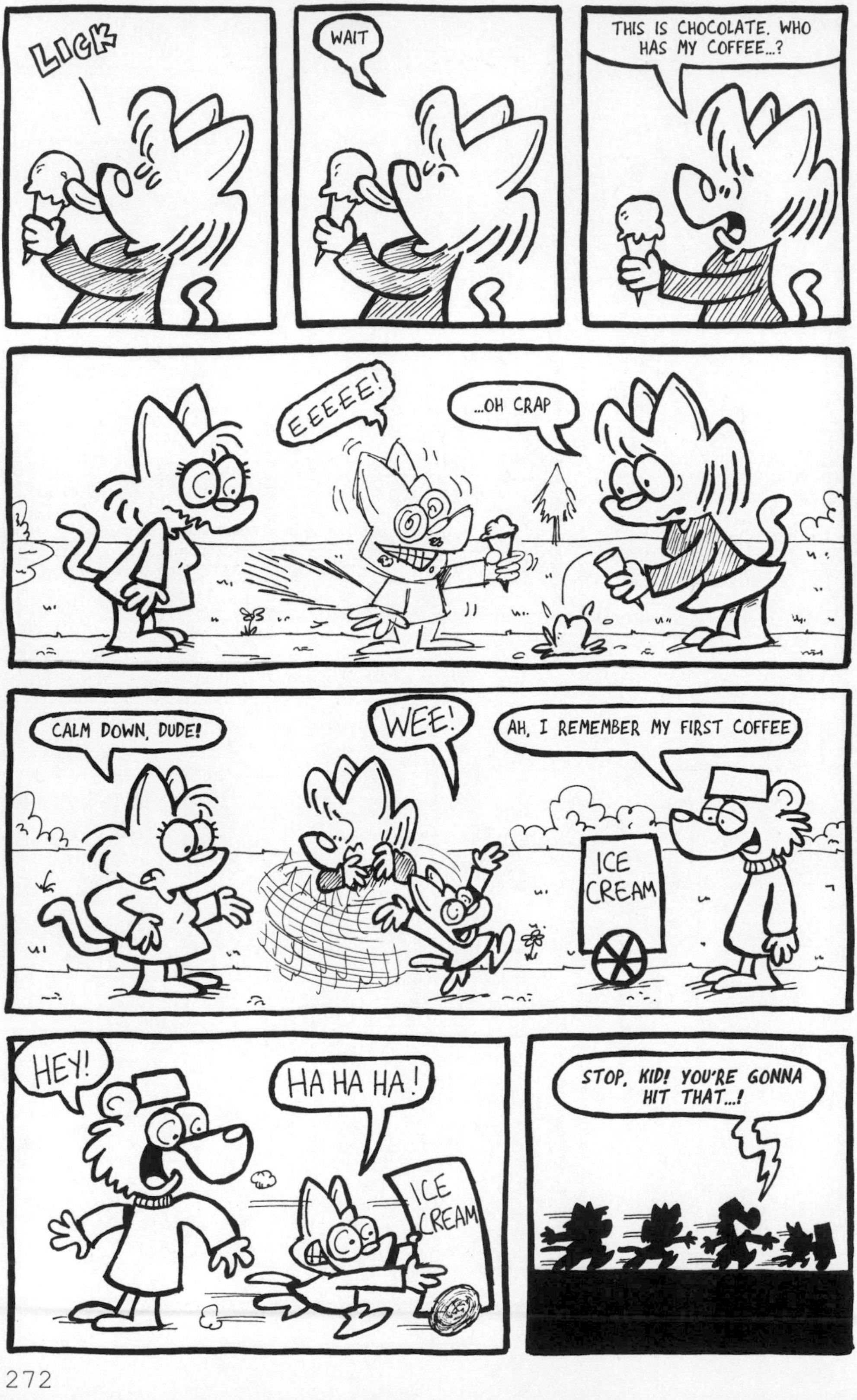
LICK
WAIT
THIS IS CHOCOLATE. WHO HAS MY COFFEE...?
EEEEE!
...OH CRAP
CALM DOWN, DUDE!
WEE!
AH, I REMEMBER MY FIRST COFFEE
ICE CREAM
HEY!
HA HA HA!
ICE CREAM
STOP, KID! YOU'RE GONNA HIT THAT...!

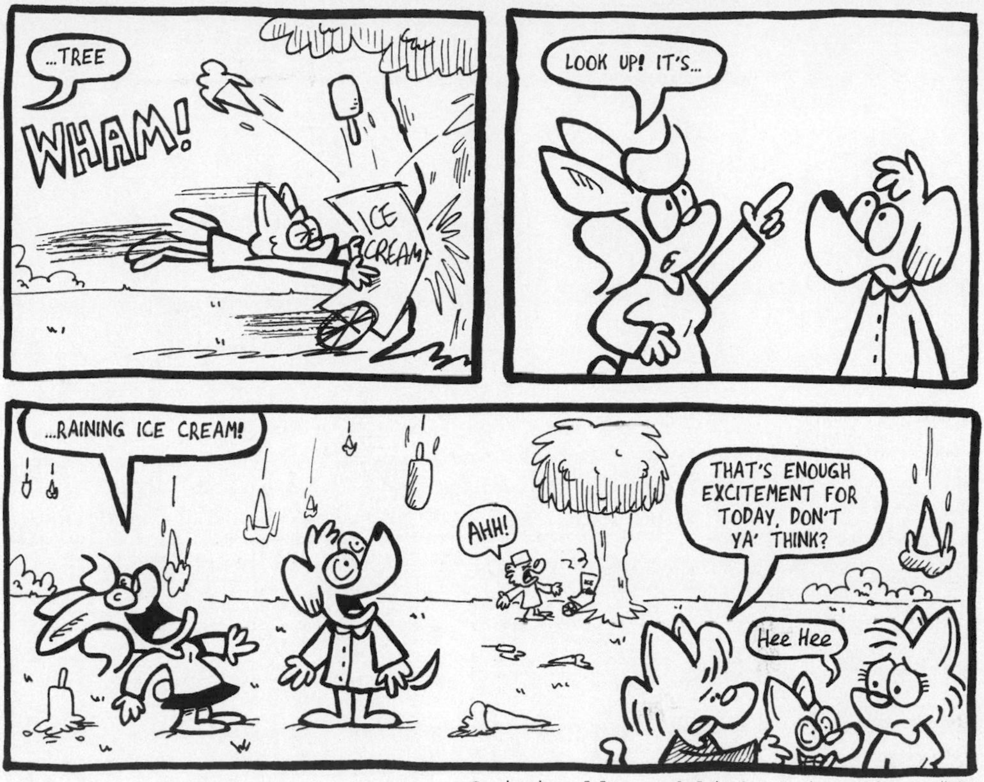
...TREE
WHAM!
ICE CREAM
LOOK UP! IT'S...
...RAINING ICE CREAM!
AHH!
THAT'S ENOUGH EXCITEMENT FOR TODAY, DON'T YA' THINK?
Hee Hee

Originally published in *Pico #2*.

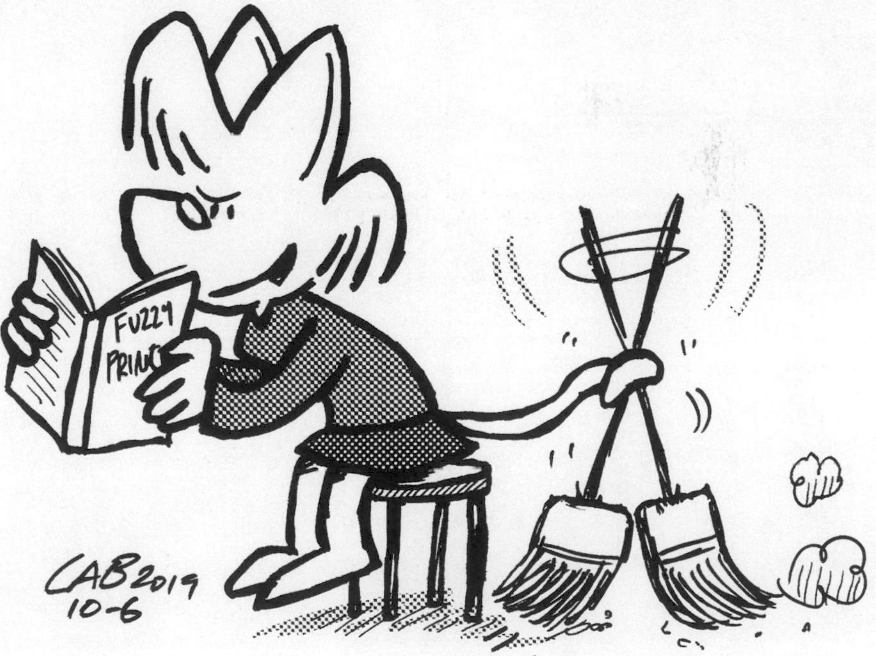
FUZZY PRINC
CAB 2019 10-6

"You can never truly multitask without a tail!"

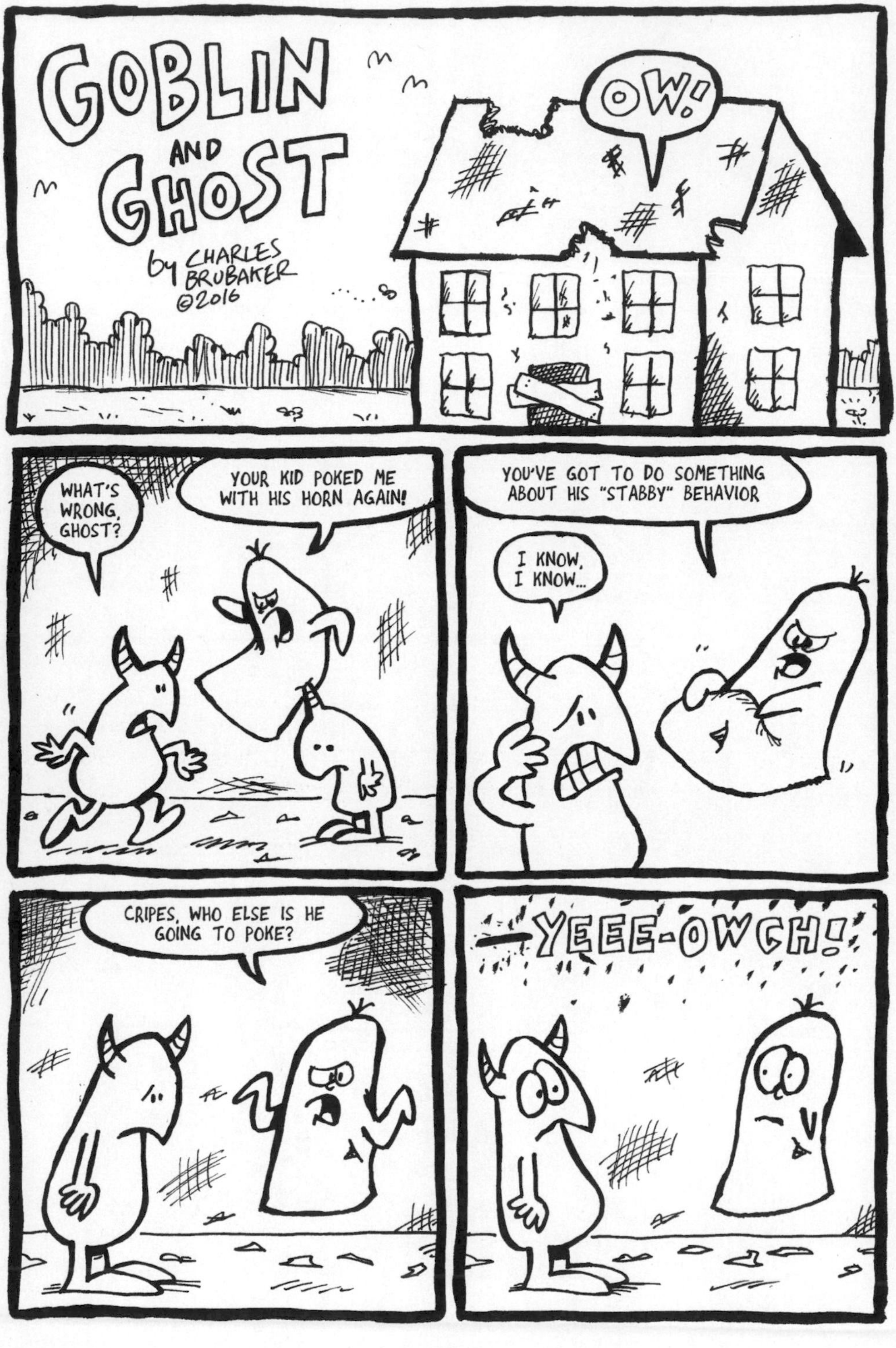
GOBLIN AND GHOST
by CHARLES BRUBAKER ©2016
OW!
WHAT'S WRONG, GHOST?
YOUR KID POKED ME WITH HIS HORN AGAIN!
YOU'VE GOT TO DO SOMETHING ABOUT HIS "STABBY" BEHAVIOR
I KNOW, I KNOW...
CRIPES, WHO ELSE IS HE GOING TO POKE?
YEEE-OWCH!

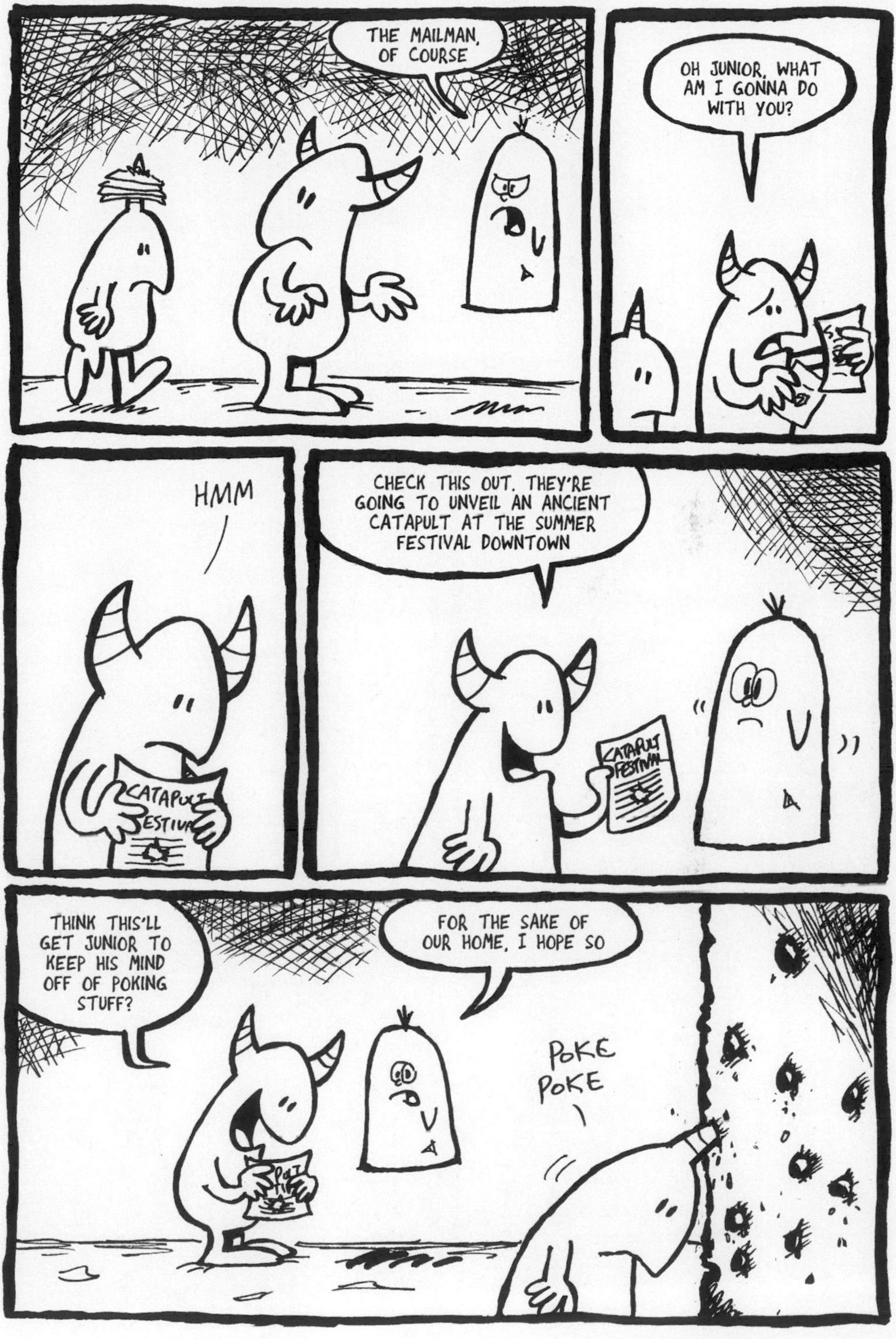
THE MAILMAN, OF COURSE
OH JUNIOR, WHAT AM I GONNA DO WITH YOU?
HMM
CATAPULT FESTIVAL
CHECK THIS OUT. THEY'RE GOING TO UNVEIL AN ANCIENT CATAPULT AT THE SUMMER FESTIVAL DOWNTOWN
CATAPULT FESTIVAL
THINK THIS'LL GET JUNIOR TO KEEP HIS MIND OFF OF POKING STUFF?
FOR THE SAKE OF OUR HOME, I HOPE SO
POKE POKE

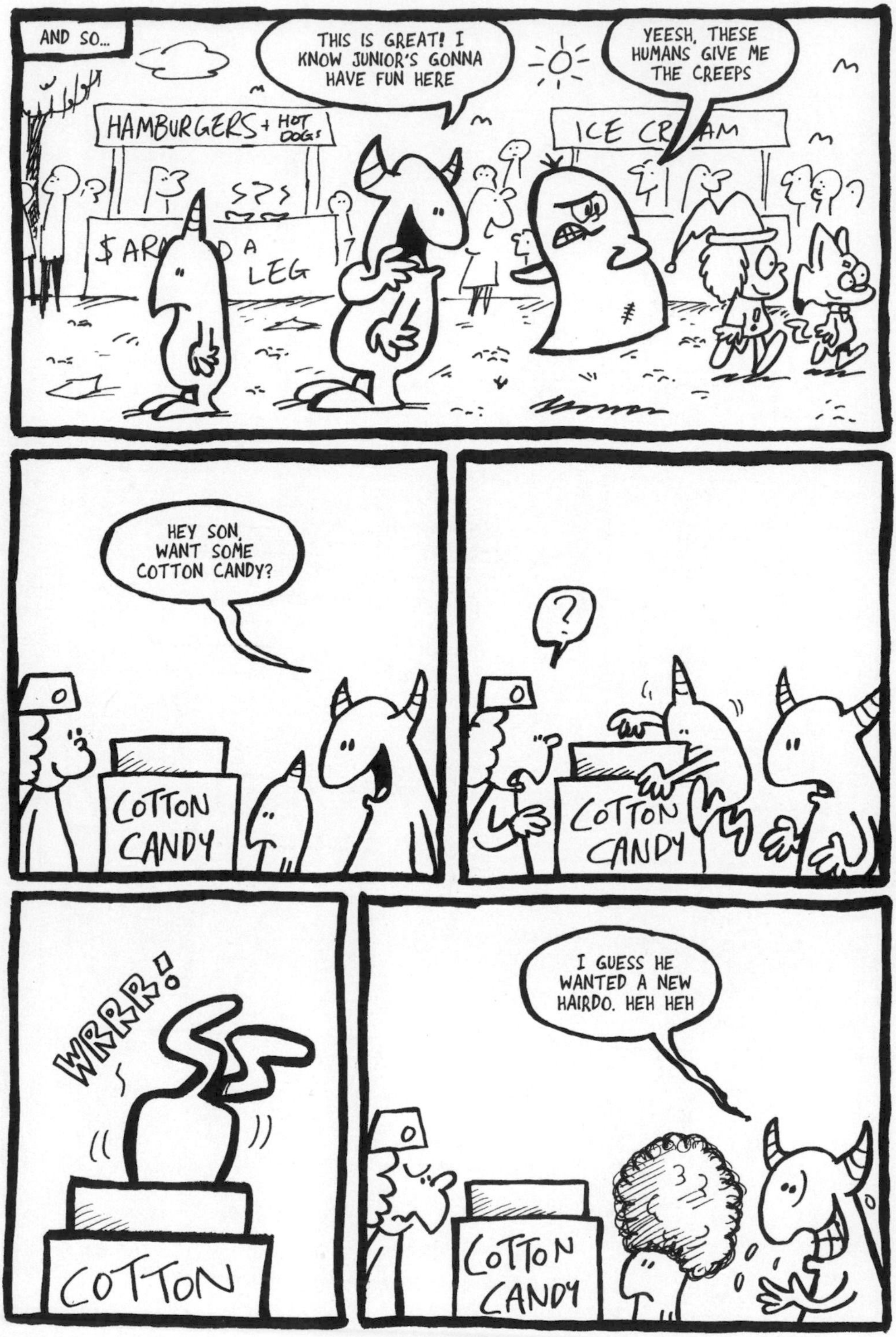
AND SO...
THIS IS GREAT! I KNOW JUNIOR'S GONNA HAVE FUN HERE
YEESH, THESE HUMANS GIVE ME THE CREEPS
HAMBURGERS + HOT DOGS
HEY SON, WANT SOME COTTON CANDY?
COTTON CANDY
?
COTTON CANDY
WRRR!
COTTON
I GUESS HE WANTED A NEW HAIRDO. HEH HEH
COTTON CANDY

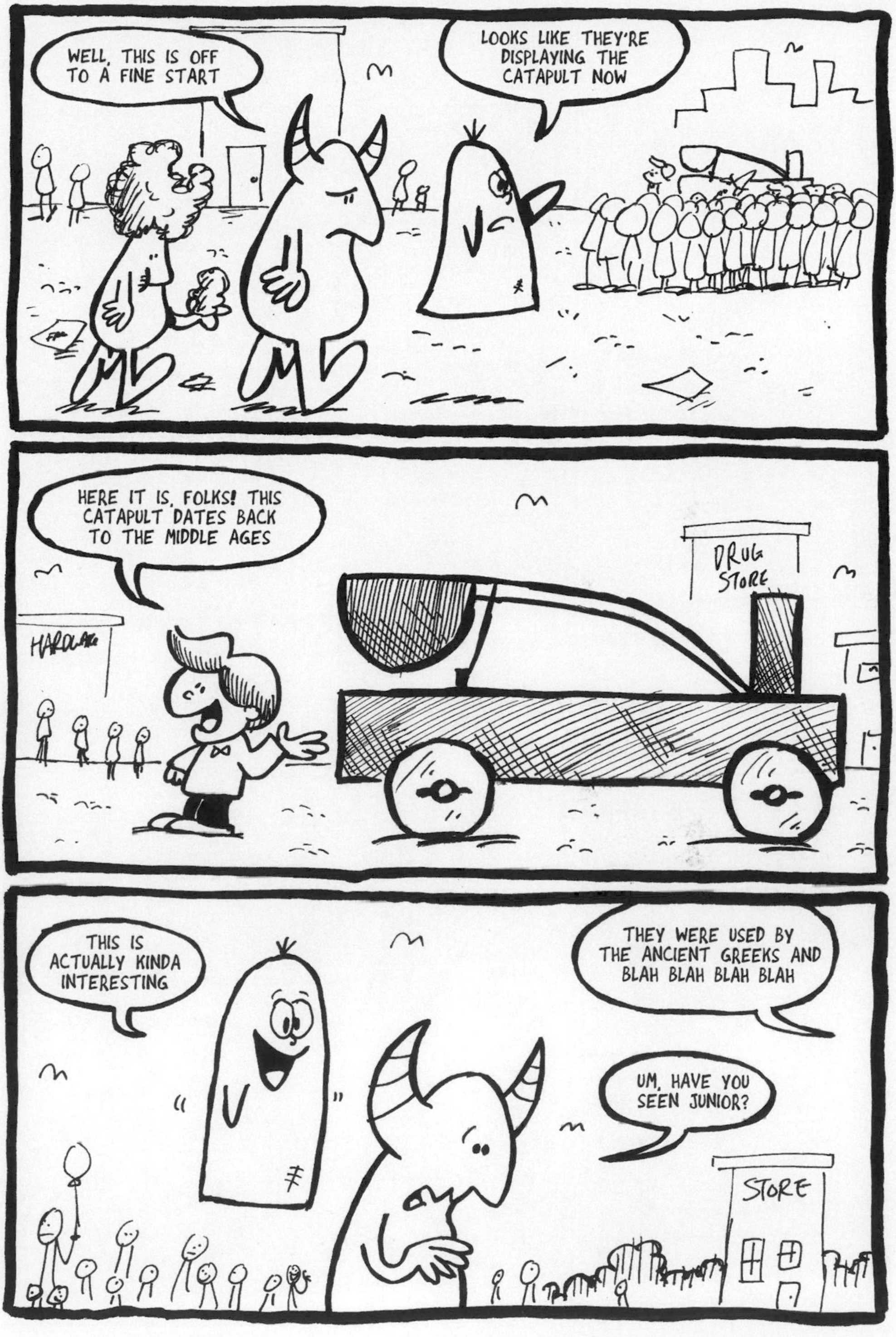
WELL, THIS IS OFF TO A FINE START
LOOKS LIKE THEY'RE DISPLAYING THE CATAPULT NOW
HERE IT IS, FOLKS! THIS CATAPULT DATES BACK TO THE MIDDLE AGES
DRUG STORE
THIS IS ACTUALLY KINDA INTERESTING
THEY WERE USED BY THE ANCIENT GREEKS AND BLAH BLAH BLAH BLAH
UM, HAVE YOU SEEN JUNIOR?
STORE

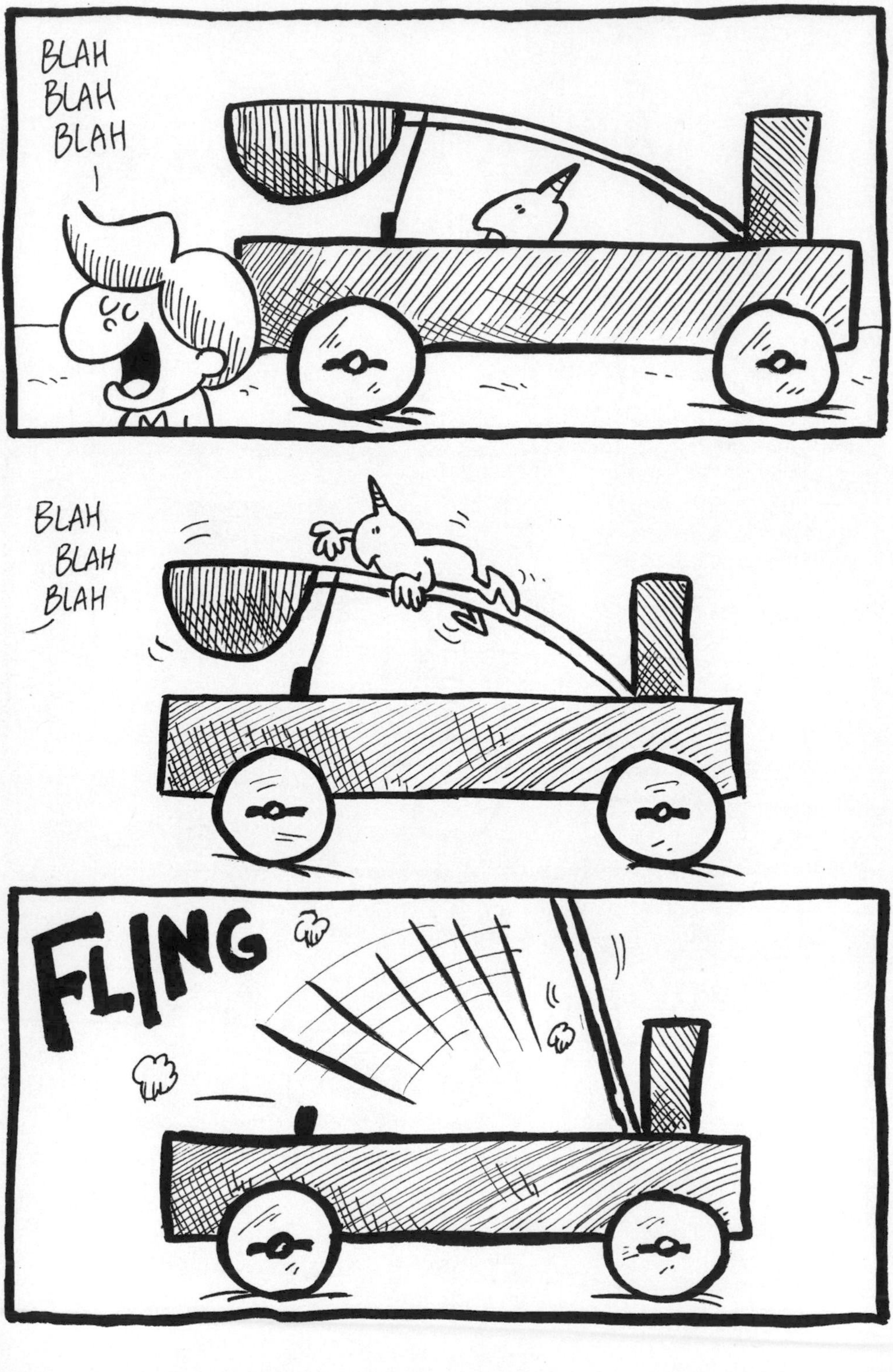
BLAH BLAH BLAH
BLAH BLAH BLAH
FLING

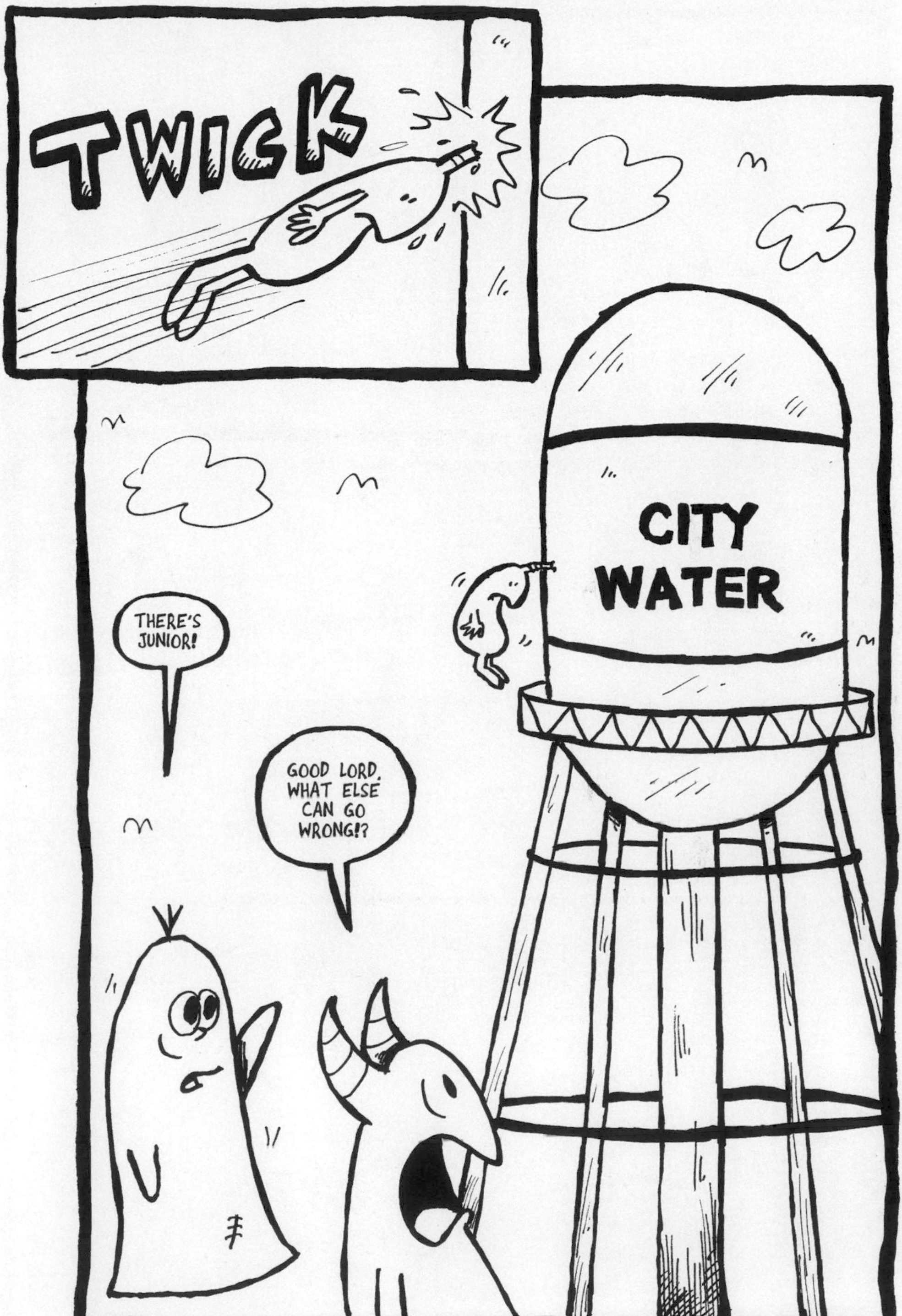
TWICK
CITY WATER
THERE'S JUNIOR!
GOOD LORD, WHAT ELSE CAN GO WRONG!?

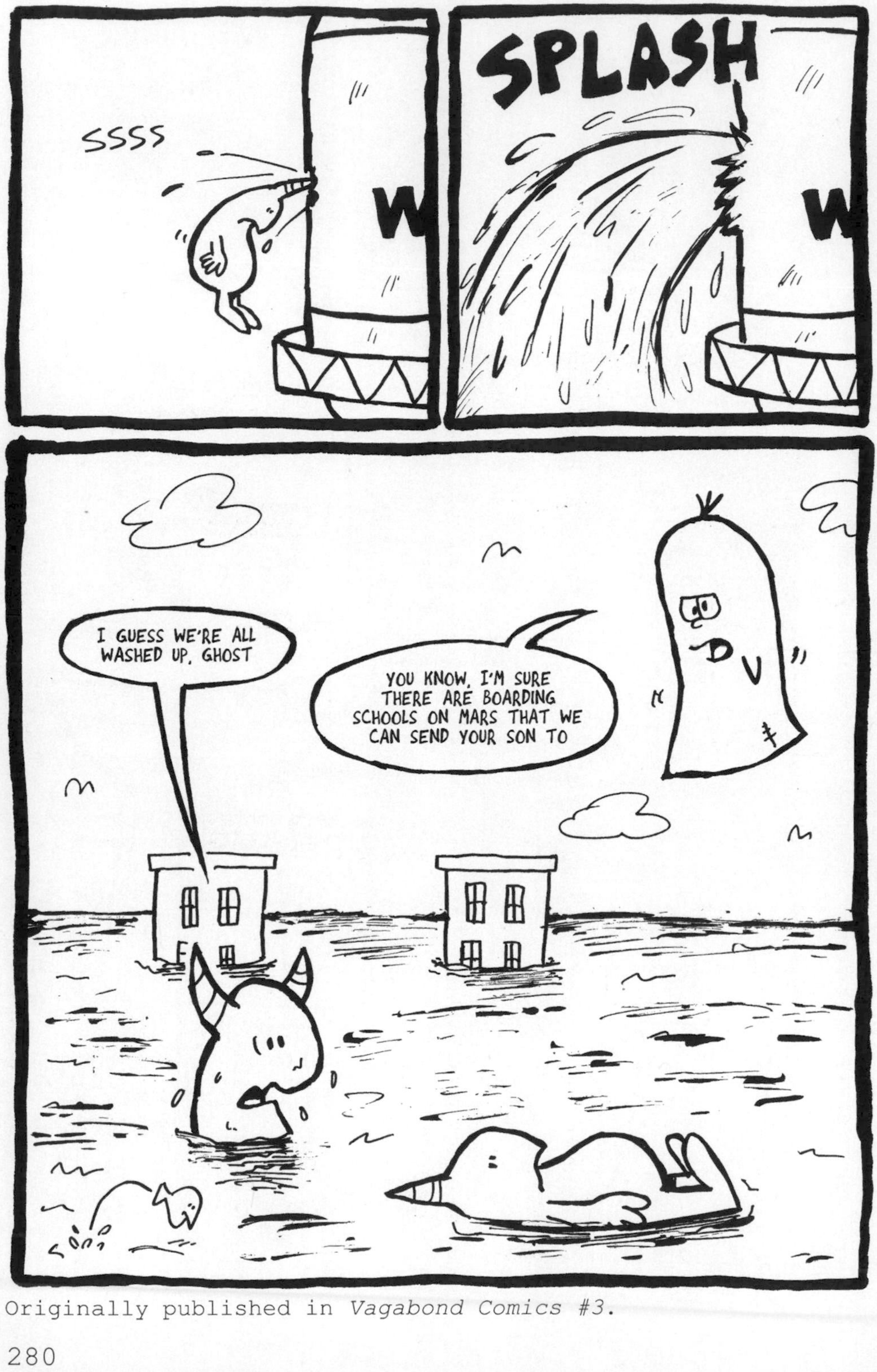
SSSS
SPLASH
I GUESS WE'RE ALL WASHED UP, GHOST
YOU KNOW, I'M SURE THERE ARE BOARDING SCHOOLS ON MARS THAT WE CAN SEND YOUR SON TO

Originally published in *Vagabond Comics #3*.

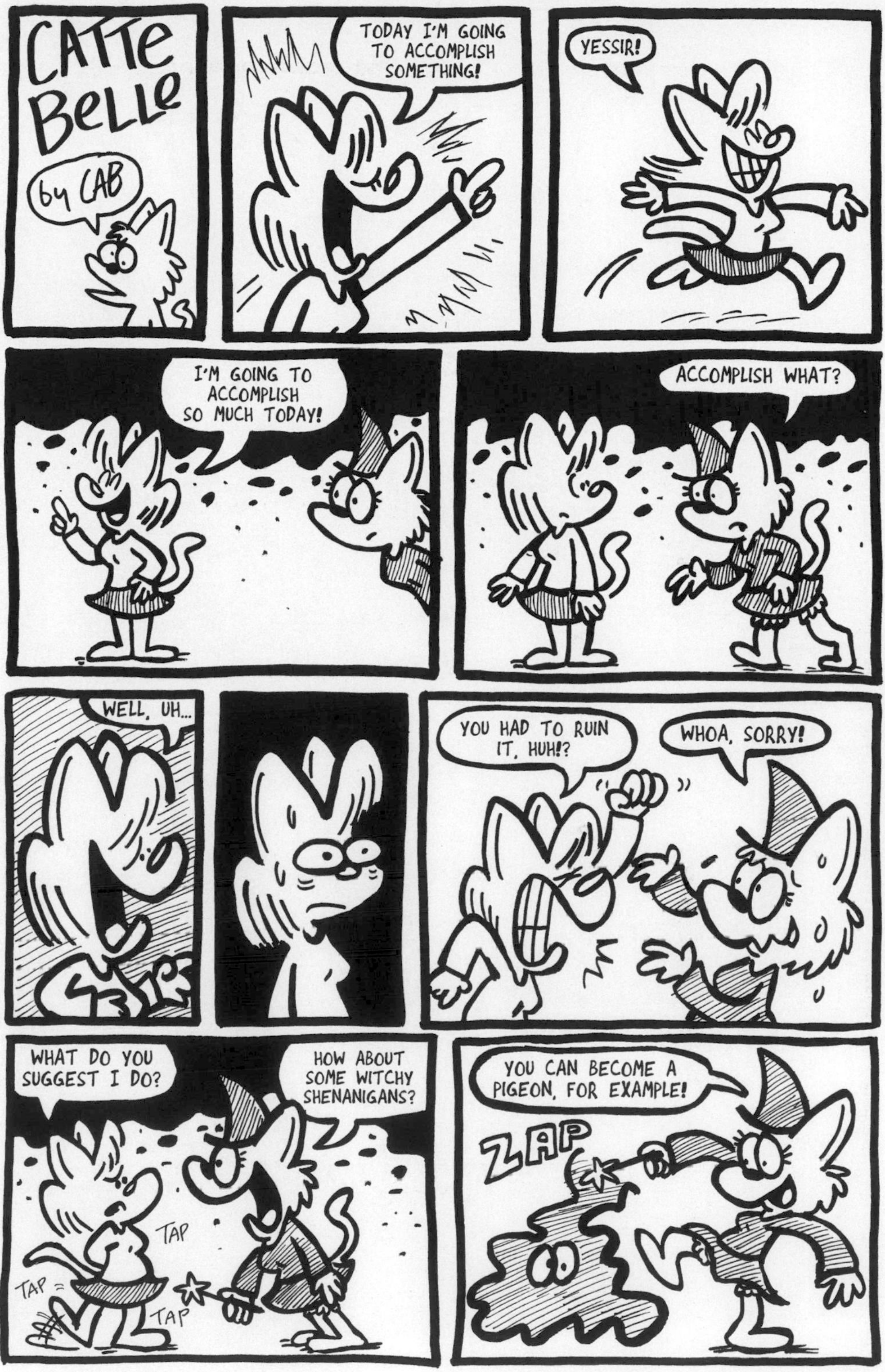
CATTE BELLE
by CAB
TODAY I'M GOING TO ACCOMPLISH SOMETHING!
YESSIR!
I'M GOING TO ACCOMPLISH SO MUCH TODAY!
ACCOMPLISH WHAT?
WELL, UH...
YOU HAD TO RUIN IT, HUH!?
WHOA, SORRY!
WHAT DO YOU SUGGEST I DO?
HOW ABOUT SOME WITCHY SHENANIGANS?
TAP
TAP
TAP
YOU CAN BECOME A PIGEON, FOR EXAMPLE!
ZAP

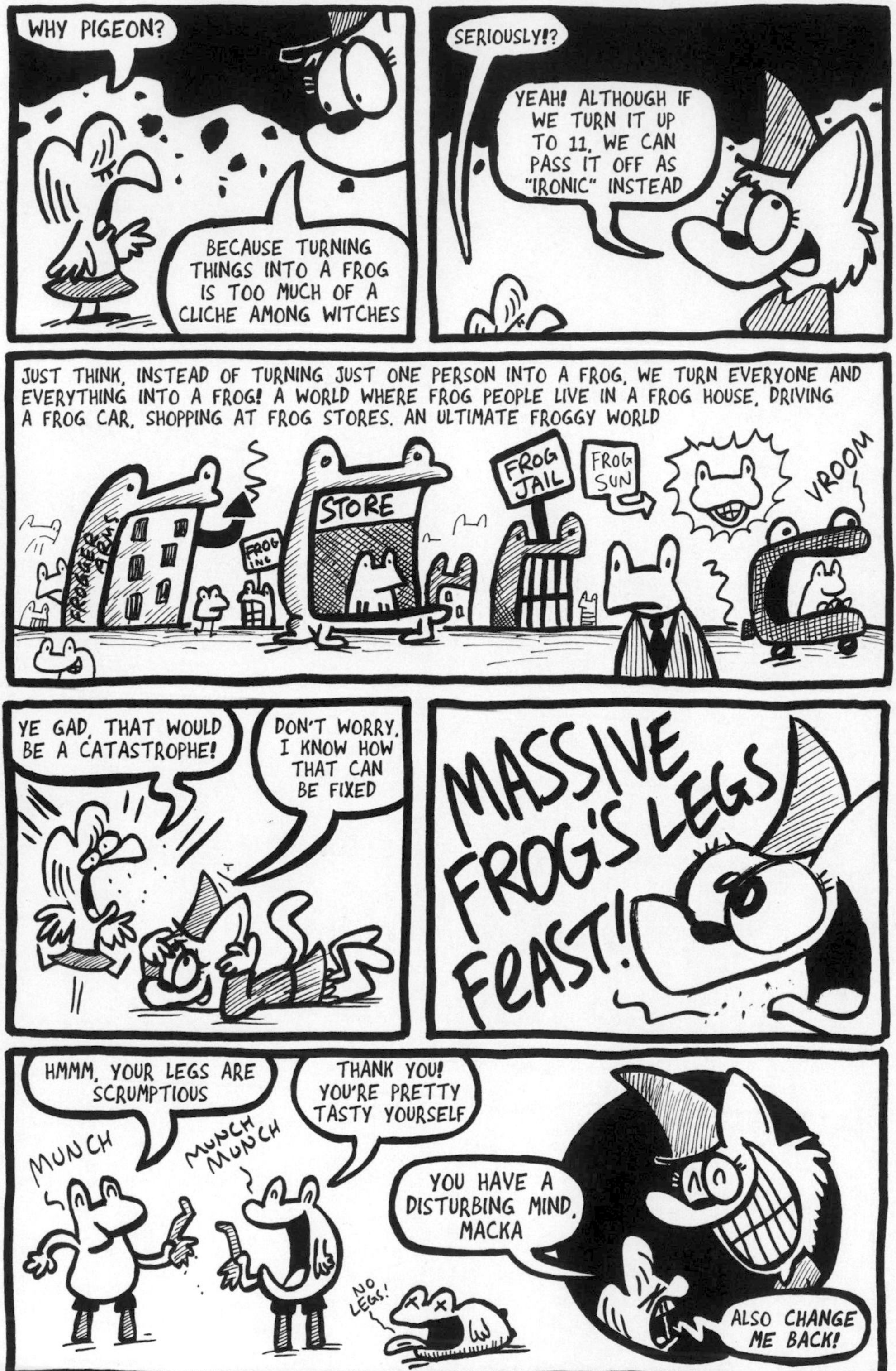
WHY PIGEON?
BECAUSE TURNING THINGS INTO A FROG IS TOO MUCH OF A CLICHE AMONG WITCHES
SERIOUSLY!?
YEAH! ALTHOUGH IF WE TURN IT UP TO 11, WE CAN PASS IT OFF AS "IRONIC" INSTEAD
JUST THINK, INSTEAD OF TURNING JUST ONE PERSON INTO A FROG, WE TURN EVERYONE AND EVERYTHING INTO A FROG! A WORLD WHERE FROG PEOPLE LIVE IN A FROG HOUSE, DRIVING A FROG CAR, SHOPPING AT FROG STORES. AN ULTIMATE FROGGY WORLD
FROGGER ARMS
FROG INC
STORE
FROG JAIL
FROG SUN
VROOM
YE GAD, THAT WOULD BE A CATASTROPHE!
DON'T WORRY, I KNOW HOW THAT CAN BE FIXED
MASSIVE FROG'S LEGS FEAST!
HMMM, YOUR LEGS ARE SCRUMPTIOUS
THANK YOU! YOU'RE PRETTY TASTY YOURSELF
MUNCH
MUNCH MUNCH
YOU HAVE A DISTURBING MIND, MACKA
NO LEGS!
ALSO CHANGE ME BACK!

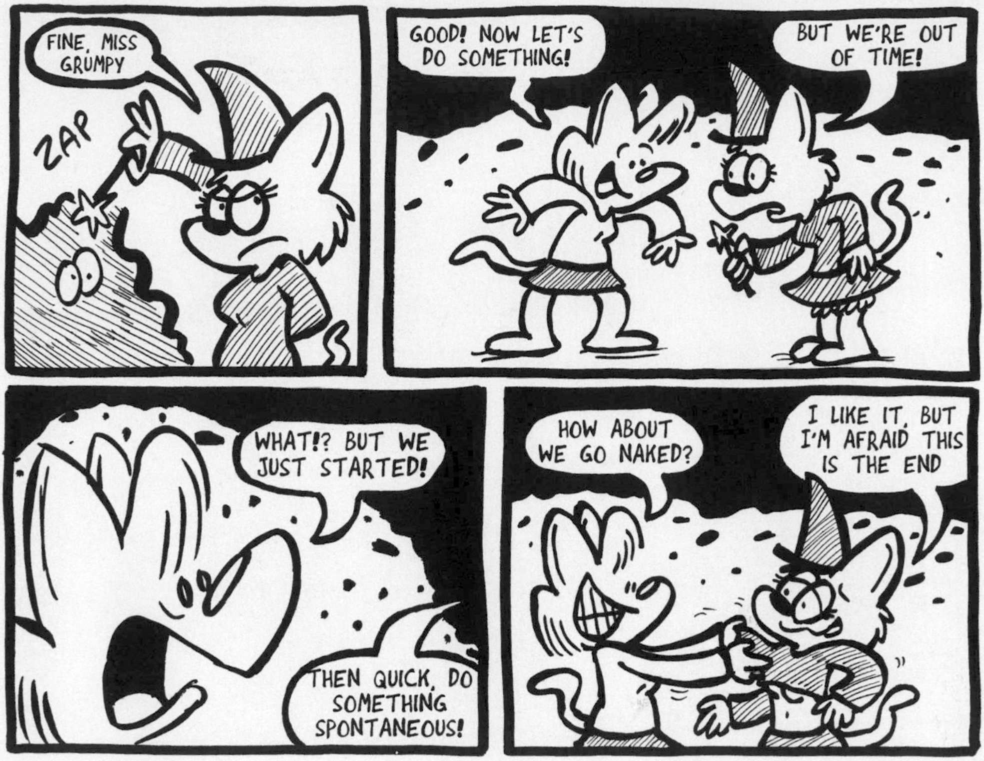
FINE, MISS GRUMPY
ZAP
GOOD! NOW LET'S DO SOMETHING!
BUT WE'RE OUT OF TIME!
WHAT!? BUT WE JUST STARTED!
THEN QUICK, DO SOMETHING SPONTANEOUS!
HOW ABOUT WE GO NAKED?
I LIKE IT, BUT I'M AFRAID THIS IS THE END

Originally published in *Pico #6*.

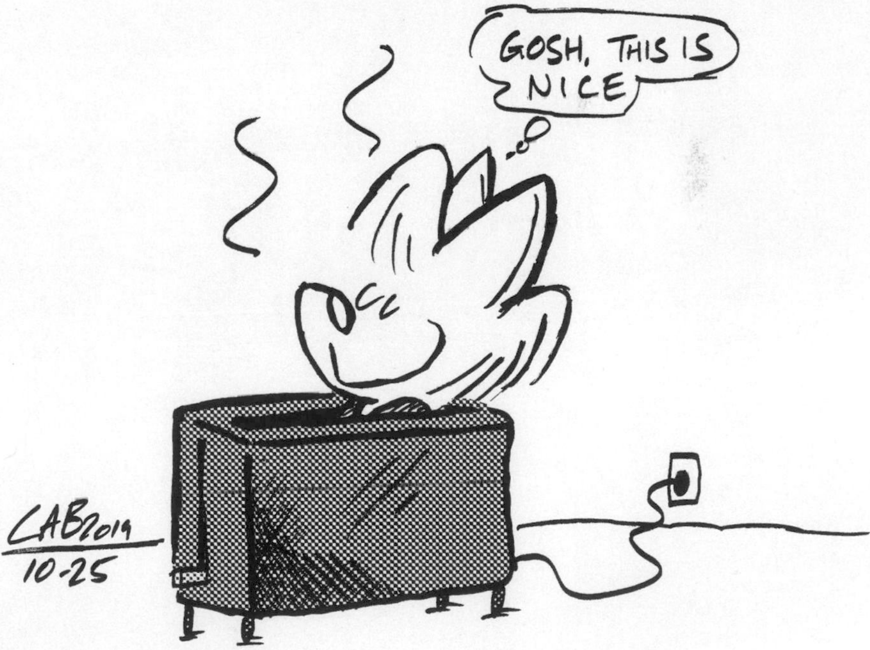
GOSH, THIS IS NICE
CAB2019
10-25
HAPPINESS IS A TOASTY CAT

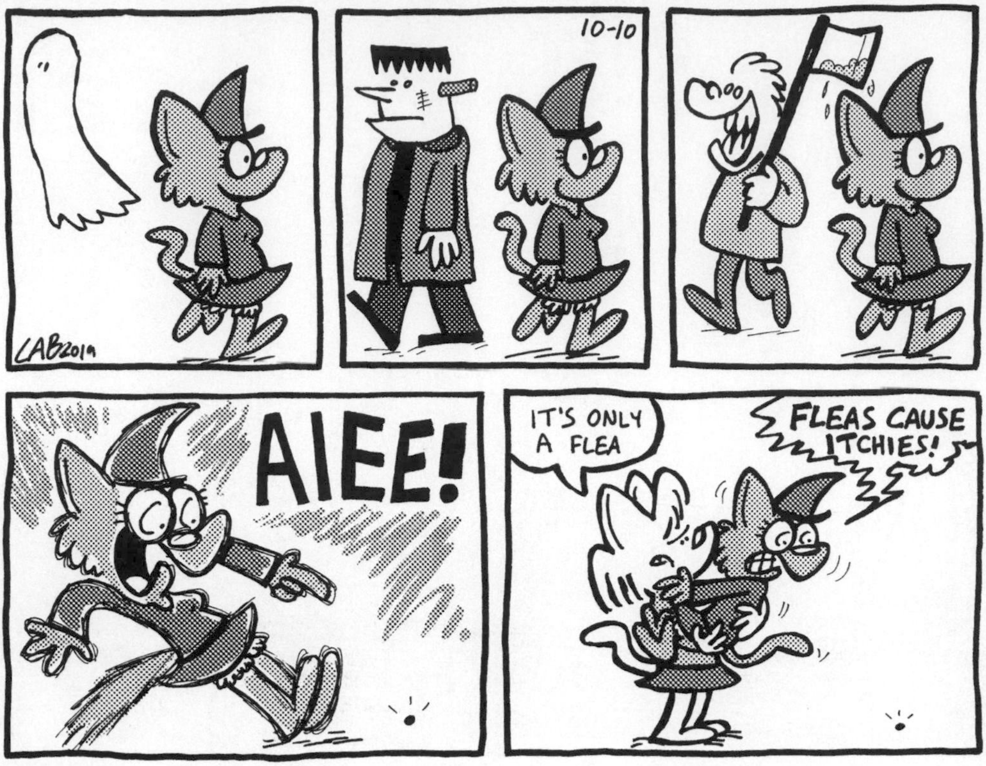
10-10
LAB2019
AIEE!
IT'S ONLY A FLEA
FLEAS CAUSE ITCHIES!

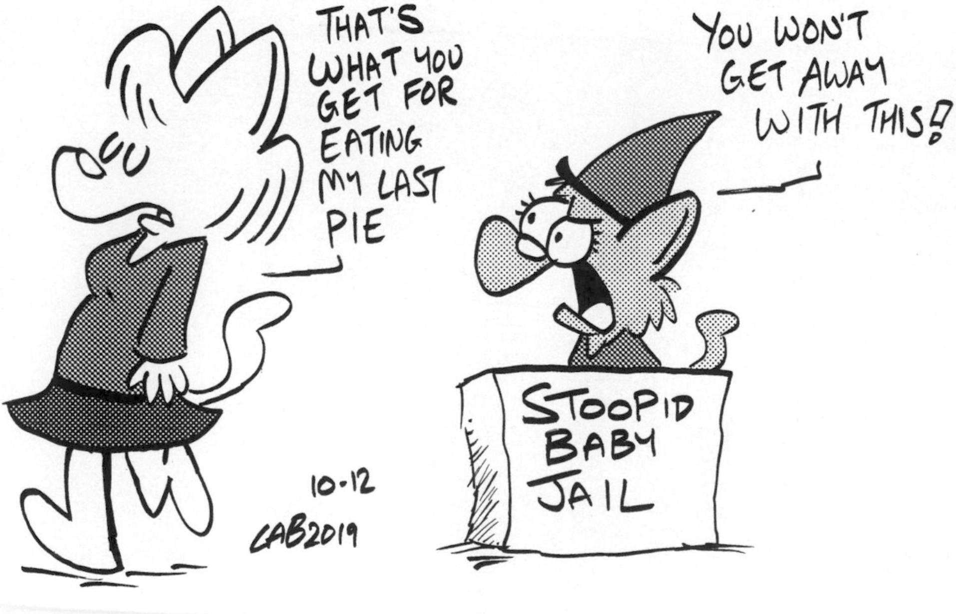
THAT'S WHAT YOU GET FOR EATING MY LAST PIE
YOU WON'T GET AWAY WITH THIS!!
STOOPID BABY JAIL
10-12
LAB2019

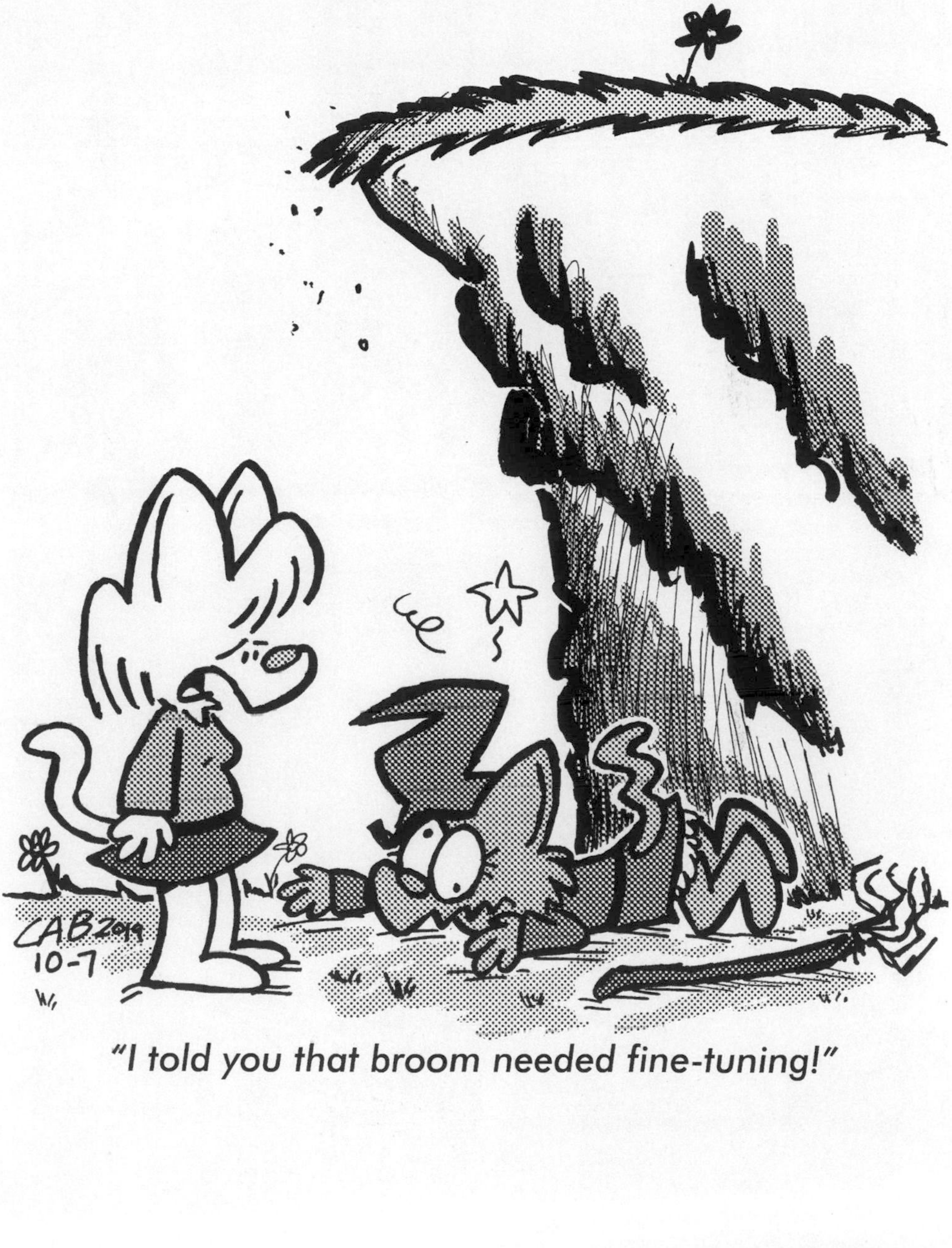
CAB 2019
10-7

"I told you that broom needed fine-tuning!"

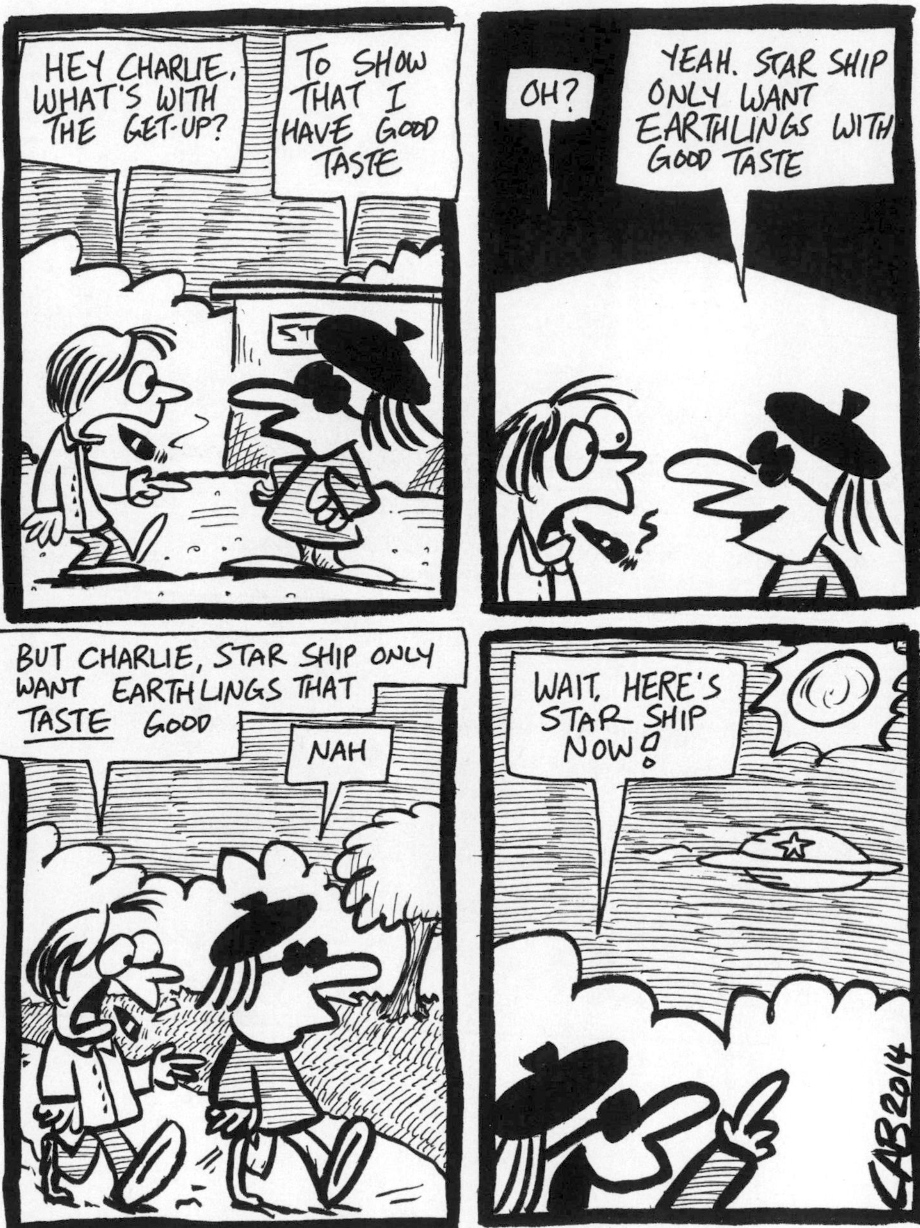
HEY CHARLIE, WHAT'S WITH THE GET-UP?
TO SHOW THAT I HAVE GOOD TASTE
OH?
YEAH. STAR SHIP ONLY WANT EARTHLINGS WITH GOOD TASTE
BUT CHARLIE, STAR SHIP ONLY WANT EARTHLINGS THAT TASTE GOOD
NAH
WAIT, HERE'S STAR SHIP NOW!
CAB 2014

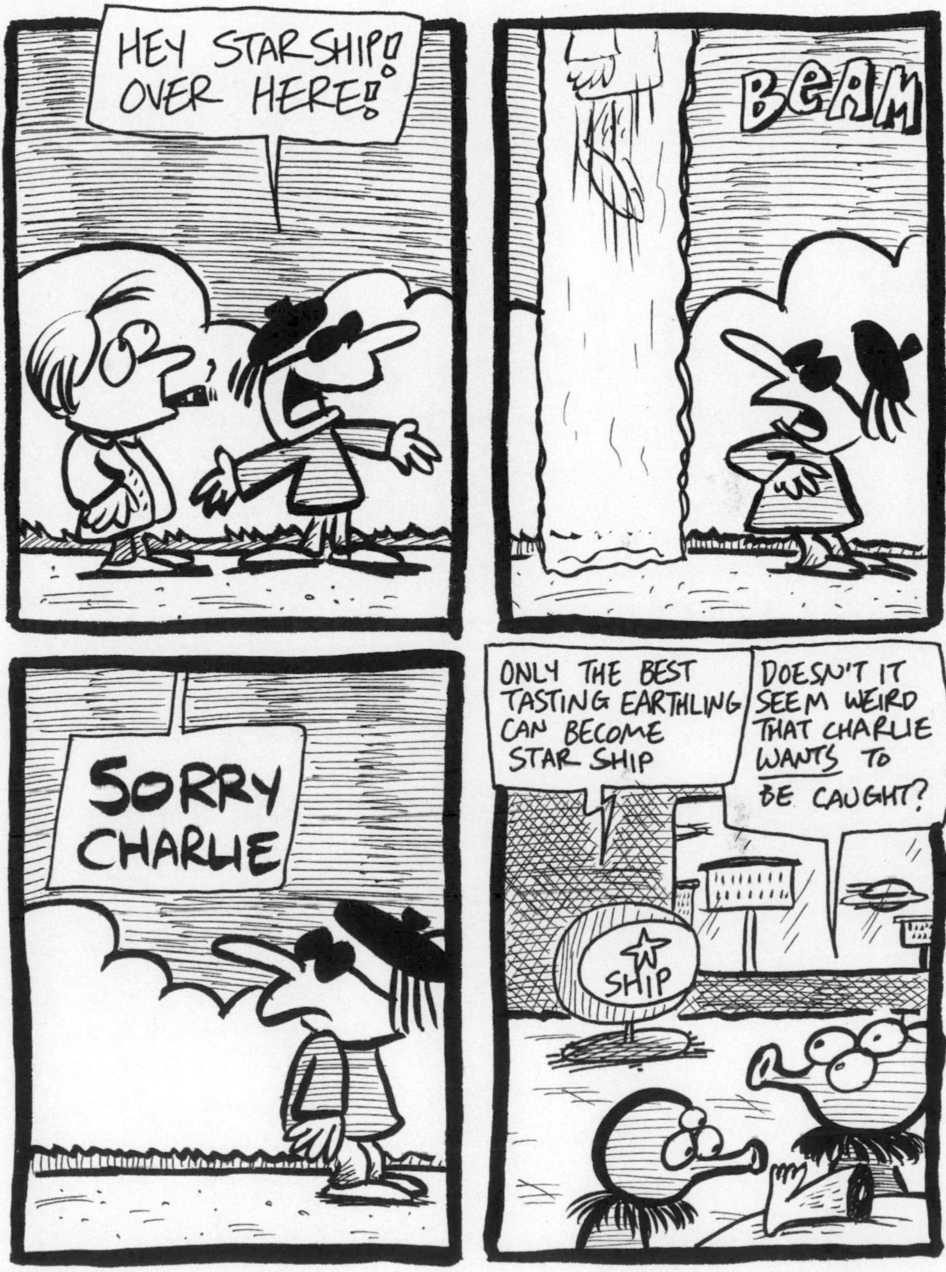
HEY STAR SHIP!! OVER HERE!!
BEAM
SORRY CHARLIE
ONLY THE BEST TASTING EARTHLING CAN BECOME STAR SHIP
DOESN'T IT SEEM WEIRD THAT CHARLIE WANTS TO BE CAUGHT?
SHIP

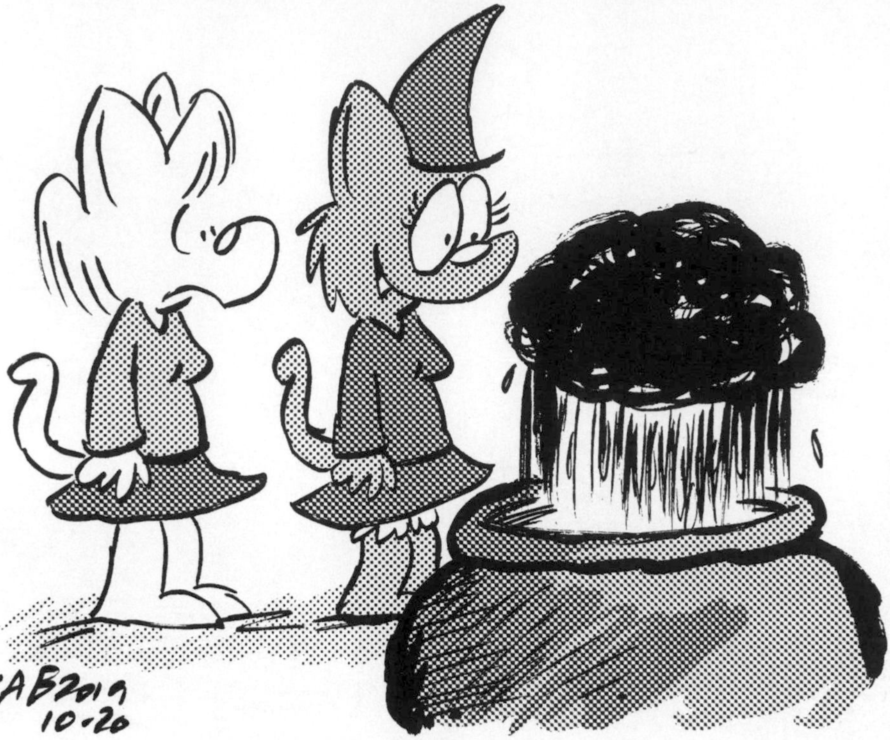
CAB2019
10-20

"I have a good feeling about this potion."

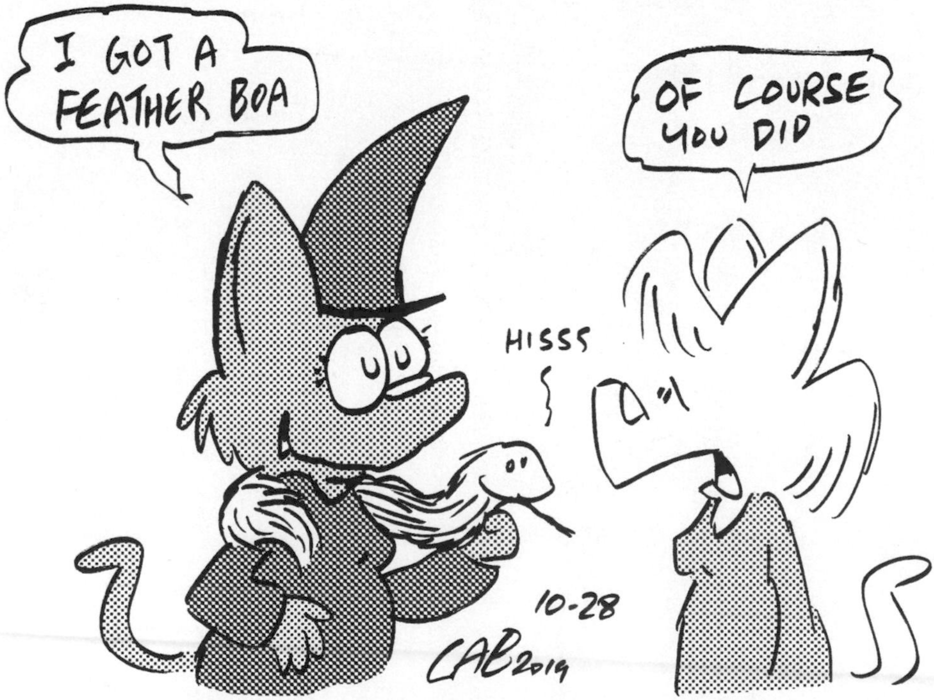
I GOT A FEATHER BOA
OF COURSE YOU DID
HISSS
10-28
CAB2019

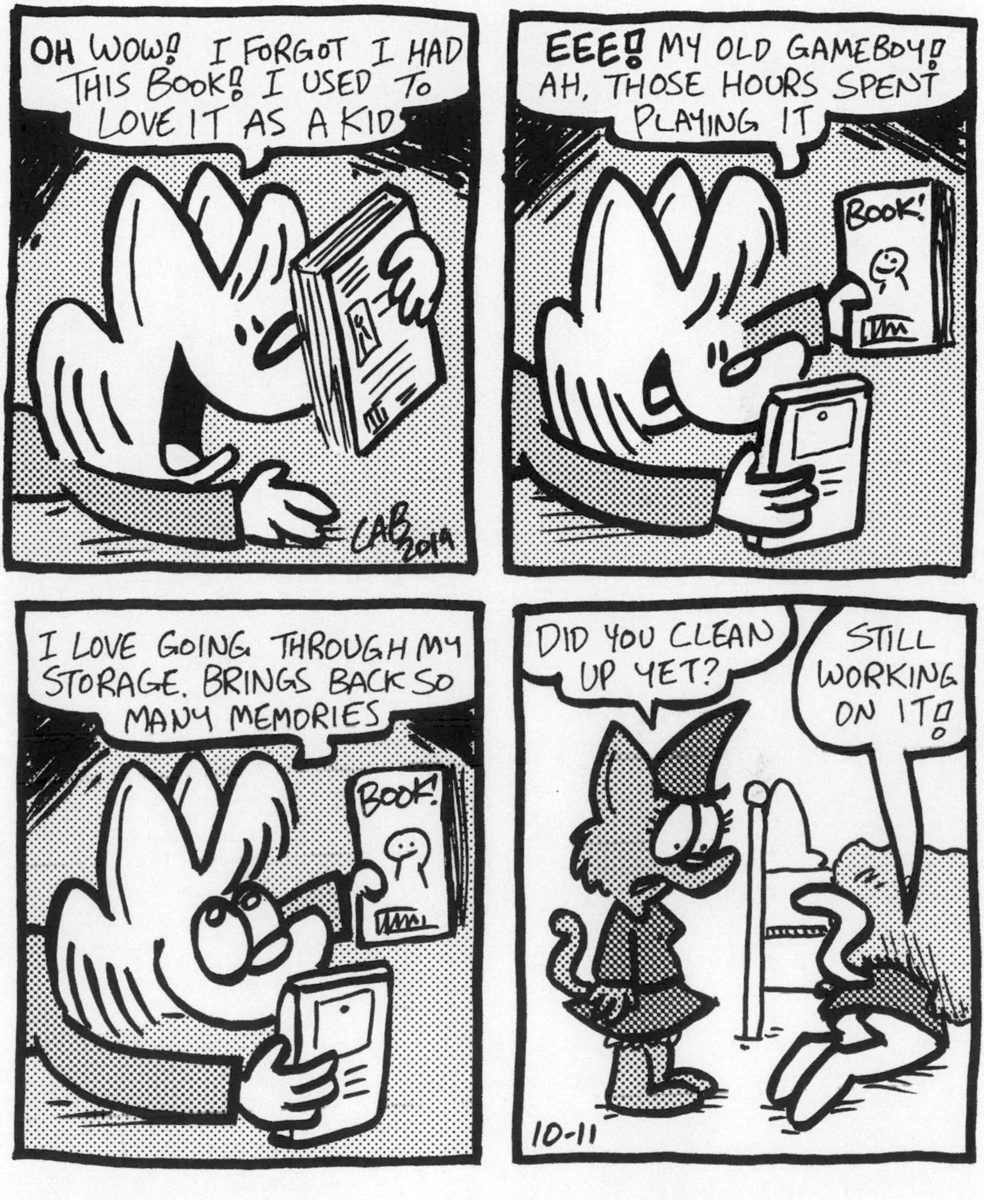
OH WOW! I FORGOT I HAD THIS BOOK! I USED TO LOVE IT AS A KID
CAB 2019
EEE! MY OLD GAMEBOY! AH, THOSE HOURS SPENT PLAYING IT
BOOK!
I LOVE GOING THROUGH MY STORAGE. BRINGS BACK SO MANY MEMORIES
BOOK!
DID YOU CLEAN UP YET?
STILL WORKING ON IT!
10-11

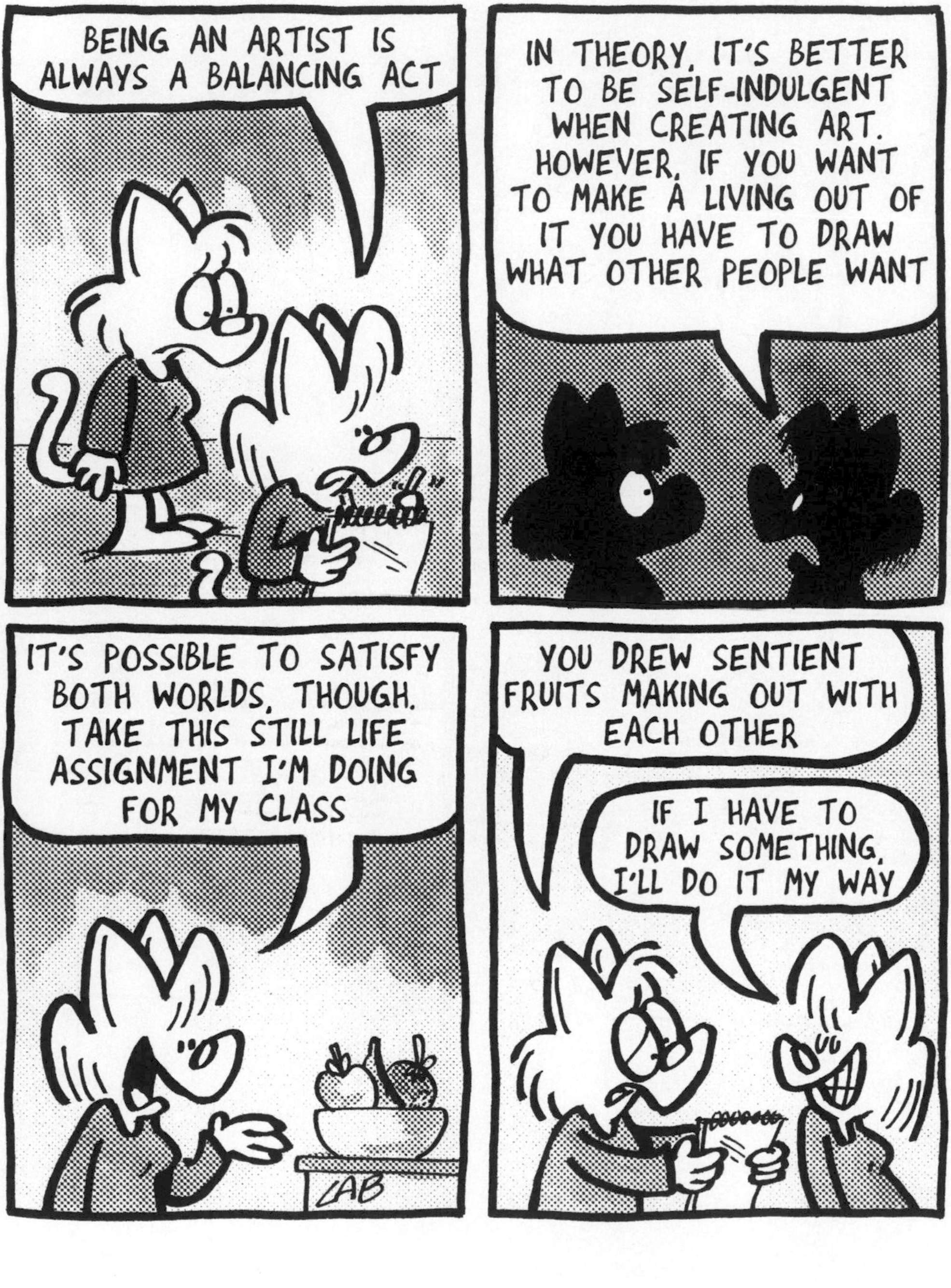
BEING AN ARTIST IS ALWAYS A BALANCING ACT
IN THEORY, IT'S BETTER TO BE SELF-INDULGENT WHEN CREATING ART. HOWEVER, IF YOU WANT TO MAKE A LIVING OUT OF IT YOU HAVE TO DRAW WHAT OTHER PEOPLE WANT
IT'S POSSIBLE TO SATISFY BOTH WORLDS, THOUGH. TAKE THIS STILL LIFE ASSIGNMENT I'M DOING FOR MY CLASS
LAB
YOU DREW SENTIENT FRUITS MAKING OUT WITH EACH OTHER
IF I HAVE TO DRAW SOMETHING, I'LL DO IT MY WAY

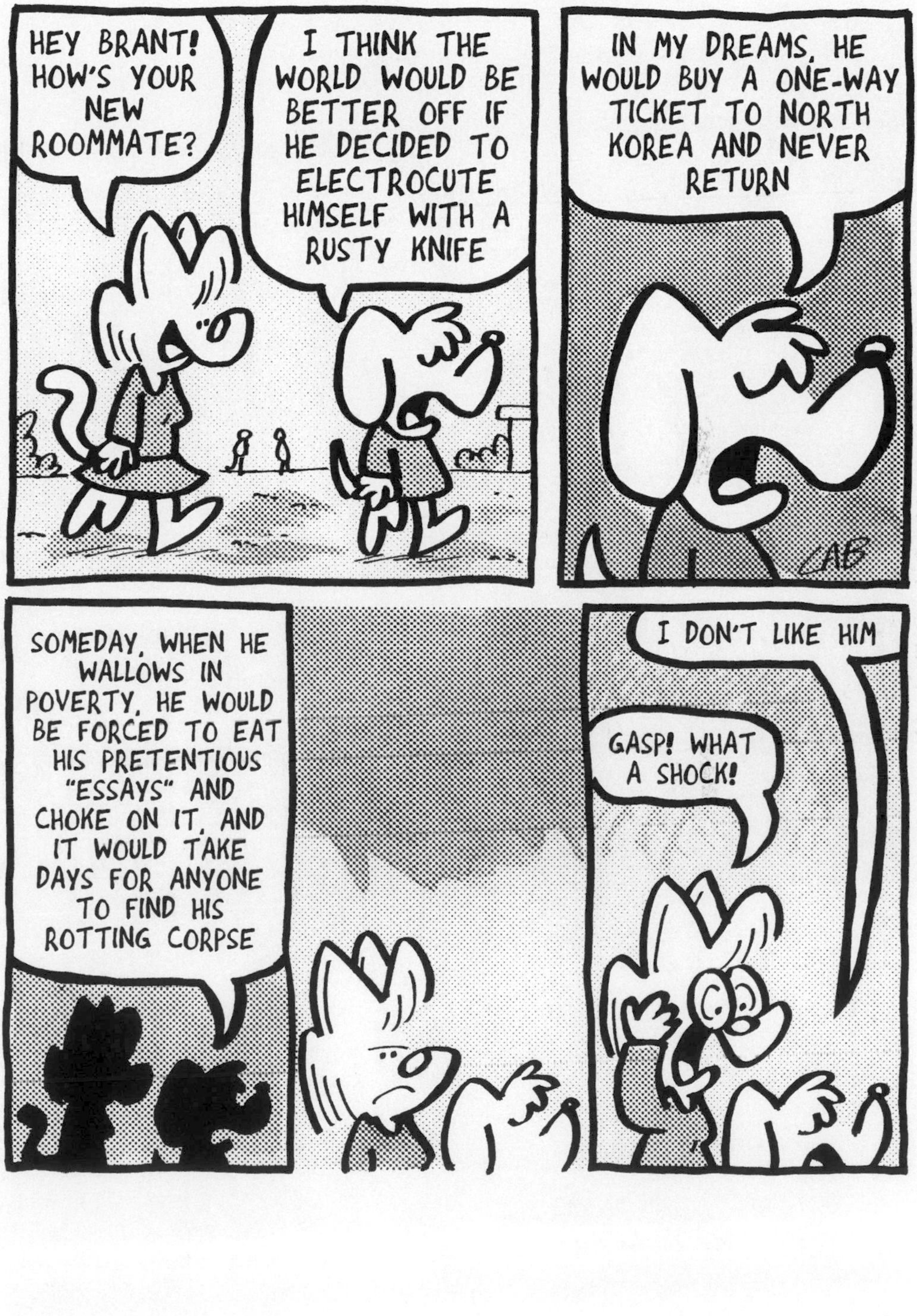
HEY BRANT! HOW'S YOUR NEW ROOMMATE?
I THINK THE WORLD WOULD BE BETTER OFF IF HE DECIDED TO ELECTROCUTE HIMSELF WITH A RUSTY KNIFE
IN MY DREAMS, HE WOULD BUY A ONE-WAY TICKET TO NORTH KOREA AND NEVER RETURN
CAB
SOMEDAY, WHEN HE WALLOWS IN POVERTY, HE WOULD BE FORCED TO EAT HIS PRETENTIOUS "ESSAYS" AND CHOKE ON IT, AND IT WOULD TAKE DAYS FOR ANYONE TO FIND HIS ROTTING CORPSE
I DON'T LIKE HIM
GASP! WHAT A SHOCK!

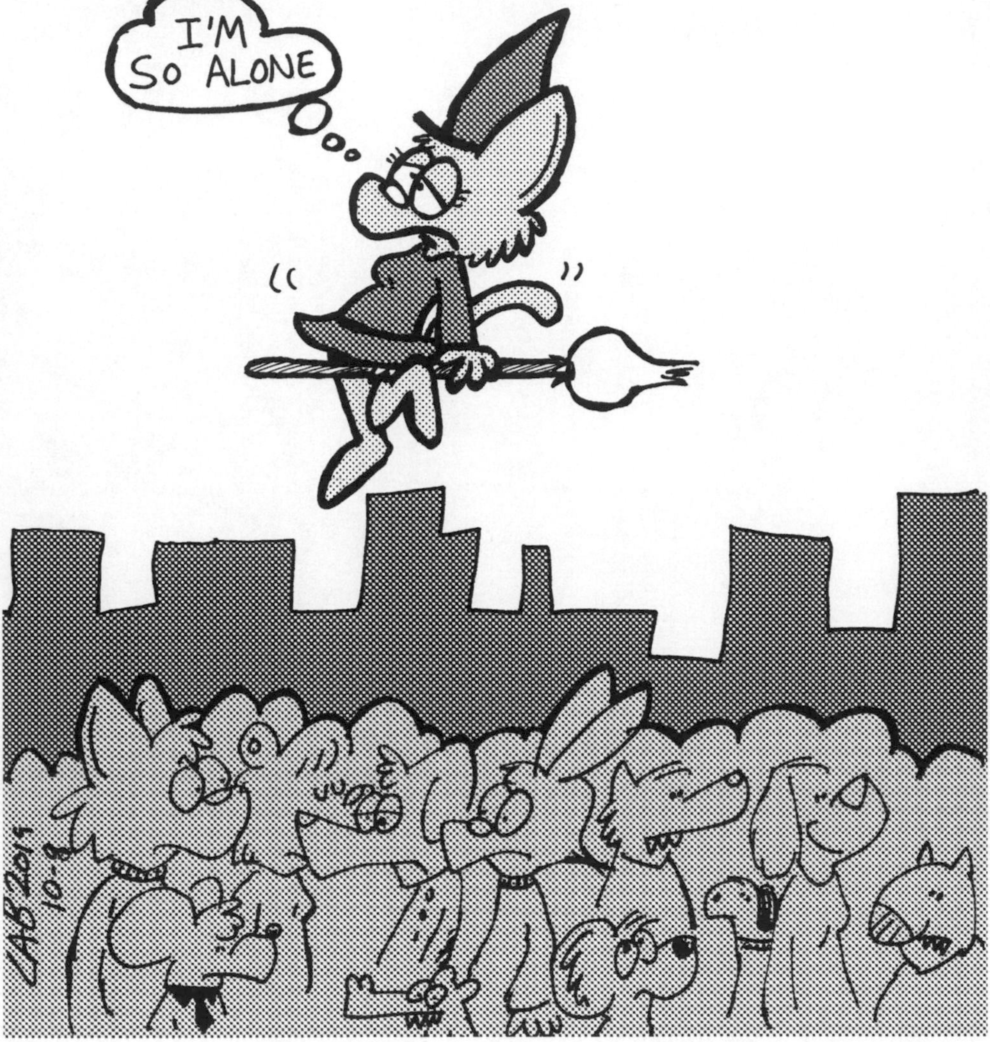
I'M SO ALONE

ANIMATION

"Ask a Cat" lives on in animation.

I am not done with "Ask a Cat". On the contrary, I have big plans for it.

While I was drawing the strip I picked up work doing storyboards for an animation company. The company's management turned out to be anything but perfect, but my years with them gave me a desire to produce my own animation. In 2018, I wrote a pilot script for a series of "Ask a Cat" shorts because I heard from the producer that he was looking for a new series concept to upload on his YouTube channel.

 Ultimately he decided not to greenlight anything, which proved to be a good thing in hindsight. Still, the script was in the back of my mind, waiting for an opportunity. The opportunity came during, of all things, the COVID pandemic. With my convention plans canceled I started tinkering around with Krita, an open-source art software that has an animation function, and decided to animate something with it.

That animation came out pretty good, so I played around with it more and more. Motivated, I decided to dig out the script and make the pilot myself, recruiting my friend Ty Konzak, a freelance voice actor, to do all the voices.

Upon completion I uploaded the "Ask a Cat" cartoon on YouTube and Newgrounds on July 16, 2020. The 2.5 minute-long short was just the beginning.

Since then I have released more cartoons, including two more "Ask a Cat" shorts: ***Cat and Kat*** (2020), a crossover between "Ask a Cat" and my other comic, "The Fuzzy Princess", and the imaginatively titled ***Ask a Cat #3*** (2022). I see a strong potential in animation and I hope to create more shorts, including new "Ask a Cat" cartoons. I hope you can join me on this journey.

For this part of the book I am reproducing the complete set of storyboards for ***Cat and Kat***. You can see the finished cartoon at **catandkat.smallbugstudio.com**.

START: 9.5.2020.
FINISH: 9.7.2020

Title: ASK A CAT 2 = KAT AND CAT   Page: 1

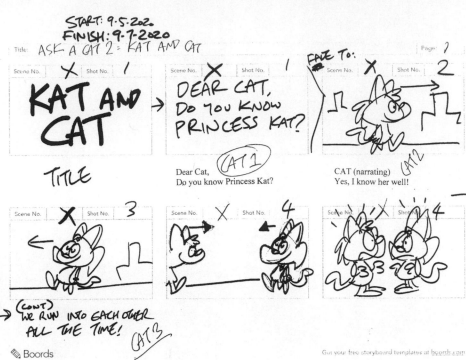

Scene No. X Shot No. 1

KAT AND CAT

TITLE

Scene No. X Shot No. 1

DEAR CAT,
DO YOU KNOW
PRINCESS KAT?

Dear Cat,
Do you know Princess Kat?   CAT 1

FAZE TO:

Scene No. X Shot No. 2

CAT 2

CAT (narrating)
Yes, I know her well!

Scene No. X Shot No. 3

Scene No. X Shot No. 4

Scene No. X Shot No. 4

→ (CONT)
WE RUN INTO EACH OTHER
ALL THE TIME!   CAT 3

✎ Boords

Get your free storyboard templates at boords.com

Title: KAT AND CAT   Page: 2

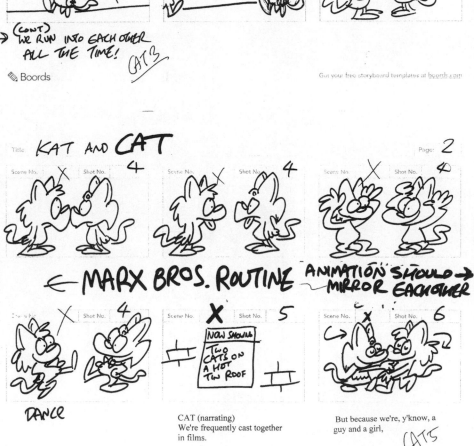

Scene No. X Shot No. 4

Scene No. X Shot No. 4

Scene No. X Shot No. 4

← MARX BROS. ROUTINE

ANIMATION SHOULD →
MIRROR EACH OTHER

Scene No. X Shot No. 4

DANCE

Scene No. X Shot No. 5

NOW SHOWING
TWO
CATS ON
A HOT
TIN ROOF

CAT (narrating)
We're frequently cast together
in films.

CAT 4

Scene No. X Shot No. 6

But because we're, y'know, a
guy and a girl,   CAT 5

✎ Boords

Get your free storyboard templates at boords.com

296

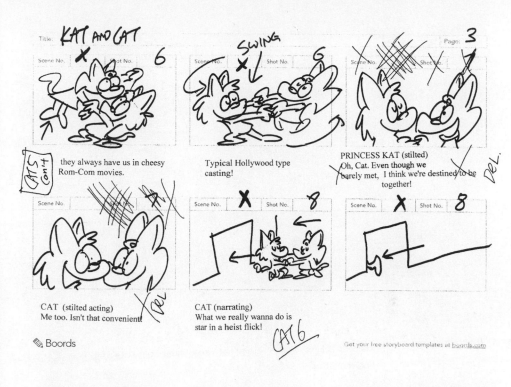

Title: KAT AND CAT

Page: 3

Scene No. — Shot No. 6

they always have us in cheesy Rom-Com movies.

SWING

Scene No. — Shot No. 6

Typical Hollywood type casting!

Scene No. — Shot No. —

PRINCESS KAT (stilted)
Oh, Cat. Even though we barely met, I think we're destined to be together!

DEL.

CATS Cont

Scene No. — Shot No. —

CAT (stilted acting)
Me too. Isn't that convenient!

DEL

Scene No. — Shot No. 8

CAT (narrating)
What we really wanna do is star in a heist flick!

CAT6

Scene No. — Shot No. 8

Boords

Get your free storyboard templates at boords.com

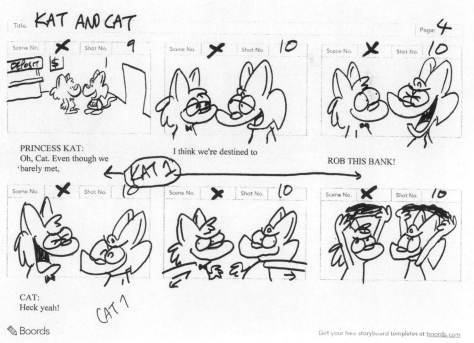

Title: KAT AND CAT

Page: 4

Scene No. — Shot No. 9

DEPOSIT $

PRINCESS KAT:
Oh, Cat. Even though we barely met,

Scene No. — Shot No. 10

I think we're destined to

KAT 1

Scene No. — Shot No. 10

ROB THIS BANK!

Scene No. — Shot No. 10

CAT:
Heck yeah!

CAT 1

Scene No. — Shot No. 10

Scene No. — Shot No. 10

Boords

Get your free storyboard templates at boords.com

297

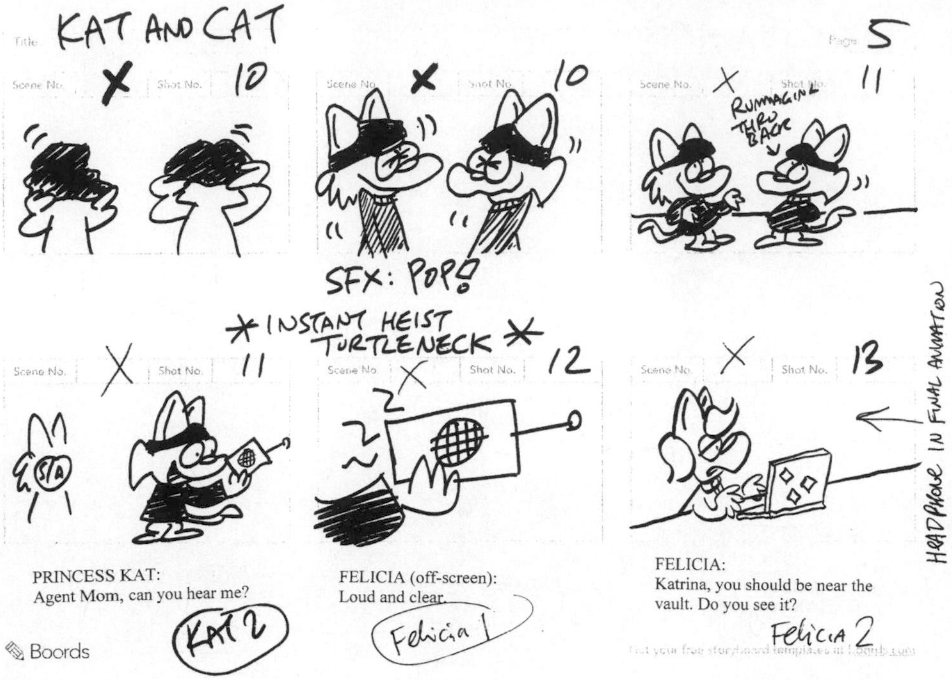

Title KAT AND CAT
Page 5
Scene No. X Shot No. 10
Scene No. X Shot No. 10
Scene No. X Shot No. 11
RUMMAGING THRU BACK
SFX: POP!
INSTANT HEIST TURTLENECK
Scene No. X Shot No. 11
Scene No. X Shot No. 12
Scene No. X Shot No. 13
HEADPHONE IN FINAL ANIMATION
PRINCESS KAT:
Agent Mom, can you hear me?
KAT 2
FELICIA (off-screen):
Loud and clear.
Felicia 1
FELICIA:
Katrina, you should be near the vault. Do you see it?
Felicia 2
Boords

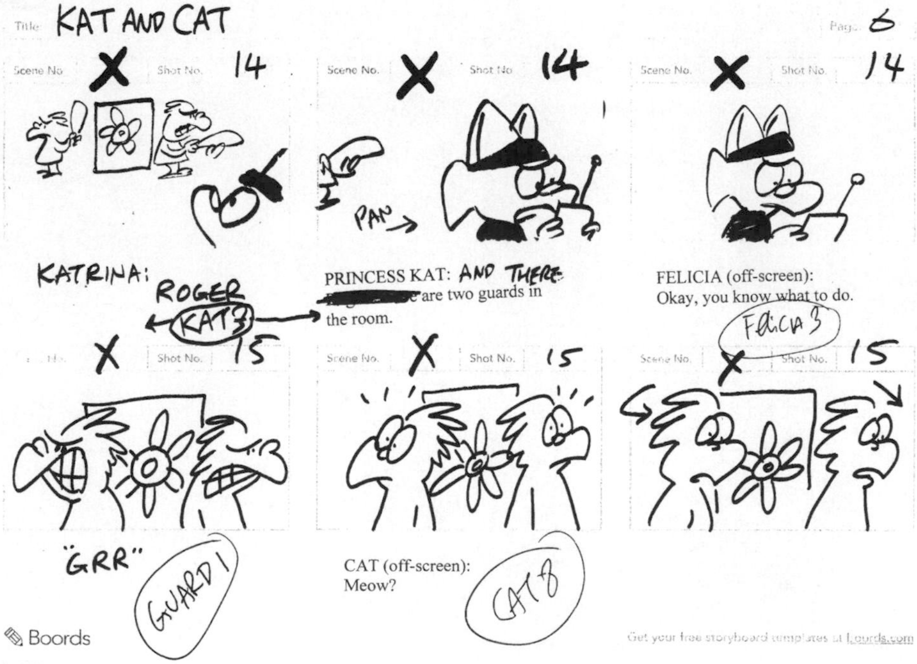

Title KAT AND CAT
Page 6
Scene No. X Shot No. 14
Scene No. X Shot No. 14
PAN
Scene No. X Shot No. 14
KATRINA: ROGER
KAT 3
PRINCESS KAT: AND THERE [redacted] are two guards in the room.
FELICIA (off-screen):
Okay, you know what to do.
Felicia 3
X Shot No. 15
Scene No. X Shot No. 15
Scene No. X Shot No. 15
"GRR"
GUARD 1
CAT (off-screen):
Meow?
CAT 8
Boords
Get your free storyboard templates at boords.com

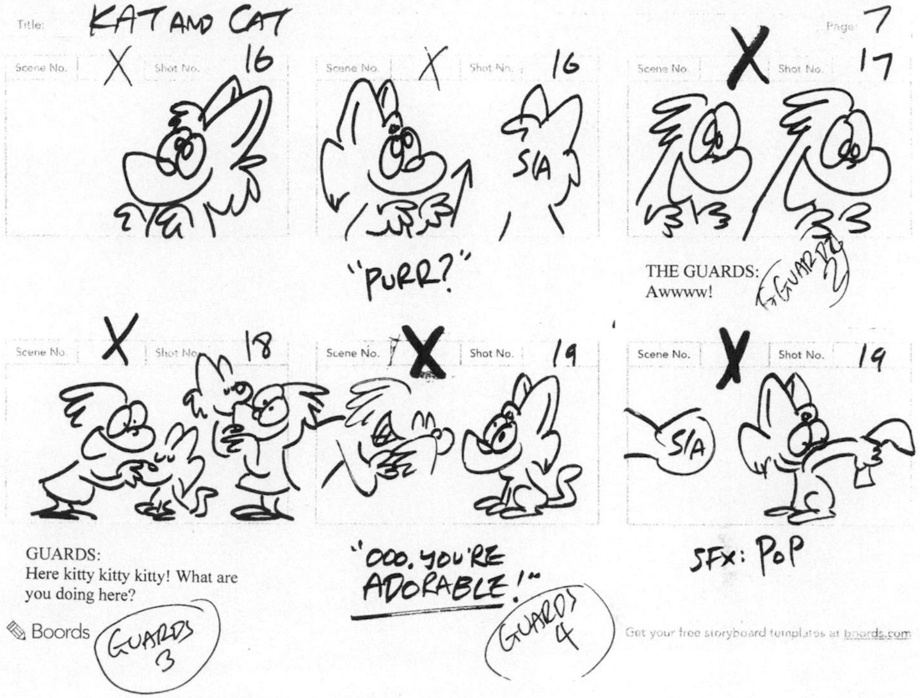
Title: KAT AND CAT
Page: 7
Scene No. X Shot No. 16
Scene No. X Shot No. 16
S/A
"PURR?"
Scene No. X Shot No. 17
THE GUARDS:
Awwww!
FX GUARDS 2
Scene No. X Shot No. 18
GUARDS:
Here kitty kitty kitty! What are you doing here?
GUARDS 3
Scene No. X Shot No. 19
"OOO. YOU'RE ADORABLE!"
GUARDS 4
Scene No. X Shot No. 19
S/A
SFX: POP
Boords
Get your free storyboard templates at boords.com

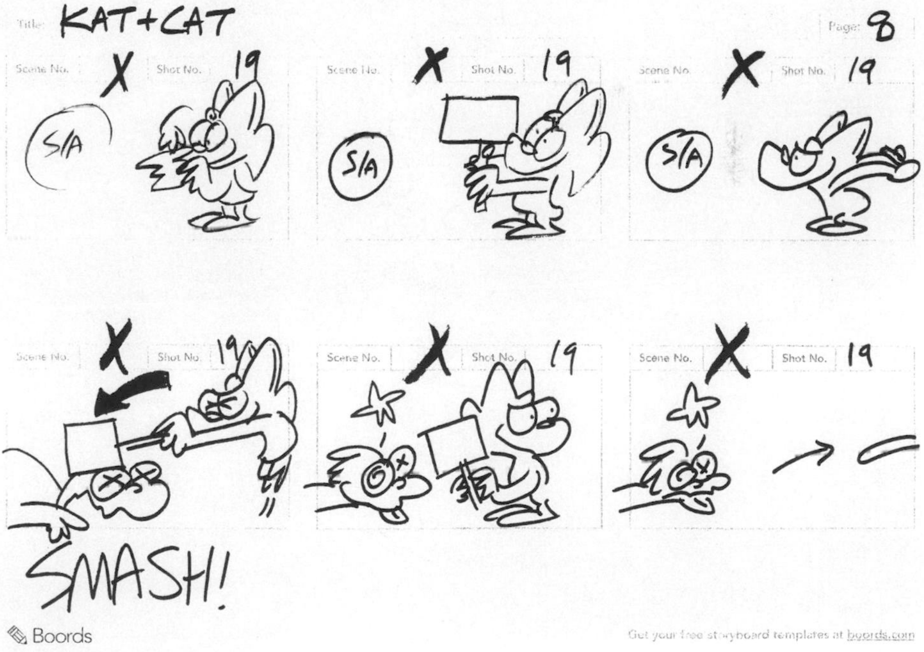
Title: KAT+CAT
Page: 8
Scene No. X Shot No. 19
S/A
Scene No. X Shot No. 19
S/A
Scene No. X Shot No. 19
S/A
Scene No. X Shot No. 19
SMASH!
Scene No. X Shot No. 19
Scene No. X Shot No. 19
Boords
Get your free storyboard templates at boords.com

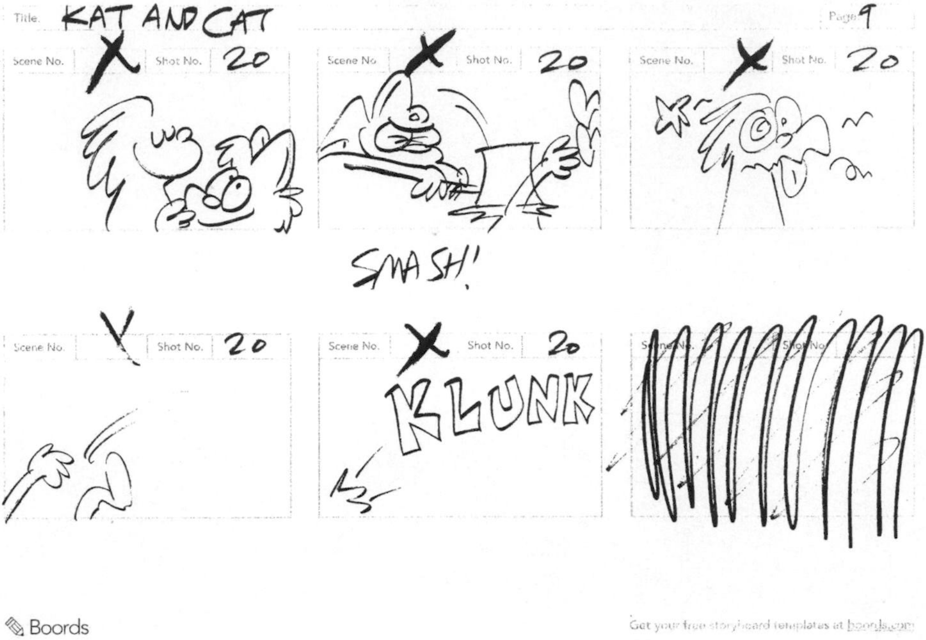
Title: KAT AND CAT
Page 9
Scene No. X
Shot No. 20
Scene No. X
Shot No. 20
Scene No. X
Shot No. 20
SMASH!
Scene No.
Shot No. 20
Scene No. X
Shot No. 20
KLUNK
Boords
Get your free storyboard templates at boords.com

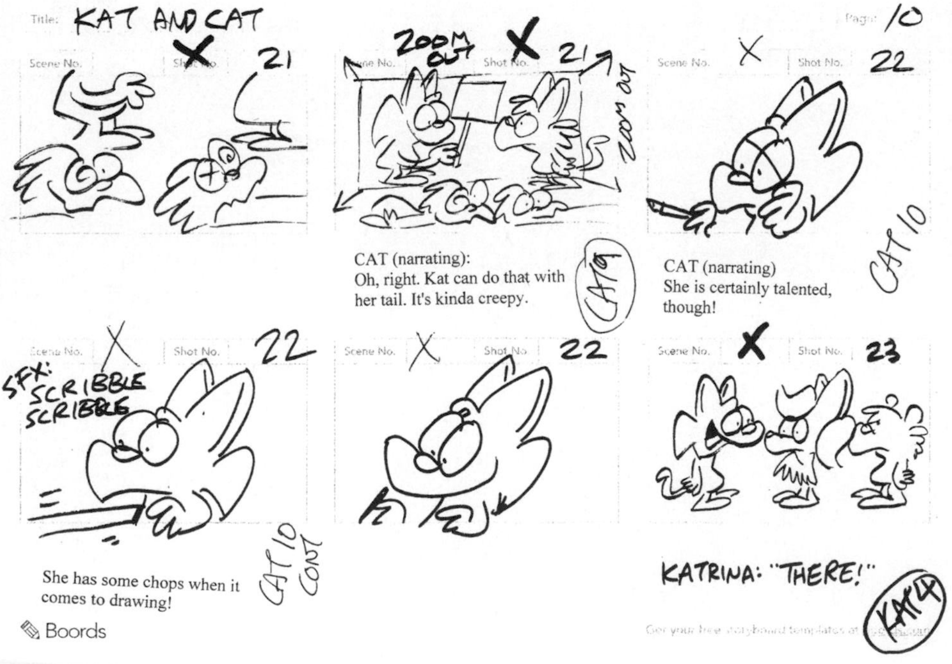
Title: KAT AND CAT
Page 10
Scene No. X
Shot No. 21
ZOOM OUT
Scene No. X
Shot No. 21
ZOOM OUT
Scene No. X
Shot No. 22
CAT (narrating):
Oh, right. Kat can do that with her tail. It's kinda creepy.
CAT 9
CAT (narrating)
She is certainly talented, though!
CAT 10
Scene No. X
Shot No. 22
SFX: SCRIBBLE SCRIBBLE
Scene No. X
Shot No. 22
Scene No. X
Shot No. 23
She has some chops when it comes to drawing!
CAT 10 CONT
KATRINA: "THERE!"
KAT 4
Boords

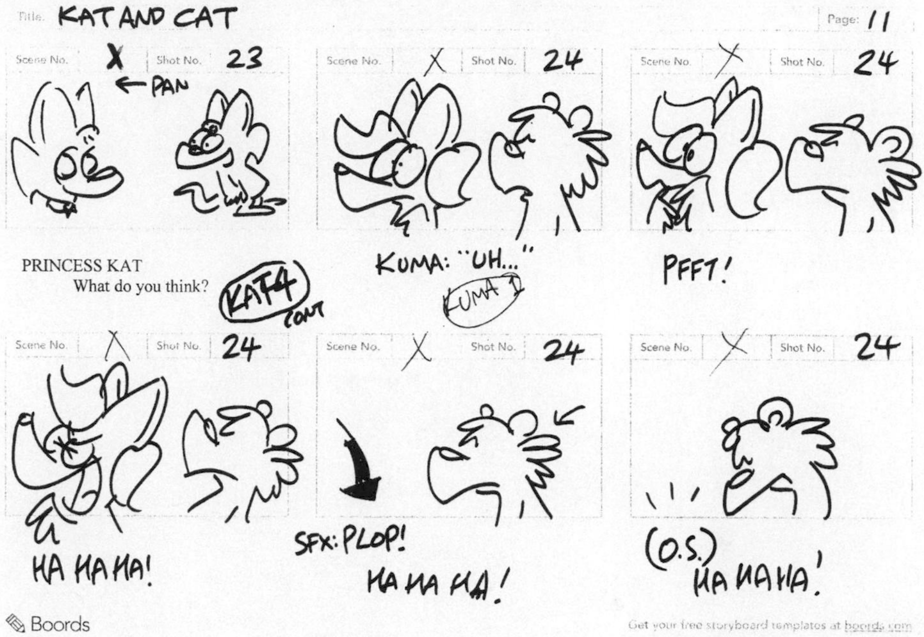
Title: KAT AND CAT
Page: 11
Scene No. X Shot No. 23
← PAN
Scene No. X Shot No. 24
Scene No. X Shot No. 24
PRINCESS KAT
What do you think?
KAT4 CONT
KUMA: "UH..."
KUMA 1
PFFT!
Scene No. X Shot No. 24
Scene No. X Shot No. 24
Scene No. X Shot No. 24
HA HA HA!
SFX: PLOP!
HA HA HA!
(O.S.)
HA HA HA!
Boords
Get your free storyboard templates at boords.com

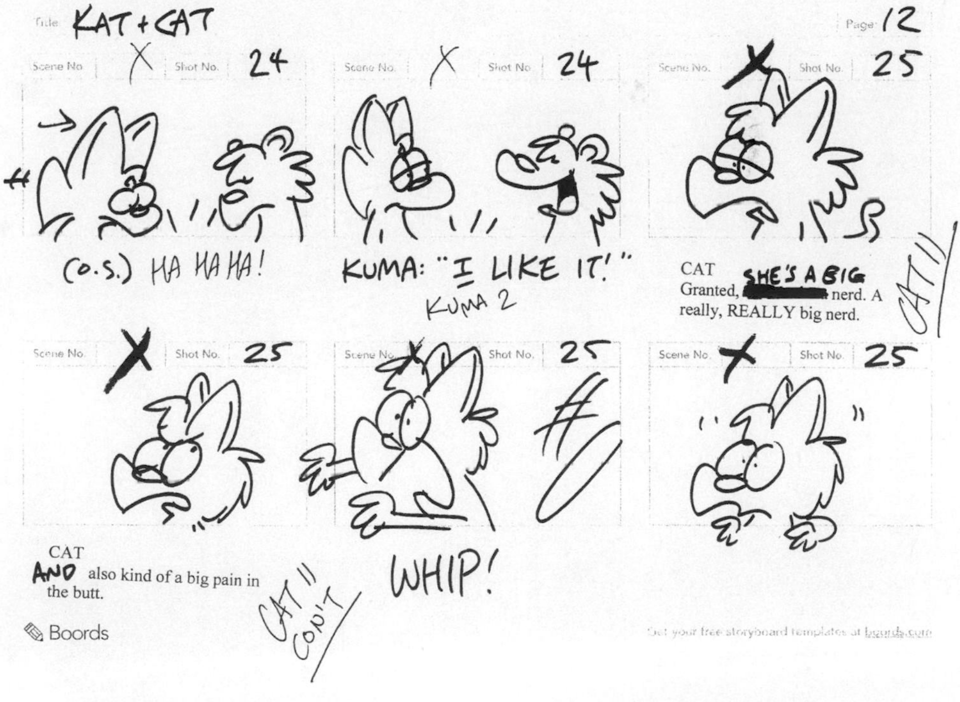
Title: KAT + CAT
Page: 12
Scene No. X Shot No. 24
Scene No. X Shot No. 24
Scene No. X Shot No. 25
(O.S.) HA HA HA!
KUMA: "I LIKE IT!"
KUMA 2
CAT
SHE'S A BIG
Granted, [redacted] nerd. A really, REALLY big nerd.
CAT 11
Scene No. X Shot No. 25
Scene No. X Shot No. 25
Scene No. X Shot No. 25
CAT
AND also kind of a big pain in the butt.
CAT 11 CON'T
WHIP!
Boords
Get your free storyboard templates at boords.com

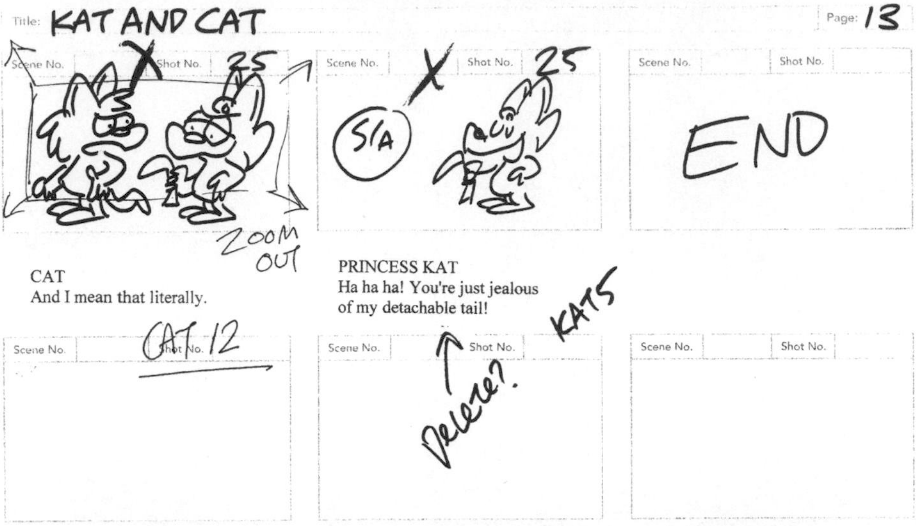
Title: KAT AND CAT
Page: 13
Scene No. X Shot No. 25
Scene No. X Shot No. 25
S/A
Scene No. Shot No.
END
ZOOM OUT
CAT
And I mean that literally.
PRINCESS KAT
Ha ha ha! You're just jealous of my detachable tail!
KATS
CAT 12
Delete?
Scene No. Shot No.
Scene No. Shot No.
Scene No. Shot No.

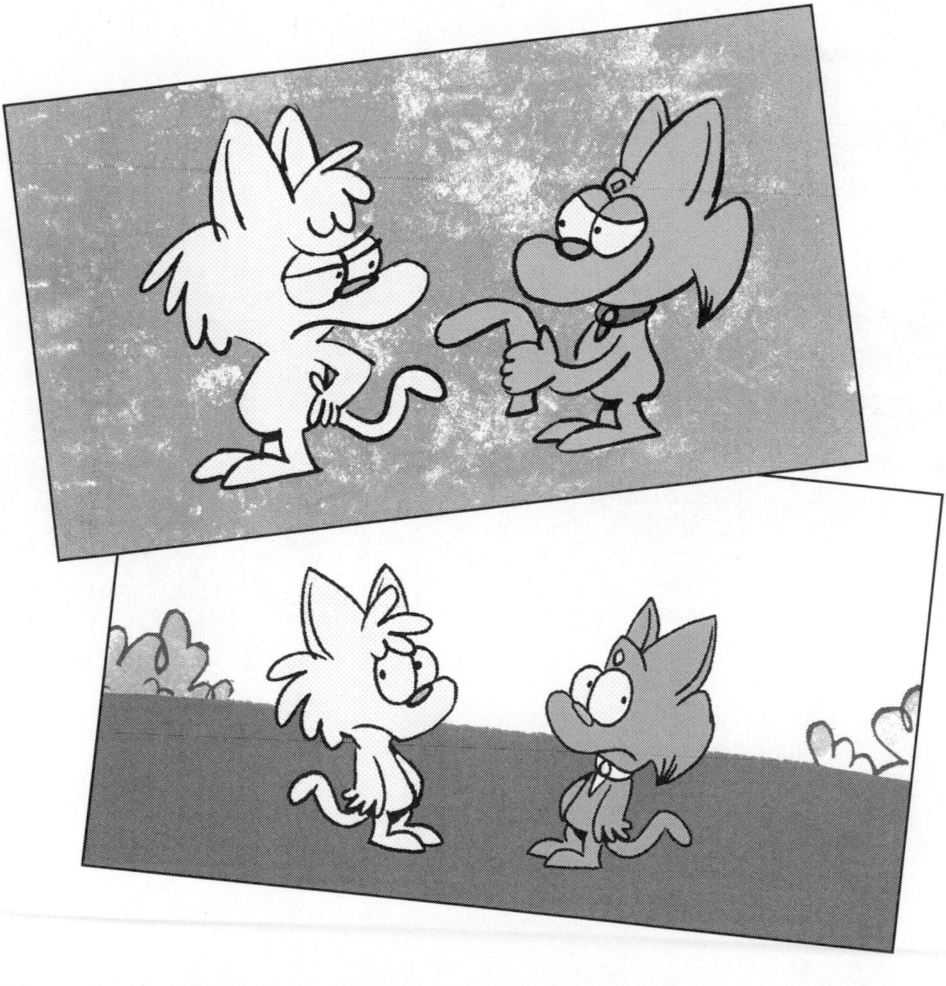

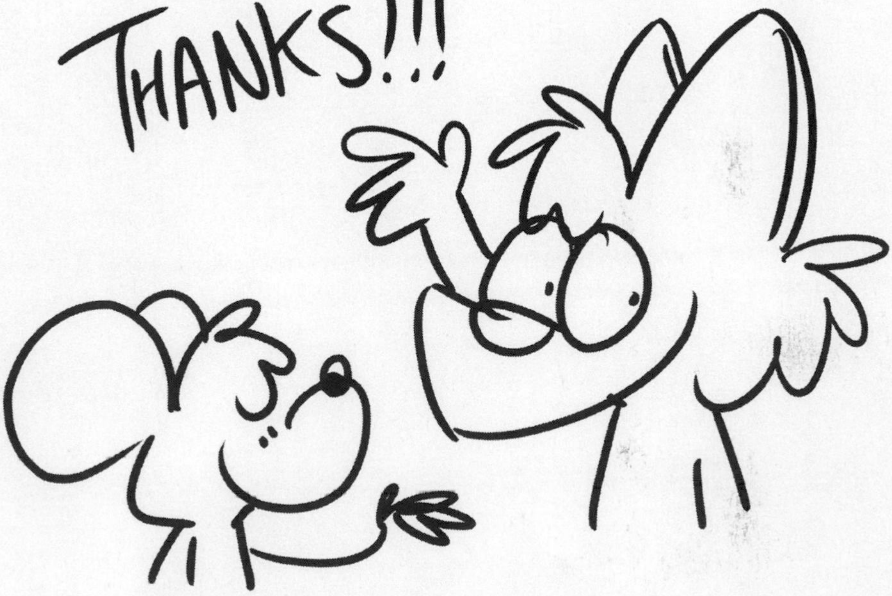
THANKS!!!

Made in the USA
Middletown, DE
05 March 2023